Editorial Board:
Luzhkov Yu.M. – Chairman
Patriarch of Moscow and All Russia **Alexius II**
Belov L.A.
Vinogradov V.A. – Editor-in-chief
Kezina L.P.
Kirichenko E.I.
Moleva N.M.
Muravjov V.B.
Resin V.I. – Deputy Chairman
Trofimov A.S.
Shantsev V.P.

Reviewers:
Kirichenko E.I.

«Moscow. 850th Anniversary» – jubilee edition in two volumes (under the general edition of V.A.Vinogradov). – II volume 272 ps.: ill. 446. Publishing House AO «Moscow Textbooks», Moscow – 1997.

    The edition touches upon the formation of historical Moscow, combination of Eastern and Western traditions in the city's artistic image, succession of symbolics of Jerusalem, Rome, Constantinople, Kiev and Vladimir. The basic principles of town-building art are shown in the planning, composition, building-in, landscape, toponymics, connected with the key historical events of Moscow kingdom, imperial Russia, the USSR and the Russian Federation.
    The edition is for the general public.

The edition is dedicated to the 850th anniversary of Moscow with financial support of Moscow Goverment.

ISBN 5-7461-0051-x(2)
ISBN 5-7461-0052-8

МОСКВА
850 ЛЕТ

ТОМ II

Foreword

The jubilee edition devoted to the 850-th anniversary of Moscow has been published in two volumes. The first volume includes two books: «Ancient Moscow» and «Images of Moscow in the 18th – early 20th Centuries». The second volume consists of book three – «The Socialist Reconstruction of Moscow. 1917 – 1992» and book four – «Renaissance of New Russia's Capital».

As compared to the previous volume the contents of the two books in volume two cover a relatively short time span – from the fall of the Russian Empire to the end of the current century. As in the second half of the 1980s and in the early 1990s the country lived through a radical transformation that can be compared only to the one that took place in 1917, and as mankind is approaching the threshold of the third millennium AD, the volume pays much attention to the comprehension, judgement and evaluation of both overthrows.

The main subject of the volume is the evolution of Moscow's city-building image in the 20th century, the disclosure of its imagery and symbolism and principal stages of its forming; the influence and role of historical Moscow upon the development of the state, society, personality.

An attempt was made to present and to describe what Russia and Moscow as its capital went through over the bigger part of the 20th century from a different angle, unlike the one that in the past was dictated by the authority and supervision of the communist party of the Soviet Union (CPSU). The third book chapters demonstrate the evolution and special features of the Soviet architecture, its spiritual and ideological roots, and later on they show the growth of the new ideas whose gist is described in brief. The chapters trace how they were reflected in such a special field as architectural and city-building activity, in projects and actual construction work, and through this vital function of the state – in new images of Moscow.

The comprehensive introduction to the third book draws the reader's attention to the pre-revolutionary development of the city and depicts the panorama of its cultural life in the late 19th – early 20th century. Among those described are the problems of nature's ecology, culture, noosphere, from whose height it is possible to assess the most complex and tragic events and phenomena of Moscow's «radical reconstruction» that took place during the socialist epoch.

The third book chapters indicate the main watersheds in the transformation of the capital's city-building image: the first years of the Soviet era (1917 – 1930s), Stalin's reconstruction of the USSR capital (1930 – 1953), the way to the exemplary socialist city (1954 – 1985), reconsideration of city-building values in 1986 – 1992.

Two contradictory processes in Moscow's city-building that went on concurrently are described in this book: the radical reconstruction versus the protection of cultural heritage; their clash has formed the capital's image. Which is natural the book represents the viewpoints of numerous authors who see and assess this epoch differently. However the views in question are united by the pathos of the entire publication – the restoration of historical Moscow and its role in Moscow of the future.

The fourth book titled «Renaissance of New Russia's Capital» acquaints the reader with the transition to the new epoch of democratic transformations in Moscow's image with the rebirth of the lost city-building values.

The fourth book chapters describe the panorama of the city's life on the eve of its 850-th anniversary, at the threshold of the third millennium of the Christian civilisation and lighten the search for the city identity in the architectural invitation to the 21st century.

No doubt, it is impossible to tell the reader about all the facets of the capital's versatile city-building. Only principal features of the city identity are described: its shrines, cultural monuments, its centre main ensembles – the stone manuscripts of the city-building tale in the capital's life.

The editorial board thanks officials from the Mosproekt-2 Institute; from the research and development institute for designing objects of culture, recreation, health care; from the Russian Academy of Painting, Sculpture and Architecture; from the Moscow Architectural Institute; from the Experts-Consultative Public Council to the Moskomarchitektura; from the Department of State Control over the protection and use of monuments of history and culture; from the Institute of «Spetsproektrestavratsiya» – for the materials presented in order to prepare this publication.

B. Iofan: Project of the Palace of Soviets. 1930

Demolition of the Cathedral of Christ the Savior on December 5, 1931. This act marked the beginning of mass destruction of Russian temples and cultural monuments.

The «Moskva» swimming pool at the place where the Cathedral of Christ the Savior once stood. 1980s.

Recreation of the Cathedral of Christ the Savior. 1996.

K. Alabyan, V. Simbirtsev: The Theater of the Soviet Army. 1934 – 1940.

L. Rudnev, S. Chernyshov, P. Abrosimov, A. Khryakov (architects),
V. Nasonov (engineer), N. Tomsky (sculptor): The Moscow State University on Vorobievy Hills (former Leninskie Hills). 1949 – 1953.

Fountain «Friendship of the Peoples». All-Russia Exhibition Center. 1954

A. Rukhlyadev V. Krinsky: Khimki (Northern) Steamer and Water Bus Terminal. 1937.

A. Kibalnikov:
Monument to V. Mayakovsky. 1958.

A. Faidysh-Krandievsky, M. Barshch and A. Kolchin:
Monument «Conquerors of Space». 1964.

M. Posokhin, A. Mndoyants, G. Makarevich, B. Tkhor, Sh. Ayrapetov,
N. Pokrovsky, Yu. Popov, A. Zaitsev: New Arbat Avenue. 1963 – 1968.

M. Posokhin, A. Mndoyants, E. Stamo, P. Shteller, N. Shchepetilnikov
(architects), A. Kondratiev, G. Lvov, I. Kochetov (engineers):
Palace of Congresses in the Kremlin. 1959 – 1961.

M. Posokhin, L. Aranauskas, B. Tkhor (architects), Yu. Lvovsky,
Yu. Ratskevich and others (engineers):
The «Olympiisky» Sports Complex. 1977 – 1980.

D. Chechulin: Hotel «Rossiya». 1964 – 1967.

M. Posokhin, A.Gutnov, Z. Kharitonova:
Walking-zone «Old Arbat».

D. Chechulin: The House of the Government of Russia –
«The White House». 1980.

N. Bondarovitch, N. Leonov, S. Firsov:
Avenue named after A.D. Sakharov (former Novokirovsky Ave.).

B. Ul'kin, D. Lukaev: Culture-Business-Trade Center on the Manege Square.

G. Astaf'ev, B. Klimov, A. Dzershkovia, I. Vinogragskii: The State Tretyakov Gallery after restoration and reconstruction. 1996.

Polyansky (architect), Z. Tsereteli (sculptor): The Great Patriotic War 1941 – 1945 memorial on Poklonnaya Hill. 1996.

The Moscow International Business Center – «The City» in Krasnaya Presnya. Project designed under B. Tkhor. 1991 – 1994.

BOOK THREE

Socialist Reconstruction of Moscow 1917-1992

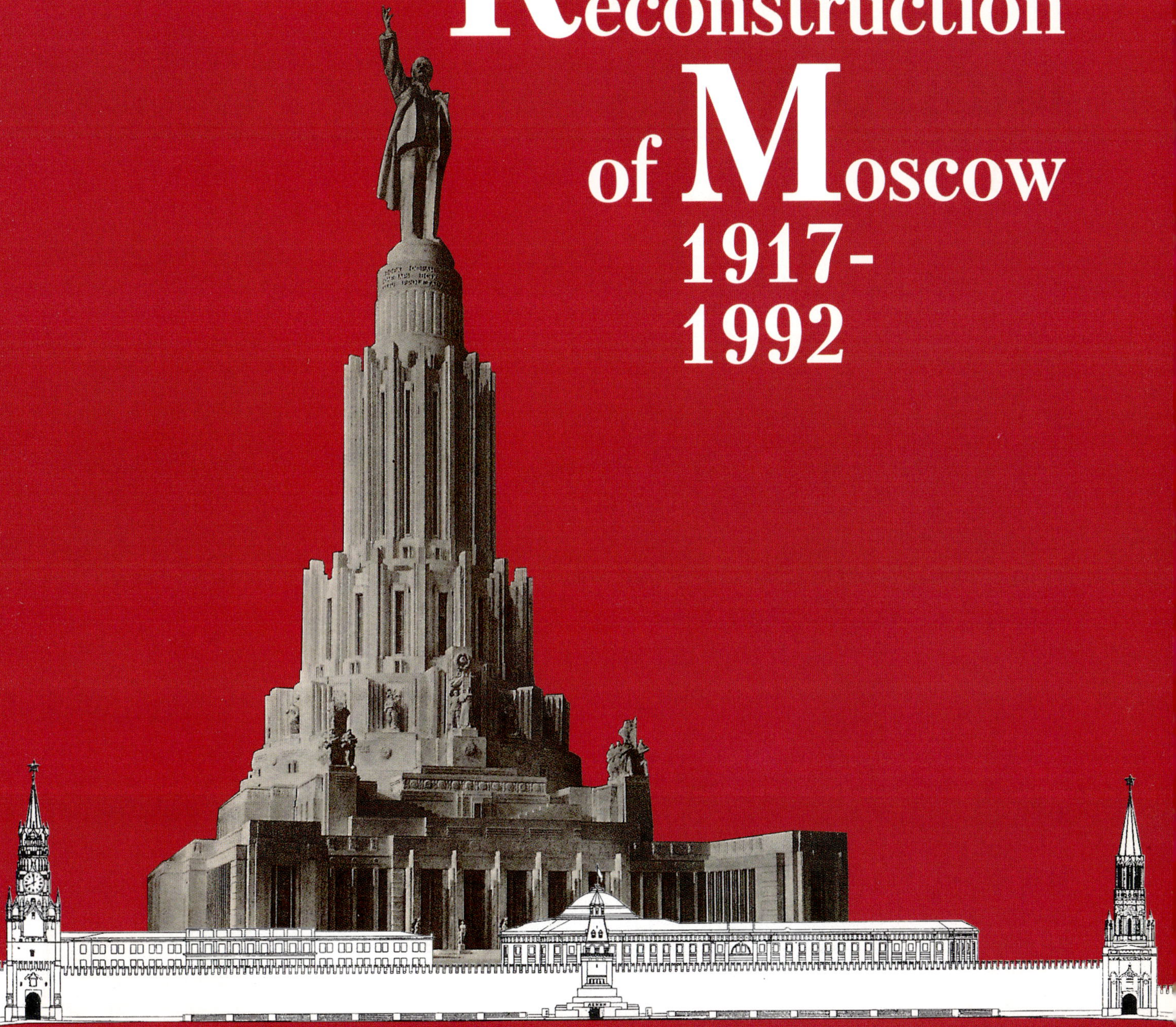

«Prayer about Russia». Artist: Hieromonk Stephan (V. Linitsky).

Introduction

Icon of Our Lady with the Orb

Icon of Crucifixion of Christ

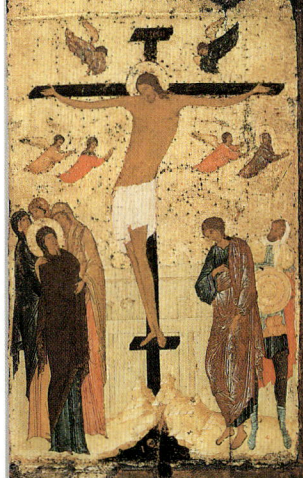

His Beatitude Patriarch of Moscow and All-Russia Tikhon

Cathedral of Christ the Savior which is being recreated. Model

The Emperor of the Russian State Nicholas II

To see and perceive the centuries-old, multi-layer image of Moscow from a city-building angle one should cast a glance back from a time perspective long enough to make out the grandiose phenomenon of the city's form evolution. As a matter of fact, the issues highlighted in the first volume of this edition pertaining to the phases of development, transformation and growth of the city from its birth to the reign of Peter I, and further on until the Revolution, have been viewed exactly from such a perspective, allowing for a time span to analyze complex processes of city building. It is far more difficult to single out and comprehend what was acquired and what was lost looking at a qualitatively new image of the 20th century Moscow, i.e. the city image of the era of revolutionary quakes, which is very different and opposite to that of the ancient times.

Not to be captured in the anniversary year by a multitude of Moscow's eternal but omnipresent everyday social, economic and technical problems it is necessary to rise above the ocean of day-to-day bustle to see the true role of Moscow, to feel the sense of its majestic image, opening up the purpose of its social development, its place and meaning in both the world of today and the history of civilization.

Two major problems have been outlined by life itself. They are ecology of nature and ecology of culture. As a notion ecology emerged owing to a growing concern about the critical situation of our natural and cultural heritage without which normal and healthy development of any society is inconceivable. Besides, the degeneration of state, society, family and man is a direct consequential effect of the infringement of social and natural «genetics» incorporated in the processes of natural and cultural ecology. If these development fundamentals enter as principal organic components into government programs, if only they are there, it is from this point that a revival will begin, i.e. a process to regenerate a living medium which is a shell, embracing society, family and man, and accumulating, like an aura the potential energy from structural social and cultural elements of the city. It is true, because today we can witness for ourselves these processes, regenerating historical, cultural and natural medium at work alongside with the revival of public consciousness, or, in other words, the return of «prodigal sons» to their fathers' home, to the sacred capital.

The third major problem is the ecology of noosphere (i.e. of Logos, of Mind). It is only starting to take shape to replace the collapsed communist ideology. It cannot exist without either ecology of nature or ecology of culture for it focuses on formulating targets for social development on the basis of the entire previous evolution cast in natural and cultural monuments that make up the principal treasure of any society or state.

Centred specifically on natural landscape evolution, the Introduction to the second volume first pictures the cultural panorama of the early 20th century Moscow, then highlights its super problem, i.e. the problem of existence, preservation and development of historical Moscow as part of future Moscow, and presents it as the central problem of ecology of noosphere.

The insight of these aspects will allow everyone, as N.V. Gogol put it, to open up «a spring of great possibilities» through which we shall be able to make out and comprehend the fate of sacred Moscow and a place for each of us in this grand co-creation cut and expressed in stone as such are the chronicles of the Russian capital.

Natural Landscape Evolution

The unique town-planning layout of Moscow has been inherited from earlier periods when a unique city structure was shaping up, embedding almost perfectly in natural environment, and leaving the cycles of nature practically intact.

Geological and atmospheric medium, soils, vegetational associations, surface and underground waters, flora and fauna make up together a natural component of Moscow as an urban phenomenon. The complex of natural conditions is characterized by instability, susceptibility to rapid changes alongside with adaptability as a result of over a millennium landscape development. It has a distinctive feature which is a close interaction between city impact and the response of natural factors.

The city area development has been fairly different in terms of time: about seven thousand hectares were under development for 750 years, 4-5 times as much – during the following 50 years, and up to 100 thousand hectares – in the last 30 years. Analyses show an important difference in the state of the whole range of natural conditions in different parts of the city.

In ancient times all Moscow area must have been woody and rather swampy. Spruce and birch forests spread from the northern interfluve to Neglinnaya River ending in Kuchkovsky forest. Pine and birch forests edged in from the east, and platyphylous forests spread from south up to the primary terrace of the main-stream right bank of Moscow River.

The development of the area had started long before Moscow was founded. The sites of prehistoric man speak for earlier settlements on the river banks. Crom-towns took shape in the 8th- 9th centuries. There were portages between the basins of Klyazma and Moscow rivers. So, the main settlements took root along these rivers, – a fact backed up and confirmed by man-made hills, mounds, fortification remains that now look at as natural landscape.

Open cleared areas along the rivers started to expand as far back as in the early pre-Moscow period. But Moscow had been a rural area amongst woody and swampy land before the beginning of the 13th century. Then, in the midst of this already cultivated and mainly open space there formed a nucleus – a Moscow fortress surrounded by suburban gardens and villages. The Kremlin stone walls were built in the 14th century, and later in the 16th century first the Kitay-Gorod walls, then the Bely-gorod (White Town) walls were built. The suburbs spread around at the same time. Lower riverine areas were cultivated following the upper ground. The differentiation of population and building densities in the Kremlin, Kitay-Gorod and White Town, and later in the 17th century in the Zemlyanoi-gorod (Earth Town) was a natural process.

The buildup area of the city was changing according to the following pattern which is commonly accepted now: the center became more compressed, clear-cut and isolated (13th-15th centuries), it grew rather up than out (until the 17th century), surrounding villages merged together (12th-14th centuries), suburbs expanded (12th-16th centuries); spaces in the center broke up into smaller units (15th-20th centuries), the number of stone buildings increased (13th-20th centuries), hard surface streets also increased in number (15th-20th centuries), and the outlying parts of the city expanded (14th-20th centuries).

Izmailovo country-estate

Forests retreated from Moscow while and because built-up, ploughed-up, swamp drained, clay-field areas for brick production, as well as other areas expanded. The city pressed out the ancient natural forest mass, and the left-out so-called «hanging gardens» appeared in the Kremlin (13th century), on the Boulevard Ring (18-19th centuries), next to the Kremlin walls, such as the Alexandrovsky Garden (19th century), and in some other places.

The 16th-17th centuries period is characterized by making large «country-side» park-and palace complexes such as the Izmailovsky ensemble stretching from Yauza River to Pehorka River, the Moskvoretsky ensemble having two centres in the villages of Kolomenskoe and Ostrov, and on Skhodnya River, as well as in New Jerusalem. This period is note-worthy for a vigorous transformation of these areas into the so-called «promised lands» consistent with ethical and spiritual ideas of the time: be it «the Garden of Eden» in Izmailovo, be it «the Lord's Land» in New Jerusalem. Land preservation was inspired not only by pragmatism but also and in large part by spiritual and ethical aspirations, (e.g., «sacred groves», «precious forests», etc.). A canal network was built, rivers were placed under control, large drainage systems organized (in such villages as Bogorodskoe, Knyazhino, Alekseyevskoe, and Izmailovo), river banks were reinforced (in the villages of Kolomenskoe and Ostrov). A tremendous number of reproducer-plants from other countries and geographical zones were brought into the city. Even today one can see them in Moscow «woodlands» and forest parks, such as Izmailovo, Sokolniki and Kuskovo.

The so-called «city-woodlands» that have held out until now such as Bitsa Park, Izmailovo, Petrovsky Woodland (kept under the auspices of the Timiryazev Academy of Agriculture), Kuzminki, Losiny Ostrov (Elk Island), Pokrovsko-Streshnevo, Dubovaya Roscha (Oak Grove), etc., are to a great extent man-made anthropogenic areas which absorbed an enormous human effort aimed at their purposeful arrangement, upkeep and preservation during the period of the 17th- 19th centuries.

Owing to the expansion of open arable lands, the process which went on continuously until the end of the 16th century – the number of settled population in the Moscow area was much lower than that of today (20-25%). At the beginning of the 17th century, i.e. after the desolation of the Time of Troubles the number of forests on deserted lands grew up to 52 %, and it went down slightly during the whole of the 19th century before it settled finally at the present-day level.

By the 17th century the built-up four-wall private space had not exceeded 16-18 square kilometres while surrounding country-side had occupied 3-4 times as much.

The Kremlin and Kitay-Gorod being the most densely built-up areas, provided impetus for the change in the natural setup, mainly hydrological, geological and later microclimatic. However, the «transparency» of building, its country-estate-like character, the incorporation of meadows, groves and gardens, which singled out Moscow from the stone-clad cities of Europe, provided for necessary humidity, air circulation, soil aeration, natural water circulation cycles, leading finally to lesser heat and dryness in summer. As early as in the 17th century the contemporaries and travelers pointed out that they felt «warmer and less windy» within Moscow walls, which speaks for the fact that a special «microclimate» had set up there.

By the early 18th century a new water piping network had been built. It was fitted with water pumps designed primarily for fire-fighting purposes, which accounted for increased water consumption. At the same time new boggy seats and pollution pockets appeared in the city center because of unorganized surface water drain. In the post-Petrine time, first all fundamental works were carried out to dry up the city center, then embankments were built for the first time, and hydro-technical and land improvement operations were performed, entailing large-scope earth-moving works. While building became denser and paved areas expanded, engineering construction acquired full swing: water-towers, dams, and bridges were built, salt-water disposal wells were drilled, vigorous underground works were conducted, and a tunnel under Moscow River was attempted – in short, all this testified to the intensive transformation of the city medium.

In the 18th century the government center shifted to Yauza River area entailing the development of the adjoining territories, which in itself constituted a tangible factor in changing the natural setup. New brick works and various mills were opened in the suburbs and along rivers. First industrial pollution, though insignificant, started to appear at the end of the 18th century. The city numbered up to three thousand stone buildings, 1144 streets and 463 lanes at that time.

There had been 600 gardens and parks, and over 300 ponds by the beginning of the 19th century, a large portion of «groves» had been used as public pleasure grounds. A gravity flow water pipe was constructed (1805). Wood remained a major construction material: only one-fourth of houses in Moscow had been stone-made before 1812. In the after-the-fire period building became more congested, which had a certain effect on the whole range of natural conditions. By the end of the first third of the century many streets had already been widened and straightened, roads were paved with cobble stone, drainage provided.

Forests retreated by wedges, selectively. In between built-up areas there were territories which belonged to the country-side rather than town, but gradually they were changing their functions subject to its permanent influence: field – ridge – meadow – garden – sloboda (suburb). It was not by mere chance that M.V. Lomonosov wrote of Moscow as of «many towns merged in one» as early as in the 18th century.

Country-house estates were forming up, each of which being, as planned, a unique corner of transformed nature. The transfer of

Kolomenskoe Country-Estate.

Kuskovo Country-Estate.

Vasilievskaya Country-Estate on Vorobiovy Hills.

country-style forms from near Moscow to Moscow gave birth to such masterpieces as the estate ensembles on the Yauza banks and the gardens in Lefortovo. The forms of park arrangement were superimposed on «groves» and ponds. The economic use of rivers secured bank stretches for serf-manned landlord-owned and royal mills first, factories and works then.

A network of small gentry estates was formed around Moscow united by a common road and alley network together with compulsory ponds, flour mills, country-houses, bathing places, farmsteads and parks gradually changing into woods. A system of present-day national historical and cultural as well as natural territories around Moscow that are specially protected now, was founded.

Wood cutting near the city has been prohibited since the 17th century. An edict on protection of certain wooded areas was issued in 1703, followed by another one in 1714 on hunting rules, and another one in 1722 on regulations for wood cutting and forest protection, including clauses on natural reservoir water protection zones and prohibiting wood cutting in the radius of 10 kilometres from Moscow. In 1804 yet another regulation on better preservation of government-owned groves adjacent to the city, and on forestry reserves in 1805.

The functions of territories had to be measured and complied with natural capabilities of rivers proper and flood-lands. So, more pressure was applied to primary terraces, but their usage was strictly regulated. Restrictions of the 16th-17th centuries concerned erecting such water polluting facilities as soap works and cattle washing sites. It was natural that water consuming production activities such as flour mills, works and factories had to be set up on river banks. As they emerged, rules and restrictions were adopted. Secondary terraces and open watersheds were used for construction. In short, should it be a selection of a site for a temple, market, fortifications, or ditch digging or converting it into a small canal, or water intake arrangement, or selection of a place for a well or a construction site, or should it be building an embankment with high water level to be considered, or a new street with fire-safety to account for, or road laying either through lowlands or watersheds, or site selection for dams and bridges – all this, in a word, the development of the city areas was carried out according to those resources that were intended to be used.

Low density, a country-estate building traditional approach, a must for house gardens and the building of Royal Gardens in Zamoskvorechie, i.e. all what distinguished Moscow from European «stone-jacketed» and densely built-up capitals was nothing else but the realization of a big city experience to commensurate its effort with its specific natural features which it had to comply with.

By mid 19th century plenty of gardens disappeared, built-up areas closed in, ditches, holes, rivulets and other features causing inconvenience were filled up. The weakest elements vanished not affecting the main aspects. By that time the results of the 17th century transformation had already become «natural» components, specifically, the Alekseyevskaya Grove as well as the parks in Kolomenskoe, Ostrov, and Izmailovo had turned into «woods». The built-up area structure had changed too. The foundation for pre-industrial Moscow had been laid. At the end of the 19th century Moscow began to receive public utilities of a qualitatively new engineering level: a sewage network built in 1864, and a new Mytishchi water pipe laid in 1892 in addition to the already operational Khodynsky, Preobrazhensky and Andreyevsky water pipes. In 1870 a large-scale government-sponsored work began to drain the city land, construct drainage systems, and water drain ditches, which entailed filling up ponds, garden cutting and river bed changing. The city incorporated great railroad terminals and networks of Nicholaevskaya, Yaroslavskaya, Kurskaya and Kazanskaya railways with production sites grouped in alongside.

Qualitative changes took place in the whole complex of natural conditions at the end of the 19th and the beginning of the 20th centuries. The population growth brought about a radical improvement of public utilities (water supply, sewage, power supply and railway transport). This explains vigorous paving, increased underground water usage and general growth of resource consumption. The growing number of production facilities resulted in a sharp increase of earth works and affected noticeably the city environment. Thus, the transformations in city-building entailed negative and unexpected consequences.

As a result of land transactions with government participation and sponsorship as well as bank credits a new form of settlement started to take root out of city bounds. It constituted country-house (dacha) settlements organized either in the English «garden-city» manner or just as «public parks».

By the end of the 19th century the ecology situation had been affected by a radical increase of acreage and volume of building in the previously vacant land, reduction of green-belt

Kuskovo Country-Estate.

Tsaritsino Country-Estate.

areas and emergence of chemically active agents in the air. However, both smoke and carbon black had been blown out by north-west and south-west winds. Intensive development of the Podmoskovny (Near Moscow) coal field, its coal having high sulfur content, put its imprint on typical «working outskirts». Civil and industrial construction began to use more and more metal; gas and then electricity for the city lighting and transport were introduced.

One can call the end of the 19th century a critical point in the balance of forces of the city and nature. The balance in favor of the unforeseen consequences has been upset, and it has been gaining momentum ever since. The results of the interaction of these forces are mirrored by the ecological situation in Moscow. Three main trends have been definitive to it since the turn of the 20th century. They are: air pollution, increased acreage and density of building and public utility infrastructure development.

At the turn of the new century Moscow embraced 7,250 hectares, its population density being 210-270 men per hectare. The Eastern industrial area, i.e. the eastern watershed between Yauza and Moscow Rivers, had been developed to incorporate industrial construction and a railway junction by the late years of the 19th century. At the turn of the 20th century a north-western watershed, stretching to Likhoborka tributary stream was built up completely. Moscow's spatial structure comprised the densely populated Sadovoe (Garden) Ring area (570-600 men per hectare) embracing blocks in Kitay-Gorod (1.0-6.0 ha), on Boulevard Ring (1.5-6.1 ha) and in Garden Ring proper (1.5-2.0 ha).

This period which lasted until 1941, turned out to be a real hard blow to Moscow ecology, affecting not only the city center but also suburban outskirts. The Moscow underground, or subway, was built during this time. Its construction marked a large-scale development of the underground space. It was soon filled in with electric fields, and great amounts of earth were removed from beneath the surface to the city's south-west for filling up plentiful ravines on the highgrounds in Teply Stan, which has led in our days to serious damage of surface drainage. It was during the same period that water-carrying communications sharply increased in number and reached tens of kilometres (only central heating networks aggregate length exceeded 60 km). Asphalt covered one-fourth of the total city area. This fact together with other infringements of the hydrogeological situation, brought about serious changes to the city geology medium. Streets in the north-western and north-eastern sectors (Gorky and Kirov streets) were rebuilt, some streets and yards were widened, new spaces were cleared for central squares. The reconstruction period of 1936-1940 with respect to ecology laid down the foundation for a disproportion between the transformation effect and the transformation consequences.

The pre-war period could be characterized by a wide range of transformations of Moscow natural surroundings. A complex Moscow-Volga canal and reservoir system was built, so, finally, the capital started to take water only from the river. The idea of «parks of culture and recreation» for broad masses was realized, the utility communications spread over the whole area within the Garden Ring and partially abutting the Kamer-Kolezhsky (Chamber Collegiate) rampart. The ideology of the «proletarian capital» and «the transformation of nature for peoples' benefit» brought about an outburst of «unplanned consequences» which had a particular impact on suburbs where the idea of «working people settlements», «working people outposts», «recreation zones for broad masses», «mass show sites», «mass beaches» and the like, was gaining predominance over anything else.

Created in 1935 the forest and park protective green belt became not only a «continuous chain of forests and parks» but also a place for working man recreation, a system of the «people's sanatoriums» of which a greater part was arranged in the expropriated suburban country-house estates. This meant that prerequisites for the development of an immense technical infrastructure extremely close to Moscow were created, which predetermined the construction of future industrial complexes.

As a result of intensive urbanization the remnants of the suburban («near Moscow») forest ensembles together with birch groves that emerged in lieu of the original woods cut down during the «fuel hunger» of 1918-1919, as well as neglected, desolated and turned-back-into-wild parks, that once had been part of much cared for estates, with lakes and ponds, namely, Kosino, Dolgoe, Vinogradny (Grapes) Pond, Kuskovo «Circumnavigation» Pond Chain, became a natural complex of a giant city, just as Aleksandrovsky Garden, Boulevard Ring, Gorky Park and many other territories.

Today Moscow and Moscow Region make up one of the largest urban areas of both Russia and Europe where 47 thousand kilometres sustain 15.7 million people of which number 8.6 million live within the city acreage being 99.4 thousand hectares.

Every day up to 700 thousand commuters come to Moscow (and 200 thousand go out). 2.5-3.0 million people from other regions of the country and from abroad stay in Moscow every day, some coming in, some going out.

Dwelling blocks and micro-districts occupy 28% of the city area (i.e. 27.8 thous. ha), industrial area makes up 18% (or 18.0 thous. ha) and green complex territories constitute 23% (22.8 thous. ha). Moscow's public use centers make up 6 % of its area, but mixed polyfunctional sectors occupy one-fourth, i.e. 24.8 thous. ha. Today's housing is characterized by 170.0 million square metres of living space (planned to be brought up to 220.0 million sq. m.), and by 30.0 million square metres of functional space (70.0 million sq. m are yet required). Arterial highway length is over 1,230 km, with aggregate length of surface transport network exceeding 2,340 km, and arterial highway transport length deficit being not less than 250 km accounting for an estimated populace mobility of up to 1,300 trips per year per person in the near future. All Moscow water supply systems work at daily capacity of almost 7.0 billion cu. m of water (Moscow's water consumption is rising); water daily discharge amounts to 6.2 billion cu. m per day, its network length being 6.0 thous. km, and the length of street drainage net is over 5.0 thous. km. Central heating is provided by more than 3.0 thous. km long arterial hot water pipe network, which will have to be extended.

So, the scope of transformation activity in the Russian capital, which is home for 10.6 percent of its population, is indeed tremendous. The changes, that have taken place in the habitat medium of multi-million populace, are irrevocable. Intensive anthropogenic pressures with relative instability of environmental components produce a variety of «secondary» and «tertiary» effects perceived as both negative and factual negative, which is only to be expected with regard to so large a city. And it is these spontaneous effects that shape up the ecological situation in Moscow.

Moscow's ecology of the 20th century's last decade is considered critical and, what is more, it retains a tendency for the worse. Like 17 other Russian cities with highest levels of air pollution, Moscow's air is badly contaminated with such agents as petrol vapors, nitrogen dioxide, ammonia, formaldehyde, etc. In 1995 the aggregate discharge in the atmosphere accounted for 1.8 million tons (of which amount 90 % fall on transport vehicles). The acreage of warmed-up land is 42% of the city area, incorporating about 30 large industrial enterprises including some that are key in defining the degree of environmental risk for Moscow. Altogether, there are more than a thousand high-rate raw consuming and environment-hazardous enterprises. The total area of anomally high and bad pollution embraces almost one-fourth of the city.

The development of large agglomeration complexes such as Korolev – Mytishchi – Ivanteyevka – Schelkovo, Lyubertsy – Tomilino – Balashikha – Reutov, Podolsk – Klimovsk –Scherbinka, Krasnogorsk – Nakhabino, etc., has resulted in a complete devaluation of «natural surrounding» as a notion. And what is more: pollution tails, underground water depression zones and other negative effects have been registered 70 – 120 kilometres from Moscow.

Within city limits the general pollution boundary has moved 15 kilometres from south-east to north-west during the last 30 years. 2/3 of city forests are degrading, and no city reservoir can meet the standards of a 1st degree reservoir for water consumption. As a result 3.3 million Muscovites live in the zone of extremely unfavorable ecology, and only one-tenth of the city populace enjoy relative environmental comfort.

The role of natural factors has always been assessed exclusively in a positive way. This approach is based on a conviction that not only the capability to regenerate, but also the sanitation capabilities, i.e. the ability to enhance city ecology, are retained under any conditions. But the analysis of Moscow ecology proves the opposite. The scope and diversity of pollution, the scope of destructive changes have transformed the initial properties around the greater part of Moscow area (up to 40 thous. ha) and have suppressed the sanitation capability of the natural complex. So, today man is sick, water is «sick» and soil is «sick».

It is only through altering the character of production and changing technology figures, liquidating the sources of pollution, including toxic transport discharge, on the one hand, and through environment-friendly city area building transformation, as well as setting up technological and technical protection and establishing proper infrastructure, on the other hand, that is possible to give back healthy ecology to Moscow to support its fragile nature.

Herewith, the Moscow historical structure will have to be considered. The development of interfluve high-grounds which started at the end of the last century, led to the situation that the historical center «on seven hills» found itself to be in the lowlands of the Moskvoretskaya valley and, thus, became exposed to all types of impact coming from the other parts of the city, i.e. water run-offs, pollution tails, etc.

The Moscow historical center, which today represents 1/12 of its total area, was surrounded in the 18th century by the so-called «working people outposts» set up to mark the city limits. They were reconstructed in the '30s to become the so-called middle zone for a five-story building to take shape and swing around in the 50s, this is where the «near» belt of industrial zones settled in, this is where reconstruction is badly needed today.

The near «cramp» of industrial belt is supplemented by another two zones in the north and a vast Eastern industrial area linked with the Southern industrial area developed during the last decades. These hypertrophied industrial areas in the Moscow periphery are the result of the idea prevailing in latest decades of an even distribution of labor sites and their proximity to the city residents living quarters.

The siting of the industrial zones farther to the city boundaries expanded outward the pollution source area, failing to resolve the issues relevant to the organization of the city medium. The photographs made from outer space picture these Moscow's industrial areas as unbelievably large spaces covered by smoke, which makes it possible to rightfully state that the remaining gaps are being filled with industrial waste residue. No European capital has so large industrial zones emplaced in their residential areas in the second half of the 20th century. In Moscow this naturally led to the enhancement of all technical communications supporting approximately seventy industrial zones.

Historically, manufacturing production facilities – works and factories – were attracted to the rivers, so, the conservatism in industrial siting has led to the situation that today's industries are crammed along Yauza and Moscow Rivers. The industrial zones expanded into enormous technogenic sectors almost devoid of living space. Thus, living (only living!), industrial (only industrial!) and recreational (city forests!) zones alternate in the Moscow periphery, having relatively independent transport communications networks.

The today's concept of city-building does not presuppose Moscow's further expansion. Major reconstruction will take place in the city's mid-zone, and that will include the removal and replacement of the five-story buildings, the reconstruction of the lesser railroad ring, the rehabilitation of small watercourses and the expansion of the natural green-belt areas. The polyfunctional city area where living and environment-friendly industrial, as well as recreational and other sites of public use and value are located, will also have to be enlarged.

The historical center, which must squeeze out not only the industrial zones but also the «consumer market» activities foreign to it, shall imperatively become the most precious and preserved core of this city where man shall recreate the lost and create new parks and embankments.

Panorama of Moscow
Life in the Early Years of the 20th Century

«I have seen wonderful cities, I was greatly impressed by Prague and Budapest, but Moscow is something unworldly, something from a fairy tale!.. There are about four hundred and fifty churches and chapels in it. When all their bells begin to chime, the air over this city of one million citizens trembles with a multitude of different sounds. A sea of beauty opens up when you look at it from the Kremlin. I have never suspected that such a city could exist on Earth: it strikes one's eye with green, red and gold of its domes and spires. Everything, I have ever dreamt of, put against this mass of gold on the bright sky-blue background, pales into insignificance».

Knut Hamsun. «In the Fairy Land».

In the early years of the 20th century Moscow did impress and astound foreign eye with the sight of its bright individuality in which tens of smart temples began their fantastic dialogue with trade and rented houses, offices and modern shops. At the same time this «asiatic» diversity of colors combined with its vast unevenly built up territory gave the reason for St. Petersburg residents to call Moscow «a big village». (We must give tribute to the Muscovites for never having offended for this nickname – a fact that today it is still used in Moscow speaks for it). On the other hand, the Muscovites have been known for their vanity from time immemorial as they have been certain that «one can hardly find another capital as their Moscow».

What did the second capital of the Empire live by on the eve of the formidable forthcoming revolutions? Let us try to describe some of the most interesting events that happened in Moscow during the reign of the last Russian Emperor Nicholas II.

According to the ancient tradition the ceremony of Russian tsars' and (beginning with Peter I) emperors' coronation was to take place in Moscow's Cathedral of the Assumption, which had been the principal sacred site of the Russian state. The splendid coronation ceremony, for which the whole city prepared in advance, consisted of various public prayers, processions and outdoor activities. In 1896 Nicholas II with his wife Alexandra Feodorovna, former Princess of Hesse-Darmstadt, as the custom prescribed, came to Moscow and stayed at the Emperor's Petrovsky Palace situated at the side of St. Petersburg Avenue. After several days of rest on May 14 a gigantic procession started out along decorated streets to the center of Moscow. The coronation procession was to pass through the Arc de Triomphe by all means which had been erected in Tverskaya Street to commemorate the victory over Napoleon. Then, accompanied by the chimes of thousands of bells the Emperor to be with his wife and retinue entered the Kremlin where the coronation proper was held in the Cathedral of the Assumption. After the coronation the new Emperor went to another Kremlin cathedral – the Cathedral of the Archangel – to pay tribute to the ancestral tombs, for all the Russian tsars of the Ryurik dynasty and those of the Romanovs up to Peter I had been interred there. (Peter the Great and other

Pleasure-ground in Mar'yna Roshcha.

Russian emperors that followed were buried at the Sts. Peter and Paul Cathedral in St. Petersburg).

Coronations, as the custom prescribed, were usually accompanied by public celebrations with free refreshments, gifts, and money give-outs. During the last coronation such celebration festivities took place on May 18, 1896 in a vast Khodynka Field used at other times for military exercises, horse-back races and other sporting contests. Lavish tables with free refreshment and give-out pavilions were prepared for the poor and low-income Muscovites, but the number of the willing was so great that a good intention turned into a tragedy. In the throng that occurred during the give-out of gifts 1,400 people were squeezed to death, which all the Russians took as a bad omen for their new Emperor.

In the 1900s the Emperor's family visited Moscow a few more times, usually trying to time their comings to coincide with the Easter festivities, as they did, for example, in 1900 and 1903. They also came to Moscow in 1912 to celebrate the anniversary of the

The Kremlin. General view.

The Kremlin Embankment.

I. Veiss: Ilyinskie Gates of Kitay-Gorod with Church of Nicholas the Big Cross. 1852.

Battle of Borodino, and in 1913 when the whole country was grandly celebrating 300 years of the Romanovs dynasty.

Easter festivities, i.e. the Resurrection of our Lord Jesus Christ, have traditionally been central in the Orthodox Church calendar. Therefore, Easter celebrations in Moscow which had a reputation of the most pious city in Russia, were usually arranged with special scope and splendor. New dresses sewn, Easter cakes baked, Easter eggs painted and special delicacies cooked for the holiday, so that later in the evening the people with Easter cakes and eggs would go to their temples to attend the matins, and then at midnight the crowds would line up for the Easter procession and march holding lit candles headed by priests with icons and banners. The Emperor would listen to the matins at the Kremlin palatial Church of the Savior behind the Golden Lattice, and on the Easter Day he together with the people would attend the Easter service administered at the Cathedral of the Assumption. In 1900 and 1903 this was almost a theatrical performance for all the ladies of the court retinue with the Empress at the head wore luxurious national style dresses and high kokoshniks, a traditional Russian head-gear. It was usual to illuminate Moscow in a beautiful way for Easter night and further on through the Holy week. The Kremlin was also illuminated in a big way: the Cathedrals and Ivan the Great Bell Tower – with special care.

The Church had always had a great influence in Moscow on many a human activity, bending the order of life to its pace and tempo all through the year. Christmas holidays were usually the culmination of winter as they were known for their picturesque fir-tree market on Theater Square, public merry-making in the Manege (riding school), Christmas masquerades and balls that went on to the Epiphany. The next holiday was Shrove-tide. The Manege was the center for Shrove-tide merry-making as well. «The Shrove-tide walk» went around the Manege building. At the head of the procession they carried a giant pancake followed by a crowd of cook-boys, wearing white caps and aprons, carrying the attributes of the Shrove-tide menu, i.e. pancakes, caviar, butter, sour cream and fish. This was a special week in a year dedicated to gluttony which ended in Shrove Sunday when according to the ancient tradition it was customary to ask each other forgiveness. After that came the Lent which ended in Holy Week. During this week even the best Moscow restaurants that usually did not strictly observe the lenten fare menu to please the tastes of the new generation of merchants who were not as strict as their fathers in observing church traditions, served only fish and vegetable soup, pickled mushrooms, open-top fish pasty and other lenten dishes. After Easter and Holy Week there came St.Thomas' week – that was the time for big discount sales of goods to the people. After the spring merry-making on May 1 the city began little by little to become deserted as some people went to the country, others to the Caucasus or the Volga, still others abroad. This was the time when all manifestations of noisy Moscow life subsided and died down including those of the Church.

Apart from these annual holidays the Russian Church marked a few important anniversaries during this period. In 1903 it marked 600 years since the death of St.Daniil, the Prince of Moscow, the forefather of the Moscow princes, in 1907 – 500 years since the death of St. Efrosinya, the Princess, and 500 years since the foundation of the Voznesensky monastery in the Kremlin which housed the burial place of grand princesses and tsarinas.

However, the most important event in the church life at the beginning of the 20th century was undoubtedly the Imperial Manifesto of October 17, 1906 which repealed the ban on Old

I. Veiss: Nikolskie Gates of Kitay-Gorod and Church of the Icon of Our Lady of Vladimir. 1852.

Belief followers and on some other Christian sects. The history of Old Belief in Moscow is a striking retrospective of stoic adherence on the part of the Old Believers to their convictions. The two principal trends of Old Belief centred around two Moscow cemeteries: Preobrazhenskoe and Rogozhskoe. The Old Belief followers who had returned from Austria where some of the Russian Old Believers fled in the years of persecutions in the 17th century, settled around and close to these cemeteries. It is worth mentioning that it was from among the Austrian Old Believers that the priests for Moscow were usually chosen in the 19th and at the turn of the 20th century. The Old Believers proved to be useful for the city as almost all Moscow merchants and industrialists of substance and renown came from their circle – the Morozovs, the Ryabushinskis, the Guchkovs, the Rakhmanovs, the Shelaputins, and many others. After the unsealing of existing Old Belief altars in 1905, they started to build new Old Belief temples, and an All-Russia Old Belief Congress was held in Moscow in May 1907.

The Russian-Japanese war became a memorable milestone in the life of Muscovites. The surprise attack on Russian war ships based at Port-Arthur rocked all the country. A grandiose manifestation of people's indignation under patriotic slogans took place at the footsteps of the governor-general's house in Tverskaya Street on January 29, 1904. On the 27 of June 1904 Red Square received the people for a special public prayer for God to confer victory and peace. Elizaveta Feodorovna, the Grand Princess who was also the wife of the Moscow governor-general, volunteered to head the Committee of Assistance to the Wounded. The halls of the Imperial Grand Kremlin Palace and the Rumyantsev Museum turned into workshops to make all sorts of items badly needed in hospitals. Various public funds collected donations for the front.

There was hardly an office in Moscow, hardly an agency or a man in those days that did not give out part of his salary or allowance to the «Red Cross» sections. The Moscow gentry formed up a special medical detachment, organized nurse training, and sent special hospital trains to the front.

The noble patriotic impulse of the Moscow citizens found its expression in enthusiastic meetings of seamen and soldiers returning from the theater of operations. For example, to honor the heroes of the sea battle fought at the Chemulpo (Inchon) harbor, an Arc de Triomphe was erected in the district of Khamovniki near the Spasskie (Savior) Barracks. Ended in 1905 the war brought much suffering that found its reflection in the form of new buildings for orphan children of soldiers killed in action and almshouses for the invalids.

Though fought in the far east, the Russian-Japanese war as well as the events of January 9 in Petersburg started a tragic series of political events both in Moscow and in Russia, i.e. the revolution of 1905. On February 4, 1905 a certain terrorist, Kalyaev, killed Moscow's governor-general Grand Prince Sergei Alexandrovich. Same year an All-Russia strike shook the country in October. The response to these events was the Imperial Manifesto of 1905. It proclaimed personal immunity, freedom of speech, freedom of worship, freedom of unions and meetings. The election system became substantially more democratic. But it could not avert the growing crisis. In December Moscow witnessed an armed uprising of workers which lasted 12 days. Barricades were set up in the streets during the uprising. To suppress the resistance of their defenders the government had to bring in troops from St. Petersburg and shelled them with artillery fire. Later, a series of Moscow post-cards was issued to illustrate that a

I. Repin: The royal couple near Petrovsky Palace on Coronation Day, 26 May 1896.

number of buildings had been destroyed in the clashes. Incidentally, among them was the printing house which belonged to a famous publisher, I.D. Sytin. This may serve an indirect evidence of the unprecedented nature of these events and of the general public interest they inspired.

Apart from the political cataclysm of 1905 and mass riots against the tsarist regime that swept all over the country, bad natural disasters befell Moscow. The hurricane of 1904 was of tremendous power: the wind tore off roofs, many church domes were damaged. Eye-witnesses said that some houses had been «lifted» high up in the air just by sheer force of wind in the outskirts of the city where most buildings were wooden structures. In the spring of 1908 another calamity, this time a flood, befell the capital – a rare phenomenon to account for the calm nature of the Moscow River. Streets in Moscow's central part turned into canals, like those in Venice. The Aleksandrovsky Garden was also flooded. At that time it served a reminder of medieval Moscow when Neglinnaya rivulet had flown in its place. That year the flood coincided with the Easter festivities, so some resourceful citizens of the inundated districts had to have their traditional meals with their families sitting around on their roofs. The list of natural disasters that shook Moscow in the first decade of the 20th century would be incomplete without a reference to a number of great fires that had always been a traditional plague for Moscow. Thus, on the 14 of December 1901 a big fire occurred at the Metropol hotel which was being built at that time, then the Solodovnikovsky theater burnt down in 1907, and the roof of the Olympia theater collapsed same year.

Notwithstanding the complexity and ambiguity of the political situation in the country in the 1900s, Moscow could boast of vigorous and diverse cultural life. As new theater companies emerged, new theater halls were built for them. So, one of these was the Moscow Arts Theater founded by K.S. Stanislavsky and V.I. Nemirovich-Danchenko: in 1902 it moved to a building in the Kamergersky Lane which had been reconstructed by a famous Moscow modernist-architect F.O. Shekhtel. Well, it has been there ever since. In 1913 K. Marjanov and A. Sanin set up the Free Theater which won the following enthusiastic response on the part of the visiting Belgian poet Emile Verhaeren: «I have come to a firm conclusion that I wish to share with you: «Well, Moscow's been destined for high theatrical arts blossom. Neither Paris, nor London, nor Berlin could be a match for such a festive spirit, or could they give one so beautiful, so bright and «highly artistic» impressions as one can get in Moscow».

These flattering words spoken of the most innovative stages in Moscow in no way meant that the remaining eight theaters did not stage up interesting and fresh in spirit productions. The Korsh Theater, for example, was popular with the middle class, students and schooling youth. Of course, the Bolshoi Theater was very popular too. Performances were also staged by the Moscow Peoples' Houses for the low-income public. The cream of society – the gentry, the bourgeois and the military – were enticed to go to the halls of the governor-general's house and those of the Noble Assembly to listen to a concert or to take part in a party or a masked ball. Operas staged at the S.I. Mamontov's private opera house attracted artistic intelligentsia. Sketches for the scenery-work were provided by such famous painters as V. Vasnetsov, K. Korovin and some others. In these years the new Big Hall of the Moscow Conservatoire was opened, and a wide range of music lovers that immediately responded to new creations of N.A. Rimski-Korsakov and A.P. Borodin, A.K. Glazunov and A.K. Skryabin gratefully welcomed touring performers, all of them, not only just as famous as Pietro Mascagni who came to visit Moscow in 1904.

Ceremony of arrival in Moscow of the Emperor Alexander II on Coronation Day. (From the album dedicated to the coronation of Alexander II).

The tempo of Moscow's everyday cultural life can hardly be perceived without mentioning a great number of exhibitions organized in the capital at the turn of the century. They were extremely varied in terms of subject matter: medicine, electrical engineering, fishery, bee-keeping, navigation, photography, etc., including those dedicated to many anniversary celebrations. An exhibition held in the premises of the Historical Museum in 1899 dedicated to the 100th birthday anniversary of A.S. Pushkin was part of a wide program of Pushkin celebrations. It culminated in a mass rally at the foot of the Pushkin monument on Tverskoy Boulevard. A wonderfully sculptured monument on Arbat Square to another outstanding Russian classical author, N.V. Gogol, was unveiled on the 50th anniversary of his death. A special exhibition was also held to commemorate this event. The delegations from Vienna, Rome, Lyon, the British Academy of Sciences and Sorbonne saluted the Moscow public in their address during the ceremony. Apart from these big nation-wide celebrations a good many of other memorable dates were marked such as 200 years and 100 years of city hospitals, gymnasiums, institutes, etc.

The series of benchmarks that went down in history of both Moscow and Russia the cultural life would be incomplete without pointing out two tragic dates: July, 2, 1904, i.e. when A.P. Chekhov passed away, and November, 7, 1910, the day of L.N. Tolstoy's demise. Tolstoy's death in particular shook the whole of Russia, giving rise to a mighty wave of spontaneous meetings, many a student and worker demonstration. Lots of works and factories stopped to work on the day of the funeral.

At that time the artistic life in Moscow and in all Russia was an active part of the European artistic process. Moscow painters, architects and patrons of art used to attend the Arts Salons in Paris and took part in art exhibitions organized by the Darmstadt painters' union, Munich and Vienna Secessions. In 1908 Vienna became the venue of the 31st Secession exhibition specifically dedicated to modern Russian art. V. Serov, B. Kustodiev and N. Roerich were elected full members of the Vienna Secession. And at the turn of 1902-1903 Moscow held an exhibition in Petrovka Street named «New Styles in Architecture and Artcrafts». The builder of the Vienna Secession Hall Joseph Maria Olbrich himself came to attend the opening ceremony. Among the participants were Charles and Margaret Macintosh, Peter Berens, Henry van de Velde, Ian Cauteras, Hans Christiansen and some others. In 1908 and 1909 the exhibitions of the «Golden Fleece», for such was the name of one of the numerous artists' unions of the time, showed the works by Cezanne, Degas, Gauguin, Van Gogh, Matisse, Bourdelle, Maillol, Rodin, Braque, Derain, Rouault and others. Another artists' association, «The Jack of Diamonds», also held exhibitions in 1912 and in 1913 with the participation of Gleizes, Delaunay, Kirchner, Leger, Marc, Picasso and Metzinger.

Moscow artists, men of letters and poets debated endlessly on what ways the Art should take in the future and discussed the works of cubists, fauvists, Italian and Russian futurists, verbal declarations and creations of the founder of abstract painting, Vasily Kandinsky, musical experiments of A. Shenberg and A. Skryabin, and novelties of European literature. Quite often painters and composers whose creations attracted everybody's attention came to Moscow as guest-visitors. For example, a Swedish painter A. Zorn came to visit Moscow in 1897, Maurice Denis worked here in 1909, Henry Matisse visited Moscow in 1911 and E.F.T. Marinetti the famous leader of Italian futurism, came to deliver lectures in 1914. Gustav Mahler came to play in the concerts three times.

M. Tsikh: Pleasure-ground at Khodynka, 1856.

Some talented architects and artists grouped into a special circle in Moscow at the turn of the century. Such institutions of higher learning as the Moscow School of Painting, Sculpture and Architecture and the Stroganov School of Artistic Crafts played a major role in forming it. The graduates of these schools managed to shape up the distinctive identity of the Moscow artistic school. Its historical impact on Russian culture was also in the fact that it was in Moscow that the new «modern» style (Russian Art Nouveau) had evolved to complete its cycle. The penetration of new elements of the architectural language from such acknowledged European centers of artistic life as Vienna, Brussels and Paris coupled with the findings in the field of new aestheticism made by Russian artistic rotaries (as, for example, the roterie of S.I. Morozov, a talented businessman and patron of arts, in his country-mansion «Abramtsevo») found the most obvious expression in Moscow architecture.

One cannot imagine Moscow's cultural life without patronage. As far back as in 1873 P.M. Tretyakov, a merchant from Zamoskvorechie, opened the doors of his house for the lovers of art to come and see his gallery of Russian painting. He officially presented the city with his own collection, when it had grown up considerably, together with that of his deceased brother in 1893. Thus, the Moscow city Gallery named after the Tretyakov brothers – Pavel and Sergei – has been working ever since. The public response to this gift was enormous. It happened to be the first museum of Russian art in the country. (It was the opening of the Tretyakov Gallery that stimulated collecting Russian objects d'art and brought about the inauguration in 1898 of the second gallery of this kind in St. Petersburg, i.e. the Russian Museum). Some other patrons and collectors followed Tretyakov's example who had donated the city the whole of his house with the collection of paintings in it. Thus, another merchant, I.E.Tsvetkov, also gave his private collection to Moscow as a present placed in a house specially designed for the purpose by V.Vasnetsov. A rich industrialist, M.A. Morozov, donated his private collection to the Tretyakov Gallery too in 1910.

Many Moscow merchants went in for collecting paintings, some of them managed to make up exceptional collections, among them were Soldatenkov, Ostroukhov, Mamontov, Kharitonenko, etc. Many a private gallery was open for the public. It seems to be worthwhile to single out two most interesting collections of modern Western art, i.e. those of S.I.Tshukin and I.A. Morozov. Moscow had to thank these two expert merchants and expert patrons of art for having one of the most substantial collections of the French art of the end of the 19th and the beginning of the 20th centuries which includes many masterpieces by E.Manet, C.Monet, Renoir, Pissarro, Sisley, Degas, Cezanne, Signac, Van Gogh, Matisse, Toulouse-Lautrec, Marquet, Leger, Picasso, etc.

There had been 30 museums in Moscow by the beginning of the century, the most representative and beautiful among them being the Museum of Fine Arts. Opened in 1912, it also came to exist owing to, in large part, to wealthy merchants. The construction of the building was funded mainly by an industrialist, Yu. Nechaev-Maltsev. Some other patrons of art also made their contributions. The construction work commenced not far from the Kremlin in 1898 at a place specially chosen for the future museum. But it was opened only 14 years later. It's first director,

Unknown artist: A Walk at Ostankino. First half of the 19th century.

Professor I.V. Tsvetaev, proved to be a real zealot in the long course of its construction. Owing to his self-sacrificing effort, the museum, which had been initially intended to house a collection of the copies of the Moscow University for its students to be able to familiarize themselves with these copies of some world art treasures, began, as it was constructed, to turn into a remarkable storage place for European works of art. One of the first big collections of originals was the collection of the artifacts of Ancient Egypt which belonged to V.S. Golenishchev. These art treasures were bought and turned over to the museum by the Grand Princess Elizaveta Feodorovna who was the wife of the Moscow governor-general and also the sister of the Empress Alexandra Feodorovna.

Based on the collection of yet another merchant, A.A. Bakhrushin, a unique museum of theatrical art, the first in Europe, was founded in Moscow in 1913.

Philanthropy in Moscow at the beginning of the 20th century appears to be a special page in the city history as it literally embraced all aspects of life. Apart from object d'art collecting and opening museums, the efforts of the Moscow bourgeoisie were also focused on various educational institutions, hospitals, asylums for the old, orphans and invalids, cheap apartment houses for the poor, free-of-charge canteens for students, workshops and a good many other things. Thus, the opening of the so-called People's University in Moscow shall always be associated with the name of a gold prospector A.L. Shanyavsky. In the 1910s this university changed its location for a new building on Miusskaya Square. This was the second university to be opened in the city as the first one had been founded as far back as 1755 by M.V. Lomonosov. The People's University also became a place for numerous debates and public lectures with free admission. The Bakhrushins' Schooling House acquired well deserved popularity at that time as it united a number of educational institutions in an association. A certain rich lady, V.Morozova, funded the opening of a free municipal reading hall. A lot was done for the public weal that time in Moscow: clinics built with the Morozovs' money who were a famous merchant family, a hospital set up by another merchant Soldatenkov, a nursery orphanage opened and funded by Abrikosov, almshouses organized by the Medvednikovs, Tretyakov and Nechaev-Maltsev, free-of-charge apartment houses opened by Soldatenkov, the Bakhrushin brothers, the Mazurins, and Rakhmanova. Generous philanthropic investment coupled with the care of the city administration made Moscow hospitals and medical service the best in Russia at the beginning of the 20th century.

The city Duma and municipal administration also paid great heed to public education in the form of assistance to expand existing educational institutions and to build new ones. In 1901 a new building to house the University library was constructed, and in 1902 the Moscow Zoological Museum joined the complex of University buildings, yet another block, that of the Institute of Geology was added to it in 1914. This was also the time when the Institute of Physics and Geography, the Pedagogical Institute, the Institute of Archaeology and the Morozovs' Technical College opened their doors to receive first students. Great interest to natural sciences, agriculture and economy and their vigorous development produced a number of specialized museums such as the Museum of Hygiene, the Museum of the Russian Society of

Festivities on occasion of the 300th anniversary of the House of Romanov. Military parade in front of the Cathedral of Christ the Savior. 1913.

Poultry Farming and, to crown it all, the Polytechnic Museum, of which the first phase of building was finished in 1907.

Another important issue in the field of education was that of higher and secondary education for women opposed strongly by conservative-minded circles. Although the first educational institution to prepare women-pedagogues was established as far back as 1869, and the Higher Women's Courses were opened in 1872, these institutions of higher learning did not last long. The situation changed only in 1900, when the influx of Russian women to European universities became immensely large, and the Higher Women's Courses were opened again. These Courses expanded and had over 5000 students as early as 1911. Same year, i.e. in 1900, another courses for women were established with the Petrovskaya Academy of Agriculture, and in 1902 architectural courses for women were organized. This is how women's education commenced to develop at the turn of the century, embracing gradually ever more and new fields.

All these plentiful and diverse successes in business, culture, education, production and house building could not overshadow the other side of the city life. No matter how hard some educated works and factory owners tried to improve the life of their workers by opening canteens and kindergartens, staging concerts and theatrical performances, making contributions to their education, the way of life of workers' outskirts differed substantially from that of an average citizen. The reason was not only in that the outskirts were far less provided with essential services and utilities than the center – the streets were unpaved, there was neither gas nor electricity, no sewage, no water-supply, no trams – the only existing public transport in those days. The matter is that the need for living space was all there, there was insufficient affordable medical service, labor conditions at production facilities were extremely hard, and the percentage of physical labor was high. All this stirred up both spontaneous protests and organized riots against the government. It is not by mere chance that the workers' district of Presnya became the main stronghold of the 1905 uprising. The people's resistance there was suppressed only after a series of full-scale street combat.

Working days were relieved by holidays only, when people went out into the streets for merry-making. The most popular and populous festivities with swings, merry-go-round, puppet and farce booths, and wax figure «panopticums» were those on Shrive-tide and Easter. But gradually new kinds of entertainment were coming into being, i.e. cinema, motor rally, bike

A. Opekushin (sculptor), P. Zhukovsky, N. Sultanov (architects): The monument to Alexander II in the Kremlin. 1898. Demolished in 1918.

A. Opekushin (sculptor), A. Pomerantsev (architect): The opening of a monument to Alexander III near the Cathedral of Christ the Savior. 1913.

races and aeroplane flights. As early as 1896 N. Ryabushinsky, a Moscow millionaire, set up an aeronautics station in Moscow suburbs which gave rise to serious aviation activities. Although among sports, games and sport shows horse-races were traditionally the most popular, people also liked to play soccer and ice-hockey. But still Moscow could hardly be called a sporting city at that time.

But the most terrible was the life of Moscow slums whose inhabitants were not only tramps, cripples and dregs of the society but also peasants who had come to the city to earn for a living, but, having no profession, failed to get a job. The Khitrov Market was exactly such a sewer. The dweller of this very densely populated place had literally to struggle daily for a piece of bread or a space to sleep in a communal bunk shared by his like in a doss-house. Located not far from the city center, the Khitrov Market was a sharp contrast to its ebullient well-dressed bustling life subsiding usually by 2 or 3 o'clock in the morning when smart looking public was going out from theaters, cinemas and restaurants into the streets lit by electric lamp posts to finally get home. At the same time the miserable, drunk and sick people of Khitrovka wrapped in dirty rugs were creeping in to their cooped-up bunks to fall asleep instantly. Such slums attracted all sorts of criminals, thieves of every stripe, gang leaders looking for a place to hide at doss-houses, as well as ruined clerks, prostitutes and beggars. There were many beggars in Moscow: in the 1870s, for example, they numbered beyond 25 thousand, and this number did not go down at the turn of the century. Their ranks were continuously replenished by the numerous unemployed, which was an obvious consequence of the Russian-Japanese war and the 1905 revolutionary uprisings. The life of this social layer was an interminable tragedy: to get from this «bottom» up to a more comfortable social level was virtually impossible.

So, such is the general panorama of how the Muscovites lived in their city at the turn of the 20th century. Despite social contrasts and political crises, this period was a happy time for the city as it was the time of city renovation, economic growth and cultural blossom. Unfortunately, the World War and then the Revolution cut short this creative process, leaving many social, economic and cultural undertakings unrealized. Only now Moscow was able to attend to some of them.

Pokrovka near Armyansky Lane.
Colour-retouched photograph from the collection of E. Gautier-Dufayet.

Preservation of Cultural Heritage

The process of study, restoration and protection of historical national monuments in the pre-revolution Russia began in the second half of the 19th century. It was inspired by the emerging interest of the public towards the history of Russian culture. It happened after the war against Napoleon which gave rise to strong patriotic feelings in the Russian society.

The recognition of the services performed by the Russian people for their Fatherland found its expression in the edicts of Alexander I and of Nicholas I to erect a memorial complex of monuments in the field of Borodino, and to build a memorial temple, i.e. the Cathedral of Christ the Savior, to perpetuate the memory of the heroes of the 1812 Patriotic War. Some new museums, providing a systematic impression of Russian historical and cultural development, were opened under the patronage of the Imperial court during this period. An album of pictures depicting ancient samples of household utensils, weapons and architectural forms of Moscow, Novgorod and Kiev compiled by F.G. Solntsev, the Academician of Painting, was published in 1830. In 1862 a well-known scientist A.V. Viskovatov prepared a monumental thirty-volume work with 4000 tables entitled «The Historical Description of Russian Military Uniforms and Weapons» which is a priceless source for a military historian, artist and scientist even today.

The Imperial Archaeological Society opened sections of Russian and Slavic archaeology in 1851. Laws to protect the ancient Russian painting and architecture against damage and destruction were passed. In 1859 the Imperial archaeological commission was established to supervise archaeological excavations in Russia. It exercised its authority until the Revolution.

Collectors and devotees of local lore, history and economy who belonged to a very well-to-do circle of Russian society, played a major role in finding, describing and studying Russian antiquities. For this we should pay due tribute to such families as the Sheremetevs, the Golitsins, the Rumyantsev, the Uvarovs, the Bobrinskys, the Stroganovs, the Yusupovs, the Vorontsov-Dashkovs together with the numerous representatives of the Royal House as well as the following representatives of the Russian merchants: the Postnikovs, the Bolshakovs and the Rakhmanovs, these to be joined a bit later by the Soldatenkovs, the Morozovs, the Tretyakovs, the Tsvetkovs, the Bakhrushins, the Mamontovs, the Ryabushinskys and the Rukavishnikovs who made rare artistic collections of great value. Many ancient paintings from their collections were later described, reproduced and edited for the broad public by the historians of Russian art of the second half of the 19th century and the beginning of the

Strastnoi Monastery. Demolished in the 1930s.

20th century, namely F.I. Buslaev, I.E. Zabelin, V.V. Stasov, N.P. Kondakov, D.A. Rovinsky, I.E. Grabar and P.P. Muratov.

First steps undertaken by the Russian society to protect and restore historical monuments were rather rough and, unfortunately, entailed substantial losses incurred due to ignorance and lack of knowledge of the persons who were responsible for these monuments of Russian ancient art at the time.

Many wall paintings were lost in the renovation of ancient temples some of which underwent radical rebuilding. The frescoes of the 12th century's Temple of the Protection of the Virgin on the Nerl river were completely destroyed. Practically all frescoes of the 12th century in the Cathedral of the Savior's Transfiguration in the Mirozhsky monastery in Pskov and those similarly dated in the Cathedral of the Savior's Transfiguration in the town of Peryaslavl-Zalessky perished at the end of the 19th century. All this happened despite the repeated instructions issued by the Holy Synod prohibiting self-willed and unauthorized restoration works.

Whereas in the first half of the 19th century restoration was based on the existing practices which did not have substantial scientific traditions and were only beginning to evolve, in the late 19th and the early 20th centuries restoration acquired a true scientific character: architectural measurements were taken, frescoes to be restored were copied, and some steps were taken to keep historical monuments from disintegration.

Nikitsky Monastery. Demolished in 1935.

Varsonofievsky Monastery. Demolished in the 1930s.

Vozdvizhensky Monastery. Demolished in the 1930s.

Zlatoustovsky Monastery. Demolished in the 1930s.

Ivanovsky Monastery.

The 1st Congress of Archaeology held in 1869 produced a draft law on protection of monuments. The Moscow Archaeological Society established a special commission to protect ancient monuments in 1870. The Ministry of Education prepared a draft law on protection of monuments in 1876. Exclusive rights for excavations and supervision over ancient buildings and their restoration were delegated to the Imperial Academy of Arts and the Archaeological Commission by government's resolutions of 1889 and 1893.

The perception of the Russian society of its cultural heritage changed considerably at the end of the 19th century. The creative talent of the artistic master craftsmen of Ancient Rus was universally recognized.

In 1904 the government of the Empire established a commission to revise existing laws and resolutions pertaining to the protection of historical monuments in Russia with the Ministry of the Interior. These issues were also discussed at the All-Russia Congress of Architects held the same year and at the 2nd All-Russia Congress of Artists in 1912.

During the second decade of the 20th century anarchic tendencies inspired by new revolutionary theories came to existence and began to develop. These anarchic ideas were professed by certain individuals of whom many came to power after the October coup. It is from this time that the age of confrontation between the cultured and patriotically-minded public on the one hand, and the official authority composed in large of those individuals who were alien to Russian cultural heritage, on the other hand, commenced. The beginning of this strange and double entendre play is marked by and expressed in one of the first decrees of the Soviet power. It addressed to the people as follows: «...Fellow-citizens, do not move a single stone, protect monuments, buildings, old things, documents as all this is your history, your pride. Remember, that this is also the soil which will bring to life your own, new people's art».

All is right and correct. This decree seems to have a profound idea of protection and further development of national culture. It could and did inspire idealists and credulous people and put faith in them for the forthcoming spiritual renaissance of Russia. In fact, it could be topical today if it were issued today.

On November 3, 1917 in compliance with the resolution passed by the Presidium of the Moscow Soviet of workers' soldiers' and peasants' deputies a Commission on protection of art monuments and relics of the past was formed with P.P. Malinovsky as chairman. On its foundation it comprised 17 members, but as early as January 1918 it was 70 man strong as it had included new members from the professional Union of artists, sculptors, graphic artists and decorative art painters. So, it embraced prominent professionals capable of ensuring further development of scientific restoration in Russia.

Georgievsky (Voskresensky) Monastery. Demolished in the 1930s.

G. Afanasiev: Simonov Monastery. 1823. Demolished in the 1930s.

Spaso-Andronikov Monastery.

Novodevichy Monastery.

In this way a favorable situation was formed for establishing a central scientific institution designed to study, plan and direct all and any restoration works on historical and cultural monuments. In 1918 the initiative of the Commission with the People's Committee on Education (Narcompros) of the RSFSR resulted in opening the Central State Restoration Workshops under the leadership of I.E. Grabar, a prominent artist and a public figure. During the period of their existence these workshops carried out a great number of expeditions to study and mark for future restoration the most ancient monuments of Russian architecture in Moscow, in the village of Kolomenskoe, the Troitsko-Sergiev Lavra (monastery of the highest rank), Yaroslavl, Smolensk, the Boldino Monastery near Dorogobuzh, Samarkand and in other towns. The expeditions sent to the Upper Volga, Vologda and Archangelsk regions discovered a number of priceless architectural monuments that had been unknown before to historical science.

However, the triumph of scientific and artistic public was short-lived. Soon a reverse process to protection and preservation of Russian historical heritage began. The appeal passed in 1917 by the Executive Committee of the Soviet of workers', soldiers' and peasants' deputies was consigned to oblivion. Everything that had been restored during the period from 1918 to 1933, was destroyed. Not only the historical center of Moscow was affected but also other cities and towns of central Russia. A time of open, ostentatious destruction of historical monuments and at the same time of necropolises began. It is hard to say now what blame found the new authorities with the dead, but everywhere they provided all sorts of explanations referring to general development plans of Moscow and other cities which instructed to eliminate old cemeteries for laying out parks for working people to rest and recreate, or stadiums for their physical development with plentiful public toilets and strong drink stalls nearby. It was hard to imagine the degree of memory desecration of the passed generations.

The apotheosis of this anti-cultural policy was the instruction passed by the Soviet government to the Narcompros of the RSFSR to close down the Central State Restoration Workshops, which left the Soviet Union without any scientific organization that could lead the studies and restoration of monuments.

During the Great Patriotic War the protection and restoration of Russia's cultural heritage became a political issue though for a short time. Service was resumed in some churches and temples that had been previously closed and devastated, in Moscow and some other cities. Many priests were returned from exile. The Theological Academy opened in the Troitsko-Sergiev Lavra, and a journal entitled «Bulletin of the Moscow Patriarchate» started to be published. A campaign of appeals to the patriotic feelings of the Soviet people who had just lived through mass repressions and a series of planned annihilation activities targeted on unique monuments of national culture in Moscow and other historical cities, all in peacetime, began. These appeals contained the texts of orders issued by the German nazi command reflecting merciless attitude towards historical and cultural monuments. The notes of the People's Commissar of Foreign Affairs V.M. Molotov of January 6 and of April 28, 1942 underlined that alongside with monstrous crimes of the German nazi invaders there had been acts of vandalism of German troops and authorities against historical and architectural monuments in the occupied Soviet territories.

The first day of the war opened a new phase in the struggle for the protection of the historical heritage. This turn of development of the national self-consciousness among the cultured public undoubtedly contributed to the rise of patriotic feelings and hopes for the better. But as the war ended in victory, the initiatives displayed by the masses were very soon discontinued because the political aspect began to lose its urgency and topicality in the eyes of the leaders of the communist party and the Soviet government.

1941 is the year in which the Commission on protection and restoration of architectural monuments under the USSR Academy of Sciences was born. The Commission began to work immediately. In the first days of the war it started to examine the damage of the monuments of Russian architecture inflicted by German bombardment of Moscow and nearby towns and villages, i.e. Kalinin (Tver), Kaluga, Mozhaisk, Volokolamsk, Bogoroditsk, Yaropolets. The Commission was chaired by the associated member of the Academy of Architecture, Doctor of Architecture, Professor D.P. Sukhov, and comprised the most prominent scientists of the country such as the associated members of the

Donskoi Monastery. Engraving by P. Picard. 1714.

Academy of Architecture, Professors D.E. Arkin, N.I. Brunov, Professor S.A. Toropov, architects S.Ya. Zabello, P.N. Maximov, M.P. Tsaienko, and its expert team included architects I.E. Bondarenko, N.D. Vinogradov, V.I.Gridin, V.N. Podkluchnikov, N.P. Travin and A.S. Fufaev.

The Commission not only examined and measured the damaged or destroyed monuments but also worked on problems of their protection against incendiary bombs in close contact with the Moscow air defense headquarters, camouflage teams and firefighting squads. The government act of July 7, 1942 placed it under the newly organized Commission on «Registration and Protection of Art Monuments» answerable to the Committee on Arts of the Soviet of Peoples' Commissars of the USSR.

After the war ended, planning and building in Moscow resumed on the basis of the general plan for its reconstruction approved by the government in 1935 adjusted to meet new requirements. The post-war construction was based on old technique without making allowance for preserving precious historical heritage. As was expected the destruction of historical buildings started with the city center in full compliance with the traditional approach which had taken shape with the reconstructors of the capital. First, in 1945-1946 the walls and the gates of the 17th-18th centuries Bogoyavlenski Monastery were dismantled, then in 1947 a very big mansion-house of the late 18th century in Bolshaya Ordynka Street, plot No. 24 where prominent Russian musicians A.G and N.G. Rubinstein lived, was destroyed; later, in 1951 the southern portion of the Kitay-Gorod wall was demolished in Zaryadie together with the Prolomnie (Breach) Gates and the south-east Tower (1535-1538), the Temple of Nicholas the Wet of the 15th-17th centuries, the «Korchma» (Tavern) of the 17th century and a whole complex of civil architectural buildings of the 17th-19th centuries having medieval planning that had not been examined by either historians or archaeologists. In 1959-1961 trading rows on Kaluzhskaya and Taganskaya Squares were removed (first quarter of the 19th century, architect O.I. Bove).

Vysoko-Petrovsky Monastery. Temple of St. Peter, the Metropolitan.

All this was the beginning of the grandiose pogrom of Russian historical heritage which in terms of scope in no way was inferior to that of the 1930s and was growing, gaining momentum with each decade threatening to transform Moscow into a «model» communist city – the city of high-rise multi-story barracks deprived of slightest trace of history and high cultural spirit.

The Icon of Our Lady with the Orb

According to the Chronicles it was St. Prince Vladimir, after his baptism in Christianity in 988, who received the first Icon of Our Lady, called the icon of Jerusalem, from the Byzantine Emperor Leo IV the Philosopher. When Andrei Bogolyubsky went to sit as prince in Vladimir and Suzdal principality in 1155, he took the Icon of Our Lady from Vyzhgorod (Upper City of Kiev) along with him. Later it came to be known as the Icon of Our Lady of Vladimir. Since that time all Russian history has been under the continuous protection of icons of the Mother of God for a thousand years now.

When the Emperor Nicholas II abdicated, a certain Icon of Our Lady appeared miraculously in Moscow and the people began to call it the Icon of Our Lady with the Orb.

Feeling constant patronage of the Mother of God, the peoples of Russia glorified more than half thousand of such icons with the likeness of Our Lady. There were very many temples and altars sanctified in the name of the Mother of Our Lord Jesus Christ. Every Russian family had its own icon of Our Lady. Praying in front of her various icons, the Orthodox people saw not her likeness but the Mother of God Herself, their all-the-time Protector.

Some of the icons were glorified as Protector of the Russian State as was the Likeness of Our Lady with the Orb, others as Deliverer and Protector from illnesses and sorrows.

Despite a short historical period, this miraculously appeared Icon of Our Lady with the Orb, has a long and complicated legend. The first evidence of its miraculous apparition was published almost right after it had happened on March 2(15), 1917, i.e. of the day of the abdication of Nicholas II. A short one-page leaflet can be recognized now as the first of such publications. One side of it contains «The brief narration...» and the other – «The Prayer» addressed to the newly brought to light Likeness of Our Lady[1]. Same year in October the «Dushespasitelny Sobesednik» (lit.:Soul-Saving Interlocutor) published a more detailed «Narration» of which the language was treated by Nicholai Likhachev, a senior priest of the Temple of Ascension in Kolomenskoe where the icon called «The Icon of Our Lady with the Orb» made its reappearance[2].

The text of the leaflet narrates as follows:

«On February 13, 1917 a woman Evdokia Andrianova, p. of vil. [peasant of the village] of Pochinok, Bronitsky uezd (district), Zhiroshkinskaya volost (region), living at Pererva sloboda (outstanding group of houses), which is not far from Moscow, had a mysterious dream. As if it were for real, she heard a voice saying: «There is a big black icon in the village of Kolomenskoe, it should be taken, turned red, and prayed in front of it». This message impressed Evdokia Andrianova strongly as she was a religious woman. She could not help thinking of the voice she had heard all the time as if it were very close, so she began to pray hard, asking the Lord to send her another dream and it was sent to her. Now Evdokia saw a white church, and in it a woman sitting on the throne in all her glory. And she felt she was looking at the Heavenly Queen, Our Lady, though she could not see the face of the Mother of God.

This second dream captured so strongly the soul of Evdokia, and she set out for Kolomennskoe after the day of her Angel, i.e. on March, 1. On March 2 she came to see the priest and told him about all she had so mysteriously seen and heard. She begged of him to find that holy likeness revealed to her by the Lord. The Father lead her into the Temple and showed her all the honored saint icons but she did not recognize the one she had been told about in any of them. Then the priests remembered that there were some old icons in the basement of the white church. So the Father asked his men to bring a big icon from that basement, if any, consistent with what had been revealed to her. Nobody knew what that icon was. All those present thought it was the icon of the Ascension. Only when the icon had been cleaned and the centuries-old dust had been removed, all who stood there were strongly moved by the sight of the likeness of Our Lady, the Heavenly Queen, sitting in glory on her throne wrapped in a royal mantle and with a crown on the head and with the scepter and the orb in the hands and infant Christ on her lap giving blessing. With great joy and emotion Evdokia Andrianova fell in awe in front of the Likeness of the Virgin and then asked to administer a public prayer of gratitude with acathistus. So, this was the likeness which had been shown to that woman in her dream.

The news of the revealed likeness spread fast, so the Christian people went to see it to address all their sorrows, asking the divine Protection of the Virgin in the time of troubles and receiving the miraculous good and help from the Mother of God. The people unanimously began to call the miraculous icon «the Icon of Our Lady with the Orb» because it was the likeness of the Holy Virgin, the Heavenly Queen with the scepter and the orb».

The other side of that leaflet carries a prayer reflecting both the confusion and at the same time the hopes of the people in that hard year.

«O Our Lady, Most Holy Theotokos, holding in Thy hands the King of Heaven, supporting by the palm the whole universe! Grateful to Thee we are for Thy mercy unspoken by the word of mouth, that Thou favored to bring Thy holy miracle-making likeness of Thee to our sinful eyes in these crafty cruel days that have, as a whirlwind, as a windy storm, befallen our native land, in these days of shame and disgrace, in these days of destruction and profanation of our sacred values by the those senseless people who not only by their heart but also by their bold mouths say: «There is no God!» and who show absence of faith in all they do. Grateful to Thee we are for Thou have looked from the High Heaven upon sorrows and misfortunes of Thy Orthodox children, and as a bright sun Thou put joy in our eyes tired of grief so that they can see today the Likeness of Thee with the Orb! O Blessed Mother of God, Mighty Helper, Strong Protector, we thank Thou with fear and awe and as Thy miserable servants we fall down in front of Thee with emotion and distress in the heart, with tears in the eyes, and beg of Thee, and wail to Thee: Save us! Save! Help us! Help! See, we are perishing! Our lives are coming closer to hell, let many sins, many troubles, many enemies escape us. O Queen of Heaven, hit with that scepter of Thee bearing God's Powers and turn our enemies both seen and unseen into dust, into smoke, for they fight, for they slander our Orthodox Faith and Church, for they are willing to ruin our Native Land, please disrupt their vain plans, please forbid them! Please plant the truth, peace and joy in our hearts, O Our Lady! Please restore calmness, prosperity, serenity and love to each other devoid of hypocrisy! Use Thy Orb, O Holy Virgin, to stop the turbulent streams of dishonesty and lawlessness that are threatening to throw the Russian land in the terrible abyss! Please help us, for we are weak and faint-hearted, feeble and depressed, put strength in us, please lift up our hearts! Save us who under that Orb of Thee have always been saved, and shall always sing, extol and glory Thee the Mighty Protector of the Christian race, now and for ever and ever! Amen».

In this prayer addressed to their Protector the Orthodox people in the face of the forthcoming troubles, «... to ruin their native land» seeing the «vain plans» of the new rulers of the beheaded state, asked Her to destroy the enemies who were slandering their Church and essential ethics of human communal life.

I.M. Andreyev whose memoirs were published in Jordanville in the middle of this century and who had witnessed the appearance of this icon, described the initial impact of this event on the Russian people: «The news of the appearance of the new icon on the day of the Tsar's abdication, i.e. March 2, 1917, spread around very fast, first in the suburbs, then in Moscow, and finally throughout Russia. A great number of people started to come to the village of Kolomenskoe. And the icon began to make miracles of healing body and soul ailments – a fact of which evidence was based on the reports of those who had been cured. So they began to show the icon in nearby temples, factories and works, returning it to the Church of the Ascension of the village of Kolomenskoe only on Sundays and holidays»[3]. They also made several copies of the icon on orders that came from the parishioners of some churches. One copy was made especially for the Cathedral of Christ the Savior.

«Knowing the exceptional power of faith and prayer of the Emperor Nicholas II and his special awesome worship of Our Lady (let us remember the cathedral which had the Feodorovskaya Icon of Our Lady in Tsarskoe Selo), we can have no doubt that he managed to persuade the Heavenly Queen to take from him the powers over the people which had rejected his tsar – the anointed sovereign. So the Virgin came into the «House of Theotokos» prepared for her by the whole course of the Russian history at the hardest time for this God-chosen people at the moment of its deepest inner degradation, and took upon Herself the succession of the powers of the Russian state», – continued Professor Andreyev[4].

After taking the revived patriarchate Patriarch Tikhon gave his blessing to prepare the Acathistus for the Icon of Our Lady with the Orb. «For which he ordered to collect part by part from each available in Russia acathistus that had been written for other icons of Our Lady before, and to name the work as «The Acathistus of the Acathistuses», – remembers one of the worshippers of this icon[5]. Initially, this Acathistus was published in Russian in Paris[6], and with the blessing of His Beatitude the Patriarch Alexii II it was published in Moscow in 1995[7].

The newly appeared Icon soon disappeared... «Severest repressions befell the heads of its worshippers who prayed in front of its copies throughout Russia. Thousands of believers were arrested, priests who composed the service and canon were shot, and icons proper were removed from all the churches. Today, the service with the acathistus of the Icon of Our Lady with the Orb is performed only in the catacomb Church in the Soviet Russia because the official Soviet Church in its attempts to please the theomachist rulers forbids these prayers», – this is what was written in the «Narration...» which ends the Acathistus published in Jordanville in 1984[8].

Today, the legends of the miracle-making icon that allegedly vanished in the years of the Soviet rule, have been shattered. It has been established documentarily that after divine service was abolished in the Temple of Ascension in the village of Kolomenskoe (in 1922), this icon together with other icons of the Temple was placed in custody of the State Historical Museum. In 1988 the icon was temporarily turned over to the Publishing Department of the Moscow Patriarchate (as that was the pretext). Then, in compliance with the resolution of the government on returning the Church property to its legal owner, the icon, on request of the Patriarch of Moscow and All-Russia Alexii II, was to be kept in Kolomenskoe. Thus, on July 29, 1990 the Icon of Our Lady with the Orb was met in Kolomenskoe by the religious procession of the clergy and the people of the parish. So, the miracle-making icon is now placed at the right choir in the main part of the Temple of Our Lady of Kazan[9].

Icon of Our Lady with the Orb

Moscow's Super Problem

«The savage, mean and ignorant do not have respect for the past, and they grovel only before the present».

A.S. Pushkin

The «super problem», as it has been agreed to be called, is a problem of preservation of the city of the past in the city of the present and of the future. It is eternal and at the same time it is sort of an «addition» (over and beyond) to a multitude of everyday, topical, bustling, absolutely «earthly» problems of a modern city. Be it a problem of preserving ancient Athens in the present and future Greek capital, or ancient Rome in the Italian capital, or a medieval London in the British capital, or the old Beijing in the capital of China, ... and finally old or as agreed ancient Moscow in the capital of Russia.

A city with a long past is unusual in particular. It has absorbed centuries-old cultural and spiritual heritage of the people and thus has become a storage of its artistic and architectural values. In becoming such, it has transformed into a new quality and cannot be compared with any modern city irrespective of its size. One should not make such a comparison because essentially different phenomena will have to be collated. This difference, their incomparability can be clearly seen if we take Moscow for example.

All Russians who come to see Moscow do not normally go to its new high-rise multi-story glass and concrete precast panel micro-districts. They go to the center instead to pray in front of its holy likenesses (as if they have come home), to see the people's and the state's values, to have a look at ancient relics, places of interest... and just to walk in «the good old and dear streets». All the visiting people see is theirs, and they feel it, all they look at is as if it were their native home, in fact it is a feast for their soul, it is a buttress of their self-consciousness. Strange but when they leave Moscow, they think that they have seen all and know what Moscow is. And all this is absolutely true. The people have always meant by Moscow its historical center, and be it known that the outlying districts have already their own names.

The word combination «super problem» also contains a hue of something «burdensome» and not only that of something of a «surplus». Herewith this «burden» should be understood as something polysemantic. As an «economic burden» of a modern city and a state, for example, it is linked with the volume of heritage (in this case we have an absolute «burden»). And if this heritage has been badly preserved and is numbered in terms of just a few monuments, or be it a few architectural ensembles that have survived, the super problem does not seem to encompass any economic burden (in this case there is no problem at all). And what if that heritage has survived relatively well and in «plentiful» numbers, and the architectural monuments make up complete complexes of ancient buildings and one can see ancient town-building structural schemes and systems?.. Then, it is not just architectural, but town-building heritage, and a task to preserve it becomes actually an economically «burdensome» problem.

But we must bear in mind that this «burden» of the super problem can depend upon a ratio of the ancient town to the modern town expressed in percentage (relative «burden»). In the 1930s the ancient Moscow area, being in the center, made for about 15 per cent of the total city area (there was «plenty» of heritage then). During the reconstruction and renovation of Moscow this percentage badly affected its fate: more than half thousand unique architectural monuments were destroyed.

Today, ancient Moscow accounts for only 2 per cent of the total area of the Moscow agglomeration – a fact that has practically reduced to nil all the former causes of its destructive reconstruction. This is why Moscow's super problem, even if judged according to this «percentage» criterion, ought to be set forth and re-examined with regard to the 21st century!

This super problem may turn out to be a «super burden» not with respect to its economics, but in terms of city-building when it is aggravated by clumsy incompetent (ambitious) and perhaps even ill-intended deeds of previous city-builders (in this case we shall have an «artificial burden»). Thus, in 1935 a grandiose radial traffic-relief grid system of the city of five million was intentionally «superimposed» upon ancient Moscow and its medieval streets! Just think: 15 multi-kilometer radial avenues were cut to join the old city – today's 2 percent of the total city area – from all sides(!?). This done, not a single of the four planned «traffic-relief» rings to lessen the «suffocating» center have been constructed so far (even through at one time empty stretches) (?). Meanwhile the city grew to eight and the megapolis to ten million people. The dynamic pressure upon the historical center is increasing. It is becoming stronger and stronger proportionally to the increasing number of individual transport of the whole agglomeration.

As a result, Moscow's super problem has become infinitely more complex and much heavier as it has interwoven with the artificially complicated transport problem of this multi-million city as a whole. If even the worst comes to the worst and all of ancient Moscow were destroyed, the burden of the transport problem would still be there because of the «funnel-type» radial system of the whole agglomeration chosen in 1935.

To disentangle ancient Moscow from the gigantic radial traffic system, to save the sacred city from the fetid engassed «traffic maelstrom» is a super hard problem for the Muscovites to solve in the 21st century, our foremost duty being to develop the ways for its solution.

What is more, this super problem is not only a problem of economics and city-building but also a problem of ethics and morals... If we draw an analogy, it is sort of akin to the responsibility of the grown-up children to support their old and for this reason weak folks, or to the sacred responsibility of the descendants to always remember their ancestors and to keep memory of them (including material in the form of relics). Such practice has been traditional

Strasnaya Square. Church of Demetrios Solunsky (of Thessalonika). 1791. Demolished in 1933.

Built-up area at the place of today's Manezhnaya Square. Second half of the 19th century – beginning of the 20th century. Demolished in 1932.

and indisputable from time immemorial in Russia. Only a «Herod» or an «alien» who entered the family by this way or another and who thought himself freed of his «blood responsibility» could refuse to support his old men.

In the last instance the explanation is that the city community newcomers, thinking themselves not bound by the responsibility to preserve the heritage as they are alien to it, are active in trying «to write off» the super problem in their own way. All sorts of pretexts, excuses and vindication are invented to justify their destructive effort. And the best time to most obviously and tangibly realize this, as the reader will see later, was the Soviet period – the period of the reconstruction of historical Moscow under the leadership of the internationalist power.

The super problem is also linked with aesthetics of the highest order. The ancient city makes the modern city look more beautiful. It can also do the same with the city of the future. If «the beauty is supposed to save the world», this beauty should be taken care of, it should always be seen, felt and emotionally comprehended... This is what is required from the coming generations in particular. The youth ought to be fostered in it through artistic education to see it, feel it and comprehend it emotionally... particularly with respect to the beauty of national art and architectural treasures. And since any national culture cannot spring up in wilderness, for it is something inherited, the descendants ought to continue the traditions passed over to them by their ancestors guided by their vision of the world and its beauty.

Finally, the super problem is closely linked with the love to the native land, the ancient city being a tangible symbol of this land as a whole for each fellow-citizen. Should we spend more time on proving the obvious that this love ought to burn unquenchably in the hearts of all forthcoming generations? But only if this love is there, a mighty movement of people capable of self-sacrifice for their Fatherland can emerge and once again one can here: «Though vast is Russia, but there's no place to step back for Moscow's behind!»

* * *

There are three possible ways to resolve this super problem.

The first way is to preserve the ancient city as much as possible to use it mainly in the function of an open-space museum center. One should not look at this approach condescendingly or scornfully (which is generally expected from the demagogues as they always do so). The old city is always bigger than a museum. It is a storage battery of the generic ancestral memory continuously «feeding» the descendants so that they would not turn into «Ivans with ancestry unknown». What is more, the old city is the essence of the spiritual potential of the people, it is a vault where its «cultural and genetic core» is stored. And, finally, the old city is a city-building symbol of the nation and the state. This is why Moscow should be a traditional place for key functions of the capital city: public meetings, government and Orthodox Church activities; it should be a place for regional and foreign representations. The best variant for the functional existence of the old city in the modern city is a separation of the former in a special city unit. This will allow it not only to live in a special way but also to improve, to restore shabby buildings and reconstruct technical utility infrastructure without additional «hindrance».

The Resolution «Regarding the General plan of reconstruction of the city of Moscow» of 1935 had the following declarative lines: «The CC of the VKP(b) [All-Union Communist Party (of bolsheviks)] and the Soviet of the People's Commissars of the USSR reject the projects pertaining to preservation of the existing city (actually, the ancient center was meant – Author) as the country's secured museum-city and suggesting the construction of a new city beyond the limits of the existing one»[10]. This looks like a right-wing position.

The second way is to destroy the old city completely, and through it the super problem is done away with all by itself. The destruction of Moscow has always been a longed-for dream of the Russian people's «open» enemies. We can remind our readers of

Lubyanskaya Square. Beginning of the 20th century.

Moscow's complete ravaging by Batu Khan in 1238, or by Tokhtamysh Khan in 1382 or Mengli-Guirey in 1571. Later, united into multilingual hordes, the external enemies were coming up to the city not under national colors but under «multinational». In the Time of Troubles at the beginning of the 17th century Moscow was jointly burnt by the Catholics – the Polish, the Lithuanians and the Germans, in 1812 Napoleon brought the army comprising contingents of almost all European nations under the masonic leadership, and in 1941 Hitler did the same but under the fascist colors, the slight difference being that whereas the Catholics and masons tried to burn Moscow down to ashes by fire, the fascists wanted to drown it by water. But it stood all the same having gone through fire and water!

The aforesaid Resolution of 1935 proceeded with the following: «The CC of VKP(b) and the Soviet of the People's Commissars of the USSR either reject proposals to dismantle the existing city and to build a city with a radically different plan in its place». These words look as sort of a left wing position.

The third way is to destroy the old city on a selective basis and it can be destroyed during a long time by portions. Its carcass shall provide the foundation for a new modern city. As a result, we shall have «neither one thing nor another», not even an ill synthesis of old and new for the simple reason that a new city is usually built without the old one in mind but according to a new general plan.

So, the Resolution of 1935 proclaimed the third way, and a new general plan had to be developed: «The CC of the VKP(b) and the Soviet of the People's Commissars of the USSR think that in formulating a plan for Moscow we should proceed from the preservation of the essentials of the existing historical city but on the basis of its radical re-planning through decisive streamlining the network of its streets and squares...» So, this was the «general» line.

A more detailed and elaborate story on how the capital of the Soviet country was re-designed and then reconstructed will follow

Prechistenskie Gates' Square. Beginning of the 20th century. Church of the Descent of the Holy Spirit. Demolished in the course of the construction of the first lines of the Moscow subway.

further in the book. Here we shall confine ourselves with a note that ancient Moscow was dealt with in a barbaric way. No professional feasibility study was carried out and naturally they started to destroy it, not knowing what they were destroying and, perhaps, not wishing to know it at all. Suffice it to say that the ancient city planning was not a combination ring-radial, but only the outer build-up ring was radial which had formed as capitalism evolved. It looks as though having accepted the radial system of the city of capitalism they started to build a city of socialism, while destroying the city of feudalism. Many things were really very strange not to say «insane».

First millions of rubles were spent to escheat and bring down the old living space, then billions were spent to build new living space practically of the same scope and area in the same place. The surplus space for living was almost zero, and the people's money was wasted for a senseless «wheel-spin». Anyway, it appeared as if the principal aim was to wipe the ancient sacred city off from the face of the earth.

The third way had to be chosen, because it was the only one that could be used openly by the international forces in a national medium. This is the root of all strange features of Moscow reconstruction and its result – «neither one thing nor another». Thus, by the beginning of the historical regeneration of Moscow in 1993, we had been living in a crippled ancient sacred city and an unfinished monster.

Life itself proved this way of resolving the super problem to be senseless and singled out the only possible alternative which is the revival of the lost quality of the city's historical medium because armed with a new vision of this problem expressed in a word – regeneration, one cannot rely only upon the diminishing remnants of the national heritage.

* * *

What have we lost so far?

In essence this super problem of Moscow showed itself as early as the beginning of the 18th century after the capital of the Russian State had been moved to the banks of the Neva River. Having reigned in Moscow for 20 years altogether, Peter I came to hate it for its patriarchality and strong traditions which stood as an insurmountable barrier in the way of all his undertakings and novelties. He had strong concerns that all the transformations in Russia might fade out after his death. Personal negative emotions added up to the tsar's attitude towards Moscow. As a result, as Fokkerot wrote in 1737: «His hatred towards Moscow for what had happened to him there in his green years, was so sharp that he would have willingly razed it to the ground if only that could have been possible under a plausible pretext and without great irritation on the part of the people. Thus, under the pretext that mason workers were in great demand in Petersburg he forbade under fear of severe punishment to build new or to repair old buildings in Moscow no matter how big or small they were, which lead to the situation that a multitude of the most beautiful buildings collapsed and turned into ruins»[11].

In 1718 the tsar forbade to have domestic churches in Moscow, later this prohibition was also re-affirmed in 1762 and 1800[12]. If we remember that there were more that 200 domestic churches in the old capital at the turn of the 17th – 18th centuries, we can only imagine what great damage was caused to Moscow's many-cupola cityscape.

In the 1760s the Senate and the Synod carried out a revision of church and monastery staff organization throughout Russia. As a result of this secularization, a certain number of churches in Moscow was to be closed down and demolished. In this way during the whole of the 18th century the traditionally multi-templed gold-domed silhouette of the old capital was growing poorer and poorer, the process being rather active.

The walls of Bely-gorod (White Town) were dismantled and the ramparts of Skorodom were removed at the end of the 18th century. And the beginning of the 19th century was marked by a gigantic conflagration of the whole city in the time of the invasion of Napoleon's multi-lingual army of many a European tongue. After that Moscow was restored on the basis of classicism. This explains why it wore new «European architectural clothes» in the middle of 19th century. However, hundreds of rebuilt churches and belfries, thousands of golden domes and crosses rose again over the sea of traditionally low classical buildings. The good old Kremlin with its indented walls, marqueed towers and golden domes stood in the center as before. Moscow of that time still retained its unique panoramas, joyful appearance and national «image», a combination of its ancient picturesque plan, with «organic» streets and lanes, cozy yards and small courtyards, and low dwelling houses.

To transform such a purely «Russian image» of ancient Moscow into an average European or Americanized something, it would have been required to carry out another something, almost unthinkable, i.e. to pull down its plentiful temples, having taken away all the gold from their domes, and to substitute high buildings for low ones. Such an opportunity appeared only at the beginning of the 20th century when our «kinfolk» Soviet power took over.

The active destruction of ancient temples in Moscow began outright, i.e. in 1918, and continued practically all through these 70 years. According to the latest calculations, 433 unique churches were destroyed (excluding side-churches). This figure accounts for 2/3 of all existing churches in the city. Such a loss, on the one hand, in combination with the hastily launched active invasion of «high-rise architectural bad taste» into the city center, on the other hand, has naturally affected the capital. It began to lose its «individuality». In the 90s the process reached a dangerous line beyond which «the disappearance of historical Moscow» would have been irrevocable. Even the Kremlin already dismantled by 1/3 found itself surrounded from on all sides by «mastodon buildings», a theater and a palace of congresses let alone other smaller structures had been dragged into it. Almost everything was done with a merry slogan: «One cannot go ahead, looking backwards!»

* * *

What has been left of the priceless Moscow's architectural and building heritage, especially that of the ancient and medieval city, by the 21st century? What makes us all the same, though «having made calculations and shed tears», speak of the ancient heritage of this city in a positive way and set forth its super problem once again to be resolved through the «first way» only?

– First of all, it has already been mentioned that historical Moscow makes up 2 % of the total modern city-agglomeration area (and together with the area within Kamer-Kolezhskie ramparts it is 6%). The demagogy based on the premise that the Muscovites living in semi-basement quarters and slums must be provided with decent modern living space, has disappeared. It is not possible at the expense of these 2 percent to rectify the chaot-

Red Gates' Square. Demolished in 1927 – 1928.

ic layout of production facilities, or liquidate over-cumbersome crammed-up network of warehouses and depots, or streamline railways and other elements of the city economy and utilities as it was declared out loud in 1935. All this demagogy has irrevocably gone down into the nightmarish past. So today these two percent of our «Grandmother-Moscow» need 100 percent of attention and care for its «reanimation and rehabilitation».

– Only architectural monuments have been counted in Moscow until recently[13]. Now we also began to add and count built-up areas constituting the frame for these monuments, both valuable and not as valuable but traditional and low which make up the historical medium. All this, i.e. monuments plus medium, makes up 60 percent of all the now existing buildings in the old city center. Even this still looks rather discouraging because high and high-rise buildings do not let us see those temples that have survived, you cannot see even their cupolas as «mastodon houses» embedded into old blocks «suppress» older buildings.

– Why does then Moscow even in such a state still continue to look distinctive almost in any of its corners? It is still distinctive, as a matter of fact, because its city-building monuments continue to exist (some of them in good condition) alongside architectural monuments and historical built-up medium enframing them.

A special professional study of ancient Moscow development was carried out within the last two decades (70s-80s) by M.P. Koudryavtsev, T.N. Koudryavtseva and G.Ya. Mokeyev – scientists of the Russian Architecture Sector of the Central Architectural Theory and History Research Institute. The results of this research are presented in the first book of this anniversary publication. It seems practical to briefly remind the readers of them but with regard to Moscow's super problem.

Two notions were formulated in the course of the mentioned study of ancient Moscow: «city designing and building monuments» and «city designing and building art monuments», the classification being somewhat conventional as city-building monuments are not completely deprived of «art». But still...

– According to the study the city designing and building monuments include mainly layout systems and city formations. The «form and function» criterion has been formulated to outline them. Thus, the following has been found to constitute these monuments of ancient Moscow: the developed urbanized city landscape; the system of towns and villages of Muscovy of the 8th-12th centuries; the fortress (Kremnik) and three open suburbs (Veliky, Zagorodie and Zarechie) of the 12th-15th centuries, and then of the 16th-17th centuries; the system of fortresses (the Kremlin, Kitay-Gorod, Bely-Tsar Town and Skorodom); city development (the Kremlin, Kitay-Gorod, Zaneglimenie and Zamoskvorechie); trading quarters (the Upper, Middle and Lower Rows of Kitay-Gorod, Okhotny [Hunters'], Kuryatny [Poultry] and Obzhorny [General Foods] Rows of Zaneglimenie, Nogai market place of Zamoskvorechie and trading grounds at most gates of fortress system); street junctions (sector, semi-circular and circular); fan-branched streets of phased layout development; the whole of spiral-fan layout of ancient Moscow[14].

As the ancient city suffered great destruction caused both by time and by man, and as it was partially transformed in the 18th-20th centuries, a greater part of the ancient city designing and building monuments comes out only in an «archaeological» form. However, such monuments as the Kremlin, Kitay-Gorod, Zamoskvorechie, fan-branched street system, street junctions and ancient city layout system have generally survived in a fairly good condition (some of up to 70-80%) and allow us to speak today of their preservation, restoration and regeneration as a must for now and for the future.

According to the aforesaid study the city designing and building art monuments include mainly composition town formations. The «content and form» criterion has been formulated to outline them. The following has been found to constitute these monuments of ancient Moscow: the Cathedral Rus monument; the Military Glory monument; and such symbolical monuments as «Moscow – the Home of the Most Holy Theotokos», «Moscow – the Second

V. Bazhenov: Pashkov House. 1786. Church of Nicholas Streletsky. Demolished in the course of construction of the first lines of the Moscow subway.

Jerusalem», «Moscow – the Third Rome», «Moscow – the Symbol of the Heavenly City» as well as ancient Moscow designing and building pyramid (formal) composition; and «Moscow – the City of Gold Domes» as a structural and imaginative monument of ancient Moscow on the whole.

These monuments of city designing and building art are in large part structurally connected but scattered formations. They can be compared with scattered «patches» of different species of trees in a mixed forest: «islands» of spruce, pine, oak, birch, maple... All these trees of different species share their beauty with each other especially in autumn, and this mixed forest taken as a whole is the beauty of all Rus-Russia.

The architectural monuments, constituting the scattered «patches» of city designing and building art monuments, neither emerged spontaneously, nor were scattered at random. They were mainly placed at a certain time with a very clear idea in mind, i.e. consistent with the hierarchy of building structures, pyramid composition concept of city building, separate compositional systems, complexes, ensembles, which is explained in the first book of this edition[15].

The ancient Moscow monuments of city-building art suffered great losses and particularly in the Soviet period. So these «patches» of monuments of the Cathedral Rus, the Military Glory, the Symbols of «the Home of the Most Holy Theotokos», and, especially, of the «Heavenly City» have been decimated, mildly speaking. They took their time to topple down «these trees» and they cut them down mercilessly like barbarians, we might say, for, on the one hand, they did not know what they were doing, and, on the other hand, they were trying to raze everything to the ground to build their new world. However, the architectural monuments that make up the basis and foundation of the pyramid (formal) composition of ancient Moscow, have survived. Therefore, not everything even with regard to the city-building composition has been lost.

The monuments of city designing and building revealed through extensive research have added up considerably to the total volume of sacral heritage of ancient Moscow and have brought this heritage up to so complete a perception that is well deserved by our priceless and sacred city. But it seems necessary to say a few special words about the last of all these monuments.

* * *

«Gold-domed Moscow» is a well known poetic expression widely used to describe ancient Moscow.

The greatest «density» of golden domes has always been the Kremlin's most distinctive feature. It looked as if it were a enormous «candle stand with candles in it», its sun-shine domes burning like fire in the midst of Moscow upright towards the Heaven.

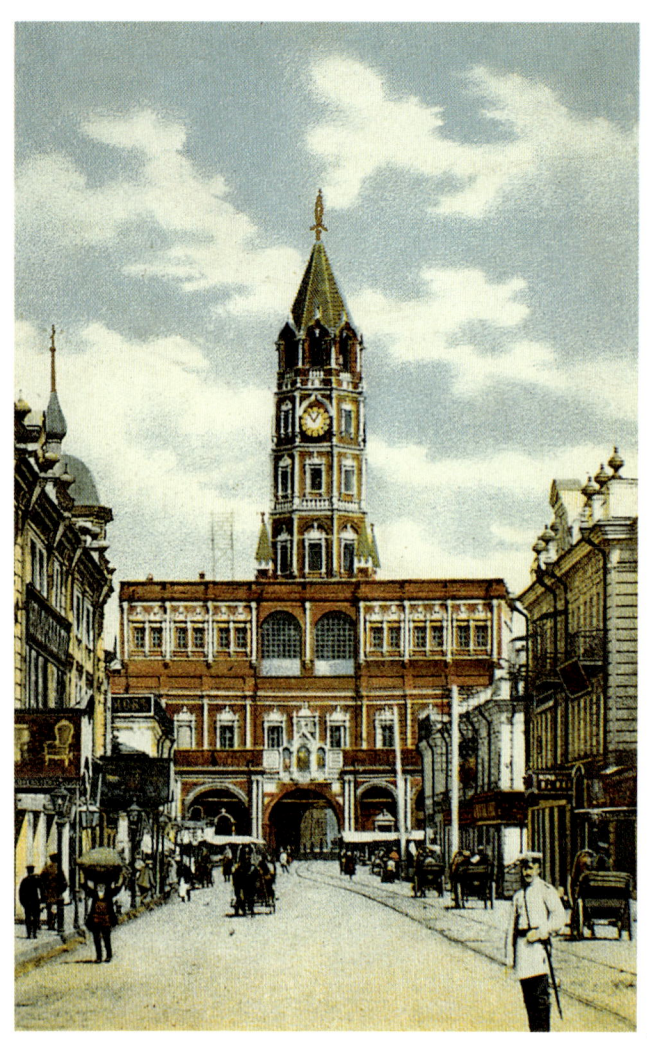

Choglokov: Sukhareva Tower. 1695. Demolished in 1934.

70 of more than a hundred domes and cupolas in the Kremlin were covered with gold leaf. Even now having lost half of its «gold», the Kremlin still looks like a gold-domed city. Unfortunately, this impression is produced owing to a contrast to faded and, therefore, dull golden-cupola temples of the ancient capital, or to those shielded by high modern buildings.

«Gold-domed Moscow» is also an image of the city unique to this world and, of course, an outstanding city-building phenomenon. The «fires» of golden domes of its Orthodox temples that shone in the sun also supported their «fiery tops» (about three hundred «fiery» temples had been built in Moscow, nearby villages and in country-palaces by the beginning of the 18th century). Cupolas of plentiful domestic churches and yard churches added to Moscow's «gold-domed» looks. Even without a precise count of the number of cupolas this speaks for the fact that Moscow has been making that special, unforgettable «golden-cupola» impression since the 16th century.

«Gold-domed Moscow» is not just a unique image of our sacred capital, past but not forgotten. It is also one of the goals and a criterion of the future regeneration of ancient Moscow. It is a goal to strive for continuously, it is a criterion to commensurate daily our activity to what has been done with respect to future city-building. Ancient Moscow's 2%, being so small a value, will allow to bridle the ambitions of irresponsible present-day and future barbarians with architecture and to defend the city from their wild invasions or wedge attacks.

The methods of the regeneration of gold-domed Moscow are simple. If it has been actively destroyed for the last 70 years, time has come to actively restore it. But this must be done on the basis of a «humane» approach which is, in essence, rigid implementation of two contrasting processes that should take at least 50 years. The first process is the lowering of multi-story buildings or their complete liquidation, and dismantling high-rise structures after the expiry of their amortization period (to prevent the danger of collapse). The second process must be focused on the restoration of the gold-dome panorama throughout the whole of the ancient city, adding «gold» to all necessary new constructions (not exclusively to temple buildings). By the time these two processes come to an end, the gold-domed city must emerge once again in the center of the Moscow agglomeration. Besides, it is also necessary to resolve the problem of easing traffic overload in the historical center of Moscow. As it is a very special subject it will be dealt with in the fourth book of the second volume of this edition.

---

[1] The leaflet was printed on ordinary newsprint sized 35.5 x 28 cm. It has «The brief narration of the Icon of Our Lady with the Orb which miraculously appeared at the village of Kolomenskoe in the suburbs of Moscow» on its front side; the following is printed on the left bottom margin under the printed frame: «Printery of the Ryabushinskis' Partnership». The back side contains the following: «Prayer to the Most Holy Theotokos in front of her miracle-making icon called «Our Lady with the Orb»; the following is printed under the frame: «Published by the Varnavinski People's Society of Sobriety. Moscow, Semionovskaya zastava on the square, Tram No. 22».
[2] Likhachev N. Narration of the appearance of the Icon of Our Lady in the Church of Ascension at the village of Kolomenskoe of Moscow uezd // «Dushevny Sobesednik», October 1917, pp. 314 – 315; reprinted in «Moskva» magazine Nos. 5, 6, 1992.
[3] Cited according to: Russia before the Second Advent. (Compiled by Sergei Fomin)., M., 1994, pp. 223 – 227.
[4] Same as 3, p. 226.
[5] Madam E.B. Same as 3 with reference to «The Orthodox Rus» magazine, 1967, No. 6, p.6.
[6] The complete acathistus or the Acathistus of the Acathistuses to the Most Holy Theotokos on the occasion of the miraculous apparition of her Icon with the Orb at the village of Kolomenskoe near Moscow on March 2, 1917. Compiled from different acathistuses with the blessing of His Beatitude Patriarchate Tikhon. Edition stored at: Librarie, E. de Sialsky, Rue Pierre-le-Grand, Paris (8), France.
[7] Acathistus to the Icon of the Most Holy Theotokos with the Orb. M., 1995.
[8] Narration of the apparition of the Icon of Our Lady with the Orb, in edition entitled Acathistus to the Most Holy Theotokos on occasion of the apparition of Her miracle-making Icon of Her Likeness with the Orb. Printery of the Reverend Job Pochaevsky, Svyato-Troitsky Monastery. Jordanville P, 10, 1994, p.40.
[9] Filatov V.V. Notes on the second acquisition of the Icon of Our Lady with the Orb in Russia // «Mir Bozhii», 1996, No. 1, pp. 82 – 89.
[10] The Joint Resolution of the Soviet of the People's Commissars of the USSR and the Central Committee of the All-Union Communist Party (of bolsheviks) «Regarding the General Plan of the Reconstruction of the City of Moscow» of July 25, 1935 // «Stroitelstvo Moskvy», 1935, No. 1.
[11] «Lectures of the Moscow University Society of Russian History and Antiquities». M., 1874, vol.II, sec. V, pp. 93 – 100.
[12] PSZRI under the years indicated. Also MIAS, Moscow, vol. I, p.589.
[13] Architectural monuments of Moscow. The Kremlin, Kitay-gorod, Central Squares. M., 1982; Bely-gorod. M., 1989; Zemlyanoi gorod. M., 1989; Zamoskvorechie. M., 1994.
[14] For more detailed information refer to the first volume of this edition, pp. 36, 72, 108.
[15] For more detailed information refer to: Kudryavtsev M.P. Historical Moscow – a Monument of City-building Art // «Pamyatniki Otechestva», 1980, No. 2. Same author. The Experimental Transition of the 17th century's Moscow to an Idealized Scheme // «Arkhitekturnoe Nasledstvo», No. 30, 1982. Same author. Moscow – Third Rome. M., 1994.

CHAPTER ONE

Moscow in the First Years of the Soviet Era 1917-1930

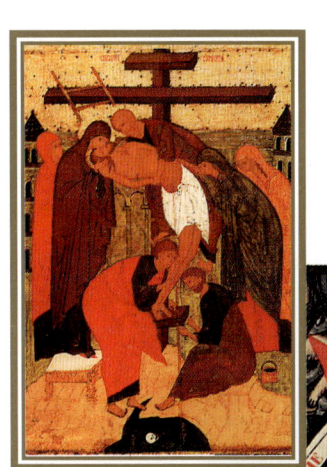

Icon: The Descent from the Cross.

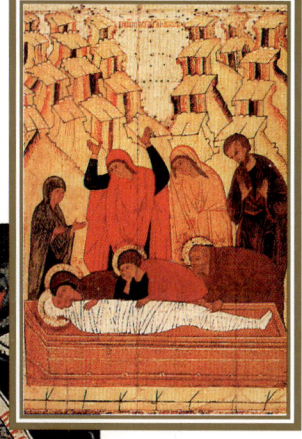

Icon: Burial of Christ

Hieromonk Stephan (Linitsky): Shroud of Christ.

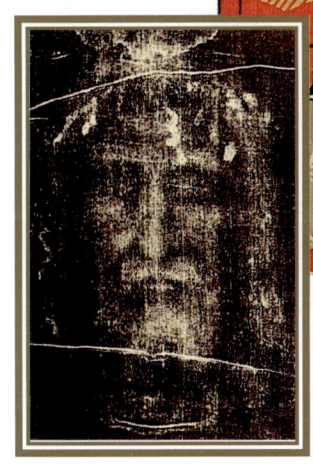

Icon: Descent to Hades

D. Moor: Poster. 1919.

V. Shilov: His Beautitude Patriarch of Moscow and of All-Russia Tikhon.

I.S. Glazunov: Crucify Him! 1994.

I.S. Glazunov: Fires of October. 1986.

N.Vsevolzhsky: Monument-obelisk to the outstanding thinkers and leaders of the struggle for the liberation of working people. 1918.

S. Konenkov: Memorial Plaque «To those who gave their lives for the cause of peace and fraternity of peoples». 1918.

A. Trofimov: View of the Kremlin in the First Years of the Soviet Power.

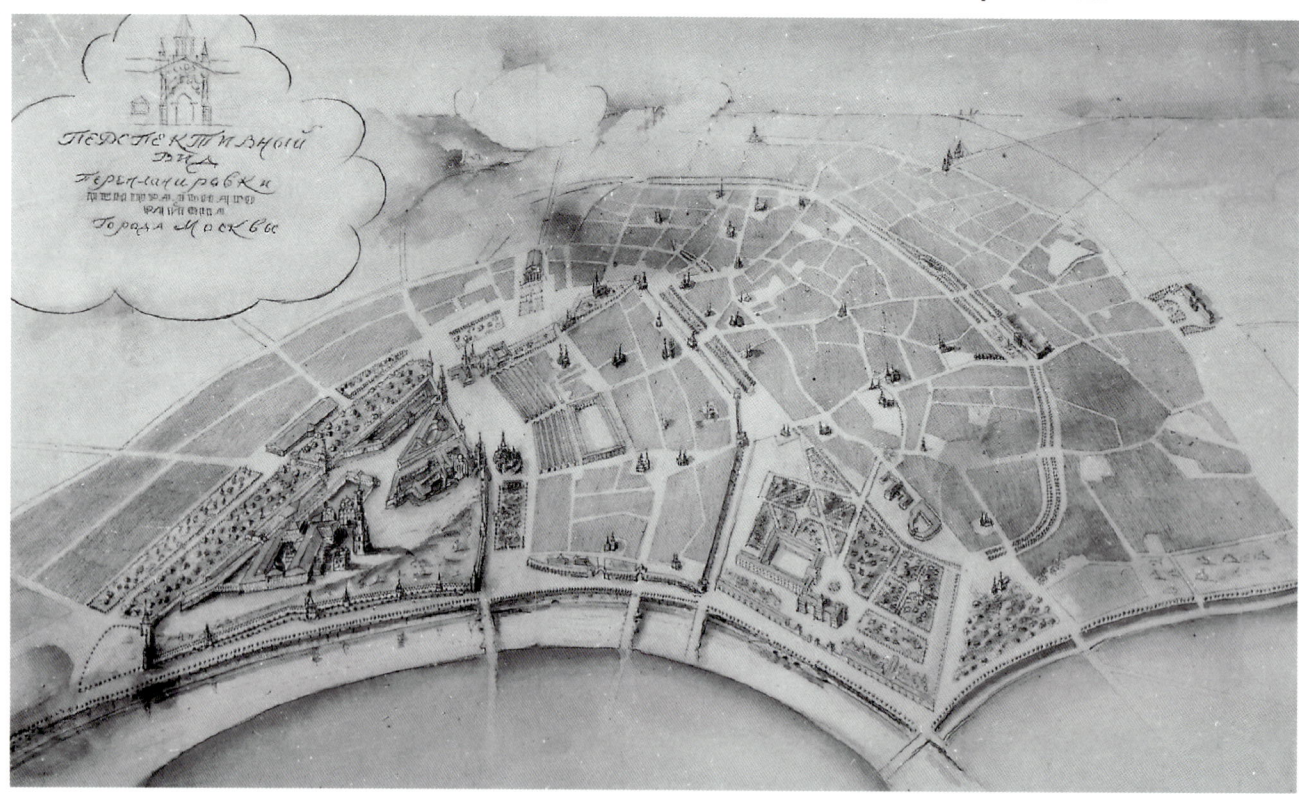

A. Shchusev: A detail of the plan «New Moscow» with the monuments in the historical center to be preserved. 1923.

A. Shchusev: Plan «New Moscow». 1923.

Тов. Ленин ОЧИЩАЕТ землю от нечисти
ДА ЗДРАВСТВУЕТ МИРОВАЯ РЕВОЛЮЦИЯ
Парвус
ДОЛОЙ САМОДЕРЖАВІЕ
БРАТАНИЕ
ПРИКАЗ
ТЫ
ПОМОГИ!
ВСЯ ВЛАСТЬ СОВЕТАМЪ
1613
1913

I.S. Glazunov: The Great Experiment. 1990.

Two Worlds:
the Bolsheviks Versus the Church

Oh, God the Creator, give us the patience
In these turbulent and gloomy days
To weather the public persecution
And endure our wardens' cruel ways.

Oh, God the Righteous, build up our spirits
To forgive thy neighbor's evil deeds
And have this heavy and lethal Cross
Be welcomed with due humility.

Oh, Jesus Christ the Savior, please help us
In these days of mutinous outbreaks
To survive the disgrace and insults,
With our slanderers reigning unchecked.

Oh, Lord the Almighty, the Most Gracious,
Have our humble souls
Divinely blessed and securely saved
In this insufferable hour of our demise.

And as we come to face the grave,
Have Your devoted slaves filled
With superhuman capacities
To humbly pray for the enemies.

Poem copied by members of the imperial family at
Tobolsk and uncovered after their assassination.
(S.S.Bekhteyev, October 1917, Yelets)

Every Christian city is known to epitomize two patterns of service. One seeks to emulate the Primordial Heavenly Urbs embellished just like the Bride of Christ through the filial duty of Christians before our Heavenly Father. The other archetype, which is after the apocalyptic seducer of Babel, «sitting on many waters», is maintained through people servicing the prince of this world with his adoration of the «golden calf». The first way is redolent of salutary visions of Noah's ark, the tabernacle of the Lord, the Lord's tomb, the Temple of God, the earthly and heavenly Churches. The second option is reminiscent of the persistent effort to have the defiled or destroyed divine shrines replaced by some godforsaken satanic structures. This dichotomous path has, in fact, been traveled by all Christian cities, each bearing its own Cross.

The old Moscow is one of the brightest memorial cities of the Sacred Russia, a precious icon for the World of God. Having succeeded to the supreme Christian symbols, thereby becoming the bearer of divine energies and revelations of the World and Image of God, the city of Moscow then had been subject to desecration, blasphemy and crucifixion with a new regime seizing power in Russia.

***

The year 1917 brought a revolutionary turnabout in Moscow's evolution and appearance. With Emperor Nicholas II abdicating the throne in March 2, 1917, power in Russia was assumed by the Provisional Government formed by the State Duma in February of the same year. On the eve of the Tsar's abdication, Chief Procurator of the Holy Synod Rayev urged the Orthodox Church to call on the people of Russia to come out in support of the imperial authority. However, the top Church leadership declined the appeal, citing the pointlessness of such a move.

The February 1917-vintage policy officials, that chain-replaced one another in ministerial positions, as a matter of fact, had their schemes to introduce a new policy based on sandy grounds. The rank-and-file people, seduced by the talk of liberties, had come to perceive those freedoms in the way totally different from the ideas pursued by the academic-landlord community. At that point in time, the governance began to disintegrate irrevocably, with the front line troops getting out of control. Separatists in the country's remote locations with no prior arrangement proclaimed their autonomies and independent government without even waiting for the Constituent Assembly to convene. Both central and local governing authorities were wholly paralyzed. Property expropriations then were rampant, with the pan-Russian plunder and looting getting afoot. Given the scene, developments culminated in the October Bolshevik takeover. Conversely, it was then that the Orthodox Patriarchy was restored.

Archpriest K. Zaitsev in his «The Orthodox Church in Soviet Russia», released in 1947 in Shanghai, writes, «The Orthodox Church came to confront the revolution while being fully equipped in terms of canon law. The long-lasting preparations had eventually resulted in convening the National Assembly of the Russian Orthodox Church held in the days of the Provisional Government's rule. The God's miraculous benevolence being readily acknowledged, the make-up of the delegates turned out to generally measure up to the challenges brought to the fore by the collapse of the centuries-old governance in Russia Notably, the election of delegates for the Church national event was conducted while the new rulers were still in the heat of hangover from their successful coup d'etat.

The Bolshevik coup, that came to pass in the initial stage of the Orthodox Assembly sessions, could not but bolster conservative elements within the Church and consolidate the delegates' sentiments that tended towards establishing the hierarchical unity of authority... The Assembly resolved to restore the Patriarchy, abolished by Peter the Great over two centuries earlier, in order to enable the Church to emerge vis-a-vis the newly-established governing structures as a most viable institution wholesome in its canonical singularity.

God willing, enthroned as Patriarch of Muscovy and all Russia was the humble and merciful Metropolitan Tikhon. The inauguration of the new Patriarch, conducted within the walls of the Red Kremlin, had nonetheless had a heavy measure of foreboding about it. The event was organized to feature a specially devised procedure to emulate the old modus operandi. The new Patriarch took office amidst the relics reminiscent of the past patriarchs and surrounded by large numbers of the clergy, with the entire splendor and grandeur of the Russian Orthodox religious service being fully in evidence. The festive ceremony was conducted in the Assumption Cathedral, with all eyes glued to the patriarchal throne filled at long last after two centuries of desolation.

Alas, standing right next to it was the now-orphaned throne of the Russian tsars, anointed sovereigns. At that moment, one just could not help being tormented by the specter of an awesome danger generated by that unfilled throne. After all, the godless Council of People's Commissars (Sovnarkom), the Tsar's replacement, had already been installed in the Kremlin, while the stark wounds of the sacred memorials were most indicative of the defiant violence that was the price of the Kremlin's recent seizure by the Bolsheviks.

Sinister realities of the day could be read quite easily: rather than just like some awe-inspiring ghost, the Red Kremlin was clearly a fact of life that was destined to have the Partiarch's inaugural held against the backdrop of tall grey-overcoated Red Guards turning their backs on the clergy whenever an encounter was unavoidable. Moscow was obviously split into two camps, which was only emblematic of the rest of Russia. Admittedly, crowds of Muscovites came out to welcome their Patriarch, but those could hardly be called «all Moscow». There were other people that no longer took the Patriarch to be their treasured asset! And it mattered little that those folks had in no way been supportive of the Bolsheviks. What really mattered was that they were not wholly with the Patriarch. While the Bolsheviks had nearly universally been perceived as alien invaders, the anti-Bolshevik Russia remained ambivalent about the Orthodox Church.

As the new Patriarch was enthroned, he had these words to say in his inaugural address, «It is in the times of God's wrath and in the days of many sorrows and hardships that I take this venerable position of Patriarch. Our homeland is being torn apart by the debilitating war, destructive discord, outside incursions and internecine conflicts. However, the soul-consuming spiritual discord comes to be the most devastating. The public conscience appears to be somewhat imperceptive of the Christian guidelines for state and societal building and inattentive to the belief itself, with the ruthless ways of this world reigning supreme as a consequence»[1].

***

Prior of the Candlemas Monastery in Moscow Georgy Shevkunov, compiler of the book of addresses by the Saint Patriarch Tikhon, emphasizes this point in the preface: «The patriarchal duty by the Saints Iov and Tikhon happened to be done in the times of troubles. It was precisely in the periods of state authority getting too feeble to manage the Orthodox nation that God arranged for the Patriarchy to be installed in the Russian land. Notably, the striking similarities about the fates of these two Saint Patriarchs continue to be uncovered.

They both survived civil wars. The internecine battles and Polish-Lithuanian intervention of 1606 – 1612 unleashed by Muscovy's adversaries and fanned by the traitors had been waged to exterminate the Orthodoxy in our homeland. The civil war and foreign intervention in the 20th-century Russia came to be in sync with the first days of service by Saint Tikhon. This time, the civil war had to do with the onslaught focused on achieving total elimination of the man's communication with God and with the attempt to secure abolition of Orthodoxy.

The Patriarchy in Russia has both initially and repeatedly been initiated by the two tsars, the sovereigns that were regarded as saints by the Orthodox Russian people. Those are Tsar Theodor Ioannovich and martyr-Tsar Nicholas II.

Patriarch Iov left his fascinating «Tale of the Honest Life of Tsar Theodor Ioannovich», while Patriarch Tikhon responded to the assassination of the imperial family by coming out with his sermon designed to expose and identify the true assassins.

Both patriarchs have witnessed such watershed developments in the evolution of Russia as terminations of the great dynasties. Patriarch Iov saw Tsar Theodor Ioannovich, the last Riurik descendant of the Kalita clan, while the Romanov dynasty was brought to an end under Patriarch Tikhon.

Both patriarchs were in office when an innocent tsarevich of adolescent age was assassinated, the developments having tremendous impacts on the psyche of the entire people in either case. Tsarevich Dmitry was knifed to death in May 15, 1591 at Uglich, while Tsarevich Alexei was shot to death on the night of July 16 – 17, 1918 at Yekaterinburg.

Both patriarchs survived the seizure of Moscow and witnessed the outrages of the iconoclastic invaders inside the Kremlin. Patriarch Tikhon, in fact, was elected to head the Patriarchy to the thunderous artillery shelling of the Kremlin. Under Patriarch Iov, Moscow's sacred site happened to be profaned by the Polish aggressors and Tsarevich Dmitry the impostor (Lzhedmitry).

Soldiers of the Revolution in Moscow streets. February. 1917.

Troubles within the Church have likewise served to bedevil the duties of the two patriarchs, either one being declared deposed and replaced as head of the Russian Orthodox Church. In 1606, the Catholics, motivated by the desire to introduce the supremacy of the Roman Pope in Russia, joined ranks with the clergy, that had sworn their allegiance to Lzhedmitry, and arranged for the impostor Ignaty to be elected Patriarch of the Orthodox Church. Patriarch Iov was assaulted and pilloried in the Assumption Cathedral, his sacred robes being torn off. The threats notwithstanding, he would not take an oath to be loyal to a mountebank... Under Patriarch Nikon, hitting the Church had been the so-called «renovation rift». Just like three centuries earlier, many bishops were apostatized, and they zealously attacked the patriarch with their slanderous accusations. Articles and sermons by those renewed prelates are still there to be found...

On the eve of the times of troubles, God not only had bolstered Russia with the patriarchy being restored but also had her supremely backed up by the Mother of God, Tsarina of the Heavens. The Mother of God of Kazan Icon had come to be uncovered shortly before Saint Patriarch Iov was elected, while in March 2, 1917, the day Nicholas II abdicated the throne and a few months before Tikhon was elected Patriarch, the Mother of God Icon («Sovereign») was miraculously retrieved at Kolomenskoye, near Moscow. Both of the images, that we know only too well, are not merely of local but also of tremendous Church-wide and all-Russian relevance.

Saint Iov and Saint Tikhon fulminated anathemas on the powers-that-be engaged in mocking at the Orthodox Church, the people and the Russian homeland.

Either patriarch had been incarcerated: Patriarch Iov – in Staritsky Monastery and Patriarch Tikhon – in Moscow's Donskoy Monastery and then in the VChK (State Secret Police) internal prison on Lubianka.

The imposture phenomenon manifested itself under both Patriarchs. Lzhedmitry's cheat has been broadly known, just like the ruses he had used to come to power in Russia. The way he ended his days has remained no secret either. Admittedly, the Lzhedmitry scenario appeared to have had its remake under Patriarch Tikhon. The patriarch was clearly aware of the people and entire nation charting misconceived objectives and stood out to fight until he realized the people and society would not alter the chosen course! And as it had occurred on numerous occasions in the past, the Church opted to proceed with the people toward the predictable abyss in order to come to the very brink of the void and wrest to safety the elements that would finally be sufficiently equipped to see things in their true perspective and understand... This is positively the challenge for the Church, though it obviously holds a major inherent danger of unavoidable compromises.

A triumph in countering the evil is merely tantamount to being true to the behests till the last, and it can hardly be measured by some external feats. Patriarch Tikhon had sought no external deeds. He would view such frames of mind to be un-Christian. «...but he who stands firm to the end will be saved» (Mark, 13:13). While trying to achieve this measure of patience bequeathed by the Saint Patriarchs, the Russian people have been seeking the salutary fortitude that is known to have been made from the willingness to endure and stand for the axioms of Orthodoxy. This, in fact, has been the lot of Russia, the Cross that the Russian people were chosen to carry a thousand years ago.

Patriarch Tikhon's messages are known to have featured the very special quality inherent in the prophetic divinely-inspired word, which gets the attention of not only the speaker's contemporaries but also of the whole Church at all times: «...all of these dislocations and inadequacies come from the Russian State being built with no God for guidance. Have we ever heard our rulers mention the name of God in the numerous council, parliamentary and preparliamentary sessions? Not once, for they have chosen to be exclusively reliant on their own capacities while seeking to canonize their names, which is wholly at odds with our pious ancestors working to glorify the name of God rather than their own monikers. This is enough to know that Lord the Almighty will just scoff at our earthly schemes and do away with all our councils. Oh, God, You truly had the foreknowledge about our sort «being too unruly to take Thy Word» (Lamentation I; 18;1918).

The fates of these two Saint Patriarchs came in confluence, just like the critical features of their periods, or the ways of the modern times and the present-day Church, which through the Holy Spirit had these very saints engaged to back up the divine service today.

As he assumed the Cross of his responsibilities before the Church, Patriarch Tikhon observed, «From this day on, placed in my care shall be all Russian parishes, and I am to wear away for all of them each day»[2].

* * *

As far back as early 1905, members of the Holy Synod headed by the First Metropolitan of Saint Petersburg Antony (Vadkovsky) were received by Emperor Nicholas II who is reported to have said,

«Word has reached me that there has now been much talk amongst you in the Synod and in the public about the need for restoration of Patriarchy in Russia. The issue has also struck a cord in my soul and got me quite excited. I have thought it out for quite a while, looked through the current publications on the question, come to know about the history of Patriarchy in Russia and its relevance in the times of interreign troubles, and come to the conclusion that the time is now right for Russia, going through the times of troubles anew, as well as for the Church and state to have the Patriarchy restored. You at the Synod seem, no less than myself, to have been concerned about this matter. Should that be the case, what is your thinking on this question?»

«We, of course, rushed to respond to the Sovereign that our judgment was wholly in line with what His Imperial Majesty had just voiced».

«If that is so», said the Emperor, «you may have already picked out a patriarchal nominee?»

«We somewhat hesitated and left the Emperor's implied query unanswered».

«Well, inasmuch as you have not yet made your pick of candidate or have difficulty doing so, what do you say to my giving you a name?»

«Who is he?», we asked.

«The candidate is myself. Under a special arrangement with the Empress, I shall abdicate the throne in favor of my son and establish the due regency made of the Empress and my brother Mikhail. Then I will take the monastic vows, be ordained priest and offer my name for the Patriarchy. Would you be ready to accept me, and what is your reaction now?»

«That was so nearly like a bolt out of the blue, so much removed from all our ideas that we were just at a loss for words. As he got no response from us for a few fleeting moments, the Emperor threw his glance over us rather indignantly, rose, bowed politely, and left us dumbfounded. We then felt like tearing our hear for not being smart enough to provide a dignified response to the Emperor. We positively should have dropped on our knees to acknowledge the greatness of the commitment he was about to make in order to save Russia. However, we just remained mum».

The right opportunity had been forever lost, with the great moment being left unrecognized and unused: «...because you did not recognize the time of God's coming to you» (Luke 19:44)[3].

Following his subsequent deliberations and discussion of the differences within the Church community, in March 31, 1905 the Emperor had the following decision left on the Synod's report on the Patriarchy issue, «Deem unfeasible in today's troubled times to accomplish the challenging undertaking of convening the Church national assembly, the job requiring both the societal tranquility and balanced judgment. At this juncture I can only visualize the right time when the good old examples of Orthodox emperors would be taken up to pursue the matter and convene the all-Russian assembly of the Orthodox Church in order to address the questions of belief and church management in full compliance with the standing canon law»[4].

Notwithstanding this policy position, as early as December 27, 1905, the Emperor dispatched this ordinance to Metropolitan Antony (Vadkovsky), «At this point I fully recognize it to be expedient to carry out some shifts in the structure of our domestic Church. I suggest you determine the timeframe for this kind of assembly»[5].

The pre-assembly conference, that opened March 6,1906, culminated in the 1917 – 1918 National Assembly and the restored Patriarchy.

* * *

«The Church has been growing militant of late», noted Archbishop Anastassy of Kishinev in the initial stage of the Assembly sessions as he touched upon the question of Patriarchy, «hence, it must be enabled to protect itself not only against its adversaries but also against its pseudo-members. Assuming that eventuality, the Church definitely needs a leader».

As the historic act of Patriarchy restoration was completed, the Assembly got the first word of the Petrograd takeover. Arriving then from Petrograd was S.A. Kotliarevsky to tell that the Provisional Government had been taken into custody, with the power seized by the Military Revolutionary Committee.

October 28,1917, internecine clashes broke out in Moscow. Military officers, cadets and rapidly called-up students, that remained loyal to the Provisional Government, were deployed to defend the Kremlin. The rest of Moscow was soon in the control of the rebellious Red detachments.

At dawn of November 3, 1917, the Kremlin was surrendered by its defenders that did not want to see the sacred buildings and sites destroyed by artillery shelling. Arrests, firing-squad executions and soldier-staged lynchings followed immediately. The Russian Orthodox believers were also heavily chagrined by the destruction and damage within the Kremlin. Right after the Kremlin assault, an Assembly-authorized team headed by Patriarch Tikhon headed for the Kremlin to assess the damage sustained by the Church buildings. As they reached the Nikolsky Gates, the clergy were stopped with the question, «What is your need?». They explained they wanted to look at the Kremlin's shrines, but all they got in return was, «You will go in when the right time comes!». There was a soldier who even quickly interjected, «Let them in and then we will have them up against the wall!».

Cadets guarding the Kremlin. 1917.

V. Shtein: Carrying the Cross. Golgotha. 1994.

The prelates then turned to walk toward the Spassky Gates. As they proceeded, they spotted broken panes in the windows of the Pokrovsky Cathedral. The delegates made quite an effort to talk the guards at the Spassky Gates into letting them go inside.

In the first place, they hurried to examine the Assumption Cathedral. A huge black hole in one of the Cathedral's domes immediately caught their worried attention. When inside, they saw an unexploded artillery round that landed right between the patriarch's and tsar's seats, with the floor window panes broken to pieces. The Twelve Apostles Cathedral was most heavily damaged: one shell pierced the Saint Martyr Germogen Icon, while another one hit the crucifix and knocked off the Savior's hands, the mutilated body remaining on the cross.

The Chudov Monastery took hits in the metropolitan's quarters, with one round detonating nearly a minute after Metropolitan Veniamin left the building. The Saint Alexi Icon was totally destroyed, while other icons were unharmed. The flame on the Mother of God Icon-lamp miraculously stayed on.

The Reds buried their dead at the Kremlin wall on Red Square to the singing of revolutionary songs, with the burial services and prayers remaining unread. A relation to one of the killed asked for the body to be released for a Christian interment, however the plea was rejected. There was nonetheless somebody who contrived to bring in an icon and carry it at the head of the funeral procession. For years afterwards Muscovites would talk of the impenitent souls of the dead moaning through the nights at the Kremlin wall for being devoid of the due burial service.

On the very same day, the Russian Church Assembly issued an appeal to the Orthodox believers to do penance for their sins and expose the pseudo-prophets:

«...The pseudo-teachers' promises of building a new life for the people are now being phased out by the builders' bloody discords, while the espoused peace and brotherhood of the peoples are being replaced by the mingle of tongues and bitter hatreds amongst the brothers. The people that rejected their God are nearly like hungry wolves assaulting one another. They have their hearts and minds universally eclipsed. It has already been some time since the Russian soul began to be permeated with anti-Christ motions and the heart started to be poisoned with the teachings designed to sap the belief in God and plant the seeds of envy, greed, larceny... While shooting at the Kremlin's holy places, Russian cannons thereby hit at the hearts of devout Orthodox believers. However, no earthly kingdom can rationally be built upon the groundwork of godlessness: such a structure would disintegrate from internal strife and political party hassles. This explains why the Russian nation is breaking up from this unbridled paganism. What we are witnessing today is God's just trial of the people that has come to reject its holy institution. Those elements, that exclusively seek to build their authority on a single societal segment using violence with regard to the entire people, feel no need either for the homeland or its holy institutions... Unfortunately, we have not yet seen any new and truly popular authority which would qualify to receive the Orthodox Church's blessings. And in the Russian land, it is unlikely to come until we address our mournful prayers and bring our humble repentance to the One that the new city builders are now vainly toiling without».

As he delivered his message in January 1, 1918 at the Christ the Savior Cathedral before embarking on the New Year service, Patriarch Tikhon likened the past February- and October-launched attempts at building the state to the dismal experience of erecting the Tower of Babel. «And our local builders», he pointed out, «are likewise willing to canonize their names and through their ill-conceived reforms and decrees do good not only for the unfortunate Russian people but also for the entire world... This haughty venture of theirs would inevitably go the way of the Babel Tower builders' scheme, with good intentions merely producing an utter downfall.

While desirous of making us all rich and having no need for a thing, they are, in fact, turning us into «the wretched, pitiful, poor, blind and naked» (Revelation 3:17). They have transformed the great and powerful Russia, that had until recently been feared by her adversaries, into a heartbreaking name of the desolate land fragmented into isolated pieces and engaged in destructive internecine battles. As you read Jeremiah's lament, you quite habitually apply the prophet's words to bemoan our dear homeland».

While lamenting over the plight that befell Russia's Orthodox people and seeking to protect his God-given parish, Patriarch Tikhon issued an address to anathematize the perpetrators of the bloody massacre of the innocent, the iconoclasts that attacked the Church's holy shrines and clergy,

«The Holy Orthodox Church of Christ in the Russian land is now going through the times of severe hardships. The true Word of Christ is being violently attacked by the overt and covert enemies of the Word of God... You, the crazy lot, come to your senses! Stop your bloody carnage! Beware, for what you are now doing amounts to much more than cruelties. Your activities are obviously the work of the Devil that will assure you Gehenna's flames in the afterlife and unatoned curse of your posterity in this life. Having the God-given powers, we herewith bar you from being administered the Sacraments and anathemize you even though you might bear Christian names and belong to the Christian Church by the virtue of birth. We also adjure all of you, the truly dedicated children of the Orthodox Church of Christ, against communicating in any way with suchlike scum of the

V.I. Lenin attending the reservist parade under the General Military Compulsory Education Program (VseObuch) on the Red Square. 25th of May 1919.

earth. «Expel the wicked man from among you» (1 Corinthians, 5:13). The Holy Church of Christ has been made the target of the most intense persecution, with the Sacraments declared useless, holy shrines plundered, looted or even blasphemously abused and ruined. The long-revered sacrosanct cloisters are being commandeered by the godless masters of this age's darker forces...».

The patriarch's address served to bolster the spiritual stamina of the believers as well as urge them to display patience in adhering to their creed. But then, the cup of God's wrath and ire continued to plague the blameful Russian people. In January 20, 1918 issues of national newspapers carried the Decree on Separation of the Church from the State and of the School from the Church. The Decree not only symbolized a formal and codified rift in the long-lasting union between the Church and the State but also had the ongoing iniquitous Church persecutions and harrassments legalized. God's shrines, holy icons and sacrosanct artifacts continued to be sequestered, with the Church thereby losing all of its properties. «No religious association», read the Decree, «can be authorized to have properties. Neither of those can be registered as legal entities».

Any and all bishops in the Russian Orthodox Church and even its chief-priest, the patriarch, then were suddenly under the real threat of being taken into custody and executed at any time. Given the scene and motivated by the desire to preserve the Patriarchy unscathed and assure succession of the pontiff's powers, the Church Assembly, in January 25,1918, issued an emergency edict to confirm a procedure under which the standing Patriarch should name a few caretaker patri-archs authorized in the order of their seniority to execute the supreme duties and succeed to the office should the incumbent Patriarch happen to pass away, be taken ill or be prevented from being functional by any other circumstance. Under the ruling, the Patriarch was supposed to personally pick out his successors and keep their names secret for security reasons, with the candidates however being privately notified of the choices made. Shortly afterwards, the Patriarch appeared before the Assembly, that gathered in a closed session, and reported he had accomplished the will of the top-governing body.

* * *

In March 3, 1918, at Brest-Litovsk the Soviet delegation signed a peace treaty with Germany, thereby getting committed to honor all terms of the German ultimatum. Under the Treaty, Poland, Finland, the Baltic Region, Lithuania, part of Belarus, Ukraine, the Crimea and Georgia were separated from Russia, with the cities of Batum, Kars and Ardahan being transferred to Turkey. All of a sudden, Russia came to lose quite a few of her industrial and cultural centers, to say nothing of the organized defensive lines. The nation had indirectly been forced to pay an indemnity to the amount of DM 6 billion. Ethnic Russians in the German-occupied areas were compelled to toil like slaves in specially-tailored work teams.

On the day, following the Treaty signing, Patriarch Tikhon appeared with a public address to say, inter alia, the following, «...The Holy Orthodox Church, that from the times immemorial has been assisting the Russian people to build up and consolidate the Russian state, now cannot afford to sit on the sidelines and see the nation degrade and disintegrate. This new peace treaty, signed in the name of the Russian people, is not about to produce a friendly community of nations. The treaty holds no assurance of tranquility and appeasement, it rather has sown the seeds of animosity and hatred, as well as engendered the specter of new wars and ills for the entire mankind...

For you, the seduced and unfortunate Russian people, my heart is now filled with the burning compassion that will last through my lifetime... To survive God's horrible trial of our country, we all need to rally around Christ and His Holy Church».

The Brest-Litovsk peace treaty, that cut to the quick the national sentiments of Russians, as a matter of fact, precipitated the turning of nearly the whole of Russian land into some ugly fratricidal battlespace. The unfolding civil war was only made worse by foreign powers joining in the fray, with Germany and its allies supporting one side and the Entente countries backing the other force. In 1918, the Czechoslovakian Corps mutinied on the Volga and in Siberia. And while the principal battles for the control of Russia were fought along the frontlines separating the Reds from the Whites in the south and east, the palette of political interests involved in the internecine warfare, particularly in the nation's remote regions, had throughout been fantastically varied.

By early June, 1918, victimization of the Orthodox Church had grown to become unprecedented in scale. In-house shrines and religious educational institutions were ordered to be closed across the board, with the in-school teaching of the Word of God being totally banned, privately-funded programs making no exception. The Church properties and furnishings were inventoried and expropriated in favor of the State. In the tragic summer months of 1918, the clergy had now been made to face the firing squads by the hundred. The Synodic Roll of priest martyrs and martyrs of the Church of Christ, that lost their lives in the days of the Russian troubled times, had soon grown to be as endlessly long as the martyrology of the first martyrs whose spilled blood became the spawning grounds for the Ecumenical Church.

In July 17, 1918, Emperor Nicholas II together with the family were assassinated by the Bolsheviks at the Ipatyev House in Yekaterinburg.

In July 18, 1918, Grand Duchess Elizaveta Fyodorovna together with nun Varvara, Grand Duke Sergei Mikhailovich, Princes Igor Konstantinovich, Konstantin Konstantinovich, Ioann Konstantinovich and Vladimir Pavlovich Palei were executed 15 miles from Alapayevsk in the Urals. Grand Duke Sergei Mikhailovich was shot dead, while all others were thrown into a mining pit alive, with rocks and assorted debris dumped on top. The investigation, conducted under Admiral Kolchak, revealed that Elizaveta Fyodorovna had remained alive in her grave for some time before she finally expired. Though badly injured, she managed to dress Prince Ioann's wounds. For days, the sounds of religious chants from the pit's deep could be heard in the neighborhood.

On the night of July 12 – 13, 1918, Grand Duke Mikhail Aleksandrovich, the Emperor's brother, was shot dead in Perm.

In January 29, 1919, Grand Dukes Pavel Aleksandrovich, Nikolai Mikhailovich, Georgy Mikhailovich and Prince Dmitry Konstantinovich were executed in Petrograd.

As he was informed of the Tsar's execution, Patriarch Tikhon completed the mass at Moscow's Kazansky Cathedral and briefly delivered this message to the parishioners, «The other day, a horrible crime has been committed. Our former sovereign Nikolai Aleksandrovich has been shot dead, and our top leadership and the Central Executive Committee have approved of that action and passed it as lawful... However, guided by the Word of God, our Christian conscience refuses to comply. We must take the Gospels for our direction and have that action condemned, for otherwise the blood of the executed would have us incriminated along with the executioners. Let them brand us counterrevolutionaries, throw us in jail or put before a firing squad. We are poised to persevere all those trials in the hope of coming to see the Savior's words «Blessed rather are those who hear the word of God and obey it» (Luke 11:28) attributed to us.

The family of the Emperor Nicholas II.

We have ventured to build a Paradise in this world in defiance of God and His Holy Testaments. But God can never be defamed. And now we are desperately striving, hassling and persisting in shortfalls on this beautiful land fabulously rich in natural resources, with the very human labors and all enterprising endeavors bearing the stamp of curse. The vicious and unrepented sins had accumulated to bring forth the Devil that now is blaspheming God the Almighty and Jesus Christ and coming to attack the Church in the open».

In August 30, 1918, the Assembly issued the following ruling on protection of the religious shrines: «Holy shrines and chapels with all of the dedicated artifacts and furnishings shall be regarded as God's assets exclusively operated by the Holy Church of Christ through the agency of all Orthodox believers and the supremely-established hierarchy. Any attempt to alienate the Church's assets shall be viewed as an act of blasphemous seizure and violence».

At its concluding September 7, 1918 session, the Assembly ruled for the next all-Russian Orthodox Church Assembly to be convened in the spring of 1921. The Assembly then was terminated, with the building, where the sessions were held, being immediately expropriated without much ado.

The Assembly's canonical definitions provided a solid groundwork for the Russian Orthodox Church to proceed on its laborious path and made an unshakable spiritual beacon for the effort to find good solutions to most complex issues that emerged in large numbers in the years that followed. Given the restoration of the unity of authority within the Church and reinstitution of the Patriarchy, the Russian Orthodox Church's canonical framework became to be invulnerable to any subversive schismatic ploys.

«Things have come to be shaped so that in the godless state, devoid of any built-in nationwide cementing structure at that and being profoundly alien to the historic tradition of the Russian people, the Church, its victimization and deprivation notwithstanding, managed to not only stay functional but even grow and expand, while exclusively operating off its own resources. A totally new arrangement of «the Church separated from the State» became a fact of life never assumed by any theorists in the past. The godless State discriminated against the «hateful and doomed to extinction» Church, which for its part called for God's wrath to befall the State authority and anathematized its public servants and stooges»[6].

In October 13, 1918, Patriarch Tikhon sent this message to the Council of People's Commissars:

«All who draw the sword will die by the sword» (Matthew 26:34).

This is the prophesy of the Savior that we address to you, the current rulers of our homeland's destinies that label yourselves people's commissars. For nearly a year now you have been at the helm of the State and are already preparing to celebrate the October Revolution's first anniversary. But the rivers of blood shed by our brethren, mercilessly massacred at your behest, are now calling upon Heaven, thereby compelling us to tell you these words of truth.

While seizing power and appealing to the people to place trust in you, what pledges did you then make and how have you lived up to those?

Indeed, «you have given them a stone in place of bread and a snake instead of a fish» (Matthew 7:9, 10). You promised a «no-annexation-or-contribution peace» to the people exhausted by the long and bloody war.

What gains could have been sacrificed by you, the ones that have maneuvered Russia into a shameful peace arrangement whose humiliating terms came to be too hard even for you to have them fully released? With your «no annexations or contributions» pledge cast aside, our great homeland has now been conquered, downsized, fragmented, and you are secretly engaged in the transfer of gold, that you had not secured in the first place, over to Germany as payment for the tribute Russia has been compelled to meet.

You have left the warfighters bereft of everything they had until recently courageously fought for. You have taught them, the brave and invincible breed just a few years ago, to abandon the defense of the homeland and flee from the battlefields. You have extinguished in their hearts the inspiring thought that «greater love has no one than this, that he lay down his life for his friends» (John 15:13). You have substituted the heartless internationalism for the homeland, though you realize perfectly well that, whenever it comes to defending the homeland, workers worldwide come to be devoted sons of their lands rather than traitors.

Having refused to defend the homeland from external adversaries, you nonetheless keep raising the forces.

Who will you lead those forces against?

You have split the entire people into antagonistic societal groups and had them involved in the unprecedented and ferocious fratricide. You have had the Christian love openly phased out by hatreds and the peace supplanted by the class struggle. The war, you have engendered, has no end in sight, for you seek to use Russian industrial workers and peasants to have the specter of a world revolution come alive in triumph...

You do not seem to be satisfied with getting the Russian people to have fraternal blood on their hands. While using the assorted notions of contribution, requisition and nationalization, you have pushed the Russian people to be readily engaged in the overt and shameless plunder. You have engineered for lands, estates, plants, factories, houses, cattle, money deposits, personal belongings, furniture and clothes to be impudently commandeered, appropriated or just looted. The first ones to be robbed were the well-to-do individuals branded the «bourgeoisie» that were soon followed by the «kulaks», the propertied, landed and hardworking peasants, with the growth of the impoverished masses being thereby only stepped up. You can not possibly be ignorant of the fact that ruination of large numbers of individual citizens merely erodes the national wealth and brings about a downfall of the country itself.

Having lured the unsophisticated and ignorant people with opportunities for easy and unpunishable gains, you have obscured their moral values and eclipsed their perception of the sin. But regardless of the cover tags for your evil deeds, murders, assaults and robberies shall forever be viewed as grave crimes, with the victims calling upon Heaven to be avenged with yet new sins and crimes.

You promised freedom...

Freedom is a great boon, provided it is seen as the freedom from evil, which hampers others in no way and stays short of degenerating into tyranny and arbitrary rule. However, you stopped short of allowing such a freedom, for your brand of freedom amounts to an all-out connivance at the brutish passions of a wild crowd, unpunished murders and robberies. Any and all manifestations of truly civic and predominant spiritual human freedoms have come to be ruthlessly suppressed. Could freedom ever be found where you need to be specially authorized to be able to earn your bread or lease living quarters, where separate families or even tenants of whole apartment buildings can offhandedly be ordered to move house, with private possessions forcefully thrown out, and where citizens get arbitrarily categorized, some social groups being left out to face the reigning famine and devastation? Could that situation be called freedom when no one would dare voice his judgment for fear of being labeled a counterrevolutionary? Where are the freedoms of speech, the press and religious preaching? Already, many a dauntless priest have shed their blood of martyrdom, while the mouthpiece for public and state censure of illegalities remains heavily constrained, with merely the Bolshevik perspective allowed to appear in print...

«And what more shall I say? I do not have time to tell about» (Hebrews 11:32) all the misfortunes that have befallen our homeland. I will not talk about the breakup of the once great and mighty Russia, about the total collapse of the communications network, the unheard-of degeneration of the produce distribution effort, the deprivation and cold that threaten to produce massive lethalities in larger cities, as well as about the lack of supplies that peasants badly need to efficiently work their land. These calamities are there for all to see. Indeed, we are going through the horrors of your rule that will impact the Russian psyche to only dim the image of God and bring forth the instincts of the beast. In fact, coming to life are the prophetic words: «Their feet run to evil. And they make haste to shed innocent blood: their thoughts are thoughts of iniquity; wasting and destruction are in their paths» (Isaiah 59:7).

We are, of course, aware that our accusation would merely arouse your fury and outrage and that you would readily take advantage of the

A. Trofimov: Lubyanskaya Square in the 20s.

current hardships in order to charge us with conspiring against the authorities, but mind you, the higher the «pillar of your rage» builds the better it testifies to the veracity of our denunciations»[7].

On the night of November 24 – 25, 1918, Patriarch Tikhon was ordered by the All-Russian Emergency Commission (VChK) to be put under house arrest with no charge filed. His residential quarters were thoroughly searched and placed under watch.

* * *

Lenin directly initiated four massive drives against the Russian Orthodox Church. The first one, November 1917 – 1919, upstarted the closures of monasteries, convents and some shrines, as well as requisition of the Church properties. The second dash, 1919 – 1920, was predominantly focused on uncovering holy remains and depriving the clergy of political rights. The third campaign, late 1920 – 1921, was conducted to split up the Orthodox Church and have it eroded from the inside. And the fourth strike, launched in early 1922, was mainly aimed to loot or, using Lenin's lingo, «clean» all of the churches and execute most of Orthodox priests in the process (the Bolshevik leader actually had plans for each hanged «cleric» to be taken as a feat worth a prize of R100 thousand, with the operation being devised so that the blame could be easily put on the «Greens»)[8].

In March 1919, M. Svet, brother of the Saint Alexei Community, turned to Lenin with a letter to ask for the remains of Saint Alexei, known to be in the Kremlin's Chudov Monastery grounds, to be transferred to the Community. Lenin scribbled this order for the attention of the people's commissar of justice: «Cde Kursky! I suggest you turn down the evacuation and proceed instead to assign a team and have it open up the tomb with witnesses in attendance»[9]. And the letter also carries Kursky's directive: «Urgent. Care of P.A. Krasikov, 8th Department. Have instructions issued to get the remains uncovered, with the Moscow Soviet of Workers' Deputies (MSRD), the People's Commissariat of Justice (NKYu) and the People's Commissariat of Internal Affairs (NKVD) representatives brought in to witness the procedure». This order of Lenin incidentally failed to be included in the leader's complete works.

...To no avail had been Patriarch Tikhon's April 27, May 10 and August 9, 1920, messages to Lenin with a request to prevent disdain over the remains of Saint Sergy Radonezhsky, Saint Patron of Russia, and cancel the plans to move those from the Lavra (monastery of the highest rank) to a museum, which act would be taken by Orthodox believers as utter sacrilege. And all references to the Soviet Constitution-proclaimed liberty of conscience had no effect. In his letter, Patriarch Tikhon also rejected the charges of the shrines being engaged in «profiteering with candles», which allegation made the grounds for the authorities to file a criminal case against the Patriarch.

In June 15, 1920, Lenin signed the ruling of the Council of People's Commissars (Sovnarkom) passed to approve the dedicated interagency commission report on turning the Trinity-Sergy Lavra into a museum. The revolutionary leader would not receive the Patriarch on the grounds that «the Chairman of Sovnarkom is busy discussing crucial issues and an audience can not be granted over the short term». The Sovnarkom's official message to the Patriarch actually read, « Citizen Belavin's (Patriarch Tikhon) May 10, 1920, appeal against the resolution by the Moscow Regional Executive Committee on the transfer of the remains in question from the Trinity-Sergy Lavra over to a Moscow museum shall be left with no further action. Pursuant to the People's Commissariat of Justice's circular of August 25, 1920, the MSRD Executive Committee shall be committed to complete relocation of the remains of Sergy Radonezhsky, thereby executing the

March 26, 1920 resolution of the Moscow Regional Executive Committee on the move of the remains to a Moscow museum».

One of the rulings, passed by a mid-June, 1920, Sovnarkom session chaired by Lenin, read: «The People's Commissariat of Education (Narkompros) shall be committed to draft a scheme for an all-Russian removal of the holy remains». In about a month, in July 20, 1920, while conducting a regular Sovnarkom sitting, Lenin made this notation: «Pending the forthcoming session (against Item 12) on the procedure for Russia-wide removal of the remains». The question was then addressed by two other Sovnarkom sessions chaired by Lenin.

In July 29, 1920, following the deliberations «on the Russia-wide removal of the remains», Sovnarkom passed this ruling: «The People's Commissariat of Justice's (Narkomyust) suggestions on the issue shall be in principle confirmed, and Narkomyust shall have the remains of 58 unearthed bodies briefly attributed and described»[10].

In December 3, 1920, Dzerzhinsky dispatched to VChK's covert operations division a directive to prepare a VChK policy position report on the Church, while making known his own stand: «In my judgment, the Church is disintegrating, and this trend needs to be given a push. In no way the Church should be allowed to reemerge in the traditional fashion. Hence, it is precisely VChK, rather than some other agency, that should be tasked to pursue the Church disintegration policy. The Bolshevik Party's official or semiofficial contacts with the clerics should be ruled out. We stake on communism rather than on religion. Only VChK is equipped to engage in maneuvering, the whole purpose being to engineer a demise of the clerics. Any other government agency's links with the clerics will merely serve to cast a shadow on the Party, which would be a most dangerous thing»[11].

While he resolved to have VChK entrusted with the challenge of pursuing active measures against the Orthodoxy, Lenin personally undertook to theorize on the matter. As early as May 1920, he most carefully looked through N. Bukharin's «Economics of the Transition Period», underlined some points and scribbled «True!» against the author's observation that «the clergy, ill-educated though some of them might be, should be treated as the societal segments, classes and groups apriori engaged in countering the proletariat, with the political hegemony being normally provided by the generals...». To approve of the suppression policies pursued against those social groups, the leader proceeded to underline more points and jotted down «Precisely!» against the concluding remark that «the proletarian coercion across the board, starting from shootings and all the way through labor conscriptions, paradoxically as it may sound, has been proved to make the techniques to help produce the communist mankind out of the human material left by the capitalist era...»[12].

* * *

The Church struggled hard to survive. Over the Civil War years, Russia's episcopate had radically dwindled: some of the prelates died from natural causes, others perished, while still others left the homeland. The Church National Assembly ruled for the numbers of archbishoprics to be significantly increased, with each diocese establishing a few parishes. The seemingly insurmountable barriers notwithstanding, the Assembly's edict was effectively implemented. In the course of 1918, four prelateships were ordained, which was roughly the pre-Revolution annual average. In 1919, 14 new bishops were installed, while in 1921 the number of such ordainments shot up to as many as 39.

In the summer of 1921, the Russian people, ruined by the Civil War and ravaged by the internecine strife, were hit by yet another calamity: the Volga, the Urals, the Caucasus, the Crimea and the southern Ukraine were devastated by a most severe drought. Famine set in to engulf Russia's thirty-four regions. By May 1922, nearly 20 million people had been starving. About a million died, with two million children getting orphaned. While seeking to flee from their deadly famine areas, crowds of dwellers of the dying villages just walked away to safety or traveled in their horse-drawn carts to only get utterly exhausted and drop dead by the roads in large numbers. There appeared press reports of cases of cannibalism and cadaver-eating.

In the meantime, the Communist International (Comintern) headquarters had been busy nurturing another bloody strike at the Church of Christ. To provide the right verbal excuse, it was alleged that the Church had been too scantily helping the famine-stricken areas, that the clergy remained deaf to the moans of the dying and that they cared little about the people's calamity.

In February 19, 1922, Patriarch Tikhon issued an appeal to the Orthodox flock to call on parishes and local church communities to make donations of unfunctional precious church plates and artifacts to support the starving.

The high priest's appeal, motivated by the fatherly and charitable love for the suffering children of God, was responded with a radical upsurge of attacks on the Orthodox Church through the press and public appearances. Eventually, in February 23, 1922, the All-Russian Central Executive Committee (VTsIK) issued a decree on forceful confiscation of Church treasures to allegedly satisfy the needs of the starving.

To respond to that illegal decree, Patriarch Tikhon issued the address that particularly reads: «From the Church's perspective, the decree has been a sacrilegious act, and we generally consider it our duty to pass it that way and let it be known to all of our true followers. Given the extreme hardships in the nation, we found it appropriate to give out for charity the assorted religious artifacts that have not been consecrated or used to conduct Mass... However, we refuse to go along with expropriations, «voluntary donations» though they might be termed, of the consecrated articles that are barred from being used for other-than-religious-service purposes under the Ecumenical Church's canon law and are punishable as sacrilege, with lay persons running the risk of excommunication and the clergy confronting the threat of laycizing or defrocking (Rule 73 of the Apostolic Rules, and Rule 10 of the Two-Session Assembly Rulings)».

The Patriarch's address was sent out to all of the diocese (eparchy) bishops to be then multiplied and distributed further on to the parishes. But the government authorities viewed the high priest's message as an illegal action and proceeded to toughen their pressures on the Church.

As the Church assets were expropriated throughout Russia, there were 1414 cases of bloodshed amongst the believers, with the pogrom-style horrible harvest producing hundreds of fatalities, with thousands of other victims being either injured or thrown behind bars.

* * *

In March 19, 1922, Chairman of Sovnarkom Lenin wrote a letter that through the agency of the Secretary of the Central Committee of the Russian Communist Party of Bolsheviks (TsK RKP (b)) Molotov was then secretly distributed to all the Politbureau members. Prefacing the message's main body was this instruction: «The request is to absolutely exclude making copies of the letter. Each Politbureau member, Cde Kalinin included, should leave their notes on the received document».

«The events at Shuya», read the letter, «should necessarily be traced to the communication recently distributed by the Russian Telegraph Agency (ROSTa) to the national newspaper offices for in-house consumption, the report being about the Petrograd-based Black-Hundreders preparing to stand out against the decree on expropriation of Church treasures. Should that report be linked with what the press writes about the clergy's attitudes towads the decree on expropriation of Church treasures and should it then be compounded with what we already know about Patriarch Tikhon's illegal appeal, we could safely deduce that the Black-Hundred clergy together with their high priest have been purposefully scheming to unleash a decisive battle against us at this very moment.

Obviously, the leading Black-Hundred clergy members thought through that scheme of theirs most carefully and have now been firmly sticking to it. The Shuya events evidently make a link in their comprehensive plan of action.

To my knowledge, at this point our acknowledged adversary is committing a grave error, as he seeks to get us involved in the fray when he appears to be hopelessly disadvantaged. Conversely, at this particular point in time we seem to be extremely well equipped, the chance possibly being the best or standing at 99 percent in our favor, to totally rout the enemy, achieve a triumphant victory and secure the desired positions for decades to come. It is precisely now and only now, with cannibalism still rampant in the famine-stricken regions and the dead strewn along the roads by the hundred or possibly thousand, that we can (hence, we must) proceed with expropriation of the Church's treasures most aggressively and relentlessly, while unhesitatingly putting down any and all protestations. It is exactly now and only now that the overwhelming majority of the peasant masses will come to be either on our side or, at worst, unable to meaningfully come out in support of the tiny handful of Black-Hundred clergy and reactionary urban philistines that nonetheless are willing to forcefully oppose the latest Soviet decree.

Whatever it takes, we need to have Church treasures expropriated in the most resolute and speedy manner in order to build up the funds to the tune of several hundred million rubles in gold (suffice it to recall the fabulous riches possessed by some monasteries and lavras). Unless we achieve that, no government-sponsored effort in general, no development project in the national economy in particular and no substantive backing of our foreign policy positions, particularly those held at the Genova talks, would appear to be practicable. We should exert every imaginable effort to secure those treasures reported to be several hundred million (possibly, several billion) gold rubles worth altogether. And it is at this juncture that the objective could securely be achieved. All considerations appear to be indicative of the fact that the effort would not succeed at any later stage, for no other circumstance but the extreme famine across the land would enable us to take advantage of the sentiments of the broad peasant masses, which would either make those masses receptive to our policies or at least allow us to neutralize the masses in the sense that they would be convinced of our unquestionable and utter win in the struggle aimed to secure the treasures.

So, I come to positively conclude that it is today that we must mount a decisive and uncompromising battle against the Black-Hundred clergy in order to quell their resistance with the extent of brutality which they would be recalling for decades. This is my vision of the campaign to achieve the goal.

V.I. Lenin. Photograph, 1920s.

Appearing formally with any kind of policy measures should exclusively be Cde Kalinin, while Cde Trotsky should never and under no circumstances appear in the press or make any other public pronouncements on the matter.

The directive circulated in behalf of the Politbureau on the expropriations being temporarily frozen should not be disavowed, for it could help make the enemy believe we are vacillating or feel scared...

...The forthcoming Party congress should hold a closed-door session... and pass a classified resolution to the effect that the expropriation of Church treasures, particularly those held by the wealthier lavras, monasteries and churches, should necessarily be carried out resolutely, mercilessly and within the shortest possible timeframe. The larger numbers of reactionary bourgeois elements and reactionary clerics we manage to shoot while we at it, the better. It is exactly today that we need to teach that breed a lesson, which should be hard enough to make them hate the very idea of launching any form of resistance for decades to come.

To assure the appropriate oversight of the expeditious and effective execution of the said measures, the congress should hold a secret session and without much ado set up a dedicated commission, with Cde Trotsky and Cde Kalinin having to be made the commissioners. No mention of the commission should be allowed in the press, for the subsequent operations should be devised and managed along the regular-Soviet or regular-Party lines and should never be attributed to the commission. Highly trusted and most competent operatives should be involved in the effort, which is expected to cover the wealthier lavras, monasteries and churches».

In March 30, 1922, at its sitting the Politbureau passed the Lenin-initiated scheme aimed to eliminate the Church as an institutional structure: «Arrest of the Holy Synod and the Patriarch should be viewed as necessary... The press should be frenetically engaged to support the drive... Requisitions should be conducted throughout the nation, with the churches holding no treasures of relevance being left untouched»[13].

In the course of State-versus-Church trials, launched across the country, the defendants quite obviously cited the Patriarch's message taken as their guidance whenever they refused to go along with illegal requisitions of consecrated articles held at the shrines. Hence, the tribunals kept passing the rulings demanding that Patriarch Tikhon be brought to justice.

Then came the day when the Izvestiya daily carried this announcement: «The just-completed Moscow Tribunal trial of a whole batch of Moscow-based clerics and other citizens charged with opposing the requisition of Church treasures, with Patriarch Tikhon and Archbishop Nikandr taking the witness stand, has come to quite clearly and explicitly determine that the latter headed the organization Orthodox Hierarchy, drafted a plan of action as part of the campaign to resist the expropriation of Church treasures and used the organization's local chapters to have that plan distributed amongst the broader masses, thereby provoking numerous public disturbances. Given the evidence, the Moscow Tribunal ruled to have Patriarch Tikhon (Citizen Belavin) and Archbishop Nikandr (Citizen Fenomenov) duly prosecuted, the appropriate materials to help proceed with investigation being forwarded to Narkomyust)».

The long-hatched scheme finally came to fruition: the Patriarch was turned into a defendant and placed behind bars, while the bishops and priests were outlawed. Indicative of the scale of the pogrom, that hit the Russian clergy in connection with the organized drive to expropriate Church treasures, would be the following statistics: shot and tortured to death – 8,110 persons, 2,691 out of that number being the secular clergy and 5,409 being the regular clergy that included monks, nuns and novices of either gender.

The concentration camp on the Solovki Isle was made the principal location where counterrevolutionaries in general were confined or incarcerated. Held there were over two thousand captives at any one time, including bishops, priests and layman believers. Making the most horrifying location on the Solovkis was the retribution site at the Calvary-Crucifixion cloister on the Anzer Islet. There, the convicts would all be dying from hunger, cold, penal servitude and beatings.

Two centuries before the Solovki concentration camp was established, in July 18, 1718, Solovki Celibate Priest Iov was on top of the

Anzer Hill and had a vision of the Mother of God that said, «From now on, this hill shall be called Calvary and it shall hold a chapel and Crucifixion Cloister. And it shall be filled with innumerable sufferings».

Today, students of history are fully justified while concluding that the 1921 – 1922 famine in Russia was engineered by the Bolshevist regime. Testifying to that observation, inter alia, are some of Lenin's messages. In that period, he used to repeatedly indicate the grains in the country were to be found in plentiful amounts: «Not far away from Moscow, in the Kursk, Orlov and Tambov Regions, we continue to maintain an estimated inventory of 10 million poods (one pood roughly weighing 16 kgs) of excess grains»[14]. Hence, it had always been a question of politics rather than of food shortfalls. «The bread monopoly, bread voucher slips, all-out labor conscription need to be wielded by the proletarian government as... the most effective tools of audit and oversight. These vehicles of assuring oversight, multiplied by forced labor, appear to be much more relevant than the French Convent's regulations or its guillotine. We not only need to intimidate the capitalists through giving them a sense of the full extent of the proletarian severity, thereby preventing them from scheming any active moves of protest, but also ought to do away with their passive protestations, which are obviously more consequential and destructive in the longer run... Let nine out of ten Russians perish, should that be what it takes to enable the 10 percent to live to see a global revolution in!»[15].

By July 1922, the following amounts of treasures had been expropriated from the shrines of the Russian Orthodox Church: 26 poods and 38 pounds of gold; 21,137 poods and 11 pounds of silver; 82 poods and 10 pounds of other precious metals; 33,456 gem stones and cut diamonds to the overall value of 1,313 carats; 10 pounds and 76 zolotniks (one zolotnik roughly weighing 4 grams) of pearls; 72,383 other precious stones weighing at 1 pood and 29 pounds; 19,064 rubles and silver coins; 1,595 rubles in gold coins; 29 poods and 24 pounds of garments and furnishings laid with precious stones.[16]

The presidential commission on rehabilitation of the victims of repressions in the former Soviet Union recently perused the period's documents and in November 27, 1995 press-conference made the following announcement: «Priests and monks were crucified on the altar holy gates, shot and strangled to death, turned into ice columns. In the early 1920s, 2.5-billion-ruble-worth of Church treasures were requisitioned under the pretext of helping the famine victims in the Volga valley. Admittedly, we have come to find out that merely one million rubles out of the Church «donations» had been expended to purchase food supplies for the starving, with the rest of the funds being either directed to settle in the foreign bank accounts of Party bosses or committed to meet the needs of the world revolution». So, the Bolsheviks merely spent several hundredths of a single percentage point of the funds generated from auctioning the looted Church treasures.[17]

* * *

Evidently, the Bolshevik leaders' goal had been to totally root out the Orthodox Church, but inasmuch as the challenge could not possibly be met within a short term, Trotsky advanced a scheme which, once implemented, would allow to no longer take the Orthodox Church as a domestic policy factor in Russia.

For the scheme to be successfully carried out, there had to be a rift in the Church, with the Patriarch being removed, the very patriarchy eliminated and the renewed leadership installed to head the Russian Orthodox Church. The available renewed prelates had by then quite positively displayed their willingness and ability to serve as the new regime's dutiful and even obsequious tool, for they appeared to be smart enough to quickly see what their masters required of them.

However, staking on the Church renovation had been a short lived idea in the first place. At the March 30, 1922, Politbureau session, Trotsky pointed out that «as early as today we need to set out to design a theoretically-sound propaganda drive to counter the renewed Church. It has to be turned into an abortive brainchild.., while the Black-Hundred clerics should, of course, be made to face a reprisal».

The persecutions against the Church of Christ – executions, jailings and banishments of Orthodox priests – clearly played into the hands of the schismatic renewal advocates. Part of the clergy, while remaining wholly unsupportive of the «revivalists's» reform projects but nonetheless being demoralized by the reigning bloody terror and, motivated either by the fear of death or concern about the future of the Church, that appeared to be fragmenting under the VChK axe, wavered in the long run and opted to join ranks with the revivalists through extending their recognition of the schismatic Supreme Church Authority (VTsU). By May 1922, half of the functional 73 diocese heads had come to report to the revivalist VTsU.

By early 1923, the counter-Christian propaganda drive had grown to be even more fierce and frenzied. Heading the Church-bashing now, was the TsK RKP(b) Antireligion Commission established in 1922. The Commission had for many years been chaired by E. Yaroslavsky (Gubelman).

To better counter the Christian belief and assure the so-called «scientific» remolding of the people, the magazine Bezbozhnik (Atheist) began to be released in 1923. The magazine's opening issue carried an absolutely unbridled introduction by Bukharin, a Comintern executive. The Party official's tenor was readily taken up by the magazine's editors that allowed the publication to include most filthy sketches. Any and all Bezbozhnik pieces used to make outlandish and bizarre reading matter: while authors sought to prove that there was no God, they would simultaneously ferociously rant and rave at God that was officially declared nonexistent.

The magazine likewise carried «theoretical» or «scholastic» materials whose themes and «scarlet threads» would always be focused on proving the animal nature or «beastliness», as the godless scholars chose to term it, of the human being. The article «Materialistic Perception of History» (No. 6, 1923), in particular, reads: «Man is a gregarious animal living in a community, be that a primordial horde, a bourgeois society or the Soviet political system». The magazine's author appears to have been carried away with the realization of his beastly status: «Where does the human being get all these beastly qualities and abnormalities should he actually descend from Adam and Eve? Now, when we have come to see that the humans, as a matter of fact, originate from animals, all things seem to fall into their proper places... According to all indications, the human descended from the beast rather than from Adam and Eve, as claimed by the Bible».

To maintain canonic procedures in the Church and the mandatory apostolic continuity, numerous priests were ordained bishops, like in the previous years. In the course of 1923, 49 ordainments were held, and in 1924 – 23, which had had no precedent in the prerevolutionary Russia. Receiving a priest order, a bishop order the more so, then nearly spelled a sure jail sentence or displacement. Still, thousands of selfless Christians would embark on this thorny path to serve at the holy altar, which continued to be reviled and defamed by the authorities. At the Specialized State Political Administration (OGPU), a fresh file was opened to initiate action against Patriarch Tikhon. However, in June 19, 1925, «Case No. 32530 containing charges against Citizen Belavin Vassily Ivanovich under Articles 59 and 73 of the Criminal Code» was terminated «on account of the death of the individual under investigation».

Our Saint Patriarch Tikhon expired at 23.45 hours on Virgin Mary Day in 1925 at Moscow's Bakunin clinic on Ostozhenka in the 61st year of his pious and burdensome life.

Bolsheviks Take Care of Cultural Heritage

A painter – a boor with a sleepy brush –
Is wrecking the work of a genius
As he freely puts his pointless sketch on top.
But the alien colors drop away with time,
Just like some crumbling scales,
And the work of a true artist comes alive
In all of its pristine beauty.
                    A.S.Pushkin, «Renaissance».

The triumphant Russian revolution precipitated the destruction of the nation's cultural heritage and gave rise to nihilistic attitudes towards any culture, the domestic tradition in the first place.

Providing a solid testimonial to that effect is the Communist Party's anthem explicitly revealing the intentions to tear down the old world and then build a new one, which would have radically different features. The anthem's message had been translated not only into the sphere of societal relationships but also into the effort aimed to build a new civilization. Making the true champion of the resolute global restructuring was founder of the IIIrd Communist International, its leader and theorist, ideologist and arranger of the October Socialist Revolution, head of the Bolshevist government V.I. Lenin.

Lenin maintained that, with the Bolsheviks coming to the seats of power, the bondage of the artists to the customers and their whims would eventually be broken up and the era of free expression of ideas and sentiments would set in.

However, while recognizing the educational utility of arts, Lenin nonetheless held that those should be appropriately channeled in support of the Party, thereby countering one of his own crucial guidelines about the freedom of creative endeavors and the personality of an artist operating under the conditions of an evolving socialist society.

The class struggle, that the Marxist teaching is based upon, could hardly be viewed as a moral phenomenon, for it espoused the supremacy and violence of one social segment with respect to other groups. Hence, the works of art promoting the new political system and justifying the crimes could in no way be passed as moral and truly humanistic creations.

As the Soviet regime matured in its first years, all government agencies had been involved in the overall effort to eradicate the former Russian Empire's heritage across the entire palette, as was demanded by Lenin's teaching on the dictatorship of proletariat.

The drive in that direction was launched with closures of a whole array of periodicals, the move provoking the immediate protestations from V.G. Korolenko and A.M. Gorky that appeared in the Social Democrat daily. April 14,1918, the decree, signed by V.I. Lenin, A.V. Lunacharsky, I.V. Stalin, G.V. Chicherin and V.D. Bonch-Bruyevich, was issued to close down the world-known Saint Petersburg Imperial Academy of Arts and Moscow School of Painting, Sculpture and Achitecture that had played a great role in the growth of Russian national arts. The measure quickly produced an erosion of the established school of fine arts, the void being rapidly filled by the home-grown leftist waves in painting, sculpture and architecture. Chaperoned by Commissar of Public Education Lunacharsky, those fresh currents were introduced in the newly-established free-wheeling Petrograd and Moscow studios of fine arts that had no points of contact with the Russian tradition.

Architecture, which is instrumental in creating human habitats responsible for shaping much of a human being's mood, happened to be placed at the core of the ideological agenda pursued by the Bolsheviks and their leaders. Given that architectural environments carry a very special educational value, right after the October Revolution Lenin initiated the monument propaganda drive and the plan for general rebuilding of Moscow.

Lenin's conversation with notable British «scientific romances» author Herbert G. Wells reveals the whole essence of the Bolshevist policy position on the architectural heritage. In response to Wells' tricky question about old cities incrementally dying away, Russia's new leader said, «Except for isolated historical monuments, the bulk of built-up areas in today's cities will be torn down... Russia needs to be radically renewed and recreated...»[18]. These Lenin's words are starkly demonstrative of complete rejection of the priority of cultural heritage in the Communist society.

Indeed, one had to hate Russia and her people real hard to seek a radical redo of the millennium-old culture!. A whole range of archival materials and witness accounts indicate how bitter, painful and even tragic at times that rebuilding drive had been.

As he entertained his visions of a world revolution, «the Kremlin dreamer» never assumed what fatal consequences could be produced by his calls for elimination of «the exploiters» and expropriation of their assets. Those invitations were sufficient for some elements to launch free-for-alls, plunders, rapes and murders, with the right conditions being thereby created for molestations and burglaries to go unchecked.

Fortunately, given the firmly rooted religious tradition, not all of the people turned out to be villainous and immoral. Suffice it to recall the incident at Uzkoye near Moscow where the local peasants took to arms and opened fire in order to prevent the «requisitioners» from coming in to Prince Trubetskoy's estate. Shortly afterwards, the estate was placed under state protection and opened as a Commissariat of Public Education rest home.

Owner of suburban-Moscow Ostankino, Kuskovo and Ostafyevo estates Pavel Sergeyevich Sheremetev requested his artist-friends S.Yu. Zhukovsky and A.M. Vasnetsov (members of a governmental commission on preservation of the old relics and monuments) to help turn over those properties to the State for the invaluable collections of paintings, sculpture, china, manuscripts and books, domestic and foreign applied arts to be securely maintained. While Ostankino and Kuskovo were made museums, with P.S. Sheremetev named head curator, Ostafyevo was turned into a country house (dacha) for People's Commissar of Education Lunacharsky that graciously permitted the estate's former master to live in one of the service houses (Sheremetev's Moscow city palaces and mansions having been nationalized).

Following the expropriations, huge amounts of historical and artistic treasures were moved to foreign countries either by auction or through Soviet foreign trade offices that were established in later years. The protests by commissioners on preservation of the old relics and monuments notwithstanding, part of the valuables were allowed to be melted down at a specially-built facility at Mytishchi near Moscow.

Closures of churches, monasteries and convents across Russia had not infrequently been followed by their demolitions. Moscow proved to be particularly badly hit: out of the city's 846 churches, cathedrals, chapels and other shrines merely 25 percent of the buildings can be found intact today.

In April 12, 1918, Sovnarkom passed the Lenin-initiated decree «On Removal of Monuments Erected in Honor of Tsars and Their Servants and on Creating Designs for Monuments to Honor the Russian Socialist Revolution». And it so happened that the revolutionary leader was the first one to be personally involved in implementing the decree.

Erected at the site of Grand Duke Sergei Aleksandrovich's assassination in the Kremlin was a large bronze cross featuring Virgin Mary kneeling at the feet of the crucified Christ and the legend reading: «Father, forgive them for they do not know what they are doing». The monument was designed by the great Russian artist Viktor Vasnetsov.

Commandant of the Kremlin P.Malkov recalled: «May 1, 1918, broke with an overcast and gloomy morning... VTsIK and Sovnarkom officials and staffers gathered at 9.30 a.m. at the former Judicial Chamber building in the Kremlin. Within minutes coming out was Vladimir Ilyich, looking cheerful, dropping jest remarks and laughing away. As I came up to report, Ilyich welcomed me with a handshake, wished me a happy holiday, and suddenly shook his finger at me.

«All is good, my dear, all is good», he mimicked me and pointed towards the monument built at the site of assassination of Grand Duke Sergei Aleksandrovich.

I just signed ruefully and then replied, «My fault, Vladimir Ilyich. I have not had it removed for lack of work hands».

«Well, what an excuse you are giving me! You say you lack work hands? You know, to do this job, those can be found this very minute. Well, what do you say, comrades?» queried Vladimir Ilyich as he looked at his entourage to only draw a chorus of supportive voices.

«You see. And you are telling me you lack the work hands. Well, as we still have some minutes to spare, go fetch the ropes».

I quickly ran to the storage room, picked up the ropes and was back in a jiffy. Moving quite swiftly, Vladimir Ilyich made a noose and smartly threw it over the cross. Then, everybody joined in and within a few minutes the monument was nearly enmeshed.

«»Now, all together!» came Vladimir Ilyich's animated command. Lenin, Sverdlov, Avanesov, Smidovich, other VTsIK and Sovnarkom leaders and staffers, plus a few people from a small government office, harnessed themselves with the ropes, pulled, then tugged a bit harder, and the monument toppled onto the cobble stones.

«Away with it! To the scrap yard!» went on Vladimir Ilyich.

Dozens of hands took over at the ropes and the monument was seen rumbling towards the Tainitsky Garden».

**Monument at the place of assassination
of Grand Prince Sergei Alexandrovich in the Kremlin.**

On another occasion, commandant P.Malkov reminisced, «In general, Vladimir Ilyich just could not stand any monuments dedicated to tsars, grand dukes or distinguished generals glorified under the past tsars. Repeatedly, he would make the point that the victorious people should tear down all those loathsome vestiges of the imperial autocracy... Under the express orders from Vladimir Ilyich, coming down in 1918 in Moscow were the monuments to Alexander II in the Kremlin, Alexander III at the Christ the Savior Cathedral, and to General M.D. Skobelev»[19].

Following the Russia-wide discontent of the broad masses with the policies of military communism and terror, the need was definitely there to resort to the well-proven appeasement ploy applied through a set of focused propaganda drives and decrees that for the most part were only wishful thinking and wholly at odds with realities. To provide an example, pronouncements were made and decrees issued to show the Party and the government were concerned about restoration of the Kremlin's historic and architectural monuments damaged in the course of artillery shellings by the Red Guards (only to have many of those totally razed within a decade).

On the night of November 1 – 2, 1917, the Bolshevist artillery shellings destroyed or badly damaged: the Smaller Nikolayevsky Palace (formerly, the quarters of Metropolitan Platon), Miracle of the Archangel Mikhail Cathedral, Annunciation and Alexei the Blessed Churches, superior's quarters at Chudov Monastery, Twelve Apostles Cathedral, Cathedral of the Ascension Convent, central dome of the Assumption Cathedral, southern porch of the Annunciation Cathedral, belfry of the Ivan the Great Tower, a dome of the Pokrovsky Cathedral on Red Square (Vassily the Blessed Cathedral), roof of the marqee atop the Beklemishev Tower, marquee and wall at the Nikolsky Gates, face and clockwork of the chiming clock on the Spassky Tower.

Following surrender by the cadets, that chose to save the Kremlin from further shellings, and seizure of the Kremlin grounds in November 2, 1917 by the Red Guards, the Moscow Soviet of Workers', Soldiers' and Peasants' Deputies, while being apprehensive about the safety of the treasures held by the Kremlin museums, ordered the Narkompros' Artistic Education Department to immediately set up a commission tasked to protect the old relics and monuments.

In the initial stage, the Commission included just 17 members. By January 1918, however, with more artists, sculptors, architects, historians, museum curators and other experts getting enrolled, the total number of commissioners had grown to seventy, which allowed to establish more dedicated branches and divisions.

Restoring the Kremlin architectural monuments made the Commission's top-priority objective. In early 1918, the Council of People's Commissars earmarked R450 thousand for the purpose, a huge amount in those days. The governmental directives, in fact, stipulated that the Kremlin's magnificent architectural assemblage should be restored to its prerevolutionary splendor, with the tough deadlines being set to have the rehabilitation completed as early as possible, within a single building season at best. But the rebuilding effort had to be protracted on account of the ongoing Civil War on the one hand and because of the archeologists and arts historians uncovering major alterations of the Kremlin structures' original designs on the other hand.

With the Kremlin renovation work completed, the Narkompros' Commission proceeded to draft a grander scheme of city restoration projects. Work was launched to rebuild the Kitay-Gorod walls and towers, V.V. Golitsin palace, Paraskeva the Friday Church on Okhotny Ryad, Kazansky Cathedral on Red Square.

Most unfortunately, the benign policy in the area of culture did not last long, with the funding for research and restoration projects phasing out. Then, a reverse drive was initiated to eliminate what had been intact. In 1922, torn down was the Alexander Nevsky Chapel on Manezhnaya Square, in 1927 – the Red Gates (designed by D. Ukhtomsky, 1757), and a year later – the Three Holy Bishops Church (1699) near the Red Gates. The year 1928 marks the beginning of scheduled demolition of the age-old religious architectural clusters and stand-alone churches throughout the city. The just-completed restoration work in the Kremlin, which proved to be tremendously costly in terms of human and financial resources, did not prevent the authorities from giving orders in 1928 – 1929 to detonate the Ascension and Chudov Monasteries with their Ascension of the Christ (20th century) and Miracle of the Archangel Mikhail (16th century) Cathedrals; Great Martyr Catherine church (17th – 19th cen-

**P. Samonov: Monument to General M.D. Skobelev. 1912.
Demolished in 1919.**

Bearing-out of sarcophagus from Vosnesensky Cathedral of the Kremlin. 1919.

The chambers of V.V. Gagarin in Okhotny Row. Process of restoration. 1919.

turies) Holy Mikhail of Maleya Church (17th century), Annunciation of Our Lady and Holy Bishop Alexei Churches (15th – 17th centuries). Slated to be seen no more were the Konstantin and Yelena Church (1651) on the slopes of the Kremlin Hill and Annunciation of Our Lady Church (1731).

The Kremlin's destructive cycle was completed with the demolition of the Transfiguration of the Savior on the Bor Cathedral (1328), the oldest structure on the Hill, in 1933. The bitter irony, generated by the extreme degree of cynicism, used to be part of the psyche of Soviet leaders. «One day», recalled N.P. Gushchin, the former deputy commandant of the Kremlin, «after he had given me a new task, Stalin lit his pipe, came up to the window and, while no longer spotting the familiar domes of the Transfiguration of the Savior on the Bor Cathedral, remarked in mock surprise, «Something seems to have been there before?», as if he had wholly forgotten about his recent orders for the cathedral to be demolished within the shortest possible time. As he proceeded making his points on the cathedral, he lifted his hands in dismay and, addressing no one in particular, concluded quite indignantly, «You just let them have a go, and they would break the Kremlin Palace to smithereens the very next day». His long-lasting habit of impunity fostered by the blind fear of the toady go-getters around him had Stalin totally oblivious of the true perception of his illegal undertakings. He would invariably be seconded and even emulated by most of his Party associates.

That sort of policy was deeply rooted in Lenin's attitude to the heritage of past generations. Architectural monuments were perceived by the enlightened Sovnarkom chairman as nothing more than historical lumber. «How can you», he reproached Lunacharsky, «attach such importance to that or other old building, no matter how valuable it can be, when we are on the verge of breaking into the social system that would be capable of creating things of beauty by far transcending the dreams of the past?»[20].

Lenin also entertained most unusual ideas about replacements for the religion. In his remarks at an early 1922 TsK RKP(b) Politbureau session, M. Kalinin mentioned, «As I talked privately with Vladimir Ilyich one day, in answer to my question about what the religion could be phased out by, he said the challenge should wholly stay with the theater, which must wean the peasant masses away from ritual assemblages». That truly had been the policy stand of the revolutionary leader: the preliminary punitive measures by VChK detachments were supposed to be followed up by the theater, which would be entirely engaged to pursue the assigned goal. But that job was yet to come. For the moment, the leader gave Lunacharsky these orders, «I suggest all theaters be interred for now. It is the literacy problem rather than the theater that the people's commissar of education should handle in the first place» (53:142). In the meantime, when the question of national electrification came under discussion, Lenin argued that the peasants would see God replaced by electricity, which they would pray to and sense the might of central authorities rather than Heaven. The absurdities that the philosophizing Soviet leader dropped in his lifetime could hardly ever be inventoried![21].

The schemes to primarily demolish monuments of religious arts and architecture had been appropriately underpinned by the Party's cognizant bodies with the propaganda that pushed those barbaric actions as radical measures to fight the religion.

Desolate shrines and closed monasteries could nearly freely be separated from their treasures, which then were offered for sale in foreign markets. In April 1922, while being heavily concerned about the

D. Ukhtomsky: Red Gates, 1757; Church of the Three Prelates. 1699. Demolished in 1927 – 1928.

Church of the Savior on the Bor in the Kremlin. 1328. Demolished in 1933.

Subbotnik (a day of voluntary unpaid work, usually a Saturday) to dismantle Simonov Monastery. 1925.

catastrophic state of things with the former Church properties, noted members of the Russian arts and literature community approached the government with a plea to take urgent steps to save valuable articles worthy of being kept in museums. That delegation of Moscow historians, archeologists and museum researchers included Professors D.N. Anuchin and M.M. Bogoslovsky, Directors of the History Museum N.M. Shchekotov and I.E. Grabar. Following that solicitation, the museum department of the VTsIK's main science directorate (Glavnauka) issued a directive barring elimination not only of Church valuables dated earlier than 1725 but also of any other items passed as having superior artistic value. However, the government could easily override Glavnauka's directives and the flow of Church valuables to foreign customers had incrementally been on the rise.

The «new Russia» did not seem to appreciate the intellectual assets of the past. In the years of the War Communism, the class struggle had been pursued as far as to cast off as ballast part of Moscow's population that included the nobility, merchants and clergy. As early on as March 1919, Lenin shared his far-reaching plans with American journalist Lincoln Steffens and said, «We just need to devise some way of getting rid of the bourgeois and upper social classes. They would not let us achieve any economic shifts other than those they would have welcomed before the October Revolution. So, they have to be knocked out of here. Personally, I do not see how they could be frightened into fleeing from Russia without massive shootings... To me, the only effective solution is for the threat of Red terror to sow the seeds of trepidation, thereby compelling them to get away».

The Civil War, its fatality count reaching 13 million people, was finally over. The terrifying famine of 1921, that took more than five million human lives, appeared to have become a thing of the past. First indications of the rebirth of spiritual life began to be evident across the spectrum of Russian society. Clubs and interest societies reemerged, with noted-scientist public appearances and open disputes drawing huge audiences. Independent writers unions and partnerships of poets and artists came to be established against the backdrop of «proletarian culture». Larger provincial capitals started to grow their own philo-

sophical, historical and psychological societies. The Moscow Soviet, for one, had registered the Free Academy of Spiritual Culture created by N. Berdyaev. Attracted by the initial projects launched under the New Economic Policy, dozens of thousands of refugees of the Civil War began to return to their homeland.

However, in May 15, 1922, Lenin directed Minister of Justice D. Kursky to enter into the Criminal Code a number of additions stipulating the legal procedures for deportation of the antagonistic intelligentsia. In particular, the leader directed «to add the right to have the sentence by shooting commuted to a deportation to a foreign country for a fixed span of time or without duration, subject to confirmation by the VTsIK Presidium, and also add the sentence by shooting as punishment for unauthorized return from abroad» (45:189). And four days later, Lenin sent a letter to the «Iron Felix» to substantively describe what sort of preparatory training the punitive organs should undergo to be best equipped to handle the issues in question.

Eventually, in August 31, 1922, the Pravda daily carried the front-page «First Warning» material on the deportation «by the dedicated State Political Administration (GPU) decision of a batch of more militant counterrevolutionaries, mostly the professors, medical doctors, agronomists and writers, to the Republic's northern provinces, with part of those individuals being expelled from the country». Since the article made no mention of either the numbers or names, it was not clear which of the two punishments, «banishment to northern provinces» or «deportation abroad», was to be taken as the most severe. The phrase about «the deported individuals nearly including no big names», as a matter of fact, amounted to an outrageous lie. Big names were there to be found, and quite a few, too.

Declared enemies of the people were members of almost all intelligentsia communities (liberal arts, science and technology) that the leader as early as September 1919 in his letter to M. Gorky explicitly branded as «petty intellectuals, lackeys of the capital, imagining themselves to be the brains of the nation. But the fact is that they make the dung rather than the brains» (51:48).

The sentiments notwithstanding, deportations of intellectuals had not been allowed to escalate to reach a large scale. The deported could not be brought to face the charges that the West could accept. Then, the communist leadership came to conclude that it would be more affordable and predictable to «let the brains of the nation rot domestically either on the Solovkis or the Kolyma»[22].

Thus, Moscow became one of the last major European cities where the Jacobin experience of destroying the national culture has been fully replayed, as brought against the past trials of Rome, Paris, London, Madrid, Vienna and other older cities.

For some yet-to-be-grasped reason, Moscow kept its name, while Saint Petersburg and many other historic cities of Russia did not. Demolitions of historic monuments and renaming of cities have obviously made the links of a single chain, the whole purpose being to get the posterity to be fully oblivious of past memories.

In the late 1920s – early 1930s, the effort to preserve the cultural heritage had been particularly ineffective, which only served to put in doubt the feasibility of any further projects pursued by the Commission on the Preservation of Old Relics and Monuments and the All-Russian Research and Restoration Facility. In 1934, I.E. Grabar resigned from his position as head of that official body. In fact, the Commission on the Preservation of Monuments, set up as far back as 1918, ceased to be functional on account of many of its authoritative and influencial members either passing away or emigrating. Leaving Russia for good in those years were many outstanding artists that so enthusiastically volunteered their services to help keep the Russian cultural heritage: I.Y. Repin, S.T. Konenkov, S.Yu. Zhukovsky, K.A. Korovin, F.A. Malyavin, L.O. Pasternak. Dying within a short order were: V.Ye. Makovsky, V.M. Vasnetsov, V.D. Polenov, A.S. Stepanov, A.Ye. Arkhipov, A.M. Korin, M.Kh. Aladzhalov, A.M. Vasnetsov.

The 1930s witnessed the apogee of the domestic culture destruction drive, which went totally unprotested by any public voice, for such a voice could be found nowhere. Engineered and activated then was a smoothly-running destructive machinery finely tuned by the Bolshevist ideologists and bolstered by the lower-level unscrupulous and ignorant masses of people that awakened to only be involved in the whirl of the self-consumptive «dance macabre», with the enthusiasts absolutely unaware of the nation's millennium-old spiritual heritage remaining the only one value that the living and future generations should work for.

Anyway, it has to be concluded that the general plan for rebuilding Moscow was based on the idea of preconceived demolition of historical and cultural monuments.

Moscow – Capital of the Soviet Russia

The seizure of power in Moscow by the Bolsheviks was announced from the balcony of the former Moscow governor-general's mansion on Skobelev Square, the location of the Moscow Soviet of Workers', Peasants' and Soldiers' Deputies since the victorious 1917 February Revolution. In Petrograd, holding its first session then was the All-Russian Constituent Assembly convened in order to define Russia's new political system with due regard for the interests of all societal segments. As he sought to consolidate his power, Lenin promised to adhere to whatever ruling would be passed by the Constituent Assembly. But it turned out so that the vote was carried by the left socialist revolutionaries (SRs), with the Bolshevik-deputies being by far outvoted. Upon coming to know that the people's deputies were not supportive of the Bolsheviks, Lenin ordered the armed sailors to have the Assembly disbanded. The Russian society was on the verge of confronting the specter of disintegration and civil war as a result. Given the risks, the Bolsheviks were compelled to merge with the left SRs and other political parties and leave Petrograd. Headquartered at the heart of European Russia, they felt better placed to counter the White armies deployed in the Baltics, Ukraine, the Don-river, the Volga-river, the Urals and elsewhere throughout Russia. Being primarily based in Moscow enabled the Bolsheviks to enjoy a fair degree of maneuver and capacity to quickly shift and lift Red Army contingents to most threatened areas, for the recently-built railroad network had turned the newly-chosen capital city into a huge hub of transportation links. Preparations to move the Soviet government to Moscow had been conducted under the conditions of utter secrecy.

In March 16, 1918, the 4th All-Russian Special Congress of Soviets declared Moscow capital of the Russian Soviet Federative Socialist Republic (RSFSR). In the initial stage, Party and government officials and their families had to be accommodated at hotels in the central Moscow. Larger hotels with restaurants and movie houses, located on squares semi-circling the Kremlin and the Kitay-Gorod neighborhood, as well as those up Tverskaya Street were labeled Houses of Soviets and Houses of Unions numbered 1 through 28. The largest place was the Second House of Soviets (Metropol Hotel) that temporarily served as Russia's main government building. Housed there, were the VTsIK of Soviets of Workers', Peasants', Cossacks and Red Servicemen's Deputies; numerous officials and staffers headed by the VTsIK Chairman Sverdlov. Lenin was accommodated at the First House of Soviets (National Hotel).

The Delovoi Dvor hotel at the Varvara's Gates was turned into the Fourth House of Unions. The First House of Unions was located at the Nobility Assembly building on Okhotny Riad, the new name of the building holding for more than seven decades now. The Peterhof Hotel at the corner of Vozdvizhenka and Mokhovaya was named the Fourth House of Soviets that was filled with the VTsIK reception office and apartments of the Party and Soviet officials. The Eighth House of Soviets on Manezhnaya Street was assigned to house the Comintern Executive Committee. Numerous Comintern functionaries, that arrived in Moscow in the early 1920s from all over the world, were accommodated at the Lux Hotel (then Tsentralnaya Hotel) on Tverskaya Street.

The newly-established Soviet office buildings were scattered along the city's principal arteries, which included:
– the semi-circle of central city squares from Lubianka Square via Teatralnaya and Manezhnaya Squares down to the Christ the Savior Cathedral at the Prechistenka Gates;
– the main thoroughfare originating from Red Square and running up Tverskaya Street all the way to the Khodynka Field in north-westernly direction.

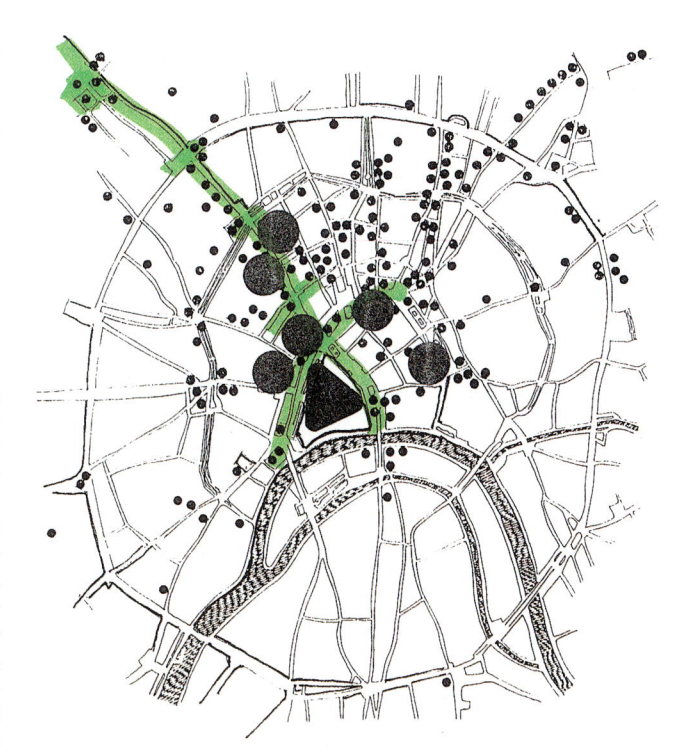

Hotel of the Soviet of People's Commissars in Moscow. 1918.

Those formed sort of a bow and arrow rested against the Kremlin and aimed at Petrograd. The traffic, coming from the Khodynka Field in the reverse south-easterly direction would go past the Vassily the Blessed Cathedral, across the Moskva-river and further on into the Zamoskvorechye areas. Making the capital city's main plaza now was Sovetskaya Square (former Skobelevskaya Square).

Inasmuch as Muscovites displayed no special liking for VKP(b) leaders, Lenin thought it best to shelter behind the Kremlin walls as early as possible. The Senate building was quickly renovated to house top Party and government officials, with second-tier buildings assigned to accommodate staffers, security elements and support personnel.

As it was turned into a closed governmental residential area, the Kremlin was actually made off limits to all city-wide functions. However, all large-scale events then began to be held on the Red Square. Soon, quite a necropolis emerged at the Kremlin wall to honor the new Russia's heroes. Installed over the common grave at the Senate Tower was a dedicated plaque-composition by sculptor S.T. Konenkov, the reliefed mural featuring a figure of the genius of glory and the legend reading «To those who have fallen for peace and brotherhood of the peoples». In 1919, buried next to it was the VTsIK Chairman Sverdlov, in 1920 – Commissar for Posts and Telegraph Podbelsky. The row of graves had stretched too far, and since 1925 only urns with ashes have been placed in the Kremlin wall, thereby turning it into sort of a state columbarium. But the most distinguished Party officials continued to be interred at the wall.

In May 1, 1918, the new regime's first festivity was staged by a team of avant-garde artists headed by A. Vesnin. The Kremlin towers were draped in red, with a grandstand for the leaders being put up at the Senate Tower facing the mid-section of the Red Square. A few military elements, that paraded from Tverskaya past the grandstand and down to Vassilyevsky Slope, established the precedent for all further parades and public rallies.

A portentous event occurred in the course of the first parade. The red cloth on Nikolskaya Tower burst open to reveal the Nicholas the Miracle Worker Icon placed just above the gates. That happening was taken as a major auspice by all Muscovites. In May 9, 1918, the Saint Nicholas Day, religious processions carrying cross and banners were held by all Moscow parishes willing to visit the Nikolskaya Tower. Thousands of Orthodox believers with icons and standards

Necropolis of the heroes of the Red Russia. 1922.

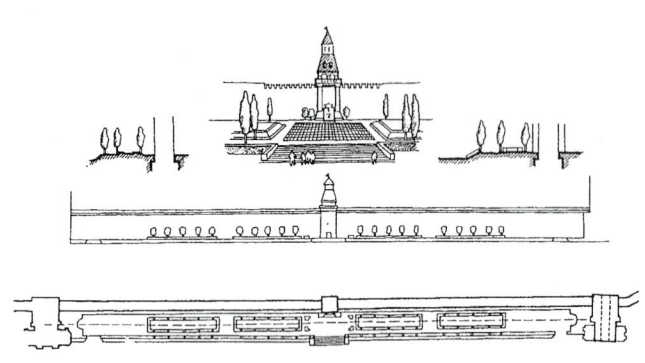

Layout project of communal graves at the Kremlin wall on the Red Square. 1918.

flocked to the Red Square to be welcomed by the newly-enthroned Patriarch Tikhon. The event's massive character and beauty, with religious hymns performed by the marchers, most positively dwarfed the 1st of May parade. The confrontation between the capital city's population and new authorities, between Lenin and Patriarch Tikhon then clearly came into the open.

Passing through the Red Square in religious processions on that day were about 400 thousand people, according to rough estimates by the Bolsheviks. Standing on top of the Kremlin wall in the company of Chinese security guards, Lenin viewed the square entirely filled with people[23]. Admittedly, Lenin-initiated rallies would draw no more than 80 – 100-thousand-strong crowds, the promotive effort being exerted each time, too. It was obvious that Moscow would not rush to recognize the new authorities.

To pursue its external and domestic policy goals, the central government began to take urgent steps. The challenges were to put at ease the world community, show that the Communists care about the national cultural heritage, secure international recognition and attract foreign loans on the one hand, and remove the Nicholas the Miracle Worker Icon from the Nikolskaya Tower, ostensibly for restoration

Procession to the Icon of Nicholas the Miracle-maker on Red Square. 9 May 1918.

purposes, thereby putting an end to the ongoing religious services on the Red Square, on the other hand.

The effort was then launched to restore the country's historical, cultural and architectural monuments, with the decrees issued in the meantime to tear down the monuments dedicated to the former tsars and their servants, promote the culture of newly-built monuments, etc. Notably, Lenin personally ordered the Nikolskaya Tower to be urgently renovated, with the double-headed eagles on top kept intact.

In that period, A. Lunacharsky publicly appeared on the issue of monumental propaganda in Moscow as «one of the many vehicles used to carry out the global propaganda of ideas» of the new proletarian culture. For the Red Square to be closed to religious ceremonies and for «the sacred symbols of the Soviet politically-charged mass»[24] to be subsequently installed, it was deemed essential to:

– utilize the Red Square, formerly a market place, to exclusively stage political rallies; (In 1922, a brickwork grandstand was put in place there (designed by Mayat);

– have the state funeral rites conducted on the Red Square rather than in the Kremlin, and have a necropolis laid out at the wall;

– have state ceremonial functions moved from Sovetskaya to the Red Square;

– have the Alexander IIIrd Monument at the Christ the Savior Cathedral replaced by the Liberated Labor Monument;

– have the symbols of Orthodoxy and tsarist autocracy banished.

The symbols of Orthodoxy and tsarist autocracy had been eliminated against the backdrop of the efforts to do away with local governments in the provinces, pursue forced collectivization in the rural areas and enable Party elements to consolidate all power. Coexistence of historic and socialist values in Moscow had grown to become a problem. Demolition of the old fabric grown from the Byzantine Christianity and its replacement with the newly-created myth made a standard element of the emerging architectural utopia. State monopoly on land and real estate in general served to simplify the task of destroying the old built-up areas Besides, the arbitrary «red line» strategies would not be predicated on any previous clearances or compensations.

The buildings evacuated by the owners, were left to grow decrepit, with log structures being taken apart for firewood. Larger buildings heavily suffered from the individual heater-stoves that could never be evenly stoked to avoid destructive temperature extremes. The nationalized apartment buildings of the rich, rapidly filled by large numbers of working-class tenants that were not required to pay the utilities, soon dramatically degraded.

Lenin Plan for Monumental Propaganda

No more penny-worth truths,
Cast away the old values.
Streets shall make our brushes,
Squares shall be our easels.
V.Mayakovsky, 1918

In April 4, 1918, the People's Commissar of Education A.V. Lunacharsky had a scheduled meeting with V.I. Lenin in the Kremlin. «It has been for quite some time since I began to be haunted by the idea that I am now going to expound to you», said Lenin. «You remeber Campanella in his «Sunshine State» describing his imaginary socialist city's walls bearing the murals that served graphic lessons in natural and political histories and promoted civic duties, that actually had a role in educating and nurturing the younger generations. In my judgment, that approach is not so naive and we could improve on it and proceed to some immediate applications...

I would call what I have in mind the monumental propaganda. To work to that end, you should first make arrangements with the Moscow and Petrograd Soviets, while simultaneously seeking to mobilize the needed artistic resources and pick out the right city locations. Our weathers would hardly be friendly to the kind of murals Campanella dreamt about, so I mostly have in mind the visions to be filled by sculptors and poets.

Assorted vantage sites could be chosen where building walls or specially-erected structures could be used to bear brief and expressive logos containing the core principles and values of Marxism as well as apt and succinct judgments on those or other major historical events... I am not talking about eternal things or any timeframes for that matter. But let all those creations be functional for the time being.

But the logos to me are less relevant than monuments: bust or complete figures, possibly, reliefs and groups.

A roll should be compiled to include all progenitors of socialism or its theorists and practitioners, as well as those luminaries of philosophical thought, science, arts, whatever, that truly make the champions of culture though they can hardly be regarded as direct precursors of socialism.

Use that roll to have a team of sculptors commissioned to design short-lived monuments that could be fabricated either from plaster or concrete. It is essential that they should send a clear message to the masses, that they should be made to catch the eye...

Attention should particularly be focused on monument dedication ceremonies. Some of us, other comrades and noted experts could be asked to make public remarks at those events. Let all of those ceremonies be turned into propaganda actions and small festive events. Afterwards, as jubilee dates come to be celebrated, words of praise to honor the given great personality could be said again and again, with the remarks being clearly traced to our revolution and its tasks each time...».[25]

This conversation, as a matter of fact, holds all of the essential guidelines for a plan of monumental propaganda.

In April 12, 1918, Sovnarkom confirmed the decree «On Monuments of the Republic». Signed by the Sovnarkom Chairman V.I. Lenin and the People's Commissars A.V. Lunacharsky and I.V. Stalin, the decree reads:

«To commemorate the great takeover that has transformed Russia, the Council of People's Commissars hereby rules to have:

1) the monuments, erected in honor of the tsars and their servants and designed to have neither historical nor artistic value, removed from city squares and streets...

2) the dedicated commission, made up of People's Commissars of Education and Republican Properties and head of the department for fine arts with the Commissariat of Education, make arrangements with the fine arts boards of Moscow and Petrograd and determine the monuments to be slated for removal;

V.I. Lenin and Ya.M. Sverdlov attending the ceremony of unveiling the memorial plaque «To the those who gave their lives for the cause of peace and fraternity of peoples» on the Red Square. 7th November 1918.

Inauguration of the monument to K. Marx and F. Engels on Theater Square. 7th November 1918.

3) the said Commission tasked to mobilize the artistic resources and organize a large-scale contest for projects to design monuments aimed to commemorate the great days of the Russian Socialist Revolution...».[26]

In July 17, 1918, Sovnarkom heard the report by the Chairman of the Moscow Sculptors Union S.T. Konenkov on the plans to arrange a contest for monuments to the outstanding personalities as well as the report by the Deputy People's Commissar for Education M.N. Pokrovsky on the installation in Moscow of 50 monuments dedicated to «great men in the areas of revolutionary and public activities, philosophy, literature, arts and sciences».

In July 30, 1918, Sovnarkom considered the finalized list of monuments to great men and added the names of Bauman, Ukhtomsky and Heine, while striking off the name of the Russian philosopher Vladimir Solovyev. The ruling called for the monuments to Marx and Engels to be pursued as top-priority projects.

The sculptors community was overenthusiastic in their willingness to win the orders. While sparing no effort, they sought to speedily craft the desired figures and even whole groups of figures (with the remuneration being the same either for less-sophisticated or more labor-consuming projects).

In October 7, 1918, dedicated in ceremony on Triumphalnaya Square was the bust-monument to A.N. Radishchev, the composition making a sample of the realistic approach in the area of monumental plastic art.

B. Korolev: Monument to M. Bakunin. 1918 – 1919.

B. Korolev: Project of monument to K. Marx. 1919.

In November 3, 1918, four other interim monuments were unveiled. The grotto in the Alexander Gardens had a concrete sculpture of Robespierre (designed by B. Sandomirskaya) installed on the pad right in front of it. Built along the Kitay-Gorod wall were monuments to the poets I.S. Nikitin (designed by A. Blazhevich) and A.V. Koltsov (designed by S. Syreishchikov). Large contingents of workers from Moscow and near-Moscow plants and factories brought along their banners, choirs and bands to attend the dedication ceremonies. Appearing before the crowds was Sergei Yesenin who made some heartfelt remarks that were followed up with more speeches and poetry recitals. Simultaneously, the monument to T.G. Shevchenko was then dedicated closer to Trubnaya Square on Rozhdestvensky Boulevard. The latter sculpture was designed by S.M. Volnukhin, who also created the broadly-known monument to printing pioneer Ivan Fedorov. Coming to appear with the opening remarks was A.M. Kollontay. In November 7, 1918, V.I. Lenin attended the opening of the K. Marx and F. Engels Monument on Revolution Square. Massive rallies were held to unveil the monuments to: Jores on Novinsky Boulevard, Stepan Khalturin and Sophia Perovskaya on Miusskaya Square, M.Ye. Saltykov-Shchedrin at the Serpukhov Gates, Heinrich Heine on Strastnoy Boulevard, F.M. Dostoyevsky on Tsvetnoy Boulevard.

The central event, however, was made by the unveiling of the memorial plaque over the common grave of Red Guards that had fallen in the battles to defend the Soviet authority. This is how S.T. Konenkov, the plaque designer, describes the dedication ceremony: «In the morning of November 7, 1918, the Red Square began to grow filled with delegations from plants, factories and Red Guards units. The day was clear and cold. Vladimir Ilyich was expected to arrive at Red Square together with a column of delegates to the VIth Congress of Soviets.

...As the veil came off the plaque, the military band struck the first note and the Proletkult Chorus performed a cantata written for the occasion... To the sounds of the cantata, all the attendees walked closer to the Kremlin wall to carefully inspect the memorial plaque in silence.

The imaginative winged figure of the Genius of Glory, personifying Victory, was sculpted to hold in one hand the dark-red banner featuring the Soviet State Seal and in the other – a green palm branch. Seen at the figure's feet were broken-up sabers and rifles stuck in the ground and belted with a crape band. Rising over the domineering figure's shoulder was the sun, with the golden rays hitting the words «October 1917 Revolution». Featured at the bottom was the dedication «To those who fell for peace and brotherhood of the peoples». Those words made the credo of my lifetime effort...».[27]

Lenin persistently demanded that public buildings should as soon as possible be made to feature «revolutionary and socialist logos». The Narkompros architectural department, headed by I.V. Zholtovsky, suggested that legends and catchwords be reinforced with the appropriate relief adornments. The idea was duly backed up and within a relatively short order many of the public buildings in Moscow were embellished with fresh reliefs and catchwords.

Just a few relics from the triumphant revolution days are still in evidence: the «Worker – the Creator of New Life» cast-iron plaque, designed by M.G. Manizer, on the wall of the Petrovsky Passage shopping mall; the relief «Worker and Peasant», designed by G.D. Alekseyev, at the front entrance of the Central Lenin Museum, and the plaque on the wall of the Izvestiya-daily office building. Most of that era's monuments also had limited lifetimes, with nearly none of those surviving to the present day. First statues and compositions were fabricated from short-lived materials, such as wood, plaster or cement, which was the principal reason for the monuments degrading early.

The approved list of great men «in the areas of revolutionary and public activities, philosophy, literature, sciences and arts» handed over by Narkompros to the Sculptors Union included 67 names, with nearly 20 monuments being actually erected in Moscow in the first years of the Soviet era.

Lenin's idea of monumental propaganda «perfectly met the needs of the revolutionary masses bent on the desire to not only destroy the remains of the pathetic tsarist arts but also see the revolutionary pathos translated into the statues of their leaders and great precursors».

N. Andreyev, D. Osipov: Obelisk to the Soviet Constitution (monument to Freedom) on Sovietskaya Square. 1919.

In November 7, 1918, the temporary Monument to Soviet Constitution was unveiled on the square in front of the Moscow Soviet (Mossovet). And in June 27, 1919, the monument was replaced by the Statue of Freedom, one of the most inspired revolution monuments, with its noted designer N.A. Andreyev evidently being enthused by the values of the ancient world. As one looked at the statue, one just could not help recalling the ideal shapes of the all-powerful soaring Nike, the Winged Victory of Samothrace. However, the creation could in no way be passed as some regular imitation. Andreyev came to be really great in this admirable and truly enthusing piece of art in that he managed to use his plastic art capacities to convey the very spirit of the Great October Socialist Revolution.

As the later years had shown, Lenin's agenda for monumental propaganda was proven to be something more than just a passing craze, for it had grown to become the mainstream of the Soviet monumental art for decades to come.[28]

Defining the Guidelines

I welcome our giant plans
And the giant strides in the making.
I rejoice at the march we maintain
To engage in labors and battles!
               V.Mayakovsky

Following the move in March 1918 of the Government of the Soviet Russia from Petrograd to Moscow and in the dramatic period of the Civil War up to 1922, the city's economic life had petered out to a complete standstill. Given the large-scale emigration of the nobility, upper classes and intellectuals, the city's social makeup had meaningfully changed. Plunders, violence and shootings sent the city life into the state of chaos and depression. Lenin continued to demand that Russia's social segment, antagonistic to the Bolsheviks, should be exterminated. In particular, he argued, «There should be no clemency for those enemies of the people, enemies of socialism, enemies of the working masses. There should be fighting maintained to root out the rich and their toadies, bourgeois intelligentsia, crooks, spongers and criminals... The rich and the racketeers are the two faces of the same coin, they are the two principal categories of parasites bred by capitalism. Those make the principal enemies of socialism, and they should especially be overseen by the entire people. Should they commit the slightest misdemeanor under the conditions of a socialist society, they must be dealt with most ruthlessly. Any partiality and hesitation, any sentimentality in this regard would amount to the greatest crime before socialism». (This is an excerpt from one of Lenin's more misanthropic works quite innocently titled «How to Organize an Emulation Drive»).

Examples as to Ilyich's willingness to pursue the policy of «scorched earth» and demolish Russian towns and cities do abound. To provide an example to this end, this is his September 10, 1918, telegram to Trotsky: «Surprised and alarmed over the deferral of the Kazan operation, particularly so, if the message, that I received, is true about your unquestioned capability to use your artillery fires to destroy the enemy. To my mind, you can not afford to take pity on the city and postpone the hostilities. You need to proceed and mercilessly exterminate the defender, especially if it is true that Kazan is held within an iron ring»... After that, Trotsky's directives have been phrased to be in line with Lenin's guidance. Here is one example: «...With the Czech-White-Guard hordes getting established in Kazan, the city has been turned into a counterrevolution nest. This nest must be ruined. Should the resistance persist, the city's counterrevolutionary blocks and neighborhoods shall be razed to the ground...». The warfare techniques espoused by Lenin were aptly branded as «the school of brutalities» by the Russian populist N. Mikhailovsky.

Russia's rebuilding period for the most part had to do with the adopted New Economic Policy (NEP). After the October Revolution, interests of the city dwellers, heavily impacted by the lack of badly needed food supplies, had increasingly become focused on plots of cultivated lands. The NEP strategy and local government budgets were implemented to create a wholly fresh set of circumstances to bolster the growth of city economies and streamline land management. City land properties had particularly grown in value. At that juncture, the most complex trend was initiated to have city land properties separated from agricultural lands, with landowners getting their plots delineated. The process had been saddled with most painful problems.

Given the lack of a sufficiently powerful federal budget, the funding commitments for the most part used to be assured through identifying well-to-do businesses, that initially were allowed to grow in order to secure solid positions in their individual industries, and getting those to be subsequently engaged in raising local budgets and determining the relevant spending levels. But inasmuch as local budget appropriations had to be in line with the federal guidelines and targets, the core enterprises and businesses were increasingly perceived as economic hubs. To provide for growth, any budget would have to be built by the enterprise in question with due regard for the inherent capacity to meet the center-prescribed production targets. Need for the smooth economic management envisioned a margin of latitude regarding budget authorizations and required that authority be centralized. This is what actually happened with the municipal services.

In the Kommunalnoye Delo monthly (Issue No. 6, 1929) in his article «On the Issue of Designing Targets for 1929 – 1930» V. Vesselovsky reasons: «Over longer term of the socialist construction, the problem of cities should be raised and resolved with the use of a comprehensive plan-based approach tied to the idea of total rebuilding of the cities, social reconstruction of the entire national economy and living conditions of the working people...». In the same Kommunalnoye Delo journal (1930) in his material «On the Issue of Building a Socialist City» I.Lehrman argues: «...The tasks of rebuilding the USSR national economy by far go beyond not only the goals of recreating the country's industrial base but also beyond those of reconstructing the infrastructural services of the entire national economy... The rebuilding effort reaches much further to engulf all of our culture and everyday support services... And for this effort not to be haphazard and spontaneous, the whole set of projects should best be put together on the basis of a single plan».

As G.I. Krzhizhanovsky made a critique of the discussions on the matter in the Planovoye Khoziaystvo monthly (Planned Economy) (No. 3, 1931), he concluded: «It is only their industrial growth (meaning larger cities that made the nation's industrial centers) that can enable us to effectively spawn industrial facilities across the entire country, for no new capacities could be seeded by the enfeebled economy. Admittedly, billion-ruble infusions in our large industrial centers have not yet been committed to assure the socialist rebuilding effort. And each time we begin to tackle the questions relating to radically improved cooperation of the existing plants and factories, we come to be particularly convinced that this drive is still in its embryonic stage».

The magnitude of the effort, that the best of the new Soviet intelligentsia applied to address the problems of rebuilding the entire national economy, was indicative of the profound shifts in the fundamentals of economy and in management strategies. The challenge then was to identify the thrust of development, with the contemporaneous tasks requiring the maximized involvement of the available talents and resources.

In the meantime, the late 1920s – early 1930s marked the crested struggle in the top tier of authority in the Soviet Union. While serving as VKP(b) secretary on organizational matters and then general secretary, I.V. Stalin had been using his dependable information links to be fully knowledgeable about the political and economic status of the nation. With Lenin still alive, Stalin somewhat got hold of a copy of the leader's letter containing the latter's brief evaluations of the principal contenders to the Party's top-leadership position. The letter posed the risk of L.B. Trotsky getting the supreme authority. As early as December 1923, Stalin launched a political campaign against Trotskyism and by the time Lenin died, the former had held all control levers in the Party. With the Party leaders in the provinces being replaced by his proteges well in advance, Stalin had thereby secured a dependable «claque» force that would vote for him at the forthcoming Party congress. In addition, the central authority over local budgets, with the prescribed assignments being disbursed on schedule under the orders from the Politbureau and VKP(b) Secretariat for the most part, enabled Stalin to build a solid funding base needed to better handle personnel questions in the provinces. As early on as the mid-1920s, the chief «puppeteer» started his horrid shows at the theater named the USSR. For the shows to go unchecked, the following two crucial provisos had to be met: unconstrained political power and total economic authority throughout the nation.

The dictatorship of the first leader of the Revolution with a «beastly face», as labeled by Holy Patriarch Tikhon, was followed up by the dictatorship of yet another leader featuring a «beastly face», who made the people worship the first one. And as recorded in the Revelation, he who refused to worship him would be killed. An anti-shrine, the mausoleum holding the proletarian leader's mummified body, was installed for general and prospectively global worship. «The grave of Lenin is the cradle of freedom for the entire mankind» was written on the banners carried by the working masses in the days of mourning rallies. The subsequent galvanization-based treatment of the leader's dead body and the ongoing rallies and parades with their «Lenin lived! Lenin Lives! Lenin shall live!», «Lenin shall live forever!» only served to heavily hypnotize the participants of those massive events. The national media used to be wholly engaged to make any and all citizens seek to emulate that great genius of the mankind, the most humane of the humans, leader of the global Socialist revolution. The comprehensive effort had been focused on molding a new genotype, the Soviet people, expected to be involved in building Communism, a paradise on earth, in the name of the best of humans, leader of the proletarian revolution, a new antigod – great iconoclast Lenin, rather than in the name of the divine Progenitor.

Lenin's funeral. Mourning columns on the Red Square. 1924.

Transformation Gets a Boost

Comrade Lenin, reporting to you
With my heart, rather than formally.
Comrade Lenin, the Herculean job
Shall be done.
In fact, it is already under way.
                    V.Mayakovsky

In March 1918, Moscow regained its status of the national capital city. In February of the same year, VTsIK issued the decree «On Socialization of Land», under which all of the so-called «slave-labor businesses» were expropriated, with thousands of estates being ruined in the process. Coming to be issued shortly thereafter were the decrees on demolition of monuments to tsars and their servants, auditing of safes, elimination of private commodity markets, dictatorship in the area of food supplies deliveries, labor mobilization (blue and white-collar workers being denied the right to quit their jobs and seek employment elsewhere).

In April 1918, the Presidium of the Moscow Soviet, that had its jurisdiction cover the city and the region, passed the ruling on tightening up the living space in the apartments populated by «nonproletarian elements», while in August of the same year, VTsIK issued the decree on abolition of private ownership of real estate within cities. All buildings and structures, valued at or generating the revenues «in excess of the ceilings established by local authorities», were subject to expropriation. In theory, any property could easily be confiscated. Devoid of scheduled care and maintenance, the nationalized housing assets quickly fell into the sorry state of disrepair.

The newly-installed authorities appeared to be particularly aggressive and consistent in their effort to concentrate in their hands the key levers to control the society's life support capacities. Any hitch in the implementation of decrees would immediately be passed as sabotage, with the sad consequences taking their course. Crucial enterprises would be turned on a war footing (militarized), with the employees being regarded as mobilized personnel, while other businesses, unrelated to the defense sector, would be closed down by the hundred.

As it moved to Moscow, the Soviet government radically boosted its impact on many aspects of the city life. In the very first months of its operations, with Mossovet being circumvented, Sovnarkom resolutely moved in to quickly requisition the buildings, furniture and assorted assets needed to adequately accommodate a multitude of the just-arrived central government agencies and organizations. By 1921, their numbers had grown to be so large that Sovnarkom, as requested by the city authorities, created a dedicated commission made up of officials from the People's Commissariat of Internal Affairs (NKVD), Workers' and Peasants' Inspectorate (RKI) and Mossovet to take on part of the governing responsibilities.

In 1917, the Moscow Soviet divided the city area, as it was determined in May of the same year by the Moscow Duma and roughly delimited by the Ring railroad, into eight districts. In 1921, that number was reduced to six, with the centrally-located Gorodskoi District eliminated and split to be shared by the two adjoining peripheral territories.

In January 1918, pursuant to the decisions of the last conferences of the Soviets of Moscow and Moscow Region, the effort was completed to form the single Mossovet Presidium authorized to manage vast territories (the region then included today's Moscow Region and the adjacent regions). Though the range of economic and social responsibilities was immense, the new leadership at least did well to efficiently handle the questions of city survival. To provide one example, as early as 1918, free lunches were provided at Moscow schools and specialized dining facilities for children, the size of their parents' «class-based remuneration» not having to be accounted for under the circumstances. Within a year the number of free meals for kids had grown to exceed 200 thousand. In the fall of 1919, dozens of kilometres of narrow-gauge railroad lines were laid to reach out into Moscow's environs for firewood to be rapidly supplied to the city consumers at the peak of the most severe energy crisis. It was then that work was incrementally resumed to restore the housing assets, the projects to complete the semi-ruined buildings getting the foremost attention.

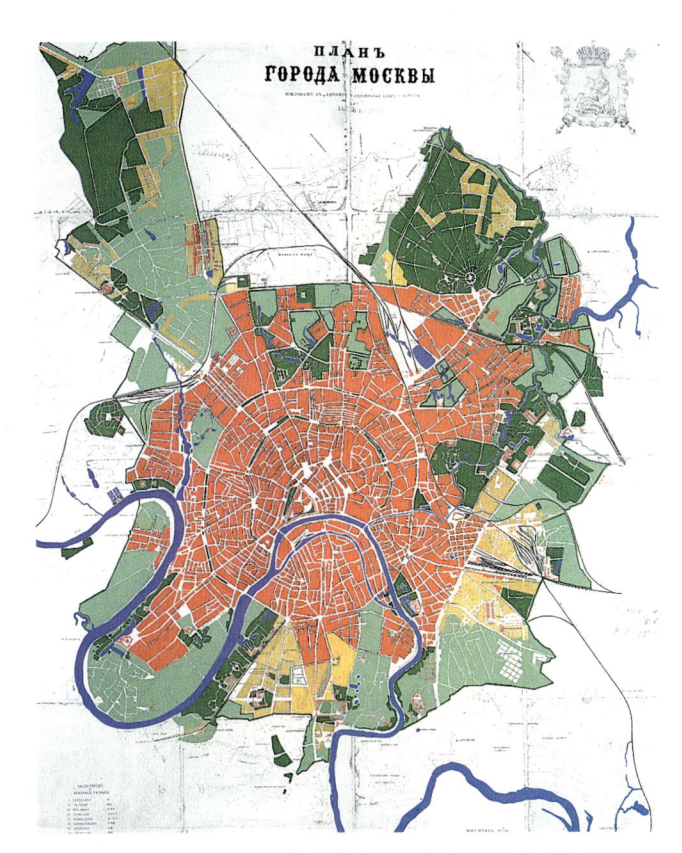

Plan of Moscow. Beginning of the 20th century.

The Moscow Soviet officials, that largely had been the old-vintage specialists, were less captivated by the «romanticism of the New World» and were mostly concentrated on the concrete tasks of restoring and building the city. In 1918, for one, Mossovet came out to back up the ideas voiced by a group of architects (G.D. Dubelir, V.N. Semenov and other names) to unload Moscow by way of creating a number of country-style settlements on the land around the city. Initially, company settlements were mainly conceived as garden-townships featuring the appropriate social and environmental attributes. In April 1918, the Moscow Soviet was reelected for the first time in the post-October period, with the Bolsheviks winning more votes than the SRs and Mensheviks. Elected chairman of Mossovet was P.G. Smidovich, a former Iskra distribution agent. He was a man of great learning and, which was particularly consequential, capable of thinking historically (later, in the 1920s, he would be named to head the Central Bureau of Local History Studies, the body initially known to be most active in safeguarding the architectural, historical and natural monuments and preserves). It was under his leadership that the Mossovet Architectural Workshop was set up. Involved to carry out large-scale projects then were numerous «old-schooling» architects, Academicians I.V. Zholtovsky and A.V. Shchusev in the first place. They should primarily be credited for the Mossovet-released documents that started to carry the ideas of mandatory preservation of architectural monuments and high-value historic ensembles. But the most outstanding accomplishment achieved by these masters was their hard-won perception of Moscow as a single phenomenon, sort of an organism evolving under its inherent laws and demanding a most careful and sound approach.

To alleviate the acute municipal services problems, the local industrial, transportation and energy-producing facilities and businesses needed to be given a boost, just like more restoration projects had to be launched. Establishment in April 1918 of Moscow's first municipal architectural workshop, designed to precisely accommodate the Zholtovsky (neoclassicist) and Shchusev (neoromanticist) city-building strategies, seemed to amount to recognition of a special status of the arts that would not be swayed by any political weathers.

A. Lentulov: Peace. Triumph of Liberation. 1917.

Sovietskaya Square. 1920s.

Of course, the move was not welcomed by all. In the very first months following the October 1917 Revolution, the «proletarian interests» in the sphere of liberal arts had been rabidly championed by the avant-garde protagonists. They came to be particularly fixed on the idea of designing all sort of huge structures, towers for the most part. And the tower-like Palace of Soviets, designed in the 1930s and looking very conservative, can nonetheless be traced to V.Ye. Tatlin's Third International Tower backed up by the People's Commissar of Education Lunacharsky.

The whole thing, as a matter of fact, went beyond personal likings. The avant-garde champions in the realm of arts proved to be «natural allies» of avant-garde dealers in politics. «The leftist artists became to be friendly with the leftist politicians as their shared outlooks were known to be extreme, persistent and destructive... The «futurism» actually makes an artistic form of Communism, for a communist in arts can hardly be anything else than a «futurist», writes A. Efros. In the first years after the October Revolution, the leftist artists were treated as the «select caste»: they would be picked to head artistic schools, get state orders for monuments to revolution leaders and heroes, decorate streets and rallies on the newly-established national days. The formally-declared atheism in the Land of Soviets intrinsically implied the creation of a new cult of role-models, staging of dedicated rituals, gatherings and rallies.

The contemporaneous arguments, debates and discussions, that Moscow-based architects were drawn to take part in, came out of the wholehearted desire to create fresh means of expression and find new solutions to outstanding social challenges. The goals of architecture were then understood as «creation of an environment», transformation of the living conditions and shaping the personality.

The importance of Moscow as the nation's economic and political «center of gravity» had been on the rise. With the society being heavily politicized throughout, the task of pursuing powerful non-stop graphic propaganda drives was top-priority. Shop windows were filled with ROSTa posters, streets were liberally decorated with banners reading catchphrases of the day, while May 1 and November 7 rallies were turned into unprecedented smartly-staged massive shows. In keeping with the Lenin-signed June 1921 ruling, the city's six largest squares were outfitted with loudspeakers to issue «oral newspapers». A specially-designed radio station was soon installed to broadcast Soviet government decrees and statements and then lectures, talks and literary presentations. In September 1922, the station broadcast its first concert of the Russian music.

However, the grander were the ideas committed to paper the lesser were the capacities to have them put into effect. This circumstance was especially painful in the early 1920s when the prime task was to provide people with housing, its quality being of secondary consideration. Notwithstanding the economic hardships, first post-revolutionary apartment buildings built to new designs came to rise in 1923. Completed in construction the following year was Moscow's first skyscraper – the eleven-floor (in its mid-section) Mosselprom department store building on Kalashny Lane (designed by D. Kogan, executed by V. Tsvetayev).

Housing construction projects in the 1920s were to the highest possible degree funded by the consumers or enterprises where those people were employed. In late 1923, for one, there was established the Moscow Worker Housing Construction Joint-Stock Society that launched a project to put in place eighteen light-grade apartment buildings. Mossovet issued housing-construction bonds to raise money for more projects. Given the acute lack of building materials, particularly, brick and cement, coming to be widely used were building blocks holding varied fillers. Engineer P.G. Galakhov came up with the idea of getting a wooden framework filled with the compressed «warm rocks» or thermolytic blocks made from sawdust, peat and a mixture of alabaster and lime. In July 1924, work was completed on the first settlement of single-floor thermolytic homes for the Krasny Bogatyr plant's employees on the edge of the Sokolniki Wood.

A year later, the Moscow Architectural Society (MAO) was commissioned by Mossovet to hold a contest for the best project of a communal (having a state-of-the-art everyday services capability) two-three-floor fireproof apartment building, and in 1926 – a tender for apartment buildings each designed to house 750 – 800 residents. Those buildings were required to feature a centrally-run catering facility including a kitchen, dining area, boiling-water rooms, shower booths, laundry rooms, reading rooms, club, nursery school, storage area, janitor's quarters, back office and central-heating control room. However, very rarely those attractive schemes had been translated into full-sized buildings containing the complete set of above-described services. For the most part, those were government-funded projects carried out to build hostels or dormitories for singles or small-family couples, such as a cluster of buildings on 1st Baltiysky Lane or a student dormitory on Ordzhonikidze Street (designed by I.S. Nikolayev). Condominiums had nearly always been built to feature conventional designs.

Representatives of all schools of Moscow architectural design readily shared one another's ingenious solutions or findings. Quickly applied were the dynamic shapes by I.A. Golosov: nontraditional facade discontinuities and corner-embracing balconies, or bakery plants featuring «spiral conveyor belts» to achieve large economies of shop space.

In the mid-1920s, many of the city's streets began to feature solidly-built buildings containing five, six and even more floors. However, fully-integrated compound projects were rather rare, with the approach being mostly applied to build housing in industrial suburbs. Making one of the first post-revolutionary public buildings in Moscow, expressly designed to confirm the new ideology monopoly, was the V.I. Lenin Institute erected in 1926 at the site of the former Tverskaya police precinct (designed by S.Ye. Chernyshev). In 1931, the V.I. Lenin Institute merged with the Marx and Engels Institute, with the building then being used to also hold the Central Party Archives. In 1927, The Central Telegraph building (designed by I.I. Rerberg), so recognizable by any Muscovite, was completed in construction. Playing a big role in the life of the city also were automated telephone exchanges built to the standard design by V. Patek on Bolshaya Ordynka, Arbat, Nemetskaya and other streets.

By the late 1920, the numbers of big apartment buildings could already be counted by the dozen. For example, put up at the Soymonovsky Lane and Ostozhenka corner was an apartment building with a large dining facility (then turned into a cafeteria) on the first floor; the condominium at the upper end of Arbat was designed to have a huge grocery store. That category of constructions also includes buildings on the Boulevard Ring: the new building on Nikitsky Boulevard, which is shielding the Theodor Studit Church (the parish church visited by A.V. Suvorov); building No.8 on Gogolevsky Boulevard; a large residential compound at 14 Pokrovsky Boulevard; the Moscow Avionics Engineering Institute at the Petrovka corner... .

Spaced by a time span of two years are buildings Nos. 37 and 41 erected on Pokrovka. Making nearly a similar couple are office buildings Nos. 21 and 27 put up in 1930 on Pokrovka. Two five-floor buildings constructed as far back as 1928 for the People's Commissariat of Foreign Affairs could be found at 25 Trubnaya Street. A tall residential building of that period can be seen at 24 Bolshoi Golovinsky Lane.

Singled out of the set of unique structures should be the Dynamo Sporting Club building (designed by I. Fomin) on Furkasovsky Lane, Ptitsepromsoyuz office building at the lower end of Maroseyka (used for decades to house the Komsomol Central Committee), the «Za Industrializatsiyu» editorial offices building on Tsvetnoy Boulevard (occupied by the Literaturnaya Gazeta and the Literaturnaya Rossiya weeklies since the 1950s). The Narkomfin building (designed by M. Guinzburg and I. Milinis) on Novinsky Boulevard, the former dormitory for students of the Communist University for Minorities of the West on Petroverigsky Lane and, finally, the «House on the Embankment» (designed by B. Iofan and D. Iofan in 1928 – 1931) continue to be of positive interest to the casual viewer. Found in Moscow could also be large-block-construction samples aged close to seventy, the best example being made by the seven-floor apartment building at 51 Bolshaya Polyanka (engineered by G. Krasin).

However, all those isolated projects were pursued to satisfy local needs rather than respond to the city's multidimensional challenges. The exigency to devise a single integrated plan of operations had by then grown to be obvious.

The General Plan «New Moscow»

In April 1918, the Moscow Soviet established the Specialized Architectural-Artistic Workshop, with I.V. Zholtovsky appointed «senior architect» and A.V. Shchusev «head master». The facility's leaders were granted «broad rights to initiate architectural-artistic projects aimed to provide for construction of best-designed and integrated townships in the city's suburbs and in-town compounds, with individual buildings engineered to feature state-of-the-art furnishings and attributes in terms of support equipment, hygiene and esthetics». In addition, they also were entrusted with the task «to carve out Moscow's lands into industrial areas, garden-towns, trading and shopping sections, etc.». The guidelines for the «New Moscow» general plan were drafted by A.V. Shchusev, and in 1925 the draft-plan was passed by Mossovet.

The political dimension of the draft was to use architectural tools in order to bolster the myth about legitimacy of the Bolshevik regime that forcefully succeeded the All-Russian Constituent Assembly, which was supposed to rule on Russia's political system with due regard for the interests of all societal segments.

The «New Moscow» plan, put together to cover the territory of 20 thousand hectares, reflected the long-lasting city-growth tradition and was aimed to have the social and governing functions separated. The historic center was supposed to be spaced from the newly-designed political center, which was supposed to be represented by the new Government House on Khodynka. The Kremlin was securely safeguarded, while many of its architectural monuments were restored. Underpinning the plan was the idea of the Soviet and historical Moscow displaying the continuity of evolution.

Zholtovsky and Shchusev, named to head the Specialized Academic Moscow Replanning Commission, summoned the services of the best architects capable of offering solutions to city-building challenges. The Commission included I. Golosov, P. Golosov, N. Dokuchayev, A. Yefimov, N. Kolli, B. Korshunov, G. Lavrov, N. Ladovsky, K. Melnikov, E. Norvet, A. Poliakov, A. Rukhliadev, S. Chernyshev and other noted designers.

In January 1923, the general plan «New Moscow» was for the first time debated by members of the Moscow Architectural Society. The effort to update the plan took a little over a year, and by the summer of 1924 it had nearly been finalized. The crucial part about the new city-building strategy, that for the first time ever was to be translated into construction projects under a single plan covering the city and its environs, was the motivation to preserve the established structure of the urban territories representing the old and the new, industrial and residential areas, with the idea of «separated centers» being strictly adhered to.

The «New Moscow» was confined by the city ring railroad. The Boulevard Ring was expected to be made complete with the construction of bridges across the Moskva-river and the Water-Supply Canal. The city's functional A, B and C (Boulevard, Garden and Kamer-Kollezhsky Val) rings were supposed to be complemented with the D Ring measuring 100 metres wide and stretching out to 60 kilometres. The newly-planned ring was expected to connect the following environs: Ostankino, Sokolniki, Lefortovo, Vorobyovskoye Shosse, Fili, Serebrianny Bor. They had all been intended as residential gar-

I. Rerberg: The Central Telegraph Building. 1927.

the Cathedral of Christ the Savior. the Kremlin the Palace of Labor the Foundling Hospital

M. Krinsky: View of Moscow River embankment with the Palace of Labor. 1922.

den-townships. The city's principal industrial area, including port facilities and adjacent factory-worker settlements, was supposed to be put in place on the south-eastern edge of the metropolis.

The entire city was supposed to be encircled with a two-mile-wide vegetation band where built-up areas would not be allowed to exceed 25 percent. The green belt was to be linked with the city center via the specially-tailored wedges of park-land to help improve the local environmental conditions. The per-resident vegetation benchmark was raised to stand at 26 square metres. For Moscow to have the sustainable water supply and for the Moskva-river to remain navigable, a number of dams and water basins were supposed to be constructed in the upper reaches of the river.

Moscow's older section was kept unaltered though some of the radial thoroughfares were supposed to be made broader, and isolated private orchards turned into larger public gardens. For the architectural monuments to continue making the city's skyline and be viewed better, the architects suggested that graded constraints should be placed on the heights of new-builds so that the city's landmarks would be neither overshadowed nor dwarfed.

The Christ the Savior Cathedral was invariably featured by all of the New Moscow Plan's panoramas as the principal site completing the Lubianka-to-Prechistenka Gates passage. To balance out this grand ensemble, Lubianka Square, Moscow's highest elevation, was expected to carry the All-Russian Council for National Economy (VSNKh) skyscraper. In 1922, the contest for the project had a team of the Higher Arts and Engineering School (VKhUTEMAS) students, headed by M. Krinsky and N. Ladovsky, inspired to come up with a number of extravagant designs that could hardly be put into effect for lack of resources.

In the course of the 1920s, restoration work was completed on the Kitay-Gorod walls, with the towers being rebuilt and the lean-to vending and other motley structures removed altogether. Under the New

**M. Krinsky and A., V. and L. Vesnin:
Project of the Palace of Labor in Moscow. 1922.**

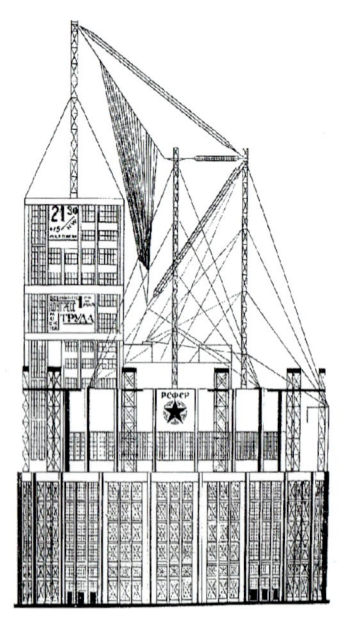

Moscow Plan, the governmental buildings in the Kremlin and ministerial headquarters turned out to be within sort of a Kitay-Gorod citadel hedged by liberal green spaces. As it appeared to come too close to the Kitay-Gorod walls, even the Polytechnical Museum was under the threat of being torn down. The newly-established trend of the major government departments settling their employees in the neighborhoods assigned to be close by is certainly of some interest. Office buildings began to be surrounded by departmental housing, shopping malls and clubs, that were supposed to phase out the Church. As a matter of fact, church buildings had initially been used for club activities (for example, the People's Commissariat for Military and Naval Affairs Club was housed in the Miraculous Apparition of the Virgin Mary Church).

The project was then finalized to have the overcrowded built-up area on Okhotny Riad totally torn down, the plan being eventually executed in the 1930s. The space between the prospective Palace of Labor and the Manege building was assigned to serve as parade grounds. Manege Square would thereby acquire classical proportions, and for the impression to be reinforced even more, the Memorial Pillar in the Aleksandrovsky Gardens was expected to be moved and planted at the square's center-point.

The Palace of Labor was intended as the city's principal and powerfully-domineering structure. The contest, whose requirements had been written by Shchusev, was won by the Vesnin brothers. The winning project was designed for the Palace to house both Mossovet and Moscow Bolshevik Party Committee, thereby concentrating all governing functions at one place. The building was also expected to include an eight-thousand-seat theater to conduct massive gatherings, as well as accommodate Moscow's social history museum and a number of smaller organizations. Kept intact near the Palace of Labor would be the Paraskeva the Friday Church and the restored Golitsyn and Troyekurov Mansions – rare examples of the 17th-century mansion architecture.

The city in those years was intended to be a multipole structure, with the Kremlin, expected to be turned into a museum complex, making the whole network's nucleus. Red Square was to be linked with a few centrally-located squares and Okhotny Riad, which via a boulevard would be connected to a new square to be built opposite the Rumyantsev Museum (now Borovitskaya Square). The government center was supposed to emerge on Petrogradsky (now Leningradsky) Shosse. Zariadye was assigned to be a shopping area, Khamovniki – an educational segment and the Vorobyovi Hills – sporting grounds.

Ring thoroughfares were intended to divide the city space into zones featuring the skylines that would taper off towards the periphery. The city center was allowed to hold seven-floor buildings, with the second zonal belt being constrained by five-storey buildings and the third belt only featuring two- or single-storey houses. Most of the buildings were supposed to feature just a few stories.

Detailed plans had been drafted to launch construction projects in Tsentralny, Zamoskvorechye, Alekseyevsko-Rostokinsky, Sushchevsko-Maryinsky, Khamovnichesky districts, south-eastern industrial zone and other territories, with the designs for the most part being heavily romanticized and removed from reality. The city's entire architectural community was invited to be involved in drafting specific project designs, and a few contracts for buildings and civil engineering complexes were even brought up to be publicly contested.

One of the first contests to be conducted was the July 1920 bidding for bridge contracts, for Moscow then was to put in place 18 new bridges under the city transformation plans. Particularly crucial were the bridges upstream from the Christ the Savior Cathedral and the Large Moskvoretsky Bridge extending Bolshaya Ordynka further into town. Concurrently, there arose the issue of rebuilding the Bolshoi Krasnokholmsky and Krymsky Bridges that had nearly been falling apart. The contest produced most exciting results. For example, the innovatory Krymsky Bridge design by Professor N.S. Streletsky featured a single-span chain-suspended framework, which then attracted a lot of attention but, for lack of the right technologies, could not be implemented in the 1920s. (However, the design was later improved upon and used in the 1930s to build the currently-functional Krymsky Bridge).

Authors of the General Plan kept transportation issues in the focus of their attention, too. In the initial stage, Professor V. Obraztsov, responsible for the Moscow railroad hub designs, suggested that a few rail lines should be allowed to come deeper into the city. Conversely, designer of the Moscow underground system L. Bernatsky cautioned against any rail lines crossing the city areas. A few years later, the city underground project draft, commissioned by Mossovet and the Municipal Railroad Authority, was also effectively drawn up. The first Moscow metro construction phase was expected to include the following three lines: Sokolniki – Miasnitskaya – Center (5 km); Tverskaya Zastava – Tverskaya Ulitsa – center (4.2 km); Smolensky Rynok – Arbat – Vozdvizhenka – Center (3.5 km). The finalized plans had metro lines crossing the city north-west to south-east and south-west to north-east, stretching out far enough to connect to the second ring railroad.

While the Moscow-transforming General Plan was still in the works, some of its components already were off to be implemented. One of the first projects in that regard was the effort to rebuild Sovetskaya Square. The question on having it reshaped came up as early on as 1918 when the General Skobelev equestrian statue was replaced with the Russian Constitution Monument (designed by D.P. Osipov) under the Lenin-initiated monumental propaganda drive. In 1919, the monument was complemented with the Liberty Statue (designed by N.A. Andreyev) and became to be generally known as the Liberty Pillar measuring 25 metres in height, with the figure rising to stand at 5.5 metres. The three-surfaced pillar was built to grow out of a three-surfaced platform featuring concave sides to form stylized arches holding bronze plaques reading excerpts from the first Constitution of Soviet Russia. At the feet of the Liberty figure was a stump with a semi-circled fencing featuring the emblem of the Russian Republic. The figure's left arm embraced the globe, while the right one was raised in a cautioning gesture. The monument's features were meant to convey the young republic's ideals being redolent of those of the French Revolution. The Constitution Pillar was similar to the obelisk adorning la Place de la Concorde in Paris, while the Liberty figure could easily remind one of the Statue of Liberty donated in 1916 by France to the United States to become America's symbol.

In 1922, A. Shchusev and I. Golosov drafted a plan to rebuild Sovetskaya Square. The plan implied both engagement of the space around the Pillar and extension of the square away from Tverskaya towards Bolshaya Dmitrovka, with a few graded stone terraces, greenery hedges, guard railing and fountains added for adornment. All this spatial composition was to continue into a drama theater building. The square was supposed to feature two green bands: one stretching towards the Conservatory building on Bolshaya Nikitskaya, while skirting the Resurrection and the Smaller Ascension Churches on Uspensky Vrazhek; and the other one running towards Petrovka along the right-hand side of Stoleshnikov Lane, while linking the Kosma and Damian Church in Shubino and Nativity of Virgin Mary Church in Stoleshniki.

The project began to be implemented in the summer of 1923. The effort was started with clearing the ground adjacent to the Tverskaya Fire Department. Then, a classical portico was erected to face Sovetskaya Square, which was followed by a subsquare built in place of the removed fire department. The local guardhouse was renovated, with a summer pavilion being added to it for the sake of a more pleasing appearance. «This project», the newspapers then pointed out, «marks the beginning of Moscow's transformation carried out under the revolution-inspired guidelines for building a new Moscow».

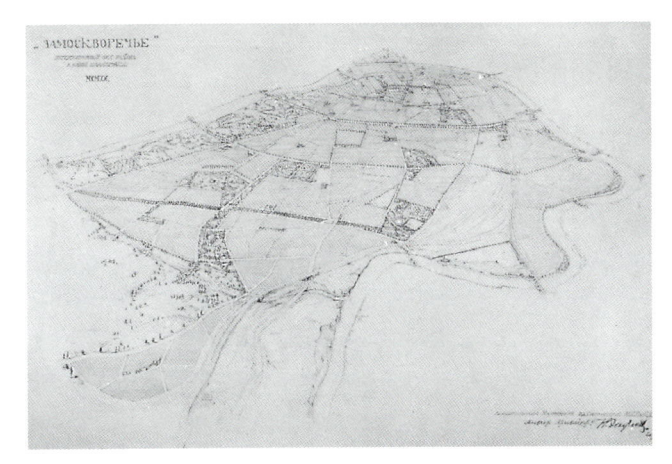

N. Dokuchaev: Zamoskvorechie. View of the future district. 1920.

By the mid-1920s, the Party leadership decided to erect a new building for the V.I. lenin Institute opposite the Mossovet headquarters, with S.Ye. Chernyshev's design getting the top-level confirmation. Despite Shchusev's protestations, the original colonnades had to be eliminated, which only served to have the square's proportions and balanced style heavily distorted.

The upper Tverskaya Street zone beyond Strastnaya Square, that under the Shchusev plan required no major alterations except for removal of minor structures and clearance of the approaches to the Dimitry Solunsky Church, was expected to feature a broad green boulevard along Trekhprudny Lane from the Nativity of Our Lady Church in Palashi up to the Epiphany Church and the Aquarium Gardens on Sadovaya-Triumphalnaya Street.

The historical architectural sites, that stood out in their neighborhoods, were in no way demolished. They were preserved and even restored. Many of those were turned into museums, that at times symbolized the opposite of the original builders' goals. For example, the English Club on Tverskaya was made the Revolution Museum, while the Monastery of Our Savior's Passions was transformed into the Antireligion Museum, etc.

Triumphalnaya Square with its Buff and Aquarium Drama and Comedy Theaters, Nikitin Circus, Khanzhonkov movie theater was perceived as the opening cluster of entertainment facilities. The square, as a matter of fact, was a nodal point connected with other squares along the Boulevard Ring via broad tree-lined avenues.

Making a particularly critical crossroads was the intersection of Tverskaya-Yamskaya with Bolshaya Gruzinskaya and the passage

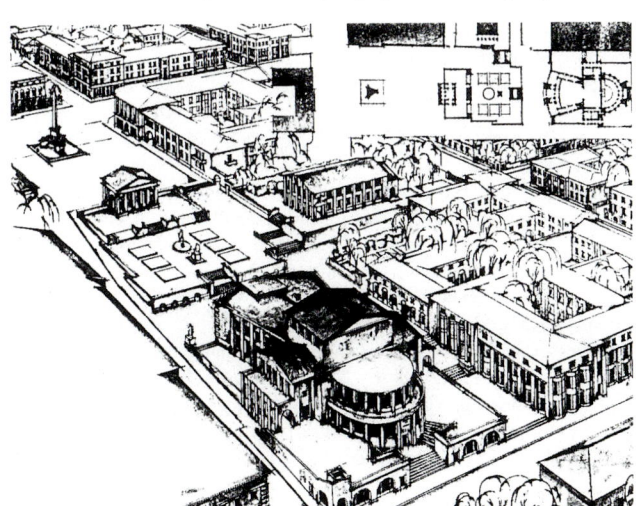

A. Shchusev, I. Golosov: Layout project of Sovietskaya Square. 1922.

The Institute of V.I. Lenin on Sovietskaya Square, the middle of the 1920s.

running toward Miusskaya Square, with the Alexander Nevsky Cathedral at the center. The multidome cathedral was supposed to crown the straightened-out Bolshaya Gruzinskaya Street running from its Saint George Church in the former Georgian settlement.

The Shaniavsky Public University on Miusskaya Square in 1919 was turned into the Sverdlov Communist University, that in the 1920s received a few more buildings and became to be known as the TsK VKP(b) Higher Party School. The Alexander Nevsky Cathedral (designed by Dushkin and Mordvinov) was expected to be rebuilt into the Radio House with a tall tower on top. The attempt, however, failed, and the cathedral eventually was torn down to vacate the spot for a Young Pioneers House.

Tverskaya-Yamskaya Street at its upper end featured the Triumphal Arch with the mandatory corps de gards at the sides, which provided a sense of style to those entering the Russian capital's main thoroughfare.

The ongoing religious processions to the Nicholas the Miracle Worker Icon on Red Square, which the Bolsheviks were so concerned about, made Shchusev think of the plan to move the governmental center away from the Kremlin's holy Orthodox shrines. Under the New Moscow Plan, the government buildings were supposed to be spread along the Tverskaya-Petrogradskoye Shosse axis, with the squares in the way being cleared and adorned in keeping with the esthetic requirements of the newly-established ideology. The factor, that the Moscow – Saint Petersburg highway once used to be Russia's principal road, was duly taken into account. Russian tsars, arriving for their coronation ceremonies at the Kremlin's Assumption Cathedral, would always make an overnight stop at the Petrovsky Palace before proceeding the next morning to the heart of Moscow along Tverskaya Road.

Since Catherine II, who the Petrovsky Waypoint Palace was actually built for, the nearby Khodynka Field had traditionally been used to hold festivities and parades in honor of Russia's war victories. The field was encircled by barracks and camps. In 1910, a large plot of the field adjoining Peterburgsky Shosse was transferred to the Moscow Aeronautical Society. Close by, on Begovaya Street, there was the Dux aircraft plant, and the first domestic flying tests were conducted on the Khodynka airfield. Notably, the first Soviet military parade of May 1, 1918, started on the Red Square and ended with a flying demonstration on Khodynka. V.I. Lenin, who was there to inspect both parades, attached special importance to the growth of aviation, while underlining its military relevance. In 1923, the Petrovsky Palace building and grounds were handed over to the Zhukovsky Air Force Academy. In the same year, scheduled flights began to be launched from the Khodynka airfield to service the Moscow – Nizhny Novgorod route.

The Shchusev-designed government center (to house VTsIK and Sovnarkom) was placed a bit south of the airfield and covered the grounds of the 1882 national industrial show. The center was meant to be a huge complex of impressive buildings wedging into the Khodynka Field off Petrogradskoye Shosse. The location appeared to be just perfect for the planned government center: the nearby military bases were on hand to assure safety of the government on the one hand, while the airport and a high-powered radio station in the southwestern corner of the Khodynka Field were available to provide the needed logistical support on the other.

However, with the party and government leadership choosing to remain in the Kremlin, the Khodynka location in the 1920s had incrementally been filled out by the burgeoning aviation production facilities that expanded off Begovaya Street. Within a few years, coming to be established there was an aircraft design bureau led by N.N. Polikarpov that raised a number of noted aircraft builders.

In September 12, 1920, the Main Administration for Universal Defense Training (Vsevobuch) announced a contest for the All-Russian Stadium Project on the Vorobyevi Hills. While being unsatisfied with the results of the bidding, the Stadium Building Society in March 1924 called for a new contest. Within two months, the visions submitted by the students of MIGI and VKhUTEMAS architecture faculties were considered as part of the standing practice required to maintain links between the practitioners and the academic community. Design and implementation of the stadium building project, in fact, made the first and nearly exceptional undertaking by the Association of New Architects (ASNOVA) in those years. In December 1924, the draft was completed, with the stadium's mockup traveling to the 1925 Paris World Fair and fetching a Grand Prix there.

In 1922, there was held a contest for an integrated housing project for industrial workers. The following two objectives were pursued: to create a state-of-the-art apartment building that would meet the needs of the working class, and develop detailed plans to support housing projects slated for the Simonovsky and Zamoskvorechye segments that had been expected to undergo rebuilding. The MAO contest, initiated by Mossovet, carried the flat requirements for density and heights of buildings as well as for integrated utilities and communal services facilities. The project called for the housing to be balanced out both in terms of space organization and logistical support. The best designs were picked out to contribute to the general plan of Moscow's transformation.

In 1919, the Mossovet Architectural Workshop called a contest for the common house project primarily intended for suburban townships and settlements. Making the reference option for the bidders was the idea of a trade union club. Generally, building assorted clubs around Moscow amounts to a most exciting page in the history book of architecture. The very first union club was designed by A.V. Shchusev himself. Today, the club is known as the Central House of Culture for Railroad Workers making part of the Shchusev-built Kazansky Railroad Station complex. The spirit of the times is particularly evident in the clubs built to K.S. Melnikov's designs in the late 1920s.

The newly-erected or rebuilt clubs became integral parts of all plants and factories in the city. Those «Ilyich Houses», as a matter of fact, reflected the desire of state ideologists to sanctify and enshrine the leader's image, particularly, after he passed away. «Neither constitution, nor family, nor even Communism would stand without a religion», claimed Russia's last prophet K.N. Leontyev as far back as the 1880s. A new religion was already in the making.

In the first post-Revolution years, the so-called home-communes had increasingly been made the order of day. Not infrequently, the young proletarian tenants, crammed in large numbers in the nationalized large apartments of the pre-Revolution well-to-do families, quite spontaneously would set up «communist forms of home-living» such as shared shopping for groceries, caring for kids or doing the washing. Inasmuch as the phenomenon seemed to persist, the architects began to develop the kind of housing projects that would best suit the requirements of «commune living».

Quite a few buildings had been constructed to those designs. They normally would include a kitchen and dining area, laundry room, club room, and often nursery schools. The rub, however, was that the tenants rarely came to fall in the same age group, have a comparable family status or job. Given such discrepancies, conflicts and inconveniencies would inevitably arise to spoil the living.

In 1925, Mossovet held a tender for the communal house project. Though the winners were granted contracts to build that kind of hous-

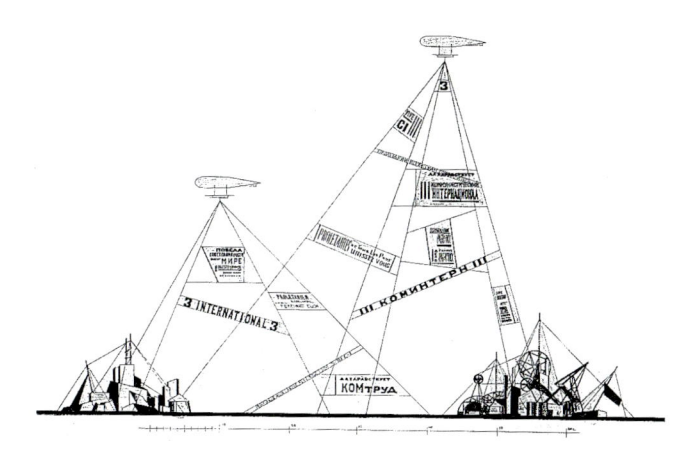

A. Vesnin, L. Popova: A sketch for the decoration of a mass show entitled «Struggle and Victory» in the Khodynskoe Field dedicated to the 3rd Congress of Comintern. 1922.

The First All-Russian Agricultural Show

Under the dedicated ruling of the 9th All-Russian Congress of Soviets, in the fall of 1922, Moscow was to host the First All-Russian Commodities and Handicrafts Show. However, given the deadliest drought and extremely poor harvest of 1921, which caused the unprecedented famine in the Volga valley, Ukraine, Crimea and Northern Caucasus, the event was deferred. But in December 1922, a large-scale construction operation, partially tied up with the New Moscow Plan's objectives, was launched to cover 65.5 hectares of land on the grounds of today's Gorky Park of Culture and Rest. The prospective show's territory was located where a green wedge was supposed to be created to link the Neskuchny Gardens with the city center.

The show's general plan was to be secured through open bidding. Unfortunately, none of the 27 projects offered by the contestants was good enough to leave the panel satisfied. Though I.V. Zholtovsky submitted his design belatedly and could not formally be treated as a contestant, his paper nonetheless was received and, what is more important, passed as worthy of application. In principle, his landscaping strategy was to create a huge parterre-like area with lots of open space. The entire arrangement was anchored on the Moskva-river that was intended to reinforce the magnitude of the tract of land extending to the water's edge.

The main gates were built on Krymsky Val that visitors passed through to find themselves on a vast square-shaped pad nearly as large as the city's Teatralnaya Square. Adjoining that open space was the territory's most elevated spot carrying the Show's research and propaganda office whose structures were built to form rather a large internal yard. The yard's principal axis and radial openings allowed one to have a view of the Vorobyovi Hills on the right and observe the old public hospital buildings on the close-by elevations on the left. The 200-meter-wide parterre enabled one to enjoy an unobstructed panorama of the century-old gardens of the Golitsin Hospital that bordered on a group of province pavilions. The Show's riverside segment held samples of old and new rural housing. The area along Krymsky Val next to the central pavilion contained a small-sized natural pond where the livestock exhibit was deployed with a race track making its main attraction. There was also a riding-house whose dome provided a vertical dimension for the entire exhibit. The next-in-line area was filled with a large gear-shaped concrete pavilion holding agricultural machinery and implements.

Apart from being commissioned to work on the Show's general plan, Zholtovsky was likewise entrusted with the job to design a whole range of dedicated pavilions and structures. In particular, he designed the entrance arch for the main research and propaganda pavilion, auditorium, theater, as well as agricultural machinery (jointly with artist I.I. Nivinsky), market-gardening, meadow cultivation and land improvement, livestock pavilions (the last ones developed together with N.D. Kolli).

Nearly all of the pavilions were made from assorted woods, truly Russian building materials for rural construction projects. Rather than replicating brickwork buildings, Zholtovsky sought to show the exceptional qualities of wood by using it resourcefully to implement classical designs (triumphal arch, portico, pediment, portals), bring the exquisite open-work items in contrast with rough paneling, take advantage of the leading-edge technologies to erect oversized wooden structures and risk wholly untried approaches in creating fresh proportions and covered spaces.

Appointed to be head architect of the show was A.V. Shchusev who oversaw the construction of 225 buildings and sites in the area. «Moscow is not equipped to handle the project of that magnitude! Given the circumstances in today's Russia, the Moscow Show amounts to a sheer fantasy, an utopian scheme!» blared the Western media. In the meantime, work was in full swing in Moscow, with no effort being spared. Taking part in completing the project had been over a thousand builders – farm and industrial workers, college and university students. The momentum of operations had been unprecedented, with the pace of construction being reported by the press and the radio on a daily basis.

ing, the newly-erected buildings for the most part were transition-type structures, with single-family apartments being supplemented by shared support services facilities.

Making an effective garden-township project was the drive to plan and put in place the Sokol settlement. Under the New Moscow Plan, Sokol was regarded as a link in the chain of garden-townships making the fourth ring around Moscow. In July 1923, Mossovet assigned a tract of land for the Sokol cooperative home-building society north of Vsekhsviatskoye-Village and next to Serebriany Bor station on the Ring Railroad. Given that under the New Moscow General Plan, the Ring Railroad was held to be of paramount importance to Moscow's environs, the township's major roads were laid to originate like rays from a single source made by the railroad station (now non-existent).

Taking part in designing and building Sokol in 1923 – 1931 had been N.V. Markovnikov, V.A. Vesnin, I.I. Kondakov, N.Ya. Kolli and other architects. The township's five-ray pattern featuring a star-shaped central square holding together the ends of straight and curvy streets clearly lacked the geometric precision of Western garden-townships and enabled varied homes to be placed at the customer's will, which only contributed to the overall artistic irregularities. Sokol's one- or two-storeyed single-family homes blended well with four-six family buildings assembled from modern building materials. Those were Russian-style, five-wall log homes, British-style filled-in-frame cottages as well as German-fashion brickwork houses with the built-in attics. As they sought to vary their tasks and designs, the architects achieved an unprecedented diversity of styles, thereby making Sokol a singular preserve of rural housing of the 1920s – 1930s period maintained to the present day.

Moscow's civil engineers, that spent two-three years being only focused on log or filled-in-frame structures, as early as 1925 switched to erecting exclusively brickwork four-six-storeyed multi-entrance buildings, which could be seen rising to form whole blocks of housing. Making the earlier example of the strategy is the Usachevka neighborhood, formerly a company settlement located between the New Virgin Convent and the Kauchuk industrial facility on Pliushchikha. Similar blocks of newly-built housing then came to emerge on Dubrovskaya Streets in Moscow's south-east and in Dangaouerovo settlement at the near end of Shosse Entuziastov. The relevance of that experience of Moscow's city builders has been felt in all subsequent housing projects, the current operations being no exception.

In the initial stage, as he drafted the New Moscow General Plan, Shchusev sought to soundly integrate the city's growth needs with the challenges to preserve the capital's cultural heritage. In his November 1925 Izvestiya article «New Moscow – Hub of New Culture» Shchusev explicitly defined the crucial and pressing city building challenge that essentially was the need to combine «the best relics of the hoary antiquity and top-of-the-line architectural achievements for either of those to be wisely integrated in clusters adequately balanced in terms of line and space».

The Moscow Agricultural Show was regarded as a critical state operation, particularly, given that the nationwide effort was under way to restore production capacities and create a socialist economy. The Show was called upon to display the status of the country's agricultural businesses and highlight the initial recovery results, as well as foster further growth, arrange for exchange of experiences amongst isolated entities, identify the best examples worthy of emulation. It was essential that goals for the agricultural science, engineering and automation be determined, that the nationwide electrification be proved to be the only sound strategy to promote not only industrial but also argicultural growth.

The Show was inaugurated in appropriate ceremony in August 19, 1923, with over 10 thousand guests being in attendance. The overall display area came to stand at 27,640 square metres. The exhibits were structured departmentally. One had to visit the field-husbandry, livestock and land-improvement section to be updated on the first partnerships and collective businesses. The Village exhibit featured nearly a dozen full-sized peasant homes standing for the country's different regions. They were of the following three categories – the current rural housing (improved peasant homesteads), new village and public buildings. In particular, put up for display were the communal house, agronomical station, rooming house, local administration house, nursery school, power plant, cooperative dairy milking facility. The New Village exhibit showed an exemplary Soviet collective farm featuring all necessary living and working structures – the office, club, public library, dormitory, bathhouse, machinery garage, farmyard, stable, cow-shed, sheep-fold, pigpens and other sites. The Housekeeping section included full-sized dwellings of Russia's numerous ethnic communities: Nenets pelt-tents, Yakut yurts, Caucasian mountain huts, Ukrainian thatch-roofed cabins. The Show was conducted to show the working and living conditions enjoyed by the newly-established peasant communes: in 1923, the country already had over twelve thousand assorted collectively-run businesses involved in working the land.

The display of the nation's burgeoning industries was particularly focused, the whole purpose being to show the advantages of mechanized labor. Exhibited in large numbers were most varied agricultural vehicles – chaff-cutters, cotton cluster-seeding machines, Kommunar sheafters, etc. The Show arrangers especially took pride in the first Soviet-made tractors. For example, the domestically-built tractor from the Obukhovsky Plant was seen to outperform its foreign-made Holt counterpart in terms of fuel efficiency and productivity. Brought in for the show also were the indigenously-designed Gnom and Zaporozhets tractors as well as other machinery products.

The adopted State Electrification of Russia Plan (GOELRO) created the right conditions for placing the agricultural businesses on a socialist footing, the incentive being to double the output of farming machinery. Hence, the Show likewise prominently featured the first applications of the nationwide GOELRO plan. The guests and visitors could view mobile and fixed electricity-generating plants. There was even a 30-meter-tall wind-turbine tower installed to produce electricity. The advantages of utilizing electricity to pursue a multitude of land-working tasks were shown in the dedicated proving fields at the Butyrki hamlet, the research and validation grounds of the Moscow Livestock-Tending Institution, where one could see the electric plough in operation. The Russian peasants' interest was particularly piqued by the mockup of an electricity-consuming village from the Irkutsk Region.

Displayed extensively at the Show also were the local industries' handicrafts, with the dedicated exhibit being accommodated in the former mechanical plant's building redesigned by A.V. Shchusev into a pavilion to hold over 33 thousand items.

Catching a great deal of attention were hand-made lace, linens, Vyatka dolls and toys, Nizhny-Novgorod wicker baskets and chairs, furniture, carpets, wood and bone articles.

A broad array of propaganda forms were used to handle the Show visitors, some of those including presentations, rallies, discussions, meetings, staged performances, festive ceremonies and «meet-your-partner» evenings.

...In those days, the Soviet capital seemed to be wholly preoccupied with the Show, with up to two hundred streetcars running to Krymsky Val on a scheduled basis. There would always be a large crowd of spectators at the Krymsky Bridge to watch an amphibian plane taking to the air. Interestingly enough, within a month and a half of the Show's events that amphibian aircraft performed 253 sorties to carry the eager visitors over the wonder-town that so rapidly emerged to replace the city's waste plots and dumping grounds.

In October 21, 1923, the Show was closed.

The First All-Union Agriculture, Industry and Handicraft Exhibition. 1923.

The «Greater Moscow» Plan

At the close of 1921, the Moscow Municipal Services Administration created the Commission on Development of the «Greater Moscow Plan» with engineer S.S. Shestakov at the head. Coming to be addressed for the first time ever was the goal to draft an urban development strategy for the Moscow Region for a long term and on a systemic basis.

The matter is that in the early 1920s the city's architects and economists had already made forecasts for Moscow to become one of the world's largest cities within the coming two decades. So, the «Greater Moscow» proponents had in mind not only the city's environs but also the entire region. Smaller towns were viewed as the metropolis' satellites that together with the Moscow Region would grow into a vast capital-city agglomeration. Moscow appeared to be destined to expand and be a huge city (with the population exploding to reach four million city dwellers). Understandably, Moscow no longer was seen as constrained by the Ring Railroad or confined to the Shchusev-prescribed «New Moscow» limits. The Shchusev-vision draft had duly been incorporated by V. Mikhailovsky in the «Greater Moscow» Plan, with the former now made to cover merely the central zone that in terms of size reached just 10 percent of the territory in question.

Under the Shestakov vision, the «Greater Moscow» boundaries were supposed to run via the townships of Lobnia, Skhodnia, Vnukovo, Butovo, Rastorguyevo, Shchelkovo, Mamontovskaya, all of those settlements being linked by the second Ring Railroad. Three belt highways were supposed to be built in the space between the city's

I. Zholtovsky: General layout of the All-Union agriculture, industry and handicratf exhibition. 1922 – 1923.

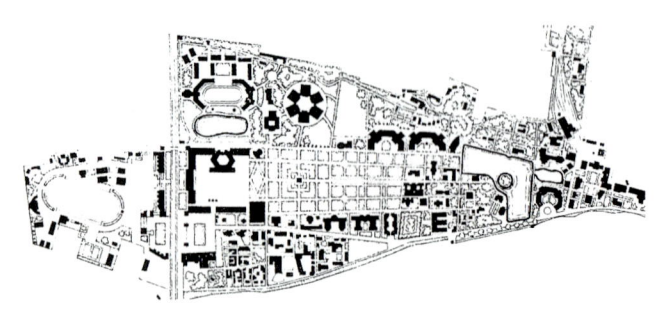

central zone and the outer Ring Railroad. The land within the belt-segment adjoining the central zone was to be split into two industrial and two park-land sectors. The next-in-line outward belt segment was supposed to be roughly divided into four housing areas interspaced with park-land. And finally, the farthest belt-segment, limited by the outer Ring Railroad, was from the very start intended to make an unbroken garden-city area with whole woods scattered here and there.

The outer belt-segment was supposed to be arranged after the fashion of E. Howard's British garden-cities featuring a developed road network, one- or two-storeyed homes with private garages, as well as plots for kitchen-gardens. For the zone not to be turned into a fully built-up area, the entire belt-segment was to hold four woods located to form the shape of a cross. Hence, the entire Shestakov scheme was dubbed the Maltese Cross. Large parks were planned to channel fresh air into Moscow's central section and help maintain a multitude of streams and basins in the capital's surroundings. Shestakov had been particularly careful about deciding the fates of suburban estates and historic mansions of the Russian nobility that would remain in place only to underscore the beauty of the landscapes. The old valuable monuments were supposed to be kept intact under the new plan.

While taking advantage of the ongoing NEP policies, the far-sighted «Greater Moscow» planners provided for a systemic approach to building and shaping Moscow and its suburbs within the territory of 200 thousand hectares, including the region's smaller towns that were supposed to function as the capital city's satellites. The satellite-towns were then believed to sort of cushion the growth of Moscow by way of maintaining businesses that would attract labor from the capital.

The «Greater Moscow» urban scheme was grown out of E. Howard's progressive garden-city ideas and those espoused by A. Piquet on the guidelines for functional zoning of cities (England, 1920). The housing problem was intended to be resolved with the public resources being merely invested to put in place the needed infrastructural facilities. Family home projects were recommended to be supported with private investments. Home-building loans were supposed to be allowed, particularly given that automobile-building projects were also in the works to help boost the New Russia's economy. Cooperatives, partnerships, land leases and other forms of entrepreneurial undertakings were expected to be introduced.

Cooperative housing construction projects had been booming throughout the NEP period. Federal agencies, departments, institutions and enterprises would throw their resources together to start condominium or partnership housing projects. They would be seen competing against municipal builders in the effort to singly resolve their housing problems. Unfortunately, the housing cooperatives and partnerships were closed down within a very short order, with their properties being appropriated by the State and single-family apartments largely tightened up to become communal dwellings.

As the «Greater Moscow» plans were drawn up, the Main Political Propaganda Administration called a contest for one- or two-storeyed worker-family home projects. The measure was part of the larger-scale effort to build garden-townships beyond the Ring Railroad, with private investments and land-leasing agreements expected to bolster the grand effort. The State was supposed to put in place the road network and support facilities. Automobile building projects were likewise regarded as a major incentive to assure growth of Russia's economy. By way of example, with merely five thousand trucks and automobiles assembled annually in the late 1920s, the annual average was expected to reach twenty million vehicles by 1940.

Starting from 1921, when the local residents pooled their resources to put up the first township in Moscow's suburbs, all other garden-settlements were cooperatively-run enterprises. People just formed partnerships, concluded contracts with home-building cooperatives or teams and had their housing built. The city authorities would merely oversee and confirm general plans and home designs as stipulated by the «Greater Moscow» planning documents.

Given the lack of the government-owned housing-building base and acute shortfalls in food supplies, the opportunity to privately own a small country house with a kitchen garden was grasped immediately. While sharp ideological debates on whether to built multi-storeyed communal houses or smaller single-family homes with complete farming cycles still continued, already rising to exist one after another had been self-styled garden-settlements put up by the employees of the Degunino chemical plant and the Dux facility at Likhobori, by the Krasny Bogatyr plant's cooperative at Bogorodskoye, as well as by other partnerships at Krasnaya Gorka on Volokolamskoye Shosse, Rykov settlement, Novoostankino and at other spots around Moscow.

Krylatskoye, Khoroshevo, Serebriany Bor, Pokrovskoye-Streshnevo and other sites were expected to be turned into model garden-townships around the capital city where Muscovites would go by streetcar, automobile, metro or even airbus at the end of their business day.

But then, the vision of garden-townships was seen running counter to the communist ideology and economic exigency to have city dwellers clustered around their work places. So, the effort was launched in the mid-1920s to construct factory-housing estates featuring four-five-storeyed brickwork buildings located close to larger industrial enterprises. It was at that juncture that coming to be introduced were state housing allocation standards and communal sharing of single-family apartments, which only caused a downturn in the socio-economic engagement of Muscovites.

Heavily focused by the «Greater Moscow» Plan were the issues of transportation. Having projected to radically upgrade passenger traffic support services on the Ring Railroad, the People's Commissariat for Transportation planned for an external rail line to be installed eleven kilometres out from the existing Ring Railroad, with the «cushion» rail line featuring assorted marshalling yards. Rail lines were likewise intended to be pushed into the city, closer to the central section, with the elevated rail tracks running over the green zones. Over the longer term, six trunk lines were expected to be laid to reach into the nation's remote areas.

However, the grand-scale rail building projects merely came to having some lines gradually powered (with the first suburban electric train being inaugurated in 1929 to service the Moscow – Mytishchi line), specialized tracks laid to go into larger factory compounds, as well as flyover junctions built to prevent traffic jams on the most heavily-traveled routes.

The Oktiabrskaya Station on Kalanchovskaya (Komsomolskaya) Square was intended to feature a set of double-level railroad platforms. The Shchusev-designed Kazansky Station nearby was crafted as a huge two-storeyed structure featuring railroad platforms to maintain sixteen through-tracks. Either the Yaroslavsky or Kazansky Station was to house a railroad museum.

S. Shestakov: Plan «Big Moscow». 1920s.

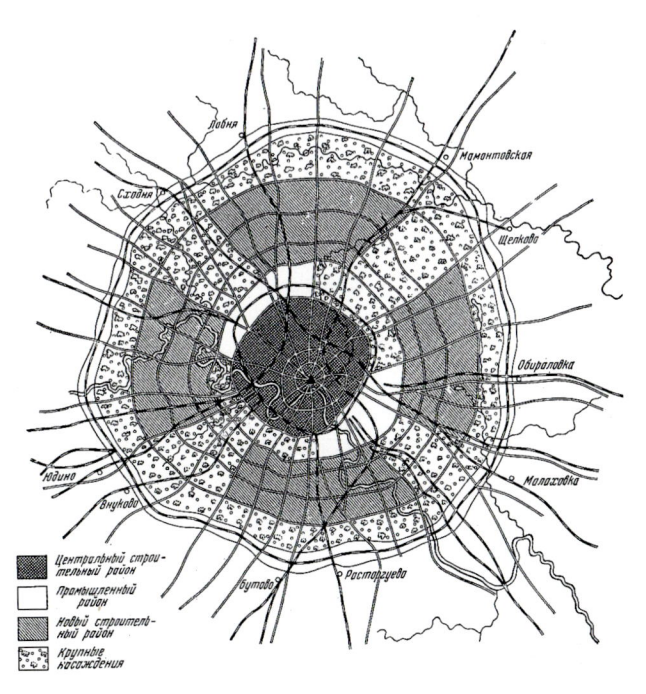

Under the Bernadsky draft, metro lines were supposed to be laid to run across the city center, thereby linking peripheral locations with «major railroad stations, shopping centers and industrial facilities». The metro was to include six diametrical lines stretching out of town, two full rings and two semi-rings. The diametricals were planned to go into all city areas, with the rings running to trace Garden and Boulevard Rings on the surface. The semi-rings were to be built under Kamer-Kollezhsky Val.

In the initial stage, the metro network was expected to stay within city limits, with streetcar or rail lines providing the requisite extensions into the suburbs. In the final stage, the metro would have two diametricals, running north-west to south-east and south-west to north-east, and reaching out to link with the second Ring Railroad.

Guidelines for the Growth of Soviet Capital

Under the conditions of increasingly bombastic rhetorics, the image of Moscow had grown to become overpoliticized, while the issues of city planning and building had incrementally gone beyond the jurisdiction of the Moscow Soviet (that governed the city and the region up to 1931). As a consequence, it was only natural for Moscow to hold center stage in the socialist-city-building debate that was launched in the late 1920s.

In mid-1929, the Moscow Municipal Services Administration (Moskommunkhoz), a most powerful city structure, made public its decision to set up a joint-stock society to build the «Green Town», a rehabilitation and residential complex for Muscovites in the area of the Villages of Spasskoye and Bratovshchina thirty two kilometres north of Moscow. That unfulfilled vision precipitated an acute debate on the questions of planning and building Moscow itself.

The first issue of «Sovremennaya Arkhitektura» (Modern Architecture) magazine, published by the All-Russian Society of Modern Architects (OSA), carried an article by M.Ya. Ginzburg, leader of the constructivists, that came up with the idea of disurbanization, which amounted to incremental elimination of large industrial centers per se, given the insolubility of this problem «generated by the capitalist era». The author, in fact, suggested that all of the capital city's problems could easily be taken out through having most of Moscow-based industrial enterprises, part of the academic and research institutions as well as government offices with no organic links to the city gradually relocated from Moscow and spread «across the Union» «on a systemic basis». The next phase was supposed to include practical measures to have the remaining city-dwellers resettled mostly along the thoroughfares linking the capital with the nearby towns and agricultural centers, the latter likewise being «proletarized». The benchmarks for the relevance of the ideas were provided by the objectives to have humans come closer to the nature and in the meantime enjoy high-level sanitary conditions of living. In the initial stage, however, it was suggested that no new housing construction should be allowed in Moscow, the rationale being that, as the city's apartment buildings degrade beyond repair, they would just be torn down to be replaced by trees and gardens. Except for a few historic fragments (the Kremlin, the «gentry» Arbat and Povarskaya, the «merchant» Zamoskvorechye, the «vending» Miasnitskaya, the proletarian Krasnaya Presnya), the rest of the built-up areas should be cleared and turned into a vast park featuring a few isolated government, research, academic, sporting, culture and propaganda institutions and facilities.

Concurrently with Ginzburg's piece, the Mossovet-funded «Stroitelstvo Moskvy» (Moscow Construction) magazine carried a material on the same issue by L.M. Sabsovich, demographer and sociologist that later wrote «Socialist Cities», a book heavily focused on the mix of urbanization and disurbanization. In his article L.M. Sabsovich mostly underscored the gains achieved in the course of rural socialization drives allegedly leading to a situation under which agricultural towns would be built. The right-sized townships should accommodate close to 50 thousand residents, according to the author. Another radical vehicle to help «disperse» larger cities was supposed to be provided by the fast-paced growth of all means of transportation that would inevitably put an end to the «provincial backwaters, insulation and destitution» in the process. Heavily pushed was rather a run-of-the-mill idea about the complete rejection of the «petty bourgeois conditions of living». The newly-built housing combine «should have no private kitchens, laundry rooms, apartments, dormitory-style rooms or family-shared rooms», according to the author. «Each working person» was to be offered a sleeping room (dubbed «cell» by other authors) measuring between 5 – 9 square metres. Conversely, communal areas were expected to be liberally spacious, with enough rooms made available for individual studies, too. Marriage was perceived to be entirely superfluous (the «unbonded marriage», meaning cohabitation with no mutual committments, used to be widely practiced in those years, particularly, amongst Komsomol members. Given the conditions, women were supposed to feel truly liberated and on a par with men), according to many of the advocates of building this kind of socialist environment. Designing rooms for children in those «brave-new-world» abodes was considered to be unnecessary, for kids would be raised in specialized facilities appropriately tailored to meet the sound needs of all age groups. The «raising», of course, was supposed to be labor-based and mostly confined to the fields, with the parents being cleared to come and see their offsprings at will.

To reinforce the political dimension of its operations, OSA in the mid-1930 was restructured into the Sector for Architects of Socialist Constructions (SASS) reporting to the newly-established All-Union Architectural Scientific Society (VANO). The SASS ideologists began to promote economy as a top-priority asset in building socialist cities, with the flows of travelers and cargoes now coming to replace the «functional qualities of isolated buildings and integrated compounds» so ardently advocated until recently. Ostensibly, the planning policy was to place industrial enterprises, introduce state-of-the-art transportation means and settle city-dwellers mostly along principal thoroughfares. It had been repeatedly stressed that the policy should necessarily be applied in Moscow. Under this updated vision, the issue of housing obviously came second to the challenges of building a whole range of «networks», starting from the transportation system and going to the so-called «educational» and «medical» ones. It was suggested that Moscow and other larger cities of the country should terminate all construction efforts, including housing projects.

Given the shift, N.A. Ladovsky, head of the Association of New Architects (ASNOVA), appeared to be more consistent in his projections than the OSA leader. After the urban-building architects had been integrated in a single organization, N.A. Ladovsky remained true to his ideas of rationalism (with the «maximized conveniences» multiplied by «modern esthetics» producing the «minimized psychological pressures»). A year later, N.A. Ladovsky suggested that the linear and radial-ring-based designs should be phased out by a totally new «dynamic city» strategy. The scheme was publicly branded «Ladovsky parabola» and «rocket-city». The growth of any city should be seen as an unimpeded evolution of an entity, with each new stage introducing some shifts of substance, according to the author. The city center should be allowed not only to rise but also to incrementally reach outwards. Under the Ladovsky vision, the city center was no longer a fixed spot but an evolutionary-mobile axis carrying growth-capable housing, industrial and green-agricultural zones. «As we break open the rings and have them shaped as horseshoes, we shall thereby enable the city center and the newly-shaped center-originated «branches» to grow, with the center actually developing to emerge like a fan... As the city keeps growing, the city center will freely deploy like an unfolding fan», claimed the project's author. When bidding for the «Green Town» project, Ladovsky is also known to have come up with the «dominant axis» idea that then got him a win. That project had already started to be implemented, but soon there occurred a radical change in the Moscow-growth plans and Ladovsky's scheme was left unrealized.

The conventional Moscow-building vision advocated by D. Friedman, Ladovsky's colleage known to have built a multitude of apartment and office buildings, appeared to be more acceptable. In the late 1930s, he appeared in the press with his article «Standing to Keep the Current Strategy for Moscow Growth». Being a highly-experienced practitioner, he succeeded in having the whole city-planning issue separated from the far-fetched visions and reduced to gritty realities by easily proving his point that, given their functionalities and

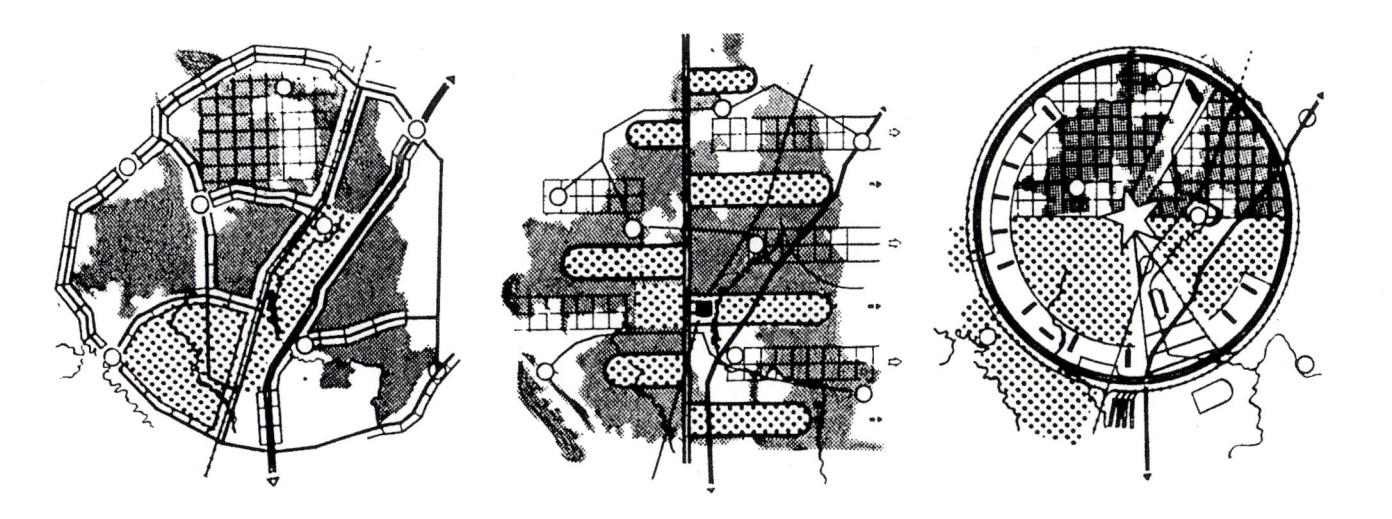

M. Gizburg, N. Ladovsky, K. Melnikov: Project variants of «the Green City». 1930.

economic exigencies, the citiy's organizations and institutions gravitate towards that or other in-town node. Hence, any Ginzburg or Gorny (Moskommunkhoz)-proposed «line» ran the risk of gradually turning into an ellipse or even a ring, which would saddle the city's civil engineers with a tremendous burden of costs associated with the installation of new water-supply, sewage, transportation and signal-communication lines. Though Friedman viewed Moscow's upward growth as the only feasible option, he nonetheless suggested that housing, industrial («labor thoroughfares») and academic-sporting axes should be amply spaced to avoid building «another New York City». As a matter of fact, the functional segments were supposed to be separated by the now-familiar green wedges.

The history of OSA and ASNOVA – the organizations actually making the two faces of the same medal of the revolutionary globalization in the field of architecture – is relevant as a good example of creative freedoms in action under the conditions of a highly-politicized society. Starting from 1923, when Professors N. Ladovsky, N. Dokuchayev and V. Krinsky established their Association of New Architects and engaged the services of many of their VKhUTEMAS senior students majoring in city architecture, they had been pushing the idea of growing some new form of art through synthesizing painting, sculpture and architecture potentialities». They sought to pursue the challenge of «rationalizing on the special character of architectural pursuits», thereby provoking the brand-name of «rationalists». Admittedly, Ladovsky would not have the architectural harmony tested with the «algebraic tool», and he merely embarked on the path of empirically creating the in-house benchmarks of clarity, perception, integrity, harmony, buoyancy, seeming vitality. Special tools had even been devised to check out 1D- and 3D-spacious qualities of the architectural forms (pro-plane viewer, pro-stroma gauger, and other implements). The students were involved in making and trying out all imaginable building-block shapes that were subject to general evaluation of the whole class. Whenever the verdicts were favorable, the «samples» were then inventoried as good findings. Overall, VKhUTEMAS, like any other school of higher learning of that period, practiced the «brigade-action» approach when the number of lecture presentations was minimized, «old-time academic» techniques (like drawing from life) were rejected, and the assignments were completed with the maximized involvement of the given «brigade» of students.

In 1928, the «proletarian architecture» came to hold center stage in sync with the ongoing, though subsiding, inter-Party struggle that culminated at the December 1927 15th VKP(b) Congress. The new policy course, aimed to assure the accelerated and comprehensive building of socialism (as perceived by the political leadership), required that long-term economic ties should also be developed with the outside world. The new policy-gaming cycle demanded that the architectural community should likewise be involved in the total effort to create an esthetically elevated image of «the new world» that got established to hold one sixth of the globe. Given the state of things in the country, joining the ranks of «proletarian architects» then were many of the former pragmatists, some of those posing in the past as constructivists and formalists.

The «class-approach» strategy, as applied to the business of architecture, had evidently been generated by the command of the times, which essentially called for large-scale and cost-effective construction of industrial workshops, depots, storage facilities and bridges, the standardization being increasingly the order of the day. The effort was perceived to be by far smoother should the «proletarian architectural community», heavily laced with Party members, be engaged to do the job.

The All-Russian Society of Proletarian Architects (VOPRA), set up in 1929, immediately set about to unleash an uncompromising struggle to come against the «idealistic and rote-based architectural schools and stand for the «class-motivated architecture», «for mastering the culture heritage in order to be better equipped to critically take advantage of the past achievements». The bashing had been so effectively organized that even the constructivists, running their own «Sovetskaya Arkhitektura» journal, were not always up to the mark while responding to the numerous challenges. The VOPRA organizational structure, its agenda and tactics were excellently thought through by the political acientists and developers of varied ideological myths and ploys «released» into the «playing field» of public life.

In 1930, VOPRA's architects got involved in the dispute on the planning and rebuilding of Moscow. V. Dolganov, a practitioner-architect of long standing, publicly appeared against the idea of «adding the rings» and laying new straightened radials, citing that the center would then within a short order «suffocate» from the growing traffic flows. Under the Dolganov vision, the city for the most part needed to be grown in the south-easterly direction where the housing construction had been heavily outpaced by the industrial development projects. The areas west of Moscow contained the Rublevo water supply system, restricted areas and land reservations, while there was scarcity of water supply to the south of Moscow. Dolganov's idea was to have a number of stand-alone and self-contained nodes built around the city's nucleus, with a ring of satellite towns grown further out.

The short-lived «revolutionary age» of Moscow's architecture had increasingly been phasing out. Until it was radically restructured, the Moscow Architectural Scientific Society, apart from its dedicated thematic divisions, included the OSA (known as the division of socialist construction architects since 1931), ASNOVA (later transformed into the Association of Urbanist-Architects), Moscow Architectural Society (branded «traditionalists») and VOPRA (labeled «proletarian achitects») sections.

Architectural Romanticism of the 1920s

In the first years of the Soviet era, the architectural knowledge had been recreated, with the «heritage» being either ignored or discarded. What is more, while being cut off initially by the frontlines and then by the economic blockade, the nation's architecture acquired wholly sui-generis features exclusively incident to the Soviet land's architecture. Today, we regard that modern architecture as a powerful revolutionary vehicle taking the people into a new world, the world stubbornly rejecting the entire universal heritage, the world seeking all sorts of novel architectural values, provided they should carry no vestiges of the «old» past of merely two-three years ago. The architectural crazes of the period contained no traces of the past techniques, with their champions having neither appreciation of «styles» nor flair for «styleshness». All of the «modern» drives in the realm of architectural design have now proved to be so hopelessly passe and outdated, so outlandish and hostile at the same time that the careful observer of the landscape hardly needs to be persuaded of that, for he would immediately come to see why the architects of the Soviet regime's first decades got aliented from the heritage that they seemed to have taken as friendly just a few years before. The planners, that until recently had conscienciously and devotedly labored under a different set of circumstances to follow their own «spirits» (as was phrased in those years), all of a sudden came to stand in awe of what they had been doing and were happy to be engaged in totally different pursuits, which they appeared to maintain with a new sense of purpose. The revolutionary shift obviously took the architectural community under total control, with the architects, just like all other masters of the arts – poets, painters, musicians and sculptors, getting enthusiastically and readily summoned to create fresh architectural designs for the new political regime in the country.

Today, we can see how the projects of those first Soviet years helped mold the perceptions of social-class-related housing and produce new ideas on building techniques and standard applications, as well as how they impacted Russia's entire architecture for decades to come. The inevitable blunders of the creative search period had luckily remained on paper and found no applications.

N. Ladovsky: Variant of the General Plan of Moscow. 1932.

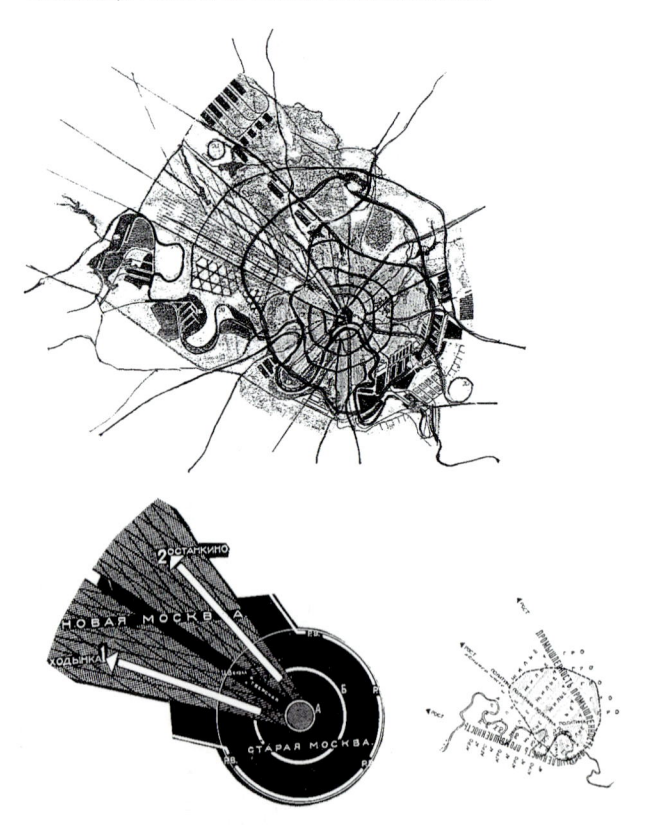

However, the innovational pursuits of that period had not been totally wasted, for they had produced quite a few promising ideas and given rise to varied schools of design. Our architectural gains are rooted in the 1920s, and the relevance of the period's projects, clearly featuring revolutionary ideas and innovative approaches, as well as fresh perceptions and unorthodox implementation techniques, can neither be belittled nor made exclusive. This observation is also true for the Soviet architecture (with the first Soviet projects getting accessible worldwide) either directly or indirectly bearing on the international architecture.

The unprecedented revolutionary tide then enabled the younger designers, that had sought to have the advanced forms meet new functions, come out into the open and make public their lofty visions, discoveries and findings.

The new and comprehensively forward-looking domestic architecture of the Soviet era's first decade had obviously advanced to take the leading edge in the world's architectural thinking and provided the guidelines for further growth of the country's school of architectural design.

Addressed by the entire architectural community then were the challenges of creating a new design theory (theories), searching for the best options to conduct research-based feasibility studies, identifying sound strategies and techniques to draft plans, balance structures and finalize shapes (it makes little difference if these terms were exactly voiced in those distant days). The important thing is that the focused effort was then under way to perceive and seek to build any structure as a whole and self-contained entity.

Architects then would try to secure their own designing strategies while profiting from the knowledge borrowed from the areas of philosophy, sociology, psychology, phisiology and mathematics. The techniques, perceived to be functional in discovering some basic laws or regularities governing the right balance of an article in general, would then most casually be applied to seek a design solution to either a city-planning or chair-building task.

But had the domestic architectural thought really turned to become wholly novel «overnight»? Had there been any spawning grounds? Any traces leading to the past? Admittedly, there had been no U-turn, which only adds to the drama of the period.

The architecture had not actually been turned upside down. After all, the inherent values of logic, ease of use, durability and beauty of the line were left to be functional. The Earth continued to be looked upon as the platform to support newly-designed structures (though, indeed, there had been ideas to have structures be literally lifted off the ground). The nature continued giving lessons to designers who were yet to discover more of its laws. The architectural designs still had been made to blend with the nature through the use of the well-proven touchstones of juxtaposition and detail, just like in the environments used by humans. The mechanics and gravity laws contunued to impose their constraints on the architectural ideas and applications.

But then, what actually had come to be novel and fresh? What predetermined the basic disparity between the emerging and old architectural philosophies?

It was the laws of societal evolution that happened to be primarily responsible for that sort of disparity. The life of Russia's society began to be based on a new set of guidelines, with the architectural community, no matter how inertial it is generally taken to be, immediately setting out to try and satisfy the newly-emerged needs. As a result, unorthodox structures began to rise. The surviving old-vintage designs had been updated radically enough to nearly appear as new builds. Part of the options had been discarded altogether. The esthetic standards had been totally reconsidered. The severity and modesty of the first post-Revolution years had left their meaningful impacts on the creative pursuits of designers. The underlying causes of novel approaches in the area of architecture had been so fundamental in character that it was precisely the socio-political influences that made the Soviet architecture undergo radical transformations in terms of functions, forms and building strategies.

The old benchmarks of durability, translated through mass and solidity; beauty, expressed as regular pleasing appearance; ease of use, taken as the value appreciated but only by a few, had evolved and mutated.

But what actually transpired in the first years after the October 1917 Russian Revolution? Directly translated into the new architecture had only been the capacities of advanced building materials and equipment that enabled more spacious interiors, sturdier support structures, larger bays and spans. And that came to be quite natural, too. The engineering gains and opportunities had avidly been absorbed by the new society's architecture. Overall, the growth of technologies had quite meaningfully augmented the capacities of developers and designers working in all areas of creative pursuits.

The newly-built industrial structures had been designed to feature unprecedented support facilities, such as dining rooms, locker rooms, shower stalls, mother and baby rooms, first-aid stations, etc., which totally transformed the interiors and exteriors of industrial buildings. Democratization of railroad stations, for one, made the designers discard the conventional strategy of dividing the internal space into the isolated standard areas differently equipped to cater to the three «classes» of travelers, as people would say in the old days. Nearly the same quantitative and qualitative shifts made the architects review their guidelines for building shopping, sporting, banking and entertaining facilities. A whole range of standard building projects had disappeared never to come back, some of those including boarding houses with their crowded and dark enclosed yards or semi-yards, factory worker barracks wholly unfit for decent living, business clubs and casinoes, innumerable churches and chapels. Coming into existence were higher-quality buildings, such as apartment buildings and factory dormitories, communal houses featuring shared properties and facilities, with all new structures boasting spacious interiors and large yards. Newly-designed public buildings began to come to the forefront with their unprecedented facilities, such as factory worker clubs, reading rooms, meal-preparation complexes, palaces of labor and even palaces of culture. As time passed by, new government buildings emerged – Houses of Soviets, executive council buildings and other administrative offices.

Throughout the years of industrialization and first five-year plans, the fundamentals of Soviet architecture had been most heavily influenced by the brisk growth rates in the area of building first small and then larger industrial facilities with their clear-cut functionalities.

And finally, playing a most crucial role had been the artistic dimension of architecture. Having been mightily enthused with the lofty ideas of the moment, the designers had wholly applied their talents and sought to support the country's aspirations with such dedication and selfless devotion that no room was left for decorative niceties of the previous era, which only served to have the architectural values transformed. Those, as a matter of fact, had so radically changed despite the circumstance that the architects had in no way generally and quickly rejected the palette of the conventional design techniques that they had perfected for decades and utilized so casually. In the initial stage, conflicts would erupt more often than not, and they used to be touched off not only by the grand-scale Palace of Labor (1923) contest but also by most regular projects commissioned to construct industrial and residential buildings, clubs and other public facilities. Overall, the architectural landscape had been made different in all of its dimensions. And as the change got under way, the need to devise a fresh theory of architecture, where the ongoing projects (though unrealized at that juncture) and new design strategies would be generalized and put into the proper perspectives, soon began to be felt in earnest.

In the first years of the Soviet era, the demand for construction was at its low. However, the architects then had achieved a lot in the way of reviewing their strategies and drawing up advanced projects. That initial period turned out to be most productive in the sense that the new Soviet architecture guidelines started to be defined. It is that singular mix of the living and working conditions of the period that created the unique creative environment and produced the matchless results, which set our architectural achievements totally apart and enabled the nation's architectural thought to secure the leading edge globally.

Not only the younger students would not be guided by any «authorities» or respected «sources», but even the more experienced designers, that had received classical educations in the old days, would be willingly, though differently, involved in researching fresh forms. Those included both the Leningraders I. Fomin, A. Belogrud, then A. Nikolsky and the Muscovites L.V., and A. Vesnin brothers, I. and P. Golosov brothers, K. Melnikov, N. Ladovsky and others. Of course, they each in their own way sought to depart from the old outlooks in order to shape and define new principles in their world of architectural design. It makes little difference at this point in time to conclude that some would wholly base their visions on the scientifically calculated forms best perceived by the viewer, others would focus on the maximized external attributes of modern structures, while still others would have the form strictly follow its function or even go as far as establish their own order-type organizations, such as «Red Dorics». What really matters now is that the old ways then seemed to be cast off for centuries rather than years or decades. What had been a fact of life just a few years before, be that the Saint Petersburg neoclassicism, Petersburg or Moscow «modern», «neo-

V. Tatlin: Monument to the 3rd International. Model. 1919.

V. Shukhov: Radio Tower. 1922.

A., V. and L. Vesnin: Project of the Palace of Labor. 1924.

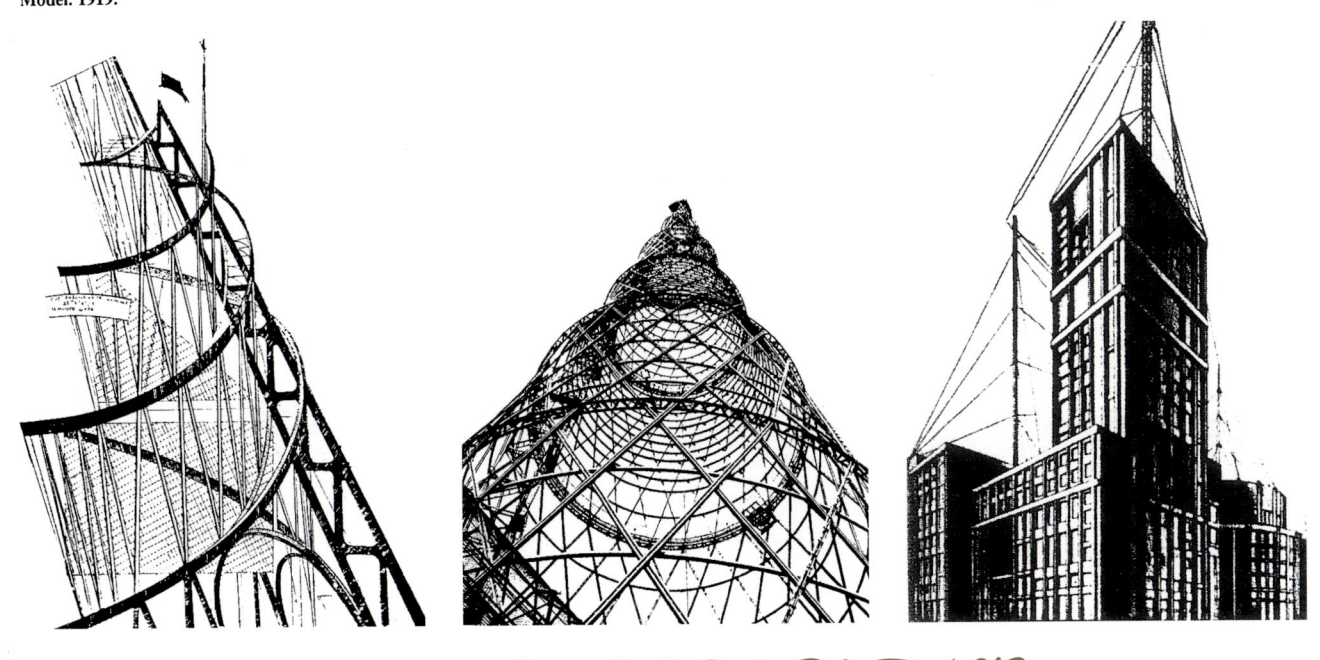

A. Shchusev: Building of the USSR People's Commissariat of Land. 1928 – 1933.

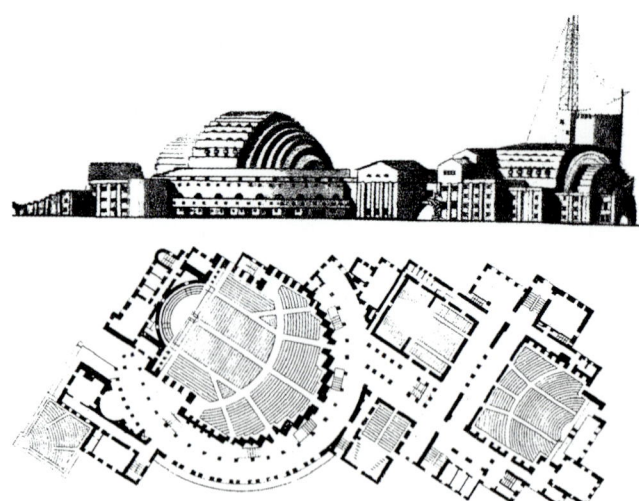

I. Golosov: Project of the Palace of Labor. 1922 – 1923.

Russe» or any other style for that matter, all of a sudden began to be nearly generally perceived as ancient as the age-old Babylonia or India, with all other «styles» from the time immemorial through the early-20th century making no exception.

What the younger designers would then be largely mesmerized by was the exceptional role of function. We would mostly be knowledgeable about just a few categories of structural composition, like measure, rhythm, symmetry (considered to be «bad form»), vitality (deemed to be «very good»), weight, mass, plane, volume. Admittedly, we did know one or two things about some nebulous, though allegedly inexhaustible, opportunities brought by advanced engineering and design solutions. What we were certain about in those days was to have the new society's needs be satisfied with the use of fresh building strategies. Was that insufficient? Well, we then felt pretty well equipped to handle the new tasks. We tremendously profited from sharing our visions and attending unending debates on any and all issues of city-building. That was our modus operandi. We would accept no shades in principle, for we would see them as pointless. And we then had not yet come to appreciate the detail. We would live in the world of contrasts: the new things should differ from the old ones (the recent ones to be more precise), and «mine» should not look like «yours».

Now, what assignments did the architects get in the first years after the Revolution? What role was the architectural community supposed to play? What did the nation expect from its architects? How did the architects receive the new regime's unconventional assignments and requirements? What tools did they intend to use to handle the tasks assigned? What gains did they achieve and what orders remained unaccomplished? What paths were charted and taken, and what progress was then made? These are the points that obviously need to be clarified.

In the first decade following the Revolution, the Russian architectural community's goal was to define new building strategies to carry out the projects wanted by the new society. The proven design techniques and prototypes of yesteryear had to be entirely reviewed. The whole methodology had to be reconsidered to create a new architectural vision both for functions and forms.

Research of the techniques used by the Russian architects in the first post-Revolution years reveals that their methodology had made a quantum leap rather than evolved incrementally. That was the period which all of a sudden produced a new set of societal challenges that would not be tolerant of any old stereotypes. This actually made the period's singularity and uniqueness.

Each time, designing spontaneously amounted to creating a wholly untried structure (even though specifications could be the same). That was the phase of Soviet architecture when everybody (or nearly all) would go about his business without looking to models for guidance. Would those designers have lasted long in their passion to remain that creative on the job? That was exactly the point in time when a new methodology or a fresh architectural school of thought needed to be introduced. Unfortunately, no such methodology or thinking had then been explicitly finalized and defined. The challenge apparently required longer than a single decade, which happened to be «allowed» by the circumstances. At some point, the societal needs brought about a shift of the Soviet architecture's mainstream and had it once again bounded by the established «stereotypes». The work to «master the heritage», as a matter of fact, went no further than prescribing the rules of growth...

What is «the old» and what is «the new»? Should a U-turn to face «the past» be necessarily regarded as a machine-type operation rather than an evolutionary phenomenon in its own right? Dividing things into «the old» and «the new» surely is debatable, for its primarily generated by a most superficial assessment of the architectural state of play.

As the reader is returned to look at the design techniques of the 1920s, it has to be underscored that architects then quite enthusiastically and effectively separated themselves from the past stereotypes. No matter what kind of assignment or project was handled at any given time, the designer inevitably considered it his duty and profession-de-fois to provide his proprietary solution to the challenging order.

Besides, one needs to be fully aware of the country's living and working conditions at the time. Like they say, when cannons are active, muses are silent. After all, the years 1918, 1919 and 1920 were filled with fierce battles that the newly-established republic had to wage to survive.

The demand for architectural pursuits had always been there. Even the first post-Revolution years were not completely void in that regard. The country had to be rebuilt and then grown. Hence, the new archi-

I. Zholtovsky: Building of the Moscow Thermal Power Station. 1927.

B. and D. Iofan: Living complex in Serafimovich Street. 1928 – 1930.

tecture first mostly dealt with notions and «ideas» rather than minor designing techniques. The new life itself, greatness of the revolutionary ideas and gains, unprecedented prospects and challenges measured in terms of the entire nation rather than some individuals, as well as other watershed circumstances made the designers be convinced about the termination of the old ways and techniques.

«...From the very first days of the October 1917 Revolution, we have known that we can ill afford to carry on with our old work habits... We came to be convinced that the past architecture stood in the way of progress and that an effort should be undertaken to create a new architecture receptive to the challenges of the new constructive era...», indicated A.A. and V.A. Vesnins as they reminisced about the past. Notably, this observation most aptly conveys the sentiments shared by the Russian architects at that time.

The functions and ways of the new times had already shaped up or could at least be anticipated. But the advanced design techniques were yet to appear. What sort of techniques? Well, any sort, ranging from engineering sequences all the way through artistic patterns. Also, there was a lack of acknowledged theoretical guidelines. But then, the pre-Revolution builders had been very familiar with such materials as metals and concretes, and the old-time housing construction companies had been appropriately equipped to take up and bring to completion any project that could then be signed up. Even a few theories were there to be followed, some of them including the neoclassicist, Russophil, modern-international and other schools of architectural thought.

Both now and then one could clearly see that the First Agricultural Show, held in 1923 in Moscow, most definitely featured the traces of classicism about its numerous pavilions so enthusiastically and freshly designed by a team of builders led by I. Zholtovsky. Noteworthy now, of course, is not the fact that V. Shchuko's international-exhibit pavilion at that show was built to feature most modernistic (by the standards of the times) lines, or that the Moscow General Plan sketches by I. Zholtovsky and A. Shchusev, the biggest names amongst the young talents at the time, did not really measure up to the vision of an ideal socialist city. Today, all those shades appear to be negligeable. What really is worthy of a mention is that all builders then had made tremendous strides to break away from the routine incrementalism that for the most part had been characteristic of both Russian and international schools of design just a few years before. Nobody could pretend to be oblivious of the «gold heritage» of the Soviet architecture that includes the superbly-designed IIIrd International Tower, Vesnin's Palace of Labor in Moscow (project), Norvert's Shatura-based power plant and a multitude of ventures pursued by Moscow higher-school students.

How then had the school of structural composition, school of new perception of functions, school of function-to-form links, school of design and techniques, even the school of graphic arts come into existence? A great role in that regard was played by the contemporaneous contests. New builders came into the limelight, matured, defined their «credos» and conducted numerous contests to teach their students. Those contests made the litmus test to check out the aspiring architects for novelty and validity of their projects. The contests were consequential in the sense that they had the capacity to make new architectural ideas available to prospective customers. Admittedly, the contesting projects had often been launched by customer specifications or orders. In general, contests and tenders made the principal competition grounds for active architects wishing to try out their mettle and have their individual perceptions expressed. Those competitive battles had been instrumental in shaping the country's best talents that in later years played a decisive role in establishing the Soviet school of architecture.

The severe hardships, that followed the post-Civil War economic dislocations, prevented any large-scale construction project from being launched. The new builds of that desperate period mostly included top-priority facilities, such as power plants, boiler works, housing at newly-commissioned factories and plants. The most pressing housing problem, that was felt nationally, was resolved through political means rather than with the use of the architectural community's services: large numbers of blue-collar workers had been relocated from unlivable and decrepit factory barracks and slums to be settled in larger cities' quality apartments vacated by the fleeing bourgeois elements.

The leap from building low-ceiling reading rooms in tiny backwater villages to designing the Lenin Mausoleum and Palaces of Labor with theaters seating thousands of spectators in the country's largest cities; from small peat-burning power plants at Kashira and Shatura to the Lenin-initiated GOELRO plan with its anticipated high-powered dams across Russia's great rivers; from small-sized factory-worker settlements to newly-built cities populated by millions; from housing featuring age-old customs and ways to tall apartment buildings holding integrated support facilities; from cities and townships with their dull unavoidable features, corridor-narrow streets and crowded blocks of housing to residential areas and large cities built to support new styles of living, both in form and substance, stretched out either linearly or parabollically, and spread liberally across the vast green expanses of our land or made to rise to nearly reach the blue skies, all this obviously inspired the contemporaneous architects to creatively engage their bolstered potentialities.

As the country's architectural thought continued to evolve, the 1920s wound up to open the door into the 1930s. In terms of calendar time, that line appeared to be no different from any other routine shift marked by yet another new year setting in. However, despite the seeming lack of major transformations on the verge of the 1930s in the Soviet Union, one can identify at least two shifts of historic proportions. Firstly, that was the timeline by which the most significant and mature projects had already been drafted by the domestic constructivists, rationalists and proponents of other building philosophies. In the meantime, the architectural thought continued to slowly move ahead, with the fresh strategies growing out of the bold ideas of the previous years.

Secondly, it became evident that it was precisely in the first years of the Soviet era's second decade that our architecture underwent a radical change of policy, which impacted the architectural strategies and applications for decades to come.[30]

K. Melnikov: The House of Culture named after I. Rusakov. 1929.

Architectural Chimeras

«I had the Revolution and Mozart».
The People's Commissar of Foreign Affairs
G.Chicherin

In the ancient Greece, Chimera stood for a fabulous lion-headed monster with a goat's body and serpent's tail. Her father Typhon, a hundred-headed fire-breathing monster, son of Tartarus and Ge, was vanquished by Zeus's thunderbolts and buried under a volcano, in his case, Mount Etna, where the eruptions were traditionally said to be due to Typhon's struggles to free himself. Echidna, Chimera's mother, made yet another monster posing as a half-woman-half-snake belching poison.

The sculptors in medieval Europe represented Chimeras as assorted grotesque she-monsters engaged to the present day (for example, the Notre Dame de Paris) to safeguard old Christian shrines, with their frightful looks keeping away the restless souls of deceased sinners hovering about the holy places and seeking to finally repose there.

Today, the term «chimera» for the most part stands for an impossible or foolish fantasy.

Moscow's architectural chimeras have nearly always featured the attributes of the above-described creatures in their entirety. Built to include starkly disparate structural elements serving antagonistic functions, they appear to be most peculiar, and, certainly, much more pleasing in appearance than their ugly medieval predecessors. However, they are, indeed, repulsive, for the purpose, they were made to serve, is both offensive and vicious. The Soviet-era architectural chimeras can be traced to all stages of a project design and implementation, from the drawing-board stage, when all sorts of fantasies begin to take shape and start their evolution into confirmed blueprints, through concrete operations to put in place buildings and varied structures.

Nearly half-a-hundred architectural chimeras are known to have been conceived in Moscow. Admittedly, those mainly have been left on paper, but a smaller part of those designs have been put into effect. Their photographic pictures can now easily be held together to research the phenomenon as a whole. For the sake of brevity, we shall only touch upon the most outstanding chimeras, with five of those representing stand-alone in-town structures and three more, in a separate section, standing for city-planning visions.

To begin, a few preliminary remarks would be in order. The architectural chimeras need to be explained to the public. First, people should have some knowledge about that sort of structures. Second, the viewer should be equipped to see the architectural contrasts of the capital city's Soviet period that contained both «honey» and «pitch». And third, a measure of «honey-treatment» is now required to safely heal the «spiritual wounds» inflicted on the psyche of our people by the chimera-builders, particularly, in the prewar years. The treatment job could, of course, be done through total elimination of those chimerical structures, but for that to be eventually achieved, our preprogrammed socialist psyche should first be made to see the destructive essence of those city chimeras in stone.

It has never been easy to talk of architectural chimeras because they are all the same in their weird appearance and yet unique in some other ways. One sometimes tends to use the metaphorical language to describe some of the chimeras as human beings with their energies and sentiments. Hence, this theme is going to be covered with the use of the tools of the «chimera-fitting» language and, hence, be unlike any other section of the book.

Normally, novels, stories and fairy tales use «the further the meaner» scheme. The story of architectural chimeras would follow a reversed sequence, with «the horrible-to-the-utmost» component being followed by «the ghastly aromatic» and eventually «the further the seemingly grander» part.

Inasmuch as many of the chimeras were designed to feature similar structural patterns or even titles, they had to be given individual nicknames to help the viewer distinguish between them. Admittedly, the architectural chimera tags have been coined to reflect the qualities of the targets, and so they can be taken as «chimerical» in their own right. The roll includes the Moloch, two Skunk «brothers», Callhouse, Rostgrave, Babedon, Brute and Starcrasher. Funny-sounding though they may seem, they all stand to be deadly-serious structures. To pro-

V. Shukhov: Radio Tower (Shukhova Tower) in Shabolovka Street. 1922.

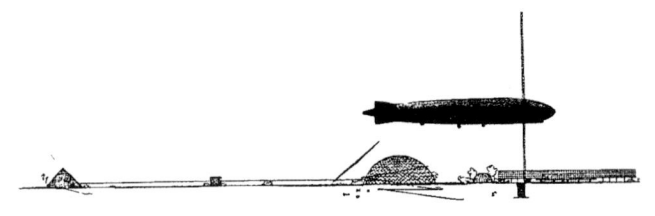

I. Leonidov: Contest project of the House of Culture at the place of Simonov Monastery. 1930.

vide an example, the ten-million Moscow might have to take the entire 21st century to fight the mighty city-building Brute that would strike to daily produce dozens of lethalities.

Understandably, the resourceful «chimeramakers» also deserve to be briefly introduced. They all shared a common city-building policy and legal base, a set of proprietary statutes and standards to govern and shape the «new world order» builders' perception of the cultural heritage. The style of chimeramakers was to have their perverse visions conform to their in-house «laws». Most of the chimera creators were just the eager greenhorns enthusiastically involved in executing the confirmed schemes. Their driving force has always come from the «just-carry-on» principle.

The architectural chimeras came to be established at the turn of the two antipodal eras in terms of their domineering civilizations – Orthodox and Communist, the trend being by no means accidental. Though the Bolsheviks labeled themselves atheists, their outlook is known to have come from their fanatical belief in the Communist idea, a wholly undefendable philosophy that made the antireligion a new form of confession. And given that one of the principal goals pursued by the Bolsheviks had been the rejection of the Christian groundwork of societal building and even the elimination of Christianity, their antireligion attitudes had primarily been directed against Christianity. It appeared to be natural for their antireligious attitudes to be mostly fueled by the long-lasting carriers of the anti-Christian outlook whose schemes provided the guidelines for the large-scale onslaught aimed to destroy Christian shrines and have them replaced by chimeras.

I. Fomin: Building of the «Dynamo» Sports Club in Dzerzhinsky Street. 1928 – 1929.

The Moscow Moloch

This architectural chimera, living to the present day, seems to have been the first one to come into existence. In the times of hoary antiquity and old Testament, Moloch was a Phoenician deity worshipped in Jerusalem in the 7th century B.C., to whom live children were sacrificed by fire. He featured a male body, arms, feet and a bull's head with a pair of big horns. Given that Moloch's red-hot-copper arms received the idolizers' sacrificial babies that would quickly be turned into a pile of tiny bones and then ashes, the term «Moloch» is now standing for a terribly insatiable monster thriving on human sacrifices.

With the Bolsheviks seizing power in Moscow, the million-and-a-half capital city was immediately confronted with the challenge of interring hundreds and then thousands of the deceased atheists. By then, the civilized and overpopulated Europe had already maintained a number of functional crematoriums. And since the Soviet Moscow experienced an urgent need for a crematory, the problem asked for an urgent fix, with the task to build a new facility being deferred for later years. The iconoclastic authorities in the form of Narkompros (!) and its architectural division (headed then by A.V. Lunacharsky and I.V.Zholtovsky respectively) embarked on the most sacrilegious course and in February 1919 suggested that one of Moscow's Christian shrines be rebuilt into a crematory. Soon afterwards, Moskomkhoz conducted an open contest for the project in question, the conditionality being for the church to be mutilated heavily enough not to show its features when commissioned as a crematorium.

The search culminated in picking out a most beautiful brickwork church on the grounds of the Donskoy Monastery, which only in 1914 was consecrated to bear the names of recently canonized Seraphim of Sarov and Anna of Kashin.[31] Under the winner-project by D.S. Osipov (with merely three contenders resolving to vie for the contract), the already-despoiled church was decapitated to put on a square-shaped chimney-tower, the floor being opened up to install a large underground furnace-facility. Shortly afterwards, that nether-facility began to receive atheist-filled coffins descended into the «hellish flames» as part of a pagan ritual. Since 1927 the newly-established Moloch has been operating to capacity.

The contest, held to secure a most sacrilegious «church-into-crematory» project, which subsequently was used to grow the Moscow Moloch, was certainly indicative of the ritual-based function of this architectural chimera. To put it bluntly, all of those hilarious and treacherous chimeramakers, the «New Phoenicians», had quite purposefully rethought the symbolic meaning of the contest's provisions. The Christian Church, they knew, was universally perceived as the Holy Sacrament. Now, the Descent into Hell appeared to have been restaged. God was not even crucified. After the revolutionary fashion, the Church was beheaded to be given the rectangular-shaped Moloch head. The shrine's subterranean space was expanded to hold the hellish flames eager to receive the unending line of the dead bodies, with the church thereby being transformed into an antichurch, sort of a satanic den with a throne for Devil.

The boldly and smartly engineered chimera of a crematory can still be viewed in all its ugliness on the green grounds of the Donskoy Monastery graveyard. But a monastery is generally regarded as the Christian symbol of a Heavenly settlement, a Paradise garden. The Moscow chimera has been carefully serviced and maintained to stay functional without a hitch and turn bodies of the dead atheists into small piles of ashes, while making fat profits out of catering to one's «nearest and dearest». The ashes have no longer been committed to Mother Earth, which had for centuries been the way of the old Arians, Slavs and Russes. The ashes are kept suspended in the columbarium urns arranged in numerous levels. Under the time-tested belief, the lost soul finds itself restlessly migrating between the Heaven and the Earth.

The Donskoy cemetery has been closed for burials of Orthodox Christians for quite some time now. But no constraints or bans have been placed on the local chimera operations. Planted on the grounds of the Paradise-emulating garden, the chimerical plant has now for seven decades been working to lovingly ring itself with new rows of urns, held by the thousand in the columbarium (it all sounds like an ominous joke about Columbus, an Arian, being dumped into Hell). Thousands of lost souls appear to be hovering about the place while building an invisible aura of anxiousness. The chimera's east-facing side seems to obscenely show its three «breasts» (the former shrine's apsides), and its boxlike top appears to feature eye-sockets revealing the flashes of unfriendly hellish flames.

What is more, that chimera is known to have the ear for good music, for nearly every day she can be seen enjoying the tunes by Mozart, Bach, Pachelbel and other catholic composers performed in recording.

The dream of Moscow Bolsheviks, indeed, has come true: each one of them had the Revolution and Mozart!

Today, Moscow is operating three more crematories, replicating the original one for the most part. Admittedly, the new builds can hardly be passed as Moloch chimeras. They are fully specialized European-class businesses epitomizing the latest advances in terms of engineering and services.

The Skunk

Chekistov to Zamarashkin:
«You seem to be odd and funny folks!
You have for centuries lived in poverty
And kept building your shrines...
In your place I would have long ago
Turned those places into latrines».
S.Yesenin, «The Country of Villains».

Standing in the very middle of the Kremlin is the 15th-century Assumption Cathedral, Russia's most sacred shrine. The Cathedral's northern wing is right next to a large-capacity public toilet installed there to offer services to the unending flow of visitors coming to do the Kremlin sights. The facility is literally two steps away from the Cathedral's northern doors. There are some religious services that call for mandatory ring-the-shrine processions when the clergy (sometimes led by the Patriarch) egress through the northern doors, proceed eastward and then southward in order to circle and then reenter the shrine via the western doors. The festive and colorful flux of marchers with their standards, crosses, icons, heavenly chants and pious prayers first are compelled to head towards the toilet, face it and only then turn eastward.

Building a huge public toilet next to the Assumption Cathedral, particularly, at a spot like that (with the doors designed to be face to face), was certainly the product of a villainous scheme. The facility of that sort could easily be placed in one of the Kremlin's remote corners, and visitors could well be directed to find their way. What we have on our hands in this particular case is a highly sacrilegious operation shrewdly hatched and arrogantly executed to hit the Christian values the hardest.

The matter is that the latrine was planted under the ingeniously-designed Cross Chamber of the former Patriarch Palace built in 1655 by Patriarch Nikon. The Cross chamber had been used by the former Russian patriarchs to hold receptions in honor of the monarchs and conduct All-Russian Church Assemblies. As Peter the Great established the Holy Synod, the Cross chamber ceased to be used for those functions. Under Catherine the Great, the chamber began to be used as the chrism-compounding chamber.

The consecrated chrism is known to have been used for anointing since the Old Testament days, the sacrament being taken by high priests, prophets, emperors, Russian grand dukes and tsars. Anointed in baptism are generally all those entering into the fold of the Orthodox Church. Understandably, the anointing has always amounted to a ritual of great relevance.

The chrism is compounded from over fifty aromatic oils, balsams and other ingredients and then distributed to churches all across Russia. Before the 1917 Revolution, the consecrated chrism had only been prepared at two places: at the Kremlin's chrism-compounding chamber and at the Kievo-Pechersky Lavra monastery.

Building the Soviet Union's principal toilet under the chrism-compounding chamber and next to the Assumption Cathedral is certainly an act of most refined scoffing at our ancestors' sacred monuments.

K. Melnikov: Contest project for the conversion of the Church of Serafim Sarovsky and Anna Kashinskaya in Donskoi Monastery into a crematorium. 1927.

* * *

The year 1936 saw the demolition of the Kazansky Cathedral on the Red Square, a unique memorial of Moscow's liberation from the Catholic expansion and Polish-Lithuanian intervention of 1610 – 1612. The sacred shrine was replaced by an open-air restaurant decorated with large flowerpots. The expanse of the Red Square was to please the eye on the one hand, while a «grand-style» toilet was made conveniently available in the basement of the nearby building on the other.

Once again, the whole scheme was ritualistic and sacrilegious to the utmost. Firstly, the commemorative cathedral was torn down exactly to mark its 300 years from the day it was founded by Tsar Mikhail Fyodorovich. Secondly, the restaurant's tables were positioned on the former cathedral's elevated floor and platform, and every time the visitors wanted to use the local toilet they had to walk over the tombs holding the remains of the heroes of 1612. And finally, the latrine was placed between the Kitay-Gorod housing and the shrine on the level of the former cathedral's groundwork, which was fully pursuant to the «skunk law».

The chimerical dimension, added to the sacrilege, was in that the toilet turned out to be integrated with the nearby apartment building's ground floor, its subterranean section going three metres deep.

Crematorium within the boundary of Donskoi Monastery. 1927.

It is precisely the spot where remains of the Kitay-Gorod's original structures of the 16th – 17 centuries make the archeological layer running up to three metres underground. That also is the site of the old Kitay-Gorod brickwork stores dealing in icons. Put otherwise, the Kitay-Gorod skunk found itself a cozy place on the grounds of Moscow's oldest icon shopping mall where prayers had been heard the most!

In the years of the 1941 – 1945 war, the restaurant was gone, with the chimera-makers' product remaining functional. As Moscow's GUM, the capital city's main department store, was declared open after the war on the Red Square, the Kitay-Gorod «skunk facility» began to be used by thousands of shoppers. As a consequence, the size and odor of the place acquired the city-wide relevance.

The underground skunk had functioned up to 1990 when it was put out of operation with the new Kazansky Cathedral being laid in construction.

The Callhouse

In 1918, the Red Square began to be used for military parades, rallies of the working people and new Soviet festivities. It all appeared to be fine except for that the square had not been equipped to offer «communal» services to participants of huge rallies and marches. Things needed to be put right the sooner the better. In 1928, civil engineer F. Gauze inspected the scene and filed a report that carried these words: «The lack of public toilets is particularly pressing in the days of May and October festivities when hundreds of thousands of people come to pass through the Red Square. We keep receiving sackfuls of letters from industrial workers, participating in annual rallies and festivities, their demands being that toilets should without delay be installed in the area. We suggest that the project, appended to this report, should within a short order be executed to have public toilets installed in the Kremlin and Kitay-Gorod area...

A toilet on Vasilyevsky Slope could either be built in the Kremlin wall's ramp or placed to take part of the store in the Vassily the Blessed Cathedral's basement. Given that the space already features the flooring, finished walls and overhead spans, revamping the place is not expected to be prohibitively costly. The facility only needs to be outfitted with toilets, urinals, other fixtures and heating. Electrical heaters appear to be the best solution, for that would obviate the need for a chimney, which could spoil the general view of the cathedral».

Frantz Gauze's draft carried a sketch of the Vassily the Blessed Cathedral against a backdrop of the Spassky Tower, with the basement featuring two toilet entrances and the legend reading: «Public toilets to replace the store rooms in the basement wall supporting the shrine». Pictured at the top of the sketch was the suggested scaled-down drawing of the area. The idea never came into effect, for it obviously was over-sacrilegious, offensive and foul-smelling. Then, thousand-strong marching columns would have been mischanneled. These considerations seem to have sealed the fate of the outrageous chimera. It had merely soared over the sacred domes of the Vassily the Blessed while spreading its lethal odors.

A few more years passed and L. Kaganovich suggested... the cathedral be torn down altogether (the 1935 general plan for Moscow was drawn up under L. Kaganovich's guidance). Predemolition measurements already began to be taken to prepare for the blast. The project had been confirmed by all agencies only to be scrapped by the top-level authority.

The Rostgrave

Planted amidst the Red Square is the Lenin Mausoleum, Shchusev's ingenious and greatest creation. The structure has gathered lots of written eulogies and tributes. Ostensibly, the place seems to be perfectly well known by everybody. However, the proprietary «graveyard» secrecy would only let you know about the facility to the extent of your authorized concern. But take a thorough and unprejudiced look at the Mausoleum as a whole and you would immediately see many of its ambiguities with an unaided eye.

The original Mausoleum was the white marble tomb of Mausolus, ruler of Caria (377 – 353 B.C.). The white Mausoleum in Galicarnassus, over 130 feet high, became one of the Seven Wonders of the ancient world. However, our granite «wonder» had not essentially replicated the original structure, for it was built to simulate still older Babylonian ziggurat terraced pyramids, temple towers of the ancient Assyrian and Babylonian (or Chaldean) priests principal compilers of the Old Testament) rather than some Hellenic tombs. And should we deal with a newly-built temple tower, it should have not only the deity's mummy (or remains) but also the wizard-priests supplicating over the «altar-grave». Indeed, our impressive tomb features a rostrum where sets of Communist «Chaldeans» from time to time could be seen inspecting the ritualized rallies flowing below. The newly-coined term «Rostgrave» appears to be the best name for the structure integrating a rostrum-platform and a grave. And what are the rites practiced by our wizard-priests, should those be viewed from the chimerical perspective.

Our ziggurat-temple amounts to something more than just a mix of opposites: the quiet of the tomb, holding the mummy of the leader of the Communist International and global proletariat, down below and the buzz of the living USSR leaders treading the «sacred» altar on top. «Dear Comrade» can hardly repose in peace because they do not and would not let him. He is doomed to taking the disparate noises amidst the central square of a large metropolis rather than to reposing peacefully. In addition to the routine clatter, on the newly-fixed national days the square has been filled to capacity by enthusiastic crowds frenetically shouting their mantras in the course of the carefully-staged witches' Sabbath-style performances. There have been times when he could hear thunderous sounds of large military bands followed by the clamor of heavy military equipment discharging clouds of noxious diesel fumes. Put otherwise, the galvanized dead body precipitated the crowds' craving to be mesmerized in the name of the deceased leader.

F. Gauze: Public toilet in the supporting wall of St. Basil's Cathedral, 1928.

The body obviously could not be placed to rest elsewhere. The Red Square turned out to be precisely the place where it was supposed to be kept for idolization. It was only there that «he» could several times a year address «the world pgholetaghiat» while appearing before the marching thousands and saluting the working people with his energizing incantations. His dead body continues to be kept suspended in mid-air, between the ground and the skies, rather than be properly interred. The leader's soul keeps soaring over his rostrum-grave, even over the whole of the Red Square. People, entering the square, seem to have ESP for this circumstance. Many are known to have been totally oblivious of their bearings: they would either respectfully freeze before they go into the Rostgrave crypt guarded by sentries or would keep yelling at the top of their voices as they saluted a clan of the living leaders to show they were soundly held together by the behests and spirit of the dead leader (with the term «demon – stration or de-monstr-ation clearly containing a chimerical dimension to it).

Built in back of the Mausoleum is a necropolis strictly arranged to honor the individual ratings: coming first are the Party leaders followed by the soldiers of the Revolution and distinguished USSR citizens. Catching one's attention in the first place is a small row of graves of the deceased leaders, with the flanks holding square-shaped common graves filled with the remains of the Moscow revolutionaries that had fallen in the battles fought to see Russia ruined. And they all have been privileged to rest in peace, with the former moat turned into a graveyard and their souls anchored accordingly.

As one looks further in the background, one immediately spots the familiar-looking wall-mounted plaques denoting the urns that hold the ashes of the outstanding people of the «Land of the Soviets». This actually is the treatment accorded by the idolizers of the newly-reigning Moscow Moloch to all those who are viewed to be «more alive than anybody else». That was the first revolutionary leader himself who suggested the 15th-century fortress wall be turned into a columbarium. But even on the Red Square the lost souls of the great talents of our half-devastated nation are not free to hover above the graveyard and the Mausoleum, for they continue to remain spellbound by the restless soul of «the greatest of all humans». They all apparently create an aura of the awfully fascinating chimera.

Placed in front of the «restless souls» and «peacefully resting» soldiers of the Revolution are numerous huge stands that on Soviet holidays would always be filled with guests readily exploding together with the rallying crowds in massive cheers of allegiance. Those pathetic mergings of Russia's «dead souls» were supposed to display the might and unity of the VKP(b), the new Bolshevist anti-church, that truly had come to pose at the apocalyptic Loose Woman of Babel.

The above-described chimera has more to it than just the familiar ideological or communist aspect. It not only came too late to join the run of ancient Chaldean terraced pyramids. The Rostgrave is certainly much more chimerical than it seems to be at first glance. And it would never have achieved the status of an accomplished chimera, had its gloomy zigguratic splendor had not exuded exotic odors to better establish its presence. Indeed, the most-high-titled chimera-makers and designers had spared no effort to satisfy the demand and make a good job of it.

To be fully compliant with the requirements of the «skunk law», the newly-built Soviet temple-tower and Moscow's three oldest neighborhoods – Kitay-Gorod, Zaneglimenye and Zamoskvorechye – by 1930 had been interspaced with three huge public toilets remaining functional to the present day. Two of the facilities were installed at the Red Square's opposite ends, with the third one planted exactly opposite the Mausoleum in the GUM building's central section (with the built-in archway inviting visitors to the local latrine rather than to the department store). All of the three facilities are placed underground to be at the level designed for the leader's subterranean sarcophagus. Hence, the chimera does not appear to be limited in scale to a stand-alone architectural monument (Rostgrave) or even some larger complex (with the nearby necropolis and the stands thrown in). It obviously pursued a larger-scale goal, for the overall chimerical complex was drafted to include two five-pointed stars atop two Kremlin towers, three public toilets to face the square, and three residential neighborhoods. But that was not where the villainous scheme ended.

The symbolic purpose of the Rostgrave-centred city-building complex appears to be even more destructive. The Spassky Tower used to be flanked with the Savior of Smolensk and Our Lady of Smolensk (Odyhitria the Counselor) brickwork chapels built in honor of Smolensk expelling its invaders. The Kremlin's Nikolsky Tower was flanked with Saint Nicholas the Miracle-Worker and the Saint Alexander Nevsky chapels. All four same-design chapels, put in place at the close of the 19th century, following the dedication of the Christ the Savior Cathedral, served to be the latter's sort-of representatives at Moscow's sacred Red Square or even «sentries» standing guard at the Kremlin's principal towers. Just like the Christ the Savior Cathedral, the chapels had been installed to stand as war memorials in honor of the Russian victories over Napoleonic hordes that came from Europe.

This is the way the idea was represented by the Saint Nicholas the Miracle-Worker chapel at the Nikolsky Tower. The chapel contained the Apostle Philip (his commemorative October 11 marking the date the French troops began to flee from Moscow) and the First Martyr Stephen (his commemorative December 27 marking the date the Russian land was cleared of the invaders) Icons. The chapel's ceiling murals featured the Saints Adrian and Natalia (August 26 marking the Borodino Battle date), Saint Apostle Thomas (October 6 marking the Tarutino Battle date), Saint Apostles and Evangelist Mathew (November 16 marking the Napoleonic army crossing the Berezina-river) and Saint Martyrs Chrisanph and Darya (March 19 marking the seizure of Paris by the Russian forces). Displayed on the chapel's door from the inside was the Our Lady of Kazan (October 22 marking the Viazma battle date) Icon.

As the Rostgrave architectural complex was planned and drafted, all those sacred commemorative chapels had been removed by 1930, with the sites now featuring public toilets. The latrines were not exactly put on the chapel groundwork. But, following the rationale of the «skunk law», they were built to fill the space between the remains of the chapel basements and Moscow's ancient residential neighborhoods. In this particular case, the chimera-makers provided a degree of redundancy for their basic «skunk law» by clearing the field of vision between the Mausoleum and the latrines.

There are some points that need to me mentioned to describe the evolution of the Rostgrave complex. In 1928, F. Gauze was busy designing the southern public toilet to be installed in the Kremlin wall ramp facing the Vassilyevsky Slope. However, by 1930, the facility had actually been moved up and built right next to the groundwork of the demolished Our Lady of Smolensk chapel to be on the same level with the Mausoleum. The Gauze-designed northern toilet had likewise initially been intended to sit further out at the Sobakin Tower and face the Revolution Square. But by 1930, the foul-smelling facility had been moved up to be right next to the groundwork of the Saint Alexander Nevsky chapel. The field of view from the Mausoleum to the third public toilet, integrated in the central section of the GUM department store, was also cleared. Originally, found in front of the prospective toilet could then be the Minin and Pozharsky Monument, with the bronze Minin raising his arm, apparently, upon Prince Pozharsky's approval, to point in the direction of the Mausoleum. To have the Mausoleum and the latrine within sight of each other, the Minin and Pozharsky Monument was then moved closer to the prospective «Callhouse» in the basement of the Vassily the Blessed Cathedral.

The large-scale architectural Rostgrave complex had eventually been put into effect in all of its entirety. The chimera's spirit had, indeed, achieved the desired explosive mix of the Soviet-style «sanctity» and chimerical sacrilege. And even that was not the whole story.

The Rostgrave is standing in its satanic splendor in the middle of Holy Russia's oldest and most sacred place – Moscow's open-air square-turned-temple – created by Ivan the Terrible, Saint Metropolitan Makary and Russian shrine builder Postnik Yakovlev, nicknamed Barma, in the image of the Heavenly City of Holy Jerusalem. The clearly outlandish and shrewd chimera came to set up shop in the building of that closed Christian shrine just like a hostess. Every day, from morning till evening, that hostess receives the crowds of domestic and international visitors coming to enjoy the marvel of Russian architecture. And as the tired spectators then spread out to use the local latrines, they apparently, either in whispering or out loud, «hail the spirit» of the leader and his retinue. That is exactly the ritual and the sequence that the chimera-makers had carefully concocted for the monstrous architectural complex to be integrated and fully operational.

The Mausoleum is going to be revisited further on, and it will then appear as a great feat of the Soviet architecture rather than as a chimerical structure.

---

[1] K. Zaitsev. Orthodox Church in Soviet Russia, Part I. Shanghai, 1947, p.p. 3 – 8.
[2] «To you, the tempted and anquished Russian people...» Address by Saint Patriarch Tikhon. Preface. G. Shevkunova, Moscow, 1996, p.p. 4 – 9
[3] Nilus S.A. On the Banks of God's River. Vol. 2. San-Francisco, 1969, p.p. 182 – 183. Quotes from «Russia Before the Second Advent». Published by the Saint Trinity of Sergiyev Lavra, 1993, p.p. 31 – 32.
[4] Oldenburg S.S. The Reign of Emperor Nicholas II. Saint Petersburg, 1991, p.276. Quotes from «Russia Before the Second Advent». Published by the Saint Trinity of Sergiyev Lavra, 1993, p.33.
[5] Same, p. 337
[6] Zaitsev. The Times of Saint Tikhon. Moscow, 1996, p. 30.
[7] Same, p.p. 40 – 43.
[8] Latyshev A.G. The Uncovered Lenin. Moscow, 1996, p. 147.
[9] Leninsky Sbornik XXXIII, p. 248.
[10] Latyshev A.G. The Uncovered Lenin, p.p. 152 – 153.
[11] The Central Party Archives of the Marxism-Leninism Institute (TsPA IML), fund 76, opus 1, file 3546. Quotes from «The Uncovered Lenin» by Latyshev A.G., p. 158.
[12] Leninsky Sbornik XL, p.p. 420, 424.
[13] Quotes from «Russian Church (1917 – 1925)» by V. Tsypin. Moscow. Published by the Candlemas Monastery, 1996, p.p. 170 – 174.
[14] Lenin V.I. Complete works, vol. 36, p. 369.
[15] Same, p.269.
[16] K. Zaitsev. The Times of Holy Tikhon. Moscow, 1996, p.101.
[17] Latyshev A.G. The Uncovered Lenin, p.p. 170, 171.
[18] Remembering V.I. Lenin, vol. 5. Moscow, 1979, p. 297.
[19] Latyshev A.G. The Uncovered Lenin. Moscow, 1996, p.p. 140 – 142.
[20] Same, p. 161.
[21] Same.
[22] Same, p.p. 207 – 223, 226.
[23] Vostryshev M. Patriarch Tikhon. Moscow, 1995, p. 103.
[24] Same.
[25] V.I. Lenin on Graphic Arts. Moscow, 1977, p.p. 318 – 320.
[26] Decrees of the Soviet Government. Moscow, 1959, Vol. 2, p.p. 95 – 96.
[27] Konenkov S.T. My Age. Moscow, 1971, p.p. 223 – 224.
[28] Bychkov Yu. Let Monuments Engage in Propaganda. Kuranty; the area-history almanach. Moscow, 1983, p.p. 49 – 58, (excerpts).
[29] The USSR Architecture, 1935, No.4, p.40.
[30] Barkhin M.G. The Architect's Techniques. Moscow, 1981, p. 9 – 90 (excerpts).
[31] Church designed by Z.I. Ivanov. Started in construction in 1904 and dedicated May 26,1914. Features three altars and a belfry over the western wing. The side-chapels are dedicated to: Assumption of the Virgin Mary and Mary Magdalene; Descent of the Holy Spirit and All Saints.

I. Toidze: May Lenin's victorious banner dawn upon us.

CHAPTER TWO

Stalin's Reconstruction of the USSR Capital 1930-1953

Radical reconstruction of Moscow.

General plan of reconstruction of Moscow. 1935.

N. Petrov, K. Ivanov: Poster. 1952.

I. Lobov and others: Project of reconstruction of Zamoskvorechie. 1935.

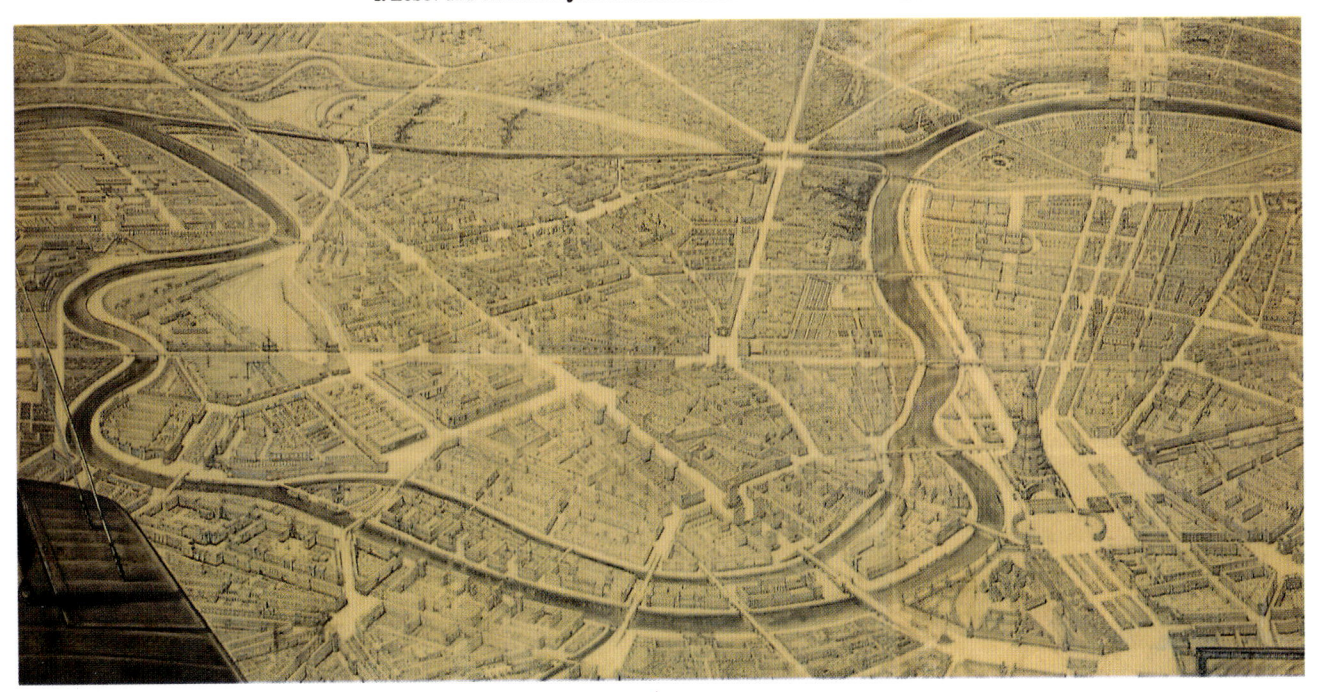

Sculptors: S. Orlov, A. Antropov, N. Shtamm; architect V. Andreev: Monument to Yuri Dolgorukii. 1954 г.

V. Mukhina: Worker and Peasant. 1937 – 1939.

Mysterious Pages of History of the 30s

«Party – is a million-finger palm,
Clenched into one crushing fist».
                              V.Mayakovsky

In his essay «Betrayed Revolution» Trotsky undertook to comprehend the course of history: «It is quite a well-known fact that until now every revolution was followed by a period of reaction or even counter-revolution, which, to be objective, never threw the nation back to the point of departure... Victims of the first reactionary wave were, as a general rule, pioneers, initiators, instigators, who headed masses during the offensive period of the revolution... Axiomatic assertion of Soviet literature that the laws of bourgeois revolutions are «inappropriate» in case of a proletarian revolution, have no scholastic backing whatsoever»[1].

Trying to specify the notions of «reaction» and «counter-revolution» using hot «facts» from the USSR life in the mid-30s, Trotsky wrote: «...yesterday's class enemies are being successfully assimilated by the Soviet society... In view of successful collectivization «kulaks' children were relieved of any responsibility for their fathers». Even more: «...now even a kulak will hardly ever believe in the possibility to recover his former dominating position in the village. It is quite clear, why the government started lifting restrictions connected with people's social background!»

Trotsky was indignant about attempts to revive family in the USSR: «The revolution made a heroic effort to destroy the so-called «family hearth» which became something archaic, dilapidated and sluggish... Family's place... was to be occupied, according to original schemes, by an extensive system of public care and support», – which was supposed «to bring actual liberation from millennium-old bondage. Since the task has never been solved, 40 million Soviet families still remain nests of the Middle Ages... It is for this reason that successive alterations of tackling the issue of family in the USSR are the best indication of the actual character of the Soviet society... Back to the family hearth!.. Formal rehabilitation of family which takes place simultaneously – what a significant coincidence – with the rehabilitation of the rouble... The scope of retreat is difficult to grasp!.. The ABC of communism has been downgraded to the status of a «leftist deviation». Stupid and insipid prejudices of low-cultured Philistines have been revived under the name of a new morality»[2].

And the other side of the coin: «When the hope to concentrate the upbringing of new generations in the hands of the state was still alive, – continued Trotsky, – authorities not only ignored the idea of the «elder people», in particular, Father and Mother, authority, – on the contrary, they did their best to separate children from the family in order to screen them from retrograde habits and customs. Not so long ago, during the first five-year plan, both school and komsomol were places where children regularly unmasked, disgraced and, in general, «re-educated» a vodka-addicted father or a religious mother... This technique meant undermining parents' authority to the very foundations. Today, a drastic change took place in this crucial sphere – alongside with the seventh (on the sin of adultery) the fifth (on respecting father and mother) commandments were completely rehabilitated, though God was still left aside... Nevertheless, care about the authority of the elder people did bring about changes of attitude to religion... Today, the assault of heavens, like the assault of family has been halted... The mode of ironical neutrality towards religion is being gradually introduced. But this is just the first stage...»[3]

Further on, Trotsky went on protesting, «the Soviet government... is rehabilitating the Cossacks, who used to be the only militia force of the tsarist army... The restoration of Cossacks trousers stripes and forelocks became one of the most eloquent manifestations of Termidor[4]. Another, even more crushing blow, was inflicted against the principles of the October Revolution by the Decree that restored the officer corps in all its bourgeois glamour... It is worth noting that reformers did not bother to invent new names for the restored ranks... At the same time they disclosed their Achilles' hill, and did not dare to restore the rank of general»[5]. (However, Trotsky, who was assassinated on August 20, 1940, had a chance to see the determination of the «reformists» – on May 7, 1940 the ranks of generals were restored too).

Thus, Trotsky defined the turn that took place in the mid-30s as «counter-revolution» (which, in the long run, apart from everything else, quite naturally led to extermination of scores of revolutionaries). It is only natural to ask the following question: isn't it absurd that counter-revolutionary changes were underway in the country, and still those repressed were called counter-revolutionaries! It was such a wide-spread official accusation that a new word of «ka-er's» was coined (that's how in Russian sounded the abbreviation of «counter-revolutionary»).

Let us consider the phenomenon of «counter-revolution» of the 1930s as viewed by another «observer». In the same 1936, when Trotsky was writing about drastic changes that took place in the USSR over a brief period of time, the same facts, though presented from a directly opposite point of view, were described by the prominent thinker Georgy Fedotov, who emigrated from the USSR in the fall of 1925, that is relatively late (which gave him a chance to understand the post-revolution situation back in the USSR better). He asserted that it was the year of 1934 that started «a new period of the Russian revolution... The general impression was that the ice had been ruptured. Huge icebergs that had been squeezing Russia by their weight over 17 years, began to thaw and fall down one after another. This was a real counter-revolution, and it was conducted from above. Since it did not shake the foundations of the political or social structure, then it could be called «household» counter-revolution. Household, and at the same time spiritual, ideological... Young people got the right to love each other and form families; reinstituted were the right of parents to their children and to a decent school, the right of everybody to «a cheerful life», to a Christmas Tree[6], and to a minimum of old-time rituals – the rituals that would make life a bit more attractive, – all that meant that Russia was rising from the dead...»[7].

Further on, he writes: «Starting from Kirov's assassination (on December 1, 1934), Russia is flooded with arrests, exiles, and even executions of communist party members. All this takes place under the banner of fighting the remnants of the Trozkites, Zinoviev-supporters and other opposition groups. But no one will ever be deceived by these official labels. As a rule, false proofs of «trozkism» are poorly masked. If we analise them we shall see that trozkism simply means regular revolutionary, class-oriented or international socialism... The struggle... was affecting the entire cultural policy. Political subjects were abolished or downgraded at schools. History was introduced instead of marxist social science. Struggle was going on in history or literature, and it was directed against economic patterns that erased cultural diversity... A question can be asked: Why can't marxist decorations be removed from the stage if marxism in Russia had been done away with? Why, having deserted it, or mocking at it at every step, do people still mutter old formulas?.. It would be ridiculous to renounce one's own revolutionary genealogy. For 150 years the French Republic has been writing at its walls «Liberty, Equality, Fraternity» despite the obvious contradiction of the two last slogans to the very basics of its existence[8]»; and really, there is neither «fraternity», nor «equality» between proprietors and hired workers or employees.

Which is typical, G. Fedotov right away recollected Trotsky: «Revolution in Russia has died. Trotsky committed a lot of mistakes, but there is one thing where he was right. He realized that his personal fall was Russian «Termidor». The regime which exists in Russia now is not a termidorian regime any more. This is a regime of Bonaparte»[9] – that is something similar to the regime of General of the French Revolution Napoleon who later became Emperor.

It is worth noting that the same understanding of events that took place in 1934 – 1936 (though with absolutely different interpretations!) was shown by two absolutely different people. No doubt, both of them exaggerated the results of «counter-revolutionary» changes, though they did it for different reasons: Trotsky was trying in a most vigorous manner to unmask the «betrayal» of the revolution, while Fedotov, on the contrary, cherished hope to see the «rebirth» of Russia as it was before the revolutionary cataclysm. Both desires interfered with objective perception of what was going on.

Trotsky's speculations quite obviously contain an «evil» contradiction – it was he who claimed that «each revolution» was followed by «reaction» or even «counter-revolution». That means that he was absolutely right when he saw an instance of the inevitable historical truth in the coup of 1934 – 1936. However, later, he began to grumble at quite «natural» consequences of this historical turn (kind of «restoration» of the past).

In his own turn, Fedotov was right when he reminded of the course of the French Revolution which quite naturally gave birth to the Napoleonic Empire; however, he right away started talking about the possibility of «rising from the dead» of pre-revolutionary Russia – though, which he knew quite well, neither «Bonapartism», nor the restoration of monarchy following it (in 1814) could «cancel» the principal results of the French Revolution (it must be mentioned that later on Fedotov «got upset» about the «counter-revolution», as he defined it, that allegedly took place in the USSR in the 1930s, and he never again tried to treat it as «the rising from the dead» of former Russia).

Still, with all possible reservations, both Trotsky and Fedotov were right in their main premise – that, starting with 1934, the country had been going through a «counter-revolutionary» coup in the very general meaning of the word.

Here we can not avoid discussing the meaning of the word «counter-revolution». In Trotsky's mouth it had the most «terrible» accusational meaning, while Fedotov was not «scared» by this word at all. This must be mentioned because until now the word of «counter-revolution» in the public opinion means something closer to «Trotsky's version» than to «that of Fedotov». There is nothing more «awful» in history than revolutions which are global catastrophes that inevitably lead to countless victims and unprecedented destructions.

Glorification of the Russian revolution that had been dominating history for dozens of years and – which is natural – of any revolutions in general has produced a lasting, though quite false, impression of the essence of these cataclysms. Mercilessness that was typical of all revolutions when they encountered any resistance can not be compared to any similar social phenomena.

Let's analise specific features of the «counter-revolutionary» coup of the mid-1930s. In this period the very attitude to the «pre-revolutionary» history of Russia drastically changed. Ten-volume «Malaya (Minor) Soviet Encyclopedia» had been published in the 1930 – 1932, whose articles, despite their utmost brevity, still found needed space to condemn the greatest historical figures of Russia in every way possible:

«Alexander Nevsky... did many helpful favours to the Novgorod trade capital... by suppressing riots of the Russian population who protested against heavy contributions to the Tatars. The «peaceful» policy of Alexander was appreciated by the Russian church which was on good terms with the Khan: after Alexander's death he was sanctified... Minin-Sukhoruk... a Nizhni-Novgorod merchant, one of the leaders of city trade bourgeoisie... Bourgeois historiography idealized him as a class-indifferent struggler for united «Mother-Russia», and tried to present him as a national hero... Pozharsky... a prince... who headed the volunteer corps organized by the butcher Minin-Sukhoruk on the money of rich merchants. This volunteer corps suppressed the peasants revolution... Peter I... was a brilliant representative of the Russian initial accumulation of capital period... who combined a strong will-power with a most unbalanced character, cruelty, heavy drinking problems, and boundless fornication»... etc., etc.

Starting with 1934, the above-mentioned historical figures of Russia were talked about in quite a different way. A little later the entire country was admiring the pathetic film-poems «Peter I» (1937), «Alexander Nevsky» (1938), «Minin and Pozharsky» (1939), «Suvorov» (1940), and others.

We can't fail to recollect that over 1929 – 1930 the majority of most prominent Russian historians belonging to different generations were arrested. They were accused of participating in a «monarchist coup» and other similar crimes. Among them there were S.V.Bakhrushin, S.K.Bogoyavlensky, S.B.Veselovsky, Yu.V.Gotie, B.D.Grekov, V.G.Druzhinin, A.I.Zaozersky, N.P.Likhachev, M.K.Lyubavsky, V.I.Picheta, S.F.Platonov, S.V.Rozhdestvensky, B.A.Romanov, E.V.Tarle, L.V.Cherepnin, A.I.Yakovlev, and many more. But a few years later all of them – with the exception of Lyubavsky, Platonov and Rozhdestvensky who – alas – did not survive in prison – were not only allowed to continue their work, but soon were granted the highest honours and awards. It should be added that in 1937 – 1938 almost all the «prosecutors» of S.F.Platonov and others, starting with the militant marxist historians G.S.Fridland and M.M.Tsvibak and ending with the state security service leaders Ya.S.Agranov and Ya.Kh.Peters were repressed. Really symbolic was the republishing in the same 1937 of the main work by S.F.Platonov who was the principal defendant and died in 1933. In 1939 former «enemies» were elected to high posts – Yu.V.Gotie was elected Academician, and S.V.Bakhrushin – Corresponding Member of the Academy of Sciences[10].

No doubt, the drastic change in authorities attitude to the pre-revolutionary history (and, correspondingly, to historians) – is only one side of the reversal in question. In order to reconstruct the entire picture it would be necessary to talk in detail about almost all the fields and aspects of the country's life in 1934 – 1936.

The most important thing is to understand that it is wrong, even pointless, to view such a crucial and sweeping turn as something that took place at Stalin's personal will and design. As far back as February 18, 1935, Trotsky quite reasonably wrote in his diary that the «triumph... of Stalin was predestined. The final result which idle viewers and morons were explaining by Stalin's personal strength or, in the least, by his exceptional guile, was hidden deeply in the dynamics of historical forces. Stalin's figure was just a semi-spontaneous manifestation of the Revolution's Second Chapter, its hangover»[11].

Having realized that the coming war would be, as a matter of fact, not a war of fascism against bolshevism, but of Germany against Russia, Stalin, quite naturally, began thinking about the «mobilization» of Russia, and not of bolshevism. That's why the primary cause of Stalin's support for the «restoration» was his realization of the above-mentioned fact. Still, it went on quite reasonably in the 1930s and involved the life of the country (it was not a reflection of Stalin's political line – the latter was just a «frame» for it).

The «rehabilitation» of the historical past was only one facet of the coup, of the «counter-revolution» that was underway in the 1930s. But it was the most vivid, the most expressive manifestation, – that's why it's appropriate to talk about it in detail. Trotsky described the 1935 «restoration» of the pre-revolutionary military ranks as «the most crushing blow» against «the principles of the October revolution». Hostility, and at times open resistance to the «restoration» was typical of the vast majority of revolutionary activists.

«Mysteriousness» of 1937 was to a great extent caused by the fact that it was actually impossible to speak openly about someone's disagreement with the turn that had been underway since 1934 – otherwise it would have been necessary to claim that the USSR government itself was making a counter-revolu-

The 8th Extraordinary All-Russia Congress of Soviets. 5 December 1936.

tion! Trotsky and Georgy Fedotov who were abroad at the time, spoke about it openly though quite differently.

It's most indicative that the «diagnosis» was repeated by many of those who, having been sent abroad with political assignments, made up their minds not to return to the USSR. For instance, one of the secret police leaders (OGPU – NKVD) Alexander Orlov (actual name – Leiba Feldbin) who in 1938 became a «defector» said later on, that beginning with 1934 «old bolsheviks» – and he used to stress that «the majority of them» – came to the conclusion that «Stalin has betrayed Revolution. They were bitterly watching the triumph of reaction which was destroying one revolutionary gain after another». In particular, Orlov explained, this was illustrated by the fact, that Stalin «in 1935 organized a purge under the pretext of checking and exchanging party membership cards, which was cynically directed against long-time party members... Next Stalin's step was the dismissal of the Old Bolsheviks Society that took place in May 1935... A month later Stalin dismissed the Society of Political Convicts and Exiles»[12].

Further on: «Stalin has restored Cossack Forces with all their privileges, including Cossack military uniform of the tsarist time. The fact that this action coincided in time with the dismissal of the Old Bolsheviks and Convicts Societies was most expressively characterizing Stalin's reforms. During the celebration of the Secret Police (OGPU) anniversary that took place in December, 1935 at the Bolshoi Theatre everybody was surprised by the presence... of a group of Cossack officers wearing defiant tsarist uniform... Those present were more and more often staring at the resurrected Atamans (Cossack chieftains), than at the stage. The former OGPU Chief who used to be a political convict before the revolution whispered, addressing his neighbours: «When I look at them, my blood is boiling! This is their job!» – and he bent his head to demonstrate a scar that had been left by a Cossack sabre». All this, Orlov concluded, was meant «to demonstrate to the people that the revolution with all its promises was over»[13].

As to those bolsheviks who remained true to the revolution principles, Orlov wrote: «...they were covertly hoping that Stalin's reactionary policy will be washed away by a new revolutionary wave..., but they kept silent about it. Still, ...their very silence was perceived as a sign of protest»[14].

Everything said above was not a personal «interpretation» by Orlov. Another «defector», NKVD agent Ignaty Reiss (actual name – Natan Poretsky) wrote on July 17, 1937, that the USSR is «a victim of open counterrevolution», and everybody who «keeps silent now, becomes... a traitor of the working class and socialism... The point is that everything is «to be started anew» – in order to rescue socialism. The struggle has started...»[15] (in September, 1937, Reiss was detected in Switzerland and shot dead by a group of specially assigned NKVD officer Shpigelglas who had infiltrated the country from Moscow).

The same was asserted in concert by other «defectors» of the time: Walter Krivitsky (Samuil Ginzburg) according to whom USSR leaders «were destroying revolutionary internationalism, bolshevism, Lenin's teaching, and the entire cause of the October revolution[16]»; Alexander Barmin (Graff) who claimed that «a counter-revolutionary coup» had been staged in the USSR, and «Cains of the working class... are destroying the cause of revolution»,[17] – and there were many other similar statements.

Some of the quoted above assertions credit Stalin's personal resolve for the «counter-revolutionary» plot, but, as it was said before, this is a deliberately primitive explanation: both Trotsky and Fedotov quite correctly saw in the changes that were going on a manifestation of an objective historical law of a post-revolutionary epoch, and not a sort of individual tyranny[18].

The 1935 General Plan of Moscow Reconstruction

«...We, the working people, who were born in miserable huts,
...will walk with the great song of the Internationale
...into the magic palaces... of communism».
S.Kirov at the First Congress of Soviets.

Decrees by the Central Executive Committee «On Land Nationalization» (February 19, 1918), «On Abolition of Private Property on Real Estate in Cities and Towns» (August 20, 1918), abolition of urban self-control, proclamations of the impending swift solution of the housing problem by the government made in 1919 and 1924, and other similar documents became a legal foundation for growing interference by party and state bodies into planning and building Moscow, into curbing investors' rights, cutting down individual design and construction work.

The renounciation of the New Economic Policy, the transition to the command economy, accelerated industrialization and violent collectivization triggered an outburst of urbanization in the USSR, thus enhancing the flow of people to cities and towns. Over 10 years the urban population grew by 15 million people. The rate of Moscow growth increased by 4 – 5 times (from 2 – 3

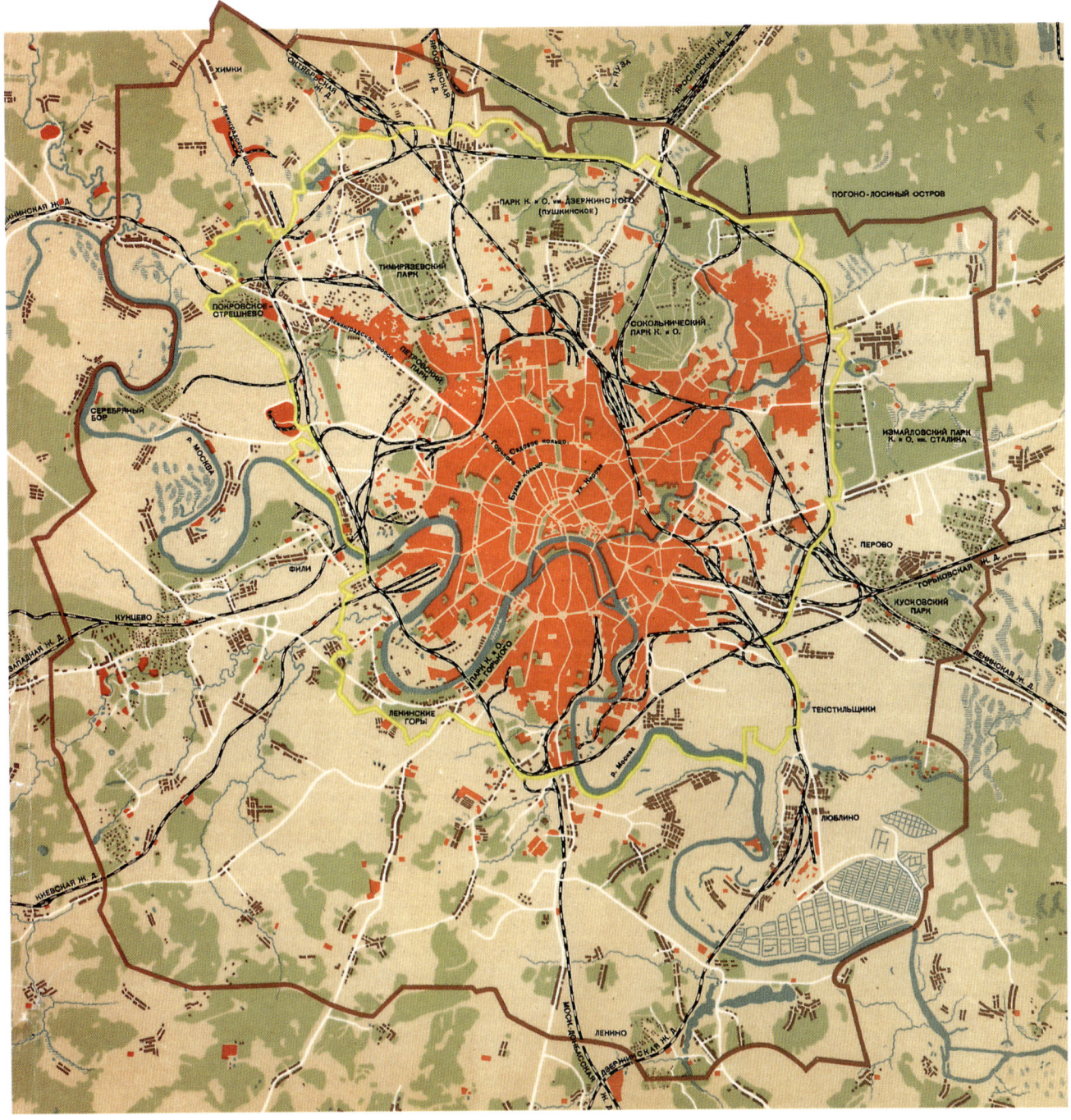

Plan of Moscow before reconstruction. 1931.

to 9 – 12 per cent annually). Houses were getting old, the density of staffing apartments rapidly grew up, up to 70 per cent of families had to share apartments. The activeness of city authorities began to depend completely on decisions by the central government, which were frequently hasty and contradictory on certain issues of city economy.

Up to 1930 Moscow did not have either perspective, or current plans of city economy. The plans of «New Moscow» (1918 – 1922) and «Big Moscow» (1920 – 1925) were found unsuitable for socialist reconstruction[19]. They were regarded as reactionary from the class point of view, since they protected churches, monasteries, estates, aristocratic mansions. Their authors allegedly «offered stubborn resistance to the destruction of historical monuments and especially churches» (for instance, the Iverskaya Chapel, the Strastnoi Monastery, the Simonov Monastery, and other monasteries)[20]. The Party urged officials to fight along two fronts in planning Moscow – against «leftist» elements who critcized the city plan that had been drafted during the feudal-bourgeois period, and against «reactionary» elements who were resisting unconstrained building by various establishments.

Under the conditions when there was no perspective for further construction in Moscow, when decisions had already been made to start constructing the subway (metro) and the Volga – Moscow Canal, the necessity to devise a General Plan of the proletarian capital was realized. Before doing it was necessary to resolve problems of socialist population distribution in the Moscow region, as well as to tackle a number of ideological and social-economic problems, such as the localization of party and governmental centres of the Russian Federation and the USSR; creation of city-building symbols of the III International Capital, and others.

It took 10 years to solve those problems. Projecting was done against the background of fighting religion, eliminating urban self-control, strengthening the power of party apparat and the system of centralized planning and distributing resources. Debates and competitions preceded the development of the General Plan.

Debates on Prospects of Moscow Construction

Since the 1920s, in view of the impending world proletarian revolution which was to be headed by Russia, its capital was regarded as the international centre of the Third International, «which will play the leading role in the cause of socialist reconstruction of the world economy after demolition of capitalism and imperialism»[21].

Since Moscow was an outstanding monument of city-building and a symbol of national state, its further destiny attracted wide interest inside the country and abroad. A wide public discussion devoted to capital's prospects was launched in view of devising the first General Plan of the USSR national economy development and announicing accelerated industrialization during the first five-year plan.

The discussion was initiated at the Communist Academy of the Communist Party Central Committee (CC VCP(b)), in State Planning Agencies (Gosplan) of the USSR and the Russian Federation, in magazines and newspapers. At conferences experts of different specialties were asking difficult at the time questions: «What is meant by socialist dissemination of population?» «What type could a socialist city or town be in general, and the capital in particular?» «Where should Moscow grow – vertically or horizontally?» «Will it be a city-agglomeration, a city of skyscrapers or a garden-city?»

During the debate many prominent philosophers and economists, repeating the views of Trotsky and Lenin, were forecasting the world revolution in the near 10 – 15 years, which was to determine Moscow's future. Part of them suggested to estimate prospects and construct Moscow for 10 years ahead, that is up to the world revolution (for instance, Professor P.Ilyashenko). Others proposed to halt Moscow's growth and to channel migrants to other areas (Academician S.Strumilin). Some experts recommended to reduce Mocow's population down to 1 – 1.5 million people, retaining there only administrative and political functions. Contrary to their views, G.Krasin asserted that the capital's size can not be forecast since it is determined by the course of history; Moscow can soon accumulate 10 million people as a minimum, and it should get ready for this well in advance. There were some extreme proposals to build Moscow in a new place retaining in the existing centre the functions of a memorial of Russian history and culture (Le Corbusier, Professor N.Sobolev, and others).

Especially heated arguments were held concerning two primary versions of Moscow development – will it be a garden-city or a city of skyscrapers? A compromise was being sought in order to combine in Moscow a business and political «city» located downtown, and garden-towns that would surround it in order to provide a house and contact with nature for every family. However, scyscapers seemed to be an offspring of the capitalist system, while family homes – alien to class conscience of proletariat because they disintegrate people. There were neither technical, nor economic conditions for building a great number of multi-storey houses, while low-storey individual construction could hardly be state-controlled, though the state had already become the principal customer, designer and builder. At the end of NEP period and at the beginning of industrialization the idea of creating proletarian garden-cities when land is leased for construction looked quite attractive, but a new principle of «maximum communalization of life» was added to it. This principle simplified control over the townsfolk, while individual apartments were meant strictly for sleeping.

It was believed that the Soviet people were to live collectively in multi-storeyed houses at a walking distance from their jobs. While supporters of the concept of garden-settlements put forward the idea of healthy environment in the green belt and an opportunity to make small personal vegetable and fruit gardens there, the backers of multi-storeyed construction spoke in favour of complete renounciation of individual households and introduction of public forms of daily life. Daily needs were to be satisfied with the help of industrialized collective kitchens, public bathhouses and laundries, 24-hour kindergartens and nurseries. The working people were supposed to spend their free time in clubs, libraries, stadiums, sports grounds and water sports centres. The slogan «eight hours of working, eight hours of sleeping, eight hours of resting» was perceived by ideologists of collective lifestyle literally. No time was left for house work in a typical daily routine. This idea found its utmost manifestation in huge houses-communes whose construction was underway in Moscow in the late 20s – early 30s.

At this period, professional city-building started to develop in the country, though it fell apart into several segments.

The so-called dis-urbanists were after relatively uniform positioning of population along transport routes that connect Moscow to nearby green towns. The end idea of this concept was to turn Moscow into a gygantic park of history and culture which will be penetrated by belts of «socialist dissemination of Moscow's population». Moscow was to accomodate remaining administrative buildings, research institutes, institutes of higher education meant for Muscovites only, auditoriums, stadiums, water sports centres, zoos, botanical gardens, tourist hotels.

The theoretician of linear cities, the author of the world-famous book «Socialist City» N.Milyutin proposed to shrink Moscow, reducing its population to 1.7 – 2.0 million people. Enterprises that were not directly supporting Moscow's needs were to be moved to areas of raw materials production. The managerial staff was to be reduced by 2.5 times. Educational centres and research institutes that were not linked to any industries in Moscow were to be moved out of the capital.

The project by M.Zhirov suggested to create a system of new garden rings around the historical city. The first inner ring was to be administrative-managerial. The second one – the ring of children's recreational facilities and sports, the third one – the ring of low-storeyed construction, further on – the ring of socialist collective agricultural farms of Moscow.

The urbanists who were frequently holding official posts in the USSR and the Russian Federation planning bodies suggested to set up compact vegetation areas with dispersed multi-storeyed «houses-communes» and «dwelling enterprises» each of which was meant for 3,000 – 5,000 inhabitants. A city area could be regarded ideal if it contained from 50 to 100 major buildings surrounded by greenery.

Unfortunately, the theories of dis-urbanisn and urbanism have never been seriously discussed or analysed. In view of condemnation of the «right» and «left» deviations in the party and demonstrative trials of «saboteurs», deviations were being looked for in every sphere, city-building included. After the decree of the Communist Party Central Committee «On Restructuring Lifestyle» both urbanism and dis-urbanism were criticized, and the debates were ended. Later, many supporters of urbanism and dis-urbanism were tried and found guilty.

In 1931 the USSR Council of People's Commissars gave its consent to convene the International City-Building Congress in Moscow, where a Charter of Moscow Development was to be devised. However, in 1932 foreign experts were forbidden to enter Russia, and in 1933 the City-Building Congress took place abroad without Soviet delegates. Links with the International Union of Designers were lost for a long time. The underestimate by party bodies of urbanism as a new theoretical and practical trend had the same grave consequences for the country as the condemnation of genetics, geopolitics, sociology, cybernetics in the 30s – 40s. City-building became one of applied branches of architechture. Architects were not ready to take into account the probable character of Moscow development, and used determinative static models.

Combination of Historical and Socialist Moscow

Combination of historical and socialist Moscow within the same city resulted in serious ideological, planning and technical problems.

First, two opposing epochs were at issue – feudal and socialist, and for this reason, as many experts believed, and first of all Corbusier, there was no way even to dream of their harmonical combination in the same spatial body. Second, historical Moscow grew in the 15th – 17th centuries as a prominent monument of Russian city-building under the conditions of absolute monarchy, and in the 19th century its population did not exceed 600,000 inhabitants. It was actually saturated with priceless monuments of Russian history. Attempts to turn it into the capital of a multi-national superpower with the population of 5 – 10 million people could bring about unforeseen results.

And, finally, third, – like many ancient capitals in Europe and Asia, Moscow grew, as experts of the time believed, on the basis of the radial-circular system meant for cartage and pedestrians. The experience of contemporary capitals of the world indicated that concentration of new business and political functions in the city's centre stimulated the concentration of traffic flows in the narrow central streets, which resulted in paralysing population mobility or in destroying the historical context. For instance, A. Borovoy noted that «no matter what train of thought is followed when searching for the best forms of planning the Union's capital, they are sure to reject any idea of using the closed, immobile, radial-circular structure»[22].

In 1928 – 1929 a new project was born, the first project of the kind, prominent because of its ideas of spatial and planning combination of historical and socialist Moscow. It was put forward by the leader of the reestablished amalgamation of architects-urbanists (ARU) Professor N. Ladovsky, assisted by E. Iokhles and I. Dlugach.

Ladovsky rejected the idea of curbing the growth of the largest state of the world capital, and suggested the following:

1. To break the circular system at one of its sectors in order to give the centre a chance to grow freely. The city's centre should be not a statistical point, but a dynamic line-axis, which, as the city functions get more complex, can expand freely.

2. To concentrate construction in one of Moscow's sectors which will become a pioneer sector of the new socialist reconstruction of Moscow. This will ensure the massing of principal objects under construction, will set up an extensive engineer infrastructure, reduce specific cost of construction work and ensure better compositional opportunities during Moscow construction.

3. To establish a new public centre along the axis of Tverskaya – the Leningrad Highway, utilizing the territories of Khodynka and Ostankino. This proposal developed the idea of the new Russian Federation's capital centre in the project of «New Moscow» and took into account vast vacant areas at the closest range to historical Moscow centre where there were fewer natural and artificial barriers on the way of development.

4. To reorganize transportation, moving the central railway station to the site of the Byelorussian Railway Station, while the remaining district stations were to be positioned along the circular railway. To organize traffic at several levels, using the natural landscape, all kinds of terrain cavities.

5. To preserve the system of «red» lines only for the new sector, in order to avoid destroying valuable buildings.

According to the urbanists concept, Moscow will consist of four zones: political-educational; housing; industrial; and agrarian – arranged as a parabola open in the north-west and located from the Kremlin to the Kamer-Kollezhsky Rampart.

For the urbanists «the spatial dynamism» was the main feature of contemporary city-buiding that defined not only its expressiveness, but social effectiveness. The concepts of continuity, dynamic development, «flows of the city's space» opposed the traditional esthetic guidelines of classicism with their cult of pompous immobility of empire ensembles. The factor of «time» was introduced into the theory of city-building.

Moscow's centre was «the museum-city» whose territories ceased to be a static planning point; the penetration ensured the free westward growth. The centre's planning horseshoe was turning into a fan of gradually expanding flow of highways. The three-dimentional city was getting a fourth dimension – the time that became a leading component of the new organization of socialist Moscow. Overcoming spatial immobility, the «museum-city» was not replanned, but was kept, like the medieval Vienna, within the Ring. Similar to every city founded in the Middle Ages (Vienna, Zalzburg, London) «a dual city» would have existed on Moscow's territory: the static historical city and the new socialist one that was developiong dynamically. Quite long main political-educational, cultural and governmental centre along the axis of Tverskaya – the Leningrad Highway was a counterweight to city-building projects that offered to concentrate the establishments of the administrative-political centre in the Kremlin and its close vicinity.

However, the scheme of Ladovsky was not accepted by his contemporaries, and was called «formalistic». The principal critics of the dynamic project of architects-urbanists were engineer A.Borovoy and architect V. Semyonov. The latter wrote: «Ladovsky decided that the socialist city is just a city of industrial proletariat, and that's how he had designed his scheme. His capital, as it is, died. Its brain has been destroyed, it becomes a major industrial centre»[23]. Later, the Moscow «parabola» was widely recognized abroad (in Greece, Denmark, Australia, Pakistan, Ghana and other countries).

Competition for the Capital's Planning Concept

In view of the condemnation of both urbanism and disurbanism by the Party Central Committee, in 1930 the Department of Municipal Economy of the Moscow Council announced a competition for a new concept of capital's planning. Soviet and foreign experts participated in it. Eight projects were offered.

1. The project designed by S. Boldyrev, L. Goldenberg and V. Dolganov under the guidance of Professor V. Semyonov in the Planning-Land Department of the city executive council. It proceded from the fact that Moscow would become the world's proletariat centre. Main attention was paid to the development of industries and to the reconstruction of the system of population dissemination and distribution of jobs in the Moscow region. «The task was to eradicate the contradiction between the socialist content of industrial and daily life processes in the proletarian capital and the principal city planning scheme which was basically pre-capitalist, feudal»[24].

The following two probable methods were proposed to reconstruct «the Moscow spot»:

– capitalist replanning of Moscow, that is cutting highways through the existing districts, which would finally mean that Moscow would turn into «a second Paris»;

– socialist replanning of Moscow, that is scheduled disintegration of the historically formed city spot into a system of city-complexes situated around the old centre; they were to have a significant measure of independence (their own industries, their own district council).

It was estimated that Moscow population would amount to 3 million people; its future growth would go eastwards where its main industries were located. The radius of the Centre – Kalanchovskaya Square was to emphasize the domination of the north-eastern direction where heavy industries were supposed to grow. The textile industry was considered to be decisive among light industries.

The designers believed that a significant anomaly of the Moscow planning system was the misalignment of the city's planning centre with its transport (railway) centre. For this reason it was proposed to align them in the same spot. A deep rail-

Istorichesky Thoroughfare. Demonstration. 1940.

way penetration was designed that would have crossed the city diametre at Lubyanskaya Square. This railway diametre was supposed to become the boundary of the out-of-town living.

V.Semyonov used to treat Moscow as the capital of industrial proletariat. «Moscow, – he wrote, – as compared to European big cities, from the architectural point of view is in a handicapped position – it lacks cultural heritage»[25]. He regarded Osman's reconstructional projects in Paris made in the second half of the 19th century as a model; at the time wide avenues were cut there through historically formed districts.

2. The main idea of the project by the German expert Kurt Mayer prepared at the Planning-Land Department of the Moscow Executive Council in April 1931 was a proposal to reconstruct the capital as «a star-city» to symbolise «democratic centralism» as a principle of organizational structure of communist and working parties according to Lenin's teaching.

The party's hierarchy structure where the majority had to report to the minority was ideally matching the structure of the medieval feudal city whose centre formed at the period of absolute monarchy. Kurt Mayer as a representative of the Comintern's German fraction defined the political situation very accurately, and reflected it in his planning scheme of the Third International Capital.

The existing centripetal planning structure was used as a basis of Moscow's reconstruction in which governmental objects were concentrated at a certain place. The would-be city's population was estimated at 4 million people occupying the territory of 56,000 hectares. The governmental bodies of the world, union and republical levels were located within the boundaries of the «B» Circle. They were Comintern, the Communist Party Central Committee (TsK VKP(b)), the Central Executive Committee (TsIK), buildings for congresses, governmental bodies, commissariats (ministries). «These buildings are organically linked to Red Square and the Kremlin; they are the constructional elements that are supposed to enhance the significance of the Soviet Union embodied by Moscow which will be its city-building expression»[26].

It was proposed to widen the «A» Circle up to 120 metres and position administartive objects at its hubs, the way it is done in Vienna along the Ring. A business «city» was to be set up in Kitay-Gorod. Beyond the «A» Circle the city was disintegrated by green wedges into ten complex planning zones with the population of 300,000 – 450,000 each. Major industrial districts were to be deconcentrated; links were to be provided with the Moscow Region.

K.Mayer proposed to lay tangential thoroughfares (chords) which were to bypass the centre. In addition to radial metro lines, special straight surface lines of mass transportation means were to be laid in order to link the biggest south-eastern industrial area with the housing districts of Moscow's northwest. It was proposed to start construction work in the southwestern direction, and to set up an integral network of parks and gardens, directed from the outskirts downtown; they were to form a single hub.

The project contained a number of new technical and planning solutions, but its main idea – concentrating all the USSR governmental bodies and power structures in the centre of the historically formed ancient city threatened to destroy the monuments of Russian culture dating back to the 14th – 19th centuries.

3. The comprehensive project by G.Krasin was prominent for its principally different approach to future Moscow. It envisaged the probability of its population growth upto 8 – 10 million people, while its area was to grow by 3 – 4 times (up to 100,000 – 110,000 hectares), which opened new prospects for the city development.

Krasin objected to limiting Moscow's size, «slowing down» its growth to a voluntarily pre-determined level. «The political, administrative and cultural centre of the country will develop and is to develop to the size that will be determined by the course of history, – and that, certainly, can't be either foreseen or, moreover, prevented».

The whole star-pointed plan of Moscow development was based upon the system of improved transportation. It stressed the time factor (as opposed to distance). The centre of Moscow was supposed to include everything that is located at a distance of 10-minute travel from one point to another. By the capital was meant everything that is located within 50 – 60 minute travel from the Moscow centre. As a result an integral Moscow agglomeration was to be formed based on outgoing lines of electrified railway transport. Krasin was insistently raising the question of creating a system of two-level transportation hubs in the

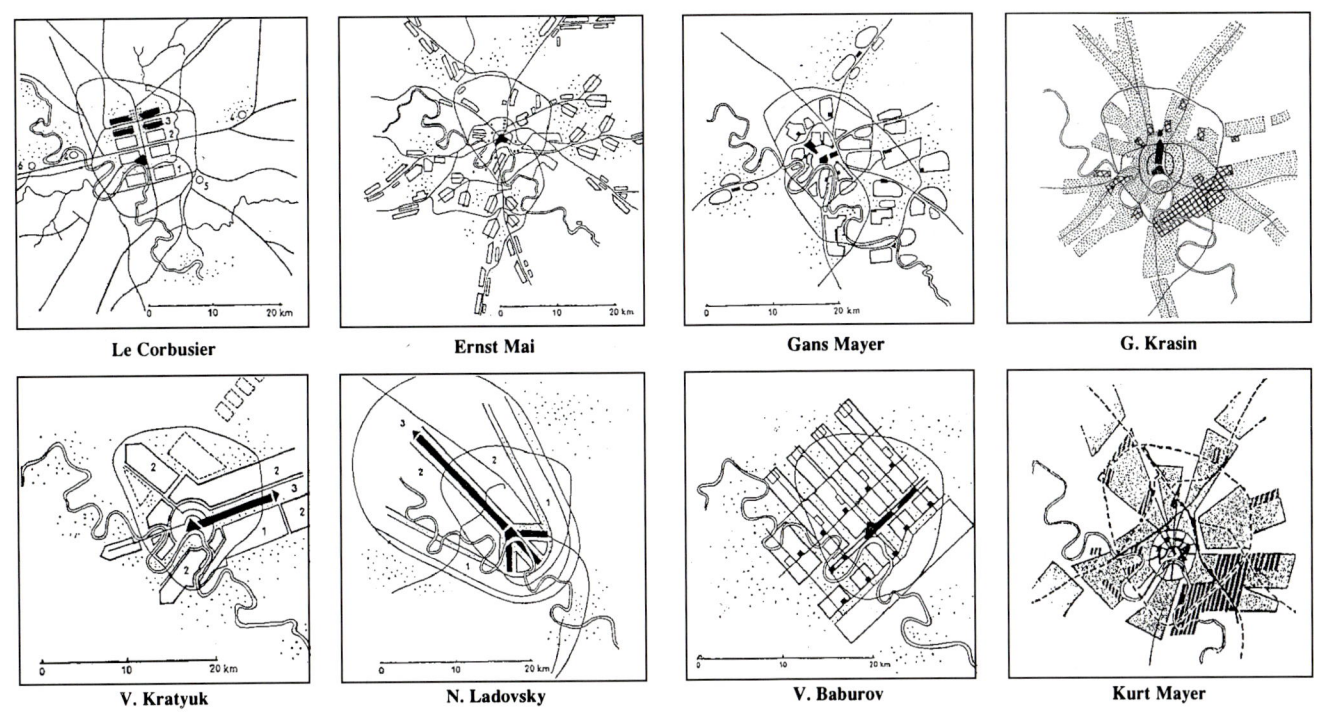

Le Corbusier	Ernst Mai	Gans Mayer	G. Krasin
V. Kratyuk	N. Ladovsky	V. Baburov	Kurt Mayer

Moscow layout diagrams. 1929 – 1932.

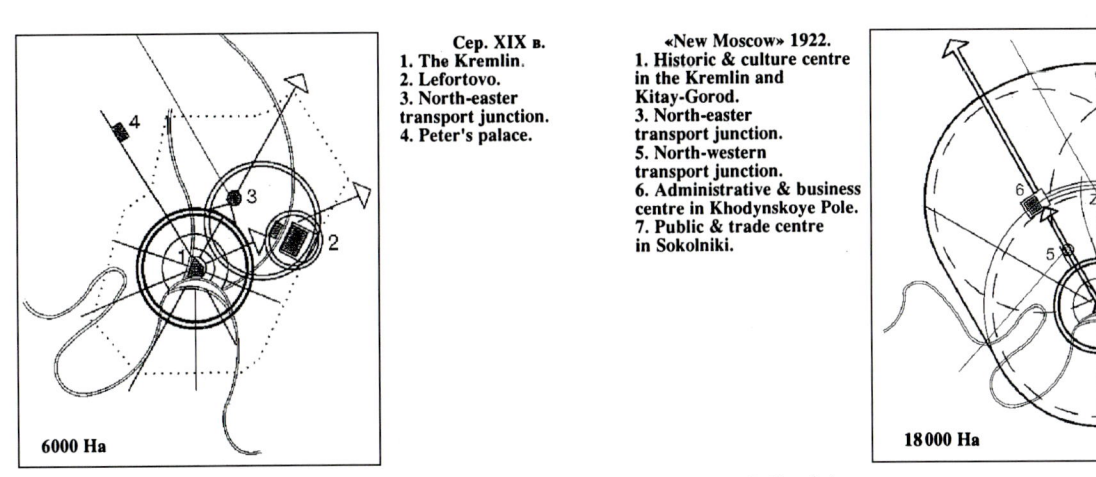

Сер. XIX в.
1. The Kremlin.
2. Lefortovo.
3. North-easter transport junction.
4. Peter's palace.

«New Moscow» 1922.
1. Historic & culture centre in the Kremlin and Kitay-Gorod.
3. North-easter transport junction.
5. North-western transport junction.
6. Administrative & business centre in Khodynskoye Pole.
7. Public & trade centre in Sokolniki.

6000 Ha

18 000 Ha

Moscow planning development (E. Sirenko).

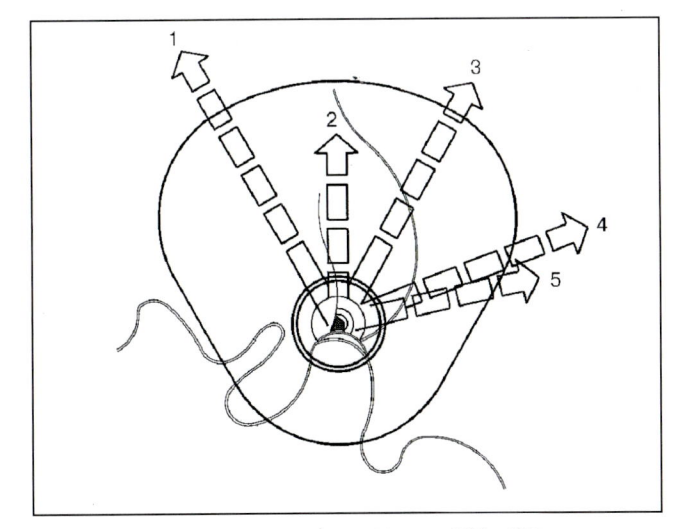

The conceptions development of the centre Moscow. 1929 – 1932.
1 – N. Ladovsky, 2 – G. Krasin, 3 – V. Baburov, 4 – V. Kratyuk, 5 – V. Semyonov

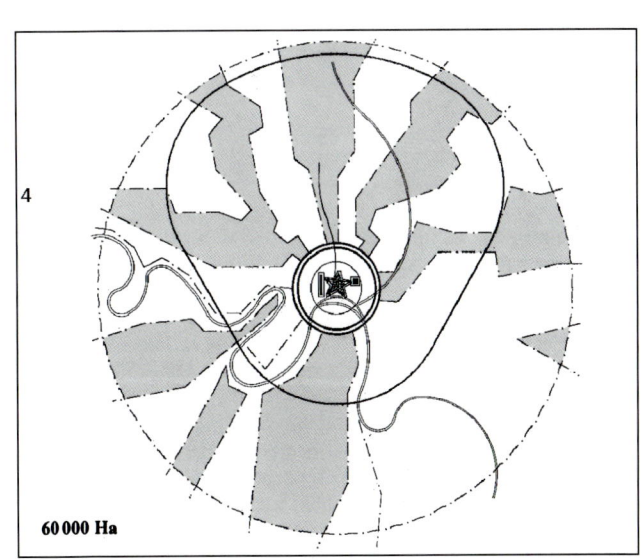

60 000 Ha

General plan of Moscow. Kurt Mayer. April 1931.

main thoroughfares; he was insisting on accelerated building of the subway (metro). He noted that «the growing contradictions between Moscow's growth and its transportation development typical of the late 20s was the primary threat and the root for future complications in planning the capital». It was proposed to develop the common city centre northwards from Trubnaya Square, since relief and building conditions favoured the establishment of a powerful multilevel transportation system. The project envisioned setting up back-up lines for the main thoroughfares of Moscow – first of all, the Novo-Tverskaya and the Novo-Myasnitskaya streets. A system of inner airfields was also to be constructed.

4. The scheme of Moscow by the German expert Hans Mayer implied the creation of a system of ten specialized town-satellites around the capital-nucleus that would occupy approximately 20,000 hectares. Six complex areas were to be adjunct to the centre. The USSR and RSFSR central functions were to be concentrated within the «B» Circle. The centre was supposed to grow north-east to reach for principal specialized towns. On the whole the agglomeration occupied around 100,000 hectares. Within the «B» Circle the population density was to reach 700 persons per hectare, while closer to the outer boundary it decreased by 2 – 3 times.

5. The German architect Ernst Mai suggested to limit the population of the Moscow's central part by 1.8 million people, and to keep within the «B» Circle administartive and business buildings and only those housing and supoporting objects that are linked with them. About 30 town-collectives were to be located around Moscow at relatively even distances; each of them was to accomodate around 100,000 inhabitants. The total area of the agglomeration reached 150,000 hectares with the population density within 100 persons per hectare. This scheme was widely used in Western Europe in the post-war period.

6. V. Kratyuk attempted to overcome the radial-centrical layout of Moscow by breaking it in the eastern part and creating a rectangular network of streets. The capital's centre was to be located in the area of Izmailovsky Park. «We envision the growth of the city area in several directions which are not equal as to their size and intensity, while one of the directions will be retained as the principal one, and it will be linked to the industrial factor in the east», – wrote Kratyuk.

By its planning structure Moscow was to consist of specialized districts-towns, each of which would grow along its own direction. The project envisaged a housing area-town which was to include public-administrative, industrial, agro-industrial, scholastic-research centres, as well as military, hospital, summer-recreational compounds. The industrial, housing, social and scholastic-research planning zones were designed as parallel strips which were to make up a kind of functional-streamlined town. The remaining towns were to be located along the main radial Moscow highways (for instance, the Leningrad Highway, the Mozhaisk Highway).

The general planning concept can be characterized as the territorial correlation of two types of planning – «the missile exhaust» type (the south-western part of Moscow) and the functional-streamlined type (the north-eastern part).

Retaining the Kremlin and the Kitay-Gorod as the all-union centre, the author was not satisfied with its static position that resembled a spot. He made it dynamic by developing it along the newly designed eastern expressway situated parallel to the principal industrial zone. The city's territory was reduced to 20,000 hectares. The population density was equal to 450 – 550 persons per hectare.

7. According to the project by the team of V. Baburov the city territory was reduced to 13,500 hectares, while the population density was increased to 550 – 600 persons per hectare. About 75 per cent of the territory were alloted for construction work.

Moscow was designed as an integral city, divided into five areas-complexes that included local (harmless) industries, housing estates and local centres. The areas-complexes were to lean upon the south-eastern industrial zone and to develop in the north-western direction along the diameter Luzhniki – Sokolniki, which would allow the city to grow simultaneously along the two directions. The chessboard-rectangular scheme was to be superimposed upon the existing radial-circular network following the flow of the Yauza River. The historical and revolutionary centre was to remain in the Kremlin and on the Red Square. The city's main diameter was to go from the Ilyich Lane to the Novo-Myasnitsky Avenue.

8. Le Corbusier believed that the concentric planning and dense construction were the main problem of all major cities of the world. For this reason he proposed to preserve only the central part of Moscow and to build the socialist city anew. The new city consisting of five parallel specialized zones (industrial, housing, administartive, political and business) were to form a functional system that was to be cut by two systems of thoroughfares – rectangular and diagonal. The living apartments were to be located in multi-storeyed buildings placed in the greenery, with the density of 1,100 persons per hectare; 14 % of the territory will be occupied by buildings and 86 % – by greenery. This project is close to his proposal on reconstruction of Paris (1922 – 1925).

All the proposals were considered by L. Kaganovich, the Politbureau Member, the First Secretary of the Moscow Party Committee, the Head of the Moscow Architectural-Planning Commission, and by N. Bulganin, the Chairman of Mossovet (the Moscow City Council). This was «the supreme court-martial on architectural questions», as Architect A. Mashkov put it figuratively (1934). When considering the planning schemes of Moscow, urbanists' proposals were regarded as formalistic – they suggested an open north-western structure of the city. Among those rejected were the ideas of garden-cities, of transition to an agglomeration or a group-city. The significance of the two-level transportation system was not appreciated properly.

The primary attention was caught by the political content of Mayer's scheme which, on the one hand, held an intermediate position between the other seven projects, while, on the other hand, vividly expressed the idea of concentrating the entire range of governing functions in the Party's hands, thus justifying the utilization of the planning structure of the tsarist capital under the conditions of the so-called democratic centralism. Though a number of progressive ideas were put forward in the static scheme (thoroughfares bypassing the centre, green wedges, expansion to the south-west), its implementation could result in the destruction of the historical city as a specimen of the Russian city-building art; it also limited the prospects of the capital's growth.

In June 1931 the Plenary Session of the Communist Party Central Committee (TsK VKP(b)) adopted a resolution «On Moscow City Economy, and On the Development of the USSR City and Town Economies» which proposed to use the existing historically-formed radial-circular structure of the city as a basis for its reconstruction; to set up new major squares; to intensify the circular traffic. The recommendation of the General Plan to align the political and planning centres became compulsory for all the forthcoming projects aimed at reconstructing Moscow.

After the 1932 Plenum of the Central Committee a pioneer sketch-project of Moscow planning for four million people was designed at the Architectural-Planning Department of the Moscow Executive Committee under the guidance of V. Semyonov. As a matter of fact it repeated the basic provisions of the earlier General Scheme of Moscow Development by Kurt Mayer. A team of experts was composed; it included S. Boldyrev, G. Balyan, A. Bunin, P. Didenko, M. Kruglova. The latter put forward on the competitive basis her own version of the project that capitulated on the 1931 scheme by Kurt Mayer.

The party elite chose the static scheme by K. Mayer, that actually lacked proper perspective, for the simple reason that in 1931 the Politbureau took a special decision «On Separating the City of Moscow into an Independent Administrative, Economic and Party Unit». By its modest parametres (30,000 – 50,000 hectares) the scheme was close to projects by V. Semyonov, V. Baburov, V. Kratyuk. The above-mentioned party resolution broke the integral Moscow social-economic region into two unequal parts and set a barrier for the migration of population to Moscow, since the institute of residence permits was introduced (1932). The inevitable territorial growth of the city was sure to aggravate contradictions between the capital and the region, while ancient towns and settlements of close Moscow suburbs that were included into the city were losing their relative independence, specific lifestyle, their own special architectural features.

The artificial administartive separation of the capital from the region interrupted the harmonic development of the Moscow Agglomeration as an integral system of towns and rural settlements of various ranks. For this reason the most perspective proposals by N. Ladovsky, G. Krasin, E. Mai, G. Mayer that contained options of Moscow and adjacent territories development covering the area of 100,000 – 250,000 hectares were never properly appreciated. The experience of European and Asian capitals demonstrated that these proposals were the most far-sighted and ensured relatively harmonic development of such cities as London, Washington, Copenhagen, Tokyo, and others.

In 1932 – 1934 the team of Professor V.Semyonov started to develop the General Plan of Moscow. Kurt Mayer had worked in Moscow until 1936, his later destiny has never been tracked.

The Search of the New Capital's Centre

«Fare Thee well, the custodian of the Russia glory,
You, the magnificent cathedral of Christ,
Our golden-headed giant,
That used to glitter above the capital!..

We've got nothing sacred,
For isn't it a shame,
That «the cast golden hat»
Lies on the block under the axe».
                                            N. Arnold. 1930

The 1931 decision made by party leaders to reconstruct Moscow on the basis of the radial-circular system that met the requirements of the totalitarian state capital could not be directly implemented in the General Plan. This problem arose due to the fact that there was still no concept of the new social-political centre for the proletarian capital, its future main square was not yet selected, the city-building symbols of the communist state were not yet created.

The designers of the capital centre changed frequently, the started projects of squares and buildings were seldom completed. Eight leaders of designing teams had been replaced in Moscow by 1931 (from S. Shestakov to K. Gan, S. Gornyi, and, finally, to I. Mayorov). Almost all of them were accused of attempts «to preserve at all costs old Moscow of merchants, nobility and priests». In the end, the APU was headed by M. Kryukov (who was repressed in1937).

It took more than 10 years to find a solution on the capital's main square and its city-building symbol. Moscow's destiny as a prominent monument of Russian city-building of the 15th – 19th centuries was decided. Starting with the period when Moscow was the capital of the Russian Federation, and later, when it became the capital of the Soviet Union, several crucial proposals were made to disseminate governmental objects and to create a new party and governmental centre at a distance of five kilometres from the Kremlin and Kitay-Gorod. This would have allowed to organize the manifold capital life better and to disperse social-political functions the way it is done in democratic countries.

However, the party and governmental bodies of Russia, and later, of the USSR occupied the Kremlin and Kitay-Gorod, first temporarily, then permanently. This was an incentive to concentrate within a limited area rapidlly growing commissariats (ministries) of security, industry, state planning, defence. Therefore, which was quite natural under the circumstances, the functions of the main square for parades were assumed by Red Square, while the Cathedral of Our Lady of Kazan, the Iverskie Gate, districts behind the St.Basil's Cathedral were demolished. Demolitions of the Museum of History and of the Trade Rows were proposed repeatedly. Selective work to demolish historical districts and to lay new streets and thoroughfares had been started before any decision was made concerning the General Plan concept. The starting point was that in 1932 Chief Architects of certain streets were appointed in order «to embellish them from the architectural point of view». Every expert was practically free to make his own decisions since there was no detailed project of the centre planning. The project of embellishing the thoroughfare from Lubyanskaya Square to the future Palace of Congresses was assigned to Academician I. Zholtovsky; the Gorky Street first was assigned to Academician A. Schusev, then to Academician S. Chernyshev; the embankments were given to V. Lavrov and N. Popov; the Boulevard Ring was trusted to I. Golosov; architect A. Vlasov was in charge of the Central Park, while the Izmailovsky Park went to N. Kolli.

Since 1933 B.Iophan was responsible for projects of the centre. He also participated in devising the concept of the General Plan. Orienting the project on the Palace of Soviets as the primary compositional centre of Moscow, Iophan proposed to cut five or six additional radial avenues directed at this sacral nucleus. The square in front of the Palace of Soviets covered from 15 to 20 hectares, which means that it was four times larger than Red Square. Among objects to be demolished there were Manezh, the Museum of Fine Arts, and many others. If these ideas had been implemented, about a third of the historical buildings would have been demolished in the south-western part

The symbol of destruction of old Moscow.

of the city. To form two new transportation rings some buildings and a section of the Kitay-Gorod wall were demolished. Work was started to renovate the Theatre Passage without any general project of the centre (architect I. Zholtovsky). The principal avenue of Moscow was to pass here; it was to stretch from the Lubyanskaya Square through the Theatre Passage, Okhotny Ryad and Mokhovaya Street to the Lenin Library. On personal instruction of L. Kaganovich the construction of the House of Mossovet (Moscow City Council) was began; it was to be built in the Palladian style (architect I. Zholtovsky). Concurrently a library was being built according to the project by V. Schuko, the Mossovet Hotel according to the project by A. Schusev, L. Saveliev and O. Stapran. Zholtovsky wanted «to drastically reconstruct the gate to the Theatre Passage. The upper part of the gate, built in an ugly pseudo-Russian style was to be completely removed, while the gate itself was to be renovated in the classic architectural style».

Moscow's central streets were being reconstructed to form monumental classic ensembles. The magazine «Planning and Building Cities» wrote: «No Bramante, no Mikel-Anjelo, no one of the titans of ancient architecture could even dream of the scope of concepts and deeds that in our case are measured only by the size of our construction sites and avenues to be built»[27].

Since the party supported the radial-circular planning of the centre, then Moscow was to surpass all capitals of the world in the number of radial thoroughfares. Magazines wrote: «Moscow has only 13 thoroughfares, while Paris has 14, Berlin – 15, London – 16». It meant that their number in Moscow was to be increased to 18, or even more. The old idea by Balinskiy and Knorre dating back to 1892 – 1902 to lay the Sergievsky Avenue between Lubyanka and Kalanchevskaya was reborn, with the only difference that the avenue got a new name – first, it was called the Novo-Myasnitskaya Street, then – the Novo-Kirovsky Avenue. The Novo-Tverskaya Street was conceived too, but it was later blocked by Zholtovsky's building in Mokhovaya Street.

Old historical buildings were ignored, since the private property on land and real estate was abolished. It was allowed to demolish entire streets and districts, monasteries, the Triumphal Arch. It was suggested to remove all the historical buildings in front of the Kremlin and on the island between the Moskva-River and the Obvodnoy Canal in order to create a vast water surface.

The administrative-managerial and party apparat required new buildings, and they were constructed close to Kitay-Gorod and the Kremlin. The House of Military Industry was built next to the USSR VSNKh (Supreme Council of People's Economy) located inside the former Business Yard in the Kitay-Gorod Passage. The biggest commissariats were tied to the semi-circle that embraced Moscow's centre. The new building of OGPU – NKVD (Secret Police) (architects I. Fomin and A. Langman) was constructed at the highest point of the centre, on the corner of Furkasovsky Passage and the Bolshaya Lubyanka; it combined service, club, shopping and housing facilities. It was called the House of «Dynamo» after a shop situated on the ground floor from the side of Malaya Lubyanka. The building of the USSR Gosbank (State Bank) (1927 – 1929, architect I. Zholtovsky) is located further on in Kuznetsky Most, and one of its sides touches the semi-circle too. The significance of the new semi-circle was emphasized by the corner tower of the Central Telegraph (1927 – 1929, architect I. Rerberg). The Narkomvoenmor (the Ministry of the Navy) was built in Frunze Street in 1934 according to the project by L. Rudnev.

The choice of the site for constructing «The House of Government» (which is better known as «The House on the Embankment») is quite indicative; the house combined all the functions necessary for living. Built in 1927 – 1931 according to the project by brothers Iophan[28] for the party and governmental nomenclature, it was located on an island, cut off from the rest of the city. Almost complete life cycle in the house-town by

L. Rudnev, V. Munts: The M. Frunze Military Academy. 1937.

B.Iophan made it unnecessary to leave it – the only travelling needed was to the job place inside service cars. The dwellers of its 500 apartments turned into inhabitants of a citadel whose life was hidden from an inquisitive eye, though it was closely watched by security police possessing the right to execute or to show mercy.

In the late 30s the population of the house was considerably renewed – the previous hosts had been arrested, and their apartments were given to other people.

New Sacral Buildings of Moscow

Watching the activities of the Soviet state from abroad after he had been expelled from Russia philosopher N. Berdyaev noted that under communists the perception of Moscow as the Third Rome was replaced by its perception as the centre of the Third International, while the Messiah idea of the Russian people had been transformed: «the Russian atheism, nihilism, materialism were acquiring religious colouring».

This became especially obvious during the struggle against the Orthodox teaching, that was accompanied by the total destruction of cathedrals and historical monuments with subsequent construction of new monuments at their sites. The new stage of development of ideologically-coloured sacral objects with ceremonial space around them started during the construction of the tomb of the prophet of the world proletarian revolution. Lenin's mausoleum became the first «sacral object of the entire Soviet political liturgy» (N. Berdyaev).

Lenin's funeral demonstrated genuine sorrow of millions of people who believed that their chief could have led them to the happy future. The press carried workers letters: «It is necessary that Ilyich should stay with us physically, that boundless masses of working people could see him». It was suggested «not to bury Lenin's body, but to balm it». This reminded onlookers of the cries of Egyptian crowds who gathered on the banks of the Nile when the mummy of the deceased pharaoh was floating along the river to the tomb pyramid.

«Meeting the desire expressed by numerous delegates and in countless appeals, the USSR Central Executive Committee decided to do the following:

1. The coffin with Lenin's body shall be kept in a vault, and the vault shall be open for visitors.

2. The vault shall be erected at the Kremlin wall among the common graves».

The decision to construct the Mausoleum to eternally demonstrate Lenin's body accelerated the transformation of Red Square into a site of «political liturgy». Trade functions were replaced by political ones. On the days of revolutionary holidays almost religious rites took place here resembling a religious procession. Military parades were gradually turning into a special kind of sight that was made more attractive by the advent of newer weapons which required a larger area for their demonstration. Not only the Voskresenskie Gate with Iverskaya Chapel had to be demolished because of this, but the Kazan Cathedral as well – a monument to driving the Poles out of Moscow. All the transformations of Red Square were essentially subordinated to the task of staging all kinds of mysteries there, including official funerals of deceased chiefs whose bodies were carried on gun carriages from the direction of Okhotniy Ryad, from the House of Trade Unions.

The first mausoleum on the project by A. Shchusev was wooden. In 1925 various projects were offered at the competition of the «eternal mausoleum», some of them looking like a pyramid or a cube as a symbol of eternity, the Pantheon, the Halicarnass Mausoleum. One of the projects in the competition imitated Lenin's figure 15 to 20 storeys high. Apart from the tomb located inside it were top state authorities, libraries, concert and rally halls. At nightime Lenin's eyes – two huge searchlights – were to dispel the shadows and to «lighten the way» to communism.

Architect Rudnev suggested to make the mausoleum in the shape of a huge cube. According to one of Iophan's versions (1926) the mausoleum was like a tall stepped hipped roof embellished by figures of chieftains holding the globe. Soon after the first wooden mausoleum had been built the myth was created about the «immortal Messiah» of the communist paradise. In February 1924, in his article «Architectural Immortalization of Lenin» the devoted bolshevik G. Krasin proposed a programme of merciless demolition of existing buildings from Okhotny Ryad to the Lenin Hills in order to set up vast squares and parade avenues. «The first task is to build a permanent tomb in the place where Lenin's body is staying now... This will be the place whose significance for mankind will surpass Mecca or Jerusalem».

The Institute of Artistic Culture approved the proposal to immortalize the chief's memory and to construct for this purpose a colossal building for which even Red Square was too little. It was proposed to demolish the Trade Rows and the Museum of History and thus to increase the square by 2 – 3 times which would have completely destroyed the existing ensemble.

Anticipating the total reconstruction of the centre El Lisitsky wrote in his article «The Forum of Socialist Moscow»: «We are participants of an exceptional epoch when the new history of human community is being written. Such a tremendous construction programme is facing us now that, as to its scope and significance, it surpasses everything that had ever been done at the best times in our pre-history when cultures flourished».

Contest project of eternal V.I. Lenin Mausoleum. 1925.

As the new sacral object appeared in the USSR – Lenin's Tomb – it became more and more obvious that the symbol of the Orthodox religion dominating Moscow, the golden-headed Cathedral of Christ the Savior, was out of place. The capital city of the international proletariat needed a new main avenue that would lead people to the new main square with the main architectural symbol of the approaching communism. This was to be done with the help of the biggest building in the world – the symbol of not only Moscow or the entire country, but also the symbol of the impending triumph of the world proletarian revolution.

In spring 1924 V. Balikhin was the first to make a proposal in the State Commission for Immortalizing Lenin's Memory to erect a monument to the formation of the USSR and a monument to Comintern together with a monument to Lenin at the site where the Cathedral of Christ the Saviour was located.

According to V. Balikhin the Palace of Soviets was to look like a huge cube, the symbol of eternity, with the sides of 100 metres by 100 metres by 100 metres (by its volume it would have exceeded the Cathedral of Christ the Saviour, and its hall, like the cathedral, could accomodate 15,000 people). «The cube's plane with the size of 10,000 square metres and a figure of Lenin (approximately 70 – 75 metres high) is interpreted as the honour board of the World Union of the Soviet Republics which will carry the names of the new republics that will eventually join the World USSR. Starting with the date of forming the USSR the list of republics that joined the Union will be added from the bottom to the top by the names of new Soviet republics until the moment when the date of the final world revolution beams in the upper line – the date of forming the Union of Soviet Socialist Republics of the World».

In 1928 – 1929 L. Komarova develops a project to construct a Comintern building at the site of the cathedral with the highrise component that will surpass the belfry of Ivan the Great in the Kremlin. In early 1931 one of the leaders of the Association of New Architects proposed to set up a huge square at the site of the cathedral (which would be many times larger than Red Square) for mass manifestations of representatives of Moscow, Union Republics and Red Army units. A Palace of Soviets was to be erected in the centre of the square – the integral artistic-architectural monument to the Third International, the USSR and Lenin, which would characterize the epoch when the will of the working people to construct socialism was demonstrated.

In summer 1931 a competition was announced to design the Palace of Soviets. On December 5, 1931 at 12 o'clock the Cathedral of Christ the Savior was exploded in order to free the site for the biggest quasi-religious building in the world.

A. Lunacharsky wrote: «When it was decided to remove the Cathedral of Christ the Saviour which due to its huge size and golden dome was attracting sights if Moscow was observed from a distance (especially from the Lenin Hills) this was done not only because that was the best place for the gygantic Palace of Soviets we needed, the building that would accomodate numerous people's assemblies typical of our true democracy. This was done to give Moscow a kind of exemplary building, in order to give Moscow – the red centre – an obvious architectural backbone».

The competition on the Palace of Soviets lasted three years. There were several rounds, representatives of many countries took part in it, about 400 projects were presented – symbolic, functional, temple-like, restorative. The final victory was won by B. Iophan[29] who in his project of the Palace of Soviets as a monument to Lenin created the symbol of «resurrection» of the world revolution Messiah. Architects V. Gelfreikh and V. Shchuko, authors of the monument to the chieftain in Leningrad, joined the project at its final stage.

Iophan who actually became an architect of the Politbureau (his office was located inside the Kremlin) developed his own idea of the Lenin's mausoleum as a stepped hipped roof crowned by figures supporting the globe. In doing so, he leaned upon the project of his mentor Armando Brazini (Italy) proposed at the

Architectural team of ASNOVA:
Contest project of V.I. Lenin Mausoleum. 1925.

first round of the open competition. Brazini interpreted the palace as the Ascention Cathedral in Kolomenskoye with Lenin's figure at the top. Brazini proceeded from the fact that the act of Resurrection was the most important one for Orthodox Christians of Russia (the main holiday for the Russians is the Easter, not Christmas as for catholics). Lenin's statue at the top of the building and the five-pointed star inside the dome of the grand hall were new symbols emanated by the idea of Man-God and by sacralization of the principal values of the socialist doctrine according to Marx and Lenin. But they also were the symbols resulting from reinterpretation of religious traditions of Orthodox church-buiding. The cross on the cathedral symbolizing Christ was replaced by Lenin's statue. The Holy Trinity traditionally placed inside the dome was replaced by the five-pointed star.

The verticalism of the monument, its high-rise character are important features of Orthodox religious architecture. It is easy to see in the stepped tower-like composition of the Palace of Soviets deeply comprehended tradition, reborn on absolutely different foundation, of constructing independently located tower-like high-rise multi-layer belfries of Moscow: the Belfry of Ivan the Great, the belfries of the Novodevichiy and Simonov Monasteries, Menshikova Tower, and others.

By its size and height which was equal to 415 metres (1/30 of Moscow's radius) the Palace of Soviets surpasses the greatest buildings of the ancient world (Kheops Pyramid – 137 metres), the Medieval gothic cathedrals (the Keln Cathedral is 160 metres, the Amien Cathedral – 126 metres), all the monuments of the Renaissance (St.Peter's Cathedral in Rome – 143 metres), the biggest structures of the capitalist epoch (Eiffel Tower in Paris – 300 metres), and even the highest building of the time – the Empire State Building (a 407 metre high skyscraper in New York).

Correlation between the grandeur of the idea to be expressed and the size of the building in question was apparent in the architecture of the Palace of Soviets to the fullest extent. This correlation had been known since time immemorial, and it was typical of Russian architecture too. The grandeur of the communist epoch whose symbol was the Palace of Soviets correlated to the grandeur of its size that was bigger than anything ever built. The destiny of the Palace of Soviets was more than merely becoming the biggest building in the world. Lenin's statue on its top was to become the world's biggest statue – The Statue of Liberty in New York is 46 metres high, «The Worker and the Peasant» that was on top of the Soviet pavilion at the 1937 World's Exhibition in Paris – 34 metres. Lenin's figure author S.Merkurov believed that it would live for a thousand years if covered with a two-millimetre coating of a special alloy[30]. Taking into account Moscow's weather, frequent clouds and a low number of clear days, the figure of the proletarian Messiah raised as high as the clouds could regularly either disappear in the fog, or reappear – thus symbolizing «the resurrection» of the mummy kept eternally on Red Square.This could have been the biggest show of the 20th century created at a tragic period of Russian history and meant to divert the country's attention from actual problems of everyday life.

Both in its appearance and architectural ideas the Palace of Soviets had been conceived and was supposed to become an antipode to the Cathedral of Christ the Saviuor. The first one was erected for the sake of God-Man – Christ the Saviour – the second one – of Man-God – Lenin. The very fact of building the Palace of Soviets on the site of the Cathedral of Christ the Saviour was to symbolize the triumph of communism over the ideas of Orthodox church.

Being antipodes in their meaning, according to E.Kirichenko, both buildings were typologically similar concerning a number of their specific features. This is caused by the role each building was to play in the spatial system of Moscow – which means by the complex of ideas whose carriers and illustrations were the

Cathedral of Christ the Savior.

Demolishing the Cathedral of Christ the Savior by explosion. December 5, 1931.

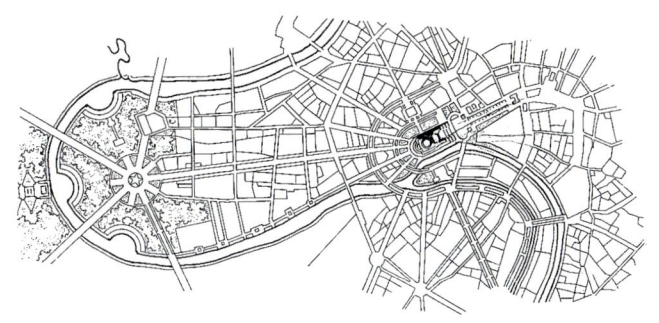

Project of the Palace of Soviets.

monument to Lenin and the Cathedral of Christ the Saviour. That explains the exceptional attention paid by the top state figures to the construction of each building. That explains the exceptional richness of artistic means used to assist architecture to express more vividly the ideas underlying each project[31].

Both buildings were in a way united by their significance in the hierarchy of ideological buildings and by similar conditions under which they were to be erected: they were built in the centre of Moscow, of Russia, of the world. In one case it was under the conditions of the absolutist monarchic state in the 19th century, in the other – of the totalitarian state in the 30s – 40s of the 20th century. The project of the Palace of Soviets sort of sanctifies the coming turning point in social life – the consolidation of the entire power in Stalin's hands.

It was planned to make more than 70 major sculptures, about 700 busts and minor sculptures, 20 sculptural groups whose size would be from 10 to 14 metres. The square of the outer and inner bas-reliefs would have equalled 11,000 square metres.

Radical architects of the West were appaled by the official approval of the gygantic project of the Palace of Soviets prepared by architects B. Iophan, V. Gelfreikh, V. Shchuko... «Some day the architects of Soviet Russia will have their hangover» – wrote G. Shmidt. «It is not easy to agree with the fact that the thing to be built will be so extraordinary (clumsy, inappropriate, fanciful) as the thing that is described in journals now» – Le Corbusier wrote to A. Vesnin. Addressing the First Congress of Soviet Architects in June 1937, F. Wright saw the falseness typical of US skyscrapers. «This construction, – he said, – which I hope will remain just a project for ever, could be acceptable if we needed a contemporary version of St.George killing the Dragon».

Thus, the decision was made in Moscow to build the second sacral construction to support the myth of the «eternally alive» Lenin and to organize around it the largest square in the world whose size would surpass the Kremlin's size. This idea served as the starting point for forming the main prospect of the capital – the Avenue of Ilyich, that was to connect Red Square where the chieftain's mummy was lying in peace, with the new capital's square.

Contest projects of the Palace of Soviets. 1931.

Contest projects of the Palace of Soviets. A. Brazini

Under the motto «Mayak» (Lighthouse)

Under the motto «Trud» (Labor)

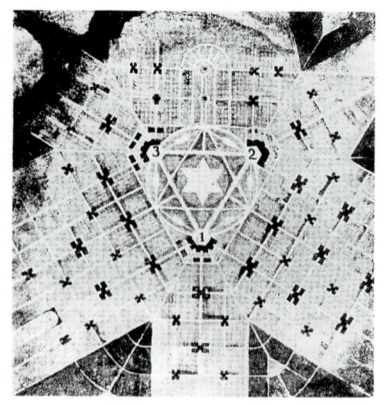

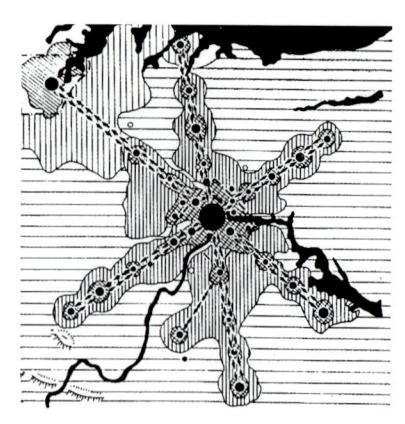

H. Ferriss: The city of the future. 1 – Arts Center. 2 – Layout diagram. 3 – Variant of reconstruction of Washington.

The entire new social-political centre of Moscow was completely subordinated to the grandiose monument that was suppressing not only Moscow, but its close suburbs. The squares of Nogina, Lubyanka, Sverdlova, Revolution were to form a single whole, where million-people strong flows of demonstrators would accumulate in order to move in orderly columns to the main square of the Palace of Soviets.

Here is a quotation from materials to the scetch project of the centre: «Red Square if to expand twice due to the demolished GUM building. Kitay-Gorod shall gradually be freed from all minor buildings, and the vacant territory will be occupied by several monumental buildings surrounded by greenery meant for state functions.

Traffic in the country's main square will be organized at two levels:

1) at the level of the square – the continuation of the Boulevard Ring will cross the square, the Kropotkinskaya Embankment, and then it will proceed along the Novo-Kamennyi bridge to Ordynka.

2) below the surface of the square – traffic will go in the gallery running along the embankment open from the river-side.

A monument to hero-Cheluskintsy (polar explorers) will be erected on the opposite bank of the irver, at the spit.

The 415 metre high palace crowned with Lenin's statue will become the embodiment of the victorious epoch of proletariat dictatorship. The monumental 200-metre-wide staircase of the Palace's main facade will lead visitors to the gala collonade of the main entrance.

Going around the Palace of Soviets on both sides, the Avenue of Ilyich will proceed as a powerful 120-meter wide speedway to Lenin Hills. In every respect it should surpass the best prospects in Berlin, Vienna, Paris and other cities»[32].

By its size the new centre of Moscow was to surpass the main thoroughfare of Washington which accomodated the centres of legislative, executive and judicial power; national monuments are also located there. (Iophan paid a special visit to Washington to study in detail the US capital social centre).

The ideology of Moscow's new centre was created under the guidance of B. Iophan. If the new centre and the Palace of Soviets had been put into life to a full extent, then it would have been necessary to reconstruct 1,100 hectares, while 40 percent of buildings within the Garden Ring were to have been demolished.

The General Plan of Moscow of 1935

The General Plan was approved by the USSR Government and the Party Central Committee (TsK VKP(b)) after the victory of socialism in the USSR had been proclaimed at the 17th Party Congress (1934). The government of the Russian Federation did not participate in approving this plan; Moscow's functions as the capital of the Russian Federation were not mentioined in the plan.

The General Plan of Moscow was conceived as an ideal supermodel of future communist society. The city's structure was subordinated to the palace of Soviets which symbolizes the «resurrection» of the Messiah of the world proletarian revolution. The plan was based upon the completed radial-concentric scheme, whose centre was meant for million-strong public manifestations surrounded by monumental buildings, a system of green plants, parks, forest-parks, numerous water rings and stadiums.

Obeying the party directive and rejecting the achievements of the world city-building and district planning of the 20s – 30s, the architects were planning the capital as a monumental static ensemble. Twelve wide avenues were directed at the Main Monument of the city. Tough centralization replaced democratic city-building trends. Functionalism and rationalism of Russia's architecture of the 1920s were replaced by political rhetorics and embellishment. The coexistence of the historical and socialist cities was problematic, since the demolition of the old context (hundreds of valuable historical and cultural monuments were to be destroyed) and the creation of a new myth to replace it represented a typical element of the architectural utopia.

The city was estimated for 5 million people. Its territory was to grow from 28,000 to 60,000 hectares. The expansion was to go first of all to the south-west due to inclusion into the new city boudaries of 16,000 hectares between Kuntsevo and Tsaritsino. The expansion was also to spread in the directions of Izmailovo, Perovo and Kuskovo to include 5,000 hectares, to Tekstilshchiki – 3,000 hectares, to Lyublino – Nagatino – 4,500 hectares, to Khoroshevo – Shchukino in the western part of the capital – 1,700 hectares, and in the north-western direction to Tushino, Khovrino, Medvedkovo – 3,000 hectares.

The Khimki water reservoir was included into the city boundary and together with the Yauza River was to set up the inter-city water ring. The outer water ring was to go from Klyazminskoe Reservoir along the Vostochny Canal through Tekstilshchiki and Southern Port along the Moskva-River to the Khimkinskoe Reservoir.

The General Plan stipulated the expansion of Red Square twice, while the central squares – Nogin Square, Dzerzhinsky Square, Sverdlov Square, Revolution Square – were to be reconstructed and embellished architecturally. The territory of Kitay-Gorod was to be cleared from existing minor buildings, and several monumental state-scope buildings were to be constructed there. The river-bank of Zaryadye was to be cleared for constructing a huge (120 – 150 metres high) building of Narkomtyazhprom (the Ministry of Heavy Industry) which together with the Palace of Soviets would have suppressed the Kremlin thus decreasing sharply its compositional role in Moscow.

It was planned to enlarge squares and to embellish them thematically. Thus, Kommuna Square was to become Red Army

B. Iofan, V. Shchuko, V. Gelfreikh (architects), S. Merkurov (sculptor): Palace of Soviets. Project. Variant. 1942.

Square, Pushkin Square – «Literature» Square, while Trubnaya Square was to symbolize the «fusion of the city and the countryside».

It was proposed to increase the size of dwelling areas by 6 – 7 times (from 1.5 – 2 hectares to 9 – 15 hectares) with the average population density of 300 – 400 persons per hectare. The first priority thoroughfares and squares were to accomodate buildings 7 – 10 – 14 storeys high.

The parks were also to become thematic: Ostankino – a zoo; Sokolniki – «transportaion»; Izmailovo – «energy production»; Fili – «military park»; Kuskovo – «metallurgy»; Kuzminki – «machine-building».

It was proposed to make within a 10-kilometre radius a protective forest-park belt consisting of vast woods that start in the nearby countryside forests. They were to serve as a reservoir of fresh air for the city. The woods were to occupy the following

General plan of reconstruction of Moscow. The 30s – 40s.

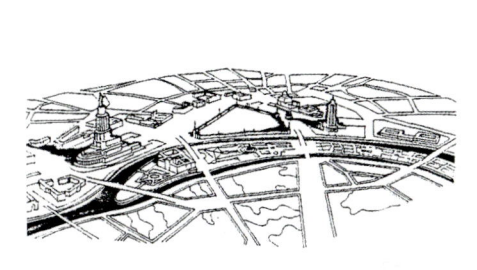

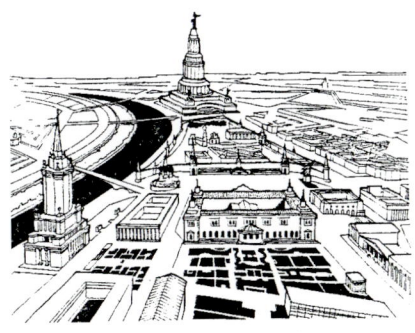

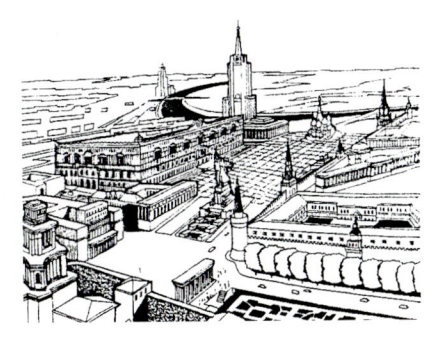

Plan of Moscow after reconstruction. Project. 1936.

I. Fomin: the House «Narkomtyazhprom» on the Red Square. Project.

areas: along the banks of the Yauza River; from the Lenin Hills and Gorky Park along the embankment of the Moskva-River; from the Ostankino green area to Samotyka and Neglinnaya.

The plan also took care of the suburbs that are adjunct to the capital. They were to accomodate industrial and agricultural enterprises that met the city's needs. The same territory was supposed to serve for locating air transport depots, technical and other communal services to be moved out of the city. The green areas – the Pogonno-Losiny Ostrov, the Rublevo Water-Protection Zone, Tyoply Stan, Sviblovo – were to be united into a single system.

The decision of the Central Committee – TsK VKP(b) – to limit the city's population and its territory was in conflict with the actual scope of urbanization, population migration, industrial development. In case the business and political functions were concentrated downtown, the static project could have been implemented only on the following basis:

– tough regulating migration of population and introducing strict residence permits;

A. Mordvinov: The building of the People's Commissariat for Heavy Industry. Project. Photomosaic. 1936.

— curbing private cars ownership (25,000 cars per 1,000 population) and developing mass transportation network;

— banning any individual housing construction; enlarging residential districts; sharply increasing the number of storeys in houses to be built;

— destroying the historically formed size and structure of private residential property.

Architects were attempting to turn the city into Mecca of the international proletariat, and to surpass Paris, London and Berlin in the number of radial avenues; Washington – in the size of the social centre; all the cities of the world – in the height of the main monument; all the sculptures of the past and the present – in the size of the Moscow statue (75-metre high Lenin's statue).

The social utopia was on the march. The 1935 General Plan approved by Stalin was an attempt to put into life the political myth of the 20th century by means of architecture. It did not bother to take into account the context of Moscow as an outstanding monument of Russian city-building of the 14th – 19th centuries.

The very style of devising projects when working on the General Plan at the Architectural-Planning Department of the Moscow Council couldn't but turn into a mechanism of «tracing Politbureau instructions». Kaganovich was «creative» in developing them. The personnel of the Department was thoroughly selected and therefore loyal; moreover, they were put into tough ideological framework. At the same time the structures of Mossovet, NKVD (Secret Police), MPS (Ministry of Railways), Narkomtyazhprom (Ministry of Heavy Industry) and other influential power structures had lots of opportunities to affect specific designing projects directly. For instance, the NKVD always made decisions on its own as to where in Moscow to have its buildings

The remains of the monument to tsar Alexander II, the Liberator. 1918.

Destruction of the monument to Alexander III. 1923.

Palace of Soviets Avenue. Project. Perspective.

and residential complexes erected (first of all, around Lubyanka). The standards of comfort and the norms of distribution of personal apartments in the «security houses» were the highest in Moscow.

In the course of realization of 1935 Stalin's General Plan Moscow went through radical changes. The standards of engineer support, services and utilities grew up, but Moscow's functions as the capital of the Russian Federation were set aside. The city suffered heavy losses in its historical and cultural heritage. Over 400 valuable monuments of culture and history of the 14th – early 20th centuries were demolished. Which is paradoxical – before the demolitions many of them had been renovated – the Kazan Cathedral (P. Baranovsky), the Sukhareva Tower (V. Ivanov, N. Vinogradov), the Kitay-Gorod wall and the Krasnye Gate (N. Vinogradov), and so on. The site of Museum of History was meant for a grandiose sculpture on the subject of International.

In 1935 Professor S. Chernyshev was appointed Chief Architect of the Mossovet Planning Department; he described the content of the General Plan at a Politbureau session. According to the main directions set in the General Plan, specified workshops were established where people held personal responsibility for appropriate architectural decisions. Architect V. Dolganov was in charge of the workshop responsible for designing approach lines to industrial giants (in particular, to the Stalin Plant) on the territory of more than 9,000 hectares. Professor G. Barkhin headed the planning efforts of the Dzerzhinsky District on the square of 4,000 hectares with the population of 400,000. Professor N. Ladovsky was designing Zamoskvorechye, while Kurt Mayer planned the area of Izmailovsky Park named after Stalin. Professor Polyakov was responsible for the north-eastern freeway to the Sokolniki District Centre on the territory of more than 11,000 hectares. Architect A. Mashkov was responsible for the freeway from the Kremlin to Fili on the territory of about 5,000 hectares; Professor B. Kondrashov – for the freeway Sverdlov Square – Khimki, I.Nikolaev – for planning the Lenin and Frunze Districts. The implementation of the General Plan increased the concentration of governmental and social buildings in Moscow's centre and stimulated the growth of transportation flows.

Unfortunately the forecasts by N. Ladovsky, A. Borovoy and Le Corbusier made in 1928 – 1930 concerning the drawbacks of static solution of the city development and combination of the historical and socialist cities here came true. A. Borovoy used to write the following: «The Kremlin is an inspired artistic fairy tale about the past. Even together with Kitay-Gorod and adjacent districts it can not accomodate the huge central regulating official structures of the international, union, republican and regional levels. There is no chance to design it correctly, and locate on the territory properly».

However, the experience of 1931 – 1948 was not assessed critically. In the post-war period the guidelines of reconstructing Moscow according to the General Plan of 1935 were used in a number of communist capitals, first of all, in Bejing under Mao Tse Tung, and in Bucharest under Caushesku. In Bejing the General Plans of 1954 and 1958 were designed with participation of Soviet experts. The plans envisaged laying five circular roads and ten radiuses leading to the centre where the historical («forbidden» city) and the new political centre were to coexist.

The building of the People's Commissariat for Heavy Industry. Projects.

Architects: V. Shchuko, V. Gelfreikh.

Architects: B Iofan, A. Baransky.

Dzerzhinsky Square. Project of reconstruction.

In Bucharest historical districts were demolished, and a monumental ensemble suppressing Man was created in the northern part of the city's central part.

The First Steps of Reconstruction

According to the plan of reconstruction the main idea of Moscow's composition was to create three powerful diametres.

The first diameter was to go from Northern Izmailovo through Preobrazhenka, Myasnitskaya, Volkhonka, Ostozhenka to Luzhniki. It became a priority issue at sectors in the city's central part. However, the required demolitions of robust buildings in order to straighten the future thoroughfare were to become so large-scale that the deadline of their implementation was constantly postponed. The buildings in the area of Ulansky Bypass where the projected back-up street for Myasnitskaya— the Novo-Kirovsky Avenue – was to pass were demolished partially. Myasnitskaya itself remained practically intact. The earlier constructed buildings of Narkomats (Ministries) of Land Cultivation (later – the Ministry of Agriculture) on the corner of Orlikov and Sadovaya; Light Industry (later – the Central Statistical Department erected by Corbusier), Defence Industry, Aircraft Industry and others happened to lie along the «red lines» of the future project. More demolitions took place in the Teatralny Bypass and in the Okhotny Ryad; as a rule, they took place before the General Plan had been adopted. The buildings that occupied the present day Manezhnaya Square were demolished completely. Among those gone are the former Loskutnaya Hotel, the buildings of the Moiseevsky Monastery, the Chapel of Alexander Nevsky. There was not enough time before the war to maim Volkhonka along which the Avenue of the Palace of Soviets was to pass.

The second diameter – from the settlement of «Sokol» to the Stalin Plant – during the pre-war years was constructed to a greater extent. A number of impressive buildings were erected in Gorky (Tverskaya) Street. First of all those were huge residential buildings with lengthy facades – Houses No.4 and No.6 (architect A.G. Mordvinov). «The scope» of Mordvinov's houses set the pace that was here and there beyond «the historical context» of the dense network of streets and by-streets that made Moscow so cosy at any season. A part of old houses was shifted deeper into the residential blocks. The bottoms of the new buildings that were coated with roughly processed stone with deep embrasures of windows were not lower in size than two storeys; thus pedestrians were separated from residential storeys which changed the life rhythm typical of Tverskaya street before.

Architect A. Burov «put in» a multi-storey residential building into Gorky Street (between Pushkin Square and Mayakovsky Square) in a more sophisticated way. He didn't make the lower part of their walls heavier; to the contrary he in a way «made them lighter» by introducing the tiers of double windows, a pilaster with stucco moulding and «renaissance» arches. The facade decorations included insets in the ancient technique of sgraffito (deepened pattern on colored plaster) that were made by the prominent engraving artist V. Favorsky. The new ensemble of Gorky Street was completed on the left side by the building of the Theatre named after V. Meierkhold (the experimenting director himself took part in devising the idea of its project) that had been under construction since 1932. The complexity of the idea and meagre financing delayed the construction work, and it was completed in 1940 only (architects D. Chechulin and K. Orlov).

The third diameter was designed from Ostankino through Maryina Roshcha, Samoteka, Red Square and Ordynka up to Serpukhovskoye Highway. Before the war construction work here was fragmentary. The most interesting object here was the grandiose building of the Theatre of the Red Army. It embodied the idea of utilizing specific artistic symbols in architectural shape-forming. The plan of the building was put inside the trace of a five-pointed star that could be seen as such from a high altitude only. The idea of completing the tier composition with three halls situated one above another and with a figure of warrior was never realised. The right side of Kommuny Square was fixed in the new red lines by constructing a multi-storey hotel of the Central House of the Red Army.

Apart from mass construction work along the principal «rays» and secondary radiuses, large-scale buildings were being erected along the red lines of the Boulevard and Garden Rings. In 1937 «the House of Writers» was built in Zamoskvorechye, next to the Tretyakov Gallery. It was meant for the most prominent members of the creative union. This building was tied to the red line of the «completing part» of the Boulevard Ring which was to be laid between the Bolshoi Ustyinsky Bridge and the western «spit» of the island.

Moscow that was named the spiritual centre of socialism «built» in 1934, in reality was rapidly turning into a unique «empire of bureaucrats». Governmental departments were divided into categories with corresponding privileges. Apart from their own residential buildings with mandatory autonomous boilers, they arranged their own shops- «distribution points», «special canteens», tailor's shops, repair shops,

Okhotny Ryad. End of the 20th century. Photograph from the album of N. Naidenov.

pharmacies, hospitals and clinics, recreational and sports facilities.

Construction of cinema houses acquired great importance; they were regarded as educational and propaganda centres. The cinema house «Rodina» («Motherland») on Semyonovskaya Square became the biggest building of the kind for many years to come. The would-be Meierkhold Theatre was turned into a concert hall named after Tchaikovsky (before the war the theatre company was dissolved, and Meierkhold himself was arrested and repressed soon after that).

Over the period of 1935 – 1940, more than 400 secondary school buildings were constructed in Moscow (there were more than 15 model projects of them).

The 1935 General Plan that initially was published quite widely, ten years later was actually made secret as to comparing it to the real city structure that emerged by the 1930s. The reason was simple: if the General Plan was superimposed on the network of historical streets, then any sober person would have emotions far from delight – the planners left almost nothing from the centuries-old city fabric. Fortunately, for objective reasons, quite often the expansion of the central streets was not put into effect on the scheduled scale (it was planned to expand Arbat from 20 to 32 metres, Kuznetsky Most from 17 to 35 metres, Bolshaya Lubyanka from 20 to 42 metres, Pokrovka from 14 to 42 metres).

Leaning upon ideas by Engels and Lenin on overcoming contradictions between the town and the countryside, the Plenum of 1931 recommended creating new industrial centers in rural areas; starting with 1932 their construction in Moscow and Leningrad was prohibited. This provision was confirmed in the General Plan. However, from the very beginning it was not put into life. In 1933 the first five-year plan was completed (within four years). For more than eight years the capital was accumulating its industrial, and research and development potential, and when Hitler's regime seized power in Germany the Country of Soviets made a sharp turn to strengthening defence industry. Naturally, the industrial output of automobile, machine-building, tool-building, bearing, instrument-building plants was growing... Dozens of new research and development centres and educational facilities were founded in Moscow and its close suburbs, and not in any «peasant areas». The number of their graduates was dozens times higher than in the late 20s.

The expansion of industrial enterprises that was usually done «as an exception» was becoming a process hard to control; it affected the dynamics of population patterns in an unfavourable way, it aggravated the housing problem and strained transportation networks. The category of construction workers was becoming quite numerous. Many unqualified workers were invited to Moscow on a temporary basis, for instance, to demolish buildings inside the Kremlin, in Kitay-Gorod and along the thoroughfares to be widened. People who escaped from the kolkhoz village were happy to get any wages. On the whole Moscow which before the revolution was reasonably regarded as the capital of Russian textile industry was becoming a major centre of heavy industry.

The governmental departments were given certain annual «limits» to import the working force to Moscow, and for this reason a considerable part of capital's inhabitants went on living in semi-cellar and similar dwellings that were poorly suited for living. The major portion of apartments in new houses were inhabited by several families – a room to a family. A kind of echo of recent passion for houses-communes was constructing apartments with numerous rooms, including those in houses located along the parade city thoroughfares which were intended for shared apartments or «communal» flats as the people used to call them.

Problems that were hard to overcome arose with the stipulated by the General Plan reconstruction of the Moscow railway hub. As a matter of fact, the requirement to free the city from marshalling yards and technical railway stations, to remove all the railway storehouses was not fulfilled. Over 60 years of construction work Moscow acquired nine railway stations, seven out of them were deadlocked (except Kursky and Byelorussky). Since 1908 the transition of railway carriages among the railway lines was done primarily through the Circular Railroad. The General Plan authors suggested to free a significant portion of territories occupied by railroad facilities by digging tunnels in the central part of the city; it was proposed to build a new railway station in the area of present-day Mira Avenue in order to operate trains of the Leningrad and Yaroslavl directions; to free the centre from the flow of transit passengers due to constructing periphery railway stations – the Southern, the Kolomensky, the Kuntsevsky ones, and others (this idea survived till the 70s). However, the actual reconstruction of the railroads amounted to their gradual electrification, construction of railroads to many major plants and factories, and erection of different level hubs at the crossing points with the most loaded highways.

Bridge-building was more successful. Over three years from 1936 to 1939 seven big bridges were constructed instead of those demolished, and a significant number was reconstructed, since a considerable share of the old ones did not meet the new requirements to city roads; besides, they were not able to ensure free passage of big Volga ships that appeared in Moscow due to the construction of the Moscow-Volga canal. In 1937 the new Moskvoretsky Bridge was commissioned – the only central bridge built of ferro-concrete (engineer V.S. Kirillov, architect A.V. Shchusev). Its total length is over 550 metres. The Bolshoi Ustyinsky Bridge was constructed in 1938 at the Boulevard Ring which was to be completed through Zamoskvorechye (that's why a considerable «reserve» of its capacity was envisaged). The suspended Krymsky Bridge is the only bridge in Moscow where transport moves below the piers (engineer B.P.Konstantinov, architect A.V.Vlasov). All the new bridges within the city boundary were designed to cross the embankments at different levels with the help of special bank sections. The bridges' size was increased considerably too; in certain cases their width reached 40 metres.

The General Plan stipulated an important city-building solution to construct embankments on a large scale in order to build later impressive houses that would «open» on waterways. By 1939 the banks of the Moskva-River within the city boundary were coated with more than 40 kilometres of granite embankments (before that only 18 kilometres had been constructed all in all). At the same time eight kilometres of the Drainage Canal were also coated with granite (with asphalted streets-lanes), granite also covered 20 kilometres of the Yauza-River banks. The plan to build a bridge over the Moskva-River and a canal near the spit (close to the confectioner factory «Krasny Oktyabr» – «the Red October») was never implemented. It was supposed to connect the Boulevard Ring from the Soimonovsky Lane with its continuation in Zamoskvorechye. It was planned to erect in 1938 a monument commemorating the rescue of the Chelyuskintsy – polar explorers – at the very spit.

The construction of the Moskva-Volga canal was of extreme importance for supplying Moscow with water, for improving transport communications as well as for city-building. Even Peter the Great intended to build a direct waterway from the Baltic Sea via the Volga River to the Moskva-River. In 1932 «the Dmitrov version» of the canal was approved, with its starting point to be located close to the village of Ivankovo on the Volga. 240 major buildings had been constructed along the canal during incomplete five years. As compared to the Byelomorsko-Baltiysky Canal various equipment and machines were rather widely used here. Nevertheless, the labour of the prisoners was used on a large scale too (prisoner camps were set up along the canal). In July 1934 Stalin and his close aides visited the canal under construction.

Designers found optimal solutions that have been ensuring effective operation of the canal for more than 60 years now. The water level at the Khimkinskoye Reservoir is 36 metres higher than in the Moskva-River in summer (stationary) period. It is also about 36 metres higher than the water level in the Ivankovskye Reservoir. Ships from the Volga overcome the Dmitrov Ridge, pass through five locks, and descend to the Moskva-River with the help of two locks. The Khimka-River valley situated lower than the reservoir level possesses a unique ecosystem, and from the very beginning of the canal construction was a protected zone. The Khimka-River within this zone flows in the old river bed, and gets additional water supply from the resevoir.

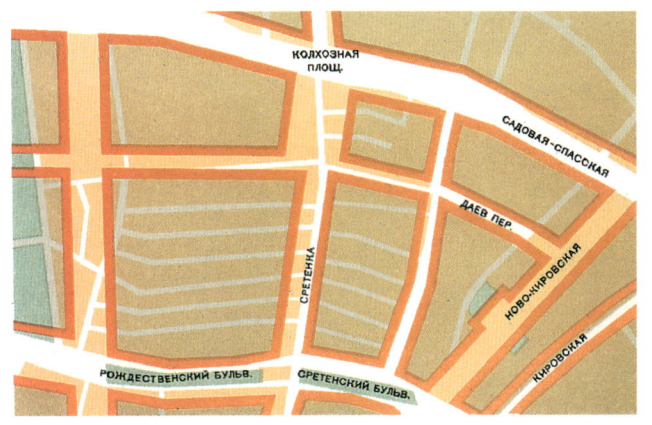

Replanning of an old block of buildings. General Plan. 1935.

In September 1935, the government took a decision to form a new passenger fleet for the first navigation, and 18 months later a flotilla of ships of various types came to Moscow; all of them had been built at the «Krasnoye Sormovo» works. Until the late 1950s only home-made steamships and motor ships were sailing in the Moscow-Volga Canal (since 1947 it has been called «Canal Named After Moscow», or the Moscow Canal). Later, some of the ships were bought in Czechoslovakia and the GDR. The steamships of «the tsar class» had been sailing there for many years. They were constructed by the companies of «Samolyot» and «Caucasus and Mercury» to commemorate the 300-year anniversary of the Romanoffs Dynasty (though they were renamed «Spartak», «Volodarsky» and «The Paris Commune»).

The first navigation started on July 15, 1937. A multi-metre figure of I.V. Stalin was erected near Lock Number 1, the first one from the Volga side (it was demolished in the 1950s). Lock Number 3, close to Yakhroma, is the most interesting structure from the point of view of its architecture. Its graceful towers are decorated with copper caravellas (architect V.Ya. Movchan).

A part of the second turn concept that envisaged constructing navigable «circular» canals was not realized. The northern canal was to start from the southern part of the Khimki Reservoir and proceed eastwards – through the ponds in Timiryazevsky (Petrovsko-Razumovsky) Park to the Yauza-River north of the Sokolniki Park. The eastern canal which was to be more full-flowing and lengthy was to be laid from the Klyazminskoye Reservoir (in the vicinity of Pirogovo) along the eastern boundary of Moscow to the Southern Port. It was to

**A. Vlasov (architect), V. Konstantinov (engineer):
Krymsky (Crimea) Bridge. 1938.**

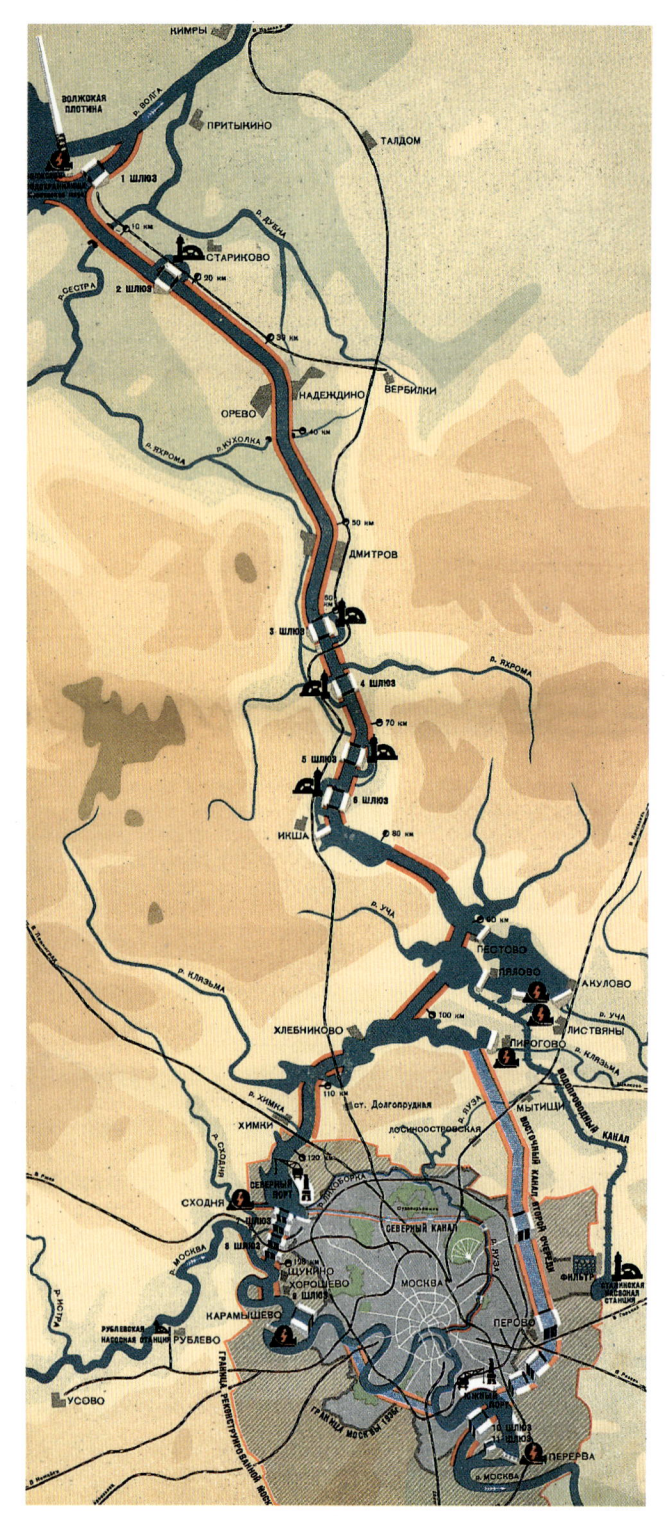

Architect V.Ya. Movchan: Moscow Canal. Lock No.3 tower with copper caravellas.

Canal Moscow-Volga. 1937.

become the main line for transit ships sailing by the Moskva-River to the Oka.

Actually, the following objects were built: the subsurface waterpipe canal that supplied the Eastern Station (formerly the Stalin Station); the Likhoborsky Spillway (also subsurface) that was supplying additional water to the Yauza through the Likhoborka River; the Karamyshevskoye and Khoroshevskoye Straightenings that «cut» the curved loops of the Moskva-River. Another staightening was conceived from the Andreevsky Monastery, at the outer side of the Circular Railroad in the direction of Nagatino.

On May 15, 1935 the first turn of the Moscow Metro was commissioned; it ran from Sokolniki to the Park of Culture and Recreation named after Gorky. There was a passage made from the «Biblioteka Imeni Lenina» Station to the «Komintern» Station (its present name is «Alexandrovsky Sud»); at first, the trains went up to Smolenskaya Square, and later, as the metrobridge was built in 1936, to the Kievsky Railway Station. Almost all the stations of the first turn were constructed by the method of excavations when trenches were dug first. The halls of the «Kirovskaya» («Chistye Prudy») and «Dzerzhinskaya» («Lubyanka») metro stations which were laid at a considerable depth due to geological conditions had minimal size of their «initial halls» that were connected to the passenger platforms by side tunnels (the central halls were constructed in the 1960s only). In March 1938, at the second turn stage, the line from the «Kievsky Vokzal» Station (the name at the time) was extended to the Kursky Railway Station. The primary work of the second turn was underway along the line from «Ploshchad Sverdlova» («Teatralnaya») to the settlement of «Sokol» whish was commissioned in September 1938.

From the architectural point of view each station is a real subway palace, a unique specimen of architecture and monumental art. For instance, «Ploshchad Revolutsii» (architect A.N.Dushkin) was decorated with more than 70 bronze sculptures of revolutionary fighters, soldiers, seamen, engineers, students, tractor-drivers, young pioneers – that were supposed «to tell the tale» of the epoch (sculpturer M.G. Manizer). The «Sokol» Station (architects brothers K.N. Yakovlev and Yu.N. Yakovlev) is prominent due to its combination of complex forms with laconic embellishment. The most interesting station is evidently «Kropotkinskaya» (until 1957 it had been called «The Palace of Soviets»). Architects A.N. Dushkin and Ya.G. Likhtenberg paid more attention to the architecture of supporting pillars that look like strict and graceful big torches made of grey-white marble. The playing of light and shadow strips, the restrained spectrum of coloristic solutions make the station's interior inimitably exquisite.

In the ideal case, the specific buildings in the historical part of Moscow were to frame the straight radii of thoroughfares. But in reality, a great number of buildings and ensembles could not be disregarded; they did not fit the straight «rays». For this reason, «the red lines» were more frequently «linked» with the existing pre-revolutionary and Soviet structures. For instance, that was the case with the buildings by I.Zholtovsky, the premises of Moscow University and Manezh in Mokhovaya Street, with the buildings of the former «Petergof» Hotel and the Kremlin Hospital at the beginning of Vozdvizhenka (the hospital's building is a lucky instance of renovating the former one-

Canal Moscow-Volga. Longitudinal section.

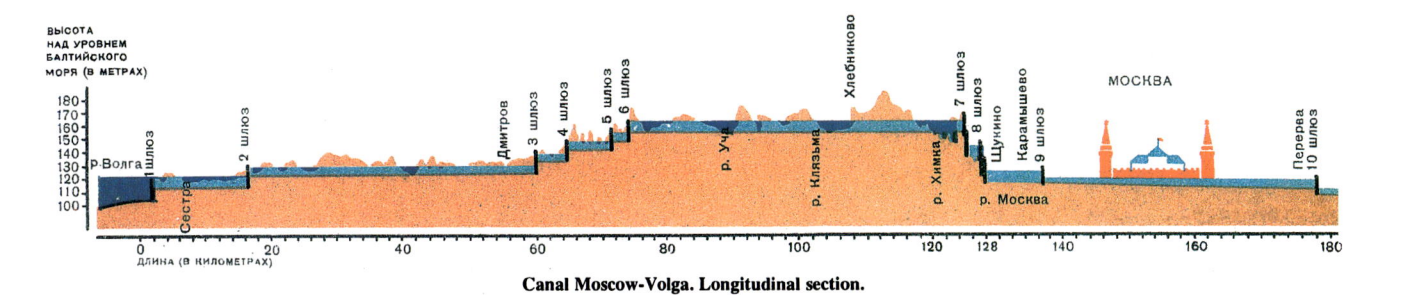

storey structure, with the complete change of style, with building a superstructure and expanding it – architect Goffman). Volkhonka Street was under the threat of complete destruction: according to the B. Iophan project only the Museum of Fine Arts was to remain there, the other territory was meant for organizing «open space» in the vicinity of the Palace of Soviets.

Lubyanskaya Square (Dzerzhinskogo Square) suffered heavy losses. A lengthy span of the Kitay-Gorod wall with Nikolskie Gate was demolished; the same happened to the majestic chapel of St.Panteleimon (the 1880s, architect A.S. Kaminsky) that was located behind the gate inside Kitay-Gorod. It used to be part of the complex of the church in town

Watercourse ring of Moscow. General Plan. 1935.

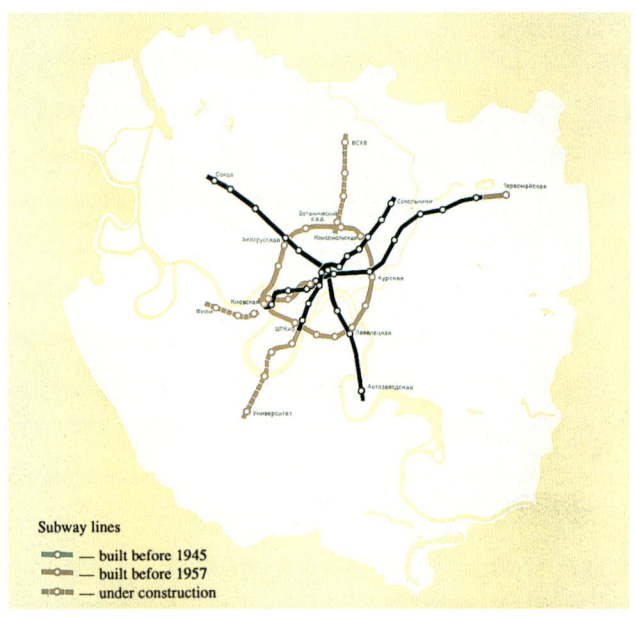

Moscow subway diagram.

K. and Yu. Yakovlev: Subway station «Sokol». Platform Hall. 1938.

of the Russian Afonsky Panteleimonovsky Monastery (at our time the Afonskoye church in town was resurrected at the Cathedral of Nikita the Martyr in Zayauzye). The water-distributing fountain was removed; it used to function after the revolution (sculptures by Vitali were moved to the former tsar's Neskuchny Palace on the Kaluzhskoye Highway). From the first days of the Soviet government, the Lubyanskaya square was favoured by the Extraordinary Commission, then OGPU and NKVD (different names for security or secret police). The main NKVD building on the square, that earlier belonged to the «Rossiya» Insurance Company was repeatedly expanded and renovated. The monument to Vorovsky was erected in the corner of Bolshaya Lubyanka and Kuznetsky Most, at the site of the demolished Introduction (vvedeniya) Cathedral.

The Boulevard Ring and the territory inside it were actively built on at certain sectors: in the vicinity of Arbatskaya Square, on Suvorovsky Boulevard where in 1937 «a house of polar explorers» emerged built for Glavsevmorput (the Chief Department of the Northern Marine Lines) during the polar drifting of the Papanin group (architect Iokheles). In 1936 a house in the style of «Stalin's» Empire was built on Khokhlovskaya square; apart from everything it accomodated a tailor's shop and a privileged-access shop (recently a monument to N.G.Chernyshevsky was erected in front of it). The house on Yauzsky Boulevard became an interesting specimen of the epoch; it was located at the end of Podkolokolny By-Street (1936, architect I.Golosov). The entry arch is decorated with the figures of the worker with a pneumatic pick and a girl with a rifle. The house for creative elite shall also be noted; it is located in Tverskaya Street, 25 (architects A. Burov and B. Blokhin). A good many houses in the centre of Moscow were added storeys. A special trust named «Mosnadstroi» («Moscow's Added Storeys») was even established that conducted this work simultaneously at hundreds of buildings. Moscow was turning into a city with elite residential buildings as related to the rest of the country, with relatively high telephonization and gas-supply rate, with relative abundance of food at shops (other cities and towns were deprived of all this). The image of Moscow was taking shape; it concentrated the potential of the daring and creating epoch, of the epoch of irreconcilable struggle against the «entrenched» class enemies, and preparation for the struggle with the foreign enemies.

The Destiny of Sukhareva Tower

> «It's something awful! Crimson, red,
> Lit by the ray of sunset,
> Turned into a heap of alive wreckage.
> I can still see it the way it was yesterday –
> A proud beauty, a pink tower...»
>   V. Gilyarovsky

For the Sukhareva Tower the year of 1926 began happily: after the renovation an exposition of the Moscow Communal Museum opened here on January 6. The museum's director P.V.Sytin wrote: «The Sukhareva Tower which many Muscovites could not even imagine in the past otherwise than in scaffolding, thus hidden from sight and curiosity, two years ago was freed from that historical scaffolding and is now open in all the beauty of its ancient garments; it is embellished inside, and the Moscow Communal Museum occupies it now».

Its future was also bright – the Mossovet Presidium took a special decision to withdraw the remaining alien services from it and to arrange there a book storage area for the rich library of the museum, its reading and lecturing halls. It was planned to set up «the Museum of the Sukhareva Tower» in one of the premises, while its upper gallery was to serve as an observation site so that the public could enjoy the views of Moscow. «It is planned

A. Dushkin: Subway station «Square of the Revolution». A part of the platform hall. 1937.

to arrange several model public gardens around the tower, – wrote Sytin, – with trees, flower-beds, lawns, children's playing grounds... There is an urgent need to set up the public gardens here, as there are no public gardens nearby where the numerous working population of the Sretensky and Meshchansky Districts could have a rest after daytime work and to breathe relatively fresh air in summer heat... On the other hand, the public gardens will make a wonderful background for demonstrating the architectural merits of the two outstanding monuments of Russian architecture situated here in all their beauty – the Sukhareva Tower and the hospital (named after Sklifosofsky)». In 1926 – 1927 the public gardens were made, and the pictures of the early 1930s show their large, well-kept flower beds.

However, in 1933 a decision was made to demolish the Sukhareva Tower since it interfered with the traffic. Academician I. Fomin and other prominent Soviet architects devise projects of the square planning and convincingly prove that there is a possibility to resolve the problem without destroying the tower. M. Gorky speaks in defense of the Sukhareva Tower. The realization of the decision was somehow postponed.

On September 4, 1933 L. Kaganovich addressed the conference of Moscow communist architects. He interpreted «the protest by the group of old architects against the destruction of the Sukhareva Tower» as an example of «fierce class struggle»: «There is not a single delapidated church about which there are no written protests. It is clear that these protests are caused not by the care about preservation of ancient monuments – they are caused by political motives, they are just trying to reproach the Soviet government with vandalism».

On September 18, Stalin and Voroshilov sent a telegram to Kaganovich: «We have studied the question of the Sukhareva Tower and came to the conclusion that it must be demolished. We suggest that the Sukhareva Tower should be removed and the traffic area expanded. The architects who object to its destruction are blind and lack any perspective».

In April, 1934 the demolition of the Sukhareva Tower was started, and again the most prominent workers of culture K. Yuon, A. Shchusev, A. Efros, I. Fomin, I. Zholtovsky write: «Dear Iosiph Vissarionovich! We address you with alarm and bitterness, since we consider you to be a man of the utmost authority who can stop the act that is being done most obviously in a wrong way...»

This letter was sent on April 17. Stalin responded quickly, five days later, on April 22, 1934: «I have received your letter with the proposal not to destroy the Sukhareva Tower. The decision to destroy the tower was made at its time by the government. I consider this decision to be correct believing that the Soviet people will be able to create more impressive and memorable samples of architectural creativity than the Sukhareva Tower. I regret that despite all my respect for you I don't have a chance in this very case to render you this service. Respectfully Yours – Stalin».

Those days, V.Gilyarovsky wrote to his daughter: «...the magnificent Sukhareva Tower which used to be called the bride of Ivan the Great is being broken... You shouldn't think that it is breaking its word to Ivan the Great – no. It is being actually destroyed».

The demolition of the Sukhareva Tower was admitted to be an error when its ruins were still lying in the middle of the square that soon after that was renamed Kolkhoznaya. But the physical destruction of the monument that embodied spiritual, moral ideas could not destroy the people's memory about it, could not downgrade its influence on the architectural and city-building thought: for more than two centuries it had taken too prominent a place in forming the special appearance of Moscow. Its image is revived in the high-rise buildings of the 1950s. No

Sukhareva Tower. 1930s.

I. Fomin: Project to preserve Sukhareva Tower. 1934.

G. Barkhin: Project to reconstruct Sukhareva Square. 1933.

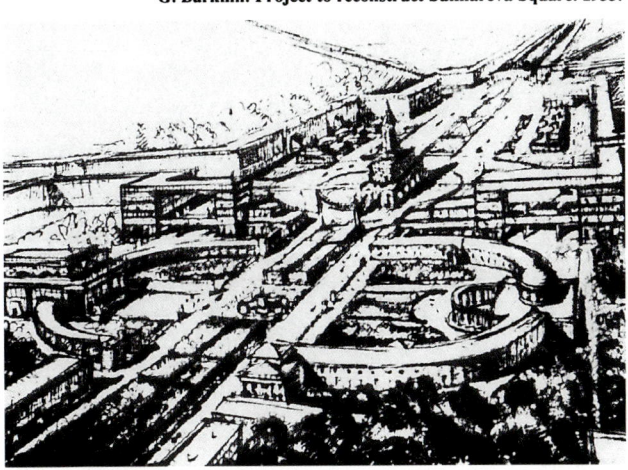

Sukhareva Square. I.Fomin, A. Velikanov, M. Minkus, L. Polyakov: Project of its reconstruction. 1934 – 1935.

matter how much they differ from each other, they represent variants of its silhouette and play a similar city-building role – they organize space around them, act as a reference point for a certain part of the city.

The demolition of the Sukhareva Tower was admitted to be an error. But the admittance of an error entails a moral obligation to correct it in deed. Speaking of destroyed monuments, it is logical and natural to nurture the idea of their reconstruction. This idea, it should be mentioned, is not new to Moscow: say, in the late 18th century, four Kremlin towers and a section of the wall between them were built anew, though they were completely destroyed in the 1770s due to the would-be construction of a new palace in the Kremlin by V. Bazhenov.

The more time elapses from the day when the Sukhareva Tower was destroyed, the clearer it becomes what an important place it occupied in the city's structure; it's clear that nothing can replace it until now.

Dismantling of Sukhareva Tower. 1934.

On May 21, 1980, the «Literaturnaya Gazeta» published a letter by a group of workers of culture and science. Among them there were architect-restorator P. Baranovsky, writers L. Leonov and O. Volkov, artist I. Glazunov, academicians D. Likhachev, P. Petrynov-Sokolov, B. Rybakov. The letter was titled «To Reconstruct the Sukhareva Tower». «Our architects and restorators are sure to be able to raise the spire of the historical building above the city again, – the authors concluded their letter. – We are sure that our appeal will be enthusiastically and widely supported by the Soviet public». After that letter the issue of the Sukhareva Tower reconstruction was discussed in mass media on a wide scale.

In 1982 construction engineer P. Myagkov and architect P. Ragulin, at their own initiative, without any financial rewards, started to work on the project of the Sukhareva Tower reconstruction. Three years later the project was ready. The designers suggested that the tower should be used as the Museum of the Navy and Merchant Marine; the idea was supported by the former Ministry of Merchant Marine. It was ready to participate in financing the work.

The 1984 publication about the project by the above-mentioned enthusiasts heralded a new, more extensive stage of discussing the problem that led to an official competition for an architectural-planning solution of Kolkhoznaya Square with the reconstruction of the Sukhareva Tower.

The first prize was awarded to the project by the Moscow Architectural Institute: according to it the Sukhareva Tower was to be reconstructed at the former site, at its own former foundation; a transportation tunnel was to be laid on both sides of the foundation. Technically it is possible to start the reconstruction work right now, without waiting for the tunnel construction.

Moscow's Municipal Economy in War Years

The image of Moscow as the city-construction site did not change in 1940 and in the first half of 1941. In the pre-war years the main emphasis was placed upon residential construction, since the most powerful industrial complexes and hydrotechnical systems had already been built. The term of «speedy construction» got an official status. The speedy-line method consisted in devising a tough schedule of well-coordinated operation of lifting cranes, concrete-mixing points, storehouses, transportation, and workers «link-ups» (at sectors of the construction work where different stages of the technological cycle take place simultaneously).

In 1940, for the first time, an entire side of a thoroughfare was built – the right side of the Bolshaya Kaluzhskaya Street. Typical houses were constructed here according to the project by A. Mordvinov, G. Golz, D. Chechulin; certain buildings were at a distance from the axis line; there were breaks between houses which made it possible to ensure better illumination of apartments and to grow vegetation inside the yards. The range of brand-new buildings completed immediately before the war included such «individual» objects as the State Lenin Library, a residential house in Bolshaya Polyanka (architect A. Mordvinov) that «opened» the street from downtown, from the newly-built Bolshoi Kamenny and Maly Kamenny Bridges. In spring 1941 Moscow architects moved to the new building of the House of Architects in Granatny Bystreet whose facade was created by A. Burov on the motifs of «semi-gothics – semi-renaissance». Simultaneously the finishing work of the assembly-block house by Burov was underway in the Leningradskoye Highway (today it is Leningradsky Avenue, 25). More and more frequently monumental motifs were used in the projects of public and residential buildings initiated by I. Zholtovsky in his residential «palazzo» in Mokhovaya Street and «tested» on the VSKhV – the All-Union Exhibition of the National Economy Achievements – pavilions.

Since 1940 the structures of the Palace of Soviets framework started to be erected (the mightiest ferro-concrete rings of the foundation had been mounted on rocky soil at the depth of 20 metres since 1937). «The storming of the sky» was going on only for a short period – war interfered with it. The construction of the colossal building in Zaryadye was approximately at the same stage – though it did not any longer belong to the Narkomat (Ministry) of Heavy Industry (it was decided to construct the latter on the site of GUM), but to the Second House of the Sovnarkom (Council of Ministers). The project by V.A. Vesnin and A.A. Vesnin resembled the then traditional scheme of administartive buildings that had been initially realized in the building of the Council of Labour and Defence in Okhotny Ryad: the stepped silhouette of facades, several storey high pilasters, strict symmetry, state emblems on the pediment and towers with flags. The complex in Zaryadye was to become unique in its size; still the Vesnin brothers were «merciful» to the Kremlin: from the riverside the building in its middle section had only 17 storeys – a bit lower than the previously projected building of Narkomtyazhprom; what's more, even the flag-post of the main facade did not surpass the height of the Spasskaya Tower spire.

On December 18, 1940 Hitler signed «Order Number 21» – «Operation «Barbarossa» – attack against the Soviet Union». As far back as in 1937, a new structure was formed – the Moscow Local Air Defence Department. Numerous appropriate services were established on the basis of Mossovet departments and sections; they were to start working in case mobilization was announced. Numberless exercises that were held in districts involved more than 500,000 people and gave priceless experience that in real combat conditions saved thousands of lifes and hundreds of buildings from perishing.

In September, 1939 the USSR Supreme Council adopted the law «On Universal Military Duty» according to which the duration of active duty in the army was increased to three years, whille in the Navy it was five years. An army corps was formed to provide air defence of Moscow that included antiaircraft artillery and machinegun units, barrier baloon units, searchlights, air surveillance and signal units (radars were not used at the time).

Since June, 1941 the entire communal life of Moscow was organized according to the Mobilization Plan: the plants and factories were starting to manufacture military equipment, many metro stations were equipped as air raid shelters, all the automobiles of Moscow were mobilized.

The command assigned six air fighter regiments to defend Moscow (more than 300 crews for daytime sorties, and about 100 – for night-time). The «Kauchuk» Plant and the «Krasnaya Roza» Factory were urgently organizing the manufacturing of air barrier baloons which were lifted to the sky at night-time.

Moscow architects were designing projects of camouflage and concealment for major buildings, constructions and ensembles, for instance, Red Square. They adapted various underground premises for air raid shelters, worked at destroyed objects. On July 22, more than 250 bombers took part in the first German air raid; they were flying at an altitude of 5,000 – 6,000 metres. The raid cost the fascist Air Force 22 downed aircraft; only individual planes managed to reach the target.

The raids took place almost every night, and the penetrating aircraft were literally pouring Moscow with incendiary bombs. Thanks to skilful and staunch air defence – both army and local – Moscow's losses during the raids were not catastrophic. The system of centralised blackout had been organized a few months before the outbreak of hostilities; when needed, the city became dark within 30 seconds. But even the bombs that were dropped at random, at times, caused considerable damage – mainly to residential areas. The Book Chamber was burnt due to a direct hit – it was located in a magnificent monument of Russian classicism – the former Gagarin house on Novinsky Boulevard. The Vakhtangov Theatre in Arbat was destroyed completely, the Bolshoi Theatre was damaged a lot. During one of the first raids a bomb penetrated through several floors of a publishing house in Chistye Prudy where a regular issue of the newspaper «Moscow Bolshevik» (later – «Moscow Pravda») was being printed, and got caught in a printing machine. There was no explosion, and soon after the removal of the bomb work continued. There were some tragic occasions when destroyed German aircraft fell onto residential areas. During one of the first raids the building of the Museum of Fine Arts was hit by a series of incendiary bombs. Selfless fire-fighters crawling along the eaves of the glass roof above the storming flames (the glass was broken) succeeded in extinguishing the fire quickly.

Hitler planned to destroy Moscow completely; he regarded it as a symbol of Russian culture and spirit. He planned to flood it so that «it would perish from sight of the civilized mankind». But Moscow kept on living. Even during the highly dangerous periods the municipal economy worked smoothly. Streets were being repaired, new tram and trolley-bus lines were being laid (the buses were mobilized), the gas supply, waterpipe and other systems were operating faultlessly. Cargo trams and platforms were built in great numbers; annually they carried millions tons of cargoes.

V. Shchuko, V. Gelfreikh: The State Library of the USSR named after V.I. Lenin. 1939.

Ack-ack battery on the square near the All-Union Exhibition of Economic Achievements. 1941.

Barrage balloons over Moscow. 1941.

The construction work of the Moscow metro was going on. On January 1, 1943 a new sector of the Zamoskvoretsko-Tverskaya Line was commissioned between the stations of «Paveletskaya» and «Avtozavodskaya». On January 18, 1944 a sector of Arbatsko-Pokrovskaya Line was commissioned from the Kursky Railway Station to Izmailovo.

Housing construction was renewed in Moscow since the summer of 1944. There were not enough materials and mechanisms for large-scale work; for this reason, two or three-storey houses were mainly built at the city's outskirts. Until now there are many houses of the kind in a number of Izmailovo streets, at the beginning of the Khoroshevskoye Highway, in Perovo and in other districts.

The Wartime Moscow

We shall not waver in combat
For our capital,
We cherish our dear Moscow.
As an impenetrable wall,
By the steel defence
We'll destroy, we'll crush the enemy!

It is so beautiful, we are so used to its beauty that at times fail to notice it. But try to leave it for half a year, for a month, for a week, and it will grow in your memory in the morning, at daytime, in the evening. It's magnificent, unusual, it's almost a fairy tale.

The cold pink dawn rises behind the Kremlin, over its walls merlons and conical spiers of its towers. The dark November water is noiselessly flowing under high bridges – the Moskvoretsky, Kamenny, Krymsky, Borodinsky ones. If you stop on the Borodinsky Bridge, whose heavy sections are crowned with granite emblems of wartime glory, 100 miles behind you there lies the Borodinskoye Field, and ahead is the Kremlin. From there you can view Moscow, its empty morning embankments; behind the river curve there rise the airy silver chains of the Krymsky Bridge...

German soldiers were reading in the «Fölkischer Beobakhter»: «Moscow in on fire, – it was written there, – it's burning from five directions». Lean German women were listening to the German radio: «We have bombed Moscow, – it cried, – we have done it! What is still left there will soon belong to us». In 20 languages, in German and French, Dutch and Polish, in Italian and Finnish, in Romanian and Hungarian, the triumphant bare-faced radio was shouting, was roaring over Europe that was lying flat on its back. In 20 languages Moscow was said to be burning, Moscow was being destroyed, Moscow was about to fall to the Germans.

But a little more than a year later we enter the Vorobievy Hills along a strictly straight path, like a ruler, with yellow falling leaves, and look at Moscow from above. It's still beautiful, it's still great. The same pink dawn is still rising above its gates. And the old bronze of the domes is still shining in the rays of the rising sun, and the chimes are still sounding on the Spasskaya Tower in their heavy, thick voice. Muscovites, no matter where your wartime destiny sends you, check your watches, and let the long Spasskaya Tower chimes sound in your ears for a minute, let Moscow open before your eyes the way it is today, – working, strong, ready to resist the aggressor. The city that resembles a Russian is as invincible as a Russian, a Soviet Man is.

If you have a free hour, if you came on mission from the frontline, from far-away Karelia or from the Northern Caucasus, from Stalingrad or from Staraya Russa, – take a walk along the streets of your city at dawn, you, a Muscovite from the frontline. Do you remember how other Muscovites came to the frontline from Moscow in July, October, December last year? Do you remember how we worried and asked them: «Well, how is it? Is it still there?» And they used to answer: «It's safe and sound!» Yes, it's there, and it's as beautiful, as it was on the day when you left it.

The monument to Timiryazev shaken by an explosion is again at its proper place, and only the different shades of asphalt in the streets can indicate the places where there were craters. Yes, it's intact! You can walk in the streets for hours and you won't notice any traces of bombing raids, of a siege. Only at times with a share of surprise will your absent-minded eye notice an empty asphalted site somewhere in Balchug or in the Garden Ring, and something will seem wrong to you. Yes, there used to be a house here. A terrible burst roared here, hundreds of hands worked here, and soon an even asphalted site occupied the place where the house stood some time before, and where we are sure to build a new one some time later. But when you look at new houses, you will never believe that high-explosive bombs burst next to them or inside them, that incendiary bombs blazed up on their roofs, that fire was raging here, and fire-fighters, risking their lives, were climbing up the squeaking ladders. The houses stand the way you left them when you went to the frontline...

The first days of the war were the days of fierce battles and heavy losses, especially at the Western Front, the closest to Moscow. Not a single bomb was dropped on Moscow yet. But Minsk was in flames, Smolensk was on fire, Dorogobuzh was blazing. Still, everywhere the fighting was for Moscow proper, for Moscow first of all. The German tanks were crawling to Moscow, their armored personnel carriers moved there, motor-cyclists rolled over to Moscow, infantry walked there. But the Red Army soldiers, who were dying near the railway station in Smolensk, were dying for Moscow. At the river crossing on Berezina our guns were firing for the sake of Moscow. The regiments that were defending Mogilev to the last cartridge were fighting for Moscow.

Columns of people dressed in semi-military, semi-civilian clothes were forming on the road that led from Moscow westwards. They were singing «Internationale», they were singing «Be Brave, Comrades, and Walk in Step», they were singing «Along Valleys and Hills», they were singing all the songs that were appropriate to sing, that were calling them to fight, that inspired courage in their hearts. The first bombing raids began in late July. The Muscovites who had already sent their best sons to the front started fighting the Germans inside the city. At nighttime, hundreds of searchlights crossed their rays in the black sky. The muffled bomb explosions shook the streets. Fires started here and there. It was real fighting, like on the frontline, fighting to the death, fighting for their native city, and we had to be the winner.

Day and night the guns on duty were ready to open fire instantly. Day and night people did not sleep, they were staring into the sky with their red sleepless eyes. The fire brigades localized and extinguished dozens of simultaneous fires.

The Germans dropped a whole series of bombs on the area where there were principal stocks of bread for entire Moscow. One of the grain elevators caught fire. The emergency brigade of fire-fighters under the command of Pavlov rushed to the site. The raid still continued. The German planes descended and tried to interfere with the fire fighting, their machineguns were shooting at the area. The elevator was burning like a huge pillar. The heat was so high that it seemed that all the surrounding storehouses would catch fire too. Tremendous upward thrust developed inside the huge pipe of the elevator. The temperature around the site was so high that people's clothes started burning all at once. Hoses were laid to the fire site, but they started burning before water was supplied to them. Still, it was necessary to put out the fire, it had to be done at all costs. And the fire-fighters went forward, into the fire, they unrolled their hoses. Gradually, step by step, they filled the hoses with water, and the operator who was walking behind was pouring water on the operator who was ahead in order to extinguish fire that appeared on his clothes.

The whole Moscow was working next to the fire-fighters. Those were real combat operations. The people who at the peacetime attended the air defence clubs, studied there, saved every free hour for the purpose, during the war were becoming daily heroes – housewives and workers, old men and youngsters.

Now you can not find any trace of the wartime bombing raids or destructions, but we do not owe it to the Germans. They did their best to destroy Moscow and to burn it. They were trying really hard. If our air defence troops hadn't protected the city in numerous rings, with walls of fire barrages, if our pilots hadn't met the Germans far away from Moscow dissipating and destroying them, if the Muscovites hadn't perceived Moscow as their frontline, if they hadn't fought bravely and fearlessly – then Moscow would have been a black site of fire now.

War brings about new professions. The air raids against Moscow also produced a new profession. A battalion appeared in Moscow after the first air raids whose commander was Captain Pedaev, – the battalion that was responsible for discharging unexploded bombs. This profession is both dangerous and challenging, it required courage, accuracy and cold blood.

N. Dolgorukov: Poster. 1934.

The military parade on Red Square of November 7, 1941.

At times the unexploded bombs weighed 1,000 kilograms. One of the bombs fell in Tverskaya Street, next to the «Nationale» Hotel. It penetrated into the ground to the depth of 8.5 metres.

The Muscovites who stayed in Moscow were defending the city inside it at the very time when the Muscovites who went to the frontline were fighting for it at all the fronts.

In October, having gathered forces for a powerful strike, the Germans rushed to Moscow. Fighting was approaching Moscow – it raged at a distance of 200 kilometres, 150, 120, 90.

Plants, ministries, factories, governmental departments were evacuated from it. All the country's huge administrative structures could not stay in close vicinity to the enemy. But this did not in any case mean that those who were defending Moscow at least for a moment considered an opportunity of surrendering it to the enemy. While the trains with machines from the plants, with qualified workers, with ministries, with everything that was supposed to be in the rear and that was not particularly crucial for the defence of the capital were moving eastwards, at the same time Moscow, having mobilized all its forces, was sending westwards replacements, combat materiel, everything that was needed for defence.

The German offensive continued. New reserves had to be committed in order to reinforce our troops. More and more new units were formed in Moscow, they were Moscow units.

The 4th Moscow Volunteer Division was committed into action near Borovsk, with the mission to counter an enemy penetration. The men were not properly trained, they did not have enough assault rifles, combat materiel, but they fought selflessly.

Throughout October and November the Germans were approaching Moscow closer and closer. Their rout near Moscow began on December 5, when our troops launched a counteroffensive. The question of the future victory was solved when the whole country learnt that the State Committee for Defence headed by Stalin stayed in Moscow. The question of the future victory was solved most of all on November 6 and November 7, when according to great Soviet traditions, a special session of the Moscow Council was held, and a parade was staged on Red Square. Stalin attended both events and addressed their participants.

At the time the Germans were at Moscow's gate, somewhere they approached it to 60 – 70 kilometres. The danger was great and menacing. But it was for the reason that the danger was so great, that the parade and the Stalin's words carried great strength, confidence in the future victory, such high and calm courage that on the day every Soviet citizen on the frontline or in the rear, no matter where he or she happened to be, deep in his heart felt that Moscow will never surrender, that the final victory will be ours.

The air raids against the city continued day and night. The Germans continued seizing new villages and settlements. Their armour penetrated here and there. Tens of thousands of Moscow women were digging fortifications, trenches, tank ditches at the approaches to Moscow. They worked non-stop, in the dirt, in rainy weather, in the cold. They worked in the same clothes they wore in Moscow streets. It was cold and uncomfortable in Moscow, there was no firewood because every railway carriage that arrived from the east was loaded with weapons, and weapons only. The population number decreased. Some people went to the front, others – to defensive work. But those who stayed in Moscow worked for 3 – 4 people. It seemed that the city was on active military duty. People slept at their plants, without taking off their clothes, during 2 or 3 hours a night. The frontline was so close that newspaper correspondents had enough time to travel to the frontline and back two times a day bringing materials for the next issue. All Moscow's primary war industries were evacuated to the rear. But the Muscovites faced the task to continue manufacturing arms inside Moscow. So the Muscovites started producing weapons for troops who were fighting near Moscow at all minor workshops, at all the remaining plants. Where primus stoves had been produced before, hand grenades were manufactured now. Where household goods had been made, fuses and primers were manufactured now. The plant that earlier had produced calculating machines was the first in Moscow to produce assault rifles, and by November 7 the first lots of PPSh's (pistol-machineguns) had been manufactured as a gift to the 24th anniversary of the October Revolution. Thousands of qualified workers were evacuated to the rear. There were very few of them left in Moscow. But they were assisted by housewives, wives of the soldiers fighting on the frontline, youngsters, schoolchildren.

On those days Moscow was quiet and strict. The closer the Germans came to Moscow, the closer was the beginning of December, the more alarming it was supposed to watch the decreasing distance between Moscow and the Germans. To the contrary, the Muscovites turned more and more composed and confident. The more fiercely they were fighting at the front, the harder they worked in Moscow. The capital of the great people was displaying great examples of heroism.

The reduced divisions of Moscow defenders were fighting fearlessly. If the Germans seized some village or a new area, on those days it meant only one thing – there was not a single alive defender at the site.

Dozens of divisions and armoured brigades were hidden somewhere in endless forests of the Moscow Region, somewhere close to the frontline. These divisions and brigades were like a heavy punishing sword that Stalin had raised above the Germans head. Meanwhile the Germans were appointing logistics officers responsible for accomodating the troops in Moscow's warm houses. By December 4 the steel spring had been compressed to the limit. And on December 5 all the reserves accumulated near Moscow, everything that was thoroughly, with iron self-control, prepared for the strike, all the personnel, all the artillery, all the tanks, everything that according to Stalin's strategic plan had been assembled near Moscow and behind it to compose a huge crushing fist – all this struck the Germans. The spring had been compressed to the limit, and it straightened with tremendous force. The word that the whole country had been waiting with bated breath – the word of «offensive» – became a reality. Our armed forces launched an offensive near Moscow. The names of Moscow Region villages, settlements, towns began to be mentioned in the official reports in the reverse order. In severe frosts, on the snow, on the ice, in snowstorms the army was advancing. It was the beginning of the immense and great event that was later called the Winter Rout of the Germans near Moscow.[33]

Wonders of Kazan and Tikhvin Icons of Our Lady

When the Great Patriotic War started Patriarch Antiokhiysky Alexander III appealed to the Christians of the entire world to render prayer and material assistance to Russia. At the time, the number of our country's true friends was quite

M. Khmelko: The Triumph of the Victorious Native Land.

low. In the past there used to be great prayers in Russia, such as the celibate priest Serafim Vyritsky. For a thousand days and nights he had been praying for the salvation of our country and the people of Russia during the hardest years when enemies were attacking the country. Like in 1612, God's Providence chose a friend and prayer for Russia from a brotherly church – Metropolitan of the Lebanon Mountains Ilia (Patriarch Antiokhiysky) who was commissioned to manifest God's will and to define the destiny of the country and of the peole of Russia. He was aware of the fact what Russia meant for the world; he knew it, and for this reason he had always been praying for the salvation of the country of Russia, for the enlightment of its people. After the appeal of Alexander III Metropolitan Ilia started to pray even harder, with his whole heart for Russia's salvation from perishing, from enemy's invasion. He decided to go into retreat and to plead Our Lady to disclose it to him what can save Russia. He descended into a stone cellar where not a single sound from the earth could reach, where there was nothing but the Icon of Our Lady. The Metropolitan locked himself there, did not eat any food, did not sleep, but only prayed on his knees in front of the Icon of Our Lady with an icon-lamp. Every morning the metropolitan was brought reports from the frontline about the number of those slain and about where the enemy had advanced. After three days and nights of his vigil he saw in a fire pillar Our Lady in Person who announced that he was chosen, as a true prayer for and a friend of Russia to convey God's Definition to the country and the people of Russia. If everything that was defined is not realised, Russia will perish:

«Cathedrals, monasteries, ecclesiastical academies and theological seminaries shall be open all over the country. Priests shall be returned from the frontline and prisons, and shall resume their services. Now the surrender of Leningrad is being prepared – it's impossible to surrender it. Let them take out, – She uttered, – the Wonder-Working Icon of Our Lady of Kazan and carry it around the city in a religious procession, then no enemy will step on its sacred land. This is a selected city. It is necessary to hold a service before the Kazan Icon in Moscow; then it must be in Stalingrad which can not be surrendered to the enemy either. The Kazan Icon shall proceed together with the troops to the Russian border. When the war is over, Metropolitan Ilia shall come to Russia and tell the truth about how it was saved».

The Metropolitan got in touch with representatives of the Russian church, with the Soviet government and conveyed everything that had been said to them. The letters and telegrammes sent by Metropolitam Ilia to Moscow are still kept in archives.

Stalin invited Metropolitan Leningradsky Alexei (Simansky), the Acting Patriarch Metropolitan Sergiy (Stragorodsky) and promised them to fulfill everything that had been conveyed through Metropolitan Ilia, since he saw no other opportunity to save the situation. Everything happened the way it had been forecast. There were no forces to stop the enemy. Famine was terrible, thousands of people were dying daily. The Kazan Icon of Our Lady was taken out of the Vladimir Cathedral, it was carried in a religious procession around Leningrad – and the city was saved. Many people still fail to understand what helped Leningrad to survive. Practically, the city did not receive any assistance: what was brought was a drop in the sea. Still, the city survived. The words that Consecrator Mitrofan (Voronezhsky) said to Peter the Great were confirmed once again. They said that the city of the Holy Apostle Peter had been selected by Our Lady Herself, and while the Icon of Kazan is inside the city, and there are people who pray, the enemy can not enter the city. That's why Leningrad inhabitants revere the Kazan Icon of Our Lady so much. All the time that has passed from the city's foundation it had been its Patroness, as well as the Patroness of whole Russia. It is interesting that the Leningrad blockade was lifted on the day on celebrating the Holy Apostle-Equal Nina, the Enlighter of Georgia. After Leningrad the icon began its tour of Russia. Moscow was saved through a wonder too. The rout of the Germans near Moscow is a real wonder that happened thanks to prayers and patronage of Our Lady. The Germans ran away in panic driven by fear, left their equipment which was lying on the roads, and none of the German or Soviet generals could understand why it had happened. The Volokolamskoye Highway was free, and nothing prevented the Germans from entering Moscow. (According to a Moscow tale, the Wonder-Working Icon of Our Lady of Tikhvin from the Tikhon Cathedral in Alexeevskoye was carried in a plane around Moscow. The capital was saved, and on December 9, 1941, the town of Tikhvin was liberated. It's possible to recollect earlier facts of the Patronage of Our Lady for Russia. On the day when the Icon of Our Lady of Vladimir was celebrated

Icon of Our Lady of Tikhvin.

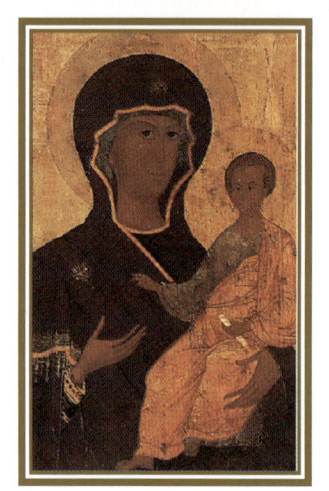

Icon of Our Lady of Smolensk.

V.V. Shilov: Patriarch Sergii.

Icon of Our Lady of Kazan.

Iberian Icon of Our Lady.

Tamerlane turned back home from Russia (1395); on the same day the famous Borodino Battle took place. The Kulikovskaya Battle took place on the Birthday of Our Lady, and the last enemy soldier left our Fatherland on Christmas in 1812).

Later, the Kazan Icon was taken to Stalingrad. Continuous service was held in front of it – public prayers, special prayers for the dead soldiers. The icon stood among our troops on the right bank of the Volga, and the Germans were not able to cross the river, no matter how hard they tried. There was a moment when the city's defenders stayed on a tiny spot near the Volga, but the Germans failed to push our warriors back, because the Icon of Our Lady was standing there (the so-called «Malaya Zemlya»).

The famous Battle of Stalingrad began with a public prayer in front of this icon, and only after that a signal was given to attack. (Archimandrite Ioann (Razumov), the Private Secretary of the Acting Patriarch Metropolitan Sergiy (Stragorodsky), recollected: «On the day of Epiphany, on January 19, Metropolitan Sergiy headed the religious procession to Iordan. Those were the days of decisive fighting for Stalingrad, and the Metroplitan was praying for the victory of Russian warriors especially vivaciously. Sudden illness forced him to go to bed. On the night to February 2, 1943 the Metropolitan overcame his illness and asked his secretary to help him rise from bed. Having risen, he bowed three times with an obvious effort, sending his thanks to God. When the secretary helped him go to bed once again, Metropolitan Sergiy said: «God of warriors, strong in battle, has defeated those who rose against us. God bless His men in peace! Might this beginning be a good ending». (In the morning the radio broadcast news about the rout of German troops near Stalingrad). The icon was brought to the most difficult sectors of the front where public services were held, soldiers were sprinkled with holy water. How touched and cheerful looked many of those who were there!

20,000 cathedrals of the Russian Orthodox Church were opened at the time. The whole Russia was praying then! Even Joseph Stalin did pray – there is evidence of it. B.M.Shaposhnikov, a former tsarist general, who did not try to conceal his religious beliefs, used to talk with Stalin for hours, and all his advice was taken (for instance, to dress troops in the old-time military uniform with shoulder boards). A.V. Vassilevsky, who was appointed the Chief of the General Staff at B.M. Shaposhnikov's recommendation as his replacement, was the son of a priest, and his father was still alive.

The Church blessed the Patriotic War of the Russian People, and this Blessing was approved in heavens. Russia's spirit got ablaze from the Throne of Our Lord! Many field officers, to say nothing of soldiers, were praying before fighting. Many commanders, including Marshal Zhukov himself, used to say before fighting: «God Bless us!» One officer, who was doing air liaison duty during combat sorties used to say that he frequently heard in his earphones how pilots of burning aircraft were shouting: «My Lord! Take my soul in peace!..»

At the same time theological seminaries and academies were opened, the Troitse-Sergieva Lavra, Kievo-Pecherskaya Lavra and numerous monasteries were revived. It was decided to carry the relic of Consecrator Alexy, the Metropolitan of Moscow and of the Whole Russia, to the Bogoyavlensky Cathedral, where the very Wonder-Working Icon of Our Lady of Kazan, that was with the voluntary corps in 1612, had been staying throughout the war. The time came to restore religion in the Russian Land, as our saints forecast.

In 1947 Stalin fulfilled his promise, and in October invited Metropolitan Ilia to Russia. He was afraid not to obey the instructions of Our Lady, since every prophecy of hers that had been conveyed by the Metropolitan of the Lebanon came true. Before the guest arrived, Stalin had summoned Metropolitan Alexy, who had become Patriarch by that time, and wondered: «How can the Russian church thank Metropolitan Ilia?» The Patriarch proposed to present the metropolitan of the Lebanon with the Icon of Our Lady of Kazan (a copy), a cross with preciuos stones and a panagia decorated with precious stones from every region of the country, so that the whole Russia could learn about this present. At Stalin's instruction, the most skilful jewellers made the panagia and the cross.

So Metropolitan Ilia arrived in Moscow and was met with an official ceremony. During the welcome ceremony he was presented the icon, the cross and the panagia. He was so touched! He said, that day and night he had been praying for Russia's salvation. «I am happy, – the Metroplotan said, – that I was a witness of restoration of the Orthodox Denomination in Holy Russia. I was a witness that Our Lord and Our Lady did not forget your country, but on the contrary gave it a special Blessing. I am really grateful to receive the gifts of the whole Russian land as a memento of the country and the people I love. I wish you, my dear, and I hope – as Reverend Serafim Sarovsky said – to sing in the middle of summer: «Christ has Risen!» That will be an immense joy all over the great land!»

At the same time the government awarded him with the Stalin's prize for his assistance to our country during the Great Patriotic War. The Metropolitan rejected the Prize saying that a monk needed no money. «Let it be spent on the needs of your country. Wc decided to donate to your country 200,000 dollars to help children-orphans whose parents were slain at war», – said Metropolitan Ilia.

...So the Icon of Our Lady of Kazan is still staying in the city that had survived the siege, with a nimbus of the Metropolitan of the Lebanon Mountains Ilia, that was presented to Our Lady to thank her for the salvation of Russia in 1941 – 1945. And today, the wonder-working icons of Our Lady and Our Patroness are still protecting the Russian Land. They are the Tikhvin Icon that is protecting and blessing the northern lands; the Iverskaya Icon that is protecting and blessing the lower lands. The Pochaevskaya and Smolenskaya Icons are protecting the Russian Land from the west. In the east, shining with rays of bliss to the end of our land, the Icon of Our Lady of Kazan is protecting and blessing Russia. In the central part of the country the Icon of Our Lady of Vladimir is radiant; it was painted by Evangelist Lukas on the board of the table where the Last Supper took place – the first holy communion that signalled the beginning of the mankind's salvation on the Blood of Our Lord, the beginning of new life. Amen[34].

The 1951 General Plan and its Implementation

Moscow still remained the biggest industrial centre of the country. «The Five-Year Plan of Reconstruction and Development of the USSR National Economy for 1946 – 1950» envisaged a great increase in Moscow's industrial output. It set serious goals in manufacturing construction equipment and developing construction industry. In the post-war years, thousands of warriors came to stay in Moscow, the young people who turned up from all over the country arrived at construction sites; still, the lack of manpower became chronic.

In the late 40s, large municipal districts started growing again; each of them inevitably affected the solution of city problems in general. The comprehensive city-building approach served as a basis for the decision made in 1947, when the 800-anniversary of the perennial capital was celebrated, concerning the construction of high-rise buildings. The highrise vertical structures were supposed to restore the perception of Moscow as a single whole; this perception was almost lost as the average buildings «grew» in scope, and many sad losses became a fact of life.

A series of high-rise buildings, «marking» the trace of the Garden Ring were sort of fixing the centre of the historical city. Other buildings of the type set directions of the capital's development to the south-west and along the Mozhaiskoye Highway. In 1950, when the construction of the high-rise

M. Posokhin, A. Mndoyants: High-rise building on the Square of Vosstanya (of the Uprising). 1948 – 1954.

D. Chechulin (architect), I. Tigranov (engineer): Administrative high-rise building in

buildings reached the stage of general «correlation» of their actual silhouettes Stalin made a decision to complete them with spires carrying similarly looking emblems (stars in various ornamentation).

The eight high-rise buildings were supposed to comprise an integral spatial ensemble together with the Palace of Soviets. However, its construction was postponed for several years, and the Department of the Palace Construction that had the status of a ministry started to build a grandiose ensemble of Moscow State University named after M.V. Lomonosov in the Lenin Hills, and in 1953 the university enrolled first students.

The entire project of the Zaryadye complex was redesigned in the same style of high-rise buildings with spire-like tops. Instead of the flat building designed by the Vesnin brothers that was to occupy a whole city block, in 1950 it was decided to build a stepped structure on the same foundation; its silhouette was to resemble «the Leningradskaya Hotel». The lower tier six-storey high looked form above like a four-pointed star, while the central part rose to 32 storeys. Ironically, this project «lived» only several years too, and remained on paper.

In the late 1940s – early 1950s the construction rate grew up sharply. The housing crisis that particularly aggravated due to the war required cardinal decisions. As to their rate and scale, the low-storey residential construction in the area of Peschanye Streets, at the beginning of the Khoroshevskoye Highway, in Izmailovo did not differ much from the restoration work in many destroyed cities and towns of Russia. In 1950, the Moscow Party Committee – VKP(b) – organized several successive conferences of builders, architects, workers of construction materials industry. The participants criticized the dissipation of materials and assets in case of low-storey construction, that caused the lengthening of communications and, consequently, higher cost of residential buildings. The problem of an integral ensemble was put forward again and again. The last pre-war ensemble of buildings on the even side of the Bolshaya Kaluzhskaya Street (the present Lenin Avenue) was criticized particularly intensely due to the fact that the rear facades of the houses were not embellished at all from the architectural standpoint, though they faced the parade Gorky Park and the Neskuchny Garden that became exceptionally popular with Muscovites.

In January 1951, the Moscow Party Committee held a scientific-technical conference on residential and administrative construction that took a decision to accelerate the transition to

Architect: D. Chechulin, A. Rostovsky: High-rise building in Kotelnicheskaya Embankment. 1952.

Zaryadie. Project. 1947 – 1949.

multi-storey ensemble construction mainly along thoroughfares that already had necessary engineer networks. Preference was given to large-panel construction.

The first experimental large-panel house was built in Sokolinaya Gora in 1947 according to the project by a workshop of the Academy of Architecture. A year later, a series of similar houses was built in the Khoroshevskoye Highway (close to present day metro station «Polezhaevskaya»). Another interesting experiment was the project of the framework-panel 8-storey building in Skakovaya Street (1952). Houses with walls of ceramic bricks were modifications of this type; they appeared in the 1st Khoroshcvskaya (Kuusinena) Street and in Levitana Street. Further experiments were aimed at creating frameless large-panel houses: the first 8-storey house was built in Levitana Street in 1951 (the «Sokol» district).

The General Plan for 1951 – 1960, approved by the government in February, 1952, was basically oriented at official «triumphant» architecture. Despite all kinds of shortages, the nation lived through the glory of Great Victory. The newly-constructed metro stations, the high-rise buidings were all monuments to the Victory; they created a new system of dominants, that in the city-building sense were in a way substituting for the lost or screened

Architects: L.Rudnev, S. Chernyshov, P. Abrosimov, A. Khryakov. Engineer V. Nasonov. Sculptor N. Tomskii. The Lomonosov Moscow State University in Lininskie Hills. 1949 – 1953 гг.

S. Andreyevsky, T. Makarevich: Surface pavilion of «Smolenskaya» subway station. Project. 1934 – 1935.

A. Dushkin, B. Mezentsev (architects), V. Abramov (engineer): High-rise building at Red Gates site. 1948 – 1953.

A. Dushkin, B. Mezentsev: High-rise building at the Red Gates site. 1948 – 1953.

Pavilion «Mechanization».

Pavilion of the Belorussian SSR.

Pavilion of the RSFSR.

Pavilion of the Georgian SSR.

Pavilion of the Ukrainian SSR.

Pavilion of the Uzbek SSR.

All-Union Agricultural Exhibition. 1953.

by new construction sites church domes and spires so typical of Moscow. The clasic heritage was being conquered; it introduced certain «tones» in the new period of Moscow architecture. The high-rise dominants with «a narrowing silhouette» were constructed along major city-forming thoroughfares more and more frequently. The large-scale ensemble of the type was to be built at the junction of the Leningradskoye and Volokolamskoye Highways according to the project of K. Alabyan and V. Petrov. The grandiose complex of the «Gidroproekt» Institute reached the square of the junction by its semi-circular 14-storey-high facade. It was crowned with a multi-metre figure that served as a lighthouse. The project was not realized.

The construction of «water rings» around the central part of Moscow envisaged by the 1935 General Plan was postponed for an indefinite period. Only the Likhoborsky Irrigational Canal was constructed; it supplied self-flowing water from the Khimkinskoye Reservoir to the Likhoborka-River and further on to the Yauza. The development of embankments as principal city freeways stipulated by the previous General Plan was continued. According to a common project it was planned to build up the Krasnokholmskaya, Krutitskaya, Simonova Embankments thus forming a park next to the Novo-Spassky Monastery, and large public gardens near the Krutiskoye Church-in-Town and the remnants of the Simonov Monastery. Like a number of other projects, this project was implemented only in part: the residential houses were built near the Novo-Spassky Monastery and in the Krasnokholmskaya Embankment. The Frunzenskaya Embankment was completed to a greater extent (architects Ya. Belopolsky, E. Stamo, and others). According to the project it was planned to build another bridge across the Moskva-River starting at the 1st Frunzenskaya street (the Khamovnichesky Rampart).

The acceleration of the housing construction rate was a top-priority issue in the 1951 General Plan; according to the governmental directive it was planned to commission 1,000,000 square metres annually.

The All-Union Agricultural Exhibition (VSKhV)

The All-Union Agricultural Exhibition that first opened in August, 1939 became extremely popular even during the short pre-war period. It was a kind of exemplary «world of abundance» whose image was linked to «the most sophisticated» ideology. The tiny paradise on the earth was forgotten for the time of the Great Patriotic War. After the war, when the nation became the main director on the stage of world policy, the former exhibition could not satisfy the country. A decision was made to reestablish the VSKhV but in immeasurably more luxurious architectural forms, and it was to become immensely richer in every respect possible. Its parade function became the leading factor in both – its general compositional structure and in individual ensembles.

The territory was increased to 207 hectares due to demoliton of the village of Alexeevskoye and irrigation of the surrounding area. The very concept of the exhibition did not change a lot. The pavillions, as it was before, were divided into groups according to the territorial and industrial branch principles; they occupied tens of hectares. By the moment of its opening in 1954, the VSKhV comprised 318 pavillions and other structures with the total capacity of more than 2,000,000 cubic metres. Like before the war, the Chief Architect of the Exhibition was A.Zhukov, and its Chief Artist was the well-known painter and monumentalist V.Yakovlev.

A new axis was laid that went from the central entrance to the Square of Collective Forms, it comprised republics' pavillions and «the Fountain of the Peoples' Friendship». The logitudinal axis divided the ensemble into approximately two equal

All-Union Agricultural Exhibition

All-Union Agricultural Exhibition. V. Andreyev, I. Taranov: Mechanization Square. 1939.

parts. The main pavillion was built anew, the second in importance named «Mechanization» was expanded and crowned with a huge glass dome that could be seen from a long distance. The Pavillions of «Land Cultivation»and «Animal Husbandry» were united around it into an integral «branch-oriented» group.

A considerable portion of the pavillions were reconstructed only to a certain degree, though a lot of them were built anew. The architectural outlook of the republican and territorial pavillions acquired appropriate national fragrance – even plants that surrounded them were typical of this or that area.

The Pavillion «The Ukrainian SSR» was practically rebuilt of ceramic units in its former shape; above the pediment it was decorated with a sheaf made of smalt. Not far from it the Pavillion of the Byelorussian SSR was erected in classic forms (architects G. Zakharov, Z. Chernysheva) with the scupture of «Motherland» atop. New pavillions of the recently readmitted to the USSR Baltic republics were built; they were created on the projects of creative teams representing each of the republics. Also opened were the territorial pavillions of «Siberia», «Northern Caucasus», «The Volga Region», and a number of others.

The centre of the Mechanization Square, where earlier a mammoth granite Stalin's statue used to stand, was now occupied by a round granite water pool. A more than six kilometer long trolleybus line was laid along the Exhibtion territory. Visitors could enjoy a complete by the measure of the time range of services: trunk telephone calls, post-office, savings bank, clinic, numerous catering facilities, tasting halls, universal food shops.

The recreational zone was expanded; it occupied a part of the former Ostankino Forest-Park. The Main Botanical Gardens of the USSR Academy of Sciences were set up nearby. From the point of view of the city-building decisions, plans still existed to unite in the future into the single «Park Ring» the green areas of Ostankino, Sokolniki and other sections of forests and parks that surrounded Moscow's central part.

Soviet Architecture over 30 Years of the Russian Federation

Each generation makes its own reappraisal of values created by the preceding generation. It is particularly explicit when ideological formations change. New assessments in the domain of city-building are no less indicative; they clearly reflect fundamental goals of the social development in the monumental forms of the principal squares, streets, ensembles. Under similar circumstances it is extremely important not to overlook the self-assessment of the predecessors made during the summing up of the results of a long way of the municipal economy development, no matter how erroneous it could look from the point of view of the new generations.

«During the majestic 30-year period of 1917 – 1947 the Soviet architecture has acquired nation-wide importance in our country.

Our entire 30-year long architectural practice was devoted to improving drastically the living standards of the working people, to making our cities and towns healthier, to upgrading their services and utilities, to making them greener and better equipped technically.

Stalin's concept of taking care of Man became the leading guideline of the Soviet architecture. This idea permeates the entire construction process of residential, public, cultural and supporting buildings; it guides the renovation of old and construction of new socialist cities and towns.

The Great October Socialist Revolution made architecture serve the people; it has put forward state-wide, popular goals that were to be achieved by Soviet architects.

D. Nalbanyan: The House for the Happiness of the Peoples.

Plan of Moscow. Project. 1935.

Sovietskaya Square. Plans before and after reconstruction.

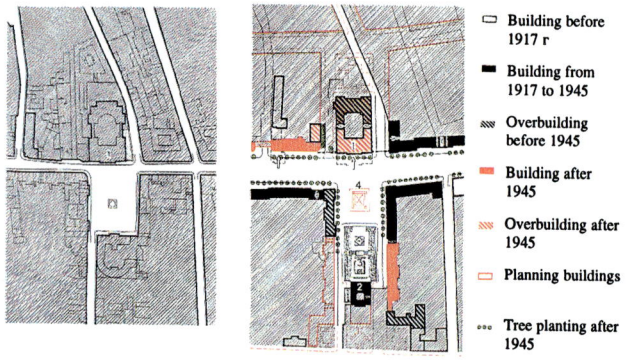

- Building before 1917 г
- Building from 1917 to 1945
- Overbuilding before 1945
- Building after 1945
- Overbuilding after 1945
- Planning buildings
- Tree planting after 1945

1 – The Moscow Soviet building; 2 – The Marx-Engels-Lenin Institute;
3 – Granite-cut sculpture of Lenin; 4 – Monument to Yuri Dolgoruky.

Clearing debris after blowing up Simonov Monastery. 1930.

Skobelev Square. 1913.

The lofty ideas of the socialist revolution, the deepest transformation that it exercised in every sphere of economic, political and cultural life of the country heralded the beginning of a new world historic epoch that filled architectural creativity with new content.

Termination of exploitation of Man by Man, liberation of labour, nationalization of major urban residential property and elimination of private property of land, socialist organization of production processes in industry and agriculture, national equality of all the peoples that populated old Russia, its transformation into the sovereign Union of Soviet Socialist Republics – all those revolutionary changes ushered in a new epoch in the development of architecture and city-building.

A vast field of creative state-oriented activities opened before architects. These activities are closely linked with the economic and cultural public interests – with the interests of the entire society, of the entire people.

The main theme of architectural creative activities became buildings that are meant for daily life, culture and work of millions of people.

The General Plan of Moscow Reconstruction was of tremendous importance in this connection; it was devised in accordance with the Decision of the June, 1931 Plenum of the TsK VKP(b) – the Communist Party Central Committee – and approved by the USSR SNK and TsK VKP(b) in July, 1935.

The General Plan of the Socialist Reconstruction of Moscow and its magnificent implementation are exceptional examples and specimens of thorough combination of the Soviet city-builders advanced scholastic concepts with practical efforts that made it possible to implement them.

Moscow has been built for 800 years. Before the Great October Socialist Revolution Moscow still remained a city of a

The church of Our Lady in Stoleshniky demolition. 1927.

Demolition of the Church of Parasceve Friday in Okhotny Ryad.

huge size, but poorly adapted for life, with a lot of one-storey wooden cabins, with suburbs built at random, with crooked streets paved with cobble-stones.

Stalin's plan opened vast perspectives for Moscow's reconstruction within the shortest historic period.

Care about Man – which is the main guideline of the Soviet architecture – has been developing widely under the conditons of a socialist city or town when residential blocks, houses, kindergartens, nurseries, schools, hospitals, and other structures were built.

New capital's freeways were created in place of suburban highways of old Moscow; they lead from the city's central districts to long-distance automobile routes – the Bolshaya Kaluzhskaya, the Yaroslavskoye Highway, the Mozhaiskoye Highway, the Lenigradskoye Highway. The principal thoroughfare of the city – Gorky Street – has been widened and lined with new multi-storey houses.

The construction of new residential blocks in place of former poorly equipped and chaotically located suburbs affected the architectural image of Moscow even deeper. These new residential districts that grew in line with the plan at different ends of the city – in Krasnaya Presnya and in the Enthusiasts Highway, in the Mozhaiskoye Highway and close to the Stalin Works, in Usachevka and in Bolshaya Kaluzhskaya – have drastically changed the city's suburbs.

Finally, Moscow metro, which is an oustanding structure of our time, became an integral part of Moscow's architecture and lifestyle. In accordance with the General Plan of Moscow Reconstruction several lines of the metro have already been completed. The metro has basically solved the problem of city transportation along the busiest directions. The layout of the metro lines corresponds to the radial-circular structure of the city's plan.

Demolition of the Church of Nicholas Streletsky on Borovitskaya Square. 1932.

Demolition of the Church of Nicholas in Myasniki (16 century). 1928.

Demolition of the Church of Spiridonias in Spiridonovskaya Street, September 21, 1930.

Architect A. Shchusev: residential house on Smolenskaya embankment. Project.

The subsurface and surface metro vestibules that are wonderful buildings in themselves have enriched Moscow's architecture.

Each metro station has its own individual appearance; however, a combination of stations forms an integral architectural ensemble. Twenty subsurface stations have been completed until now, and seven of them were constructed and commissioned during the war.

Similarly to the Moscow metro, the buildings of the Canal named after Moscow form an integral architectural ensemble – its dambs, spillways, bridges, stations, – all of them are architecturally linked with the surrounding scenery. The organic coordination of technology and art has been accomplished during the construction of this biggest transport complex. One of the leading concepts of the Soviet architecture found here its implementation, the way it was done during the construction of metro, which stipulates that buildings meant for mass usage apart from high technical characteristics should have higher artistic qualities.

Devised according to the Stalin's Plan the 120 kilometre – long Canal Named After Moscow was completed in summer, 1937. The canal raised the level of water in the Moskva-River by 1.2 metres; it linked Moscow to three seas and created a series of huge water reservoirs in the city's vicinity. The docking stations, locks, pumping stations and other canal's constructions have a strictly designed shape and finishing; they brought new architectural motifs into Moscow region landscape.

The capital's socialist reconstruction has produced new socialist Moscow, has brought new content into the 800-year old city. Moscow received a new architectural image. It became a city of spatious straight thororoughfares, vast parks, new well-equipped residential districts, imposing monumental public buildings, magnificent embankments and bridges that were constructed in accordance with the General Plan of the city reconstruction.

The Soviet architecture is assigned the task to express in the new and integral images the basic traits typical of the great creative epoch that our country is living through after the Great Patriotic War. These traits are characterized by deep optimism, the people's confidence in their strength and in their future, by buoyancy and purposefulness of the socialist world perception.

The socialist realism in architecture offers an integral unity of the most sophisticated technology, the most thorough consideration of daily and economic requirements to a building, with the high ideological and artistic expressiveness of the latter. Stalin's care about Man is the motive force of all the Soviet architectural creative activities that will open a new epoch in the history of the world architecture»[35].

On March 5, 1953 Generalissimo and the chieftain of all peoples I.V.Stalin died. His death completed a magisterial period of the capital's socialist reconstruction.

---

[1] Trotsky L. Betrayed Revolution. – Moscow, 1991. – Issue 1. – Pp.76, 77.
[2] Ibid., pp.121, 122, 127.
[3] Ibid., pp.128, 129.
[4] Termidor – one of the months of the new republican calendar at the time of the French Revolution; on Termidor 9, 1794 the extremely revolutionary government of Robespierre was overthrown and replaced by a more «moderate» government.
[5] Ibid., pp.182, 185.
[6] In 1935 it was «allowed» to decorate New Year – formerly Christmas – trees.
[7] Fedotov G.P. The Destiny and Sins of Russia. Selected articles on philosophy of the Russian history and culture. St.Petersburg, 1992. – Vol.2. – Pp.83, 84.
[8] Ibid., pp.86, 87.
[9] Ibid., p.85.
[10] See: Brachev V.S. «The Case of Academician S.F.Platonov» // Voprosy Istorii. – 1989. – # 5. – Pp.117 – 129; Perchenok F.F. The Academy of Sciences at a Crucial Turn // «Zvenya» – Historical Almanac. – Issue 1. – Moscow, 1991. – Pp.163 – 236.
[11] Trotsky L. Diaries and Letters. – Moscow, 1991. – P.91.
[12] Orlov A. The Secret History of Stalin's Crimes. – New-York – Jerusalem – Paris, 1983. – Pp.46, 47, 49.
[13] Ibid., pp.52, 53.
[14] Ibid., p.49.
[15] Krivitsky V.Ya. I was Stalin's Agent... Moscow, 1991. – P.287.
[16] Ibid., pp.284 – 289.
[17] Ibid., p.289.
[18] Kozhinov V. Mysterious Pages of the 20th Century History // Nash Sovremennik. – 1996. – # 8. – Pp.128 –141.
[19] Petrov M. To the Issue of Planning «New Moscow» // Stroitelstvo Moskvy. – 1930. – # 1.
[20] Zaslavsky A. Moscow Planning // Planirovka i Stroitelstvo Gorodov. – 1934. – # 10. – P.4.
[21] Kommunalnoye Khozyaistvo. – 1930. – # 6. – P.18 – 36.
[22] The Planning Network of Big Moscow. – Moscow. – 1930. – P.38.
[23] Semyonov V. How to Plan and Build Moscow // Stroitelstvo Moskvy. – 1932. – # 8 – 9. – P.9.
[24] Boldyrev S., Goldenberg P., Dolganov V. Moscow, the Issues of Replanning // Sovetskaya Arkhitektura. – 1931, # 4, pp.32 – 37.
[25] Ibid., p.8.
[26] Mayer K. To the Main Issues of Moscow Construction // «Sovetskaya Arkhitektura». – 1931. – # 4. – P.5.
[27] Zaslavsky A. Moscow Planning // «Planirovka i Stroitelstvo Gorodov». – 1934. – # 10. – P.11.
[28] Architecture of the Palace of Soviets. – Moscow, 1939. – P.35.
[29] B.Iophan left Russia in 1914 and studied first in Paris, then in Rome where he graduated from the Institute of Fine Arts. His teachers were E.Manfredi (one of the authors of the gygantic eclectic project of the monument to Victor Emmanuil II) and A.Brazini, an expert in the field of cult structures. Iophan was a member of the Italian communist party since the date of its foundation in 1921 and upto 1924 when he came back to the USSR. The first party's central committee meetings took place in his office; in 1971 L.Longo presented Iophan with a gold medal commemorating the 50-th anniversary of the Italian communist party.
[30] Ibid.
[31] Kirichenko E. The Cathedral of Christ the Saviour in Moscow. – Moscow, 1992.
[32] Moscow Construction. – 1932. – # 8 – 9. – P.7.
[33] Simonov K. Moscow // Pravda. November 6, 1942 (abridged).
[34] Kirillov B. The Archpriest of St.Petersburg. The Miracles from the Icon of Our Lady of Kazan. – Quoted from: Russia before the Second Coming. – Compiled by S.Fomin. Svyato-Troitskaya Sergieva Lavra. – 1993. – Pp.238 – 246.
[35] The Soviet Architecture over 30 Years of the Russian Federation. Edited by V.A.Shkvarikov. Introductory article (abridged). – Moscow, 1950.

CHAPTER THREE

On the Way to a Model Communist City 1954-1985

N.S. Khrushchev.

L.I. Brezhnev.

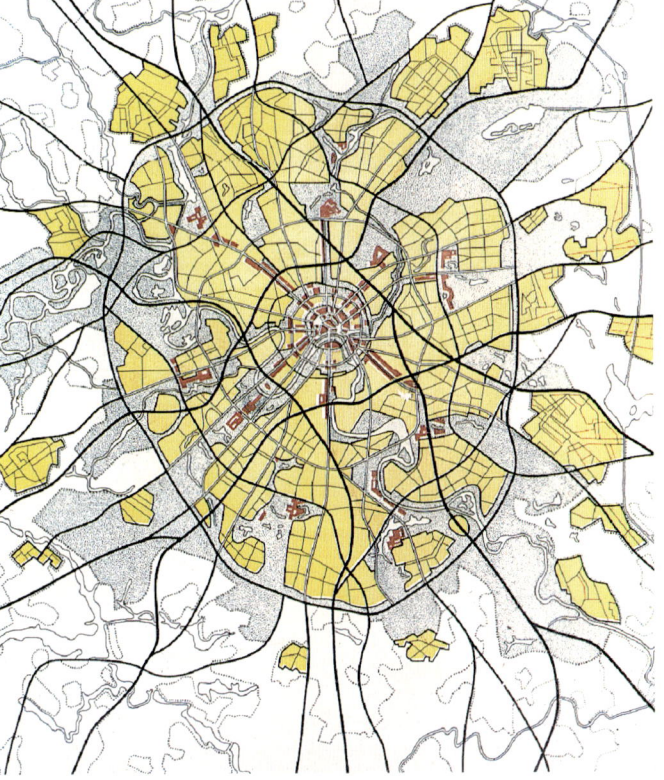

The «Rossiya» Hotel

New Arbat.

General Plan of Moscow, 1971.

Yu.V. Andropov.

The Palace of Congresses in the Kremlin.

M.S. Gorbachev.

I.S. Glazunov: Legend of the town of Kitezh. 1986.

A Pure Prayer. Priest-Monk Stephan (V. Linitsky).

His Holiness the Patriarch of Moscow and All Russia Alexius I.

Architect M.P. Kudryavstev: Reconstruction of Moscow's Centre. 17th Century.

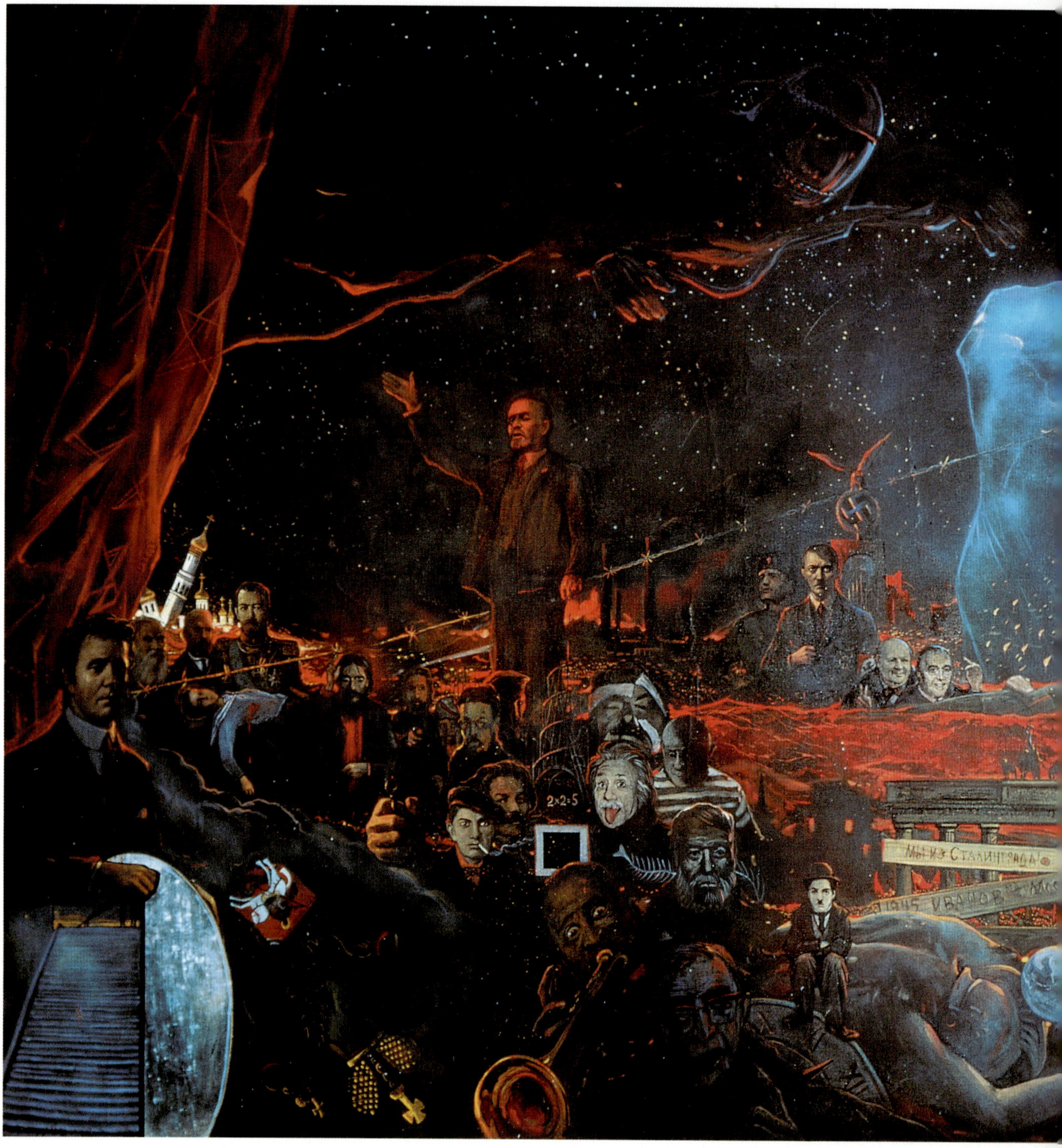
2×2=5
МЫ ИЗ СТАЛИНГРАДА!
1945 ИВАНОВ

I.S. Glazunov: Mystery of the 20th century. 1977.

Resolutions on Architectural Over-Indulgence

The years of 1930s and 1940s were the years when Stalin's personality cult began coming into shape. Soviet architects were required to produce such architecture which would be capable of glorifying the work of the Leader, his future role in the development of the country with its stately and luxuriantly decorated forms. And the architects turned to the forms of the Renaissance, Russian classicism and other national styles in their attempt to find an answer to the tasks they faced in the past. The use of expensive materials – marble, granite, valuable wood breeds – added to the overdecoration tendency. The phenomenon became especially commonplace during the years following World War II. The desire to make every building «a monument to the epoch», a monument to victory and triumph led to the situation when architecture of buildings dissociated into their structural volumes and ceremonial front get-ups. The erection of every building using unique construction elements was a drag on not only construction industry but construction as a whole.

After Stalin's death that «over-indulgence» tendency in architecture was first denounced at the All-Union Conference of Builders in December 1954. Khrushchev demanded the «lagging» of architectural art behind «the workers' needs» be eliminated. A number of speakers protested «against the trends of formalism and pseudo-decoration, against over-indulgence in architecture». Many architects including prominent ones very shortly switched vectors of their work and, moreover, plunged into theoretical research to substantiate their new views. Those who a year or two before had claimed classicism to be unsurpassed as a school of art began referring to it as antiquated, narrow and limited. Some former classicism proponents were calling for «putting an end to slavery to routine in the use of classical heritage, formalistic aestheticism recurrence and embarking on the path of innovation which met the interests of the workers to the full». Starting from the mid-1955 The Architecture and Construction in Moscow magazine was literally filled up with such appeals.

In August 23, 1955, the CPSU Central Committee and the Council of Ministers adopted a resolution «On Measures of Further Industrialization, Quality Improvement and Construction Costs Reduction». Even the title alone implies internal contradictoriness of the Resolution, so Moscow builders got down to fulfilling «mission impossible».

Newly completed building of Leningradskaya Hotel was announced a model of bad taste and wastefulness, similarly other skyscrapers were also rejected. Often times anonymous articles criticized G. Zakharov, L. Rudnev, V. Gelfreigh, D. Chechulin, S. Chernyshev, M. Rzianin and other prominent Moscow architects for their allegedly «poor role in spreading formalistic errors in both theory and practice of architecture». A.G. Mordvinov, Chairman of the Committee on Architecture, well-known author of many Moscow architectural ensembles was strongly criticized for his articles on artistic problems of the Soviet architecture, and was described as engaged in propaganda of «one-sided approach to city building».

In November 4, 1955, the CPSU Central Committee and the Council of Ministers of the USSR issued a special resolution pointing to complete groundlessness and criminal nature of spending huge amounts of state funds for the construction of decorative building fronts. The Resolution pointed out that «unworthy tower-like superstructures, numerous colonnades, porticos and other over-indulgences borrowed from the past had become common for construction of apartment houses and office buildings and as a result much state funds had been overdrawn in recent years for construction, which could have built many millions of square metres of living quarters for the workers». Criticizing the style of «over-indulgence and over-decoration» the Resolution put forward new requirements for architecture to meet, «Soviet architecture must derive from simplicity, regular forms and economical solutions. Attractive appearance of buildings and structures should be achieved through the integrity of architectural forms and purposes of those buildings and structures, their correct proportions, rational use of materials and components, as well as high quality of work rather than through artificial, expensive, ornamental decorations».

It was the tendency of architectural designing that became the focus of criticism. «In the work of many architects and

L. Polyakov, A. Boretsky (architects), E. Myatlyuk (engineer):
Hotel «Leningradskaya» on Komsomolskaya Square. 1948 – 1953.

designing offices ostentatious side of architecture with plenty of over-indulgences has become wide-spread which is inconsistent with the line pursued by the Party and Government in architecture and construction... While designing and erecting buildings and structures architects and engineers must place an emphasis on the issues of economical construction, best comfort for population, equipping apartments, schools, hospitals and other facilities with services and utilities as well as planting residential areas with trees and gardens. ...Soviet architecture must derive from simplicity, regular forms and economical solutions».

Following the passage of the Resolution at the end of 1955 the Architects' Union Moscow Branch conference dismissed nearly all the members of the Branch's governing body and adopted a resolution on radical restructuring of its work.

Engineer V. Lagutenko having submitted a proposal to master the construction of extremely cheap, compared to capital buildings, frame-free panel five-story houses, seized front pages of Moscow and national newspapers for a long time. Such houses were also built abroad, e.g. in Evron (France) but in small numbers and as experimental. However, in Moscow most of the existed production capacities were re-adjusted and large new production facilities were constructed to fabricate panels and other components used for the five-story houses' erection.

Khrushchev made construction industry and Glavmosstroi (Moscow chief construction contractor headed at that time by V.F. Promyslov who later became Chairman of the Moscow Soviet) his first priority. The Institute for Standard Projecting was earmarked as leading designing organization. Standard projects of buildings mostly for social purposes were started to be designed by Mosproyekt (Moscow Project Agency), too. In 1955 a project of five-story school made of large blocks was designed in architect Chechulin's studio and since the following year the construction of such schools was launched throughout Moscow.

Khrushchev's attitude towards the General Plan of 1935 was likely to be generally hostile as to Stalin's «creation». He agreed with proposals to move the social and political centre of Moscow to the South-West of the capital, a location between Vernadsky and Michurinsky avenues. It was planned to build there a new place of worship to revolutionary heroes – a Pantheon with subsequent transfer of Lenin's Mausoleum, as well.

The Palace of Pioneers and Schoolchildren hastily erected in the Lenin's Hills in 1961 was the first sign of the would be complex. It was a major victory for the supporters of international «glass and concrete» style. Construction of the Palace of Congresses' grandiose building in the Moscow Kremlin dates back to the same time – turning point for architecture in Moscow. Any criticism voiced was swept aside with boorishness which the new Party leadership was characteristic of.

Designing and erecting the Palace of Congresses was carried out with the pace one could not think of. Any actual archeological supervision was not even at issue. A number of archeological monuments in the Kremlin were pulled down; large earth excavations and hauling for the building of the Palace damaged the regime of sub-soil waters, so later the Kremlin hill had to be reinforced.

Initially after 1955 many people believed that industrialization in architecture primarily concerned the construction of housing. «The Palace of Soviets competition of 1957 – 1958 proved the one-sided view to be entirely erroneous. In theoretical and creative respects it played, in fact, nearly the same decisive role as the one of 1931 – 1933 only with a «reverse» mark. It became symbolic that all most critical turning points in the history of our architecture were related with the projects

A.S. Trofimov: Clearing the Place for the Construction of the Palace of the CPSU Congresses in the Historic Kremlin.

Layout diagram of the General Plan of Moscow. 1957.

of the largest, most expressive and with greatest ideological content constructions – the Palace of Labour in 1923, the first Palace of Soviets in 1933 and the second Palace of Soviets in 1957. Architects at that point departed decisively and in essence from representationalism of the 1940s-50s, which just some time back had dominated the minds, projects and practice of construction. It is natural that it seemed to be logical enough (if not the only possible way) for them to come back to the «heritage» (heritage again!), but of a different type then – the heritage of the 1920s which had been entirely ignored only recently. However, it was not so easy to do.

One has to imagine the then situation very well to realize how difficult it was for architects to work. There was no new theory, which would succeed the «classical» one: it had yet to be formulated. It was in the process of actual work that practice tried to find the right line of development. And still during the Palace of Soviets competition of 1957 – 1958 without arranging things (the projects were kept «secret») the architects managed to find some common grounds.

The concept of the Palace of Soviets' building was subject to so many ideological requirements that the use of all known means of expressiveness here seemed to be absolutely necessary. One could presume the restraint of the1920s would not allow all the requirements be met. On the other hand, however, the dramatic lessons of designing the first Palace of Soviets in the1930s – 1940s and the development of representationalism, which had followed, were only too fresh in the memory. There could be no return to those years, as well. Thus, for instance, only one project out of more than one hundred and fifty submitted for the competition was designed in the exact spirit of 1933 Palace of Soviets. Even authors of the previous project – B. Iofan and V. Gelfreigh – designed their projects in entirely different, «new» way.

Indeed, luxuriant, «over-decorative» architecture of the 1940s – early 50s was too offensive and even seemed to look «ugly». Therefore, attempts were made to provide the expressiveness by other means.

Despite creative difficulties and theoretical ambiguity one can not deny the fact that in all the projects architecture was innovative, keen and rather graphic. Such was the thirst for new architecture and based on the tendency it really became logical extension and creative re-make of both 1920s and 1940s. And by no means it could be called an architectural «hybrid». The new perception of architecture opened fresh and of full value prospects for the oncoming period... the 1970s-80s. It was the competition that made its start»[1].

Architectural environment can influence both mood and physical conditions of human beings: it either expedites or inhibits their development. Architecture and city-building have a direct impact on forming personality, being one of the most effective means for the development and perfection of hundreds of thousands people in a society. Monotonous and featureless building of our vast residential areas, once rejoicing Khrushchev-style five-story houses, undoubtedly made their «contribution» to the current state of our society with its lack of spirituality and continuous crime growth.

General Plan for Moscow Development. Feasibility Fundamentals. Year of 1961

Large-scale housing construction demanded the city territory be expanded. In accordance with the Decree by the Presidium of the Supreme Soviet of the RSFSR of August 18, 1960, Moscow ring road (MKAD) became the city's administrative border. The city territory increased up to 87.5 thousand hectares with a population of some 6.13 million people.

The 1960s – the period when a new general plan for Moscow was drawn – were characterized by significant city construction. Massive large-panel construction was launched resulting in the emergence of areas built up with the first generation five-story houses, so called «khrushchevkas», in the South-West of the capital, Cheryomushki, Izmailovo, Phili-Mazilovo, Khoroshevo-Mneovniki, Kuzminki and others. But, anyway, the priority in the territorial development of the city was given to south-western neighborhoods.

The new situation demanded a new city-building policy be devised, so in accordance with the resolution adopted by the Council of Ministers of the USSR respective organizations in Moscow began working out a new general plan with the Feasibility Fundamentals being its first stage. The Feasibility Fundamentals were based on developing the provisions of the General Plan of 1935.

The main idea behind the Feasibility Fundamentals, as well as all previous and subsequent city-planning documents, was to ensure stability in the number of population at the level of 6.2 million people, which could be achieved through balance between jobs and workforce.

Limiting the number of population and developing city-forming base was linked with significant development of the Moscow oblast (region) outer belt. It was planned to set up some centre-towns for local settlement systems, referred to as satellite-towns of the capital. The centre-towns were divided into industry-heavy towns (Dmitrov, Gzhel, Volokolamsk, Shakhovskaya, Bely Rust, Taldom), new industries towns (Kryukovo, Zaraisk, Lukhovitsy), science and academic towns (Pushchino, Mikhailovskoye, Chernogolovka), health resort towns (Istra, Zvenigorod, Ruza, Mozhaisk, Ozery, Zavidovo, Tarusa).

Issues relating to the perfection of the functional use of the territory and planning structure were recognized as an important part in the Feasibility Fundamentals. Thus, the bulk of plants and factories was proposed to be gradually assembled in industrial zones, projected in the main industrial areas of the city. That point of view was further developed in the General Plan. The industrial zones evenly spread throughout the city created pre-requisites for balanced settlement of the population and jobs' locations, while re-location of various works helped to carry out their modernization.

Much attention was paid by the authors of the Feasibility Fundamentals to structuring living quarters. A residential district (raion) was adopted as the basic element of a residential territory, which was sub-divided into micro-raions and residential blocks. It was planned to satisfy all basic needs of the

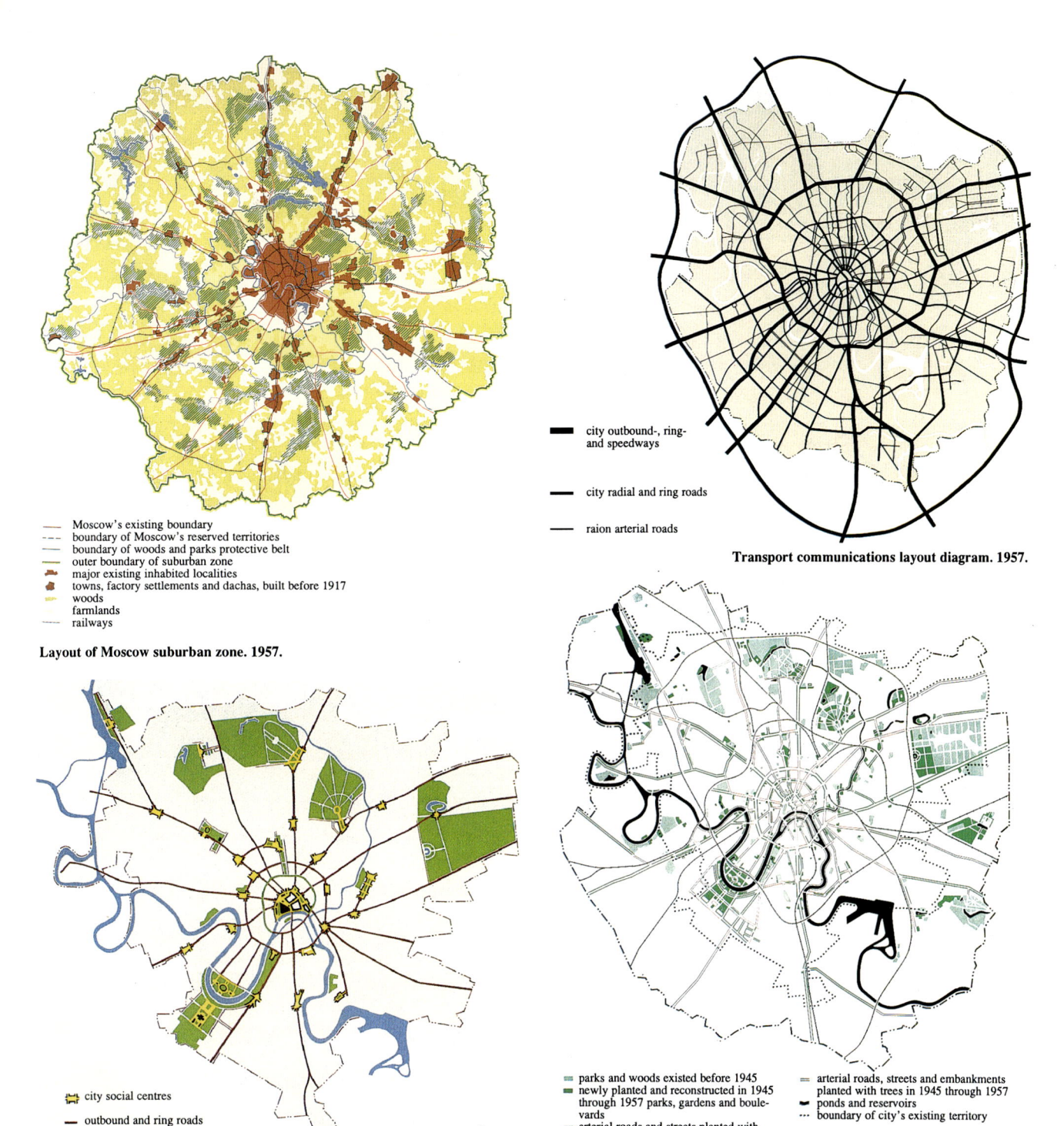

- Moscow's existing boundary
- boundary of Moscow's reserved territories
- boundary of woods and parks protective belt
- outer boundary of suburban zone
- major existing inhabited localities
- towns, factory settlements and dachas, built before 1917
- woods
- farmlands
- railways

Layout of Moscow suburban zone. 1957.

- city outbound-, ring- and speedways
- city radial and ring roads
- raion arterial roads

Transport communications layout diagram. 1957.

- city social centres
- outbound and ring roads

Layout diagram of public activity centres. 1957.

- parks and woods existed before 1945
- newly planted and reconstructed in 1945 through 1957 parks, gardens and boulevards
- arterial roads and streets planted with trees before 1945
- arterial roads, streets and embankments planted with trees in 1945 through 1957
- ponds and reservoirs
- boundary of city's existing territory
- boundary of city's reserved territories

Tree planting diagram. 1957.

population in daily (within a microraion) and periodic services within a residential raion. Social and cultural centres, shopping malls including a movie theater, a restaurant, a department and food stores, welfare and utilities offices were designed for that purpose. A park, sports facility with a stadium, sports grounds and a swimming pool were also envisaged at the same place. Such a residential raion was also composed of adequate medical facilities, specialized music and art schools, as well as a communal zone with garages and parking lots.

The Feasibility Fundamentals specified maximum distances from apartment houses to services' locations: 350 – 500 metres within a microraion, 1200 – 1500 metres within a residential raion.

Special attention was paid to the centre's system in outlying raions of the city, which were augmented with large social complexes. The Feasibility Fundamentals' prognosis read that downtown Moscow would emerge as spatially matured and architecturally integrated system of ensembles, housing top Party and governmental institutions of the Soviet Union, most important establishments of international, Union, republican, regional and the city levels. It was taken into account that the main ensembles of the centre both in the heart and along the periphery of the city, especially in the South-West and North, had already been formed. The number of residents and, to even greater degree, jobs in the downtown was planned to be significantly reduced.

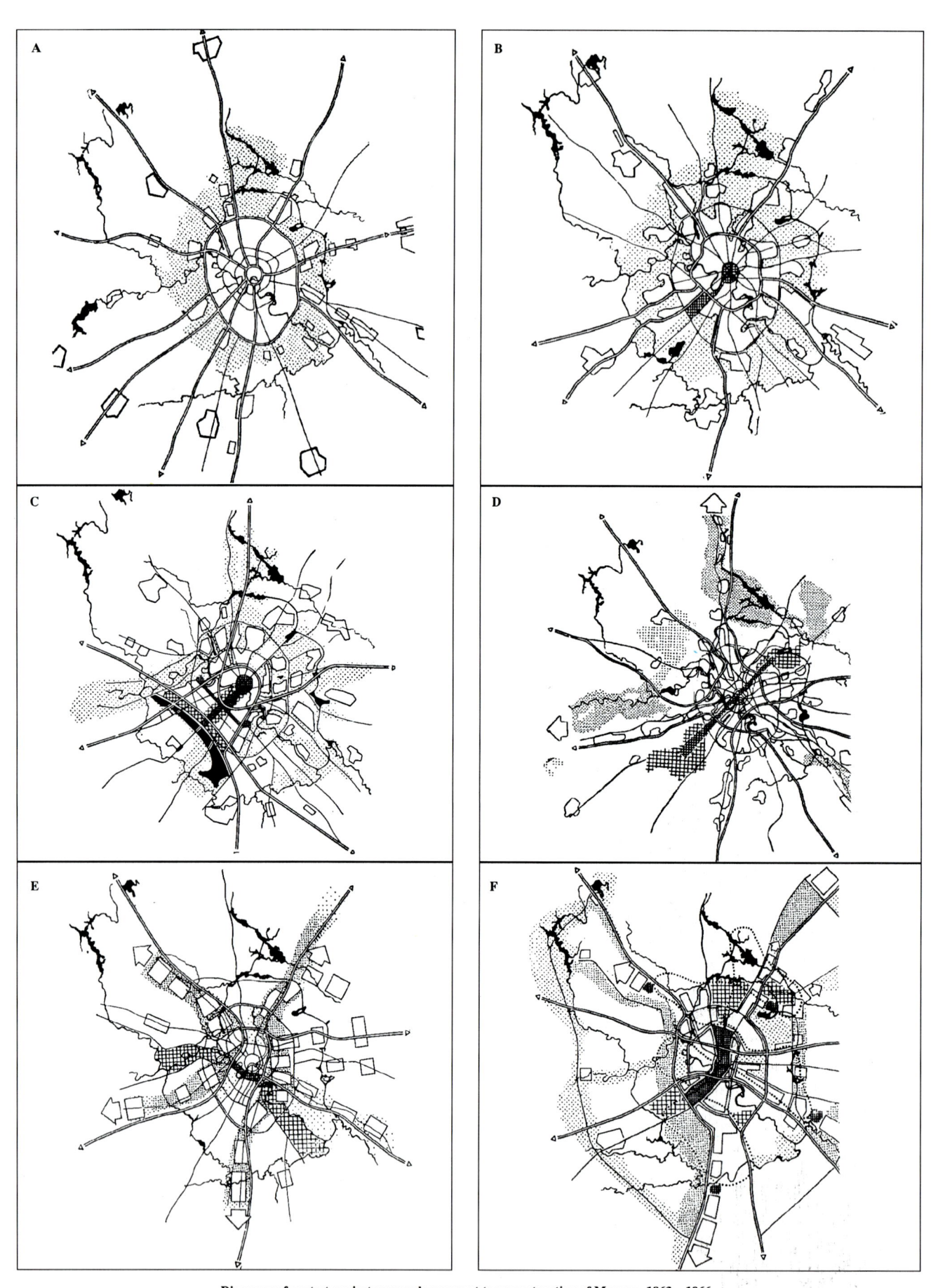

Diagrams of contest project proposals pursuant to reconstruction of Moscow, 1963 – 1966.
A, B – radial and ring solution (proposed by workshop No. 1 of the Genplan Institute of and workshop No. 4 of Mosproekt-1); C – diagram of city development to the South-West (workshop No. 3 of the Genplan Institute); D – diagram of city development in two directions (workshop No. 2 of the Genplan Institute); E, F – diagrams of city development in four directions (Moscow Architectural Institute, Central Research and City-Building Development Institute).

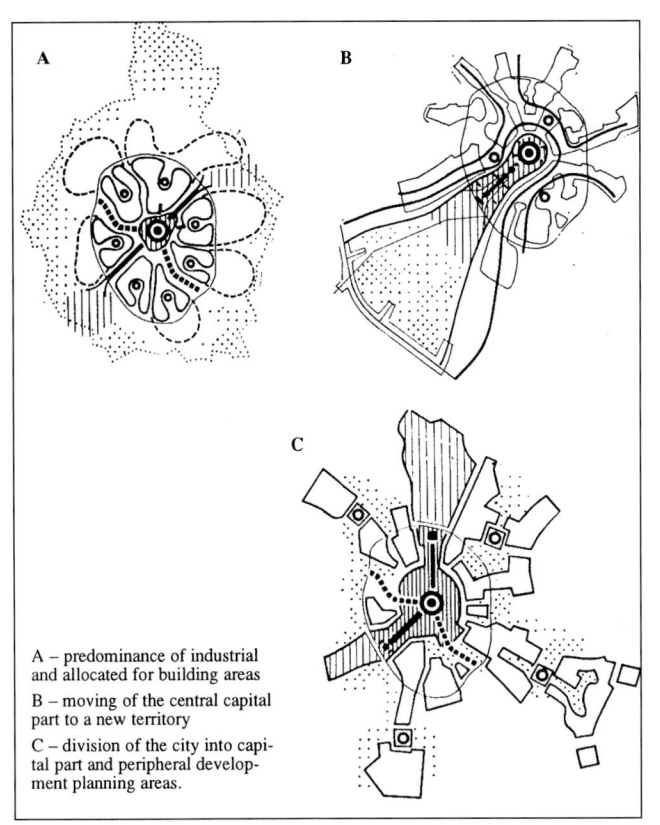

A – predominance of industrial and allocated for building areas
B – moving of the central capital part to a new territory
C – division of the city into capital part and peripheral development planning areas.

Central capital part of Moscow with respect to areas of development planning. 1967.

The Feasibility Fundamentals for the General Plan provided for the improvement of the situation with trees and gardens and territories reserved for plantations, so that per head norms were raised to 25 square metres. A task was assigned to solve the problem of unevenly spread green plantations and see to it that every raion had its parks. The woods and parks protective belt (WPPB), its protective and recreational functions were heavily relied upon. Indeed, when taking any structural decisions the city and the WPPB were considered as a single city-planning element.

Based on the calculations in the Feasibility Fundamentals passenger's transportation by the city public transport was to increase subsequently 1.5 fold and reach 6 million passengers per year. Planning of the transportation network development proceeded from the necessity to reduce the time needed to get to work from living locations down to 30 – 40 minutes for majority of the population.

In the process of preparing proposals aimed at improving arterial roads a broad discussion between major city transportation experts took place. A host of various opinions was voiced with some of them favoring radical changes in the arterial roads' structure. The authors of the Feasibility Fundamentals gave their preferences to the development of a radial-ring system, planning to add a number of ring and back up radial roads. However, there were also some proposals in the Feasibility Fundamentals based on which chord-like directions of express arterial roads were included in the General Plan.

Development of engineering equipment was recognized as one of the most important tasks. To ensure water supply for Moscow an option with the use of the Vazuza and Oka rivers was accepted. Sewerage-system provision was planned to be started with erection of the Pakhrinskaya large aeration system. In the area of power supply it was recognized expedient to unify the Moscow Energy and the Unified European Energy Systems, as well as fuel balance of the country.

Many proposals, which received their further development in the General Plan, had stemmed from the Fundamentals: setting up industrial zones, construction of chord-like express arterial roads, large-scale measures on engineering equipping, population per jobs balanced city raions (districts) and others.

The Feasibility Fundamentals fulfilled their task, having laid the groundwork for drawing the General Plan.

Development of Capital's Downtown and Competition of 1967

The program for downtown Moscow development was neither long-term nor stable. Switching concepts of the capital's structural and territorial construction took place within relatively short periods of time: in the 1940s – 50s the erection of skyscrapers consolidated the radial-ring structuring, with the construction of the MGU (the Moscow State University) and a new residential raion, as well as with projects of the Palace of Soviets and the Pantheon the development in the south-western direction was commenced, and the construction of the Kalinin avenue stimulated western direction, etc. All that served convincing evidence of the necessity to work out a clear and long-term concept for the development of the downtonw of a largest city in the world.

In the early 1960s important events took place in the rapidly growing Moscow. Its territory expanded up to 87.5 thousand hectares while the size of the population within the boundaries as of January 1, 1961, reached 6.2 million people. The woods and parks protective belt was enlarged up to 172.5 thousand hectares.

Due to the adopted decision to intensify the solution of the housing problem by means of industrialization and typification of building nearly all construction sites in Moscow moved to periphery raions so very shortly all the territories within the city boundaries were built up.

In the Kremlin at the site of a number of historic buildings and next to Ivanovskaya square massive Kremlin Palace of Congresses with 6,000 sitting capacity hall and another 800 premises was erected. That completed the damage to the historic appearance of the Kremlin and Moscow was not included in the UNESCO list of most valuable and architecturally integral historic cities and capitals of the world.

Construction of New Arbat was launched.

With the «thaw» (relaxation of ideological press) of the mid-50s reevaluation of the results of reconstruction and building in the capital began. A necessity arose to devise feasibility fundamentals for a new Moscow General Plan, that time with due account to areas adjacent to the capital, and work out a new concept for the capital's downtown development.

In the 1930s – 40s Moscow plan was considered as an aggregate of squares and arterial roads oriented to the centre of the city – the Kremlin and Kitay-Gorod with adjoining territories and sacral Mausoleum and the Palace of Soviets. Broadening the existed squares also fell under the category of main tasks. Thus, A. Bunin's project provided for doubling the width of the Red Square and clearing additional new spaces in the south at the Moscow river. D. Fridman projected the extension of the Red Square along eastern axis from the Mausoleum stretching it as ceremonial, imposing esplanade to Novaya and Dzerzhinskogo squares (the project enlarged Red Square more than four fold). In 1943 V. Munts designed a plan for downtown Moscow, including the Palace of Soviets, the Kremlin, the Historical Forum with Pantheon, Lenin and Historical Museums, Victory Colonnade and more. A. Zaslavsky and L. Rudnev proposed Arbatskaya square be expanded by 4 – 5 times and oriented to the Palace of Soviets. Projects of that period clearly underestimated the historic and architectural heritage.

In the years after World War II A. Vlasov suggested and worked at a concept of active south-western development of the downtown: on a vast vacant territory (about 600 hectares) a

The Kremlin viewed from the South.

social forum, featuring the Palace of Soviets, the Pantheon, wide esplanades and squares, were to be concentrated. Its area in terms of scale had to considerably surpass all known world analogues. The ideology of Stalin's General Plan had a long life in architects' minds as an integral and grandiose ensemble.

In the late 1950s the social centre of Moscow was started to be viewed as a corresponding to human dimension system of different in functional content raion (district) centres characterized by the community of architecture and inter-links. The rightness of those, who in the late 20s – early 30s had proposed to build a spatially developing system of the capital's centre (N. Ladovsky, V. Kratyuk and others), became obvious. It was believed that the composition of the all-city centre had to include as a minimum: the central part – the Kremlin, Kitay-Gorod and adjourning squares; the Moscow and Yauza rivers' embankments; the central part of the South-West; the system of parks – from Krasnopresnensky to Sokolniki; VDNKH (national exhibition grounds) and New Arbat.

As work on Moscow Feasibility Fundamentals to the year 2000 commenced, in 1968 a competition was announced with regard to a general strategy for the all-city centre's development. Fifteen groups of the best city experts took part in the competition, which resulted in the general conclusion that it was necessary to ensure a gradual but decisive departure from historically evolved centripetal system of the city's general structure, which further retention would inevitably complicate finding a solution to the conflict between new content of the centre and its old spatial form as a memorial to the Russian city-building art of the 14th – 19th centuries.

Within the system of Moscow and Moscow oblast (region) the development of agglomeration along two or three directions south-east and north-west or north, south-west and south-east – was seen as most expedient. In either case, it would follow a diameter line from south-west to north-east with sub-centres in north-west and south-east.

Based on singled out directions projects for the development of the capital's centre can be divided into three groups.

1. Development of the capital's centre along two predominant directions: south-west – centre – north (Lavrov's team); south-west – centre – north-east (Ullas's and Rochegov's teams); north – south and west-east (Pavlov's team).

1. Options for development of the all-city centre.
2. Options for development of Moscow's agglomeration: a) in two directions, b) in three directions, c) in five directions.

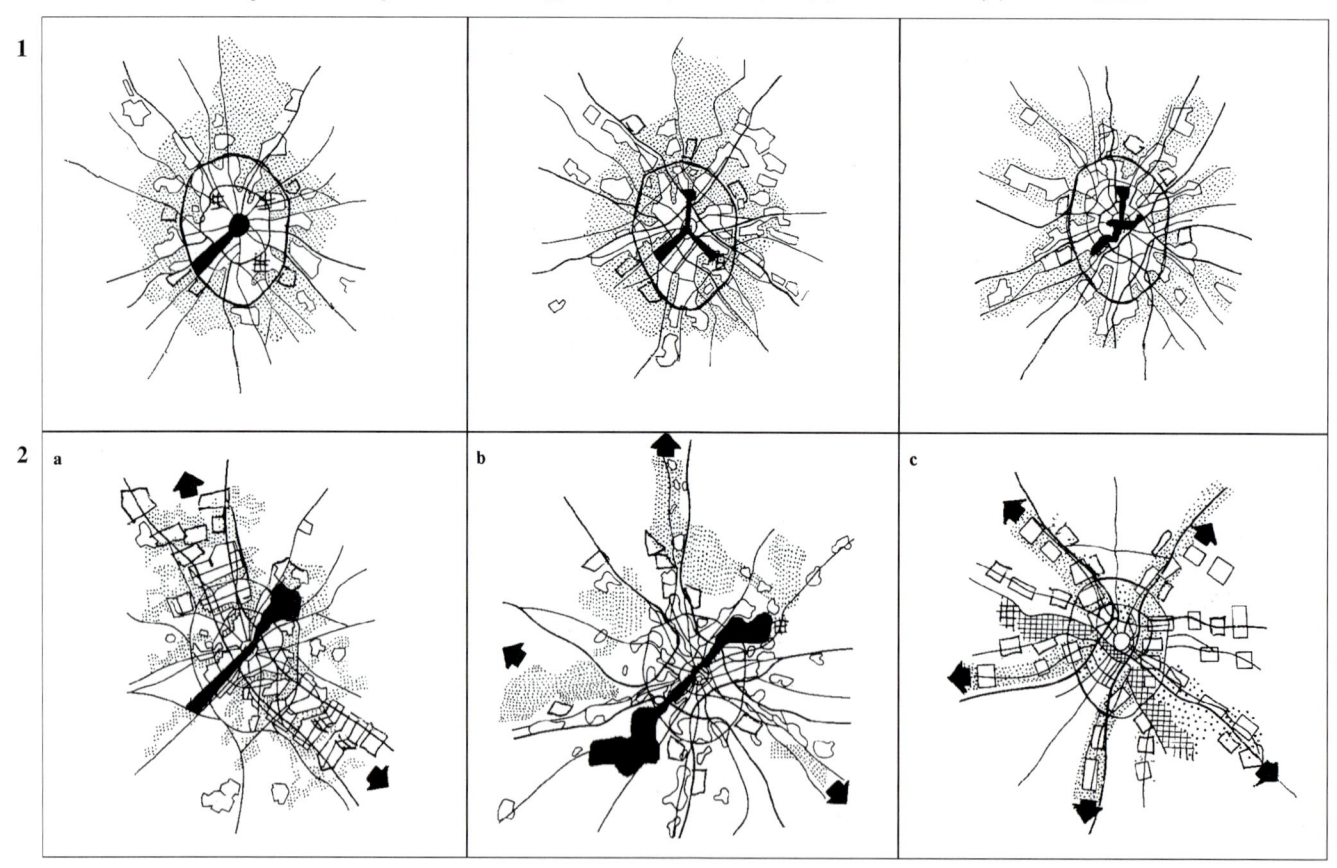

2. Development of the capital's centre along four-five directions: centre – the Moscow river, centre – south-west – north-west – north – north-east (Matveev's team); centre – west, north, north-east, south-east (Barsch's team); centre – south-west, west – east, along the Moscow river (Polyakov's, Yemelyanov's, Yeryomin's teams).

3. Even, star-like development of the capital's centre along all the directions from the historically formed city core (Kalinin's team).

Nearly all the versions divided Moscow into complex city-planning raions with their sub-centres and populated by some 500 – 600 thousand people. The majority of the projects, offering solutions for the centre's system, envisaged future development based on the perspective, which had already taken shape in the capital. The centre had to expand beyond the Sadovoye Koltso along three main directions: south-western, along the Moscow-river and northern. The proposed diametres ran from south-west to north-east in Sokolniki or from south-west to north in Ostankino. Indeed, it was impossible to accommodate everything pertaining to the capital's centre within the borders of the Sadovoye Koltso, as such concentration imposed major pulling down of existed buildings and brought about difficulties of composition's solutions, hindering distribution of buildings with city status in such a way which would provide for linkage and architectural organization of vast spaces along the main directions for development of the whole centre's system.

Examples of expedient accommodation of large buildings were Luzhniki stadium, MGU in the Lenin's Hills, skyscrapers, city air-terminus, the Kalinin avenue. In those cases large city-building scale of designing solutions determined adjourning building, approaches, system of planting with trees and gardens and open spaces. Another proposal, related to the reconstruction of Taganskaya square and accommodation of a number of administrative buildings there, was of the same magnitude. Search for an architectural-spatial solution for building along Bolshaya Tulskaya street – Varshavskoye highway was also important, although the area was least attractive in its natural features and offered little room for the construction of administrative and social buildings.

The following categories for the capital centre's zones were suggested: governmental; administrative buildings and international institutions; cultural and educational, historic-revolutionary and social buildings; scientific and academic complexes; exhibition and sports grounds, recreation facilities and green tracts.

A prize-winning project by S. Matveev's team could serve the example. Based on the premise that the basic core of the radial-ring structure of the city was its historically formed central part, the following functional and territorial development of the social centre was outlined:

– a ring zone of parks 17 kilometres long and 300 – 700 metres wide (the area is vacated with the help of gradual pulling down of predominantly dilapidated and low-value buildings) is set up. In the area of some 1000 hectares complexes of union, union-republican and republican ministries with relating departments and administrative offices, a number of international organizations, governing regional and city bodies are located;

– in the south-west within a specifically reserved area top state bodies are located;

– in the north-east already existed a major railway stations' complex in the area of Komsomolskaya square and exhibition grounds with union, republican and international status in the area of Sokolniki;

– along the Moscow river it was planned to locate main Olympic sports facilities, a Victory monument, a Kolomenskoye museum park and some unique social buildings.

The «Luzhniki» Sporting Complex. 1956.

The circular park zone around the Sadovoye Koltso would have made it possible to extend the capital's central core and draw out new large buildings from the Kremlin. The construction of 20 – 40 story buildings in parks around the Sadovoye Koltso would have opened radically new compositional opportunities for subsequent dynamic development of central

The big sports arena in «Luzhniki». 1957.

Moscow's silhouette, well observed from both inward and outward directions. And a considerable distance between the tall buildings and the centre's core would have allowed for the preservation of the historically formed placid nature of building, ensuring the Kremlin's dominating position.

The project demonstrated the radial-ring concept and was entirely opposite to the basic project by the MARKHI[2].

* * *

Demonstration of an idea for Moscow' centre reconstruction was the principal requirement in the competition. The range of proposed solutions was rather large: from complete pulling down of the centre and its replacement with structures, resembling the idea of Japanese metabolists, (Mosproyekt) to virtual preservation of the existed situation coupled to a very scrupulous account of everything planned to be constructed in the near term (winning project by the Moscow City General Plan Institute).

The MARKHI's basic or youth version exercised an entirely different approach to the competition's tasks.

First, viewing the problem of Moscow's new centre in connection with territorial and population growth of the city, as it was the period when the intensive construction of new residential areas was launched, a new idea providing for the development of the entire Moscow region, was put forward.

Second, believing that the centre of the Soviet state did not have to coincide with that of the old Moscow, rather it had to be formed on the basis of the general settlement system for the Moscow region, it was proposed to locate the new centre in the vicinity of external lines.

Third, a linkage scheme for the new linear centre and old Moscow structure, which at the same time aimed at their maximum independence, was proposed.

And finally, the centre within the Sadovoye Koltso was viewed as subject for careful restoration, but not a new construction site.

By the time of the competition New Arbat had already been built, having «swallowed» a huge piece of the old city. The construction of the Rossiya Hotel had destroyed a unique part of Kitay-Gorod. The authors of the project, rejecting such a barbaric intervention in the historic area, based their designs on the idea of «drawing transportation and construction blows aside the centre of Moscow». The new centre was to be formed in a new territory, proceeding from the principles of Moscow's agglomeration development.

The old Moscow remained radial-ring, as that lay out was a memorial to the Russian city-building. However, such a composition had its spatial limits, for the city could not grow along those lines endlessly. Giving up of the «compact city» within the boundaries of the Moscow Ring Road and linear development of Moscow's agglomeration along several directions, served the basis for the project.

Five directions were selected: Leningrad, Yaroslavl, Novgorod, Voronezh, Minsk, each being formed by large double highways with 200-thousand people satellite-towns between them. Five linear development-industrial formations were envisaged, including both city raions and a number of Moscow region's towns. Among them – Kuntsevo, Khoroshevo-Mneovniki, Timiryazevo, Tushino-Khimki-Khovrino, Zelenograd, Podolsk, Chekhov, Serpukhov, Noviye Kuzminki, Kuskovo, Zhukovsky, Perovo, Balashikha, Izmailovo, Kaliningrad, Stchelkovo-Mytistchi and others. They were planned to be separated by new or existed parks and woods, industrial areas and transportation arterial roads. Moscow was to be turned into a number of independent development formations with their own industry, as well as business, social and cultural centres, which had to result in great reduction of trips by the people to work, shopping centres and others in the Moscow agglomeration.

Two large green diametres were in the plans:

From west to east along the Moscow river, reaching woods and parks outside the Moscow Ring Road. New parks – Krylatsky, Kievsky, Pirogovsky, Zamoskvoretsky, Paveletsky, Borisovsky, Southern and Kuryanovsky – were planned to be planted;

From north to south, including the territories of Troparevo, a new park between Vernadsky and Michurinsky avenues, Kuntsevsky woods and parks, Victory Park, Gorky Park, Central park in Zamoskvorechye, parks along the Yauza river: Lefortovsky, Krasnoarmeisky, Sokolnichesky. Further on the diameter was divided into two «channels» – north-eastern (Mytistchinsky reserve) and northern with VDNKH grounds (All-Union Exhibition Grounds), Ostankino park and Botanical garden, outstretching the ring road to Klyazminskoye and Pirogovskoye reservoirs.

The centre of Moscow was proposed to be formed on the basis of two city formations: «old» city within Kamer-Kollezhsky ramparts, performing traditional administrative functions and «new» city – South-Western raion, performing scientific-industrial and recreational functions.

The two «cities» were planned to accommodate the administrative bodies of Moscow, Moscow region and Russia, while the administrative centre of the Soviet Union was proposed to be formed along the Moscow river's bends from north-west to south-east in the direction of the ring railroad.

The problems of Moscow's centre as the capital of the USSR were resolved at a new planning level: creation of a capacious linear formation, exploiting in terms of landscape most valuable Moscow river's bends coupled to opportunities for continuous development of a modern centre with its gigantic office complexes and road junctions. Thus, on the one hand, a sophisticated administrative function was being shaped, and on the other hand – the transportation and construction blow was drawn aside the historic centre. New large-scale architectural ensembles would have been added to the city, contributing to radical improvement of city-building, while no historic monuments or memorials had to be pulled down for the benefits of new construction and the unique composition of the old city could have been preserved.

It should be noted that only three projects in the competition contained region-scale proposals: by MARKHI, Genplan Youth Studio (B.K. Yeremin) and N.N. Ullas's team.[*]

Energetic Struggle for Ancient Moscow Begins

«In all that ignorant and contemptuous attitude towards everything belonging to the past one cannot see radiant aspirations for the future... But when people, being lazy and incurious, forget even most recent past and at the same time their inertness and mediocrity do not allow them even to try to think about future, then organism ceases to be living, for the organism performing only a digestive function cannot be a human being».

N.K. Rerikh

The adoption of a communist building doctrine resulted in the destruction of thousands of unique monuments and memorials to civil and church architecture (especially in connection with renewed fight against religion) in Moscow and many other towns of the USSR. In the Russian North, responding to the instructions from the Communist Union of Youth local committees, torch-marchers walked from Arkhangelsk down the White Sea coast and burned the bulk of monuments of the Russian wooden architecture. Only a few of them were saved, thanks to setting up some reserves for the wooden monuments of the North near Petrozavodsk and Arkhangelsk.

It was exactly the time, when one of the most terrible things in Moscow's history happened with demolishing buildings to

---

[*] *– The subsection is written by I.G. Lezhava*

vacate room for Kalinin, Proletarsky and Novo-Kirovsky avenues and selective pulling downs in Old Arbat. Moscow's history was literally sacrificed to protectionist strivings and a phantom of «communist tomorrow». «Devoted Leninists» in the heat of their micro victories forgot about the Leader of the revolution himself: some ten building connected with Lenin's life were destroyed in the process of reconstruction. Mansions associated with the names of Pushkin, Lermontov, Gogol, L. Tolstoi, Khomyakov, Yazykov disappeared from the place, where Kalininsky avenue runs now.

In the 1960s-70s Moscow was approaching the line, beyond which there could be neither history, nor culture. And it could quite justify the words said by the leader of the Communist Party and Soviet government, that «1917 is to be considered as the beginning of the historic evolution of this country».

In the late 50s the Monuments Protection Administration with the USSR Ministry of Culture, employing a staff of lacking initiative bureaucrats, was giving no indications of its public-oriented activities. Prominent culture figures tried to dodge too. So, at the end of his life I. Grabar admitted that he had not been energetic enough in protecting monuments, because he did not want to quarrel with the government, which was financing the Institute of Art Sciences founded by him. Active monuments protection activities were not encouraged, although one was not sent to jail or deported from Moscow for that, as it had been the case in the 30s.

Despite strong pressure by the top authorities, it was impossible to drown the voice of reason and conscience. More and more forces got involved in the struggle aimed at preserving the national culture. Artists were among the first to join the movement. In 1955 under the initiative by E.A. Rastorguyev a commission on protecting historic monuments was set up with the governing body of MOSKH (Moscow Artists' Union) including: A.M. Laptev, a corresponding member of the USSR Arts Academy, S.S. Churakov, a well-known restorer of ancient Russian paintings, S.A. Baulin, V.S. Konstantinov, A.A. Korobov, M.A. Kuznetsov-Volzhsky, V.K. Melnikov, S.G. Mukhin, A.S. Trofimov, N.S. Fomichev – painters.

The MOSKH Commission determined two basic directions for their work: propaganda of historic monuments by arranging art expositions, with the help of the press and by sending appeals to government authorities, explaining the value and significance of architectural ensembles and separate monuments to be destroyed.

In 1959 following a courageous speech at a session of the USSR Council of Ministers against the construction of the Palace of Congresses in the Kremlin by A.V. Vlasov, President of the Academy of Architecture, Khrushchev abolished the Academy. A.V. Vlasov's speech was strongly supported by the MOSKH Commission. On the instructions of the Commission painter A.A. Korobov attempted to convey an appeal to the General Secretary of the CPSU Central Committee through Khrushchev's son-in-law A.I. Adjubei, a well-known journalist. But the latter, referring to Khrushchev' view on the issue, known in advance, demanded he not be involved. The last attempt was made in the Kremlin, when Khrushchev accompanied by his bodyguards and builders was inspecting already dug out foundation ditch for the Palace of Congresses. The encounter occured in front of the Poteshny Palace, where Korobov, standing at the easel, was painting the ancient ensemble of the Teremnoi Palace. But the painter could hardly put his hand into a pocket to produce the petition, as a colonel accompanying Khrushchev pushed Korobov with his powerful body to a wall so strongly, that the latter lost his breath. When he came to, Khrushchev was far away. That is an illustration of one of the ways to convey a petition, which were many with the Commission. The struggle to protect monuments was a selfless devotion act on the part of the people, who were united by the idea to save the national culture, which elimination was very real.

For ten years of work (from 1955 to 1965) the Commission with the Moscow Artists' Union suspended the demolition of the host of historic monuments in the Kropotkinskaya (now Prechistenka) street, which was planned to be radically reconstructed in the wake of the Kalinin avenue's construction. Some lanes with historic buildings of the first quarter of the 19th century, adjourning the Krutitskoye town house were saved. Thanks to the Commission's efforts the premises of the Krutitskys' Mitropolitans former palace of the 17th century received a reserve's status. There were failures and set backs too, but they did not discourage those, who without any profit gave up everything for the sake of triumph of the patriotic

**The Prospect Mira (of Peace) avenue.
Plan and fragments of building area. 1957.**

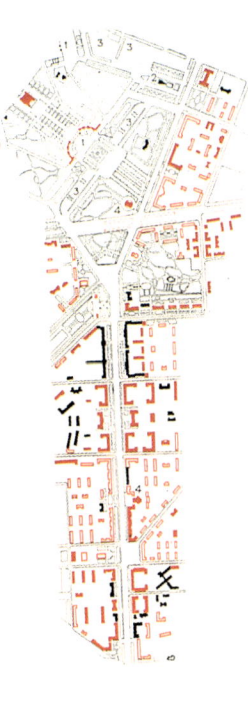

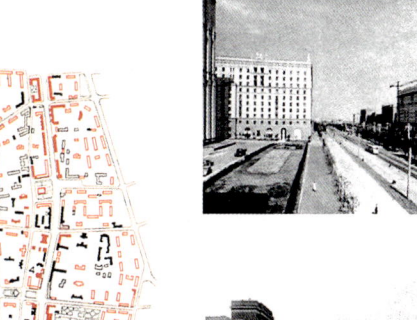

– building before 1917
– building from 1917 through 1945
– building after 1945
– planned buildings, planned bridges

1 – entrances to the All-Union Agricultural and Industrial Exhibition
2 – monument «Worker and Peasant»
3 – parking lot
4 – subway station

cause. Regrettably, at that point the policy of those, who did not realize or did not want to realize the significance of preserving the historic and that of art heritage for the generations to come prevailed for some time. But the struggle continued and here comes one of its brightest illustrations.

In 1962 the «Moskva» magazine's editorial board held a round table to discuss the issues of preserving the historic Moscow and ways for the development of city-building. To stimulate the discussion the magazine published an article by painter A. Korobov, architect P. Revyakin, engineer V. Tydman, writer N. Chetunova entitled «How to Build Moscow Next?» To better understand public concern with the destiny of our city here are some excerpts from the article.

«The face of Moscow derives from its historic monuments... a city can not be featureless, otherwise it would lose what makes it unique, unequaled and home for everyone. Love for a native city is love for one's homeland, people, its past and future. It is that love, which made the patriots of Leningrad, Sevastopol and Odessa stoically bear all the hardships of the fascist blockades and sacrifice their lives to deny the enemy a chance of outrage upon their native cities.

In frenzy the Hitlerites were destroying monuments of the ancient architecture in our land... fascists were making a desperate attempt to destroy in the hated country the material signs of its nation, its pride, a symbol of its historical dignity and turn our country into a «geographic name» without history».

Architectural monuments in any country embody the history of its nation and, thus, make up its national pride. The history of architecture more clearly than any other form of art expresses the nature, way of thinking and feelings of a people and records its evolution. Architecture as no other art is subject to a powerful creative role of the people themselves.

Architecture... is created by people, who put their dreams of beauty, best aspirations, knowledge, skills, aesthetic taste into collective consciousness. All true art has its original national features, but architecture has a clear lead here, too.

Every epoch adds something new to the appearance of a city. However, the new features should enrich the city not damaging or leveling its originality.

At our time, especially after World War II, whole raions are built according to a single federal or municipal plan. That demands special responsibility on the part of builders, for such restructuring contains a threat of destroying historic, national features of a city, its originality and turning it into a faceless «inhabited locality». Therefore, devising theoretical foundations for city-building is absolutely urgent now.

We have great experience in city-building unparalleled in terms of scale in any other country or epoch. But can you find a single theoretical generalization of that experience? Where are works, which by means of precise figures and calculations could show and prove economic, engineering, architectural, sanitary and social advantages or disadvantages of a new raion, say, in Phili-Mazilovo, as compared with another raion in Severnoye Izmailovo?

Have you ever heard that the GlavAPU published a detailed account, which could tell the public how much money was spent for designing and then constructing, say, the «Rossiya» movie theater or an apartment house in the Gorky street? How much did it cost to pull down the building, which had originally stood at that place, and build housing for the tenants to be moved. We know nothing of such accounts. And without them, however, one can not even approach the science of city-building.

City-building is determined, on the one hand, by history and, on the other hand, by the people's idea of better future, which, after all, any construction is done for. The people build their capital for centuries, as it is also the case with history. And history does not stop after us. It is just the beginning.

The duty of Moscow builders is to do away with exclusiveness and secrecy in the work of planning and constructing organizations. We can no longer tolerate it, when the General Plan of Moscow, which concerns every Muscovite, is kept «secret» from the population. We should put an end to the situation, when the Muscovites could see only «results» of city-planning, when the magic formula of «the decision has already been taken» dominated, preventing any debate on that «decision taken» and criticism, which was viewed as the infringement of Stalin's «personal» decision and encroachment upon Moscow's «watch-over» Kaganovich»[3].

The discussion failed – the right time had not come yet. In response to the article by Moscow's public figures the Pravda published a letter entitled «Against Harmful Confusion in City-Building Issues» and signed by fifteen high-ranking architects, holding a host of various titles and regalia.

This is an excerpt from the letter, «...We can not give our preference for Moscow's past at the expense of its present and future, for the sake of which we live and work. A. Korobov, P. Revyakin, V. Tydman and N. Chetunova do not understand or do not want to understand that. So in their confusion they embark on the path of opposing the past to everything new, progressive. By painting our reality black they try to discredit the creative efforts and achievements of Moscow architects and

Leningradsky Avenue. Plan and fragments of building area. 1957.

1 – Young Pioneers stadium; 2 – Dynamo stadium; 3 – indoor tennis court; 4 – indoor swimming pools; 5 – higher education establishments; 6 – hotel; 7 – subway station

- building before 1917
- building from 1917 through 1945
- building after 1945
- planned buildings, planned bridges

builders, portray them for the public as barbarians and ignoramuses, while presenting themselves as saviors of the genuine Russian traditions». Then the authors of the article are accused of having committed all mortal sins: ignorance, distortions of facts, wrong views, liberal interpretation of Lenin's behest on heritage, unprofessionalism (focusing on Dr. P. Revyakin), slander, unfair techniques...[4]

It was the first open clash between a small but brave group of old Moscow's (half-destroyed) defenders and a «legion» of destroyers. Actually the process of destroying old buildings continued. In 1960 Zaryadye was fully cleared and the oldest Moscow church of St. Nicholas, the Miracle-worker «Mokry» (the 15th-17th centuries) was leveled. The next step was the project of an overpass, leading to the building of the «Rossiya» Hotel (architect D.N. Chechulin) under construction, which was designed to link the parking lot of the hotel with Teatralnaya square. It was a nonsensical project, envisaging the demolition of Maxim the Blessed church of the 17th century, Znamensky cathedral of the 17th century, the Old Gostiny Dvor building of the 18th century (architect D. Quarenghi), the remainder of Epiphany and Zaikonospassky monasteries, which aroused strong protest of the MOSKH Commission and indignation of the Moscow public. A letter written by the Commission and signed by a number of prominent figures – painter P.D. Korin and writer L.M. Leonov among them – was sent to Khrushchev, who had to suspend that action, monstrous by its concept and wasteful for the state. The public won a victory and proved to be a moral force, which all those involved in destroying the Russian national culture would have to reckon with.

After that the remaining churches in the Razin street: St.Varvara the Megalomartyr of the 16th – 18th centuries, St.Maxim the Blessed of the 17th century, Sign of Theotokos of the 17th century with a bell-tower and cells of the 18th century (former Znamensky monastery), the Protection of the Mother of God with side-altars of Megalomartyrs St.George and St.Peter, a metropolitan at the Hill of Pskov in the 17th century, – upon the request by the Commission were taken under the state protection, although even such a measure could not guarantee their inviolability. When regulatory bodies needed to pull down a historic monument, laws were violated.

St.Joachim and St.Anna church of the 17th century, which used to stand in Bolshaya Yakimanka, serves one of the examples. It was blown up in November 7, 1972, at night counter to the protection law and despite the protests by the Commission and the All-Union Society for Protection of Historic and Cultural Monuments (established in 1966). To clear the way for ongoing construction of the Kalinin Avenue, houses and mansions, belonging to the 18th-19th centuries were demolished in the area between Bolshaya Molchanovka and Povarskaya (Vorovskogo) streets. Thus, a major part of historic and memorial Moscow was destroyed. Rzhevsky, Borisoglebsky and Trubnikovsky lanes nearly ceased to exist, while Durnovsky and Krechetnikovsky lanes were destroyed completely. House #9 on Novinsky boulevard, once owned by the great Russian artist F.I. Shalyapin, remained the last obstacle in the way for the Kalinin Avenue. Khrushchev, during one of his rides by that route, seeing Shalyapin's mansion, lashed the builders, saying, «Why does that pimple still stand in the way?» On the following day heavy tractors and bulldozers turned plafonds of the ceilings, unique wainscoting, parquet, assembled doors with bronze decorations of high aesthetic and material value (F.I. Shalyapin received guests and made his own performances in the mansion) into a formless heap of crushed stones and pieces of wood.

The house of Rimsky-Korsakov (Pushkin square, 3) also fell victim to the post-war pogrom of historic monuments in Moscow. Architect Yu.N. Sheverdiayev made a plan of erecting the administrative and production building for the Izvestiya daily at that place. It was precisely the case, when those, dealing with reconstruction, drew lines in pencil first and then in

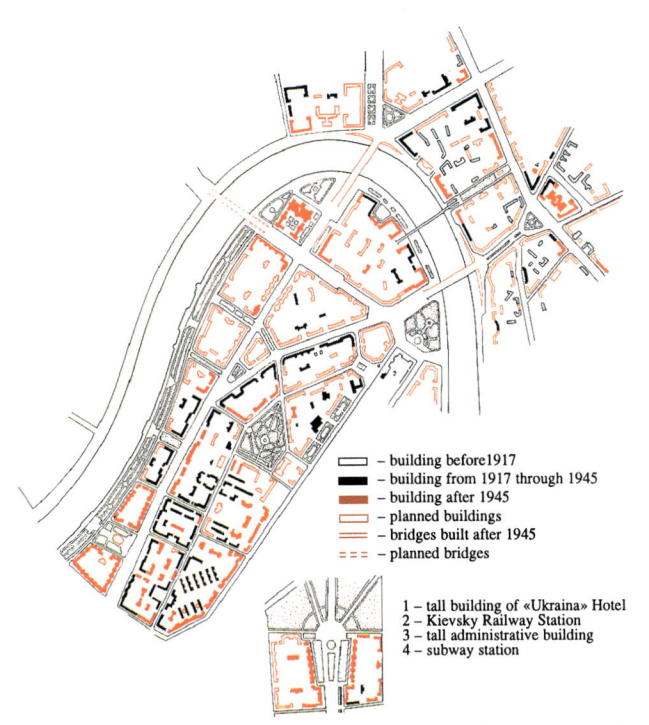

– building before 1917
– building from 1917 through 1945
– building after 1945
– planned buildings
– bridges built after 1945
– planned bridges

1 – tall building of «Ukraina» Hotel
2 – Kievsky Railway Station
3 – tall administrative building
4 – subway station

Kutuzovsky Avenue. Detail of the plan. 1957.

Demolition of the Church of Nicholas the Wet in Zaryadie.

Zaryadie. Restoration in process.

Kropotkin Square.

«bulldozer» on a living organism of the historic city. Desperate attempts were made by the Commission to prevent the demolition of that unique historic and architectural monument of Moscow, which had survived the invasion of Napoleon and been visited by A.S. Griboyedov, V.A. Zhukovsky, A.S. Pushkin, P.A. Vyazemsky, N.M. Yazykov, A.I. Turgenev, A.A. Alyabyev, M.P. Pogodin, S.P. Shevyrev and many other brilliant representatives of the Russian culture. But despite the campaign launched by the Commission in the press and appeal of acting member of the USSR Academy of Art and Chairman of the MOSKH governing body D.A. Shmarinov to top governmental officials in 1964 Rimsky-Korsakov's house was pulled down.

On Preobrazhenskaya Square same year on the eve of a religious feast one of the oldest churches in Moscow – the Transfiguration of Lord, the Savior, which had been built in 1768 with the money raised by the Guards Preobrazhensky (Transfiguration) regiment, was blown up. It was not only the people of art and parishioners of the church, who voiced their protest against that action, Lord Bertram Russell, writer M. Marshall and other prominent public figures were among them. Today, one can see a lawn at that place, which emphasizes the senselessness of the action by the Soviet and Party authorities.

As the MOSKH Commission was at work, its core was formed comprising rather well-known artists, scientists, architects, who made a great contribution to the cause of protecting the cultural heritage with their creative works, publications, scientific research, which defined the place of historic and cultural monuments in contemporary and future life. Among the most active members of the Commission were: Doctor of History, Professor N.N. Voronin, famous architect-restorer P.D. Baranovsky, rector of the Art and Industrial Design University (former Stroganovskaya Art School) Professor Z.N. Bykov, well-known writer O.V. Volkov, writer-publicist E.V. Nikolayev, engineer V.P. Tydman, Doctor of Architecture, Professor P.P. Revyakin.

The Commission expanded its activities to other cities and towns of Russia, embracing separate monuments and memorials of special value, as well. No matter what republic, region or territory members of the Commission found themselves in, they always performed their civil duty of protecting the national culture.

Following the establishment of the MOSKH Commission similar Commissions were set up with the Peace Protection Committee (1961, its first Chairman – artist I.S. Glazunov), the Board of the RSFSR Writers' Union (1962, the first Chairman – S.V. Mikhalkov), the Board of the Moscow Architects' Union (1965, the first Chairman – L.A. Petrov). Later, the Peace Protection and Writers' Union Commissions joined their effort with the MOSKH Commission.

In the late 1960s, as the General Plan for Moscow's reconstruction was being developed, the Commissions had to intensify their effort. The focus was on the plans to build a North-South arterial road, starting from the Ostankino TV tower and stretching through the Zhdanov (Rozhdestvenka) street, Moskvoretsky bridge, Zamoskvorechye to Kolomenskoye. Decisions taken by the Mossovet (Moscow Soviet) ruled out a possibility to arrange a reserve around a unique architectural ensemble of Kolomenskoye village, since according to the GlavAPU's plans the arterial road was to pass virtually by the gates of the museum. At all stages of struggle for preserving the museum all the Commissions together with the All-Union Society for Protection of Historic and Cultural Monuments (VOOPIK) were taking most active part. As a result of numerous letters to regulatory bodies, the Mossovet and GlavAPU authorities were forced to make a concession: an agreement was reached to change the route of the arterial road through Kolomenskoye.

The dispute over Kolomenskoye was followed in February, 1967, by another problem, resulting from a decision to erect an administrative building for the CPSU Central Committee (architect P. Skokan) in Ipatyevsky lane, where an ancient Borovsky town house stood. The historic monument was moved thanks to interference by the Commissions and VOOPIK, however, all the attempts to save an oldest church in Moscow that of Ipatii, the Holymartyr known since 1472 and rebuilt in the 17th – 18th centuries failed.

Much effort was made in the struggle for the Savior-Daniel monastery – a unique historic and architectural monument of the 13th – 18th centuries in Moscow, which necropolis till recently kept the graves of outstanding figures of the national culture, dear for every Russian: N.V. Gogol, N.M. Yazykov, Yu.F. Samarin, N.G. Rubinshtein, V.G. Perov, V.A. Serov and many other prominent sons and daughters of Russia. In 1930 a penitentiary for teenagers and a transit prison were set up in the monastery. The prison administration, naturally, cared very little about the preservation of the monuments and ran the premises to their complete deterioration.

In 1967 A.A. Korobov, P.P. Revyakin, A.S. Trofimov, V.P. Tydman and V.V. Filatov of the Commission, having carefully inspected the architectural monuments and murals in the Daniel monastery, made a statement, warning of the urgent need to start restoring many of the buildings due to their extremely poor conditions. They sent letters to the Ministries of Interior and Culture of the Russian Federation, suggesting the old ensemble

October Square.

be used for some other purposes (only twenty years later the monastery was handed over to the Moscow Patriarchate).

A considerable part of the Commissions' work was dedicated to propaganda of the Russian treasures of culture with the help of art expositions, publications, TV and radio programs with active participation of artists, architects, men of letters and cinematography people.

One of the first expositions – «Monuments of History and Culture of Our Homeland in Works by Moscow Painters» was arranged in the Krutitskoye town house. Some 320 artists, presenting 740 exhibits of painting, drawing, sculpture and applied art, took part in it. Such expositions made a start for a large-scale propaganda campaign of the non-governmental Commissions.

The year of 1971, when the second General Plan of Moscow's reconstruction was to be approved by the government, was at the door. And again, like in case with the first General Plan of 1935, the situation recurred. On the eve of the Plan's approval massive demolition in all historically significant streets down to Kamer-Kollezhsky rampart began. The Moscow public was indignant with yet another barbaric action.

In October, 1971, the MOSKH Commission's initiative led to establishing a similar commission with the Board of the USSR Artists' Union aimed at uniting not only artists but activists from other unions.

In 1972 in the premises of the Central Architects' House the first joint session of the monuments protection commissions – those of the USSR Artists' Union, MOSKH, Union of Literary Men, Peace Protection Committee, Architects' Union and the General Plan Institute and GlavAPU people was held. Both sides explained their positions and came to the conclusion, that unless a comprehensive research of the whole lot of problems, relating to the life of the gigantic city with millennial history was done, it would be difficult to devise a detailed plan for Moscow development. The commissions expressed their confidence that only 10 per cent of Moscow's contemporary territory were of great historic and cultural value and those 10 per cent had to obtain the status of reserve in terms of city-building regime, as it had been done with respect to the towns in the Zolotoye Koltso (Golden Ring).

In May, 1973, the commissions with the USSR Artists' Union, MOSKH and Peace Protection Committee prepared photographs with explanatory notes, illustrating the process of the city's reconstruction: unfounded demolition of historic monuments without any research and photo documentation, which ran counter to not only common sense but the Convention on Protecting Cultural Treasures both in war and peace time signed by the Soviet Union.[5]

After the materials were studied in the Presidium of the CPSU Central Committee and the Council of Ministers, the CPSU Moscow Committee and Mossovet were instructed to set up a public commission with the GlavAPU, comprising prominent people of science, art and literature, which would have a right of deciding vote. The commission was formed in December, 1975, with representatives of various creative work organizations among its members.

At a plenary meeting in the GlavAPU leading architects made their presentations, focusing on the issues of architectural-planned structure of the centre, its economy, transportation, underground urbanization, protection of historic and cultural monuments. The presentations were followed by demonstration of a new version of the detailed planning project, which made minor concessions to the public opinion. After a thorough analysis of the project the representatives of the Commission stated that the new plan, envisaging the preservation of some architectural monuments, however, was based on the old principal lines for reconstruction. In fact, that version repeated the previous one, as its implementation demanded unique buildings in a large area of the capital's historic centre be pulled down. The Commission stood strongly in favor of preserving the historic centre of Moscow and recommended the project's designers the detailed planning project be reviewed again with due regard to its remarks.

In March, 1974, prominent scientists, artists and the VOOPIK activists conferred in the Moscow House of Scientists on the subject, «Historic Centre of Moscow – Monument to City-Building Art». On the part of the non-governmental commission artist A.V. Artemyev made a report «Historic Environment and its Role in the General Architectural Composition of Moscow». Subsequent sessions made the GlavAPU officials change their tactics in implementing the General Plan of reconstruction. The latest version of the detailed planning project, based on the non-governmental commission's remarks, envisaged the formation of nine zones of special city-building regime, which would include Zamoskvorechye, where the bulk of historic-architectural monuments and memorials were concentrated.

All those positive decisions, introducing corrections into the General Plan, were late. For that period of time the historic appearance of Bolshaya Polyanka and Bolshaya Yakimanka streets was radically changed. Here comes just a short list of historic buildings, which were demolished during 1969 – 1978 there: St.Joachim and St.Anna church (1684), a clergyman's house (19th century, first half), House # 15 with gates (late 19th century), mansions of the 19th century's first quarter – Houses # 19 and 47 (A.P. Chekhov lived and worked there in

Demolition of a historic building near the Borovitskiye Gates.

1880 – 1888), the Kazan Cathedral (16th – 19th centuries), House # 18 (P.B. Ganushkin, outstanding psychiatrist, lived there in 1910 – 1917), House # 22 (S.V. Gerasimov, famous landscape-painter, lived there in 1912 – 1930), House # 24 (early 19th century), House # 26/2 (late 18th century, in 1830s great Russian actor M.S. Shchepkin lived there), House # 28 (late 19th century – premises of the Moscow Merchants' Society). From Zemskoi lane through Maronovsky lane and down to Luchnikov lane along Bolshaya Yakimanka street stood houses and mansions of merchants and gentry, which had been built in the 18th-early 19th centuries and once belonged to the Konovalovs, the Izergins, the Lepeshkins, the Okonishnikovs, the Zonovs and the Glinskies (House # 44, architect V. Bazhenov). In that row of mansions and houses there stood a unique building of the historic Moscow, # 48, which was built in 1736 during the reign of Empress Anna Ioanovna and belonged to the church of St. John the Warrior.

Bolshaya Polyanka lost about 50 per cent of its historic buildings, gone forever were many houses and mansions associated with the names of famous Russian people, such as: V.O. Klyuchevsky – historian, Professor of the Moscow University; F.I. Inozemtsev and N.I. Pirogov – Doctors of Medicine, who were the first to use ether anesthesia in Russia; A.M. Filomafiisky – Doctor of Medicine, surgeon; M.F. Spassky – Doctor of Physics and Mathematics; A. Fet – Russian poet; A. Grigoryev – poet and critic; V.A. Tropinin – painter.

Demolition of a historic building in Yakimanka. 1960s.

The non-governmental commission with the GlavAPU managed to save Pyatnitskaya and Ordynka streets, which were included into the zone of North-South arterial road, from total demolition. But other areas of Moscow's historic centre were found in a shape close to that in Zamoskvorechye.

Overall, few monuments, relating to various epochs and names prominent in history and culture, were saved in the city by the non-governmental commission's effort at that period. Among those saved were: house of V.I. Dal – a remarkable writer and etnographer (Bolshaya Gruzinskaya # 4/16); house of brothers P.M. and S.M. Tretyakov – founders of the Russian Art Gallery and prominent patrons of art (1st Golutvinsky lane # 16); mansion of the Trubetskoys, visited by A.S. Pushkin (Usacheva st. # 1); mansion of the 18th century with chambers of the 17th century, owned by V.N. Tatistchev – historian and public figure at Peter's the Great times (Malaya Yakimanka # 26); Granatny (granite) house of the 16th century (Spiridonovka # 3/5); mansion of the 18th century with chambers of the 16th century, owned by G.L. Maluta-Skuratov (Maly Znamensky lane # 7/10).

Non-governmental commissions at that point played a decisive role in saving Moscow from total destruction of its history and culture. By their courageous struggle and selfless adherence to the patriotic cause many activists of the movement deserve everlasting memory, living in the generations to come. With the establishment of the All-Union Society for Protection of Historic and Cultural Monuments many members of the commissions took an active part in setting up its precinct, district, regional and republican branches and sharing the experience of many years of struggle for preserving the national culture.

General Plan of Development of 1971

In 1971 the CPSU Central Committee and the Council of Ministers of the USSR adopted a resolution «On the General Plan of Moscow Development». An editorial in the Construction and Architecture magazine, as it was customary in those years, read that «as a result of much attention paid by the Party and Government to the issues of developing, equipping with services and utilities the city of Moscow, improving living conditions, social and cultural services for the population and also due to selfless work of the Muscovites and all the Soviet people, Moscow has become a major centre of the socialist industry, science, technology, art and culture, one of the best-developed capitals in the world». The new historical stage in the capital's existence was defined by a slogan, «Let us turn Moscow into a model communist city!» Virtually the whole propaganda machinery was engaged in promoting the new general plan, promising to demonstrate advantages of the socialist system to the rest of the world. Hundreds of architects even those, who had not been involved in devising the document, were mobilized by the Party to brief the Muscovites at special meetings held by house management committees, what kind of future awaited their home city in the near term. Mock ups and perspectives of new avenues, squares and residential areas, developed by the capital's architects in accordance with the General Plan, were installed in shop windows along major streets and avenues.

And today, when twenty five years have passed since the General Plan was approved, one can say that the document, originated in 1961, created by a large group of experts – architects, economists and engineers, incorporated all the best available at that stage in both domestic and foreign city-building practices. Yet, at the same time it triggered kind of a countdown in the process of growing crisis in economy and social-political life of the new formation country. And through life of the capital one could clearly see its focus.

The necessity in drawing the new general plan for Moscow was dictated by political reasons: the assigned task to turn the capital into a model communist city, featuring convenient layout, modern architecture, high level of services and utilities, adequate sanitary conditions and well-organized city economy. To that end it was envisaged to take all the advantages of both domestic and foreign achievements in science and technology for the purposes of city-building.

The General Plan of 1971 was devised as a follow up of the General Plan adopted in 1935 with some alterations introduced to adapt it to the changes in the situation. It was planned to accomplish the whole range of social, economic, technological and aesthetic tasks for the period of 25 – 30 years, starting from 1961. Much attention was paid to the issue of regulating the number of population. It was believed that most successively the problem could be resolved in the state planning system environment, based on the balance in the ratio between workforce size and number of jobs.

Complex-like and harmonious approach to the reconstruction was designed to prevent any deviation from the final objective in terms of both the detailed plan and deadline. Carefully outlined architectural-planning structure made up the content of the principal design for the new General Plan of the capital.

Concurrently with the General Plan, a scheme of raion planning for the Moscow region was drawn, which established borders of the Moscow-biased area. It included the suburban zone and WPPB. To avert merger of towns and inhabited localities, concentration of workforce on the same principle like in Moscow, i.e. balance in the ratio between workforce and jobs, was denied. As a result, an organic combination of built up areas and open green spaces, creating optimal living environment for the capital's population, was to be achieved.

Three things in the architectural-planning organization of Moscow to come were recognized as fundamental: making eight planning zones; convenient links between development and industrial territories; preserving and improving historic and landscape features of the city.

The historic centre became part of the core zone with other seven zones around it. Each planning zone was divided into 3 – 4 planning raions with a population of some 250 – 400 thousand people, which were further subdivided into residential raions. Integration into a planning zone suggested the establishment of its own centre with the city's status.

Common structural unity was achieved by developing the all-city centre, which included: historic centre within the boundaries of Sadovoye Koltso (Garden Ring), new capital's ensembles near former Moscow gates, an ensemble system of administrative and governmental buildings and squares, architectural monuments, existed sports facilities in combination with a system of park territories along the Moscow and the Yauza rivers and also the city-status centres of the seven planning zones.

The system of evolutionary formed radial-ring network of streets and arterial road was augmented with two chord motorways, running from north-west to south-east and from northeast to south-west, which by-passed the historic centre.

The functional organization of the zones was to be performed by setting up 66 industrial-communal zones with social centres of their own on the basis of already existed enterprises. Residential territories were to get gradually rid of old, dilapidated and small factories: only sanitarily «clean» production facilities were allowed to remain near living quarters.

The functional organization and architectural-spatial composition of the capital's development zones were conceived as an advantageous combination of large housing units and social centres' complexes. Based on the results of detailed studies and specifically held competitions, a compositional solution was selected, which envisaged the erection of tall buildings in the

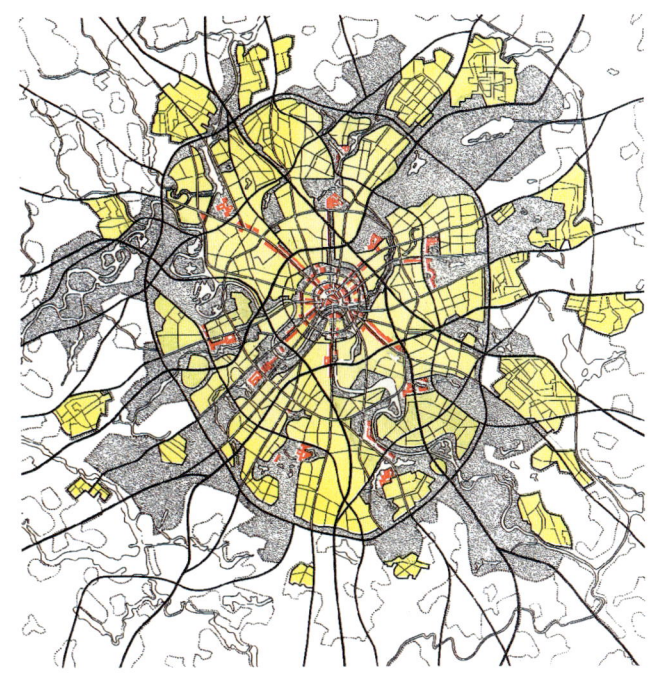

Diagram of the General Plan of Moscow. 1971.

outer perimeter of Sadovoye Ring, radial directions for the all-city centre's development and in the centres of peripheral planning zones. The bulk of housing was planned to be 9 – 12 story and sometimes – 16 story; office buildings could be as tall as 30 – 40 story and more.

An organic part of the planning structure was to become the system of planting with trees and parks, devised with due account to preserving and developing the landscape features of the city. According to the plans the norms of woods and parks territories per person had to reach the figure of 22 to 30 square metres.

It was estimated that by the deadline some 7.5 million people (8 million including Zelenograd) would live within the boundaries of the MKAD. Estimated figure for the number of

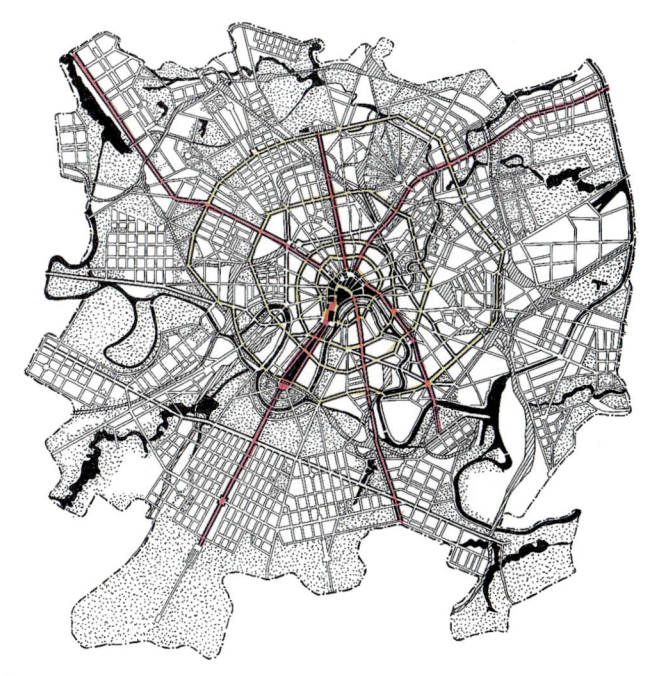

Diagram of the General Plan of Moscow. 1935.

■ system of the all-city centre.

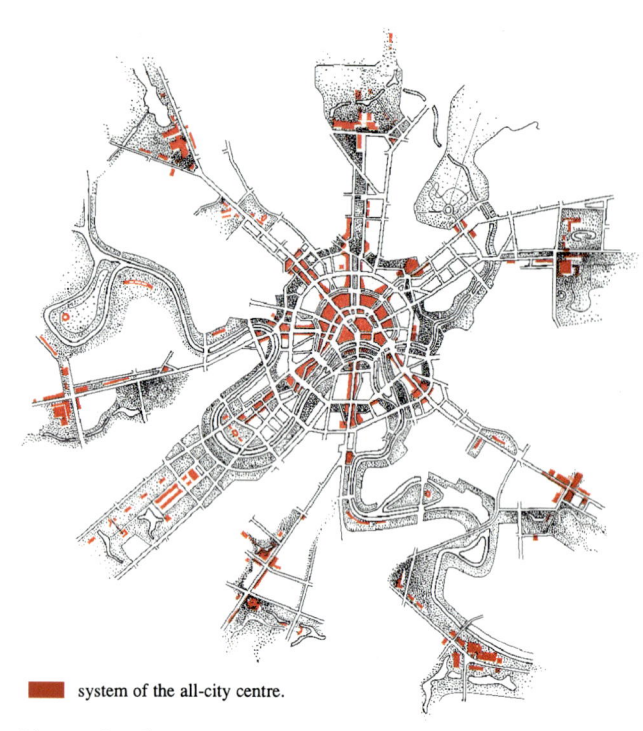

Diagram of public centre development. 1971.

the population in Moscow and the Moscow region totaled some 16 – 16.5 million people.

While defining the two regimes for the development of the suburban zone (towns and inhabited localities within the radius of 50 – 60 kilometres) and the outer belt, a reservation was made to earmark some 10 thousand hectares of reserve territories for Moscow development in the suburban zone. The adopted structure did not envisage any changes in the administrative-territorial division of the city and its region, rather it provided for exercising a city-building policy, aimed at a balanced development of the city and the region.

The enlargement of the settlement elements' system was planned, which consisted of 69 towns, 75 inhabited locations and 7,500 major villages. The action was believed to be viewed as the process of improvement, which added to the emerging trend. Thus, while in 1939 there were only 13 towns with a population in excess of 30 thousand people in the region, in 1966 the number amounted to 35. Among them there were 8 towns, which population exceeded 100 thousand people, with a special role of industrial and administrative-social centres. They were designed to ensure jobs in the adjacent area with a radius of 35 kilometres, constituting the core of the local settlement system and featuring all kinds of services. The towns of Klin, Dmitrov, Dubna, Zagorsk, Orekhovo-Zuevo, Shatura, Kolomna, Serpukhov, Naro-Fominsk, Volokolamsk and two pairs of towns – Noginsk-Elektrostal and Stupino-Kashira-Ozherelye were to become such centres. The development of those towns was planned as both multi-industry and single-major – scientific centres, recreation areas.

The implementation of the ideological doctrine, popular at that time, of gradual leveling the existed differences between urban and rural areas, raising material and cultural levels of life in the country, was also seen in reasonable enlargement of agricultural enterprises and rural inhabited localities by turning them into town-like settlements with adequate utilities and services. The program envisaged the reduction of villages, first, from 7,500 down to 1,800 and subsequently to 600 – 700. Establishing town-like central settlements was started by drawing projects of moving people from, as they put it, «unpromising» villages to those central settlements. Agriculture of the region had to major in vegetable-growing, horticulture and floriculture.

The strategy for the capital's centre development was based on three postulates: central core within Sadovoye Koltso; radial directions for the development of the all-city centre; central ensemble system with all-city status.

Taking into account the fact that business and social centre of the capital had evolved around the Kremlin – the symbol of statehood system, the General Plan reserved that zone for all top state and social institutions, which place was to be determined in the project for the all-city centre's development.

Besides, the whole area within Sadovoye Koltso had to maintain its status as the historic-revolutionary, cultural-educational and administrative-social core of Moscow. It was planned to increasingly thin out its building at the expense of pulling down dilapidated and low-value houses and their partial substitution with planted trees. Tall administrative buildings were to be erected in the outer perimeter of Sodovoye Koltso, which larger part had to be planted with trees and gardens.

By that time the radial directions of the city development were emerging as kind of linear structures with many servicing facilities. For example, the Gorky street – Leningradsky Avenue were specified as a continuous chain of the leading city ensembles. In the northern direction – the «green beam» was an extension of the Tsvetnoi Bulvar – VDNKH (exhibition grounds) axis.

Besides, more radial directions were singled out: northeast – Novokirovsky Avenue; east – complex of buildings in Zastava Ilyicha and Entuziastov Highway; south-east – based on reconstructed Volgogradsky Avenue; south-west – Ordynka, Bolshaya Tulinskaya, Profsoyuznaya streets and Sevastopolsky avenue; west – from the Kalinin Avenue to a would be park on the Poklonnaya Hill. The centre of the Southern planning zone was to be formed with due account to the historically evolved reserve ensembles of Kolomenskoye and Tsaritsyno. The General Plan included the proposals on determining the value and status of more than a thousand of monuments of history,

General Plan of the Moscow development. 1971.

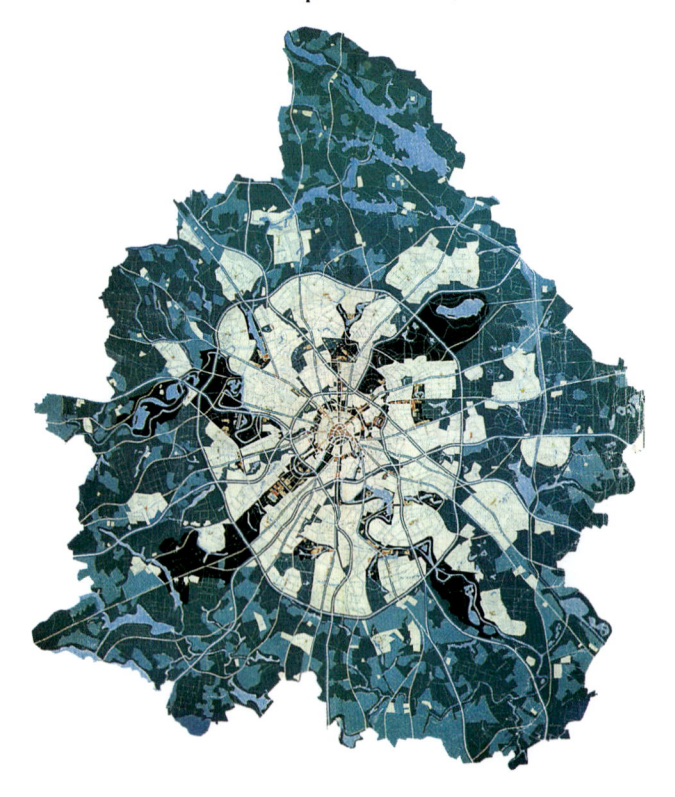

Legend:

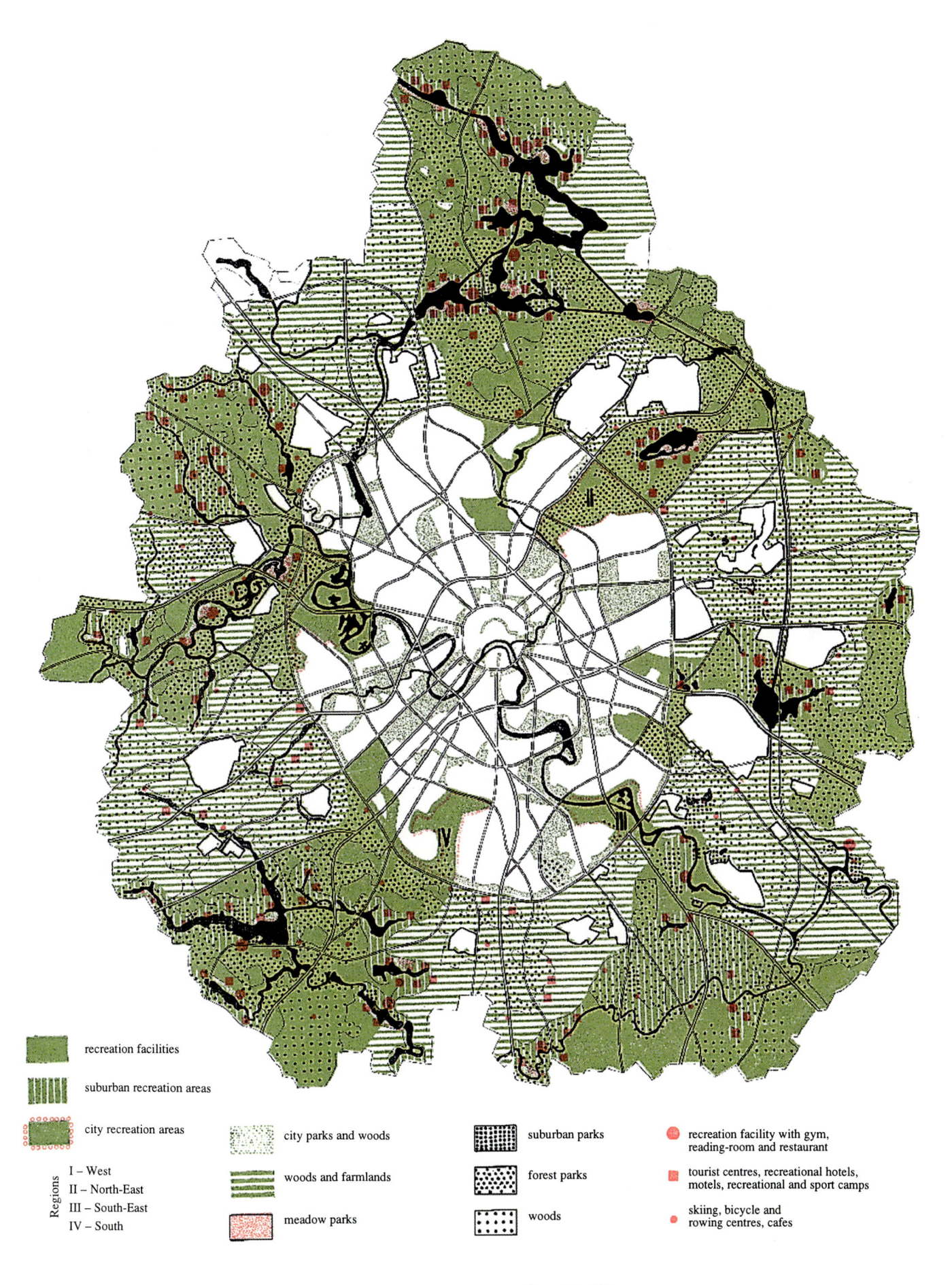

- recreation facilities
- suburban recreation areas
- city recreation areas

Regions:
- I – West
- II – North-East
- III – South-East
- IV – South

- city parks and woods
- woods and farmlands
- meadow parks
- suburban parks
- forest parks
- woods
- recreation facility with gym, reading-room and restaurant
- tourist centres, recreational hotels, motels, recreational and sport camps
- skiing, bicycle and rowing centres, cafes

Recreation setup in Park and Forest Green Belt. 1971.

V. Andreyev, N. Rudomazin: subway and highway double-deck bridge in Luzhniki. 1958.

architecture and culture, out of which 405 ensembles and individual buildings were state protected; recommendation on their subsequent functional use were written.

So-called «protective zones» were envisaged in the General Plan as a chief document designed to ensure safety for the architectural monuments and their inclusion in the composition of the buildings under reconstruction. It had a force of a law and had to prevent not only their physical elimination, but being dominated by new structures, as well.

Clearing spaces around the Kremlin, including pulling down alien buildings in terms of art in the territory, was noted as a remarkable city-building achievement. Historical continuity, saving all the best of the existed buildings were declared to be a prerequisite for preserving the originality of Moscow's architectural appearance.

The objective of the housing construction program was to provide by the deadline every family with an individual apartment with the norm of 20 square metres per person instead of previous 13 – 13.5. The total living space of houses that year amounted to 145 million square metres, so to accomplish the above task some 60 million square metres of living space with improved quality and comfort had to be built. The transition

In the South-West of Moscow. Church of Michael the Archangel in Troparevo. 1980s.

from the pattern projects to the construction based on industrial products in the Unified Catalogue was aimed at the departure from a monotonous and uniform way of the early massive building and ensuring the requirements of aesthetic and compositional tasks to improve the quality of new raions, micro raions, streets and arterial roads were met. The quality of housing was also planned to be raised by reconstructing old capital buildings.

Housing was to be constructed as a package, including a complete set of utilities and service structures organic to the respective structural element of building: starting from a residential unit and up to a microraion, raion, planning raion and, finally, an element of the all-city centre in a planning zone.

Based on the contemporary achievements in science and technology the General Plan provided for the comprehensive development of the Moscow transportation system. In 1969 it was approved by the USSR Council of Ministers as the basis for the development of rail, underground, road, air and water transportation in Moscow and the Moscow region.

It was forecast that the number of cars by the deadline would reach 550 thousand (1 – 1.2 million in prospect). However, the priority of public transport for the future was confirmed.

The street network development was planned with due account to the historically evolved structure of radial-ring streets and arterial roads, which were to be partially relieved from overload by building a system of city speedways. The system was to be composed of the ring road (MKAD) and four speedways (chords), which had to by-pass the historic centre in pairs at a distance of five kilometres from it and lead to the national highways. The routing for the new roads was believed not to affect valuable and important, in terms of city-building, parts of the city or introduce any inconveniences into its life.

The General Plan outlined a broad program of measures aimed at providing the engineering support and equipping the territory of the city.

To meet increasing water supply demands a new source, the Upper Volga's inflow – the Vazuza river, was planned to be used, while the purified water from the Kuryanovskaya aeration facility was to be supplied for industrial purposes.

The sewerage, maintained as a fully divided system, secured an overall provision for Moscow, WPPB and Moscow-biased areas in the Moscow region. A new, high capacity sewerage system with purification facilities was projected to be built in the mouth of the Pakhra river.

Power supply for Moscow was to be provided from the previous sources, those of the Mosenergo city and regional power plants and the United Energy System of the USSR. Gradual replacement of surface power lines by underground cabling was also envisaged, which would vacate large territories for the city needs.

The system of centralized heat supply by thermal plants and big boiler-houses was to meet the demands in heat and running hot water. The construction of the Ochakovskaya and Southern thermal plants was in the plans. It was believed that the future here belonged to the construction of new generation thermal plants outside the WPPB.

Gas supply from the fields in the Western Siberia was designed to increase its consumption and to make its share in the heat balance of 95 per cent for Moscow and 98 per cent for the WPPB.

The General Plan also envisaged the development of telephone communications by constructing 40 exchanges 100 thousand numbers each to provide with telephones every individual apartment, factory or office. The aggregate capacity

«Kolomenskoe» Country-Estate Ensemble.

of the network was to make up some 3.5 million numbers. The development of long distance telephone communications and invention of videotelephones were also in the plans.

The sanitary cleaning of the city suggested the construction of waste-processing and waste-burning factories and erection of the three of them started. The planned capacity of the facilities was seven (eight with WPPB) million cubic metres of garbage annually, which would allow for the elimination of open dumps of rotten waste.

It was planned to give up manual labour for waste collection, arranging for regular street watering, electro-vacuum sweeping in summer and efficient snow removal in winter.

Newspapers of those years read, «The General Plan's outlines is a multi-sided program, aimed at radical transformation of Moscow. The best aspirations of the people, following the path of building communism under the leadership of the Communist Party, will be integrated in the life and appearance of the capital».

In Defense of the Historic Moscow

Nowadays, when you meet somebody at the «top», confer with your buddies – architects or read the press you do not have to answer questions or refute assertions such as, «Why do we need to protect monuments?» or «You are responsible for defending monuments, so do it! If you, guys, are so smart, then how come you allowed the Christ the Savior Cathedral be demolished?» or «We are to build new life and you are so imposing with your demands: not to pull down buildings here or there...»

And just some 10 – 20 years ago such questions and assertions were common at both high level meetings, deciding the issues of reconstruction, debating things with all level designers and at table.

At that period unlike in preceding decades (when the majority of unique historic-architectural buildings had been subjected to either physical destruction or moral ostracism because of purely ideological considerations) the architectural heritage was beginning to be perceived by the authorities and most architects «in the background of continuous forward movement» as something, which, although had to be preserved, but being special, of elite, «a thing in itself» and, thus, standing in the way to progress, as a road block. And if you were not allowed to crush that road block or push it away, then, at least, you had to try by-pass it quickly and go ahead along «the way of progress». So, what about the «road block»? Nothing special. Let it lie about and let those «gone off the rails» art critics, renegade-architects and hysterical public persons take care of it.

As a result of the situation, by the early 70s in Moscow in its former borders (in the territory of about 900 square kilometres) only 250 architectural monuments – both individual buildings and ensembles – were registered as state protected. And the majority of them (about 70%) were in a very poor shape. However, not more than two dozens of them were under restoration at a time.

It is worth noting, anyway, that because of that above-mentioned «specialty, being of elite and thing in itself» the restoration, although slow, was done very professionally.

Assessing the situation with the architectural monuments' protection in Moscow one could come to a conclusion that a breakthrough in the public consciousness towards the national cultural heritage as a whole, having originated in the early 60s, became quite obvious by that time.

Certainly, the evolution took place not «out of a sudden» or by someone's good will, but because of a number of economic, social and political reasons.

When in the 1960s new housing was urgently built (there was no other way out) resulting in massive «rejection» of everything that looked «individual», «small» and «dilapidated» (and no wonder, for no major repairs had been done to the buildings, virtually, since 1910, just «refreshing» by painting their fronts on the eve of «great revolutionary anniversaries», which occured every five-six years) in most of our historic cities and towns, the broad public began demonstrating what was called a «rejection syndrome» to all that panel-architecture «dullness», flooding our towns and cities.

A clear discord of the «new mass architecture» with the soft middle-Russian landscape, appearances of the towns and cities evolving for centuries, their comfortable scales became so obvious, that not only individual buildings of historic value, but whole old towns with their microreliefs, original building and attractive planning were being protected from the «assembly line building». Most active part of the Russian art, letters and academic intelligentsia was literally bursting to go into action against damaging the old towns, which was gaining both pace and momentum.

«Tsaritsino» Country-Estate Ensemble. (Authors of restoration architects V. Libson, I. Ruben, G. Zyubin).
Part of a gallery with the arch of the Big Palace.
The Big Bridge.

That public movement was legalized in 1966 with the establishment of the All-Union Society for Protection of Historic and Cultural Monuments (VOOPIK).

Much was said and written about the role of that non-governmental organization, its founders – major public figures, writers, artists, pedagogues. Most praise of their selfless devotion should be attributed to the fact that they had not only to convince and win the rest of intelligentsia, the press, TV people, architects and builders, but to literally break the stereotypes of the attitude to the own culture, its history and architectural heritage with the authorities. At that time it could be referred to as nothing short of a moral heroic deed.

It can be presumed that in 1971 – 1974 the breakthrough in the attitude to the architectural heritage of Moscow finally took its shape. Its first signs were, for instance, drawing and approving «The Project for Detailed Planning of Moscow's Centre Within the Borders of Sadovoye Koltso», which was quite reformatory in 1972. The notion of «reserve streets» was introduced in the document for the first time (later, when the Project was being finalized in the GlavAPU, the notion was even extended to «reserve zones», occupying some 30 per cent of the territory within Sadovoye Koltso). The action, which may seem limited and unprofessional today, was perceived by builders and administrators as something next to a revolution in the public consciousness.

That «Moscow's early Renaissance» was completed with the approval of an additional list of architectural monuments, numbering 407 of them for Moscow alone, by the government of the Russian Federation. In the same years, first the All-Union's in 1976 and then in 1978 the Russian laws «On Protecting and Employing the Monuments of History and Culture» were written and passed.

The next 10 – 12 years (till the mid-80s) can be referred to as a period of major (for that time) changes in terms of quality of the architectural heritage's protection and maintenance. Basically, those changes meant a much greater role of the state bodies and institutions, set up to perform protective functions for the monuments of culture (architecture, in the first place) in the process of city-building; a significant upsurge in the scale of repairs and restoration (5 – 6 fold in the decade at comparable prices); rapidly growing influence of the VOOPIK and public opinion, exercised through periodicals, TV, at debates and discussions in the Artists', Writers' and Architects' Unions, in deciding the issues of the heritage protection; a flood of letters by the Muscovites to the city and Party authorities, mass media.

In the same years the state system for cultural heritage protection was being strengthened and improved. The architecture protection state body of Moscow grew from a GlavAPU's central structure into an autonomous, specially authorized organ, responsible for the protection of all immovable monuments of culture in the capital (i.e. all architectural ensembles, buildings and structures of major or unique historic or cultural value – monuments of architecture and history, works of monumental art and landscape architecture, archeological monuments). To cope with the radically increased functions the organ's status was raised respectively (starting from 1982 it was transformed into the Department of State Control Over the Protection and Employment of Historic and Cultural Monuments of Moscow (UGK OIP of Moscow or UGK), while its structure underwent the changes of principle. The UGK was composed of 18 divisions, majoring in: protection of monuments of history, architecture, landscape architecture, city-building, buildings and structures, belonging to the historic city-building environment, immovable monuments accounting, archeology, propaganda and information for the benefits of the cultural heritage protection (the latter three divisions were significantly increased by the mid-80s and grew large enough to enjoy the status of «centres» by the early 90s).

The structure seemed to better match the growing public interest in the issue of protecting the monuments of culture with that of the authorities (which was most often forced) not only in Moscow or the Russian Federation, but throughout the

М. Казаков: The First City Hospital. 1790.

«Kuskovo» Country-Estate.

Sklifosofsky Hospital (former Almshouse of Count Sheremetev by D. Quarenghi). 1792 – 1907.

Soviet Union. Like in the capital similar bodies aimed at protecting the cultural heritage were emerging in other republics of the former Soviet Union and major historic towns of Russia (Novgorod Velikii, Pskov, Vladimir, Tomsk, Omsk and others).

Let us try to conclude what was done by Moscow organizations and, primarily, the city's official body for protecting architectural monuments, for the two decades, which preceded the emergence of «market economy» and what they failed to implement.

To begin with, it should be noted that during that period a broad legislative and legal basis was adopted (with mistakes, delays, but they did it!), regulating the issue of cultural heritage: the Law of the USSR of 1976 and the Law of the Russian Federation of 1978, regulatory acts and instructions of 1980-84s. Both positive and negative lessons learned in Moscow, the largest historic city in the country, were taken into account while preparing the documents.

A successive attempt was made to let the country's leadership and people realize the importance of protecting not only individual monuments but whole historic cities and towns as well. Although it can not be said that the issues of interrelationship between the historic and architectural heritage and new construction were being actively addressed in practice, yet, they were outlined in principle and drawn in legal terms, which alone meant a lot for that rigidly regulated, kept in «blinkers» period of social life. And the biggest tribute here was to be paid to the VOOPIK, various federal bodies for protecting monuments of culture and architecture in the Ministries of Culture of the USSR and the Russian Federation, city monuments protecting inspections of Moscow and Leningrad.

Starting from 1974 – 1975, it was managed to get the Moscow authorities involved in preparing and implementing annual programs of restoration and better use of architectural monuments. As a result, the volumes of restoration work (at comparable prices) grew from 2.5 – 3 million rubles in 1970 – 1971 up to 90 – 110 million rubles by the mid-1980s.

For that period of time restorations and repairs of various kinds were carried out in 420 buildings-monuments, as well as in many historic-architectural ensembles. Among them were: the Moscow Kremlin, St. Daniel Monastery, Kolomenskoye and Kuskovo Palaces, the Column Hall of the Nobility Assembly, a great number of mansions, belonging to the 19th-early 20th centuries; some individual buildings of Novo-Spassky, Vysoko-Petrovsky and Donskoi Monasteries, Krutitskoye Metochion; «Palibin's House», «Metropol» and «Savoy» hotels and many others. It should be specifically noted that the research and restoration, conducted in Moscow, resulted in discovering a group (about a dozen and half) of monuments dating back to the Middle Ages' civil architecture of the16th-17th centuries – Gosudarev Aptekarsky prikaz (Royal Chemist's office), chambers in Ostozhenka and Prechistenka streets, Bolshoi Znamensky lane, Osipenko street.

And here, it would be worth mentioning the names of the leading at that time restoration organizations (both designers and producers), which took most active part in the work – Soyuzrestavratsiya and Rosrestavratsiya groups and Mosrestavratsiya group, having detached from the latter in 1977 – 1979 with a direct assistance from the city authorities and the Department for Protecting Architectural Monuments of Moscow. Among such organizations also were: Mosproyekt-1 and Mosproyekt-2 studios for projects and plans, Moscow Genplan's Project Institute and others.

Much restoration work completed recently had been started at that period (National Hotel, The Granite Palace chambers, St.Feudor Studit at Nikitskiye gates and St.Trinity in Kozhevniki churches), while Tsaritsyno, Razumovskiye and Yasenevo ensembles are still being restored with varying pace. Many historic buildings, such as Sytin's house, the house of the All-Union Theater Society, apartment house # 26 in Tverskaya street, chambers in Kozhevniki and many others, were first saved from demolition and later restored.

At that most complex, difficult and, yet, interesting twenty-year period of revaluing the role of heritage in our lives, discussing ways for its preservation and sophisticated use, the situation was really very tense. On the one hand, the authorities, economic planners, administrators, city- and «just»-builders were often guided by the old, time-proven principle of «down with everything, which belongs to the past, if it stands in the way to the future». On the other hand, there was an explosion of public indignation in the mid-80s, compared with shot out steam from a boiler, because of the continuing (despite all offi-

N. Oskolov (engineer), R. Klein (architect):
Borodinsky Bridge. Fragment. 1913.

cial declarations «on the protection of the cultural heritage») process of old Russian towns' destruction (regrettably, Moscow here set an example for the rest of the country). Sometimes, most radical public attempted even to stop the builders (there were cases when people lay down on the ground in front of approaching bulldozers and spent nights in the houses earmarked for demolition).

Such was the situation in which the official monuments protection bodies were doing their best to maintain their position in the middle – between the two fires, two extremes, trying not to let either the authorities or the radicals from the public or the press impose their will upon them. That does not mean, of course, that they did not have to make any concessions, like a chess-player, who often has to give up a chess-man to save the rest of the troop.

Were there losses? Certainly. However, kind of law-abidingness on the part of the authorities became the sign of the time, for the latter no longer were in a hurry to rebuild or pull down what formally enjoyed legal protection in accordance with the Laws of 1976 – 1978.

In the 1970s – 1980s a package of architectural-planning materials and regulatory documents, governing the development of historic zones based on the objective to preserve Moscow as the country's largest historic city, was prepared and approved. Some documents (ordered by the UGK OIP, which also assisted in preparing them) are still in effect: feasibility study for regulating the development of Moscow's historic centre within the boundaries of Kamer-Kollezhsky rampart; integrated historic-architectural base plan for the city's historic core within the boundaries of Sadovoye Koltso and others. Based on them and similar materials the then Moscow City Executive Committee adopted later a resolution on the regimes, governing city-building in Moscow's historic centre.

The most important document, perhaps, was the integrated program for protecting architectural heritage of our city, devised by the Moscow UGK, which drew a line under more than twenty-year period when the radically new approach to the issue of protecting immovable monuments had been taking shape. That category of monuments included: the whole of old Moscow as a monument of city-building and individual buildings, structures – monuments of architecture and history, city monuments, monuments of landscape architecture and archeology.

The program, devised in 1986 – 1988 with active participation by the city authorities (B.N. Yeltsin, who headed the city Party organization then, oversaw it personally) and named «Architectural Heritage of Moscow – Year of 2000», was approved by the Moscow City Executive Committee in June, 1989, following long and heated debate by experts, public, city management and organizations. One, who knows the Russian reality well, may not believe, but most of the program was implemented in 5 – 6 years to follow, while its methodological introductory part, defining basic problems in protecting immovable monuments and concrete ways of addressing them, is still relevant.

All-Russian Society for Protection of Historic and Cultural Monuments

Article 126 in the Stalin Constitution of 1936 allowed for setting up «workers' associations», and they were to be supervised by the departments or Soviets of Deputees, which approved their rules. In reality, it was top Party structures, which seized the monopoly in allowing any social organizations be established for many years and exercised a very pragmatic approach here, that of «minimizing the trouble». Professional or semi-professional associations – unions of creative people, inventors, hunters and the like – met the criterion best of all. To achieve educational goals within the authorized scope the All-Union Society for Popularization of Political and Scientific Learning was established in 1947 (known as Znaniye (learning) since 1965), which became well known not only for its atheistic lectures but numerous, well-done editions of popular books and brochures, focusing on actual problems of science and technology.

Such an appeasing picture of the social associations inherited from the Stalin epoch suited Party functionaries of all levels in Khrushchev's times pretty well, too. That is the reason why the proposal to establish a voluntary society for protecting monuments of history and culture in the RSFSR met with resistance in the CPSU Central Committee. The notion of «monument» implies something purely spiritual or ideological, while the notion of «protection» means potential or inevitable struggle.

It took patriots five years to have the Council of Ministers of the Russian Federation adopt a decision in July, 1965, allowing for the VOOPIK establishment. With Khrushchev in power there was no way to do that. For the Party headquarters the resistance was worthwhile. It was precisely during the time that the Palace of Congresses in the Kremlin, «Yunost» hotel, «Rossiya» movie theater, «Moscow» swimming pool were all built, let alone no-style colossus – a hotel in Zaryadye, which as if mockingly was also named «Rossiya» with a deciphering line, running across its pediment – restaurant, hotel, concert hall.

The resolution by the Council of Ministers of the RSFSR was taken just several months after an exposition «Poetry of the Russian Land», packing in great audiences, had been arranged by «Rodina» – a youth historic-patriotic club, under I.S. Glazunov's initiative in «Yunost» hotel. During the preceding year Rodina club held a number of events, mainly in higher education establishments, which were dedicated to the Russian heritage and its protection. The events, coupled normally with discussions, attracted absolutely full houses. The student youth, which «spiritual assets» since 1938 had been prescribed not to extend beyond the course in the CPSU history, all of a sudden learned about genuine Russian spirituality and its contemporary followers. The so-called «patronage group» over the «Rodina» youth club included painter P.D. Korin, sculptor S.T. Konyonkov, architect-restorer P.D. Baranovsky, writer L.M. Leonov, cosmonaut A.A. Leonov, airplane designer O.K. Antonov, opera singer I.S. Kozlovsky, engineer V.P. Tydman, writer V.A. Soloukhin and many other devotees of the Russian culture.

In thirty five years after the societies for studying the Moscow province and Russian country estates had been abolished, volunteers began coming to the country side around Moscow to examine the conditions of half-destroyed churches, take pictures of them, cut trees, growing on the roofs, and demand local authorities take elementary measures for protecting the monuments of architecture.

The VOOPIK was founded by many prominent scientists, men of art and letters, who in 1960 set up commissions on cultural monuments and museums with the influential Soviet Committee in Defense of Peace. Among them were: Academicians – M.V. Alpatov, M.D. Millionstchikov, M.V. Nechkina, I.G. Petrovsky, B.N. Rybakov, M.N. Tikhomirov, V.M. Khvostov; Doctors – A.V. Artsikhovsky, N.N. Voronin, B.P. Mikhailov, P.P. Revyakin, I.S. Smirnov; People's Artists – S.V. Gerasimov, A.A. Plastov; sculptor – V.A. Pavlov; writers – I.A. Belokon, V.D. Zakharchenko, S.V. Mikhalkov, S.S. Smirnov, and others. Many volunteers, including those who lived far from Moscow, enthusiastically assisted the commissions, forming a backbone of what would later grow into the society for protection of monuments. Ironically, it was the time of the most vicious anti-religion actions by Khrushchev and his henchmen. Thanks to their authority and much effort, the founders of the society managed to get the Party structures' (the Central Committee) and the Council of Ministers' of the Russian Federation consent and include a paragraph into the rules of the society, which entitled its Central Board to the right of participation in decision-making, concerning fates of the historic and cultural monuments. It was the first and, perhaps, the only time in the country's history that a public organization won a «right of veto» in respect of decisions taken by the all-mighty state bodies.

We can be absolutely confident now, that unless it had happened we would have already forgotten, what historic Moscow looked like. But to realize the right, the society had to study every problem much in depth and come up with perfectly argumented, scientific conclusions, which could not be disproved by «creators of the new world», bursting to the historic heart of Moscow with their projects.

The founding convention of the Society was held in the early May, 1966. No wonder, that when a division of the All-Russian Society for Protection of Historic and Cultural Monuments was opened in Moscow, hundreds of volunteers of different age groups and professions joined it, working for its various sections.

During its first years the Moscow City Division (MGO) faced a lot of natural difficulties, those of office space shortages for its sections and a conference hall for large meetings. Help came from the Znaniye society and the Central Board of the VOOPIK, which resided in a part of Vysoko-Petrovsky Monastery. In August, 1968, the «Rodina» youth club, which had occupied the premises of Krutitskoye Metochion, having restored by P.D. Baranovsky, since summer 1964, joined the MGO. Until the club was closed in November, 1972, its members worked in three main areas: restoration, examining monuments and education.

The society for protection of monuments borrowed some of Znaniye's organizational experience and placed its emphasis on recruiting more people. Even in 1966 VOOPIK members were issued «nice-looking» membership cards, and annual fee was «standard» for all public associations of the time, amounting to 30 kopecks. The number of Moscow's raions pre-determined the number of local branches, which were designed to pool members of primary cells in factories and offices in respective raions. Material financial support to the Society was rendered by its collective members – institutions and enterprises, which average annual fee made up about a thousand rubles.

Overall, funds raised in the city were partially channeled to support restoration of architectural and historic monuments.

In June, 1966, soon after the VOOPIK's founding convention the RSFSR Council of Ministers passed a resolution «On Protecting Monuments», and the special about the resolution was the fact that public involvement in its preparation was unprecedentedly significant.

Throughout the 60s and 70s the MGO in conjunction with sections and commissions of the Central Board were struggling hard against the implementation of many provisions, contained in the Feasibility Fundamentals (approved in 1966) for the General Plan of Moscow development, as well as a number of principal positions of the next General Plan, adopted in 1971, with the plans for the period through 1980.

The MGO's efforts became much more efficient when it moved in 1970 in the premises of the refectory church in Znamensky Monastery, which was located in Varvarka street of Zaryadye. Under the arch of bell-tower a large hall with wonderful acoustics was made available, which was suitable for both lectures and concerts. Staff of architectural and historical sections, which coordinated their activities with the Central Board, was strengthened. Public inspection team (headed by V.A. Vinogradov and then V.P. Apenin) was formed, which looked for and examined valuable historic-architectural buildings and ensembles and did all paperwork so that the monuments could be declared state protected. Experimental special research and restoration workshop (ESNRPM), set up with the VOOPIK Central Board, performed the following tasks: examining Moscow monuments on orders of the Society; restoration work funded by the Society; training of restorers; participation in saving from demolition and protecting individual monuments and whole historic blocks of buildings. In about six year time the ESNRPM, assisted by hundreds of the Society's activists and based on numerous archive materials and «on the spot» techniques, managed to carry out the historic-architectural survey of the whole historic area of Moscow. The importance of the accomplishment can hardly be overestimated, for neither fundamental historical research in city-building of Moscow, nor theoretical concepts for its development as an integral phenomenon and unique monument to the Russian culture and civilization were available at that point.

In 1969 the Central Board of the Society rejected, as causing unacceptable damage to the city's appearance, the «Project of Moscow's Detailed Planning», prepared by the GlavAPU, which managers kept on campaigning for the «radial-ring» scheme for Moscow's development and saying that with the «amorphous» historical texture of the capital «there would be no chance to fit it into the idea of a new communist city». But the times when criticism was not encouraged and some critics persecuted were gone, so you had to join debate with your opponents from the Society and offer ways to reach compromise. In 1972, 1973, 1975 in a row slightly modified projects for the Moscow centre's reconstruction were submitted to the VOOPIK and rejected again. VOOPIK's partial but still meaningful success came as historic-architectural reserve zones were formed in the historic part of Moscow (within the boundaries of Sadovoye Koltso). Here an entirely different approach for Russia in dealing with monuments of history and architecture as part of the city's single organism, having evolved through centuries based on its own laws, became obvious.

By the mid-80s the VOOPIK had about 15 million members and represented a formidable public organization to be reckoned with even for the CPSU, whose strength was comparable. One can say that in the place of nearly totally destroyed Russian Orthodox Church shoots of new workers for monuments of history and culture and, thus, spiritual salvation of Russia grew.

«Monuments of Motherland»

Almost a quarter of the century has passed since the Soviet Union and Russian Federation laws on protecting monuments were passed. And nearly a hundred years ago the Society for protection and preservation of art and olden times monuments, headed by the Grand Duke Nikolai Mikhailovich, was founded in Russia.

Between the two social events in the Russian history of the 20th century horrible or quoting poet Sergei Yesenin, «terrifying and bloodiest» times are known to have lain, when the old system of living was eliminated and cultural treasures, the czarist Russia had possessed before the shock of revolution, were barbarically destroyed.

Today, we express quite justified indignation to the effect of what was done by the totalitarian regime to the national relics. However, one should not forget that something very similar, except, of course, for scales, which are matchless, took place in Russia in the 19th century when without any research old frescoes were chiseled off and ancient icons were painted over anew. A hundred years earlier, in the 18th century, olden times churches were pulled down to vacate space for ballrooms, theaters and other European-style public entertainment establishments.

Actually the notion of «monument» itself was introduced in the Russian society not in the Soviet times but much earlier – during the reign of Nicholas I, who issued a decree, ordering a roster of Russian olden times treasures be compiled. Little earlier A.S. Pushkin, referring to the «History of the Russian State» written by N.M. Karamzin, said that its publication «came as a sensation and made very strong impression... Men of fashion rushed to read the history of their Motherland. Old Russia seemed to have been discovered by Karamzin like America by Columbus».

Piously-paternal traditions were obviously neglected not only in the 20th century...

The phenomenon of olden times Russian icon, which aroused so much praise and enthusiastic exclamations in all the world's languages and dialects, was re-discovered only in the early 20th century. In particular, icons painted by Andrei Rublev were found by I.E. Grabar in a woodshed near Zvenigorod in 1908, while iconography studies by N.I. Kondakov, prince E. Trubetskoi and other scientists appeared in the late 19th – early 20th centuries.

All the above said, naturally, can never justify vandalism of the Bolsheviks in the 20s and 30s in respect of the cultural heritage of the Russian people. However, it is remarkable that in different periods of the post-Peter the Great epoch under the influence of philosophical, social and other mysteries the true sacral meaning of the ancient Russian culture was not only distorted, rather its moral or physical destruction of various magnitude took place.

Nowadays, it seems that we, who are already aware of the treacherous magic of promises relating to «building communist heavens» on Earth and other innovations, begin to realize that the perception of olden times Russian cultural treasures as monuments of culture or art only is very limited and gives very little to your mind or soul, depriving the treasures of the main reason for their creation.

And yet we should not forget that very recently even such a simplified perception of the ancient Russian relics was totally banned because of those atheistic mysteries, which like evil spirits darkened, humiliated and denounced millennial orthodox concepts about the organization of the world and structure of human society.

By the mid-60s of this century social consciousness (not of everybody, but those, who did not stay indifferent to the history and culture of the Motherland), raised on the ideals of atheism and communism, came to a conclusion that their well-being – sometimes real and most often imaginary – was based on barbaric destruction of cultural treasures, unparalleled in the history of world civilization. The understanding was followed by indignation and a desire to protest and take an action. Complaints letters, which I.S. Glasunov wittily described as the «cry of pensioners», started to be sent to the «top». Then Russian Club came into existence, where stormy discussions in defense of monuments and very quite reading of Imkapress books, which were among the first on the black list of banned publications, alternated.

One sarcastic remark, relating to the existed regime, is recollected, «It's a pity a Society of fans for building communism was not set up in the Imperial Russia, so that if someone had been fond of building communism he would have joined the Society and gone ahead».

V.M. Nedelin: View of the Moscow Kremlin and Voskresenskiye Gates from the Neglinnaya river. Reconstruction of the Second Half of the 17th Century.

Churches of St. Alexander Nevsky and the Miracle-Workers of Chernigov in the Premises of Novy Prikazy (new departments) in the Moscow Kremlin. Reconstruction by V.M. Nedelin. 1996.

For the sake of fairness it also has to be said that in those years the situation with the Society for protection of monuments was very much in the line with the remark: if you were eager to protect monuments there was the Society to join, so that you could go head till getting bored. Just one taboo had to be observed and that of not disturbing the authorities, who viewed the Society as a lightning-rod or by-pass valve.

Stormy debate and complaints letters were of some use for the monuments. For example, in the late-70s the public managed to save many houses, churches and even one whole historic area in Moscow – Shkolnaya and Tulinskaya streets – which were about to be demolished.

Monuments of Motherland literary miscellany was launched during the period. Some success achieved by the public encouraged work on the magazine, despite all the obstacles put by the people, who, driven by inertia, still viewed monuments as embodiment of hostile ideology. Actually, the word «obstacle» is too soft. It was a perfect by its logical continuity multi-level system of censorship, which denied even a possibility that something, containing only a hint of criticism of the existed regime, be published. Publishing every issue of the Monuments of Motherland reminded one of walking across a mine field. And the rules of the game were not getting easier.

At the beginning of 1981 the process of printing (printing!) of a regular issue, dedicated to Moscow, was halted and from a very top level came threats to dismiss editors from publishing trade nearly for life for their alleged attempts to paint the reality black. Other accusations ranged from maniacal great-power chauvinism and ideological dissent to striving for monarchy. Sacking could be not the only punishment for such a variety of «sins».

Today, after democratic changes brought about an absolute freedom of publishing whatever you want, the arrested issue seems to be an innocent literary miscellany. In particular, it contained articles by some historians of architecture (M.P. Kudryavtsev and others), who presented their non-traditional point of view in respect of Moscow as a spiritual centre of the world, bulwark of orthodoxy, image of heavenly Jerusalem. Running counter to the doctrine of «building a model communist city», this non-traditional hypothesis stumped and frightened everybody concerned and the time-proven tactics of power pressure was instantly applied.

In his private library late His Holiness the Patriarch of Moscow and all Russia Pimen had all the issues of the Monuments of Motherland literary miscellany, which was not on his official subscription list. Today, this fact may be seen as not very significant – what is special about the Patriarch having a complete set of issues? However, for the times at issue, when one could not even think of cooperation with priests and hierarchies of the Russian Orthodox Church, when censors impudently cut out everything that favored the Orthodox philosophy, when relics of Christianity could be presented as objects of art only, this fact expressed a very special attitude of the Russian Orthodox Church to the magazine, which despite all the party-censorship restrictions succeeded in explaining the true sacral meaning of the Russian culture.

Many people could see that the issue of preserving monuments, especially city-building heritage of Moscow and ancient Russian towns, was not that simple and clear. They got convinced that destruction of the heritage could hardly be attributed (as it had often been the case) to «ignorant architects»,

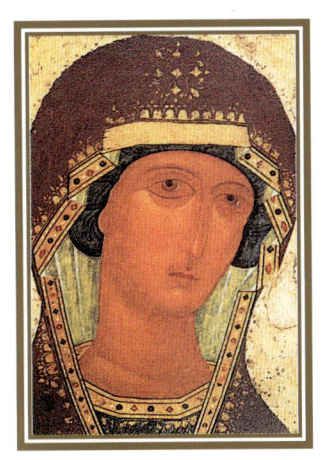

Icon. Odigitriya, the Mother of God.

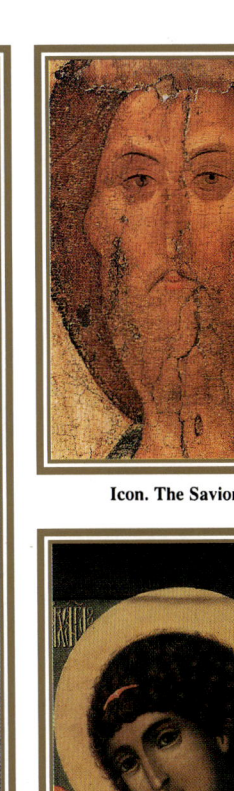

Icon. The Savior. A. Rublev.

Icon. Archangel Michael.

His Holiness the Patriarch of Moscow and All Russia Pimen. Painter V.V. Shilov.

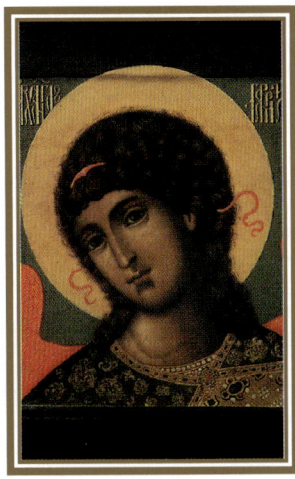

Icon. Archangel Gabriel.

«enemies of the people», bureaucrats indifferent to the historic heritage and man's will in general, let alone environmental, social-economic and other factors.

Condoling with the lost, seeing outraged beauty daily, which everybody felt pity for, the public were getting to realize that such destruction could have been caused by something extraordinary, which went beyond the ordinary and most sophisticated human ideas with regard to society's organization and that the destruction was not done by will of those in power, no matter what they were: ministers, dictators or monarchs, rather, it all happened by the will, which our forefathers, unburdened with computers, ecology and other modern concepts, had referred to as Will of God. And atheists, being irreconcilable, i.e. very proud, fail to realize that.

It was the Divine Providence that determined everything: destruction and, certainly, creation. That is why neither social-economic nor philosophical postulates can explain us how St. Basil, the Blessed Cathedral was built or the Cathedral of Christ, the Savior restored – the latter even 3 – 4 years ago seemed absolutely improbable.

Following the collapse of the communist regime and its ideology this phenomenon becomes more and more obvious, as well as the fact that there is no other spiritual and moral institution in Russia, except for the Russian Orthodox Church; no other cultural treasures, except for those, having been created for the thousand years after baptism of Russia and no other unifying popular idea, except for Orthodoxy. The moment we begin ignoring the objective truth, all attempts to give rationale for the emergence of St. Basil, the Blessed Cathedral, Protection Church upon Nerl, icons by Andrei Rublyov and frescoes by Dionisius fail.

It is only natural then, that with the downfall of the communist system the ideological concept, having evolved during the decade, of the Monuments of Motherland literary miscellany, as well as the All-Russian Society for Protection of Historic and Cultural Monuments form of existence, as an integral and organic part of the Party and state machinery, turned into nothing...

«Nasty» Commission

The debate dealt with a small house. And rather not with the house itself, but with a tiny building situated in the yard. To pull it down or not. The architect of the raion was confident: the building should be demolished. The position of the Journalists Union's representative was even more resolute: it is high time to clear Moscow from bourgeois junk, it is not permissible to bother about it because of its alleged historic value. The arguments sounded like already forgotten phrases of the 1930s. It was October 30, 1986. And indeed, what was special about house # 10 in Kalashny lane? Just the fact that it was built at the turn of the 18th and 19th centuries and survived the great Moscow fire of 1812. The fact that it was of the precise size of vanished old Moscow yards embraced by an outhouse, a stable, a coach-house and century-old spreading trees, which used to grow all around Moscow. It can be added that among its tenants, who left traces in the cultural life of the old capital, was L.M. Leonidov, an outstanding actor of the Moscow Art Theater. «Leonidov is Leonidov – V.I. Nemirovich-Dancheko used to say – he is a greatly spirited person, who explodes with breathtaking pieces of performance and then fascinates with genuine intonations of his monologues». «Years of living in Kalashnikov lane» were the years when he performed the parts of Pugachev in «Pugachevstchina» by K. Trenev, Ivan the Terrible in «The Serf's Wings», Gobsec. First, he was awarded the title of Honored and then National Artist of the Republic. And it was not the time when such awards were readily available. All drama-lovers of Moscow admired Leonidov.

Among thickly built-up areas the yard seemed to be an ideal place to accommodate a club of intelligentsia or, still better, a studio-theater, where everything was made by its actors. Here was room for sceneries and wardrobe room, there was a proper place to put a joiner's bench to repair furniture, which life was always short in the auditorium. There was a lot of volunteers to restore, fit in, maintain and take good care of the place. Many offered their both material and physical help. But the Raispolkom (executive committee) of Krasnopresnensky raion took a different decision. A drivers' school of the raion's branch of the DOSAAF (paramilitary organization) was already using the quarters. There was a flood of complaints about noise and exhaust gases it produced, so a radical decision was taken – not to change the lessee, but to pull down the buildings in the yard so that the school... could move to the house standing next.

An old house in town inevitably triggers controversy with all interested organizations involved, which usually exposes poor management, irresponsibility and strong generation-old negligence to their own past and, as a result, to contemporary population. City economy and forming a man, problems of collapsed ceilings, leaking sinks, broken doors and forming a personality – what can really the two things have in common?

A group of relatively young and very energetic people from GlavAPU got an idea to arrange pedestrian zones in Moscow, similar to those in Western cities. It was not incidental that Old Arbat was earmarked for that purpose. And it was not the alleged city traditions which mattered – Kalinin Avenue needed access transportation roads. A necessity arose to pierce a duplicate thoroughfare between the «pedestrian zone» and the new arterial road. Besides, demolition or moving to another place of the Prague restaurant to vacate space for construction of one more building was also in the plans. Projects, designed not to resolve city-building or, which is even more important, social and moral tasks, but to show who the boss was at the moment, which gave unlimited opportunities for action free from any criticism, alternated one another.

We stay short from drawing sad conclusions as to how many people, who were born and lived for many years in Arbat, died early, having moved to new residential areas. How many personal ties were severed and interaction environments destroyed. Tenants, who moved in hastily erected apartment houses of «improved comfort» and replaced the Arbat aboriginals, were not familiar with traditionally Moscow forms of personal contacts. Their problems were confined to getting a parking space or a garage, which was still better, for their cars.

The pretended completion of Old Arbat's first phase, accompanied by strong mass media campaign, could hardly be applicable to vacated houses. The bulk of them till now stand with black window apertures without glass. Destruction is taking its toll. Even if we suppose that the houses will be restored, it becomes more and more expensive with every passing day and less and less probable with every passing year. Just a few years ago the Vakhtangov Theater could have its memorable dormitory and studio in Fedotov street repaired and renovated. Now the only thing they can do is to level the building and construct it anew according to the original drawings by architect Kalugin, which are available. The Vakhtangov people still hope to save some remained interiors, unique staircases and open-work gratings.

It is worth mentioning that the alleged «reserve» status did not help house # 7 in Arbat to survive. It fell victim to construction workers' reluctance to complicate their work by laying an underground collector. House # 7 in the 1920s served the premises for a Literary Mansion where Sergei Yesenin read his «Pugachev» poem for the first time in public. Same was the destiny of house # 42, associated with Alexander Pushkin. Under the pretext of restoring the house with new materials for longer life it was pulled down and built anew. At the same time its appearance was changed by adding a multistory extension of «special purpose».

Most surprisingly, the Pushkin Museum did not believe it was their duty to interfere, although some time before they had opened their branch – the poet's apartment in Arbat – just across the street, which, by the way, had not been properly repaired and restored, rather it had also been fabricated and built anew. House # 42 was built in 1822 and first belonged to Mrs. Khvoshchinskaya – direct relation of A.M. Gorchakov's wife. Later the house was owned by Ye.N. Kiseleva, the very Elizabeth Ushakova of Presnya, who Pushkin drew numerous illustrations for in her album. Verses «You Are Spoiled By Nature» and a humorous list of Don Juan were dedicated to her. In the house on Arbat Elizabeth wrote her memoirs about the poet. Did Pushkin visit the house? Before scholars had a chance to address the issue the old walls had disappeared.

At some point house # 21/24 in Stankevich street was not viewed worth of even being put on the agenda of the Central Commission for Buildings Preserving and Demolishing. The action was put to the vote and the demolition was supported by all the architects of the Commission. The Society for Monuments Protection raised an objection, but the only concession it received was a three-day postponement (two of them were Saturday and Sunday) to prepare their historical reasons.

It was virtually nothing for any situation but for the one with the house opposite the Mossovet involved the time was more than enough. Peculiar features of its lay-out, basement, brickwork and bricks themselves dated the construction back to the 1780s. Documents from archives proved the same. The real estate once belonged to the Rayevskiyes, direct relatives of A.V. Suvorov's mother, who the great military commander maintained kind relations with. In the early 1890s the house was owned by R.P. Sablin, a representative of the famous family of Moscow cultural figures. M.A. Sablin, an outstanding statistician, who played an active part in reviving Russian handicraft industry, founder of the Handicraft Museum and one of the publishers of the Russkiye Vedomosti newspaper; no less well known book publisher V.M. Sablin; writers A.P. Chekhov and V.G. Korolenko – good friends of the family; theater figures F.A. Korsh, Vl.I. Nemirovich-Danchenko, V.E. Meyerkhold were among the habitues of the house. The «Sablins' Nights» with the participation of newly founded Moscow Art Theater's actors were very popular in Moscow. When the First Congress of the Russian Theatrical Society was being prepared some meetings took place in the house attended by M.G. Savina and N.M. Medvedeva. Even when the ownership of the house was transferred to tobacco tycoon A.I. Katyka in 1903 it only added new bright pages to its remarkable records – I.A. Bunin stayed there when in Moscow.

They managed to save the house, despite the fact it was October, 1980. A lot has changed for the past years. Multiple articles in the press, columns in newspapers and magazines, case studies on TV, round table discussions. The value of historic heritage, as well as the size of losses, which we must blame ourselves for, have long become quite obvious.

The document, signed by E.M. Chikharin, Chairman of the Council of Ministers of the RSFSR on February 27, 1987, indicated that in Moscow alone there were more than 2,900 immovable monuments – «individual buildings and structures, archeological monuments» – under the state protection. The number

Walking area «Old Arbat».

could be quite impressive should the issue deal primarily with houses. In reality houses made up only 1/5th of the number with memorial boards and signs, sculptural monuments and burial sites comprising the bulk of it.

Apart from the houses-monuments another 9,500 buildings, «forming the historically evolved building of the city's central part», were mentioned. One more number from the accounts. Starting from 1976, the year it was set up, the Central Commission for Buildings Preserving and Demolishing have considered 1,800 demolition applications, out of which «950 buildings have been preserved and are planned to be used». The statistics deserves an in depth analysis.

If we proceed from the fact that as of 1976 the total number of buildings in the historic part of the city was slightly more than ten thousands, then the GlavAPU agreed every fifth building be pulled down. Every fifth! Let us presume that the effort by the Commission reduced the number twofold. So, it leaves every tenth building of the historic environment. But to what degree the number is true? How many times decisions by the Commission, banning demolition, were ignored and pulling down took place blessed from the «top» by senior officials in the Mossovet, the RSFSR Council of Ministers, VOOPIK Central Board staff and, finally, Scientific and Methodological Board of the USSR Ministry of Culture? Divide and rule – the GlavAPU leadership had always been very skillful in exercising the tactics.

...That time the issue dealt with a block of houses located between Old Arbat, Vesnina and Lunacharskogo streets. The enlargement of the Foreign Affairs Ministry suggested pulling down some old buildings, including several blocks of one of the most valuable cultural monuments of the 19th century Moscow. Nikolai Vasilyevich Rukavishnikov, a talented pedagogue and graduate of the Moscow University, assigned himself a task of establishing an extremely humane corrective and educational reformatory for convicted children from the poorest walks of life. The reformatory was accommodated in house # 30 in Smolenskaya-Sennaya square. Additional modest brick blocks, housing a school, workshops (children were offered both educational programs and vocational training), bedrooms and living quarters for teachers were erected near the magnificent building, built in the 1780s by architect M.F. Kozakov. A free library named after A.N. Ostrovsky, serving again the poor, was accommodated in a separate building. At that time Moscow City Library # 2 had about 20 thousand readers. The one of Rukavishnikov during the first year acquired 80 thousands of them, including women and children from workers' families.

In 1888 the reformatory and the library were donated to the city of Moscow. They continued to exist, establishing the principles of humanity, trust between people and specific Russian literature orientation. Literature was the principal school subject and when former young criminals left the reformatory they were not only trained professionals but were also given a small sum of money and a collection of books by Russian writers, whom they had learned and liked. «Let it serve a lighthouse for them in their difficult life», said N.V. Rukavishnikov.

Remember or forget – today the answer seems to be absolutely unambiguous. Certainly, we must remember, pay tribute and respect our forbears for everything we owe them. At the meeting of the Central Commission the situation was different. «Bourgeois junk» – the verdict of L. Kolodny, representing the Journalists Union, was. «Ordinary building» – the conclusion of the GlavAPU's and Architects Union's experts read. The VOOPIK's Central Board fully supported that point of view. So-called Moscow Commission, part of the Board, which stopped short of participating in day to day work in the city, also found the demolition of Rukavishnikov's reformatory reasonable for the purpose of «exposing» the creation by M.F. Kazakov and making it «accessible» to the Muscovites (under the condition that the building will house the reception hall of the Foreign Ministry) at the expense of... yet another page torn out of our history. Ironically, the new block was planned to be erected behind Rukavishnikov's buildings, which virtually did not obstruct the construction. The true reason was that the buildings did not look imposing enough and besides were in a very poor shape.

There is another proven way on the part of the GlavAPU to get rid of old buildings, standing in the way, – taking a decision to move such buildings to another place. In November 20, 1978, the Mossovet took a decision on moving N.F. Von Mekk's mansion (Myaskovskogo st. 6) to align it with houses # 4 – 12. The mansion does not exist since then. House of poet A.N. Pleshcheev (Oruzheiny lane 3), dismantled for subsequent restoration, was abandoned as a heap of useless rotten wood in Kuzminki. Many other historic houses were not restored and ceased to exist. Among them: house of V.G. Belinsky in Rakhmanovsky lane 4, which gave way to a parking lot; house of S.V. Rakhmaninov in Kalinin Avenue 11; a small house of a preacher of the St. John the Warrior church in Dimitrov street 48; a mansion of the early 19th century in Gilyarovskogo street 25. A famous palace of the Ostermann-Tolstoys (Samarsky lane 24) turned into pieces of rotten wood after many years of negligence and lack of maintenance.

Moscow, having been on the verge of loosing its historically evolved appearance, needs new city-building concepts and a new architectural and plastic language badly. The city is also far from looking like a future-oriented capital of a socialist country. Featureless, without a trace of spirituality construction as an aggregate, no matter how big it is, can not result in the creation of such an appearance and formation of the adequate moral environment.

Meanwhile our Moscow can not wait. Every day can bring about new and irreplaceable losses. New ideas are in demand, as well as new people and not those, who only yesterday voted for total demolition and invented technologies for that end. What we really need is the participation of the Muscovites or, in other words, – our hearts open to all the things our History has endowed us with[6].

General Plans of 1935 and 1971 Public Criticism

When in 1935 the plan for the renewed capital was being outlined it was specified that: «...it is necessary to proceed from the premise of preserving the foundations of the historically evolved city, but with its radical re-planning by means of decisive regulation of the city's network of streets and squares»; «taking the historically evolved radial-ring system of streets as a basis for city-planning, augment it with a system of new streets, which would relieve the centre from traffic and allow direct transportation links between the raions of the city without forced passage through its centre be established».

Based on such a directive, Moscow reconstruction plan of 1935 was devised, having served the basis for subsequent draft General Plans of 1951 and 1971, without a special research on the city-planning. Till 1935 (actually till 1969) none of the city architects made a professional study of the gist of the «historically evolved planning of Moscow». Everything was farmed out to historians P.V. Sytin, S.K. Bogoyavlensky. And prior to devising the General Plan P. and B. Goldenbergs were assigned a task of substantiating the idea of «radial-ring» planning of old Moscow.

The radial-ring element of circular planning expansion during the period of capitalist development of Moscow was mistaken for the «historically evolved» city-planning system,

Traffic maelstrom instead of ancient Moscow.

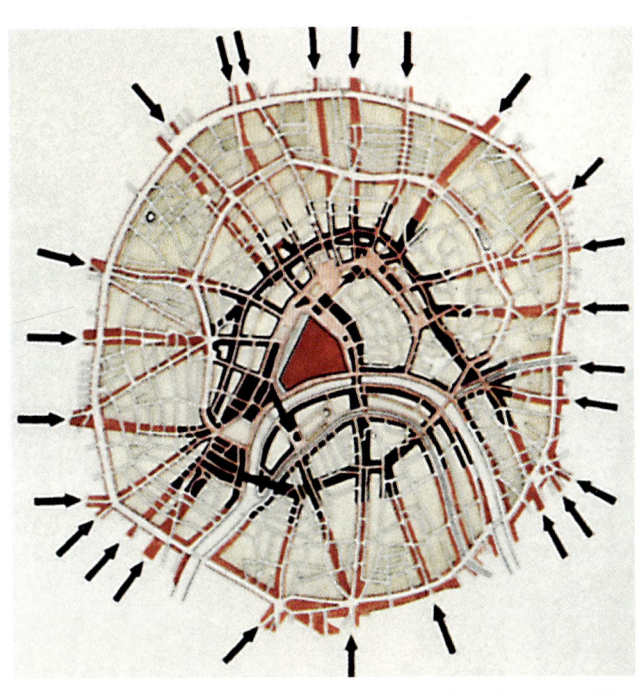

Map of the project «red lines» designed for the demolition of the old Moscow plan, buildings and composition.

which later served the basis for the formation of socialist Moscow with radical re-planning of the centre, providing for an «improved» radial-ring system. As a matter of fact, however, the centre of Moscow took shape in the times of feudalism and had an entirely different, unique fan tracery and branching planning system, which was implemented at the turn of 17th and 18th centuries as a grandiose image of a Heavens City,

recognized by the Eurasian civilization as a world Orthodox power. Excessive centralization of budget in the 30s led to the uncontrolled growth of industry, size of the population and city territory. Such a situation, despite resolutions on limiting the growth of industry, continuously postponed the resolution of the housing problem and stimulated the adoption of new ring boundaries, which were extended many times under the thrust

City centre according to the General Plan of 1971.

■ – area of the city centre for the scheduled period to 1995 along 3 diametres.

– it was planned to build 6 nodal centres with 30-storey buildings in the future.

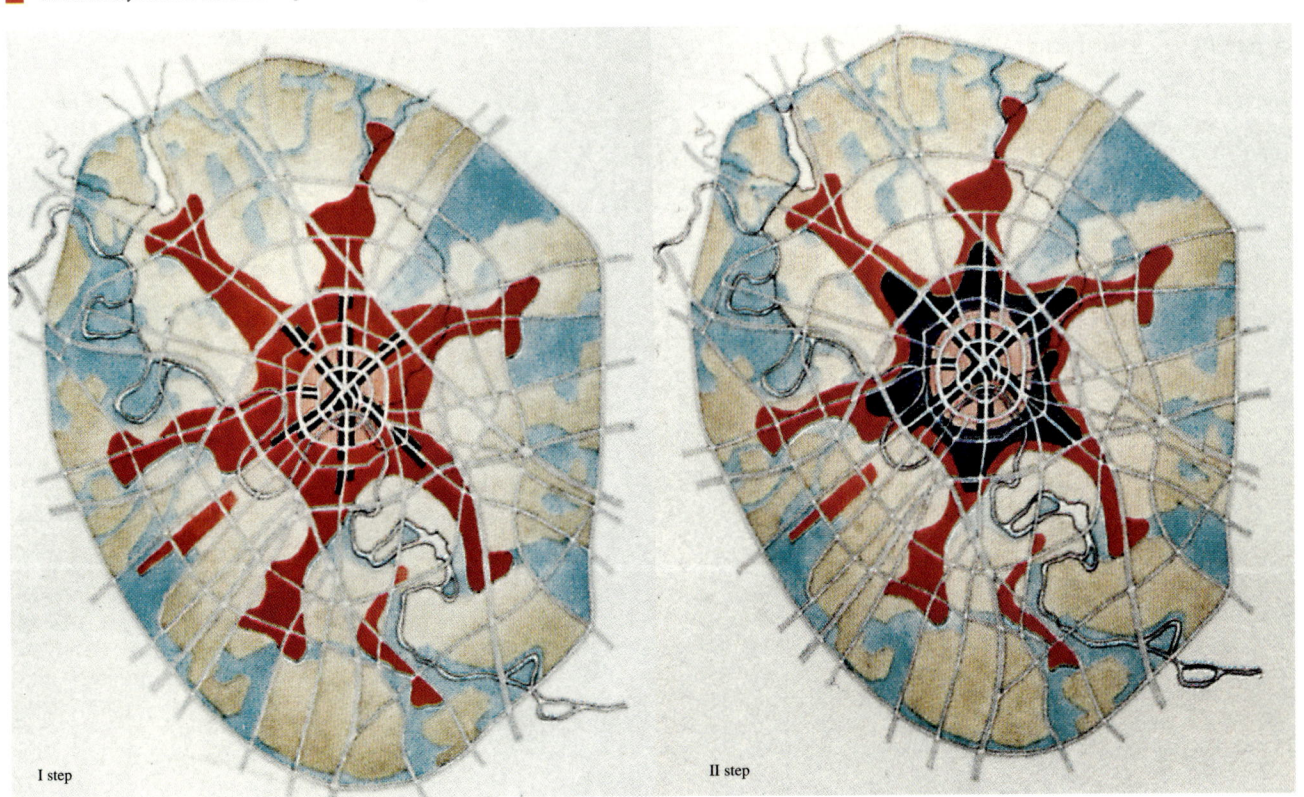

I step

II step

**The integral antropogen changes of the Moscow landscape complex.
Space shooting 1988.**

of uncontrolled growth of the radial-ring structure of the city. Increase of radii and rings is known to create an artificial pressure of transport on the centre. The main nuclei inevitably becomes denser, so the construction in the central part progresses vertically. The dynamic flows, meeting the main nuclei's streets, increase dramatically and proportionally to the new area, which grows in accordance with the rule of squares... It becomes clear that the dynamic capabilities of a city with the radial-ring system are limited.

World practice and advanced city-building theories as far back as in the 20s-30s proved the increase of the radial-ring planning structure to be absurd because of inevitable centripetal movement of all functions and transportation flows of the city, resulting in gradual destruction of its historical and city-building system, inefficient and irrational use of labour, material and financial resources, as well as inevitable expansion of the city's ring boundaries at the expense of green protective belt and farmlands.

It is precisely what happened when by libertarian methods the VKP(b) Central Committee and the USSR Council of People's Commissars approved the General Plan of «reconstruction» of 1935 and then the General Plan of «development» of 1971, which based on the concept of continuity with 1935, providing for a hypertrophied growth of the territory and population. But in the new phase the city again outstretched the MKAD boundaries, drawn by the government before.

According to the General Plans of 1935 and 1971 all the radii and one additional ring had to be pierced through the centre, accompanied by widening of red lines and demolishing street-facing buildings in the historic streets. By 1990 the projects of 12 – 15km long radii converging into one bunch in the centre were implemented by piercing Gorky street, New Arbat, Northern radius, Novokirovsky Avenue, Dimitrov street through. The completion of all the radii (along Ordynka, Kropotkinskaya, Gertsena,

Chernyshevskogo and Solyanka streets) could have led to a gigantic transportation whirlpool around the Kremlin and Kitay-Gorod. Even today one can see a thick smog «cap» over the Kremlin. Photographs taken from space show that in the city vital areas, where most federal bodies sit, – Kitay-Gorod and Bely-Gorod – concentration of harmful substances exceeds the permissible levels by 3 – 4 times and in some substances – by 10 times. The zones of «brains and heart» of the country faced a critical ecological situation, compared to the one existing at hazardous factories of Moscow, where genetic mutations can not be ruled out. According to some prognoses by 2001 the number of automobiles in the capital will have increased 3 to 4 fold. Corking of the centre is quite feasible.

Thus, in 1935 and 1971 projects were drawn for the centre of Moscow to perform the function of a gigantic road junction for transportation flows of a multimillion city of the future – the function, which it cannot be suited for. It goes without saying that the road junction was to bury the «Feudal centre», the old Moscow under its overpasses and viaducts!

Implementation of the «reconstruction» and «development» General Plans required millions be spent on pulling down old buildings and re-laying utilities networks just to clear room for erecting billions worth of new housing to substitute the demolished houses. Purposefully huge resources were spent for nothing at the time of economic hardships and external threats.

Significantly prevailing centripetal flows of functions and communications determined the irrational social and economic living standards for those who lived in the centre and periphery, which led to the extensive development of farmlands and further worsened contradictions in living standards between urban and rural populations.

Because of the fact that Moscow exported a volume of products which was approximately equal to that of imported raw materials, while the oblast had to supply goods to the city, the capital became a huge trans-shipping point with a controller's function, so instead of being self-sufficient the city relied on re-distribution of products produced in other regions of the country. The erroneous economic and city-building policies of uneven distribution of the production forces in the oblast and wrong administrative division into raions based on a formal class distinction and not on the «genuine basis» resulted in the social-economic deformation of the regional settling of the population.

The administrative division into raions, especially of the central zone, divided into 13 administrative parts, did not meet the requirements of preserving the planning structure and allow the raions to resolve a number of social tasks on their own. Meanwhile, gigantic, poorly managed central directorates of GlavkUKS, GlavAPU, Glavmosstroi, Glavmostremont, Glavmostinzhstroi, Glavmospromstroi did not provide the administrative raions with timely construction, repairs, equipping with utilities, reconstruction, laying utilities networks and other services, although the organizations worked for the benefits of other regions of the country, too. Priorities the directorates stuck to ensured the centripetal movement of labour, material and financial resources, serving the purpose of their employment on the basis of «labour-consuming mechanism», when labour-intensive work was preferred as opposed to «unprofitable» operations. It led to the construction disastrously deprived of individual features and imposing a vicious departmental city-building policy, which ran counter to the social needs of the population in the city's raions.

Under those conditions the resolution of two important tasks of providing every family with an individual flat and preserving the historic centre, given the time pressure and powerful construction industry, was being achieved to the disadvantage of the latter.

The system of administrative division into raions, introduced in the 60s on the basis of class structure of the society with due regard to the ratio between the size of the population and number of workers, as well as the implementation of plans to construct buildings along the main radii, had been in conformity with the objectives of the radial-ring planning zoning for a long time. The GlavAPU's project studios structure was also based on the principle of the centripetal radial implementation. However, already the concept for the General Plan of 1971 with eight planning zones and all-city centres in the periphery was in conflict with the administrative division into raions, when the raions were made virtually unable to take independent decisions and conveyed all their problems to the central directorates of the city. It triggered confusion and featureless construction at random. Actually, nobody was responsible for social aspects and architectural appearance of a territory – raions put the blame on the GlavAPU's designers and the latter referred to contractors. An attempt to stabilize intra-city migrations of labour in the eight planning zones failed because of an abstract determination of the planning zones.

* * *

The enormous city-building chimera was also originated as «an idea» in the draft General Plan of 1935 under the same far-reaching guidance by L. Kaganovich. The idea was further developed and specified by his followers in the projects of 1961 and 1971.

In the General Plan of 1935 it first appeared in the form of «three diametres», running through the centre in the directions of:

1 – Izmailovsky park, Bolshaya Cherkizovskaya, Kirovskaya and Okhotny Ryad streets, square before the Palace of Sports, Luzhniki;

2 – Vsekhsvyatskoye, Gorky street, Kuznetsky bridge, Pushechnaya street, Solyanka, Krutitsky rampart, Works named after Stalin;

3 – Ostankinsky park, Maryina grove, Kitay-Gorod, Bolshaya and Malaya Ordynka, Bolshaya Tulskaya, Serpukhovskoye highway.

The three diametres, running radial, made up a six-pointed star, pressing upon the city's centre (star-crasher). Despite

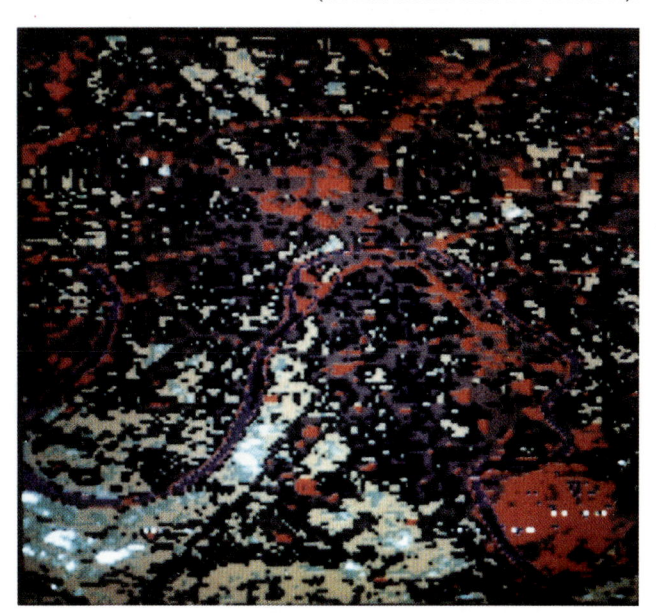

Satellite picture showing ecology situation in Moscow (the most affected areas are marked red).

setting up special studios in the system of Moscow's GlavAPU on designing and constructing the diametres, the star-crasher could not be materialized either before or right after World War II – there were other top priorities in the country much more important than the demolition of old Moscow. So it was only by the time the city project of 1968 – 1970 was being devised, that the chimeramakers began their moves again.

M. Posokhin, Chief Architect of Moscow, wrote in 1968, «Special attention in the new draft General Plan is paid to the general historic centre... The plan provides for the completion of reconstructing the historically evolved part of the city. In the future the centre of Moscow will have a star-like shape».

In 1970 a «Closed Competition on Drawing a Sketch-Idea for Prospect Development of Moscow's City Centre», based on already approved concept of star-like development of the city centre, was held. It was understood that the capital's centre would be formed as a spatially-developed and homogeneous, in terms of architecture, system of ensembles, stretching along the outer zone of Sadovoye Koltso, embankments of the Moscow river and main avenues of the city:

1 – in the west – along Kutuzovsky avenue and Mozhaiskoye highway to the Victory park;

2 – in the north-east – along Leningradsky Avenue to the complex of buildings in the vicinity of Central Air Terminus and further from the fork of Leningradskoye and Volokolamskoye highways to Khimkinskoye reservoir;

3 – in the north – along a projected park zone to the TV Centre and VDNKH;

4 – in the east – down Volgogradsky Avenue to the centre of «Yuzhny Port» industrial zone and down Proletarsky Avenue to the architectural and historic complex of Kolomenskoye and Tsaritsyno;

5 – in the south – along Tulskaya street and Varshavskoye highway to Chertanovo and Bittsa wood;

6 – in the south-west, including Lenin's Central Stadium facilities, the Moscow State University and territory between Vernadsky and Michurinsky Avenues.

The development of star-like centre was projected beyond Sadovoye Koltso, in the territory of the capitalist Moscow. These were so-called six «nodal centres». In contrast with the low houses of the old city, the nodal centres were to be built in with up to 30-story buildings. A huge star, made up of tall buildings, embracing old Moscow, would have been clearly seen from airplanes, flying over Moscow.

However, the concept of a historical and cultural role of Moscow's historic centre as a summit of the social and cultural revolution, having accumulated in the monuments of history and culture sacred things, belonging to the peoples of the world, capable of enriching human memory with the knowledge of riches created by the mankind, was not devised. The most important function of the historic centre of the capital as one of the main end products, resulting from the global activity of the society and the state and being a yardstick to measure the value of a social system of life, was disregarded. That is the reason why no sound concept for forming the historic and all-city centre was found.

Any executive manager, taking over a company, must first of all check its main assets against the balance sheet signed by auditors. The chairman of the Mosgorispolkom, however, did not have any approved list of historic and cultural monuments to be guided by in assessing all the historical-cultural stock (chief treasure of the country), as well as in appreciating the performance of his predecessors and making plans and projects of reconstruction in the new phase. Therefore, without those documents the city-building and economic activities did not have a legitimate basis.

---

[1] Barkhin M.G. «Architect's Working Technique. From the Experience of Soviet Architecture. Years of 1917 – 1957». Moscow, 1981, pp. 188 – 95.
[2] Korobov A., Revyakin P., Tydman V., Chetunova N. «How Shall We Build Moscow Next?» Moskva 3 (1962): 147 – 58.
[3] «Against Harmful Confusion in City-Building Issues». Pravda 131 (1962):4, May 11.
[4] Decree by the Presidium of the USSR Supreme Soviet of December 12, 1956.
[5] Moleva N. «The Story about an Unknown Monument». With Love and Anxiety: Articles, Essays, Stories. Moscow, 1990, pp. 182 – 95.
[6] The Encyclopedia of the Bible. Moscow: Terra, 1990, p.103.

The Kremlin Chimes in Spasskaya Tower.

CHAPTER FOUR

Reappraisal of City-Building Values 1986-1991

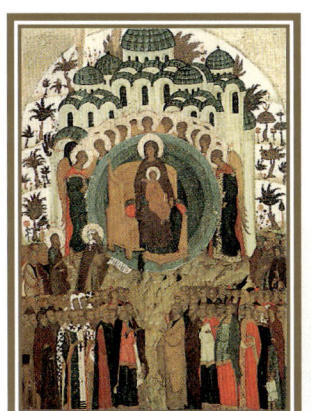

Icon. Of Thee Rejoice.

Icon. The Transfiguration.

Saint-Daniel Monastery. Celebration of the 1000th Anniversary of Russia. 1988.

Icon. St. George the Victor.

Icon. Assembly of All Saints of the Russian Land.

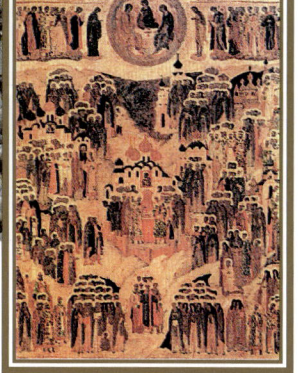

Layout of the Central Administrative District according to the General Plan of Moscow. 1987.

A New City-Building Concept of Moscow Development

September 10, 1987, the USSR Council of Ministers adopted the resolution «On Drafting the General Plan of Development of Moscow and the Moscow Region for the Period upto 2010». Actually this meant the official recognition of the fact that the General Plan of 1971 as a programme of turning Moscow into a model communist city failed to pass the test of time.

The draft copy of the new General Plan was drawn up by a creative group of design organizations of the Chief Architectural Designing Department (GlavAPU) of the city of Moscow and of the GlavAPU of the Moscow Regional Soviet (Council).

The starting point of the drastic revision of the city-building methodology that took shape over the Soviet period was the following: critical evaluation of a number of provisions of the General Plan of 1971, the disclosure of basic causes for the growing disproportion and negative phenomena in the functioning of the city organism as a result of the errors committed by the command-administrative system. The decisive factor was elimination of the former Union structures, and, first of all, of the USSR Gosplan and Gosstroi who used to outline target figures for each and every industry in the entire country concerning production capacity as well as labour productivity, personnel strength and prospective population of the country's cities. An opportunity emerged to search for the deep causes of the capital's problems, to assess the actual condition of the city's ecology. The futility of attempts to resolve the city's problems without expanding the city's boundaries became quite obvious; the prospects of Moscow development could not be outlined without taking into consideration the links with all the capital's districts and with the Central Economic Area, as well as without taking into account the capital's role in the system of the country's population distribution in general.

A variety of questions to be resolved required the involvement of a wide range of experts. For 18 months the leadership of the Moscow GlavAPU had been conducting monthly conferences devoted to every aspect of the capital's life. Those discussions held in the «open doors» mode attracted attention of practically every capital's leading expert who was involved in solving city problems and interested in Moscow's future image. Moscow inhabitants participated in the heated discussions, too; for the first time they could see how «the script of their future life was being drafted».

Efforts of the Public Council on Moscow Construction set up at the initiative of B.N. Eltsin who at the time was heading Moscow Administration helped effectively to find answers to the principal question – how the capital could avoid the state of crisis. The Council comprised almost all the leaders of the city's districts, institutions and official structures. At first, it was chaired by the Chairman of the Moscow Executive Committee V.T. Saikin, then – by the city's Mayor Y.M. Luzhkov. The Council considered, assessed and drew final conclusions on proposals born during the discussions at the sessions of the Architectural and City-Building Council of the GlavAPU (later called Moskomarkhitektura); initiated by both rank and file Muscovites and prominent public figures during all kinds of encounters; prepared by the think-tank committee on the vital, key issues of the capital and its region development perspectives.

All those organizational efforts made it possible to define a general approach to what might become a programme of crisis control in the draft copy of the new General Plan of Moscow and Moscow region development. Of exceptional significance is the fact that during the work in question city authorities of all levels who became aware of the professional efforts of city-builders and perceived themselves as part and parcel of the think-tank, which later on was of utmost importance for the successful implementation of the decisions taken.

The public spoke strongly against the destruction of architectural and historical monuments, against the elimination of the traditional historical construction style that took shape in the city's centre and was regarded as «the backbone» in the General Plans of 1935 and 1971, against the rectification of the «crooked bystreets» of old Moscow and creating prospects similar to the Kalinin Avenue and Novokirovski Avenue which threatened not only to upset the structure and odour of the historical centre but to inevitably flood the city nucleus with transport flows which even today are affecting adversely both people's health and the condition of unique architectural monuments of the Kremlin. For this reason concurrently with the drafting of the General Plan, work was underway to prepare a project of the detailed planning of the capital's centre within the Garden Ring initiated earlier by B.N. Eltsin who succeeded in lobbying a special governmental decree on the comprehensive reconstruction of the historical centre.

A wide-range discussion of the problem of saving historical heritage at the sessions of the Architectural Council, at specially held debates and scholastic-practical conferences devoted to the problems of combining traditions and innovations in the work of the city's architects made it possible to revise many provisions that directly contradicted «The Law on Preservation of Historical and Cultural Monuments» that had been adopted by the government under the pressure of the public.

The General Plan of 1935 proclaimed as its primary goal in the reconstruction of the capital's central part the preservation of the basic relics of the historically intact city. The General Plan of 1971 while stressing the need for preservation of the unique nature of Moscow's architectural image proposed to establish nine historical reservations in the central part. The new General Plan reiterated the approach to the historical city within the Kamer-Kollezhsky Rampart as to an integral object possessing the character of a work of city-building art.

The programme of the complex reconstruction of the capital's historical centre was based upon the regeneration of the functions of the capital's centre and its aesthetic features lost over the previous decades, upon the restoration of the individuality and unique nature of the architectural image of old Moscow.

Of major significance was the creation in 1987 of the Expert-Consultative Council (ECC/ECOS) – a public organization that united all the people who opposed the implementation of the destructive projects in the historical centre envisaged by the preceding General Plans. The Council enjoying the status of the advisory body to the capital's Chief Architect was made up of the VOOPIK activists, its city council, of the «Old Moscow» society, as well as of representatives of more than 40 organizations: artists, historians, lawyers, art experts, archaeologists, engineers of various specialities.

The work on the basic provisions of the General Plan was supplemented and specified by the planning of individual districts, hubs, highways, performed concurrently with drafting the project of the centre reconstruction. At the GlavAPU initiative a competition was held to find the best architectural-designing solution to prospective Moscow development joined by major design organizations such as the TsNIIP of the City-Building, Giprogor, VNIITAG, and others.

* * *

The dominating idea of the 1987 Competition was the Moscow centre development. For the first time after 1968 such a large-scale task was assigned, and again the winning projects

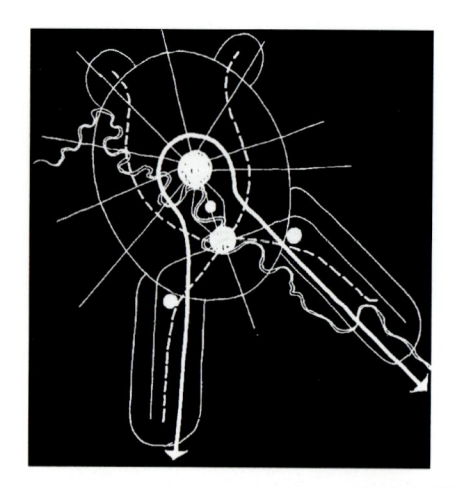

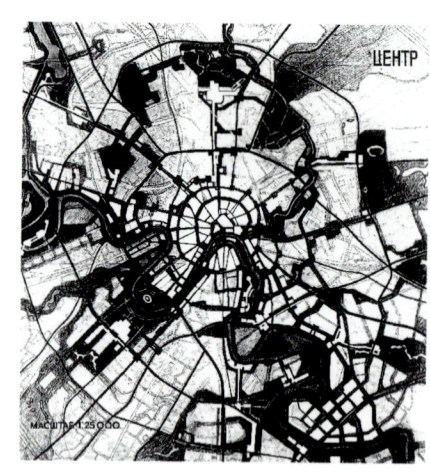

Contest of 1987. GIPROGOR (The State Institute of City Development) project.

Project of the Moscow Institute of Architecture: Ecology and retro-development of city medium. Contest of 1987.

Project of the Moscow Institute of Architecture: Four tactics of urbanization. Contest of 1987.

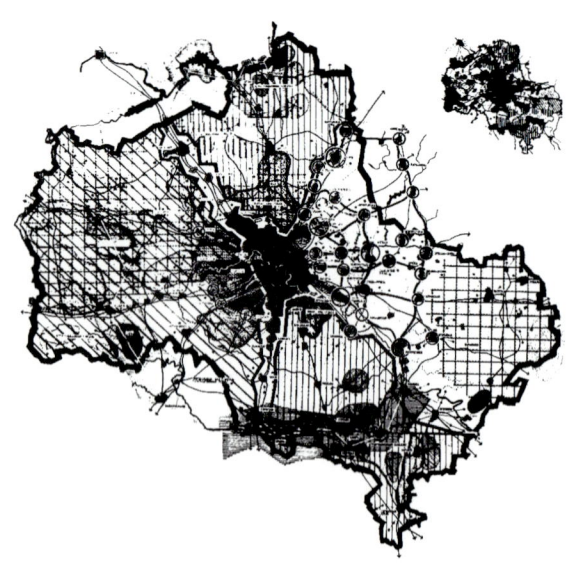

differed a lot from one another. MARKHI proposed a linear option, GlavAPU – a radial-circular one.

The first prize was awarded to the project by Giprogor, the second went to MARKHI. Authors from the Architectural Institute believed that the scope of the radial-circular planning was strictly limited to 3 – 4 kilometre boundaries. Further on the city is actively affected by the areas of surrounding habitat, and «radiality» is transformed into other spatial structures.

To better understand the specifics of the transport and human flows affecting the capital an analysis of districts planning was made. It was discovered what consequences for Moscow-building could result from the comprehensive consideration of the inhabiting system surrounding the city. Taken into account was the interrelation between the new intensively developing celiteb districts and the historical radial-circular city nucleus, whose reconstruction goals were defined.

The study of the city-building reality that directly affected the capital's development indicated that the main human and cargo flows reached Moscow from the north-east, where a lot of minor industrial towns was located. According to the project's authors, those flows actively affected the transformation of the Moscow city-building structure, therefore it was proposed to lay a powerful highway along (and over) the railway from Vidnoe to Khimki, bypassing the central zone from the north-east. That highway was supposed to stop and redistribute the flows proceeding along the Dmitrov, Yaroslavl and Shchelkovo Highways, the Highway of Enthusiasts, the Ryazan and Volgograd Highways. The proposed highway goes through the polar hubs of Kalanchev Square, from which it goes southwards to the Zemlyanoy Rampart, the Kursk Railway Station Square, to Zastava Ilyicha, Tekstilshchiki, Lyublino Railway Platform, Tsaritsino, and further on to Serpukhov through Bitsa, while northwards it proceeds through Rizhskaya, Ostankino, Petrovsko-Razumovskoye and further on through Khimki to Zelenograd. It was in those points that the authors proposed to map sites for constructing new business and trade centres. (Even today those transport-communication hubs still remain major gravity centres for people and facilities).

The south-western area of the Moscow region has quite different characteristics. It accommodates mainly recreational zones and a lower number of industrial complexes. The project envisaged laying a second highway running along the Circular Railway and bypassing the city centre from the south-west. That highway links up the Warsaw Highway, Profsoyuznaya Street, the Borovsk, Mozhaisk and Volokolamsk Highways. When the latter three cross the new highway, traditional Moscow hubs still remain there, such as the «Nagatinskaya» metro station, Gagarin

Square, Luzhniki, «Kutuzovskaya» metro station, Shmitovskaya (the vicinity of Testovskaya railway platform), «Polezhaevskaya», «Octyabrskoe Pole» and «Timiryazevskaya» metro stations, and further on through Khimki to Zelenograd. These hubs could better accumulate the centres of national authority, research and health centres than those in the north-east.

The project intentionally concentrates the construction-investment activities in the above-mentioned centres, while the city centre is subjected to thorough restoration with elements of «retrodevelopment». The term of «retrodevelopment» was introduced by B.K. Eryomin and meant active reconstruction of the lost architectural treasures of Moscow. Which is typical, this section of the project used to propose many presently implemented projects, for instance, the restoration of the Iverskie Gate and of the Kazan Cathedral.

Thus, Moscow's centre was to be enveloped by powerful transport thoroughfares similar in their shape to a «fish». In the authors'opinion, the «fish» concept was to terminate the endless radial-circular growth of Moscow. The city was to adopt a linear development system along the following directions: the town of Serpukhov – the Centre – the town of Tver (St.Petersburg – the Centre – Rostov-on-the Don). It is worth noting that active construction work is underway now on the territories stretching to Zelenograd, on the mighty Butovo bulge, while there exists a dual transport corridor in the direction of Serpukhov.

* * *

An important stage in the final work at the General Plan was heralded by the publication of its materials in the «Moscow Pravda» which triggered an all-round discussion. The debate aired demands to speed up the withdrawal, elimination or conversion of harmful from the sanitary and hygienic points of view enterprises; some participants urged to drastically reduce the capital's population in the long run due to cutting down jobs at enterprises in Moscow and Moscow region, reducing the number of higher education establishments, taking into account that most of them did not possess necessary logistics. Some proposals urged to unload the capital through setting up satellite-towns in the neighboring administrative regions, others suggested to limit Moscow proper only to its historical part to be treated as an urban relic; any construction work in this part was to be ruled out.

As a result of the discussion the new General Plan of Moscow and the Moscow Region was altered in several ways. The new city-building policy was formulated in the compact edition of the «Main Directions of Development of Moscow and the Moscow Region for the Period upto 2010», – which was an imperative component of the new General Plan defining priorities of the city development in the following succession:

1. Perfecting the city-building layout of the Moscow-dominated area as an integral social, economic, nature, landscape and city-building complex uniting Moscow and its historical centre with Moscow agglomeration including the Woodland Protective Band and the outer belt of the Moscow Region.

2. Transforming the structure of the national economy complex, priorities given to developing industries of the «third-level» sector – that is administration, finance, communications, high technologies, social and business services.

3. Raising social standards of the availability rate and quality of dwellings, health protection, trade, cultural and recreation facilities.

4. Regenerating the historical-cultural heritage of Moscow's historical centre, architectural and city-building ensembles, mansions and relics in Moscow and the Moscow Region, of his-

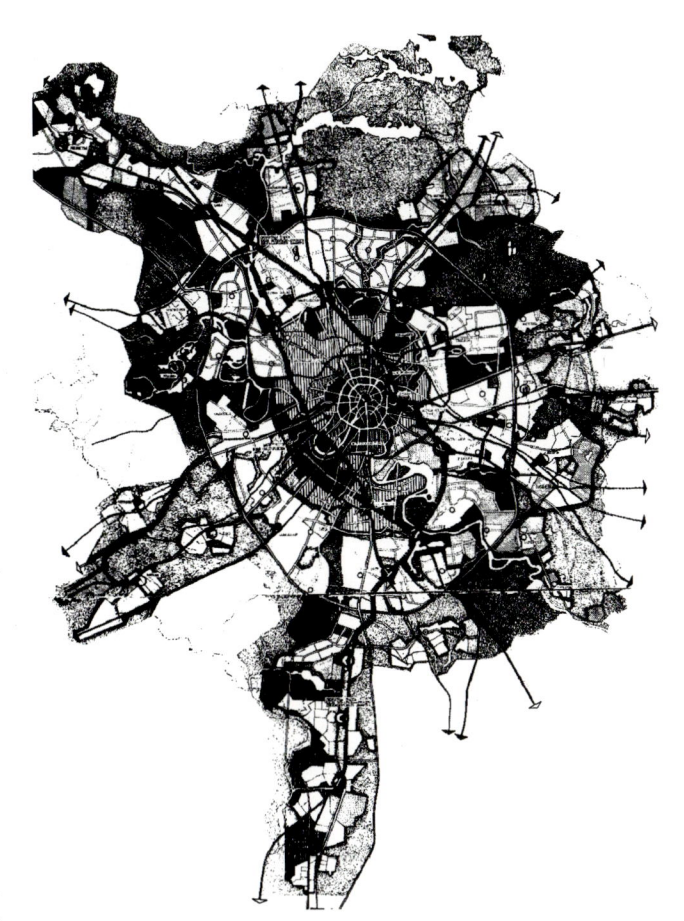

* – *Author of this section is Head of the Project by the Moscow Institute of Architecture I.G. Lezhava.*

Project of the Moscow Institute of Architecture: Traffic «drainage».
Contest of 1987.

Project of the Moscow Architectural Institute: System of four centres.
Contest of 1987.

A new bridge over the by-pass canal near Lavrushinsky Lane.

The State Tretyakov Gallery. Engineer Block.

torical settlements in the Moscow Region, preserving the architectural – spatial and landscape identity of the region.

5. Pursuing ecologically-oriented regional policy to ensure population health-protection and environmental stability.

6. Modernizing and developing the regional infrastructure in line with international requirements of ecological safety, resource-saving, quality standards and reliability of transport means, communication facilities and engineer utilities.

7. Reorganizing the construction complex in order to enhance the rate of construction work while radically modifying construction technologies, first of all meant to increase the scope of construction at existing construction sites, to expand reconstruction and modernization of existing dwellings, to accelerate low-storied housing construction, to build unique, individually-designed technically complicated objects.

8. Accomplishing successive steps to implement the goals and principles of the Main Directions, to exercise effective economic and legal regulation and stimulation of the city-building activities which would combine the mechanisms of state-control, local self-government and market competition.

A future-oriented city-building policy includes a system of top-priority programmes aimed at attracting state, private and foreign investors into the region in order to exploit the potential of the most valuable, from the constructional point of view, capital's territories:

– to renovate Moscow's historical centre;

– to form a system of new business and public centres, technoparks, free economic zones;

– to enhance health protection standards and reorganize ecologically detrimental industrial areas;

– to stimulate mass low-storied housing construction;

– to regenerate especially valuable historical-cultural and natural complexes, to create a regional infrastructure for tourism and recreation on their foundation.

On July 25, 1996, the government assessed the results of the implementation of the new General Plan over the passed three years, which demonstrated a complete coincidence of the capital's development with the forecast given in the adopted document.

Tangible structural changes took place in the social and economic development of the city as a result of the work done. The number of jobs was reduced from 5.1 to 4.8 million. The number of Muscovites working in the services sector grew by 80,000. The crediting-finance sector attracted three times more employees, minor business offered twice as many jobs, while the number of enterprises and organizations grew from 52,000 to 143,000.

Against the general background of drastic reduction of the scope of housing and cultural construction in the country, Moscow retains the leading role of a cultural centre promoting publishing business, telecommunication links, creating new theatres and picture galleries, arranging concerts, and staging exhibitions.

The rate of housing construction which remains at a regular high level of 3,000,000 square metres per year is maintained due to a commercial approach that implies a kind of balance between the sold and distributed free municipal dwellings. The restoration of the world-famous cultural centres, the restoration of the Christ the Saviour Cathedral and other spiritual centres are supported by the interested participation of governmental structures that attract budget and private money.

A major event of the past three years is the realization of the programme of Moscow's historical centre reconstruction and regeneration, according to which more than 600,000 square metres of housing, public and business dwellings have been reconstructed and built within the Garden Ring. Moscow's centre is the only Russian example of a major investment scheme implemented with the use of non-governmental investments.

The State Tretyakov Gallery. 1996. Main Entrance.

Church of Nicholas the Miracle-maker and Engineer Block.

The State Tretyakov Gallery after restoration and reconstruction. 1996.

Within the framework of this programme an important stage of the Tretyakov Gallery reconstruction has been completed, the Bolshoi Theatre reconstruction is underway, a grandiose memorial ensemble has been erected on the Poklonnaya Hill, work is close to completion on building the first in Moscow multifunctional complex with the active utilization of the underground space on Manezhnaya Square. New hotels such as «Balchug», «Aerostar», reconstructed «Savoy», «Metropole», «National» and others, numerous new cafes, restaurants, trade centres have significantly increased Moscow's appeal. Hundreds of mansions, old palaces, apartment houses have been put into order which gives reasons to speak of rebirth of old Moscow image with its unique plastic richness and colour.

The utilization of inner reserves ensures not only better housing standards for Muscovites without expanding the city beyond the Moscow ring road (MKAD) boundaries, but it gives a tangible opportunity to improve the layout of already existing districts. This work encompasses active reconstruction of five-storied apartment houses typical of the initial period of industrial housing construction. Like in new districts, individual projects of apartment houses are actively used in the above-mentioned areas, as well as modernized series of modular projects which are being mastered by existing House-Building Plants without reducing production output.

The prepared projects of reconstruction of industrial zones will provide an opportunity to significantly improve the capital's ecology due to conversion of the industrial enterprises to manufacturing other products and the subsequent reduction of their sanitary zones. A special role will be played by the historically-moulded so-called «intermediate zone» : the first stage of the programme implementation means the creation of Moscow's «City», while the utilization of the inner railway ring will give an impulse to its active revitalization. A communications corridor to be set up upon this foundation which will use all types of transportation means will make it possible to create a linear multifunctional structure on the basis of obsolete enterprises and utilities zones. A significant place in this structure will be occupied by multi-storey parking garages meant to capture transport flows heading downtown.

The reconstruction of the Moscow ring road and of the entire capital's speedway system is supposed to significantly improve transportation in Moscow.

Under the conditions of the country's general economic breakdown Moscow continues to resolve new city-building and social tasks without reducing the amount of housing construction and construction of vital objects of social and engineer-transportation infrastructure. In the course of the General Plan implementation a new crediting-financing mechanism is being created implying rational employment of non-budget financing sources such as money received from the sale of apartments, unfinished construction objects, leasing rights, securities. A market infrastructure is being formed: investment and land auc-

Lavrushinsky Lane.

The «Ukraina» Hotel and the Business Centre «City».

tions, real estate auctions, stock exchanges. A certain monopolism is being overcome in the project-construction complex, a market of project and contracting services is being created.

Successful implementation of the new General Plan main development guidelines makes it possible to speak about the fact that its preparation has practically produced a new methodology of a long-term forecast for a complex city-building system of a major city. Legal support plays a crucial role in the implementation of the tasks to be solved. The Charter of Moscow has been adopted which entitles the city to a city-building code of its own. The Government of Moscow has adopted the City-Building Charter of the city. New regulations and rules of city-building have come into effect.

Today's Moscow is vividly changing its architectural looks to the better, it is regaining the allegedly lost beauty of Old Moscow which used to be one of the most beautiful capitals of the world.

Concept of Regeneration of the Historical Moscow

«Here there will stand a city of a great size that will spread its triangular tsardom».
The Tale of Moscow's Roots

The concept of regeneration of historical Moscow was proposed in 1989 by a think-tank of city-building experts (G.Ya. Mokeev, V.A. Vinogradov, A.B. Trenin, M.P. Kudryavtsev, T.N. Kudryavtseva) as an alternative to the official version of the city and its region development.

By the time the concept was born prominent scholars of the VOOPIK Moscow City Section had been bitterly arguing with the authorities of the GlavAPU and the Moscow City Executive Committee for over 20 years. This argument at times amounted to an open confrontation on a number of emerging major city-building problems and would-be decisions. The most pressing issue had always been the preservation of the historical outlook, planning guidelines and scenery of Moscow. To this end the public have repeatedly come forward with the initiative to proclaim the historical centre of the city within the boundaries of the former Kamer-Kollezhsky Rampart to be a monument of city-building, though no official understanding and support have ever been won.

A group of scholars from the VOOPIK won the third place among 15 professional contestants in the contest held by the Moscow GlavAPU to find the best sketch-idea for the General Plan of the Moscow megapolis and for the architectural organization of the city's centre. The competition made it possible to consider alternative projects that were promoting real conditions for the preservation of the city's historical centre. The contest convinced the city leaders to single out the dominating city-building factor that would determine the city's development concept. The contest indicated that the preservation and regeneration of Moscow's historical city-building system was a quality standard in evaluating the level of the public's social development and morality, a standard of life.

As this top-priority direction was defined, a basically new approach was formulated that was different from the existing method of designing. The method was covering a 25-year span of the City General Plan with specific 5-year projects of detailed planning. It was based upon centralized budget allocations.

The negative results of the previous General Plans implementation were caused by the erroneous city-building concepts born during the Stalinist «reconstruction» of 1935 and the Brezhnev «development» of 1971.

The concept of «humanization» in the General Plan of 1990 was also based upon the centralized administrative-bureaucratic control over the city-building processes. The guideline of «humanization» remained a catchword since the very foundation of the medium humanization - the region domination, that is authoritative self-control – was based upon the old-time class structure governed by the industry-oriented principle meaning undemocratic election of the regional authorities.

The negative trends were typical of the very basis of the command and administrative approach to the planning of city life. It was impossible to raising life standards without taking into account environmental conditions. When reconstructing the city's historical districts, the standards of life are defined not only by the inner comfort of homes, the standards of services, the proximity of jobs and the speed of city traffic, – primarily they are defined by the presence of qualitative natural, historical and cultural media. The preservation of monuments acquires ecological significance since the monuments serve as public criteria for the evaluation of its development or degradation. They contribute to restoration and regulation of the balanced «multi-layer» exchange between the man, the society and their medium. The islands of nature become as valuable monuments as the masterpieces of architecture. In the course of reconstruction this factor is of decisive prominence in raising standards of the city life.

System analysis of various city-building models indicates the following: if there exists a clear-cut public ideal image of «the city», if the inhabitants of different generations actively participate in its implementation then what takes shape is not just only «funds of dwelling space» with certain demolition dates but monuments of culture worthy of Man that preserve the spiritual genesis of public morals. Historical Moscow as a monument of city-building embodied at the turn of the 17th–18th centuries the image of apocalyptic «Heavenly City» which is an asset of the entire Christian civilization. Despite even considerable demolitions the city is still an intact shrine for the inner sight of a spiritual Man. If we acknowledge its spiritual and moral value for the rebirth of an sinful person and society, if we acknowledge its ecological value for the rebirth of the environment qualitative standards, then the task of our intellectual and moral solidarity with mankind is transferred from the domain of declarations into the domain of implementation. To realize this goal and to put it into practice it is not necessary to fix any deadlines, that is to project or control this process. It is a final result, a highlight of Christian civilization and a part of the world process of moulding the human culture. What is needed is to awaken the memory and to return the lost understanding of spiritual values. Only then will it become clear, as the great Gogol put it, that «a sudden well of tremendous means» has opened. Only then the top-priority task of reconstructing Moscow relics, as well as the primary link in the chain of problems will become clear. It is possible to solve this task not through a method of projects but through qualitative improvements of the public mentality and the public's attitude towards the main wealth of the nation which is kept in threatening desolation that might result in irreversible genetic mutations and degradation of the populace and nature.

By 1990 the historical Moscow had changed its image from the «Heavenly City» into the directly opposite image of the apocalyptic «Babylon-Sinner» with the critical levels in degradation of environment, population, nature. It is for this reason that is necessary to produce a positive concept of historical Moscow regeneration with conditions provided for its survival and gradual restoration of the lost standards of life.

Under the circumstances, what is then the essence of the concept of regeneration?

At all times historical monuments have assembled national and human instances of devoted service to Fatherland, have carried the main spiritual riches of the people that the people later

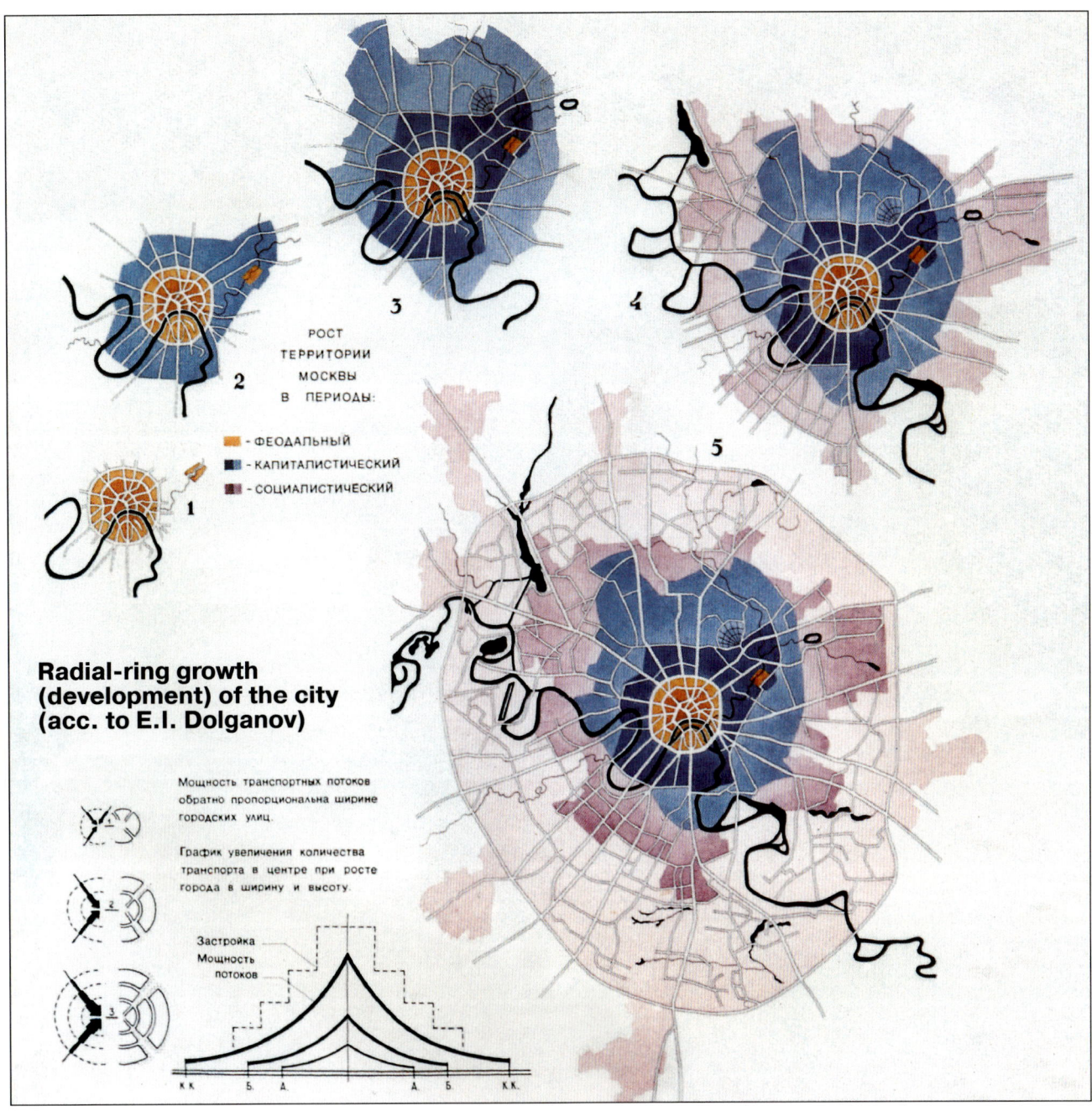

Radial-ring growth (development) of the city (acc. to E.I. Dolganov)

Concentric development of Moscow.

carried to the world, especially when such monuments were so ecologically and morally significant as historical Moscow is.

Today, when we are witnessing planetary demonstration of responsibility for the destiny of mankind, the role of monuments as the bearers of moral values is acquiring an exceptional, even extraordinary importance for the common understanding of cultural and spiritual goals of mankind. The UNESCO Charter emphasizes that «the world based only on economic and political agreements of governments can not provide a unified, solid and candid support for the peoples; it must be based upon the intellectual and moral solidarity of mankind». The exterior of monuments that organizes the harmony of the space-and-time perception of the world in the past, the present and the future – which is in a way an ecological model of culture – is an indication of the standards and way of life of a society, its prosperity or dilapidation.

Every major moral problem of the world has been focused on the outlook of historical Moscow, which became a holy storage place of the moral and social behest of mankind. As a matter of fact, Moscow embodies the assessment of the final product of activities of the entire Russia's society, its specific moral standards and spiritual influence in the world.

When casting a look at an unrestored monument made faceless due to barbarous attitude, few people will draw any historical associations, while its «dilapidation» and «insignificance» will affect one's mind and draw it to a false conclusion – there is allegedly an urgent need to demolish the building and to construct a new one at this very site in order to imprint modern age. Barbarity blindens historical memory, and one must possess an inquisitive shrewd look «enriched by the knowledge of the entire wealth» of culture in order to see and understand the imagery and historical significance of a certain historical monument. The

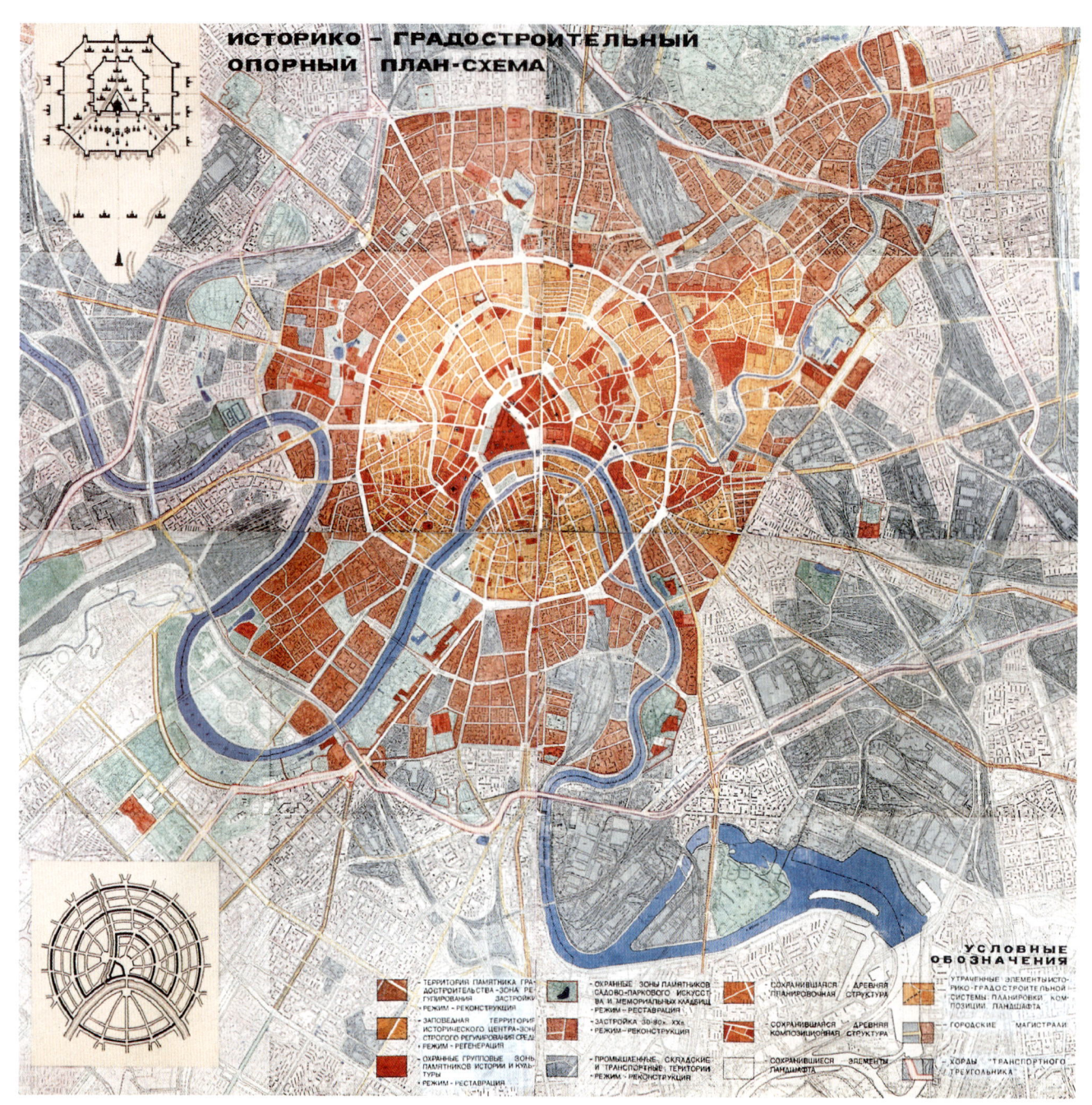

Planning systems of ancient Moscow.

same goes true for such a monument of city-building as historical Moscow, though here it takes place on a much wider scale. Many people tend to believe that they know and understand Moscow well enough, but unfortunately the course of reconstruction has demonstrated how far the people in question were away from the truth. The underestimate of historical Moscow as an integral monument of city-building is typical not only of the spheres of education, culture, communication, but of a more vital aspect of culture – its spiritual influence in the world as a catalyst of the moral and spiritual solidarity of peoples.

The attitude to this monument is to be regarded as a sample of the attitude to Motherland and Fatherland.

It is necessary to modify mentality and to re-evaluate this basic asset of the nation and the world. The regeneration of historical Moscow is first of all the regeneration of public's historical mentality. It is for this reason that historical Moscow is the most important and the most crucial factor that defines further development of the entire city.

What is then the essence of proposals on historical Moscow regeneration? It implies the three-directional development of the city which will make it possible to break the circular unstructured territorial growth and will bring about the possibility of structurally shaping three agglomerations with the complex dissemination of productive forces, population, with a special character of agro-industrial orientation, with zones of ecological balance between the environment and recreation, with zones of the historical and cultural fund regeneration and with well-balanced transformation of nature when gripping new territories.

The standards of life in district and regional centres, when the standards of commodities, information technologies and communications development become more and more uniform, may turn out to be more attractive than the standards of life in a

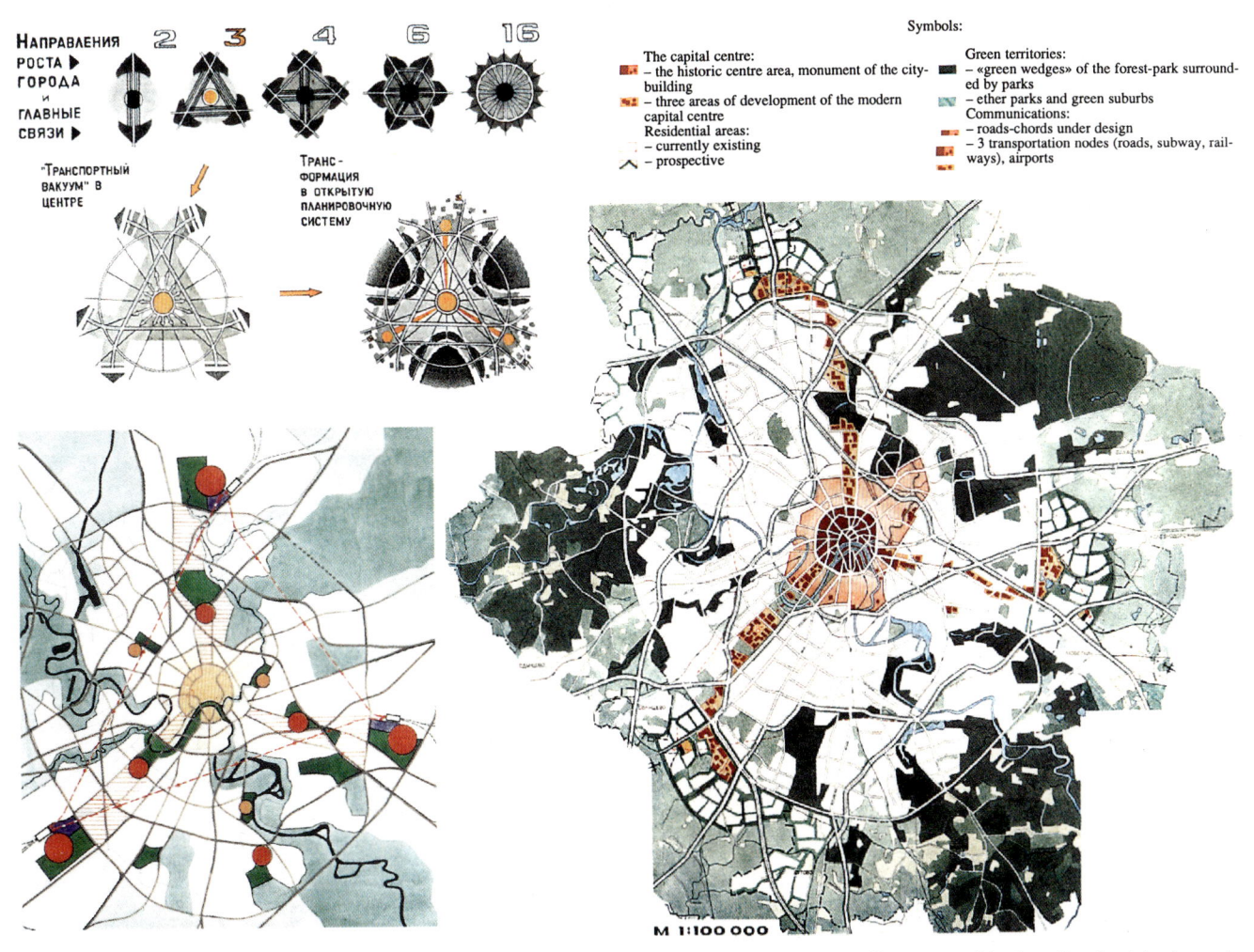

New concept of the capital city centre development. Functional diagram.

New concept of the three-directional development with preservation of historical centre.

Symbols:
The capital centre:
- the historic centre area, monument of the city-building
- three areas of development of the modern capital centre

Residential areas:
- currently existing
- prospective

Green territories:
- «green wedges» of the forest-park surrounded by parks
- ether parks and green suburbs

Communications:
- roads-chords under design
- 3 transportation nodes (roads, subway, railways), airports

---

capital city, especially at its outskirts characterized by poor environment, low-level architecture of housing and industries, transport discomfort, ecological problems, excessive density of population. The desire of city-inhabitants to own a second dwelling in the country, the development of fruit and vegetable gardening, people's co-operation in this sphere of activities will contribute to the centrifugal flows of functions and links.

Organization of the three-directional development of the agglomeration will make it possible to reduce the centripetal flows of functions, communications, links, and will still preserve and regenerate the entire historical and cultural fund, as well as will create a unified ecological system of the environment restoration. The main goal of this concept is to solve a number of problems pertaining to the following transformations: a person – into an integral personality; historical city centres that are being destroyed now – into treasure-houses of people's moral and spiritual riches, their memory and mentality; the antropogenic environment – into model samples of nature. The three-directional development of the city encompasses not only spatial but also structural organization of the population's life – in the spiritual, political, social and economic respects. It corresponds to the organic historical structure of the city development and correlates to the modules of the Kremlin and historical Moscow. Such an approach to the problem is simple, clear and comprehensible to any participant in the changes which is an incentive for its implementation – an idea seizing masses becomes a motive force.

Schemes of the city development along four, six or sixteen directions (though each of the schemes was destructive for the historical centre) were devised for Moscow according to the General Plans of 1935, 1951, 1961, 1971.

«The Triangular Scheme» is the only one in the entire figure-linked enumeration of directions that does not destroy the historical centre. It is unique from this point of view since it accumulates the achievements of the city-building thought of the 20s – the schemes of Shchusev, Shestakov and Ladovskiy. The three-directional development of the Moscow agglomeration is the only possibility to preserve historical relics in the city's centre. Its implementation provides an opportunity to launch a new city-building process.

It is advisable to launch new construction projects at the Northern, South-Western and Eastern outskirts of today's city, inside the existing districts beyond the Moscow ring road. Components of the three agglomerations steadily growing in those city areas can be interlinked by mighty chord highways forming «the transportation triangle» around the historical nucleus. As these city massives keep growing due to moving there certain functions of the capital's centre and main transportation hubs, the city's territory can be used for laying the second «transportation triangle» and, later on, the third – underground – one, outside the first «transportation triangle». The chords of the triangles for the high-speed traffic will cut the radiuses into sectors and will «consume» a major portion of traffic flows. Thus, instead of the strongest transportation pressure on the centre, it will experience

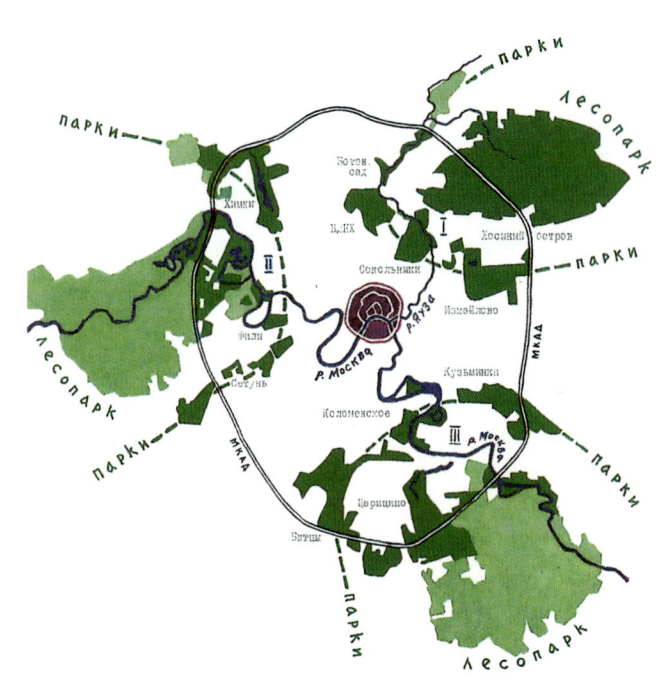

System of three green wedges (dark green stands for existing, light green shows what is planned for development).

a certain «vacuum» of transit traffic. Transportation will be only required in the zone of historical Moscow to support it and to link it with the districts of the agglomeration.

Three new centres with the functions of the capital and of the appropriate scope are to be set up along avenues from the historical centre with its functions of ideology, administrative control and representation, stretching towards new housing districts (instead of the six «nodal centres» around the Garden Ring according to the General Plan of 1971).

The scheme of Moscow's three-directional development offers an option that preserves and expands the green wedges of the city and saves green suburbs. In order to avoid the circular development of the agglomeration its growth at the sides of the «transportation triangles» is to be limited by the green wedges of the parks and forest-parks. One of them does exist already – it is the Losinoostrov forest massive in the North-East. Two others are to be grown in the North-West and in the South-West along the Moskva-river valley. The green wedges with the system of adjacent city parks and garden-park ensembles kept at a reasonable distance from the city's housing districts will serve as recreation zones for millions of Muscovites, as well as will act as Moscow's «lungs».

It is necessary to set up three hubs of metro-bus-railway stations connected by the chords of high-speed metro lines in the three new capital's centres beyond the Moscow ring road which will duplicate the surface transportation «triangle». All the downtown long-range railway stations are to be moved to those hubs while the existing railway stations are to operate commuter railway traffic. Under present day conditions the transition to the new economic models of various enterprises, corporations, agro-industrial complexes, culture and communication facilities will result in such co-operation when the enterprises will commence to merge with the administrative bodies within their city districts, and as a result will undertake to solve certain social problems. In line with this trend each administrative district will rely on self-support with basic products (food, clothes, housing), while the districts will exchange abundant and specialized products. The co-operative exchange and trade will require hundreds of new complex regional centres – for business, markets, trade,

social contacts, culture, informatics, – with the need for transportation and power supply centres, systems of water-supply, heat-supply, gas-supply. These centres will invite considerable investments, which in its turn will contribute to even wider co-operation among districts within the agglomeration. Besides, if only representative functions are retained in the historical part of the city, a number of other functions will have to be moved to those new centres.

The economy of Moscow and its region – that is transportation, administration, communications – represent a complex system of co-operation that in the course of time will be improved and rearranged. In the near future, the issue of reconstructing everything built over the past decades will become most topical, while the issue of new construction will be somehow subdued. It is most important to channel the development of the agglomeration into the right direction. If controls over its growth are lost, then the future functioning of this specific gigantic organism will become ever more complex, while some of its components will start to fall apart. The problem of growth and transformation of Moscow can and must be resolved successfully thanks, first of all, to its three-directional development.

First of all, it is important to solve the ideological and psychological problem of defining the status of Moscow as a city, and that of Moscow as a system of city conglomerations, that is as of an agglomeration. This is really a topical problem related to ideological and social-political factors. In the realities typical of our society in the past there was a disparity when the population of surrounding regions had to travel to Moscow to buy goods produced in their own regions. This disproportion and social injustice, this evil use of trade and material resources could not have been accounted for by any reasoning. Evidently, there is a need to create such a structure of administrative districts when every agglomeration exists «on its own», that is it should produce all vital products for its own needs. Only then will there be no unjustified transfer and colossal waste of assets and resources for this purpose. The circular structure of the region and superfluous centralization of the city life can not resolve this problem.

It is advisable to single out the central part of Moscow within the boundaries of the Kamer-Kollezhsky Rampart or the Circular Railway into a self-sustained capital historical city with specific functions of its own as an administrative unit subordinated to the federal centre with the status of protected zone – codified by an act of the government of Russia. The remaining territories of the city situated beyond the Kamer-Kollezhsky Rampart are to be divided into three planning sectors and linked up with the zones of the Forest-Park Protective Belt and three zones of the region to form three agro-industrial agglomerations acting as independent subjects of the Federation. In other words, the existing city within the Moscow ring road and the region (at present – two subjects of the Russian Federation) are to be structurally reorganized into the capital – historical city – and three agglomerations-regions with their own centres beyond the Moscow ring road (that is all in all four subjects of the Federation). Each of the four agglomerations is to have its own administrative bodies responsible for the development of the region according to the principle of «self-support». Along these guidelines they are to exercise co-operative administrative division into districts. In the future, the three centres of agglomeration might move deeper into the region.

These three agglomerations are to have regional names of their own. Their names, for instance, might be the South-Moscow Region, the West-Moscow Region, the East-Moscow Region (while the name of Moscow will belong only to the historical centre). Today the region's population is 6 million people, while in case of the new administrative division by 2010 each regional agglomeration will accommodate about 5.5 million people.

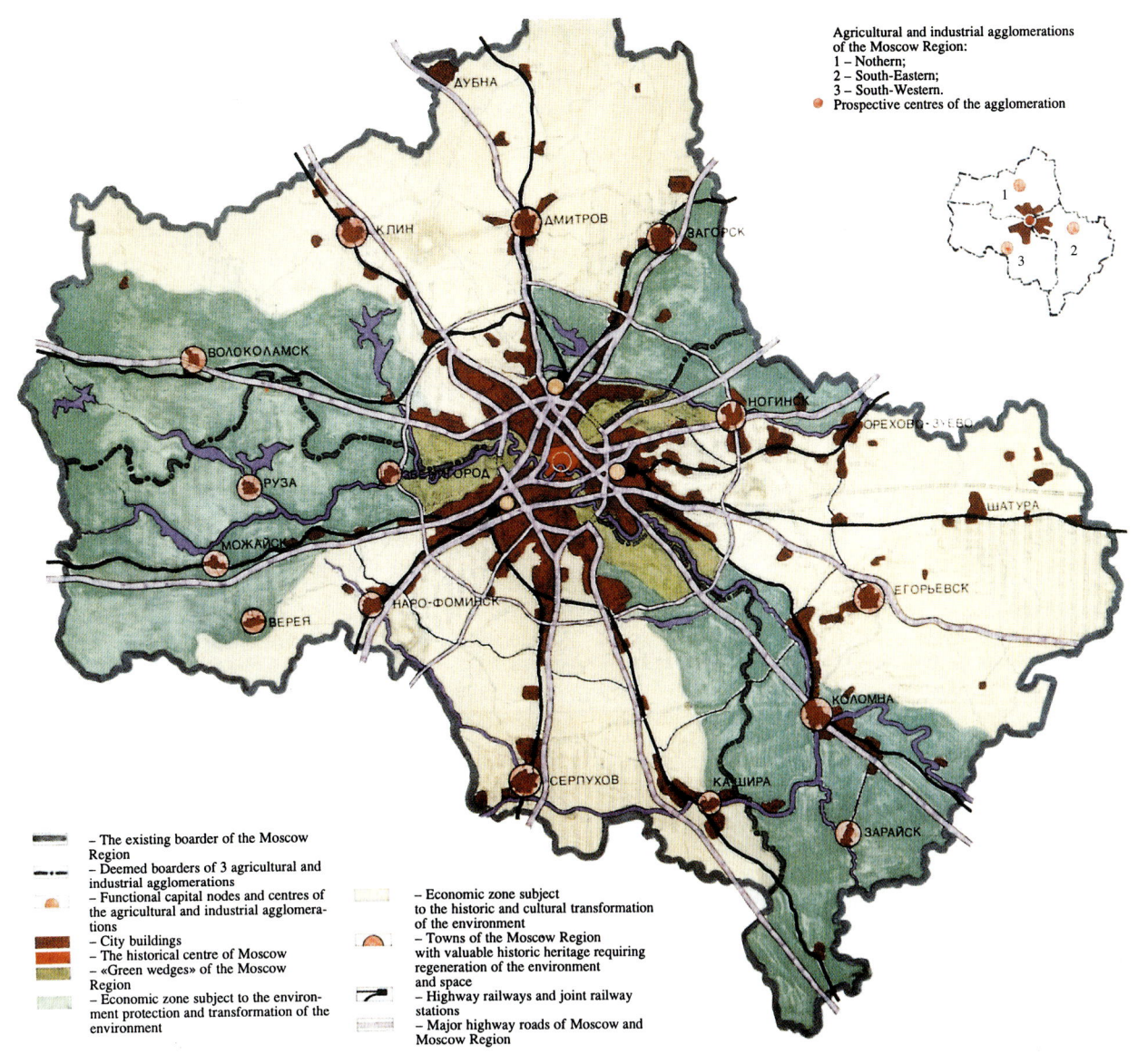

Principles of regeneration of the capital city area.

It is advisable to transfer the following broadening city functions to the new agglomeration centres: inter-city communication hubs with metro-bus-railway stations; republican, regional and territorial offices – according to corresponding geographical directions, – power supply centres, information centres and means of communication, – with their own business, trade, market, exhibition, hotel, cultural complexes.

If the historical territory of Moscow is singled out into an integral monument of the city-building, and an independent administrative city unit is created within the boundaries of the Kamer-Kollezhsky Rampart, then historical Moscow will face qualitatively new conditions for its development, with priority given to ideological and spiritual functions as opposed to economic and «command and control» ones. Both the integral city-building structure and function of the historical Moscow make it possible to precisely differentiate zones of the city-building regulation. To be selected are the zones of restoration and regeneration of sacred relics within the boundaries of the Boulevard Semi-Circle, Zamoskvorechye, to include the system of monasteries and historical-memorial cemeteries. The protected territory within the boundaries of the Garden Ring is to be singled out as a zone of regeneration of the capital's symbols. The territory within the boundaries of the Kamer-Kollezhsky Rampart is to become a zone of regeneration and reconstruction. Beyond this rampart there will be a zone of reconstruction of the industrial and celiteb territory with the zones of Moscow centre development along the three directions. The system of the chord-limited «transportation triangle» running along the tangent to the monument to city-building makes it possible to organise a system of streets in the historical centre with primarily pedestrian and limited motor traffic.

Thus, the main ideas of the concept are the following:

– remapping of districts in the city and region territory to create three agglomerations with independent bodies of government enjoying the status of Federation subjects;

– three-directional development of the city to transfer the city and capital functions, including transportation and engineering centres, out of the city to the boundary of the Moscow ring road;

– development of the «green city» around those new urbanised centres to form three green wedges directed at the historical centre and positioned between the zones of three-directional development;

– making historical Moscow within the boundaries of Kamer-Kollezhsky Rampart an independent capital-city administrative unit with the federal status; concurrent driving cargo and passenger transportation flows out of the centre through a system of chord communication ways;

– regeneration of image of the historical Moscow like the Icon of the «Heavenly City» through the regeneration of all the shrines.

The idea of these proposals is the following: to restore the state tradition of assembling sacred objects in Moscow which contributes to unification of peoples and lands, to revitalize abandoned Christian values and Orthodox Christian norms in state activities; to create a qualitative environment; to ensure a well-balanced social-economic development of Moscow and the Moscow Region.

Social Foundations of City Functioning: from the Quality of Environment to the Quality of Life

Today, major changes are taking place and are expected to take place in the Russian state system and society. The social institute of multi-form property is being revitalized; to a great extent it is independent of the state; apart from investments made from the «top» and thoroughly controlled, a growing significance is being acquired by investments from the «bottom» which are to be regulated discreetly.

The notion of «self-control» is being reinstituted, and it is intentionally or unintentionally destroying the industry-based approach to administration. «Consolidating» the integrity of the city space as a place of joint people habitation, self-control is laying the basis for better comprehension of their common interests and their responsibility for the results of all the changes underway. Industry-dominated planning is being gradually overcome by purpose-oriented strategic programming of socially-oriented development of Moscow as a conglomerate of various social-territorial administrative units.

Under similar circumstances functions typical not only of the authoritative bodies but of city-building experts are being modified and renewed, since the end-user of the strategic programmes and city development concepts is no longer the state but a community of city dwellers. Introducing taxes to resolve their own problems, this community elects trustworthy local authorities oriented at satisfying their needs. Hence comes the problem of forming concepts of socially oriented development of not only Moscow as an integral administrative unit, but of local city divisions – districts differing a lot from each other both in their level of comfort and in the composition of population. Socially significant processes are being initiated at this level of administration (self-control) which in the long run become determinative for the city as a whole. It is here that is important not to allow any «focusing» of displeasure, fatigue and stresses which are capable of growing into crisis situations of the local, city or wider scope.

Adequate awareness by the city and district administrative bodies of the whole range of problems, their understanding of the local social situation will help them avoid negative consequences (at times with the help of city and district mass media) of administrative decisions (including those pertaining to city-building) that are not properly substantiated from the social and ecological points of view, and this is a top-priority task. Only a flexible system of government and administration is capable of accomplishing this, in case it is ready to cooperate with the population in the feedback mode, ready to go as far as the alteration of the previously adopted strategy. For this reason local social-diagnostic studies are to become an inevitable and essential element of administrative activities of the city and district governmental authorities and, correspondingly, of the city-building policy pursued within its framework. The studies are to rule out any erroneous decisions affecting people's environment and, consequently, standards of people's life. In the course of time, such studies are sure to become a tradition, and will be conducted in the mode of monitoring. The time has come not only to define their technology but to ensure continuous co-operation of persons responsible for crucial governmental decisions with scholars-experts in the sphere of social diagnostics and social technologies. Today, under conditions of practical absence of tangible forces capable of representing the interests of the local population in governmental bodies – this is the only way to avoid negative consequences of the decisions that are not well-based from the social and ecological points of view.

Under new conditions the existing system of planning territorial development regarded purely as a city-building activity will have to be radically changed both conceptually and methodologically. The former system was a source of numerous social diseases including the degradation of local city communities and their social and cultural disorganization.

At present, social issues are totally absent from construction projects. Projects of new construction, reconstruction, expansion and restoration of various housing, communal and industrial objects are not, as a rule, oriented at actual demands of local inhabitants. They lack a social-diagnostic section that would allow them – at least tentatively, prior to formulating a design assignment and, later on, at the expert evaluation stage, – to assess the project not only from the standpoint of its correspondence to technical, economic and architectural, as well as ecological conditions and requirements but from the standpoint of its social significance. The latter, at least, means getting clear-cut answers to questions like the following ones: What is the local social situation? Is the project in question needed at all? If it is needed, who needs it? Whom will the implementation of the project affect? What specifically will the local inhabitants gain from its implementation, and who will benefit specifically? Will anybody have to move from the well-familiar district? Will the inhabitants including those who are ready to move be safeguarded against breaches of law, and how will their rights be protected? Will the city streets become more convenient and will the environment become more comfortable for those who will remain in the reconstructed (regenerated) zone? Will the life-support system become more accessible and convenient?

An expert will have to address all those questions to the «triune subject» of the project development embodied by the customer, the investor and the city-building designer. The questions

Building of Department of Construction at Belinskogo street.
Architects N. Pokrovsky, A. Denisov, V. Dergachyova, T. Noskina, V. Pokrovskaya, B. Solovyov.

View of the General Head Quarters Academy Buildings. Architect A. Klimochkin.

still have no answer. The latter three will be available only in case when the construction project «fits» into a concept of socially-oriented forming, rehabilitating and (or) developing an inhabited locality. The development of such a concept will need local social-diagnostic studies that are to precede the project. The results of such studies should become the most important portion of design documents that accompany any architectural city-building project. Their goal is to assess environmental conditions and actual needs of the local population of the very territory where the project in question is to «fit in».

Shaping environment means shaping a way of life. Developing a certain social quality of the environment and of the entire life support system is one of the decisive requirements to city-builders, but first of all those requirements address bodies of city government. Environment means not only nature, things and symbols. It also means people – the family, relatives, neighbors, friends, colleagues, officials, experts on infrastructure. In the course of daily human contacts the so-called «social nets» are being formed whose destruction will lead to social-cultural degradation of people and their communities, and might eventually cause outbreaks of vandalism.

A city is first of all a specially organized inhabited living space. It is created by the human activity. Daily needs of the people do constitute the social «foundation» of man-made city landscape. Any fragments of the city environment are good enough if they are «communicative», that is deliberate, if they produce in the man the feeling of comfort, the desire to stop and to look around, to sit on a bench in the park or to have a walk. If the environment does not facilitate contacts with other people, if children have no place to play their games, if people use the city space only to get to their jobs, schools and homes as quickly as possible, hastily buying daily necessities on their way, – this means that the city environment is poor.

Moscow is going through a construction boom now. Lately, it has been enriched with banks, offices, expensive hotels, casinos, restaurants and supermarkets. It has become one of the most expensive European cities. Still, its rank and file inhabitants do not have a place to have lunch, to have a walk or a rest (even with children), if we take into account their modest income.

Today our city is a poor place for its people to live in. Today's Moscow is a source of stressful life situations. Moscow is lavishly wasting its own social energy.

The stressfulness, and in this sense of the word, the «uneconomical nature» of Moscow is reflected in the figures of waste of time and, consequently, of strength on solving daily problems, on travelling in transport. According to the data gathered by TsNIIP of City Building, the average time waste on the way to the job place (one-way) has grown during the last years upto 55 – 75 minutes. The desire for self-preservation, self-realization and economy of effort is paramount for survival of any organism. A person has always met this requirement through actively affecting his or her own environment. This is proved by the entire history of people's environment-forming activity. A particular example is the creation of minor-structure landscapes in the capital's historical centre correlated to Man's size. It is not incidental that the city inhabitants rush there. Under the conditions of semi-industrial house-building which does not require high professionalism on the part of builders, the historical centre is irreversibly dying.

Industrial city-building technologies have separated people, have deprived the consumer of the right to choose his environment and to participate in its forming. Being, in the long run, the only end-user of the city environment, an average city inhabi-

Kitay-Gorod. Lower Trading Rows and the «Rossiya» Hotel.

tant, as a matter of fact, is deprived of the opportunity to affect the process of its «production». He or she cannot reject a city-building decision made by someone else, he or she cannot reject an offered place of living (as opposed, say, to a regular buyer who will never buy low-quality goods in a shop). As a result of it, certain «parameters» of their life environment are «imposed» upon the city inhabitants from outside.

Muscovites fall ill more often now. They have less time, strength and means to spend on the activities that possess socio-cultural value. Teaching children culture and sports is a problem now, since all the clubs of the kind are as a rule far away from housing areas, schools or pre-school education centres which makes their parents leave their jobs before hours, or causes additional travelling, and now requires significant expenses (the trend to abolish free handicraft and sports children activities added problems for low-income families). All kinds of recreation became a problem, as well as meeting daily needs, settling personal and family affairs. All this again and again causes city inhabitants to travel on the capital's territory, creating additional transport problems.

There are more and more disbalances in Moscow. Proclaiming democratization, we, in reality, are violating ethical norms at all the levels of the city life: from the authorized «deportation» of Arbat or Sretenka inhabitants to Solntsevo or Biryulevo to the practical absence in our houses, in underground passes or metro stations of special wheelways for children's or invalids' carts, to elimination of benches in parks, at the stops of public transportation and metro stations, to the absence of clubs for people of all ages and professions, of cafes for those wishing to have an inexpensive meal or to chat a little...

It is the city environment that is to contribute to the ethics of social communication, to upgrade the culture of human contacts. The minor-structured elegant construction in Moscow's centre seems to be able to facilitate it. However, even the unique historical centre of Moscow has become an anonymous transit territory which is daily «washed» by million-strong human flows that go under the walls and near closed doors of mighty banks, offices and ministries. There is no place for the people in the centre to have a rest, to talk, to make fun. They are offered nothing but shops which they visit arriving from far-away regions because of better supplies and service.

The declining feeling of self-value of the city's historical centre, the industrial landscape of its intermediate zone and complete lack of harmony, facelessness, disproportion of many districts of mass construction belittle the dignity of a Muscovite as a city inhabitant. Communicativity of the city space – its specific feature – is being destroyed ever more, and the cause is, on the one hand, in the disorderly utilization of the land for construction, and, on the other hand, in the simplified perception of the individual way of life of a city inhabitant – who is far from being an average person, but in every case is someone special, with his or her own requirements, views and expectations. By their very nature neither technical-economic specifications of city-building projects which underlay any General Plan nor the method of forming the architectural-spatial city environment that proceeds from the specifications actually takes into account or can take into account real conditions of the people's life. Nor is taken into account the fact that people's life conditions assessed in average figures of the statistics do relate directly to the welfare and feelings of city inhabitants. There are no direct and simple links between the social structure of the city population, the way of life of the citizens and methods of utilizing the city space. For instance, it is impossible to establish once and for ever «the right correlation between the apartments composition and demographic requirements». One and the same family have different requirements for their dwelling at different stages of their life cycle. Families are formed and fall apart, people are born, fall ill, die. Problems to be solved by people change, their well-being and life strategies are altered. It is impossible to solve any housing, transportation or other «infrastructural» problem once and for ever. It takes a flexible, softly-operating mechanism of the population, professionals and managers participation in order to permanently and specifically regulate the condition of various life support elements.

The dominating idea and the goal of any city-building decision is to preserve a person together with his or her alma-mater – that is nature. Life (of a person, of nature) is at the same time a highly cultural model of behaviour, activities, contacts and co-operation of people with one another and with the environment. The technosphere that serves the reproduction of resources and material assets, same as politics, - are only means and methods to support and reproduce life, not an end in itself. Industry can serve Man, in particular, through the rejection of the obsolescent «genre» of General Plans with their tradionally prepared Technical and Economic Specifications. Transition is to be made to flexible, continuously adjustable, prospective social programmes and methods of alternative scenarios of the social-economic and constructional development of the city. What is needed first of all is such a law on self-control of inhabited localities that will make it possible from the very start to open for every city inhabitant the process of preparing city development programmes. The law is also meant to resolve the problems of municipal property, land allocation, land use, leasing, reasonable taxes...

Any city-building decisions must lean upon certain legal foundations – which is done in the majority of civilized countries of the world. The laws should be based not on the present-day «final» rates of the TsNIIP, which crown the idea of administrative city-building planning of city life, but on the clear-cut system of bans and limitations pertaining to both qualitative characteristics of the buildings under construction (first of all, to their ecological properties and evaluation of their likely social damage) and to various aspects of legal and economic relations between city inhabitants and investors (customers), professionals (contractors) and bodies of local authority. This must be true in case of any project proposals that have anything to do with the interests of

Saint-Daniel Monastery.

local population, no matter whether they pertain to utilizing new sites, or to reconstruction or regeneration of city grounds, or to the organization of the architectural-spatial environment.

Planning the life space, and constructing objects within this space are not purely city-building procedures. For a long time science has known that a person who has lost contact with the environment is doomed either to isolation and indifference to his or her surrounding media, or to suffering and death. Similar social consequences could be brought about by the city-building practice that does not take into account vital needs of people. That means that while defining requirements to well-founded control and projecting of construction, it would be advisable to simultaneously adopt a technology of obligatory social-diagnostic studies within the scope of the projecting proper, and not only within the framework of the concept that supports it. This will gradually lead us to rejecting existing stereotyped priorities when the main city-building document that received the status of law contains such notions as «citybase» and «cityservicing» (instead of serving the needs of human beings). Instead of the primary function - life support - other functions are mentioned that are to serve the execution of city functions and leaving aside social-reproductive ones.

What is preventing managerial decisions orientation at the local level from being social-reproductive is, on the one hand, existing mental stereotypes, and, on the other hand, unprecedented and unlimited pressure of private and commercial capital on government and management.

Speaking of the first obstacle, the planning bodies and associated experts rely on the existing (or anticipated, or even desirable)

The Moscow Zoo after reconstruction. 1996.

social-professional and social-demographic population structure. In the best case, ideas that are taken into consideration are quite vague, and for this reason inaccurate, based on average statistics concerning the dynamics of natural (spontaneous) population characteristics (the succession of generations, migrations, transitions between social groups, structural typologies of families, the number of marriages and divorces, etc.). It is all the above-mentioned factors that determine the so-called social criteria concerning the territorial environment and infrastructure, which results in the attitude to people that is isolated from facts of life, that is reflected in decisions addressing organizational structures not people.

Everything said above is true for all the decisions dealing with reconstruction, or the so-called «rehabilitation» of inhabited localities.

Speaking of the second «obstacle» connected to the premature, that is poorly-supported from the legal standpoint, transition to marketplace economy, the present day dictatorship of the private and commercial capital, today's absolutely unconstrained methods of purchasing buildings and allotting plots of land for new construction have brought about deflation of the protection and projects authentication mechanisms. Projects are no longer subjected to either social or sound economic and historical-cultural evaluation since practical renunciation of financing pre-project studies does not give an expert a chance to penetrate into the local social-ecological and historical-cultural situation in the area of the proposed implementation of the project in question. The result is complete helplessness of the local population under the conditions of anarchy unregulated by any really working rules and competitive pressure of various investors on the city and district authorities in their «clan strife» for the best plots of Moscow city environment.

A vivid example is the Moscow Automobile Works named ZIL that occupies the territory which is many times larger than is needed for a technologically modern, ecologically pure enterprise. It nevertheless continues its expansion in the zone of the most beautiful valley of the Moskva-river. The factory of «The Red Proletarian» is rolling over the Donskoy Monastery. Plans were under consideration to build an industrial zone with a concrete-mixing unit and an asphalt plant in a section of the town of Dolgoprudnoye annexed by Moscow, though the territory accommodates a considerable portion of the Klyazma forest-park, the fields of Dolgoprudnoye Agricultural Test Station, the protected zone of architectural monuments dating back to the 18th - 19th centuries such as the complex of buildings of Vinogradovo estate, as well as a monument of the art of gardening in the vicinity of Dolgie Prudy (the Long Ponds), to say nothing of the protected sanitary zone of the Moscow Northern Waterpipe Station. The number of similar instances of city-building chaos on the capital's territory is so great that officials, experts and new investors should start thinking about the fact that their own well-being to a great extent depends on the system of city construction and population distribution being shaped by their own efforts. All this more and more resembles a game without rules.

The reconstruction or the so-called major overhauls with «moving away inhabitants» result in forced inter-city migrations. Native inhabitants of the centre move to alien suburbs and feel lost there. It will take some time to assess the social drawbacks of this process which looked a bit different during the «pre-market» period and is acquiring new traits under the conditions of transition to the marketplace economy. However, accumulated foreign and home experience indicates that such policy does not bring about social prosperity.

It is social prosperity that is the ultimate goal of any construction project which should be integrated into a concept of socially-oriented development of an area. Such a programme is to be oriented at vital interests and protection of inherent rights of local population, their families and existing communities. It is at this level that the uniformity and rigidity of construction norms and rules are opposed by the multitude and dynamism of life aspirations of real people.

There already exists a tested technology of social-diagnostic studies. Certain experience (though quite limited) of its implementation as part of concepts of socially-oriented development of a number of Moscow districts has been accumulated. It has been described in a number of works published by the Group of Prognostic Social Projecting, Communications and Management organic to the Institute of Sociology of the Russian Academy of Sciences, though this experience has not yet been spread widely enough.

However, the topicality of correcting traditional approaches to the general strategy in a drastic way is quite obvious. This strategy normally covers planning of Moscow's development, shifting emphasis onto humanitarian goals (those of survival and health-preservation of Moscow as a social-cultural organism). Technocratic and political goals are to play there a minor role, if at all.

It's common knowledge that when planning a city experts destroy its «natural» historically shaped morphology. Each intervention of the kind should be well-proportioned from the point of view of its socially significant consequences. The absence of an operating system of requirements and limitations that would control legally the process of regulating, planning and building on the city territory taking into account the rights of Man and Citizen (Tax-Payer) has doomed and will doom to failure any General Plans.

The Moscow Zoo after reconstruction. Opening ceremony. 1996.

Unfortunately, the technique of dividing territories into functional zones used widely during constructional projecting does contribute to those failures. Its roots, evidently, are to be found in the so-called «sphere-linked» and, in practice, industry-linked splitting of people's life into the spheres of «labour», «household», «recreation» invented by sociologists some time ago. This approach made it possible to «split» a person between departments, while life and social functions organic to him were to be replaced by functions of a limited number of elements of the so-called territorial «planning structure». As a result of this, labour turned out to be «industrial», «business» and «administrative» functions of certain territories. Daily activities of a person were reduced to such functions as «living», «selling and buying», «serving», and, at times, «bedroom», «countryhouse» ones, while rest was called a «recreational» function of the above-mentioned territories and buildings. Not a Person, but territories and buildings became «actors on the stage».

The substitution went unnoticed. Gradually, the above-mentioned «functions» that had been separated from people started to find «their place» in construction space satisfying the needs of departments, officials, all kinds of investors. Such actions were backed by perverted understanding of «state» or even «public» usefulness. As a result, the best plots of land were allotted to «business», «administrative», and «residential for the elite» functions, while poorer plots were used for «housing for the natives», «serving the natives», and «recreational».

All this causes serious social problems. People's behaviour becomes unnatural due to such an approach, since the most valuable resource is being stupidly wasted – their life energy. The time has come to think about the topicality of transition from the primitive structural and functional division into zones to the socially substantiated territory planning.

Relatively not so long ago, a report was prepared by a group of experts in the field of city policy and city environment improvement within the framework of the International Organization of Economic Co-operation and Development whose member-states are countries with a high level of urbanization such as the USA, Canada, Great Britain, France, Italy, Spain, Belgium, Denmark, and some others. Its title was «On the Policy of Improving the City Environment in the 1990s». The report proposed a concept of «supporting development». The industrial and commercial accentuation in city development became a real threat to people and their environment. Today, even non-experts came to realize that many today's problems emerged as a result of the earlier «transformational» practice. It means that mankind must learn to satisfy its present day needs without depriving future generations of the same opportunity.

Our understanding of social and ecological problems that look somewhat distantly related to the profit proper should go side by side with appropriate assessments of their actual impact. This is clearly a social-political task. In the past, harm done to the environment, to native population and social communities was a result of the lack of knowledge about the character of their dependence on political decisions, as well as of the lack of skills to assess this harm and take into account its cost while counting the total cost of a certain project. The non-interference of governments was prompted by their desire to get immediate returns. In similar cases the consideration of environmental problems and desires of local inhabitants and communities was ignored.

The idea of the new approach within the scope of cities «supporting development» is that the policy of improving the city environment and raising the standards of life of the native population is not limited to disclosing negative effect on the local scale. It also takes into consideration certain problems on the regional, national and international scale. For the concept of «supporting development» to become useful it is necessary to emphasise the equal status of both elements of this complex notion. Development is defined as a process that includes all the factors facilitating the growth of social welfare, preserving existing liberties and people's self-respect. It is much wider than mere economic growth. Support in this sense means public usefulness. Such a definition means that harm done to people and their environment is to be evaluated with taking into account all these elements.

In order to ensure supporting development it is necessary to stick to two guidelines: 1) «functional and self-adjustable growth» and 2) «minimal losses».

According to the first principle economic growth in each and every industry is to be evaluated together with the «contribution» it makes to the environment. The system of feedback will indicate how much the economic growth will cost. Cities might be used as some kind of «test ranges» where specific social, environmental and economic problems will be diagnosed before they reach the national or international scope.

The second of the above-mentioned principles is based upon the functioning of the natural ecosystem.

The key to the successful implementation of the environment «supporting development» is integration. It requires a preventing and instantly-regulating policy. The three necessary mechanisms for the success of integration are the following: flexibility, sound management with deep insight into local social conditions, and the so-called «social participation».

Flexibility means a mode of flexible approach to defining responsibility and accountability in the relationship inside the strata of government and its administrative divisions, and between them.

Sound management of a project means implementation of projects under dynamic management, while appropriate studies are to be held at a local level with the support of city mayors.

Social participation in the process of making city-building decisions should be guaranteed by the authorities at all levels, the federal government included. It is also necessary to invite local authorities and the local public to participate in the solution of these problems. In a number of countries the functions of maintaining needed standards of city's life and environment condition were shifted to the districts level, while the amount and boundaries of powers were «optimized». It is at this level that is necessary to regularly hold social-diagnostic studies and to rely upon their results when making any decisions that change people's life medium.

Engineering and Geological Aspects of Preservation of the Moscow Architectural Monuments

The need to preserve the heritage of the past is particularly obvious to us now that we have lost major physical objects. The loss of certain monuments is inevitable mainly because of negative sides of the city's economic and social development. Powerful equipment, imperfect technologies and low standards of construction work, large-scale urbanization resulted in worsening and destruction of the natural and cultural environment, brought about additional problems as far as the preservation of the cultural and historical heritage is concerned. The condition of all the monuments is to a great extent determined by processes that develop in the upper strata of the lithosphere. The latter serves simultaneously both as a medium and as a foundation of the mon-

Chambers of the Granatny (Garnet) Yard. 17th century. Restoration. Architect T. Engovatova.

uments and, being a part of nature, experiences the negative consequences of the technical progress which are significant in both scale and strength. The complexity of the problem forces representatives of the humanities, natural and technical sciences, as well as scholars at large, to seek solutions for it in concert.

During almost a century long period of social and political transformations the problem of historical and cultural monuments preservation has been connected with significant alterations of the initially adopted and maintained over many decades operational regulations and restrictions. New operational functions, the loss of traditional techniques and skills used to preserve natural conditions and to maintain functioning modes of territories, utility buildings and constructions have created incompatible interactions of the monuments with the environment, which at times were even destructive.

The spontaneous technogenesis has led to uncontrolled and dangerous evolutionary modifications of the historical natural and technical systems. First of all, it affected the alterations in the composition, structure and condition of the geological environment within the boundaries of the interaction sphere, and also caused serious transformations in the surface infrastructure that led to cardinal alterations in the balance of atmospheric effects and chemical pollution of the soil and subsurface water. Particular features of these evolutionary transformations are slow alterations that follow the laws of self-organization which are still accompanied by drastic and rapid transformations.

The city's historical territories became the scene of manifestation of numerous unfavourable engineer and geological processes that frequently have complicated paragenetic relationship.

Over late decades the absence of correct maintenance and care over the historical territories, the lack of control over them caused the formation of technogenic accumulations that have violated the initial high-rise planning, the structure of surface and subsurface currents and infiltrational water supply. This resulted in cases of territories subsurface inundation, in the worsening of the humidity mode of the monuments interior conditions and their carrying structures. As a result the processes of cryogenic soil deformations accelerated, same as the decay of the material of foundations brickwork, etc.

Apart from inner causes of processes development that are defined mainly by the uncontrolled mode of maintenance of the natural and historical territories and the drawbacks of the adopted decisions concerning construction, technology and renovation, external causes of processes development hold a prominent place in the structure of Moscow's historical natural-technical systems – all of them are connected with the expansion of the capital's megalopolis infrastructure.

The described worsening of the hydrodynamic and hydrochemical situation of the territory has created conditions for the gradual degradation and destruction of the white stone and wooden bearing constructions, buildings' decorative elements, marble garden sculptures, elimination of vegetation, and so on. The negative situation that has emerged reflects the external expansion of the adjacent territories that is gradually mounting, which until now is not taken into account properly when planning protective and restoration efforts and implementing them.

Preservation of the heritage became a task of the ecology of culture, a task of maintaining ecological equilibrium in lithosphere – that is a general task of Ecology. In this connection it seems to be necessary to introduce a notion that reflects modern problems of monuments preservation on the city's historical territories – the notion of historical-cultural space. This notion encompasses historical, archaeological, city-building values, expands their boundaries of interaction of the environment that surrounds the monument deeper inside the lithosphere – and it combines them physically.

When assessing the preservation of historical heritage it is necessary to take into account the condition of the geological environment that is in close, «intimate» contact with the monuments. This first of all relates to the architectural monuments (wooden pillars, foundation beams, foundations proper) and archaeology, since they are part of the geological environment being a component of the cultural stratum and of the upper layers of the mainland.

A lot of construction work underway now on the historical territories of the city is doomed to failure since they do not take into account the entire complex of related problems. At present, certain experience has been accumulated concerning integration of the interests of the humanities and natural sciences, engineer geology included, in order to preserve the capital's historical and cultural heritage. However, it has not yet been codified in any official regulations that would possess any legal force. If the situation does not change, then historical territories with the monuments located on them will be doomed to a slow destruction and decay, while the ecological-cultural approach will remain just a catchword.

This trend of research is aimed at studying geological conditions in connection with the preservation of geological environment as part of historical-cultural heritage, including cultural strata, archaeological monuments, attributes of ancient construction technology, bases and foundations of architectural monuments, natural landscapes, and so on.

The significance of this research trend is growing up due to the need to evaluate historical territories in a comprehensive way. Other reasons for this are the aggravation of archaeological situation, major alteration of their subsurface structure which led to the destruction of centuries-old syngenetically formed cultural stratum assets.

While considering the geological situation of the city territories as a whole, it is necessary to note that it has become a site of development and obvious activation of a number of dangerous engineer and geological processes that take place within the cultural stratum.

These processes are as follows:

a) rising of the ground subsoil waters level, surface moistening of certain territories and increase of the soil humidity in the buildings and monuments bases;

b) deformation of foundation soils in the zones of stresses growth under buildings;

c) temperature deformations of buildings structures and soils as a result of frost swelling;

d) airing of natural and artificial construction materials that are deepened into the mass of constructions cultural accumulations; the oxidising of organic materials within organic-mineral soils and the stagnation of strengthening wooden structures;

e) turning of territories into swamps;

f) increase of the soils corrosion activity.

The processes of surface moistening and frost swelling became particularly threatening on the territories of a number of architectural monuments. The cultural stratum for which subsoil waters are a kind of conservant allows for quite a limited decrease of the subsoil waters level which is linked to the effective height of capillary sucking.

The problems with the subsoil waters drainage do contribute to their level rising, which occurs due to the disruption of drainage and evaporation conditions as a result of construction activities and the expansion of asphalted areas. Together with all kinds of buildings asphalt pavements practically discontinue the following processes – on the one hand, the access of precipitation to the soil, and, on the other hand, the moisture evaporation from the airing zone.

Estimates prove it that for Moscow's weather conditions evaporation from an open surface is more than 10 times greater than that from a paved area. This fact causes the intensification of processes of thermal and dumping transition and moisture condensation, and finally results in its accumulation below the asphalt. For this reason, all the moisture that used to evaporate from the surface of subsoil waters in the past, in case of an asphalted area, stays in the airing zone, and its withdrawal is directed at open accessible surfaces of foundations, walls, and into numerous underground structures, thus causing their moistening. For instance, the actual assessment of the amount of existing paved surfaces inside the Moscow Kremlin demonstrated that it is approximately 1.5 hectares. This means that annually more than 2,100 cubic metres of water are additionally withdrawn in the airing zone.

As a result of such systematic soil moistening in the airing zone, the processes of frost swelling are sharply accelerated, which affects the condition of monuments. Moisture accumulation under the watertight pavement results in the fact that the water rushes to unprotected foundations that are made of white stone units fixed by lime mortar. Since salt has been used over late years on the Kremlin territory to melt the snow cover, the salty solutions got into the soil and subsoil waters through lawns, and from there they reached the foundations materials. Finally, they formed sulphate and sodium carbonate deposits on the outer and inner walls. The presence of sodium as a primary cation in every newly-formed mineral proves that this element is represented on a much wider scale than other cations present in subsoil porous waters.

If instead of continuous pavement a discrete paved coating composed of tiles of different forms, cobbles, etc., is made, this will intensify the process of evaporation from the airing zone. Active air exchange and humidity transition are to proceed through gaps in the discrete pavement; the mechanisms of masses transition will start to work actively, and as a result the evaporation process from the airing zone will significantly intensify which will protect foundations from moisture to a great extent.

The extensive use of radial and figure pavement made of paving stones or cobbles on the sandy bed which is quite popular abroad now seems to represent positive experience. These pavements are ecologically clean, since they lack all the drawbacks of asphalt pavements, particularly their carcinogenic effect; besides, they maintain their fixed position over long periods which allows them to effectively ensure surface drainage.

Unfortunately, similar pavements have been used in Moscow quite foolishly of late. Putting the paving stones onto the concrete bed, the builders completely ignore the «breathing» function of this pavement and retain its water drainage function only. This is a case of an erroneous use of discrete pavement; besides, it promotes conditions for humidity accumulation under the pavement and trigger subsequent negative processes that cause the deformation of the pavement.

The Poklonnaya Gora, Manezhnaya Square, Lavrushinsky By-Street and the Old Arbat are instances of erroneous use of historical territories paving. Artificial ceramic bricks were used in the latter two cases. Under the conditions of relatively severe Moscow winter this material is destroyed, particularly when the ice coating is being broken by maintenance personnel, and thus it loses its organizing and aesthetic potential.

Volkonsky's Estate at the Rostovsky Embankment.

Screening affects the forming of the paved soils humidity mode quite significantly. For this reason, promoting conditions for active water rotation between the airing zone soils and the atmosphere, particularly, at sites of swelling soils, is definitely a must. In order to disclose threatening areas from the viewpoint of destructive effect of swelling processes on different buildings there is a need to draw district maps of swelling soils for the city's historical territories which will make it possible to take required reasonable protective measures.

It is worth noting that the foundations of many Moscow architectural monuments are based on subsurface and moraine loams – soils which, when they get wet, display cryogenic swelling of the season freezing layer quite intensively.

The intensity of cryogenic swelling on the city's historical territories keeps growing since the natural structure of soils is being destroyed, their water content keeps growing too and the depth of season freezing is increasing which depends on the redistribution of snow cover and its removal. Architectural monuments are particularly sensitive to the effect of cryogenic swelling forces since their mass is smaller than that of numerous modern buildings. Besides, their foundations, as a rule, are not deeply dug in, and for this reason they fail to resist not only regular swelling forces, but even tangent ones. Besides, the process of cryogenic swelling under architectural monuments is growing stronger due to high temperature conductivity of the foundations material (rocky soils) and their increased humidity as a result of more intensive humidity migration towards the freezing soils located outside the building where the soil freezes quicker.

Special features of the engineer protection of historical territories are that appropriate efforts should not decrease the standard of comfort for the environment of all kinds of historical and cultural monuments which are particularly sensitive to alterations in engineer-geological conditions. At present, quite an effective means of reducing the deficit of carrying capacity is cement-applying which results in forming an integral wall-foundation-basis system. Its particular feature is that it offers an opportunity to restitute the geological environment if a correct choice is made of a technological scheme of appropriate work taking into account peculiarities of the present condition of soils forming the basis and the foundation.

It is in such a way that the task of stabilizing the Assumption Cathedral settlings inside the Moscow Kremlin was solved. Apart from strengthening the foundation the decomposed piles were restored using a new material due to the secondary strengthening by a clay-and-cement mortar which filled the cavities left after the piles had decomposed. The pressure of 0.2 – 0.3 Mpa was applied. Thus, the system regained its initial status but acquired a new quality. The work of eliminating the deficit of the soils carrying capacity was conducted in a similar way when restoring the Kazan Cathedral in Moscow. The piles heads and, partially, the parametral section at the remaining length of the piles had decomposed in its foundation.

The growing rate of the alterations in the environment of architectural monuments that are connected to technogenic and natural effects on the subsurface infrastructure throughout the period of their long-time existence causes the need to «reintegrate» them as a method of engineer protection which is directed at maintaining their artistic and operational value and to ensure further life of the monument.

The disruption of correlation between the architectural elements of the monuments in connection with the vertical transitions of the earth's surface causes not only a disproportion in their perception, but brings about particularly undesirable conditions for their preservation due to pits that are formed around the architectural monuments.

We shall mention but a few of similar monuments of Moscow architecture that were put into a similar «humiliating» position. This is first of all the cathedral of the late 16th century – the Cathedral of All the Saints in Kulishki whose high bottom section was hidden under the cultural layer more than 3-metres deep. A similar case is the rarest monument of the civilian architecture of the 16th – 18th centuries – the Granatny Yard – that had been «hidden» 1.5 – 2.0 metres below the present surface level. The same goes true with the mansion of the Volkonskie at the Rostovsky Embankment (early 19th century) that happened to be two metres lower than its present mark. An architectural monument of the late 18th century in Tverskaya Street – the English Club – kind of stands in the foundation pit. Its perception from the main thoroughfare of the city is somewhat unattractive because it is 0.8 metres below its surface.

The method of decreasing the soil level down to the initial marks which is used in similar cases, has a number of drawbacks. It does not eliminate the excessive dampening of the monument's lower part, it does not improve its aesthetic perception. It requires repositioning subsurface communications while special hydrotechnical protective measures should be taken. Besides, the issue of finding a compromise among different types of monuments is not always solved properly which at times endangers the preservation of archaeological objects. It is quite obvious that similar measures will inevitably result in additional protective efforts since they do not eliminate the threat to the durability of the building as a whole or to its individual elements.

The method of the monument's lifting makes it possible to restore its initial architectural looks, to promote an optimal temperature and humidity mode, to improve the foundation soils characteristics (since the foundations press in and harden the soil when the job is being done), to conduct qualitative hydro insulation, to build aired cellars and auxiliary rooms. Lifting is one of the prospective methods used to reintegrate historical architectural complexes under the conditions of contemporary environment due to their sophisticated technology.

This protective method has an important role in the monuments protection efforts since it is meant to reduce the threat of buildings destruction and to contribute to their durability. Still, in this case too the stage of lifting the architectural monument is to be preceded by studies aimed at assessing the soils of its foundation taking into account the probable additional stresses resulting from lifting stresses.

The entire picture of the city pollution forms as a result of joint emanation of highly toxic products coming from enterprises and transportation to the land surface, some of them belonging to the 1st and 2nd harm levels (lead, cadmium, vanadium, etc.), as well as their concentration which surpasses the minimal acceptable level for natural components several times. These include the soil, vegetation, organic components of the cultural layer. According to experts conclusions the ecological equilibrium in the city has been violated, and the chemical properties of the geological environment have been changed.

Even now the negative effect of atmospheric pollution on the preservation of white-stone elements of architectural monuments has been noted. A similar effect in its latent form is spread to all archaeological monuments that are present in the depth of the cultural layer. Chemical components get into the depth of the cultural layer with precipitation and water from melting snow. They are capable of significantly affecting the structure of the objects of material culture and their durability under the conditions of growing techno-genesis.

Everything that takes place in the depth of the cultural layer in the city's historical territory requires systematic studies in order to disclose the inevitable transformations of its composition and structure and to define the most dangerous trends in those alterations for the sake of adjusting the strategy of future research.

Monument of Peter the First. Z. Tsereteli. 1997.

President of Russia B.N. Eltsin. (Photo 1991).

BOOK FOUR

Renaissance of New Russia's Capital

◀ Book Four Title:

His Holiness Patriarch of Moscow and All Russia Alexius II, Prime Minister V.S. Chernomyrdin and the Mayor of Moscow Yu.M. Luzhkov are laying the capsule into the foundation of the to-be-restored Cathedral of Christ the Saviour. March, 1996.
　Altar of the Cathedral of Christ the Saviour. Model.
　Church of All the Saints on Khulishki.
　Hotel «National».
　Hotel «Metropol».
　Old Gostiny Dvor.
　High reliefs from the Cathedral of Christ the Saviour:
　　«Meeting David after his victory over Goliath»,
　　«Sergius of Radonezh gives blessing to Dmitri Donskoy»,
　　«Melchizedek meets Abraham with the kings captured by him».

I.S. Glazunov: Eternal Russia. 1988.

Introduction

The epoch of building socialist society and respective transformation of the capital was over. Formation of a new social style of life in Moscow triggered creative initiatives aimed at reviving the lost city-building values. And it was the Moscow authorities who assumed the initiatives, which had earlier belonged to the public. The Muscovites became both witnesses and participants of the exceptional events and happenings.

Emphasis on restoring the destroyed churches in the Soviet times seemed to be a dream for most activists of cultural heritage protection, which would never come true. Yet, the miracle happened before our eyes. Within the shortest possible time the church of the Mother of God of Kazan, the Resurrection gates with the chapel of the Mother of God of Iversk on Red Square were restored. Gradually, the transformation of the chief ensemble of the country took place. There, where most recently communists marched ritually on the occasions of their ceremonial rites, a new phenomena emerged – open daily religious services in the name of Jesus Christ. The people have come to from a nightmarish, lethargic dream.

It was only natural that not all the Muscovites realized that a miracle had happened, for many «were looking without seeing» what they were witnesses of, having lost the link between the times, so the old sacred things did not mean anything to them. Soviet rituals of worshipping the Leader of all times and peoples, belief in the mighty Party, being the «intellect, honor and conscience of the epoch», as well as sharing high ideals of freedom, equality, brotherhood and happiness for all the peoples were only too strong with them.

Commencement of the restoration of the Christ the Savior cathedral was a shock for many of them. At the times of nearly total collapse it looked so grandiose, unexpected and breathtaking that one could not help but asked oneself, if it could be done in reality.

Those architects and builders, who just a few years before had participated in demolishing the old Moscow, got involved in the work. It all seemed to be an unbelievable phantasmagoria. A great number of people were involved in that new whirlpool of events, opening for themselves a path towards the Temple of the Most High and the Temple of their souls. Insensibly, changes, similar to those with the cathedral, were happening to the people – an image of new reviving Moscow and Russia was taking shape. The disorder in minds of the public in the period of transition from totalitarianism to democracy, which was seen in the variety of contrasting arguments, reasoning and extremes, started unexpectedly to be transforming into something of creative nature.

The greatest «contract» for restoring the main church of Russia united different forces. Everybody realized that our only support rested in the things, which had formed us as a nation and a state and which had been embodied in the stone tables of the ancient Moscow, in the Holy Image and the Word of God, that generation after generation have been keeping the ideals of the social structure. This is the salt of Moscow's earth and holiness of the city.

The different opinions on the process of reviving and renewing the ancient Russian capital are compiled in Chapter Four of this publication. And the very opportunity to present these opinions and exchange views testifies to the fact that new times have come in the life of the city. The 850th Anniversary of the capital will not end with anniversary celebrations and respective activities by the authorities and the population. One can presume that it will be a milestone, starting the time for restoring and collecting the lost sacred things, as well as reviving renewed Russia, which is approaching the third millennium of the Christian civilization as an Orthodox power.

The totalitarian regime, based on atheistic ideology, has caused irreparable and irreplaceable global damage to the cultural heritage, environment, indigenous population and small nations. In their fight for domination the regime was destroying and plundering main sources of the country's wealth: nature, peoples, culture. It is not accidental that following World War II first environmental and then problems of ecology of culture arose, which brought to life popular movements for the protection of those main sources of life. The problem of protecting the architectural heritage was the focal point. It can be easily explained why. The architectural heritage, being a system of images and symbols, accumulates the spiritual potential of peoples and states. So, the ways of life, religions, cultures of various entities were originally encrypted and transformed in that man-made and interpreted environment. Architectural heritage, being city-building annals of the history of mankind, ensured continuity of the evolution and created adequate conditions for living. It determined the quality of life, level of culture, religious, legal, social and statehood forms of existence for nations.

It is in this sense that architectural heritage, along with nature and nations, constitutes a source of civilization, being one of the dearest treasures of every country, their principal asset and resource for the development of state, family and personality.

The role and significance of architectural heritage in shaping world civilization are also fundamental. Preservation and protection of architectural heritage is a founding principle for social structure, based on moral support and objectives. Lack of such an attitude shows a low cultural level of power, its aggressive expansion in self-imposition at the expense of cultural treasures of peoples being defiled or destroyed, which demands international control over such societies be introduced and sanctions imposed.

Architectural heritage, together with nature, culture and noosphere, takes a key position in determining the quality of life and, due to this global property, serves a foundation for taking any decision and adopting any economic or city-building programs. Its state should be the basis for objective assessment of actions taken by all branches of power (legislative, executive, judicial and information) aimed at changing the quality of life in either direction.

Architectural heritage, combining immovable, landscape and other kinds of monuments, irrespective of form of ownership, possesses qualities of irreplaceable resource, so all the owners bear responsibility for its preservation. Their rights must be limited by international community through national legislation, which has to regulate the relationships between owners and state with the help of protection agreements and ensure safety of immovable heritage.

Reconstruction and re-make of the architectural heritage destroyed by the totalitarian regime should be set forth in the form of a specific program of democratic changes, aimed at the restoration of historical justice, as well as the system of values, depicted in images and symbols. It also seems to be reasonable to introduce well-perceivable context of the lost and irreplaceable authenticity of monuments by applying the methods of museum management studies for remained documentary evidence.

Architectural heritage is not only the source of wealth, fund of genes or development resource, not only a criterion for the assessment of power in terms of environmental quality, architectural heritage is a doctrine, an ideology for God's Household Construction on Earth, it is the ecology of noosphere-Logos.

Protection of architectural heritage is becoming a corner stone for the planetary doctrine of Earth organization, based on already devised by the mankind objectives for the development, which had been realized in the cultural values of tablets – commandments of life. We are to keep the commandments in all their variety, authenticity and richness.

The direction for the regeneration of the historic city taken by the government of Moscow allows us to believe that the link of times, including a multidimensional image of Moscow in the mainstream of both national and world history, will be restored.

CHAPTER ONE

Regeneration of Historic Moscow

The Kazan Cathedral reconstructed in Red Square by the Government of Moscow. 1993. Architecht-restorer: O.I. Zhurin.

Religious procession carrying the Icon of Our Lady of Kazan on the day of consecration of the foundation of the cathedral. 1991.

The foundations of the Kazansky Cathedral in Red Square. 1991.

Consecration of the restoration site of the Kazansky Cathedral. 1991.

Democratization of the Society and New City-Building Policy

Despite its official 850 years Moscow is a relatively young city. Suffice it to compare its history with that of Paris, London or Berlin, let alone Rome – the eternal city. Phases of its evolution, closely connected with destiny of the Russian people are common knowledge. Today the capital of our Fatherland, which performed its historic mission as collector of lands, paved the way for beginning of Russian statehood, served for many times the stronghold of struggle for freedom and independence of Russia, concentrated national spiritual treasures and intellectual values, is at the point of changes. It is looking for and finds ways towards its tomorrow, following many decades of aggressive stand off with the rest of the globe, where the whole of mankind lives.

The modern appearance of today's Moscow, changing for the better before our eyes, is the evidence of radical changes in the social development of the country and its people. It is of special importance now, when the society, passing through the watershed between its past and future, faces the dramatic situations of social polarization, collapse of industrial production, complex collisions in financial world, degradation of the moral foundation, which seemed to have been reliably laid for the seventy years of the Soviet rule.

Implementing main priorities for the development of the megalopolis, determined by a new scenario, the government of Moscow has achieved tangible results in resolving major problems. In the first place it relates to easing the acute ecological situation and social tension, improving living standards, regenerating the historic centre, developing material basis for the cultural potential and spiritual revival of the capital. The aggregate achieved results can be viewed as the first stage, first steps in humanizing the living environment of the largest and most urbanized region of the country. It made up the main objective, tasks and ideology of a new General Plan of Moscow till the year 2010.

The methodological base, having resulted from 70 years of long-term prognoses for city-building development of the socialist city, proceeded from target figures in the General Plan, determining the rate of labour productivity and production volumes, on which basis need in human resources, spaces and, finally, continuously growing territory of the city was calculated.

A man appeared to be virtually a hostage to production functions, priority was placed on quantitative categories. No one not a single time actually looked up into issues, such as ecological and social consequences of excessive industrial construction, bringing about city living of much lower quality.

Negative features and contradictions of living in Moscow brought to the Muscovites' judgment enabled experts to see the picture of living in Moscow from every angle and determine the composition, list and scale of acuteness for outstanding problems, which demand most urgent resolution. This very important circumstance coupled with the results of studies in city problems, conducted by some leading experts of Moscow and other cities, as well as foreign city-builders, allowed for devising a strategy, aimed at achieving the objective of humanizing life in the capital and the region and setting forth a research-based group of priorities and main directions in policy.

«The Main Directions for the Development of Moscow and the Moscow Region for the Period Till the Year 2000» is a program of actions, which was approved by the governments of the city and the region and won universal recognition. The results, achieved during the first 3 years of its implementation, proved the prognosis to be correct. The authors in defining the long-term prognosis managed to establish a number of methodological provisions, which determine principles for a new city-building doctrine, meeting the requirements of rapidly changing contemporary living environment. They are:

First. Full and objective picture of the existing situation, based on detailed analysis of causes and effects, conclusions on major problems facing the city, general conclusion on necessity of humanizing living environment and proposals on directions in city-building policy in terms of their immediate implementation instead of parametres of development traditionally assigned by the authorities, instructing architects to produce an ideal picture of city conditions by a calculated deadline.

Second. Review of existing city-building base structure with the aim of increasing «ternary» sector's share – business, trade, service functions as leverage to excessive industrial facilities and jobs, taking into account the necessity of radical measures to be taken to improve environmental situation in the city and the region.

Third. Termination of vicious practices of expanding the city's territory, which do not resolve but add to the problems – transition from quantitative categories to those of quality. Emphasis on reconstruction as a strategy for better organizing the city area, review of methods in using spare lands of chaotically built up territories, as well as utilities and transportation infrastructure of the city.

Forth. Attitude towards historic centre as a zone of special significance for the program of spiritual revival of Russia, which demands policy of regeneration be launched, lost functions, spiritual treasures and aesthetic values be restored, replacing the simplified reconstruction doctrine of 1935, which gave a negative treatment of the heritage, when, actually, only individual monuments were restored, while old building was thinned out to broaden streets and make living conditions there closer to those of new residential areas, which in reality deprived the historic centre of its individuality.

Fifth. Democratic and public discussions of all aspects of the city and region development with participation of mass media, a wide range of experts, organizations, individual citizens at sessions of the Board for Architecture and City-Building at Moskomarkhitectura and EKOS (Expert and Consultative Public Council), while critical issues are debated at the Public City-Building Council of the City of Moscow to be approved by both experts and the city government.

Sixth. Continuous, as monitoring, work over general plans, specifying its main provisions in plans for social and economic development of individual territories and sector programs for utility systems of the city and the region as a single, integral organism. Annual reports, submitted to the Moscow government, containing assessment of current state of architecture and city-building and proposals on introducing necessary amendments in city-building policy underway. Systematic, once in 3 – 5 years, review of implementation by the government.

Seventh. Devising a new general plan, due regard to all issues, relating to prospects of development of the capital and the region in linkage with prospects of development for the Central economic region, taking into account the whole system of settlement of population in the Russian Federation, proceeding from the premise that sphere of influence and ties of the capital objectively go beyond the framework of not only the oblast and the region, but in some aspects the country itself.

This, far from being complete, list of radically new provisions on city-building prognosis, as opposed to usual methods, should be added with one more very important thing. The process of social relations' resrtructuring in the 1980s, having encompassed all aspects of life, revealed very clearly lack of legal basis for actions and interrelationships of nearly all structures. The administrative and command system of the totalitarian epoch was geared into motion by other springs and drives for decision-making process. However, by the end of the 1970s they were operating under great strain, while the process of democratization did away with the machinery.

The lack of legal basis, governing executive functions, became obvious in the sphere of city-building, where libertarian, named «will» decisions, were causing direct damage to the economy of the state. A great number of regulatory acts, rules and instructions seemed to have shown quite clearly a necessity to combine all them into a single law. However, it took the newly established Union of Russian Architects quite an effort to make the first in the history of the state law «On the Foundations of City-Building Activity» be enacted.

The strong necessity to have a solid legal basis, governing city-building activity, was realized in the form of a «City Charter», which appeared to be a basic law, regulating all relationships between the officials involved. Before that a «City-Building Charter of the City of Moscow» was devised and adopted. Today, draft laws on general plans, city-building land-survey, city-building zoning, protection of natural complex and other issues are in the process of making. As a result Moscow will have a code of city-building legislations, ensuring legal protection of the Muscovites' interests, as well as the interests of all persons and entities, participating in shaping the city and resolving its problems. All that will consolidate and strengthen the foundations of democratic transformations in the capital. All members of the Moscow government took a most active part in discussing current problems of the capital at the meetings of various boards and councils. That may be the reason, why all tasks and decisions, incorporated by the General Plan, were implemented without a delay. A special role in this multifaceted endeavor belonged and belongs to Yu. M. Luzhkov, who took over the responsibilities of the chairman of the Public Council on City-Building in Moscow from B.N. Yeltsyn.

Working over the General Plan became an important step in improving the mechanism of running a most complex system, which any modern major city is. Moscow is no exception.

Based on the General Plan studies, a team of experts made proposals on a new administrative and territorial system of the capital. It is no secret that the existed division into 33 raions (districts) pursued among other goals a policy of maintaining a desired social balance. For that end old Moscow within the boundaries of Sadovoye Koltso (Garden Ring), actually a homogeneous part of the city, was divided into thirteen pieces, belonging to adjacent raions, surrounding the centre. Fear that intelligentsia, who made up the bulk of the population in the centre, would not be balanced with adequate percentage of workers, because there were no factories in the downtown, pre-

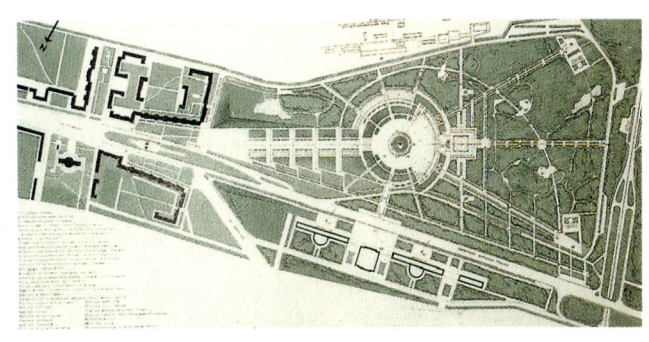

General plan of the Victory Memorial on the Poklonnaya Hill.

determined the absurd structure, but the Party and political considerations could not be argued.

The newly proposed administrative and territorial organization is based on the historically evolved structure of development territories of the city. Locations of compact settlement, originating from historical trading quarters, where people felt themselves to be a community, were used as a model for establishing one hundred and thirty seven municipal raions. Interestingly, when the list of their names was made, Moscow began speaking «its indigenous language». Yakimanka, Pechatniki, Palikha, Kutuzovsky, Lefortovo, Arbat sound much better than Baumansky, Voroshilovsky, Sverdlovsky, Krasnogvardeisky and other raions, whose names have never been accepted by the people.

To Russian Warriors. Sculptor: A. Bichugov.

The Victory Memorial on the Poklonnaya Hill. Heroes Square.
The Museum of the Great Patriotic War. The main monument. Variant.

St. George the Victorious. The monument to servicemen of law and order in Trubnaya Square. Sculptor: A. Bichugov.

The municipal raions, populated by some 50 – 70 thousand people, by its size and sense of community proved to be an apt unit for the development of self-governing systems. It was believed to be more advantageous, compared to the size of previous raions, which had up to 600 – 800 thousands of population. In this connection it is worth recollecting the old Moscow before the Revolution, when every citizen knew priests in his parish and officials by sight.

Combining the municipal raions into ten administrative districts (including Zelenograd), was determined by natural conditions, division of the city by the system of major arterial roads and its history. Such a concept was primarily embodied in the Central district, which was confined to the borders of Kamer-Kollezhsky rampart, outlining old Moscow.

Despite strong resistance by the deputies of the first Moscow Duma, who saw the new structure as a means, abolishing the Party system with its committees in every raion, the new organization was adopted and played an important part in providing utility services at the times of most acute economic crises. The structure of management appeared to be capable of maintaining the sound and efficient ratio between sector and territorial levers of control, comprising the Prefectures of ten districts and the city council.

The General Plan was developed in two principal directions. First, the sector programs were specified. Second, a number of territorial designs, containing architectural, planning and spacing solutions, pertaining to specific conditions of administrative districts and municipal raions were produced. The new approach to work in the city-building practice was of special significance and yielded important results.

Just a few years before experts were sure that the principle of self-supporting running could not be applied to a substantive program of development of a major city, such as Moscow. However, the very first concept for social and economic development of the Western Administrative District showed that some designs together with separate business-plans for individual sites pose high commercial opportunities in terms of resolving social and city-building tasks. Housing for sale and rent along with paid for entertainment, fitting and recreational centres, prospects for arranging a business-park at the Moscow State University and technological park at the economic zone of Vnukovo air terminus, opportunities for investors in reconstructing industrial and utilities enterprises, constructions of hotels, supermarkets, offices, multifunctional centres – all those things, as a comprehensive program, were a potential vehicle to attract resources doubling the resources necessary to improve housing, enhance quality of jobs, provide better services and utilities, resolve pollution problems.

The management of the District for the first time saw an opportunity to invent a mechanism, which would combine benefits for investors, as is common practice in the world, with resolving urgent problems of a district, raion, individuals. The anticipated result allowed ones to believe that part of revenues would be channeled to the city needs.

Today, all administrative districts have similar plans. Besides, more than half of municipal raions have worked out their specific programs, aimed at improving the living standards. The situation when citizens are aware of what can and should happen to their, say, backyard, house, street or block of flats under certain conditions lays a foundation for future activity of self-running bodies, when every person will be able to participate or practically control the improvement of his being.

The new system of management is based on a principle of coordinating actions by executive and legislative powers. The mayor, elected by the citizens, appoints the government composed of experts and professionals with their staff, backed by organizations and institutions, while the legislative body – the City Duma – supervises the government in accordance with the authority, received from the electorate. In a municipal raion officials, elected from most competent citizens, constitute a self-running body and are responsible for addressing all issues, confined to the raion. A concept of development, approved by the government, enables executive bodies to see to it that all decisions, vital to normal functioning of city authorities for the end of fulfilling tasks of a general plan, are observed.

The process of democratization of living in the city gives birth to a host of new problems, so the improvement of management structure becomes a day-to-day process, involving a broad range of individuals and organizations.

Special role in searching for new ways of better accommodation of the public opinion, as well as that of a group of experts, interested in solutions of preserving the historic heritage, is played by the Expert and Consultative Public Council (EKOS). This public organization with a status of a consultative body at the Chief Architectural Agency of the city combined a broad range of historians, restores, art critics, journalists, archeologists, painters, lawyers, sociologists and other experts, as well as representatives of creative unions, who cared for the protection of history and culture monuments.

The most important activity by the EKOS is attracting attention of the broad public to the issues of preserving every-

Monument to Sergei Esenin in Tverskoy Boulevard. Sculptor: A. Bichugov.

thing with historic value as a foundation for reviving national traditions, which determine the beauty and originality of the architectural appearance of our city.

Today, if the issue deals with reconstruction or restoration in the historic centre, it is a must to substantiate all designs and projects with historical base plans, giving the complete background of building in the area. Such a decision was supported by the Moscow Committee on Architecture, which made many architects reconsider theirs views and attitudes to the historical heritage.

Besides, the participation of the EKOS in sessions of the Architectural and City-Building Board of the Committee, holding conferences on promoting the traditions, publications in the press, interviews of leading architects and experts on radio and TV made it possible for the Muscovites and EKOS activists to learn more about the creative work practices, search for architectural solutions, which can further develop the traditions of Moscow architecture, meet the requirements of the new time and not just imitate Moscow's Empire style, classicism, baroque or modernist style.

The joint effort by the EKOS with Professor A.P. Kudryavtsev, Rector of MARKHI, at the head and practicing architects produced a most important document, which is an integral part of the new General Plan. It is a project for complex reconstruction of the capital's historic centre, meaning actually a program of regeneration, restoration of lost functional and aesthetic qualities of this part of the city, which image as material embodiment of the spiritual wealth of the Russian people determined the appearance of Moscow.

The devised program provided for the zones of scientific restoration and zones of reconstruction, where buildings would retain their historical appearances, while their interiors and layouts could be modified (under certain conditions) to better suit new functions. The program also allows for limited new construction, provided scales and number of stories of surrounding buildings, as well as plasticity and color solutions, facing materials are strictly observed, so that the new building can fit in the historic environment.

Indeed, the provisions open prospects for maintaining ensemble harmony between the existing historic and newly constructed buildings. As a result of correcting a number of mistakes made, this part of the capital can be regarded as a monument to the art of city-building.

One more observation should be added here. Moscow, which actually did not function as the capital of the Russian Empire for nearly two hundred years, was saved from rigid guardianship of officialdom. Many-sided Moscow, which is so different from St. Petersburg with its official strictness of ceremonial avenues and single architectural style, expresses the internal emancipation and spiritual freedom inherent in the Russian people. This may make Academician D.S. Likhachev believe that the appearance of Moscow embodies the Russian national character, so he calls Moscow a Russian city, as opposed to European St. Petersburg. The issue of building the ensemble of Moscow is more likely to be addressed in a special way, based on in-depth study of peculiar features of Moscow's architecture, trying to understand, what made a chain of architectural styles, ranging from most ancient to baroque, classicism, Empire, become a single notion of the Russian architecture.

Reconstruction of Historical City and Professional Ethics

The Expert and Consultative Public Council immediately plunged deep down in the whirlpool of emotions boiling around Lefortovo or, to be more precise, around the future of this ensemble in view of laying down the Third Transportation Ring.

The idea of this ring, being the offspring of the 1935 Genplan, has been trying to get through for so long that numerous new housing units took this time to expand and block its way so that, in order to bypass them, the highway had to knife through the living body of historical build-up area. Fortunately, the public attitude to the city historical medium has changed. All Moscow held its breath, watching the group of enthusiasts hold ground to save the Shcherbakovs' Palatial Chambers which happened to be at the cross junction of Spartakovskaya

**Russian Cultural Centre. Project.
Architects: D. Solopov, Yu. Gnedovskiy, V. Krasilnikov and others.**

Street and the Third Ring, an 8-lane highway steadily paving its way through the tunnel up to the Hospital Bridge. The Chambers that literally had been defended around the clock, were finally saved from destruction but the Ring further threatened the Old Belief Church by architect A . Zelenko – a masterpiece built at the turn of the centuries – and the Houses of Soldiers' Widows by architect V. Mashkov in Gospitalnaya Street, both were cross-cut by the red pencil lines of the highway. The unpredictability of the consequences of such a dynamic and ecological pressure on the Lefortovo historical ensemble – the second most valuable cultural monument after the Kremlin – was obvious.

The meetings of the EKOS became the site for discussions of the alternatives for laying the Third Ring through Lefortovo where the emotions were transformed into professional recommendations. At long last the project was declined by the USSR Ministry of Culture and the Soviet of Ministers of the RSFSR, and B.N. Yeltsin, then the City's first administrator, made a decision to cease the construction of this portion of the Third Ring at the meeting of the Public City-building Council pending the workout of better variants.

Regretfully, there is no happy-end in this tale, though significant progress has been made since the problem emerged eight years back. The Council asked the Institute of Genplan to work out variants for the Ring portion to completely bypass Lefortovo through the existing streets (which has been thoroughly analyzed and is deemed really possible) or to go through a low-depth tunnel bypassing Lefortovo and reckoning with hydro-geology, seismic sensitivity, impact on the foundations of the historical monuments and on the root system of the centuries-old park. The issue is still open.

* * *

Moscow has always suffered from the capital's bureaucracy and secrecy. The map of the city's centre up to the 1980s contained a host of «white spots» – Lubyanka, Staraya and Novaya squares, Kitay-Gorod – all these locations belonged to the Central Committee of the CPSU, Moscow Party Committee, the KGB, union ministries, who controlled the city on the basis of «top secret» resolutions and directives. It was very hard to stop the arbitrary rule, subordinate their expansion to the interests of the city, turn such actions into legitimate procedures. One of the acts, aimed at resolving the problem, was the decision by B.N. Yeltsyn to stop designing the project of the building for the Moscow City Committee of the CPSU on Tsvetnoi Boulevard next to the House of Political Learning on Trubnaya Square. The House, representing an obvious city-building error, gave a start for destruction of the right side background building, which remained mainly in its original shape, while the left side houses had been destroyed so that part of the location turned into an exposition of architecture of the 1960s – 1970s.

The project by B.I. Tkhor represented a monumental size, which looked like the Castello fortress in Rome. The construction site was already cleared, which aroused stormy protests from local citizens. Among them was N.M. Moleva, a well-known historian of Moscow and writer. Joined protests of the Muscovites and professional assessment by first the EKOS and then the City-Building Board finally stopped the implementation of the project. Ironically, five years later architect Tkhor designed a project of building for the Union of Russian Foreign Communities at the same site. The project was based on the historic network of streets and lanes, which unfortunately had dissappeared.

In the last years of the USSR existence one could clearly see the dissatisfaction of the Muscovites with the city-building role played by the complex of buildings at Dzerzhinsky square, which was expanding intensively during the Brezhnev era. There were strong demands to demolish the KGB building, as it had been done with the Bastille or turn it into a memorial museum (as had happened in Berlin). At the same time the EKOS received information on further enlargement of the KGB complex along Malaya Lubyanka and other adjacent streets. In doing so they were destroying the background historic building, interiors of houses with remained skillfully made staircases, plafonds, stucco moldings. All those things were disappearing and only a «mask» of a demolished building, built into new architecture, was sometimes left. It is interesting to note that the then KGB chief found it necessary to invite a group of people's deputies and discuss with them the issues of perestroika and «modernization» of the secret service. The deputies raised the issue of withdrawal of the KGB from Lubyanka, where it dominates over Moscow as an ominous bird. The answer was that the KGB underground facilities were so huge that their transfer to any other location was virtually

Diagram depicting zonal city-building regulation of the central part of Moscow. Research and Development Institute of the Genplan. Workshop No. 7.

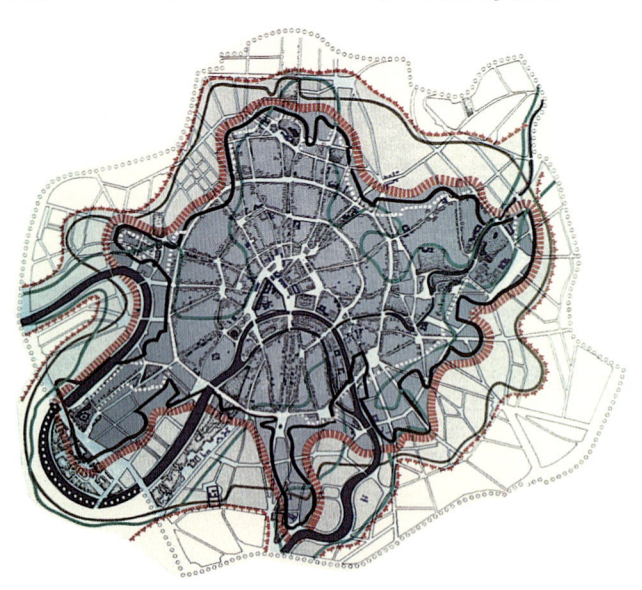

Complex of service buildings of the Ministry of Foreign Affairs in Smolenskaya (Sennaya) Square. Project. Architects: A. Klimochkin, B. Kolotov, G. Vuima, M. Novikova, S. Popov. Engineer: V. Ilyin.

Interior of the Alexander Nevsky Hall to be recreated at the Grand Kremlin Palace. Water-colour by D. Ukhtomsky.

impossible. It was simpler to move Moscow away from that ill-famed place a sad joke went. The hosts insisted on the complex being further enlarged only in Lubyanka. At that time it could be stopped. But what will happen next?

The EKOS also had very tough times resisting attempts of the Foreign Ministry to «swallow» blocks on Arbat and Smolensky boulevard under enormous pressure from its bosses. Finally, a compromising decision was made, the one which is currently being implemented.

Despite the prohibition of industrial development in the capital, a whole number of closed resolutions was passed to permit to build new structures and to add new land areas to those occupied by the plants belonging to the military and industrial complex. The EKOS managed to preserve the so-called «Anna Monce House» located within the grounds of the precision machinery plant and to make the customer allow the Muscovite if not to come up to this house but at least to look at it through the unbuilt-up area (regretfully it has been built up by now). Luckily the observant eye of the public expert working group noticed the construction of a new six-storeyed block of an incongruous size on the grounds of «Krasny Proletarian» plant. And this was really close to the Donskoy Monastery. Had it been completed, its enormous shape of a parallelepiped would have spoilt the view of the monastery from the Vorobiovy Hills. Fortunately, the construction process was discontinued, and the Moscow Institute of Architecture was directed to organize a design contest to rectify the situation. On recommendation of the Council the intensive building activity in the portion of the industrial zone contiguous to the monastery was also stopped.

Culture versus Culture

The Expert Council encountered this paradox for the first time when it was considering the development lines for the A.S. Pushkin State Museum of Fine Arts which is the pride of the capital. The model of the building itself and contiguous blocks were shining and sparkling because of perspex which covered the courtyards – the courtyards that make up Moscow's main spatial elements or Moscow's living cells, generating its special character. What was proposed was not a restoration of the architectural monuments but a «recreation» of the lost. The conversion of the whole block area, i.e. from the building with the museum to the present-day Znamenka, into a museum gave rise to doubts as it meant another step in depriving the centre of its dwelling function, in its gradual transformation into something like the City of London. Notwithstanding the decisive protest of the public expert opinion, this idea of covering courtyards transplanted from the Louvre became later a stereotype technique for augmenting the area and volume of many museums and public-use buildings – monuments of classicism, neoclassicism and modernist style that are composed as closed squares. Naturally, neither the silhouette of the building, nor the style of its facade, nor its decorum were taken into account to produce proper interior image, and – what is more – the covering attachment to the walls would lead unavoidably to their damage and distort their initial look.

Right after the Pushkin Museum of Fine Arts the Lenin Museum and the Moscow City Council put forward their proposals to cover inner courtyards, the latter proposed the covering for a business centre of the contiguous former mansion of governor-general (the Khrushchevs' Mansion belonging to the Pushkin Museum).

The reconstruction of the Lenin Library – both the restoration of the former Pashkov's House and the modernization of the buildings designed by V. Tshchuko and V. Gelfreikh – brought up the issue regarding a temporary depository for book storage and a workout of a development plan for the whole complex. More than once the Expert Public Council had to consider the proposed designs of the so-called «new blocks» of the library and to recommend again and again to bring them in compliance with the architectural monuments nearby and to fight against roof-top building in Marx-Engels Street which threatened to interfere with the silhouette of Bazhenov's creation. At that time hopes were laid on the reduction of the administrative apparatus of the Ministry of Defence that would have resulted in the utilization of the new building in Arbatskaya Square to satisfy the humanitarian needs of the country's first library. As is known, its big affair ended in the transfer of a complex of buildings in Mokhovaya Street to the library. But even this brought about another collision of the library interests with those of the Kremlin museums, mainly over the mansion-house which formerly belonged to the princely family of the Shakhovskie. Today this city area constitutes part of the sector which has been put forward for a design contest for a better planning and architectural look of Borovitskaya Square. The results of this contest will be known in 1997.

Power versus Law

When in the late 1980s the Department of Monument Protection addressed the office of public prosecutor with the case regarding the alteration which in fact was the destruction of the monument protected by the state located in Savelovsky Lane, the Moscow public actually believed in perestroika as the culprit was the all-mighty Administrative Department of the Council of Ministers of the USSR, and the alteration of that building was inherent to another step in the development of the residence of the then Chairman of the Council of Ministers of the USSR N.I. Ryzhkov. As is known, the result was zero, however, the precedent was there, and this case was made public, and it drew attention of the people to the future of Ostozhenka Street at that point desolated and degrading due to a number of different reasons. So, the Department's activity started to be discussed in the spirit of openness, the projects began to be considered «in the established order», which in combination resulted in proposing for the first time a conception of coordination between indigenous citizens and a powerful government structure.

The EKOS also repeatedly looked back into the «case» of the expansion of the building of the Supreme Court of the Russian Federation in Povarskaya Street. This project included very dense building-up of the site and erecting a multistorey tower and it was considered after the refusal of the client to shift construction to several other sites more suitable for the expansion. The tall structure came into obvious conflict with the perspectives of the Arbat lanes, and the functional pressure upon the area was clearly incongruent. But the lobbing of the project was so strong that, despite the public council's negative response and its recommendations to utilize the contiguous territories for the Court's needs, which would have made possible to significantly reduce the number of storeys, the construction began, entailing after a short while some cracks in neighbouring buildings that showed how dangerously close that building was to the architectural surroundings.

The Kremlin has always been a site for functional construction and it has been sort of a «restricted area» with regard to obtaining relevant information. So, it was difficult to obtain it about certain structures for security personnel constructed on the slope of the Tainitsky Hill. Thanks to the «excessively» vigorous public activity the issue of rebuilding the green-house near the Saviour Tower was coordinated with the EKOS.

The beginning of 1990s was the time of large works to adjust the administrative part of the Kremlin to the activity of the President and his administration. The public was informed about these works through television. The Chief Architect of the President's residence on the territory of the Senate informed the public of the refusal of the client to present relevant materials for public discussion. This is why at this point the degree of correspondence of the new implantations into the body of this architectural monument as well as the Kremlin cultural layer together with its archaeological treasures is still a mystery.

At the same time another idea emerged, the one to restore St. Andrew's and Alexander Halls that had been put together to form one hall for the meetings of the Supreme Soviet of the

USSR in 1930s (architect I. Ivanov-Shits). The documents and measurements that have survived as well as furniture, paintings and many other elements of their interior preserved in the Kremlin museums made it possible to realize this idea. It is indicative that the authorities took the right path of cooperation with the public: a council of observers and a scientific technique working group were formed. This project's path is thorny but there is confidence that its implementation will not harm the Grand Kremlin Palace. However, the atmosphere of secrecy over the Kremlin territory, lack of openness and absence of public and professional monitoring give one a feeling of concern over the condition of the ensemble which was at so big a pain put on the UNESCO World List.

Hopefully, living in a lawful state which is being formed with so many difficulties, the authorities will abide by the laws regarding the protection of historical and cultural monuments and the number of restored and reconstructed objects will not be considered as a compensation of the lost. It is common knowledge that cultural heritage is irreplaceable.

Architectural monument of the 17th century – The White Chambers in Prechistenka. 1996.

«Big Projects» of Moscow.

A number of ambitious projects (similar to the «Grand Projet» of Paris) are called this way. They have appeared on the initiative of Moscow Mayor Yu. M. Luzhkov and they are mainly connected with the Kremlin. The work that is being done so closely to the sacred place of Russia requires special professional care and responsibility.

In early 1990s Manege Square became widely popular as the place of mass gatherings. The decision to use the large asphalt-covered area with a lonely stone obelisk – which reminded that a monument to the 50th Anniversary of the October Revolution was planned to be built there – was taken almost spontaneously.

The territory was fenced. Archeological excavations began. The competition for a concept of a business and cultural centre on Manege Square was announced. The board rejected at once the French project of a six-story underground commercial centre because the historical signs of the place and its connection with the environment had not been reflected there – it means that the cultural function was totally missing. The project of architect B. Ulkin won the competition. EKOS supported the main compositional idea of this project such as preservation of the existing boarders of Manege Square, restoration of the destroyed chapel of Alexander Nevsky, creation of an artificial lake system, as symbols that would remind of the Neglinka river which used to flow here and which is enclosed now in the pipe. At the same time the Board warned against free manipulation with the boundaries of the Aleksandrovskiy Garden which is the monument to landscape art, and also advised that a six-story multipurpose underground centre should be bound in composition with the surrounding architectural ensemble. The further fate of the project is well-known: it was changed, public monitoring became much weaker and the first fragments of its implementation cause contradictory feelings.

The discussion by EKOS of the design project by I. A. Pokrovskiy to restore the Cathedral of Christ the Savior made by the initiative of the parish was fierce and equivocal. The Council in principal was not against the construction of the Cathedral on that site, but it required to carefully follow the design and approval procedure – without connecting it with certain memorial dates or anniversaries – with the development of a profound program, which would include all the stages of modern history of the Russian people. The main idea of the discussion is that the Cathedral construction should become the moral heroic deed of the people of Russia, similar to the process of construction of the masterpiece by K. Tona, which was so barbarously destroyed. They discussed the idea that the first temple should be «the monument to its predecessor» and warned not to do it «the new way» and not to allow arbitrariness when treating the interior. The important recommendations were to set up an observation board and to make the sources of financing «transparent». The position of EKOS was published in the press, it was discussed by the Committee on Culture of the State Duma, at the conference on the reconstruction of the city centre, which the Government of Moscow organized jointly with Moskomarkhitektura in 1994. It is known that a number of points were taken into account, but many issues remained unsolved, including the one whether it is permissible to have «speedy delivery» when creating the main temple of Russia.

The construction of the business centre at Krasnopresnenskaya Embankment – the so called «City» of Moscow – is plainly similar to the establishment of the Le Defense complex in Paris. Its location only one and a half kilo-

Manege Square. 1996. Architects: B. Ulkin, D. Lukaev. Sculptor: Z. Tsereteli.

St. Andrew Hall at the Grand Kremlin Palace. Architect: K. Ukhtomsky. 1849.

metres away from the Kremlin caused a lot of questions, including those about the height of the skyscrapers, their interrelation with the city landscape (especially the highest tower named RUS, proposed by a famous American company COM).

The «Big Projects» include the construction of the branch of the Bolshoi Theatre on Teatralnaya Square which goes on along with the restoration of the main building itself, projects of some coaching inns of Kitay-Gorod with possible reconstruction of the Wall, transformation of the New Arbat into walking area. They are connected with the evident desire of the Moscow authorities to establish the ideology of the famous Russian values through architecture and monumental art, to fill the vacuum which appeared in the society after communist ideas and idols were overthrown.

Unfortunately, in spite of multiple applications to the Chief Architect of the city, EKOS was not provided with the design materials on the monument to the 300th anniversary of the Russian Fleet, now known as the monument to Peter the Great, erected at the tongue of the island between the Moscow River and the Obvodniy Canal. The composition should certainly stimulate mental connections with the period of reforms, which Russia survived, and the personalities of the reformers themselves. However, the absence of normal procedures of approvals and agreements on this composition, at such an important place for the Moscow city construction, leads to a reverse idea that in a democratic country the end should not be justified by just any means. EKOS always reminds about it, often «interferes in the work», but at the same time it helps its colleagues-architects to make decisions which have their roots in the historical soil of the capital city. Thus, while designing the RED HILLS Russian cultural centre the authors proceeded from the spacious concept of the monastery. The Council drew attention of the architects to the necessity to take into account the visual ties with the Kremlin and other monasteries and recommended to use in its planning the existing historically established network of streets and the fragments of the remaining construction, which enabled to also upgrade its architectural and artistic image.

Face to Face with Muscovites

The modern history of EKOS is the expert assessment of design projects under the conditions of emerging market economy, intensive inflow of capital into the construction of objects, located in the centre, continuous decrease of the investment process period (unprecedented short terms of building construction in Moscow). The policy of the Moscow Government in attracting capital has made the impossible – the centre actually started to renew, the process of degeneration started to transform into the process of regeneration. At the same time fierce struggle started between investors for maximum profits from the so expensive land areas – the struggle for each square metre, for each floor. The rates, adopted in the capital city, which are in direct relationship with construction volumes, increased the cost of the designing by two to three times, which is, certainly, a good thing for which the Union of Architects of Russia and the Union of Moscow Architects struggled. However, the new situation brought about both fierce competition, and the struggle for the order, for the investor. The issues of professional ethics became very acute. In a number of cases the architect, struggling for the interests of his customer, again became the personification of social injustice. As a rule, it happens during the new construction on landscaped territories developed by the residents of the neighboring houses. Under these conditions, preliminary social diagnostic is required, search for compromises, involvement residents in the investment process, and, as minimum, providing truthful information at the very early stage of decision making.

As is known, the residents unite faster and closer into the self-rule committees in case of a danger of a new construction. This was the situation with the construction of new houses in Neskuchniy Garden; in Serpukhovskaya Street (construction of a house on the area of a secondary school); with the complex of the Russian-Turkish Centre in 4th Rostovskiy Lane, close to the famous house on Rostovskaya Embankment, designed by A. V. Shchusev. More than two thousand residents signed the appeal to the Government of Moscow, protesting against the violation of their rights, guaranteed by the Civil Code and the Law on City Construction. The committees of self-rule apply to EKOS for independent expert assessment of the city construction situations which are sometime already determined by all the decisions, resolutions and approvals, but made, however, without taking into account the opinion of the residents, and even putting them in front of a closed case (that is, in front of a fence, enclosing the future construction site).

It should be noted, that sometimes the interests of residents at the meeting of EKOS are defended by the architect – evidently, the role of the «social architect», so widespread in the West, is gradually becoming necessary. In the West, the process of social adaptation of the project, which takes up to 70 per cent of the whole design and approvals time, is considered normal.

Some Conclusions

The existence of EKOS for almost ten years allows to make conclusions on the changes in the professional ethics of the architect: from the representative of the totalitarian regime, of the unified state – meaning, anonymous – Customer to the representative of the wide spectrum of interests, however, with a weak sense of the social responsibility. The architect, the author of the design projects is hired only for the first, creative, stage, and sometimes without developing the working documentation, in other words, without responsibility for the final result.

We are getting more and more convinced that the profession of the architect is servile and this is proved by constant changing of one author with the other (the authors of the creative concept with the authors, which actually continue and complete it), and it is necessary to fill as soon as possible the legal and professional ethical vacuum, maintaining transparency and public control over the passing of procedures of the established order of designing and approving the design project. At the same time, the professional ethics of the architect working in the historical centre of Moscow, should include

Reconstruction works in Krivoarbatsky Lane near the architectural monument – the house of K. Melnikov. (1927 – 1929).

respect to the place of construction and to the opinion of the residents. The process of decision making should always include the work with public, both professional and nonprofessional. The architect is a transparent profession, he must ensure involvement in his work, coming down from the podium of the Messiah to the routine of the meetings of REU and DEZ service providers, not fighting with the residents, but involving them in participation in the project.

The architect can not work without knowledge of the historical city-construction foundation and general urban city-construction priorities and interests. Since the principle of regeneration of the historical environment is laid down as the basis of revival of the centre of Moscow, the architect must subjugate his creative self-satisfaction to this goal. The fact that being in the stream of this limitation, it is possible to create honorable modern Moscow architecture, is testified by the work of A. Skokan, A. Larin, A. Asadov, I. Utkin, whose project in Nizhniye Syromyatniky was recently actively supported by EKOS.

Our publication is devoted to the 850th anniversary of Moscow. Many things will be completed by the prominent jubilee, but many objects may me demolished in a hurry, in a rush, as it always happens in Russia. Let us remember about it and about our responsibility for the preservation of the wonderful, still living charm of our native city, which is guarded by EKOS – a unique phenomenon by itself.

At the meetings of the Coordinating Council on the reconstruction of the historical centre of the city on December 18, 1996, Mayor of Moscow, Mr. Yu.M. Luzhkov said: «I treat EKOS with great respect. People, who work there, want good things for Moscow. Please note, that only those projects, which did not pass through EKOS, then cause scandal, negative response of the Muscovites. We need to pass through EKOS all the most important projects to be placed in the centre».

Conservation of Woods and Parks Protection Belt

Environmental degradation observed in Moscow over the last decades has made ecology the main priority in the city development policy in the capital. However, neither significant changes nor improvement of Moscow ecology can be achieved without consideration of the territories beyond the Moscow boundaries as to a great extent it is formed by the neighbouring territories adjacent to Moscow – the so-called «close suburbs».

The ecological condition of the suburbs is of great importance for the atmosphere of Moscow to where the air flows from the environs. The condition of city's rivers which is of great concern to the Muscovites depends on their life supporting capabilities outside the city. The quality of drinking water in the Moscow water supply system deteriorates in spring and autumn due to runoff waters on the territories outside the city. The viability of city woods and parks also depends a lot on out-of-town woodlands and preservation of ecological corridors.

Pollution and construction on the neighbouring territories are not only harmful to health of the multimillion population of the city but also affects their psychics: the uniformity of vast compact construction area causes nervous tension, stresses, unmotivated behaviour.

The purpose of the Woods and Parks Protection Belt (WPPB) is to prevent pollution and haphazard construction, to preserve the nature and improve the environment around Moscow. WPPB was founded more than sixty years ago on the basis of existing woods and parks around Moscow with the aim of improving sanitary conditions and developing a recreation zone of the capital. It was assumed at that point in time that Moscow could be preserved within its boundaries independently from the neighbouring areas and its development would not have an impact on the surrounding nature.

The Istra River.

However, the formation of Moscow agglomeration changed the initial concept. The general rules of development of big cities (continuous growth of population, intensive use of territory) require other methods of WPPB formation, especially now when the need for ecologically clean environment for Moscow became more urgent.

Originally the idea of «green belts» around industrial cities was generated by the Utopian socialists in the 18th century and then it was developed by innovatory town-builders – first in Europe, then in the United States. In our country V.N. Semyonov was among the first who responded to this initiative. He wrote in 1912 that Europe only wanted to create «forest belts» whereas Russia had had them by that time (however, at that time Moscow had only forests in the outskirts, but not a green belt). Semyonov is an author of the Moscow General Plan of 1935 and the first established WPPB. His figurative descriptions such as «light towns», «reservoir of fresh air», reflected the idea of integrity of a city and its environs. This problem is two-sided: the first is the principles of suburb development when growth of the city influence provokes expansion attracting local population; the second – when a city tries to regulate the consequences of its activity in the suburban area.

The idea of WPPBs is to regulate spontaneity of suburbs development. As far back as in the 14 – 17th centuries in Russian orders and decrees the arable lands were allotted according to the number of residents; the forest areas and river fishing sites were also taken into consideration, land areas surrounding towns were determined. The rules for hunting and fishing, forest cutting,

Moscow. Serebryany Bor (Silver Forest).

conservation of rivers and their sources were long-established along with groves preservation, felling areas and land allotment regulations. It was noted that in the Moscow region «there was a large area of forests but it was kept untouched». And the more Moscow grew the larger area was under control.

Regulation of the suburb growth demands maximum efforts and resources directed not only to safeguard the nature complex but also, for the most part, to form secure environment and regulate the use of land for city development.

Time and practice showed that WPPB should be continuously developing from the impoverished outskirts – it means to plant trees, clean, improve and re-cultivate land, at the same time preserving those unique areas which remained intact.

WPPB is a zone where all types of construction are regulated as well as the use of land of all categories which is very difficult to accomplish due to a great number of land users – individuals and legal entities.

The less the territory of WPPB is, the more it overlaps with the belt of haphazardly developing suburbs and consequently the more dangerous for the WPPB are uncontrolled construction, ecologically unsafe facilities including industrial and engineering installations which are required to be close to the city but which negatively affect the suburban complex.

The WPPB was created for Moscow of 1935 with 3,5 m population and an area of 28,5 thousand hectares. Reserve territories with an area 1,2 times larger than Moscow itself were planned to be between the static WPPB of 144 thousand hectares with 0,3 m of population and the Moscow boundary line.

The WPPB layout was revised only in 1960 to implement the concept of city territories stabilization and creation of satellite towns. Since then WPPB has remained almost unchanged and in size it is close to 1935 although the population has increased more than four times whereas Moscow itself has grown three times (8,6 m people per 99,6 thousand hectares). In addition, the WPPB was inside the Moscow agglomeration – the biggest in the country. Differently from the General Plan of 1935, the General Plan of Moscow Development of 1971 provided for creation of reserve territories within WPPB near the Moscow ring road. It was accomplished in 1985. In years to come any subsequent growth of Moscow territories – due to either housing construction, the Lyuberetskaya aeration station, any water supply station or an airport will occur at the cost of WPPB.

At present, Moscow's WPPB comprises 162,4 thousand hectares of seven adjacent districts: Balashikhinsky, Krasnogorsky, Leninsky, Lyuberetsky, Mytishchinsky, Odintsovsky, Khimkinsky. 1,3 m people live within its boundaries including 1,1 m of urban population and, in addition, about 0,5 m of seasonal population in the summer time. 28 thousand hectares is the area of towns and urban-type settlements, about 56,3 thousand hectares – the lands of Goslesofond (State Forest Fund) and 38,6 thousand hectares – agricultural land. As a result of intensive housing and industrial construction the area of natural territories has reduced and their condition deteriorated considerably.

The RF Law «On the Environment Control» and literature on city development say that green zones include WPPBs. The closer they are to the source of impact – in our case to Moscow – the more stringent the regulation should be. However, in conditions of such a huge agglomeration like Moscow an idea may occur to change the woods and parks belt to a «green zone».

The green zone means only protection of forests, planted trees and shrubs, rest complexes and recreation areas located in the suburbs. Only forests and recreation areas are to be protected whereas sources of negative effect are outside the «green zone». According to the Law of the Russian Federation «On specially protected suburban territories» it is only in special cases that green zones can become specially protected areas subject to partial or complete withdrawal from commercial use. Therefore, the status of a green zone is not sufficient for Moscow suburbs.

Another alternative is to transfer the WPPB beyond the suburbs. It allows to avoid previous difficulties but creates new ones. Space environmental monitoring of the Moscow region reveals chains of towns and pollution plumes which limit the relatively clean surroundings of Moscow: from the North (Volokolamsk – Vysokovsk – Klin – Dmitrov – Sergiev Posad – Alexandrov), from the South (Serpukhov – Kashira – Kolomna), from the East (Noginsk – Electrostal – Voskresensk) and even from the West. As a result, there is no way to move the WPPB further away.

Since the WPPB is located in the Moscow region one should question if there is anything that the region can benefit from it.

In the world practice the chaotic suburbs with a low social service index and backward industries are characterized as socially unstable. Transformation of the Moscow WPPB will create a comfortable zone for the Moscow region similar to the green belts of Paris and London.

The main problems of the WPPB lie in poor coordination of activities by Moscow and Moscow region administrations. The WPPB was established on the territory of the Moscow region but the first project of the suburban zone (1931) and the project of the WPPB as a green suburban zone (1950) formed part of an integral general plan for Moscow. Traditions of this approach are reflected in the current «General Plan for Moscow and Moscow region development till 2010».

Since 1940 under the Government decree the competence of Moscow authorities was to control city planning activities and land allotment, to issue permits and approvals for construction but economical activities have been within the competence of the Moscow region. This was confirmed by Minstroy (the Ministry of Construction) in 1992 because WPPB boundaries enclose the whole system of water supply to Moscow with the most important water stations: Rublevskaya, Severnaya, Vostochnaya and Zapadnaya, and the first water supply protected belt of Moskvoretskaya and Klyazminskaya systems. Besides, within the WPPB in the city suburbs there are facilities which are of great importance for Moscow, i.e. Vnukovo and Sheremetevo airports, Lyuberetskaya and New-Lyuberetskaya aeration stations. Since 1961 according to the Government decree care of woods located in WPPB has been the competence of Moscow authorities too.

Such distribution of mandates between Moscow and the Moscow region was balanced by procedures of mutual approvals and coordination. Growth of uncoordinated activities over the past four-five years is related to legitimization of new laws, new forms of ownership and revised financing principles for legal subjects on this territory. The exclusive status of WPPB is not enforced by legislation, therefore it is subject to regulations and rules which are in force all over the Russian Federation (Moscow and the Moscow Region are its equal subjects).

The application of some provisions of the current legislation in the Russian Federation including the law on local self-government, given the lack of coordination of activities between both subjects of the Russian Federation and lack of land cadastre developed specially for WPPB, will increase dissipating of land wastefully used for cottage and small building construction and also for industrial facilities and will speed up uncontrolled construction devastating open space and woods and parks areas. It should be noted that this threat comes equally from the Moscow Region and from Moscow.

Approvals of cottage construction on the territories around drinking water reservoirs including those of the first belt are signed by region organisations and the Moscow Sanitary

Committee. Implementation of the «Moscow decentralization» concept, i.e to move part of the Moscow population beyond the Moscow boundary to elite suburbs close to nature, can become a threat to WPPB as there are no legally instituted preventive regulations on the protection of WPPB. Therefore, it is required to develop land cadastre and to control the use of land in accordance with specially developed city planning zoning.

Formation of the woods and parks belt on the suburb territories can be possible only if Moscow and the Moscow regions join their efforts either under agreements or a special Law of the RF defining the status of WPPB.

It should be a special legal status of part of the Moscow Region located close to Moscow which should be administered jointly by government authorities of both subjects to resolve ecological and social problems. WPPB should be developed as an integral suburban territory around Moscow enclosing land of all categories and performing environment protection (environment formation), sanitary and recreational functions.

A special legal status of WPPB is stipulated by its unique role in the ecological balance of the Moscow Region. It should regulate the relations with respect to the territory of WPPB between the Russian Federation, Moscow Region, Moscow city, local self-government bodies and also legal entities and individuals.

Such a legal status of WPPB enforced by a special law will be consistent with the RF Constitution (1993) establishing the people's right of favourable environment and with the Federal Laws on «Environment Protection» (1991) and «The Status of the Capital of the Russian Federation» (1993) stipulating joint activities in the field of nature protection and assistance of the Moscow Region authorities to the Moscow city and other legal norms and acts. This status of WPPB won't be in conflict with the decree of the Moscow Region Government on «Town Planning Regulation for the Central Part of the Moscow Region» (1995) and the Law on «The Rules of Construction in towns, urban settlements, villages, other settlements and recreation zones of the Moscow Region, although «the woods and parks protection belt of Moscow» concept is not defined in these documents.

The joint activities of the Moscow Region and Moscow should be conducted by way of making joint decisions, setting up joint coordinating committees including those that would be operating continuously to issue approvals for city planning, sanitary control and social programs. Moscow has already been making its financial contribution and should continue financing some of the activities. The woods and parks belt of Moscow should protect both Moscow and the Moscow Region from ecological disaster.

Renaissance of the Historical Centre of Moscow

Moscow – a city with a long and rich history – is the seat of enormous material, spiritual and cultural values which are of nation and worldwide significance. Among them are marvelous monuments of the Moscow architecture of the past centuries and the city landscape preserved within the Kamer-Kollezhsky rampart with their unique features which have become symbolic of the capital of our Motherland. Occupying the leading place in the architectural panorama of the city the downtown incorporates everything which, by right, constitutes the pride of Moscow and which distinguishes it from other cities and capitals.

The attempts to give the most precise and comprehensive definition of such a phenomenon as the city downtown have been made since the old times. One of western researchers, famous historian and expert of city building A. Vallis writes,

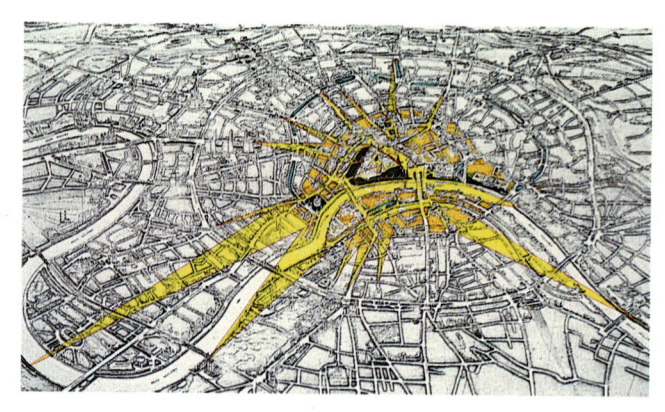

Visual-compositional links of the Kremlin.

«The downtown – often called an agora, a forum, a market, a cathedral square, the main artery of the city – has been the heart of the city life since the Bible times. It is the biggest attraction in the city». Another scientist, a prominent specialist in pedestrian traffic, P. Velev believes that «the downtown is intended to be, sort of, «a drawing-room» of a city which means to have a distinguishing quality of environment. To those who visit a city for the first time its image is associated, first of all, with its downtown». Therefore, it should not be surprising that downtown is the subject of special attention of municipal authorities and architectural institutions – indeed, judgement on a city in general is more often based on its downtown which is its face, image and «business card». The territory which constitutes a separate administrative formation – the Central District – has its own organizational structure for management and coordination of city planning, design and construction works to allow for more attention, care and consideration of the specific and rather complicated problems of the city downtown.

Currently, the development of the Moscow downtown is based on the principles of continuity with active use of traditional methods in spacious, architectural and functional approach and proportionality of the new and past centuries. Reconstruction, restoration and recreation of historical buildings have become the primary task whereas new construction is performed by techniques which allow for its adaptation to the established environment.

The main provisions adopted by the Government of Moscow for a city planning concept of reconstruction of the Central Administrative District and the project of a detailed design for the central part of Moscow are as follows:

– all city planning problems must be resolved with the ultimate goal of achieving the status of an architectural monument for the downtown part within the Kamer-Kolleguiya rampart;

– all city planning activities should be oriented at high standards of comfort for those who permanently reside downtown and for those who come there for different purposes;

– downtown should maintain the functions of the nucleus of the capital and the city centre.

The future development of downtown includes reconstruction and new construction, selective development of the social sphere, reduction of ecologically unacceptable industries and institutions including those that industrially do not fit in, development of the transportation system, upgrading and construction of new engineering mains and facilities, increase and qualitative improvement of housing and elimination of communal apartments.

Among the priorities are the following activities:

– regeneration of the main and side streets in the protected zones of the historic centre core;

– reconstruction of squares around the Kremlin and Kitay-Gorod;

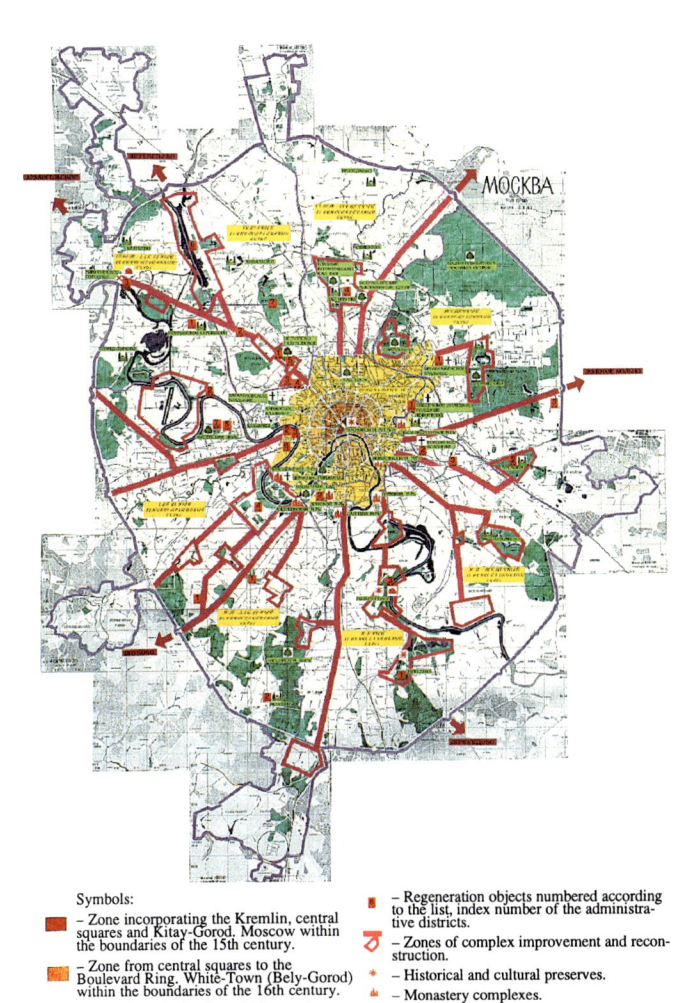

Symbols:
- ■ – Zone incorporating the Kremlin, central squares and Kitay-Gorod. Moscow within the boundaries of the 15th century.
- ■ – Zone from central squares to the Boulevard Ring. White-Town (Bely-Gorod) within the boundaries of the 16th century.
- ■ – Zone from the Boulevard Ring to the Garden (Sadovoe) Ring. Earth-Town (Zemlyanoi-Gorod) within the boundaries of the 17th century.
- ■ – Zone from the Garden Ring to Kamer-Kollezhsky Rampart. Moscow within the boundaries of the 18th century.
- ■ – Regeneration objects numbered according to the list, index number of the administrative districts.
- ● – Zones of complex improvement and reconstruction.
- ✧ – Historical and cultural preserves.
- ▲ – Monastery complexes.
- ▲ – Country-estate/mansion complexes.
- † – Necropolises.
- ▲ – Archeological monuments.
- — – Boundaries of administrative districts.
- — – City boundary.

Diagram showing restoration of architectural, historical and cultural monuments and complex improvement of the territory of Moscow.

Symbols:
- ■ – Zone incorporating the Kremlin, central squares and Kitay-Gorod. Moscow within the boundaries of the 15th century.
- ■ – Zone from central squares to the Boulevard Ring. White-Town (Bely-Gorod) within the boundaries of the 16th century.
- ■ – Zone from the Boulevard Ring to the Garden (Sadovoe) Ring. Earth-Town (Zemlyanoi-Gorod) within the boundaries of the 17th century.
- ■ – Zone from the Garden Ring to Chamber-Collegiate Rampart. Moscow within the boundaries of the 18th century.
- ■ – Regeneration objects numbered according to the list, index number of the city raion.
- ■ – Recreation of the lost monuments numbered according to the list, index of the city raion.
- ○ – complex improvement and reconstruction of city-building ensembles.
- ■ – Blocks of complex reconstruction.
- ■ – Preserved zones.
- ■ – Boundary of the Central administrative district.
- — – Boundaries of city raions.

Schematic diagram showing the location of historical and cultural monuments in the central zone of the city.

– restoration of historical, cultural and architectural monuments;

– formation of the Garden Ring squares including construction of social/cultural and commercial/business centres.

Experts from design organisations (first of all, «Mosproyect-2» which has the biggest scope of design and survey works in the city centre) fully appreciate that any upset of a fragile balance of the historical complex including nature may lead to unjustified and unrecoverable losses for Moscow. In this connection pre-design analysis of existing buildings is performed, the general concept of architectural solutions is defined, engineering and transportation problems are looked at, environmental studies are carried out, architectural-planning tasks for restoration and modification of ancient buildings are specified, programs of phased implementation of a project are set up, detailed design of work organisation under conditions of limited downtown space is developed. It should be noted that «environment» designing requires to address every problem with consideration of the whole set of problems which arise in the city centre including purely design issues such as facade colours, advertising design, street design, greenery, signs and many others. It is impossible to resolve these problems without study and application of extensive practical experience of our colleagues from big cities and capitals of other countries and also without discussions of the proposed decisions not only by specialists but also by the public.

Nowadays judgment on professional skills, an architect's culture, a sense of responsibility before the past and the future is made on the ability to work in the established environment. And it does not matter if it is an individual building or a whole area, for instance, the Kitay-Gorod preserve zone, squares around the Kremlin, the Boulevard and the Garden Rings. Radical reconstruction allows to resolve not only one of the most serious city-planning problems related to completion of the historic ensembles' system in the centre of the capital but also – which is as much important – to introduce essential functional changes in the interests of residents and visitors of downtown.

As to one of the most ancient areas which is under reconstruction now – Kitay-Gorod which has long been a cultural, trading and business centre of the capital, it shall maintain these functions which should be supported by intensive growth of museums and educational complexes as well as recreational services, mainly in the area of Nikolskaya Street which will become one of the pedestrian streets of Moscow. Modifications will cover almost all the existing buildings in this area including the Middle Age Monasteries: Monetny, Pechatny, Zaikonospassky, Nickolo-Greek and Bogoyavlensky; ancient trading and lodging buildings of Shevaldyshevsky, Sheremetevsky and Chizhevsky Podvorye («homestead»); the Upper (GUM) and Medium market rows. The concept provides for reconstruction and restoration not only of individual architectural, cultural and historic monuments but also a rebirth of a unique city-building environment in Kitay-Gorod with the outstanding role of the Gostiny Dvor undergoing intensive recon-

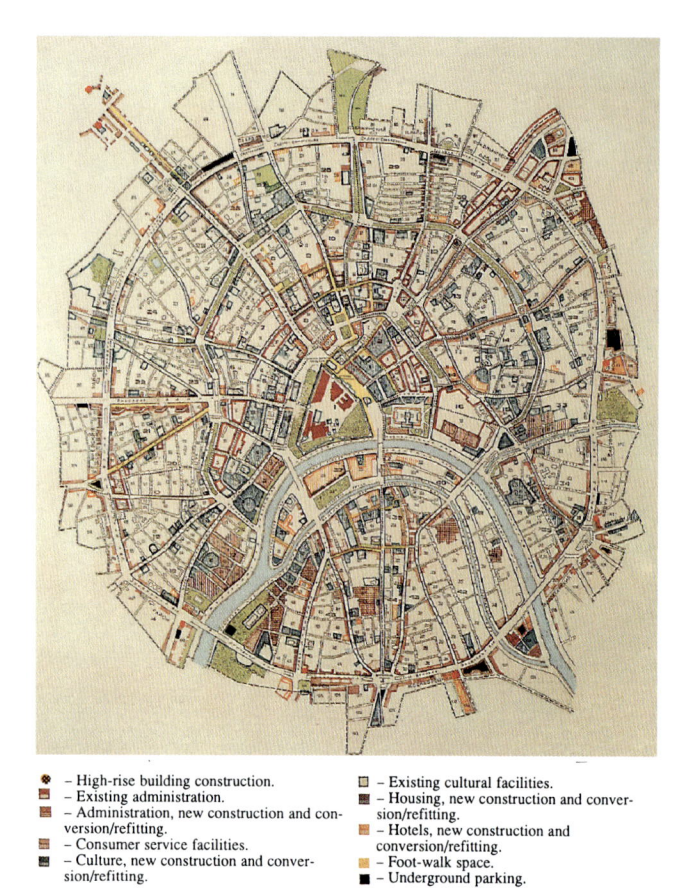

- High-rise building construction.
- Existing administration.
- Administration, new construction and conversion/refitting.
- Consumer service facilities.
- Culture, new construction and conversion/refitting.
- Existing cultural facilities.
- Housing, new construction and conversion/refitting.
- Hotels, new construction and conversion/refitting.
- Foot-walk space.
- Underground parking.

Functional structure of the Moscow centre.

struction with the unique roofed space designed for a multipurpose hall which will be the biggest in Moscow.

The basically new approach in the restoration of downtown – which causes heated debates – is rebuilding of previously destroyed remarkable monuments of the past. The Cathedral of Our Lady of Kazan and Voskresensky Gates with

Space planning organisation of Moscow's historical core.

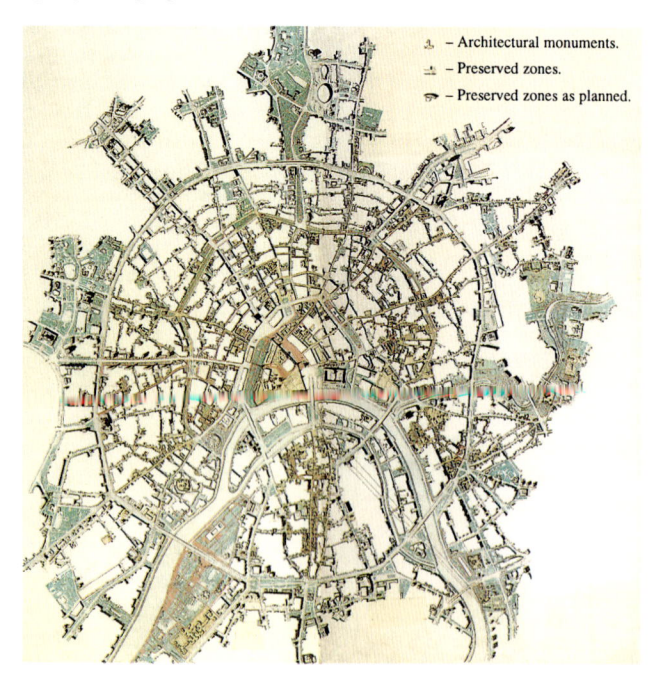

- Architectural monuments.
- Preserved zones.
- Preserved zones as planned.

the Chapel of Iberian Mother of God decorating the Red Square in the past are back again there, thus bringing back the original appearance of the main square of the country. Art lovers are again welcome to the Tretiakov Gallery, a gigantic repository of paintings by Russian artists from ancient times till present days. One of the recovered symbols of the Russian statehood is the rebuilt Red Porch of the Grand Kremlin Palace which used to be an important component of the Cathedral Square ensemble for four centuries. It was a front entrance to the main Throne Hall. It was used by the Tsars on special occasions such as going out to attend festive ceremonies and services in the Cathedral of Assumption and to meet foreign embassies' delegations. In early thirties, when a dining room was added to the wall of the Faceted Palace, the Red Porch was pulled down and now it has been rebuilt on photos and outline drawings preserved in the archives of the Moscow Kremlin museums. It is planned to restore the previously lost gorgeous halls named after Alexander Nevsky and Andrew the First Called which were as beautiful as the St. George Hall well known in the world as the place where the President of Russia meets the leaders of other countries.

In 1994 the Government of Moscow made a decision to rebuild the Cathedral of Christ the Saviour. The first foundation stone was laid on January 8, 1995, and a year after by Christmas 1996 the main bearing structures of the building were erected. Implementation of this grandiose project required enormous organisational efforts. «Mosproyect-2» set up an integrated studio and a workshop to work on the design of the cathedral, the design work was performed in parallel with construction, i.e. design documentation and work drawings were made available to builders immediately after completion by designers. There were periods when up to fifteen hundred designers were involved by «Mosproyect-2» to provide for uninterrupted construction process.

The general construction work on the site was performed by four large organisations. «Montazhspetsstroy» of Joint-Stock Company «Mospromstroy» (General Contractor) was responsible for the foundation and main structures of the building. The company «Orbit» did the stylobate part of the work, «Inpredstroy» was building the Nadvratnaya Church («Over the Gates»), engineering support facilities. «Mosstroy-16» which built the Poklonnaya Hill ensemble was responsible for interiors of the halls in the bottom part of the building. The total number of different workers employed daily in the construction was thirty five hundred.

The Cathedral will have its historical authentic appearance and size, however it will have some new features, mainly in the «sub-cathedral» space. The bottom of the stylobate part (where in the past there was a hill 18 metres high with a cathedral on top of it which was then destroyed leaving a large pit instead), of 66,000 sq.m is now a business centre and a historical/cultural complex including the halls for the Holy Synod sessions, Councils, service rooms of the Patriarchy. This area will also accommodate the lower Cathedral of Transfiguration of God with parts of the Alexeyevsky Monastery that used to be there and the gallery for Easter Processions.

The Cathedral of Christ the Saviour was an architecturally unique edifice incorporating the best patterns of the Old Russia Cathedral architecture; it harmoniously combined all arts – pictorial, sculpture, decorative-applied art and, certainly, architecture. Its paintings, murals and sculptural ornament unique in scope and complexity was a distinguished phenomenon of national and world art.

The authors of the project for recreation of the Cathedral set themselves an unprecedented and complicated task – to bring back to life everything that was lost using the preserved dimensions data, drawings, photos and other archive materials. The committee responsible for the cathedral ornament headed by Metropolitan Yuvenaly developed tender programs for all works related to decoration of the Cathedral. The tender requirements were very demanding as can be seen from the following example. Each bidder was given a technical assignment for bell casting and the data on the studied tonality of the bells from the destroyed cathedral. The winner was determined by the best bell-ringers who came to Moscow specially for this reason from all over Russia. It happened to be the Moscow ZIL which was entrusted with casting four big and ten small bells which are now mounted on the Cathedral.

The leading sculptors from Moscow and St. Petersburg – all in all about 50 people- are involved in recreation of sculptural ornament of the Cathedral. The main team of this group is the recently established Society of Sculptors of the Russian Academy of Art which includes recognized masters who have their individual style and who have already made themselves a name: T. Sokolova, A. Burganov, the Rukavishnikovs – father and son, M. Pereslavets and many others. Along with the famous masters some young sculptors are involved – postgraduates of the Academy Studio under the management of V. Tsygal. What else has to be recreated is the multifigure compositions for the «tonovsky» cathedral made by A. Loganovsky, famous Russian sculptor. As is known, three of his eight huge compositions (4 x 7,5 m) were preserved by Donskoy Monastery. They are devoted to the following events: «St. Sergius of Radonezh blesses Prince Dmitry Donskoy for the battle with the Tatars», «David going to Jerusalem after the victory over Goliath», «Abraham with allies returning after the victory over the tsars». After elaborate restoration accurate forms were made from these reliefs which will be used to make replicas in solid material. Then they will be put in the appropriate places in the Cathedral whereas the originals will be kept in the museum of the Cathedral.

About fifty sculptural compositions in total are to be made for the Cathedral of Christ the Saviour, many of them will be recreated anew. The facades of the original cathedral had representations of Christ, especially esteemed icons of the Mother of God of Vladimir, Smolensk, Iberia, the Saints and Martyrs. The masters of today when recreating the sculptural ornament of the Cathedral are guided by the works of their predecessors, icons, religious traditions and canons. A group of famous masters – the best sculptors of Russia – headed by Academician Yu. Orekhov has made models of relieves and sculpture groups which constitute the classic decor of the replica-Cathedral.

A tender was announced for recreation of paintings and murals of the Cathedral of Christ the Saviour. Fifty different teams of artists applied for participation in the tender. After thorough consideration the Russian Academy of Art responsible for this extremely difficult job recommended the most distinguished artists from Moscow, St. Petersburg, Yaroslavl and other Russian cities. The tender assignment was to make a canvas fragment of the murals of the Cathedral «Jesus on the Throne» – a central figure on the drum – within two months. The Committee for the Cathedral Decoration selected the best nine works out of 34 submitted. Among the winners are experienced Moscow artists V. Baksheev, A.Oskolsky, National Artist of Russia N. Somov, Professor V. Chelombiev, Academician Z. Tsereteli, young painter A. Ustinovich; State Prize Winners

Restoration, reconstruction and recreation of the historical core of Moscow. Diagram. 1987 – 1997.

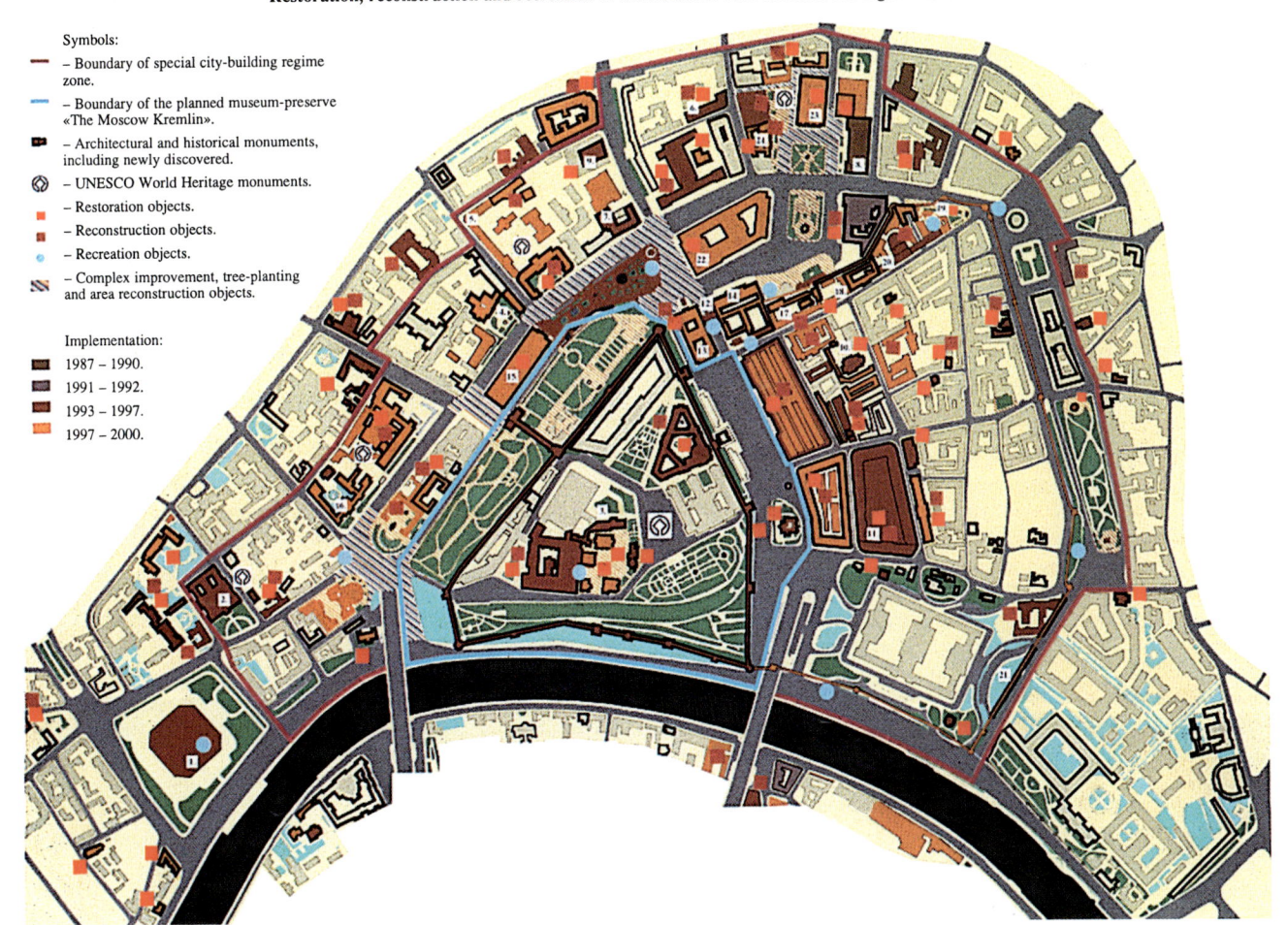

Symbols:
- Boundary of special city-building regime zone.
- Boundary of the planned museum-preserve «The Moscow Kremlin».
- Architectural and historical monuments, including newly discovered.
- UNESCO World Heritage monuments.
- Restoration objects.
- Reconstruction objects.
- Recreation objects.
- Complex improvement, tree-planting and area reconstruction objects.

Implementation:
- 1987 – 1990.
- 1991 – 1992.
- 1993 – 1997.
- 1997 – 2000.

from St.Petersburg A. Bystrov and S.Repin; N. Mukhin – famous painter from Yaroslavl. They will have to re-create the picturesque ornament and the murals of multiple interiors of the Cathedral. The International Design Centre (the manager is Z. Tsereteli, Vice-President of the Academy) won very tough competitions for recreation of unique crosses and gates.

On all issues related to the Cathedral decoration continuous consultations are held with the Project manager, Director of «Mosproyect-2», M.M. Posokhin and with the manager of the specialised complex studio designing the Cathedral – Architect A. Denisov, with experts from other institutes, organisations, museums. Yu.M. Luzhkov, the Mayor of the capital, and the Public Supervision Council chaired by His Holiness Patriarch Alexius II of Moscow and All Russia are making essential contribution in decision-making on principal matters.

By unprejudiced estimation, «Mosporject-2» has provided for the most effective and high quality designing of an outstanding in all senses cathedral ensemble and managed to involve in this work famous historians, archive experts who collected the materials by little pieces in order to re-create with the maximum degree of accuracy the Cathedral – the monument to Russian warriors.

Among the works of the «Mosproyect-2» specialised studio for restoration of historical and cultural monuments headed by L. Lavrenyov are the projects of recreation, restoration and reconstruction of cathedrals both separate and those that form part of cathedral complexes, projects of restoration of such beautiful architectural ensembles as the Moscow Kremlin, Novodevichy, Simonov, Andronikov, Sretensky, Danilov and other convents and monasteries. All this allows to preserve a historically identical appearance of Moscow for future generations.

In addition, projects of new cathedrals are being accomplished. During the celebration of the Millennium of the Christianity in Russia, according to the decision of the Holy Synod of Russian Orthodox Church, a tender was held for the project of the Holy Trinity Cathedral. Its planned location is in the area of historical-architectural complex «Tsaritsyno» in Moscow. The best project was developed by Academician A.Polyansky from «Mosproyect-2» (Moscow Project Development Agency). The studio of this agency has also developed the project of the church of St. Martyr George the Victorious on Poklonnaya Hill blessed by Patriarch Alexius II in 1995. Cathedral designing and construction earlier negligible in Mosproyect-2 activities nowadays forms a substantial part of its work.

More than three thousand Moscow buildings have the protection status and are under special state supervision. New names and addresses discovered by historians are added annually to the list of such buildings. The recreation and restoration of these buildings are carried out under strict rules which are mandatory for everyone. Additional obligations to keep them intact and to use them with special care are assumed by the leaseholders of such monument buildings.

Moscow's 850th anniversary has become a strong rallying point contributing to acceleration of all construction, restoration, recreation and city improvement works. Currently, there are more than one thousand projects under way – the edifices of well-known Moscow theaters (including the Bolshoi Theatre), museums and exhibition halls, city and suburban estates (Ostankino, Tsaritsino, Kuskovo), parks and boulevards, special programs on regeneration and social improvement of some districts in Moscow: Yakimanka, Sretenka, Ostozhenka, Pretchistenka, Zamoskvorechye. All this is being done in the interests of the perspective city development and is very important for the city's prestige – during the Moscow 850th jubilee it will be visited, first of all, by guests who will be acquainting with the history and cultural life of Moscow.

**Shopping and recreation complex under Manege Square. Project.
Architectural concept: workshops of B. Ulkin and D. Lukaev.
Design work: Mosproject-2 (M. Posokhin), Mosinzhproject (C. Pankina).**

The jubilee preparation program includes reconstruction and upgrading of some old hotels, construction of new modern first-class hotels, various business, trading, recreational and office centres in all prefectures and administrative districts. Under construction there are new large multipurpose complexes. As a rule, such construction is based on the principle of combination of historical and modern buildings with active use of underground space. An illustrative example of that can be the shopping and recreational underground complex on Manege Square. In the reconstruction program of the Garden Ring squares a special place is occupied by the project of a big hotel and a business centre on Kudrinskaya square which by its scope and style develops the ideas of the skyscraper authors (1952, architects M.V. Posokhin, A. Mndoyantz, engineer M. Vokhomsky). The new edifice (the project developed by a team of authors under the direction of M.M. Posokhin) balances the general composition of the square organically including the outstanding monument of Moscow architecture – «Vdovy Dom» («Widows' House»), 1825, architect D. Zhilyardy). The hotel and business complex includes a five-star hotel with 300 rooms and office space. The authors successfully coped with the task of providing the most comfortable conditions for both groups of users thus meeting the requirement that multifunctional facilities should form one integral unit.

Central Market in Tsvetnoy Boulevard. Architect: A. Klimochkin.

**Manege Square. Shopping and recreation complex. 1996.
Architect: D. Lukaev. Sculptor: Z. Tsereteli.**

On the eve of the jubilee among the urgent works to be done are pavement repair, improvement of residential areas, especially along the main streets, roads and places of public gatherings, renovation and construction of new subway stations, underground passages and parking places, reconstruction of railway stations and airports – the main ports of entry to the capital.

Housing is still a pressing problem. Trying to resolve it the city authorities take effective measures including use of extra-budgetary funds, control of prices for building industry products. All possible resources and efforts are used to speed up the construction and improvement of new districts : Maryino, Zhulebino, Butovo, Mitino, Novokosino and others with the names of former villages. It would be fair to say that Muscovites like these construction projects as they are based on individual design and use the world advanced technologies and besides, are orientated towards traditions of the Moscow architecture.

More attention is being paid to maintenance and upgrading of the city's housing including reconstruction of morally and physically outdated «five-storey» buildings – the first ones in large panel building construction program. This is some kind of paying off the debt to Muscovites which have had to live for many years in very small apartments with very limited space, although they are isolated but very uncomfortable for living.

**Kudrinskaya Square. Multi-purpose business centre. Project.
Architect: M. Posokhin.**

The Mayor's office and the Moscow Government are making strenuous efforts to maintain the leading role of Moscow as a great business, cultural and tourist centre. Different privileges and stimulation are granted to national and foreign investors who place money in construction of prestige buildings and facilities: offices, banks, hotels, commercial, educational, medical, sports and entertainment institutions. According to the concept of continuity of city development all new and modern projects are made part of the historically shaped city configuration which facilitates the enhancement of technical and engineering support and city improvement and makes the Moscow architecture enriched.

The resurrection of the Cathedral

The appearance of a wooden chapel in honor of the icon of Our Lady of Kazan on Red Square in Moscow, near GUM (state department store) where crowds of people are wandering the whole day was a great surprise. It seemed that worries were leaving people and many of them were coming up to find out through what miracle this tiny chapel appeared here. And one can remember: you stand and read re-read big letters on the board appealing for participation in the revival of Kazansky Cathedral which at one time was rising high here on Red Square, in front of the Nikolskie Gates of the Kremlin. You stay inside a noisy crowd resounded with voices of excursion agents.

Having crossed yourself before the image of Our Lady and having put your donation money into a transparent chest, you move aside and look at the people who follow you – one after another. People are coming and coming without any prompt and compulsion, and bringing their donations for the benefit of restoration of the sacred place of the Russian state.

The sacred place of Fatherland! The very thing that was mentioned by Alexius II, Patriarch of Moscow and All Russia, during the ceremony of laying the foundation stone of the Cathedral: the revival of the Cathedral – is the rebirth of each of us. After all, so many cathedrals were ruined and so many sacred things were destroyed but for the first time a cathedral is being restored and our fathers' sacred place is being purified.

The idea to rebuild the cathedral in honor of the icon of Our Lady of Kazan was set forth by P.D. Baranovsky. He passed away more than ten years ago but time is going and the image of this man is rising in our esteem, and his devotion to work is becoming a legend. There are courageous military leaders, scientists with challenging ideas and he was a restorer of great courage. He was a romantic and maximalist believer and an uncompromising man. It seemed that his vision penetrated thick layers of stone; through the span of centuries he could see initial forms and taste of architects and stone-cutters of the past centuries. It is difficult to say in brief how much our restoration school owes this master, expert, artist and a nice man. He started to work on the Kazansky Cathedral in 1927 and managed to reveal the contours of original ancient vaults, the design of kokoshniks (woman's head-dress in Old Russia like a crown) – true Russian and Moscow architectural form connecting the vaults with the under-dome drums. The outlines of the Cathedral of the 17th century started forming up but one year later the work was interrupted. The scientist got into argument with top authorities about the planned demolition of St. Basil's Cathedral and was exiled to building sites of Siberia. When he returned back he witnessed the destruction of the Kazansky Cathedral. It is hard to imagine but actually under the breaker of destroyers he took exact measurements, photos and made the layout of the doomed monument. It looked like a death sentence execution and the doctor was thinking how to save the life of a sentenced person.

Demolition of the Kazansky Cathedral in Red Square. 1936.

Till the very end of his life Baranovsky cherished the hope to restore the Cathedral. All materials, as a testament, he handed over to his loyal disciple-restorer O.I. Zhurin. Exactly at this time architect G.Y. Mokeev created a painted reconstruction picture of the Kazansky Cathedral of the 17th century and gave it to Peter Dmitrievich as a birthday present for his 90th anniversary on February 14, 1982. The beautiful cathedral with five tiers of kokoshniks was depicted like a fair-tale vision – a dream of Baranovsky. Peter Dmitrievich liked the picture but gave it together with his measurements records to Zhurin so that it would in sight as a symbol.

And indeed, a picture became an inspiration. After Peter Dmitrievich's decease the picture has been always shown at annual «Baranovsky Readings» initiated by All-Russia Society for Protection of Historic and Cultural Monuments, Moscow Division. The idea of the Kazansky Cathedral rebirth was finally formulated exactly here, in this Society. From year to year it captured new and new minds and shortly after that it inspired wide public movement.

In 1987 a commission on the Kazansky Cathedral revival was established under I.V. Petryanov, a well-known public activist and academician. At the very first conference of the commission Zhurin presented the Academician with the reconstruction picture of the Kazansky Cathedral – the one that he received from Baranovsky. That was the blessing of the deceased in 1984 Peter Dmitrievich to continue the work he had started.

Petryanov recollected, «Having been chosen as the chairman of such an unusual public council which was to revive the architectural rarity of the 17th century – the Kazansky Cathedral, and moreover, to make it similar to the one on the picture given to him as gift, at the first moment, to say the truth, I was bewildered with a question: what should I do?» After thinking it over but with no conclusions I took the picture, packed it accurately and went to the Central Committee of the Communist Party to meet V.A. Medvedev, chief of the ideology sector, because the circumstances urged me to hurry up: discussions on the project for reconstruction of the Lenin Museum were underway and the area of the Kazansky Cathedral was planned to be used for the Lenin Museum. As I expected he had no idea of the Kazansky Cathedral. I put the picture on his desk and told him everything I knew about the monument. Certainly, the history of the Kazansky Cathedral did impress him: my companion was surprised and asked me questions scrutinizing the picture. In short, it seemed to me that we understood each other perfectly well. Indeed, during further discussions of the Lenin Museum reconstruction project my campaign with a visit to Staraya (Old) Square led to good results: it was recommended that the Moscow Division of the Society for Protection of Monuments should begin rebuilding the Cathedral. After that Mossoviet made a decision to revive the Cathedral and turn it over to the Russian Orthdox Church...»

The old days were giving way to the new time – we finish our story. A few years ago, in the «pre-perestroyka» time (a period before the reforms), one could hardly imagine that the Party ideology sector would ever approve the construction of a cathedral of God in Moscow, particularly in Red Square!

Intensive work began. The Moscow Division of the Society for Protection of Monuments called for donations. The time-honoured Russian tradition to collect money for a cathedral «from all over the world» was reviving. Any volunteer could remit money with a note on the bank-transfer form: «For the reconstruction of the Kazansky Cathedral». Even the city authorities considered the reconstruction of the Cathedral their duty: The Moscow Government started to provide financing, material and technical support of construction works. We should express our deep gratitude to Yuri Luzhkov, Moscow Mayor, for all the good that was done to rebuild the Cathedral.

Moscow revived its ancient sacred place.

On the day when the memorial foundation stone was laid in November 1991 the Patriarch said, «The square, we are standing on, is called Red – it means beautiful. The Cathedral that we started to build, will be also beautiful. So, let our soles, our lives be spiritually beautiful, bright and perfect...»

The days we live in are looking back into the history. When the Kazansky Cathedral was pulled down in Red Square, it became different from the centuries willed. Without the Cathedral the monument to Minin and Pozharsky looked desolate. The famous masterpiece sculptured by Martos was the only reminder about the fearsome times when it seemed that after the Troubled years Russian land wouldn't be able to rise, but the light did not fade away in this country, and people's faith in Russia returned. Then, in 1612, Prince Dmitry Pozharsky entered the liberated Kremlin and his warriors brought a sacred thing into the Cathedral of Assumption – the Mother of God icon of Kazan which they carried all the way from Nizhny Novgorod to Moscow. That event occurred in Autumn, on the 22nd of October, on the Day of St.Averky Ierapolsky, and since then this day is celebrated by the Russian Orthodox Church as one of the main holidays.

How did this icon happen to be at the head of militiamen? And why was miraculous power was ascribed to it? The legend says: in the town of Kazan a maiden by the name of Matrena had a dream as the Mother of God had come to her and ordered to announce the appearance of her miraculous vision. And she pointed out the place where to find it. On the place where the icon was found a cathedral devoted to Our Lady was created and then a monastery was founded. A copy of the icon was made (it was believed that the copy blessed by the Church also

Consecration of the Cross at the site of recreation of the Kazansky Cathedral. 1991.

had miraculous power). With this copy the militiamen of Kazan came to Nizhny Novgorod. However, people believe that it was a genuine icon and it was brought to Moscow by the troops, but it was an embellished copy that was sent to Kazan. As a proof of authenticity of the icon brought in by militiamen, historians quote the chronicles which say that Patriarch Hermogen captivated by the Poles in Moscow blessed the people of Nizhny Novgorod to rise against the enemy and ordered them to take the miraculous icon of the Mother of God which he took into his hands when it appeared in Kazan. There were talks that Hermogen confined in a dungeon had a vision while praying that Sergius of Radonezh had come to him and predicted that the Russian state would be saved by intercession of the Mother of God of Kazan. With the symbol of this intercession – the icon of Kazan – the warriors led by Pozharsky reached Moscow.

When the Polish invaders were driven out of Moscow and the restoration works started the icon was transferred from the devastated Assumption Cathedral to Dmitry Pozharsky's court, into the parish Church of the Mother of God's Introduction in Lubyanka (the corner of present Bolshaya Lubyanka Street and Kuznetsky Most Street) where it stayed decorated with «a lot of utensils» under the vow of the Prince until the cathedral commemorating the icon discovery and liberation of Moscow was built in Red Square.

There is a rather wide-spread assertion in literature that the cathedral was built by Prince Pozharsky, particularly it is stated by such a connoisseur of Moscow as P.V. Sytin. However, now we have a chance to get acquainted with an interesting document – «The Historical Notes on the Moscow Kazansky Cathedral» compiled by A.I. Nevostruyev, the Cathedral's dean, in the middle of the 19th century. On the basis of written documents with factual grounds the author of the «Notes» proves with full obviousness that the creation of the Cathedral devoted to the Icon of the God's Mother of Kazan should be related to the will of Mikhail Fedorovich, the first tsar of the Romanov's family, in commemoration of the liberation of Russia from foreign invaders and a new dynasty taking the throne of All-Russia.

In short time the cathedral was erected in Red Square but a fire occurred – which was frequent in Moscow and as a chronicle says, «many God's churches in the Kremlin and Kitay-Gorod burned down». The Kazansky Cathedral did not survive either. The Cathedral was restored by apprentice Abrosim Maximov. In fact, the Cathedral was entirely rebuilt – according to the Moscow architectural canon of that time. The works were completed in 1635 – 1636. Later on, under Tsar Alexey Mikhailovich, an attachment in honour of miraculous men of Kazan appeared and a new church porch was built and a front porch was added (the temporary wooden chapel erected prior to the laying-down ceremony resembled that porch).

From that time on a tradition was established – on the Icon's holiday, the 8th of July, – the day it was found – a religious procession marches solemnly from the Assumption Cathedral in the Kremlin to the Kazansky Cathedral. The icon is carried along the fortress walls of the Kremlin and Kitay-

The Kazansky Cathedral: recreation in process. 1992.

The Kazansky Cathedral in Red Square. Recreated in 1992.

Gorod, prayers are offered in commemoration of warriors slain in the Time of Troubles and all the soldiers that never returned from the battle fields. There were so many Russian warriors who laid down their lives in countless wars, and there was not a single family that would not commemorate a husband, a brother, a son or a father. That is why such great national importance was attributed to these solemn ceremonies – religious processions and prayers which were offered by the Clergy of Moscow attended by many Muscovites – eminent residents and city people. Everyone tried to make a contribution to the prosperity of the cathedral. At that time near the Nikolsky Gate there was a stone platform with cannons built to defend the Kremlin, and the space beneath it was rented out to merchant Danilov for shops. There is historical evidence that the honourable merchant governed by the motion of his soul paid his money to build a stone protection barrier around the Cathedral.

For ages the Cathedral has been the centre of military honour of Russia. The Orthodox Christ worshipful warriors-host – these words pronounced in prayers and commemorations were associated by the Church and all others related to it with ideas of morals, duty and faith. Let's recall how Moscow blessed Kutuzov with the icon of God's Mother of Kazan to fight against Napoleon; may be, the steps of the Kazansky Cathedral became the starting point for Kutuzov on his way to Borodino, and there is something imposing in this link between the two periods of time: the year of 1812 got the behest of 1612 and thus found its place in the historical calendar of the Fatherland. From the very beginning the Cathedral conveyed the idea of Russian military honour connected directly with the idea of Orthodoxy and protection of Russ from religious and spiritual enslavement. In the time of trouble Polish and Lithuanian invaders propagated the Catholic cross ravaging Moscow and Russia. In the beginning of the 17th century the time-honoured roots of Orthodoxy – Greece, Bulgaria, South Slavs' countries were under Turkish yoke. Malorossia became tied up Roman-Catholic Uniate. The Polish-Lithuanian troops of Rechpospolita invaded the Russian muddle land – where would the Orthodox Church seek salvation, who would save the Russian people and their faith together with their perception of a nation, native home, spiritual unity of generations? That is why at that point in history, when Catholics outraged upon sacred Kremlin cathedrals, when the Orthodox Christianity seemed to be on the verge of collapse, the victory of Russian warriors over foreign invaders meant salvation of the faith adopted by Slav Russia under Holy Vladimir. And the monument to the victory of Russian people. And the monument to the victory of Russian people – the cathedral in honour of the Icon of the God's Mother of Kazan – became the monument to the victory of the Russian Orthodoxy.

But not only. Time wove precious cloth over Moscow – the cloth of unity of memorials related to the heroic history of liberation struggle for the Russian land. Devoted to the liberation of Moscow, Russia and restoration of the Russian statehood after the time of trouble in the 17th century, the Kazansky Cathedral was another monument commemorating the warriors of Kulikovo Pole along with the Church of All the Saints «on Kulishky» which survived in present Slavyanskaya Square, previously called Varvarskaya. It is not incidental that the two monuments have similar architectural forms. It so happened that the more ancient cathedral «on Kulishky» of the 16th century was rebuilt in the period of construction of the Kazansky Cathedral. And it is right that cathedrals were erected in Russia to honour the victories and to commemorate those who paid their lives for those victories! The cathedral in honour of the warriors of Dmitry Donskoy, the cathedral in honour of the warriors of Prince Pozharsky, and finally the cathedral-apotheosis in commemoration of 1812 built thanks to the patriotic movement of the Russian people and their loyalty to the Orthodox Christianity – the Cathedral of Christ the Savior. All they are the utmost expression of the national self-conscience and moral behest that passed from one generation to another throughout the centuries. And if it so, let's try to imagine the role and significance of the Kazan Cathedral from the view point of spiritual values of our ancestors. In essence, for Moscow and for Russia the Kazansky Cathedral of the Mother of God was a forerunner of the Cathedral of Christ the Saviour. And it shared the bitter fate of the Cathedral of Christ the Saviour.

The Kazansky Cathedral has deep roots in the history of Moscow and the history of Russia. In the reign of Queen Elizaveta Petrovna there was a building of the Main Drug Store located close to the Cathedral where the History Museum is now. Later on that building became the first Russian university founded through the efforts of Lomonosov. The Cathedral was a parish church for the university and it is quite possible that pupils from the university gymnasium kneeled down in front of the Icon of the Mother of God of Kazan – for example, Novikov and Fonvizin, future great architect Bazhenov and future prince Potemkin. It is another benchmark on the life tree of Russia.

Long before that time frantic Avvakum was appealing to people with his ardent speeches. From the very start of the church reforms when Nikon became the Patriarch and when the strong supporters of the old church were under severe repression, the Kazansky Cathedral was the stronghold of the Old Believers. The writing by Avvakum «Life» reads, «I'm pleased to state that Kazansky (cathedral) didn't surrender, we have been reading books to people and there were so many people coming to us». For some time the Cathedral was his home where he was hosted by priest Ivan Neronov, also a strong opponent of Nikon's reforms, «He was a Father to me; when he was away I was looking after the church». Having rejected the new rules of divine services, Avvakum left the Cathedral and since that moment, from the threshold of the Kazansky Cathedral, the rebellious priest had to go through endless misadventures. But his ardent writings calling for disobedience to three-finger crossing reached Moscow from Pustozersk, the banks of Pechora, through Mezen.

The Cathedral witnessed so many motions of people's hearts and so many prayers for the sons of the Fatherland perished in the wars which Russia had in excess. «Russia, Be a guard of yourself!» we can say quoting Nikolai Rubtsov.

***

They say that architecture is a music in stone. It is also a history in stone. Red Square is the incarnation of sounds and the march of centuries. Its magnificent ensemble was developing for centuries – from buildings of all times which eventually achieved harmony. True harmony is the essence of Red Square. It is the embodiment of history displaying a creative spirit of a great nation. It keeps the memories of centuries. Surikov said, «I can give you an example: I believe in Boris Godunov and the impostor only because there is an inscription about them on Ivan the Great». The Kazansky Cathedral was part of this belief and is now again. The Kremlin herostrats are gone but Red Square has triumphed. It was as if the original cathedral had left it for some period of time but it is back in place which looked deserted without it. The Square symphony lacked its individual unique melody without the Cathedral as if the score of the historic ensemble was missing some notes and without them the Square did not look complete.

What is the unique melodics of the Kazansky Cathedral? It does not have the solemnity of the Kremlin towers and the ornate decoration of St. Basil's Cathedral. It is simpler and clearer for comprehension, it retains the tuneful pattern of the centuries. The Cathedral of today is exactly as it is depicted in the painting by Mokeyev. The festive combination of red and white – red-brick walls and carved white stones – in the decoration of the Cathedral and even the window frames is a demonstration of the national taste – similar to the embroidery in the form of red crosses in white linen of peasants' clothes. That's why a Russian church has always been so dear to Russian people – it incorporated the people's unchangeable perception of an aesthetic ideal – spirituality and beauty. Architectural canons changed but the triumph of the spirit remained – for this reason the cathedral was built. This is how it was and how it is now – the Kazansky Cathedral. Here it is in front of you – it pleases your eyes with the spired «crowns» (kokoshnik) which rise to the domes as if the tongues of the stalled flame. This is why such cathedrals were called «fiery»: «The force of the Heavens in essence is the fiery flame». What idea did the architect put in this «flame»? May be, a feeling of being part of the Highest Truth and a perception of human beauty and unearthly beauty in the vision of «The Heavens» Town»?

As is believed by researchers of the Old Russia architecture, Moscow had about three hundred «fiery» temples built in the 17th century. Mainly, they were «posad» churches (in-town), some of them survived till present days and now form the core of a number of preserved monuments of the church architecture. The top of them and one of the first was the Kazansky Cathedral. Its five-tier pyramid of «kokoshniks» laid the foundation of a new tent-roof architecture of Moscow. We have a right to assume that Abrosim Maximov, builder of the Cathedral, could be a pupil of famous Fedor Kon, the creator of stone towers and walls of the White Town, who gave a new appearance to the Cathedral on Kulishky. Anyway, it can be assumed that an earlier creation by the senior colleague served as a model for the Kazansky Cathedral. There is evidence to the effect that Abrosim Maximov built a temple in honor of the Mother of God of Kazan on the territory of the Kolomensky Palace of Tsar Alexey Mikhailovich – that same palace which the contemporaries believed to be the eighth wonder of the world, and there may be more cathedrals in Moscow that conceal the touch of this talented master of the 17th century.

The rebirth of the Kazansky Cathedral allowed us to get a view on its previous surroundings as it was followed by restoration of the Voskresensky Gate with the Chapel of Iberia, also an ancient sacred place in Moscow. Together with the tent-roofed

Chapel of Iberia. Recreated in 1994.

belfry and the domes of the Kazansky Cathedral the tent-roofed Voskresensky Gate makes a captive sight – as if Moscow of «forty forties» rises again. You start to realize that it took Moscow centuries to build up the treasures of its architecture and it lost many of them. The feeling of bitterness can not be belittled. It is only now that we do realize that we destroyed our history. During the May or October holidays there were demonstrations marching through Red Square, orchestras were roaring, flags were flying, delighted glances were thrown at the Mausoleum whereas on the same square in the former place of the Kazansky Cathedral there was desecrated dust of the great national culture with awkward structures upholstered with red cotton or retail kiosks, or the public lavatory, and truly, the white foundation stones beneath the extraneous grounds were the grave of the history which was ruined to ashes.

One of the genuine Muscovites, and not a young one, recollects, «I was a boy when in 1936 the Church of Assumption in Pokrovka was demolished in the same way as the Kazansky Cathedral. The school and the pioneer organization made me believe that God did not exist and it seemed to me that Moscow was just getting rid of old junk. Could I realize at that time that they were killing my sense of Fatherland? Later on, in my mature age, I read that Vasily Bazhenov considered the Church in Pokrovka one of the marvelous monuments of the Old Moscow architecture!..»

It is the time of recovery now. Back to our native home. The time of blindness is over. But to whom should we confess and repent of what, whose forgiveness to ask being unwillingly guilty? What should we think of ourselves – cheated, slandered, – when in the state that proclaimed itself a successor of all the best achievements of the mankind the sacred places were destroyed by triumphant ignorance, and the people blinded by lies and evil did not see their spiritual self-destruction. This is why the rebirth of the ancient cathedral, a solemn action, that took place on Red Square, was a great relief to the people. This is why – as we see it today – the immutable real values are getting free from the slavery of everything false and extraneous which is going away: Russia exists and Russian people and the Fatherland do exist as well.

In the times of Pushkin and Gogol there was Metropolitan of Moscow and Kolomensky – Filaret who knew how to value the Russian antiquity. These are his words, «A monument is a wordless preacher which in a way is better than the one who speaks because he never drops his sermons and they reach the nation and the succeeding generations». Let's be confident that the recreated cathedral will become a preacher honoring the past times. Let's also believe that it will be a preacher for our days too – our spiritual renaissance – and in its silent preaches it will tell about us to those who will live after us.

The rebirth of the Morozovs' mansion in Spiridonovka

Quiet beautiful Spiridonovka joins the Boulevard and the Garden Rings. On it odd side there is Building 17 which for decades has been used for receptions by the Ministry of Foreign Affairs. This building is the Morozovs' mansion, Savva and Zinaida, built by F.O. Shehtel in 1893 – 1898.

The name of Savva Timofeevich Morozov (1862 – 1905) has become a symbol of the Moscow merchantry. He was a grandson of the serf and a graduate from the Moscow University, the owner of the biggest manufactory and the founder of the Russian-German chemical joint stock company, the patron of the arts and the main shareholder of the Moscow Art Theater...

His wife, Zinaida Grigorievna Morozova (1867 – 1947), was a woman of like merits. There was a legend saying that she started as a worker at Morozov's factory. However, now it is a known fact that Zinaida was a daughter of a rich merchant of the second guild, G.E. Zimin. The contemporaries called her «the Russian nugget». She was so intelligent that ministers, politicians and the intellectuals listened to her opinion. Among the Morozovs' friends were A.P. Chekhov, K.S. Stanislavsky, F.I. Shalyapin. A.M. Gorky and many artists.

The Morozovs were among the first who managed to reveal an outstanding talent of F.O. Shehtel. The mansion in Spiridonovka was a milestone in his career that brought him fame and success of an architect. Shehtel became and architect who was always wanted by the bourgeois elite.

While working on the project of Morozovs' mansion he made about 600 drawings – facades, layouts, sketches and plots of walls, chandeliers, furniture. Designing this building as a live integrated body he tried to avoid any fortuity both in details and in the whole composition. May be, the customer wanted the building to look like an English castle. Savva studied chemistry in Cambridge. The Morozovs' had business contacts with England, the most advanced weaving machines of that time came to the Nikolskaya manufacture from Manchester and Liverpool.

However, employing austere expressive forms of the English Gothic Shehtel developed a basically new architectural pattern, new layout structure. Everything in the house is subordinated to beauty and comfort. It has a complicated asymmetric layout and is located in the back of the site. It is separated from the street by a beautiful metallic fence. The lengthy front side is predominated by a corner tower-shaped structure which draws attention to the open arch of the front entrance in the yard. The angle-type facade from the yard side has a view on the garden with a fountain, sculptures and lawns. The whole building has repeated features of spired arches, vertical lines and parapets which create a harmonious rhythmic structure emphasized by plain walls colored in light ochre.

Rejection of traditional symmetrical-axial composition allowed him to create dynamic and interconnected interiors which were impressing by the variety of styles, rich colors and pictorial art.

The absence of distinct borders between architecture, sculpture, pictorial art, between functions and decoration impart the unity of plasticity and spiritual refinement to the building. These features became determining in all further

The Morozovs' house in Spiridonovka (The Reception House of the Russian Ministry of Foreign Affairs). Architect F. Shehtel. 1893 – 1898.

Lobby. Post-fire view. 1995.

View after the restoration. 1996.
Architects: Yu.P. Kalinichenko, A.I. Yepifanov.

After the restoration. Big Drawing-room and Small Marble Hall. Architects: Yu.P. Kalinichenko, A.I. Yepifanov.

Colonnade. Fragment.

works by Shehtel, a leading master of Moscow modernistic art.

It was in 1894 when the customer and the architect invited M.A.Vrubel to execute the interiors. Like Shehtel, he was not well known to the Muscovites. His complicated style was not easily accepted by his contemporaries. A. Benois said that the Morozovs' clan had given him and exclusive opportunity «to put his dreams into reality, to satisfy his «thirst for real art». The stained glass panel «Meeting with the Knight» was made on the basis of his sketches. He is the author of the sculptural group «Robert and Nuns» on the front stares, panels «The Morning», «Midday», «The Evening» in the small drawing-room and, possibly, of the picturesque frieze in the master's study.

In 1912 when the mansion was purchased by manufacturer, banker and collector M.P. Ryabushinsky, artist K.F. Bogayevsky painted the panels «Distance», «The Sun» and «The Rock» for the Big drawing room.

On August 4, 1995, the famous mansion in Spiridonovka was on fire. The interiors were severely damaged. Immediately after the fire the company «Deepcomfort» set up the headquarters to save the masterpieces. The best specialists with extensive restoration expertise were selected on a tender basis. Organizational talent and hard day-to-day work for 10 – 12 hours allowed to accomplish the restoration successfully and in an orderly manner. Scientific support was provided by the institute Spetsproyectrestoration» (Yu.P. Kalinichenko, A.I. Yepifanov). The team included technologists, engineers, art critics. Challenging tasks – methodological, architectural-design and technological – had to be solved in parallel with restoration-rehabilitation works.

Experts from the company «Preobrazhenye» restored the Big and Small marble halls, the billiard room, Savva Morozov's study, the facades of the building (the company «Antique» was involved in plastering and painting works). Joint-Stock company «Stroyservice» replaced some partitions and roofing, upgraded service rooms employing the most advanced technologies. Polish restorers from the «PKZ» company recreated the carved wood ornament of the Avanhall and the front stares. Restorers from the Tretyakov Gallery headed by A.P. Kovalev performed an elaborate treatment of the panels by Vrubel. M.F. Rozanov, Professor Assistant from the Stroganovsky institute made a sketch of Vrubel's stained glass panel destroyed by the fire. It was then recreated under his supervision by the oldest British company «Goddard & Gibbs». Reconstruction of Bogayevsky's panels which could have been lost for ever was accomplished by artists from the association «Restoration» headed by A.S. Kuznetsov. Skillful specialists lent the second life to the grand piano «Bekshtein», they also restored crystal chandeliers and wove the decorative cloth using Shehtel's sketch «The little bee».

Everyone worked with so much dedication. Restoration was completed in eleven months. The unprecedented schedule and quality of works were highly appreciated. Today the Morozovsky mansion lives it normal life.

Reconstruction of the Old Gostiny Dvor

Working on the project of reconstruction of the Old Gostiny Dvor the design engineers headed by S.B. Tkachenko set themselves two major tasks:

– to preserve it as a monument of architecture of the 18 – 19the centuries – to carry out the scientifically substantiated restoration of the facades and to maintain the perimeter layout with a vast courtyard;

– to bring back the original function of a trading and social service building and to incorporate it into the functional structure of the city centre which is in line with the general concept of reconstruction of Kitay-Gorod.

In accordance with these objectives a multifunctional concept was developed for further use of the Old Gostiny Dvor. Its role in the city architecture and the size of the building originally designed for small shops and warehouses suggested the solution. Functionally, the building is «mosaic» and is intended for a big number of lessees. The reconstructed rooms of the main three floors are expected to accommodate a social-cultural centre, shops, offices, banks, hotel rooms, restaurants, cafes and multipurpose space for presentations and other activities. There will be an underground parking place.

The idea to turn this building into a big cultural-social and retail complex required to increase the usable area and to develop proposals on a superstructure that would rise up to the ridge of the existing three-floor part of the building (due to a considerable slope from Ilyinka to Varvarka the floors' elevation of some parts of the building is different). It was also taken into account that the external side of the building should look like an architectural monument – in other words, its outside facade is maintained almost as it was originally (except there are some new dormer windows on the roof). At the same time, the courtyard space is slightly modified. It will have a transparent glass roof which makes it possible to use the space for temporary fairs, presentations, exhibitions, rest and entertainment activity. It is also proposed to build an underground parking place there. The facades from the courtyard with three rows of monu-

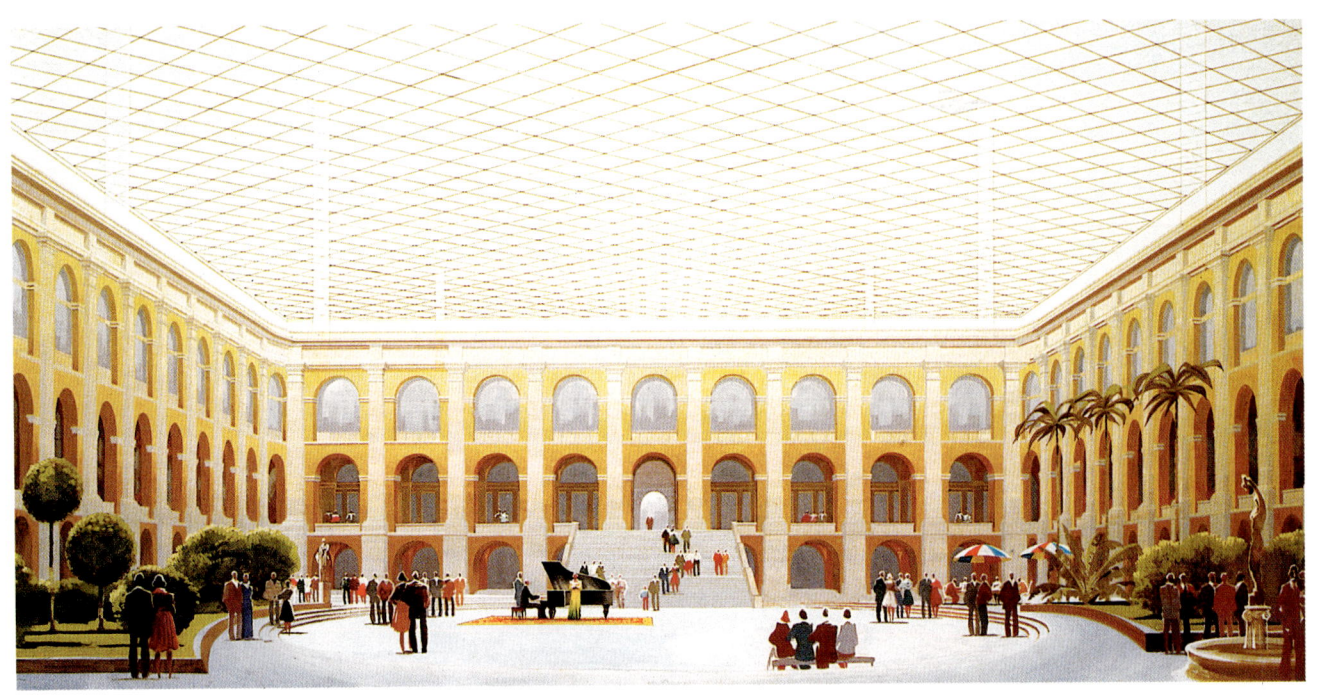

**Restoration of the Gostiny Dvor and its reconstruction to become a business and cultural centre. Inner courtyard interior. Project.
Architects: V. Kuzmin, L. Lavrov. 1996.**

mental arch openings will be restored too, two attic floors which are going to be built will be adapted to a maximum degree to the historic appearance of the building.

The transformation of the courtyard of the Old Gostiny Dvor appears to be well argumented and feasible from the view point of its future use, a variety of functions, room comfort, and on top of that it is justified historically. For the whole duration of its existence Gostiny Dvor underwent numerous modifications and reconstruction which was due to functional changes of some rooms and change of owners. Thus, required renovation and construction of a roofed courtyard can be regarded as further evolution of the historically established function.

D. Quarenghi: The Old Gostiny Dvor in Kitay-Gorod. 1805.

The Kremlin. Premises of the President of Russia B.N. Yeltsin. Artist: I.S. Glazunov; architechts: V.A. Vinogradov, A.V. Vaneev, N.D. Nedovich. 1994.

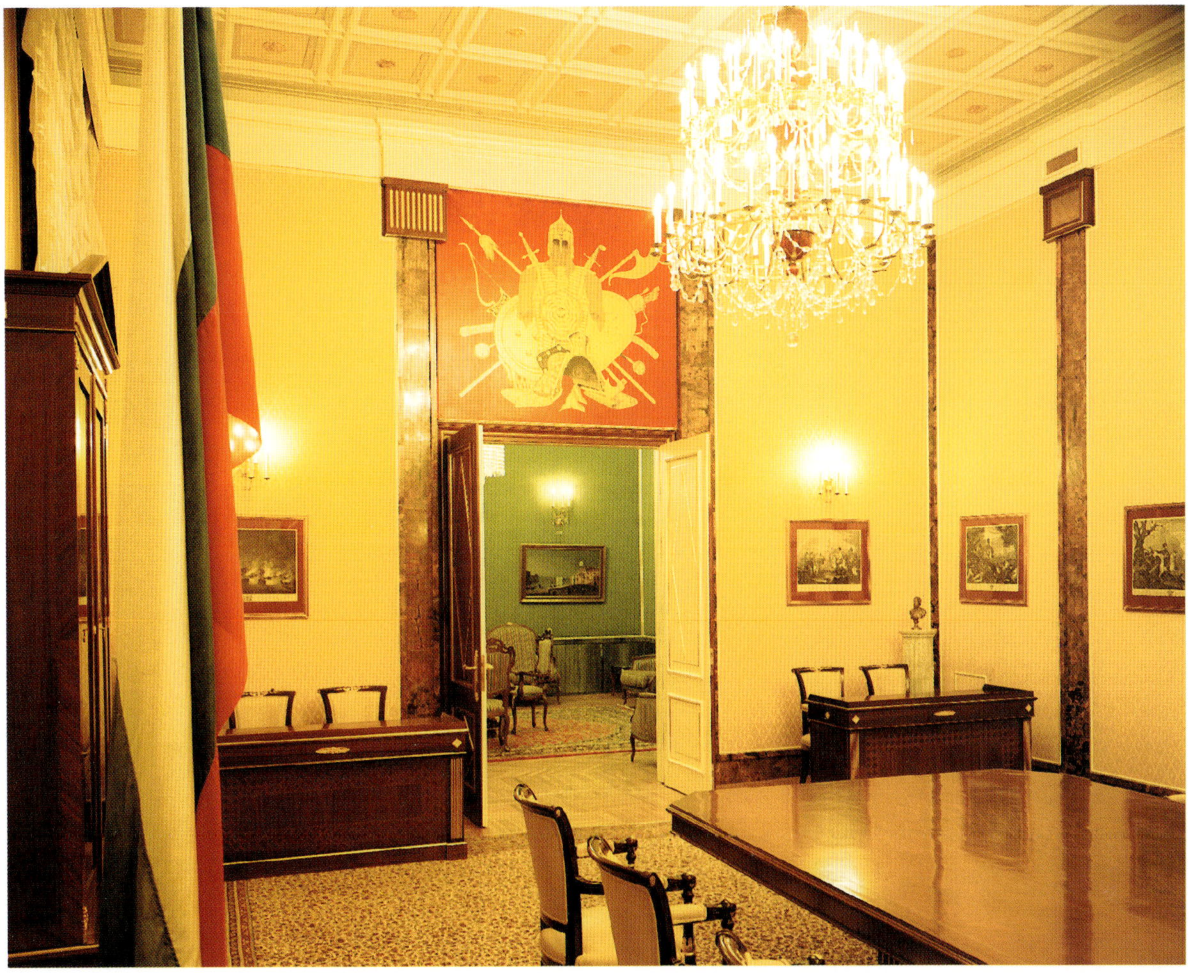

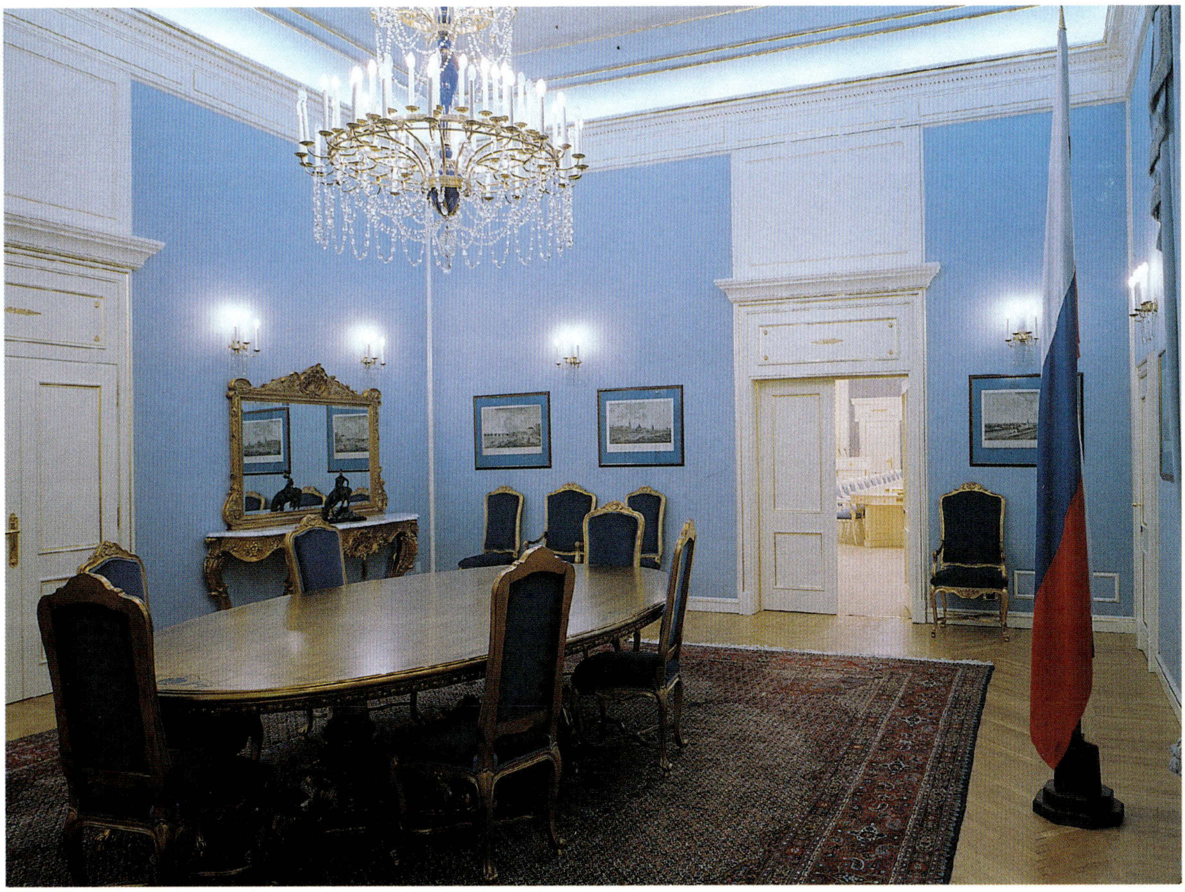

Moscow. The Kremlin. 1997.

CHAPTER TWO

Moscow on the Eye of Bimillenium of the Christian Civilization

Resurrection Gates and Iberia Chapel restored under Moscow Goverment Decree. Architect-restorer O. Zhurin. 1994.

Building New Architectural Ensembles

In Jerusalem, one of the world's most amazing cities in terms of its architectural attractions, there is a building in the old-town neighbourhood where numerous and varied shows are held on a regular basis, with one exhibit being particularly noteworthy. The exhibit's theme is «Jerusalem Unbuilt». The display contains the visions drafted by numerous noted architects to build a grand-style city, with its impressive architectural qualities being fully consistent with the role Jerusalem has played in the evolution of global civilization. The relevance of the exhibit is hard to overestimate, for it most graphically shows the utter inconsistency of the designers' fantasies with that ancient city's inimitable architectural flair.

Regrettably, Moscow can not boast of such an exhibit though proposals to that effect have repeatedly been forwarded. That kind of display would surely come to be most instructive. After all, Moscow's history is known to hold a good deal of examples of city-building visions and applications that the capital city's master builders could substantively profit from as they proceed with their efforts to correctly direct their creative pursuits.

Suffice it to recall the Bazhenov vision of the Grand Kremlin palace that Catherine the Great commissioned and ordered that the older Kremlin structures should be torn down, or the Palace of Soviets that was supposed to be erected where the Christ the Savior Cathedral had been built to stand but was eventually destroyed, the intended Government Centre that was to emerge on the Vorobyovi Hills just behind the MGU university main building, to say nothing of numerous unrealized projects to build government and administrative buildings on the city's Lenivka, Ostozhenka and many other streets, with the old structures having to be removed in the process.

Notwithstanding, the most ingenious man-made structures appear to have been miraculously preserved as if the course of history had been directed by some omnipotent manager. The undying beauty of the great ensembles erected in the olden times seems to have been able to survive through the centuries. Even the most ambitious 1935 General Plan to totally rebuild Moscow, with its implementation proceeding nearly unchecked for the Soviet era's seven decades, failed to make our capital city's distinctive features sink into oblivion. Neither the time available nor the effort applied were sufficient to raze the great structures and ensembles created over the centuries by the hard-working generations of builders and talented designers that managed to come up with the best-conceived ideas applied to have the Russian people's spiritual riches translated into unique tangible assets. Today, Moscow, the old and eternally young city, ranks high among the world's most beautiful cities, the circumstance working to have the Russian citizens' hearts filled with pride for their homeland and make the capital city's visitors display profound interest in Moscow's cultural heritage that the city administration is now effectively seeking to preserve, with the federal government being meaningfully involved in the effort.

Over the last decades, the city has grown to be much larger, the landscape considerably changing as a result. Again and again, we would be compelled to revisit the capital city's Soviet era to better learn the lessons, see the motivations behind that or other city-building scheme, evaluate the implementation strategies and arrive at the true balance of the gains achieved and losses sustained.

In this regard, the contemporaneous debates over the still-in-development capital city and Moscow Region General Plan turned out to be exceptionally fruitful. The discussions of the issues relating to preserving the tradition and continuity, applying the novelties, defining the role of aggregate strategies in shaping the city's landscape, discovering the roots of the indigenous architectural design and, which is most significant, of the Moscow school of design that made tremendous contributions to the overall drive aimed to draft a scientifically sound program for the growth of Moscow and development of its outlook in the latest stage of evolution.

Particularly productive in the course of those discussions were the exchanges between the scientific community and practicing designers. A. Ikonnikov, N. Gulianitsky, B. Thor, T. Savarenskaya, O. Shvidkovsky, V. Sarabyanov, P. Loveiko, A. Riabushin, Yu. Bocharov, A. Pokrovsky, A. Kudriavtsev, A. Meerson, I. Biriukov, V. Kuzmin, Yu. Sheverdiayev and many other architects had greatly contributed to the overall effort to review the situation at hand and assess the running trends in urban development, which eventually enabled the capital city's designers to correctly define the priorities and principles of shaping Moscow's landscape and developing the city-building strategies. Understandably, given a broad array of existing ideas and attitudes in the mid-1980s, the overwhelming desire to launch a bottom-up revision of the standing approaches, as a matter of fact, only added to the rich palette of sentiments and heated discussions. One could hear, for one, both the claims to the effect that the Russian school of design was nonexistent, that it was merely a replica of the western architecture, that the Soviet-era projects only produced a great deal of irreparable damage in the capital city, and the judgments to allege that the past architectural accomplishments were beyond any criticism. The unconstrained discussions of any and all perspectives enabled an unbiased observer to see how removed from the truth the extreme assessments of past experiences had been. It is in no way that easy for anyone to be explicit in passing one's judgment on the following transformations. With the semi-circle of squares and streets to embrace the Kremlin, Kitay-Gorod and the stretch from the Kamenny Bridge to Moskvoretsky Bridge being created, the Kitay-Gorod wall and part of the old-city structures were nearly lost. But then, that change most positively made the city centre's appearance much more attractive, for the newly-built Manezhnaya and Borovitskaya Squares allowed to have the Kremlin and its golden-domed cathedrals majestically displayed. With the degraded structures on the Vassilyevsky Slope removed, one could enjoy the integrated sight of the Kremlin and the Vassily the Blessed Cathedral in their onobstructed splendor.

In one of his public appearances in 1945 on the issue of Russian classicism in architecture, D. Arakin, a noted theorist of urban development, underscored the need for «the extended-range development projects befitting a major world city» as he pointed out the relevance of the landscaping dimension in architectural ensembles and referred to the existing large-sized city-forming blocks in Saint

**Borovitskaya Square and the Christ the Savior Cathedral.
Draft designed by V. Kuzmin.**

Petersburg's central section. While following up on that thought, D. Arakin added, «A world city's panorama is, as a matter of fact, made by the following two drivers of the extended-range city-building strategy: the city skyline and building shapes».

In the past, until the first half of the 19th century, clearly dominating Moscow's landscape of low buildings had been the Kremlin, with the numerous tall structures across the city being only made by cathedrals, churches, monasteries and convents. With the city starting to grow rapidly, buildings rising higher and higher, particularly in the decades of Russia's booming industrial capitalism, the skyline of Moscow's centre turned out to be radically changed. The city rebuilding projects of the 1930s, aimed to have the Kremlin ringed with open spaces, in fact, served to restore the crucial role of the skyline factor in urban development, with the artistic shapes of the Kremlin's cathedrals and belfries being truly highlighted as the world's unique architectural ensemble.

What is more, the work completed by V. Kuzmin and his team under the newly-approved general plan permitted to fully define the vision for the squares and openings surrounding the Kitay-Gorod. These sites could be developed to become integrated social centres to complement the leading role of the Kremlin, the principal administrative centre of Moscow and the Russian nation.

To provide an example, the currently-recreated Christ the Savior Cathedral together with the adjoining structures, sitting on the banks of the Moskva-river, come to grow into a powerful spiritual centre. The contest, called to secure the best project to rebuild and reshape Borovitskaya Square, has been aimed to eventually have the site filled with the centre of culture and fine arts integrating the State Library with its core Pashkov Mansion, Pushkin Museum of Fine Arts and new buildings, which are expected to hold exhibits from the Kremlin museums. Understandably, the newly-erected structures should be made consistent in terms of style and size with the Kremlin and Pashkov Mansion, the key features in the area.

With the Manezhnaya Square rebuilding project implemented, Moscow has now received a multifunctional shopping, accommodation, business and cultural centre, which could effectively be involved in the commemoratives to mark its 850th anniversary. For the first time in its history, the capital city has had the idea of subterranean space utilization put into effect, with the four-level complex including exhibitions, restaurants, cafes, shopping malls, archeology museum and many other functional facilities. The paved «desert», that the Manezhnaya Square used to be for decades, has now become another pedestrian area growing out of Red Square and Aleksandrovsky Garden. Manezhnaya Square is now split into the following three segments. The rally and parade part runs from Tverskaya Street up to the Zhukov Monument planted in front of the History Museum. The utility of this segment of the Square and its dedicated architectural solution come from its running into Red Square. The Square's second segment is made by the space adjoining the Manezh building, the prevalent features remaining unaltered. This section is made available to hold open-air exhibits and other cultural functions. The Square's middle section comes to be somewhat elevated above the first two segments and makes sort of a large platform for the visitors to enjoy the Kremlin view. This area is outfitted with benches, minor lawns and flower-beds, thereby providing the newly-designed Manezhnaya Square's recreational area. Some of the premises of two subterranean levels have been designed to feature arch-shaped stained-glass windows facing the Aleksandrovsky Garden and the Neglinka-river's man-made bed with sculptures scattered along the stream.

Teatralnaya Square with its Bolshoi and Maly Theatres, both being renovated, Metropol and Moskva hotels is expected to keep its utility and feature new cultural facilities, which would be accommodated in some rebuilt structures at the Kitay-Gorod wall. The Square's subterranean space will be used for garages and parking areas. An idea is currently being addressed to have a new building erected just in the back of the recreated section of the Kitay-Gorod wall to accommodate either the Moscow History and Development Museum or Moscow government reception house.

Lubianka, Staraya and Slavianskaya Squares have come to be wholly shaped up, and they are expected to continue serving their

Borovitskaya Square. Draft designed by V. Kuzmin.

long-lasting administrative, business, hotel accommodation, shopping and entertaining functions. The Kitay-Gorod rebuilding program implies a broad range of restoration projects to be carried out, with the overall character and configuration of the historic neighborhood being necessarily preserved and more comfort features provided to enable Muscovites and city visitors to enjoy state-of-the-art conveniences.

Having the Kremlin, Red Square and Kitay-Gorod surrounded by advance squares to fill out the spaces, which for hundreds of years used to be crowded with haphazard shapeless structures, would allow to achieve an artistically complete system of clustered squares around the capital city's key architectural attraction. This short-term goal is expected to demand that the city builders display their utmost skills and profound respect for the traditions of the Moscow school of architectural design. The newly-introduced elements in the given landscape should be wholly in line with the existing status, the additions only being made to take out the obvious deficiencies and improve the overall architectural scene adjoining the Kremlin. The whole idea is to have the Kremlin ensemble perceived as the hub of a coherent system of disparate aggregates destined to highlight the domineering gem in the centre.

With designer teams competing through tender bidding and open discussions being held by the Moscow Architectural Committee's Designers Council to evaluate any and all suggestions, and with EKOS and Moscow Public City Building Council now addressing the submitted visions, a major prerequisite is thereby being put in place for the capital city residents to regenerate their confidence in the expertise of Moscow developers.

The time, that elapsed since the new general plan began to be substantively elaborated ten years ago, has now enabled the city planners to see many contentious issues in their true perspectives. It has become obvious that the city developers, as a matter of fact, implement the policies of the city leaders as they seek to meet the societal requirements. It is precisely the new set of people, who recently happened to assume power in the capital city, and their radically different perception of the cultural heritage that provided the solid groundwork for the city builders to start a new phase in their professional effort.

Playing the most crucial role in these shifts that transpired against a backdrop of nationwide transformations were the people that made themselves heard. Public appearances of numerous artists, arts scholars, historians and archeologists in defence of the old Moscow made the authorities in the last years of Brezhnev rule call off their plans to tear down a whole number of old buildings and locales.

The persistent negative attitude that Muscovites have over the years maintained towards the functional city builders as the principal demolishers of the old structures would now and again produce suggestions to have the city centre given the status of a memorial city ensemble, the purpose of the idea being to keep any authority from coming in to remove even a single structure in the safeguarded area. Today, it is an open secret that a tremendous amount of work is expected to be accomplished in downtown Moscow for the historical centre to regain the balanced harmony, artistic perfection and indigenous style, with the age-old flair, recognizable shapes and attractive features of the ancient capital city necessarily being preserved.

To accomplish this highly consequential task would obviously ask for the profound knowledge of history and tradition as well as a great deal of expertise and rare talents, which would obviously have to be tapped and appropriately integrated to have the accumulated experiences, artistic content, forms, shapes and multichromatic solutions, characteristic of Moscow's structures, best translated into new builds that hopefully would perfectly blend with the historic environment.

The capital city's central part certainly contains quite a few sites that would easily tolerate some rebuilding touches consistent with the local scene in order to have major old buildings, blocks or street segments either fully restored or somewhat grown to achieve the originally conceived design. To provide an example, the projects to rebuild the Paveletsky and Savelovsky Rail Stations could certainly be regarded as big successes in that respect. The renovation work completed on the Kazansky Rail Station's second segment, with the newly-built spaces designed to be redolent of the Shchusev-created structure, admittedly, has already caused some concerns. Obviously, it would only be bizzare to see the Kremlin Palace of Congresses built after the fashion of old shrines or Kremlin walls, particularly, given that the new structure was put in place to serve a totally different set of public functions. At present, one can hardly visualize a public consensus on the idea of placing a palace of congresses within the Kremlin walls. Similarly, it appears to be beyond any doubt that the Palace builders in their times succeeded in striking the right design solution that enabled the huge structure to be harmlessly integrated in the Kremlin landscape. This achievement is indicative of tremendous creative capacities and top-notch expertise commanded by the Palace of Congresses designers. As you view the building outline, its color scheme, coating materials and modern architectural lines, you nonetheless fail to see it being out of tune with the local scene. Until that project was implemented, it was only the Lenin Mausoleum on Red Square that was generally perceived to perfectly match the one-of-a-kind historic architectural aggregate. To a certain extent, in terms of volume and configuration, the Moskva hotel likewise made the right element of the Kremlin's entourage. Unfortunately, the Intourist hotel on Tverskaya, built through tender bidding, the Rossiya hotel in Zariadye and the square-shaped CC CPSU (Central Committee of the Communist Party of the Soviet Union) office building in Kitay-Gorod, somewhat removed from the Kremlin though they are, introduced a heavy element of discord in the downtown Moscow's traditional skyline, with the locale's architectural and artistic integrity having evidently suffered as a result.

Making another major city-building blunder was the move to put in place a street of residential and office high-rises on New Arbat whose skyline now obscures that of the Kremlin when viewed from a distance. Coming to make wholly an odd couple were the Russian Government and COMECON (now the city administration building) structures on the bank of the Moskva river.

Given the scene, the current downtown Moscow rebuilding program has been drawn up to totally rule out any high-rises within the confines of the Garden Ring. Newly-built structures in the capital city's central part should be designed to best match the local scene in terms of building materials, shapes and color schemes, which amounts to the key requirement for the historic centre's architectural and artistic integrity to be maintained. It is precisely in this direction that the centre-regeneration drive has now been successfully pursued. Once the effort is completed, the question of declaring the central part of Moscow a city-building memorial zone could be readdressed.

The Moscow General Plan NIiPI research institute recently conducted a study to locate the best sites to carry stand-alone high-rises or clusters thereof, with the local conditions, landscape, mandatory nodal public centres and overall space-organization issues being duly accounted for. The study was completed to also rule out the risks of the Kremlin coming to be dwarfed by newly-designed buildings.

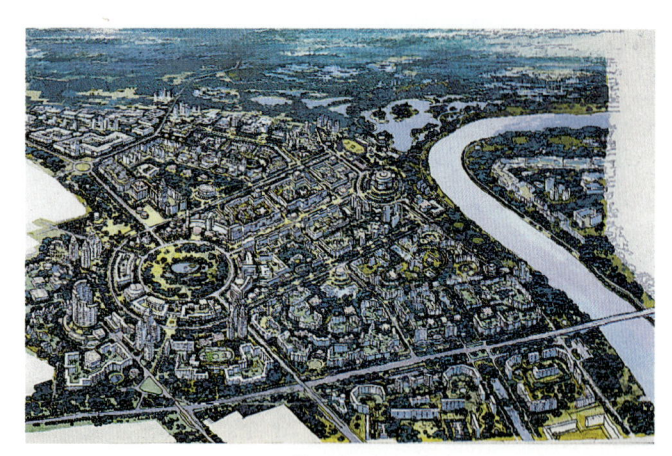

The Maryinsky Park – a new residential area.

The program for erecting tall buildings should evidently be in line with the task to have the newly built-up neighborhoods with their endless lines of same-type structures enriched with uniquely-designed structures intended to break the featureless monotony of the metropolis' peripherals. The appearance of recently built-up areas devoid of eye-catching public facilities, squares, thoroughfares and boulevards can hardly make one think of any aggregate building strategies used to implement those large-scale housing projects. The exceptions to the rule, though with a good deal of reservation, have been provided by the Olympic Village on Michurinsky Prospect, Krylatskoye and Ramenki neighborhoods. Yasenevo and Strogino could also be grown to pose as areas built up to an aggregate design.

Reshaping the capital city's peripherals appears to be the challenge, which in scale and importance only comes second to the goal of regenerating Moscow's historic centre. Admittedly, this time-consuming task is heavily linked with the need to rebuild large numbers of the 1950s–1960s-vintage mass-produced five-storied walk-up buildings filling many of the residential areas.

The effort to effectively accomplish the challenging tasks of rebuilding the featureless housing blocks in the capital city could nowadays be pursued to creatively emulate the development projects completed to grow administrative districts, municipal areas and new residential lots in such localities as Maryinsky park, Novo-Podrezkovo, Kurkino and Zhulebino. These latest housing projects have been characterized by radically improved integrated city-building strategies, with the targeted areas eventually receiving the attributes of an accomplished architectural ensemble.

Caring for the existing landscape in those areas, as well as the newly-emerged capabilities to have differently-designed modern structures put in place in order to effectively respond to the ecologists' demands to alleviate the man-engineered impacts on Moscow's green belt, just as the ongoing creative pursuits to achieve advanced and ecology-friendly city-building schemes have finally produced the desired results.

Unlike the older neighborhoods of Medvedkovo, Otradnoye, Tushino, Kuntsevo, Teply Stan, Orekhovo-Borisovo and all other housing aggregates bordering on the MKAD belt road, each newly-built-up segment is expected to have its distinctive features.

The Maryinsky Park, with its nucleus being made by the existing round-shaped garden, is expected to feature the main broad thoroughfare and a number of tree-lined streets running in parallel to the principal avenue and leading up to the parkland on the bank of the Moskva river. The area would grow into a hydropark, with the green band along the river stretching out to the Kuzminki Park, further on to Kapotnia and then continuing to the woodland out of Moscow.

The picturesque Kurkino area prompted the designers to apply the landscape-focused building strategy and put in place mostly low structures including rural-type settlements of country houses, with a complex of sixteen-, twelve- and nine-storied apartment buildings only ringing the local public centre located right next to the Novye Khimki area.

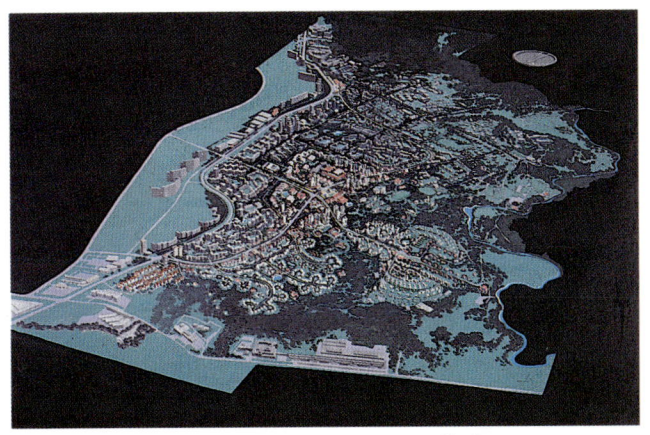

Kurkino. A new residential area in the north-western district.

The theater and hotel complex on Korolev Street. Designed by A. Akhmetov, V. Krasilnikov, M. Gavrilova, N. Nikiforova.

The Novo-Podrezkovo housing aggregate is separated from Leningradsky Highway by a strip of woodland and is designed to include a cluster of stand-alone unequally-tall residential neighborhoods and complexes, with most of those planted around a park holding a large-sized water basin that can be seen stretching out to link up with a wood preserved along the scenic local stream.

To see how the capital city's residential areas would look like tomorrow, one would be well advised to go and look at the Butovo complex where Compound 5 is about to be completed; Maryinsky Park, where the newly-designed Prizma-type buildings make the housing look more one-of-a-kind; as well as visit Minskaya, Veresayeva, Alexander Nevsky Streets and other places that now have been built to look different from one another. Given the diversity of design, the newly-erected structures have come to radically improve the habitats and make the neighborhoods aesthetically pleasing.

This philosophy has likewise been applied to grow such long-lasting districts as Mosfilmovsky and Kutuzovsky in the city's western segment, Aeroport and Sokol in the northern segment, Yakimanka in the central part of Moscow, as well as other comparable neighborhoods, with the aggregate approach allowing the city builders to introduce more individuality and improve the aesthetic qualities of the existing blocks of buildings. Holding the key position in the effort are the visions for shaping up the built-up areas along the capital city's principal thoroughfares, with the vision drafted by the A. Meerson-led team of architects providing one such example focused on streamlining and ameliorating the structures erected along the main route running from the Kremlin, via Tverskaya and Leningradsky Prospekt to Sheremetyevo-2 airport.

Paradoxical as it might seem, the rapid advance of building technologies in the second half of the current century has produced a pervasive sameness of urban environments, which have come to be wholly at odds with the older city centres. It would be in place at this juncture to refer to geometrical shapes of apartment and office buildings and nearly total introduction of flat rooftops. As he appeared before Moscow's architects just a few years ago, it was in no way accidental when Ksendzo Tange mentioned that in terms of architectural design the 20th century, which is about to phase out, comes to be greatly indebted to the mankind.

Having the New General Plan's principal stipulations translated into concrete aggregate architectural solutions makes one of the major efforts to finalize the General Plan's development projects. This important work amounts to an essential city-building dimension, with the built-up urban areas having to be reshaped and

Tverskaya Street. The subterranean-space-focused rebuilding project. Designed by V. Gostev, M. Morina, A. Asadov, V. Kozlov. Engineering support provided by V. Strizhachenko, M. Pronina.

Tverskaya Street today. 1996.

Tverskaya Street viewed from Pushkin Square. 1996.

improved to better support the integrated functioning of the multi-faceted metropolitan system. The properly-placed city-development accents, cyclically repeated to achieve the desired architectural effects, obviously serve to have the primary and secondary structures soundly counterbalanced, fresh urban development blunders avoided and new city-shaping projects soundly drafted, with individual buildings thereby receiving their unique sets of size and appearance specifications.

Today, Moscow features a good selection of aggregate-based solutions aimed to achieve well-integrated urban-development nodes, some of those including plans to develop the existing clusters of buildings adjoining Belorussky, Paveletsky, Rizhsky Railroad Stations, Triumphalnaya Square and other places throughout the capital city. The tasks to implement those designs, just like the comprehensive efforts to carry out new urban-development projects and rebuild the older neighborhoods, with the original visions being creatively extended and grown, certainly make the principal challenges for the years to come.

The Greater Ascension Church at the Nikitsky Gates

The initial design for the Greater Ascension Church at the Nikitsky Gates is reported to have been drafted by architect V.I. Bazhenov to fill out the order from Prince A.G. Potemkin of Tavria. The construction site was chosen to take part of Potemkin's land property merely located 120 – 150 metres away from the existing older Ascension Church on Tsaritsinskaya Street commissioned by N.K. Naryshkina and erected in 1673 – 1685.

The Bazhenov design featured a huge European-style structure abundantly embellished with Corinthian-order columns along the periphery and a top-tier rotunda holding the individually-crafted niches to contain the twelve apostles and their angels. Devised to look as majestic also was the nearby belfry measuring nearly 70 metres tall, which was to be connected with the main shrine building via a walkway-gallery. The integrated refectory (wintertime shrine) was supposed to be much smaller in size and devoid of embellishments.

The recovered 1800 – 1805 sketches of the given land property indicated that the main church building, refectory, belfry and walkway-gallery, as a matter of fact, had been well under construction. In keeping with the original design, the main shrine building's basement tier then was already fully faceted, the refectory completed and part of the walkway-gallery finished to look like an anteroom.

Given that the 1812 French invasion left the structures badly damaged, in 1827 Academician F.I. Shestakov was commissioned to rebuild the church complex. The existing Empire-style design has consistently been ascribed to that architect. The shrine's cube-shaped structure was made larger at the base and somewhat more squatting, with the initially-designed peripheral columns and top-level rotunda removed. The belfry was intended to be adjacent to the refectory's western wall, the walkway-gallery being made redundant as a result. The reviewed design then received some alterations and was eventually confirmed. In 1830, architect O.I. Bove had the main church building receive two four-columned porticos attached to the northern and southern entrances. As the construction got well under way, the decor furnishings and dome proportions underwent certain alterations. The development project lasted through 1848. With F.I. Shestakov passing away, the project in its concluding stage was headed by architect A.G. Grigoryev.

The 19th – 20th-century experts are known to have held the shrine to be one of the best examples of the late Empire-style architecture. The large-sized church building, nearly featuring no decorative touches and catching the eye with its laconically-designed segments, surely amounts to some impressive presence greatly contributing to the capital city's artistic value. Under the reconsidered project, no belfry was constructed...

The June 1994 Moscow government resolution ruled that a plot of land adjoining the Church's western wing should be assigned for a belfry to be built, with the existing small garden having to be sacrificed as a result. The belfry would need to match the church complex and environment on the Nikitskaya Square area.

Three options of the belfry design have already been drafted by architect O.I. Zhurin that has made an extensive use of the original end-of-the 18th-century and 1830s designs, historical analogues, completed and unrealized projects drafted by the architects that in different times had been involved in building the church complex (Shestakov, Grigoryev, Bove, Kozlovsky).

The City Development Council of the Municipal Architectural Committee and the Restoration Guidance Council of the Moscow government have passed the third option, which in terms of size and volume is seen to be best matching up with the existing church building (finalized in the 1840s) and refectory (first quarter of the 19th century).

The Ascension Church at the Nikitsky Gates. The belfry rebuilding project.
Designed by O. Zhurin, I. Izosimov, A. Zhdanov, A. Shcherbakov. Engineering support provided by V. Kurbatov.

The confirmed option features a five-tier belfry standing close to the refectory's western wall. The first square-shaped tier has been designed to feature three ionic-order porticos replicating the existing shrine's porticos. The square-shaped second tier (belfry underchamber) has been devised to contain four large-sized semicircular windows.

The elongated four-sided third tier (the principal chiming level) is framed with the coupled tapering columns guarding the chiming platform openings and holding a white-stone balustrade. The fourth chiming level is made by a rotunda designed to feature four tall semicircular openings on either of the four sides. The fifth tier is designed as a cylinder featuring four vent windows and a dome holding a spire and cross. The belfry's tiers have been designed to incrementally grow smaller towards the top. The structure is expected to be about 57.5 metres tall, with the western portico serving as the shrine's main entrance.

Apart from the belfry, the project includes restoration of the compound fencing featuring the Empire-style gates, which are expected to be placed on the 19th-century groundwork, as well as construction of a two-storied residential building for the local clergy on Malaya Nikitskaya Street to the west of the Church and of a small guard house at the compound's southern gates facing Bolshaya Nikitskaya Street. All of the newly-designed structures are expected to perfectly integrate with the existing shrine, held to be a major architectural monument. The whole compound is likewise to be improved, with the utility lines being rerouted and the remains of the belfry groundwork sites, laid at the start of the 19th century and in 1865, appropriately uncovered and preserved.

The Saint Tatiana the Martyr Church at Moscow University

In the early 18th century, located at the confluence of Mokhovaya and Bolshaya Nikitskaya Streets was the Apraksin estate including the principal mansion and two outbuildings, with one of those facing Bolshaya Nikitskaya and Mokhovaya Streets. In 1793, the Pashkovs purchased the estate and had all of the structures rebuilt. Phasing out the Apraksin mansion was a three-storied belvedere-containing palace connected through a covered walkway with an outbuilding that was designed to feature a semi-rotunda facing Mokhovaya Street and holding a colonnade and a dome. That outbuilding contained an equestrian manege, stable and carriage garage, with the hay storage space and horsemen quarters positioned just above the stable.

In 1833, the Pashkovs sold off the 1812 war-ravaged estate to Moscow University. Within 1833 – 1837, architect E.D. Tiurin rebuilt the mansion to provide the University with a new classroom and laboratory building, with the Bolshaya Nikitskaya – Mokhovaya outbuilding being turned into an in-house church and museum interconnected with a set of formally-furnished holding rooms.

The Saint Tatiana the Martyr Church makes an example of the late Moscow Empire-style architecture. The value of the shrine's interior is in the wholesome vision of its builder E.D. Tiurin who personally designed all of the furnishings, including the iconostasis.

As a matter of fact, the shrine proper was designed to be located on the outbuilding's second floor, with the altar filling the semi-rotunda held by the structure's end facing Mokhovaya Street. Domineering the interior was the classic iconostasis decorated with I.P. Vitali's sculptures. Placed opposite the altar was the choir gallery supported by a Doric-order four-columned portico. The interior's middle section featured a suspended wooden dome held between four brickwork arches resting upon four powerfully-built pylons. The wooden sail-like roofing with its ingenious girders, spanning spaces nearly measuring 20 metres across, most positively make outstanding cases of the art of engineering. In 1836 – 1837, the arches and the ceiling received the appropriate mural paintings. The main lobby or formal anteroom was designed to feature two windows, a three-step case of stairs and gallery circling the upper level.

The shrine's interior was first meaningfully altered in 1855, with the original murals being totally replaced. In 1904 – 1905, under the K.M. Bykovsky-drafted project, the anteroom's stairs, gallery and walls were partially redesigned. In 1912, the attic section of the church's colonnade facing Mokhovaya Street received the logo «God Enlightens All», with a cross placed on top of the attic.

The Church was closed down in 1918 and converted into Moscow University's club and theater. Within 1953 – 1955, the building was overhauled. It received a set of reinforced concrete girders and lost the anteroom's gallery, with the main choir gallery being replaced by a spectator balcony and a movie-projector room. The shrine's interior under the balcony was turned into an amphitheater, the altar space being reengineered into a stage featuring the sets-handling equipment. The interior's wooden decorations were destroyed, the anteroom's floor was elevated, the staircase was dismantled and replaced with a newly-designed structure. What is more, the old sound-reinforcing ceiling was replaced with a regular plaster-coated surface.

It was only in 1995, that the Saint Tatiana the Martyr Church was restored to operate as MGU's in-house church and the Patriarch's conventual church and house.

The on-site engineering, physical and chemical research as well as the study of the remaining murals allowed to find out that the building's outside walls carried the fragments of numerous alterations introduced in the course of the 18th – 19th centuries, the interior still contained some wooden pieces from the original ceiling decorations and reinforcing girders, the walls and arches still held some fragments of the mid-19th-century murals and relief decorations, the floors contained isolated patches of the old parquet and faceted flooring, as well as that the doors and windows had some sections of the original artificial-marble blocks.

The Saint Tatiana the Martyr Church's restoration project provides for:

The Saint Tatiana Church at Moscow University. The rebuilding project. Designed by O. Zhurin.

Northern facade

Eastern facade

The Saint Tatiana Church at Moscow University. The rebuilding project. The longitudinal section and cross-section.

– restoration of the 1830s-period facades, with the entire building's external appearance expected to be reestablished and original building fragments preserved and integrated;

– complete restoration of the shrine's and anteroom's original interiors, with the remaining fragments appropriately preserved, as well as recreation of the unique iconostasis, choir and gallery, and restoration of the mid-19th-late-19th century murals carried by the ceilings and arches.

Recreating the Spiritual and Enlightening Complex at Krylatskoye

The recent archeological research indicated that the Krylatskoye territory within Moscow contained traces of the 12th – 14th-century settlements of the Viatichis. The area's most elevated spot held a grove that initially had an ancient pagan necropolis and then, in the 16th – 17th centuries, a Christian cemetry. Found on the ravine slopes near the existing church were the remnants of an ancient settlement that had eventually grown into Krylatskoye, which was first mentioned in 1423 in Great Prince of Muscovy Vassily the First's edict as Muscovy's property.

The existing wooden church, that was dedicated by Tsar Ivan the Terrible, dates back to 1554. In 1681, the building was reported to be «looking frail and beyond repair». Finally, in 1713, it perished in a haphazard fire, with a new church rising in its place within the next two years. In 1785, the building was also destroyed by a fire, with yet another church being erected to replace the old one within the next year. In 1865, the wooden church structure was replaced by a two-winged stone church designed by architect Vodo. Ten years later, a tall belfry, designed by architect Stratilatov, was put in place, with a very narrow walkway connecting the new structure and the shrine. The church's and belfry's same-style facades are characteristic of the late Empire-to-Russian style transition period.

In the 1880s, the cemetery, moved at the close of the 17th century to a new site east of the existing church, was enclosed with a metal fence resting on brickwork supports.

Closed down in the first decades of Soviet era, the Nativity of Virgin Mary Church at Krylatskoye had for many years been allowed to degrade and crumble. In the years of the Great Patriotic War (1941 – 1945), the belfry was detonated to serve some tactical purpose.

Overall view of the Nativity of Virgin Mary Church at Krylatskoye – a 19th-century architectural monument and the environs. The rebuilding and regeneration project. Designed by O. Zhurin, V. Blazhevich.

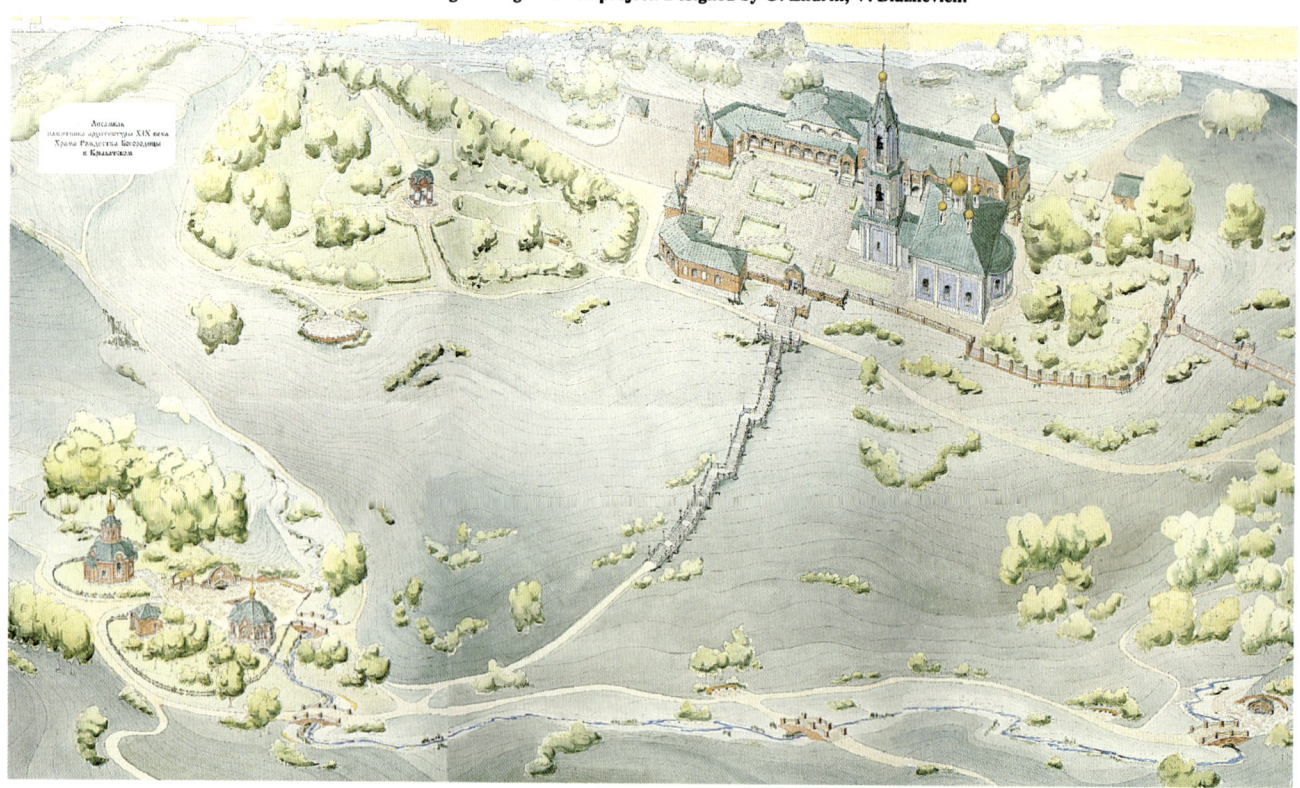

The Virgin Mary of Rudnia Chapel and the Baptistery at the greater spring. Draft project. Designed by O. Zhurin, V. Blazhevich.

Under the December 4, 1974 Russian Federation Council of Ministers resolution, the Church received the status of an architectural monument safeguarded by the state, with the appropriate memorial zone being finalized in 1981.

In 1991, the Church was transferred to the Moscow Patriarchy. Until 1995, rebuilding and restoration projects had been implemented under the so-called «self-financing strategy», which eventually led to the Church's and belfry's historic appearance and style being heavily distorted. Given their current status, the buildings no longer appear to be consistent with their original designs. The cube-shaped shrine with its five small-sized domes, showing beautifully against the tall belfry, used to be perfectly integrated in the overall symphony of chimes sounded by the «forty forties» of Moscow's churches.

The Krylatskoye village was totally torn down on account of the Olympic complex being built in the late 1970s, with the bicycle race trek, bicycle lanes, rowing canal and other structures having wholly distorted the local landscape. The natural hills south of the Tatarovsky Ravine were built up by 10 – 15 metres, the Church hill losing its domineering position in the area as a result. A large residential area, populated by seventy thousand people, has now come to emerge directly next to the Krylatskiye Hills. The architectural monument became to be dwarfed by the huge-size buildings located in the vicinity. The Tatarovsky Ravine with its springs, uncovered in 15th century, has remained uncultivated to the present day.

The Nativity of Virgin Mary Church's restoration project along with the 1995 plans to recreate the spiritual and enlightening centre stipulate the efforts to have the Church and Belfry receive their original appearance; rebuild the 1880s-style cemetry fence and the Virgin Mary of Rudnia Chapel at local spring site; as well as erect two church-related buildings to house the clergy's living quarters, refectory, workshops, parochial school, baptistery, church store with a book depository; construct an open-air baptistery and a watchman's cabin near the greater spring; put in place the flights of stairs leading from the Church to the protected and covered springs; ameliorate and improve the Church hill along with the adjoining slopes and pads at the springs, stream valley, walkways, drive-ins and parking lots; erect the memorial sheltered cross at the site of the original 15th – 17th-century cemetry.

All of the intended structures and buildings have been designed to feature the old Russian style, the building materials being the red brick and white sandstone. The shrine will keep the commanding hill location, and the support buildings are expected to be positioned in two-three tiers down the hill's northern slope. Eventually, the Church will once again be integrated in the city landscape, with the spiritual and enlightening centre receiving its due place in the newly-built architectural ensemble.

The project has been drafted to include a set of measures aimed to build and furnish the Tatarovsky Ravine natural park, which would be ingeniously integrated in the local environment.

The rebuilt Church and restored springs are expected to provide for the unity of human spirituality and natural beauty, which would certainly amount to a profoundly sacred value.

Arts and Religion

For decades the history of arts and architecture has been studied in the conditions of total separation from the long-lasting canonic guidelines and history of the Russian Orthodox Church, with the whole focus being persistently placed on the aesthetic and design dimensions of city-building. Catching the whole attention of city planners have been the shapes rather than the substance and religious content of the art of architecture.

«The aesthetic perception is generally passive, for it demands no abandon, no willpower, for it comes spontaneously», wrote S. Bulgakov and then went on, «As soon the aesthetics and its criteria develop to be superior to the current ethical standards, that phenomenal trend could only be understood as the erosion of the human spirit's remaining pillars. Coming to be particularly dangerous would be the splitting of conscience as well as the break-up of the notions of beauty and truth, which would eventually lead to the inability to perceive the outside world and all of its vital manifestations in their entirety».

«The Russian cultural elite», writes N. Berdiayev, «is positively to blame for the catastrophe that the Russian spiritual culture has suffered. The cultural elite's terrible egotism has produced its eventual isolation and disdain of the human masses' basic needs». That phenomenon has persisted to have its bearing on today's realities. For the long seven decades such a comprehensive form of public conscience as culture had been heavily tied to standardized moviehouses and houses of culture with their dancing floors. The issue of safeguarding the cultural heritage and valuable monuments had been addressed with a very special goal in mind, the church buildings and old palaces being converted for other uses.

Though quite a few years have passed since the long-lasting communist taboos on numerous aspects of our existence were lifted, the current legislation, everyday realities and even public perceptions continue to hold some vestiges of the old strategies. To this very day, most of us find it hard to come to the realization that making one of the culture's crucial manifestations is the religion that directly governs the course of principal historic developments.

The sacramental meaning of a church structure or piece of religious art is obviously by far more essential than their aesthetic qualities separated from the symbolic origins of culture perceived globally. Regrettably, given the difficulties of the ongoing ideological crisis, the above-described questions are for the most part being passed over in silence and are yet to be addressed substantively.

The works of religious arts best synthesize disparate artistic pursuits and «serve as attempts to epitomize the arts in order to help people achieve the spiritual acme that champions of the current aesthetics have been so ardently dreaming about», according to Pavel Florensky.

To get the arts synthesized, one needs to have the knowledge of how to get them appropriately integrated and sufficiently homogenized, with the individual complementing components taking on new qualities and reinforcing the given opus both in terms of form and content. Synthesizing the arts applies to more than just painting,

Religious procession heading for the Iberia Chapel at the Resurrection Gates. 1995.

sculpture and architecture. Synthesis of the arts amounts to a phenomenon that manifests itself through the agency of poorly understood and yet extremely powerful religious art, aesthetics of the religious culture in general, church environment and dedicated religious services on the whole.

But let us go back to the persisting gulf between the secular perception of the role of arts and the real problems of safeguarding numerous historical heritage monuments, the issues relating to the understanding of the relevance and value of the Russian Orthodox Church and its sacred sites and artifacts. Religious sacred objects in general make the crucial segment of such a multidimensional phenomenon as culture that definitely reflects many a societal endeavor. Hence, what should now be created is a concerted symphony of secular and religious pursuits that would generate a new set of ideological values.

As he recently declared open the «Orthodox Russia» exhibition in Moscow, his Holiness Patriarch Alexy II of Russia highlighted the need for the efforts of the Russian Orthodox Church and secular organizations to be brought together to serve the noble cause of nationwide spiritual and moral education of the people, preservation and revival of the Russian Orthodox sacred sites and cultural heritage monuments

Today, the religion has evidently become an equitable component of the nation's «comprehensive culture», and it is now absolutely essential that a focused effort should be undertaken to single out the monuments that had been built to satisfy the requirements of the established canonic rules and church tradition rather than meet the demands of the contemporaneous secular aesthetics. Obviously, those sites should be enabled to exist and find protection in keeping with their intended purposes rather than in compliance with the general rules of safeguarding the country's cultural heritage.

Let us make an assessment and find out what generally is the most relevant aspect of a religious shrine. Should that be the perfectly designed dome, the designer himself or the given dome's emergence as a model of the Heaven spreading as a canopy over the principal spots, contained by shrines and the entire Earth? Should the miraculous Vassily the Blessed Cathedral be really more important as a wonderful structure than as a monumental house of prayer built to nearly achieve the goal of an ideal shrine?

It would be in place at this moment to remind the reader that the old icon painters would never affix their names to their works done, for they would regard their contributions as mandatory jobs making an overall integrated effort, the liturgical art, which could not be attributed to individuals. An icon, painted for some church, used to be an integral furnishing of that shrine. In the olden times, the icon painters maintained that all arts could only thrive within the fold of the religion.

An icon is an important ingredient of a sophisticated system of church values defying the dogmas of the rudimentary logic. Just like a church building, an icon first comes as part of the Church and only after that could be perceived as a cultural or historic artifact. Understandably, it is the canonic rules and religion-related laws that should primarily be focused whenever the issue in question is about rebuilding a shrine.

During his first service at the Christ the Savior Cathedral, his Holiest Patriarch Alexius II of Moscow and All Russia said in particular, «...The shrine, whose flesh is seen to have been growing at such a rapid pace and so efficiently, should now acquire its soul, which is to come through prayers of God's children and activities of the local parish».

Though they are truly aware of the souls of their shrines, that now and again they can hardly articulate, many of the current church shepherds come most strongly against the demands of the cultural heritage protection officials, with the requirements often standing to be at odds with the canonic laws. To remind, the soul of each shrine also makes a substantive component of the nation's culture, and it should likewise be safeguarded by the state.

Pavel Florensky writes, «...I could understand the fanatical demand to tear down the Lavra (the Troitse-Sergiyev Principal Monastery or Lavra) in the name of the religion of socialism, but then I totally refuse to see the goal that the current culture regents are trying to achieve. Given that the experts dealing with fine arts by the dint of some accident now heavily outnumber their counterparts specializing in other arts, the aggressive cultural regents are seen coming to the rescue of icons and murals, with other no-less-precious artifacts being wholly ignored. Which is most consequential, they seem to be oblivious of the arts having to be perceived in their synthetic entirety – the supreme mission for the arts throughout...

The advocates of the aesthetics, practiced until recently, had held they were justified in treating the Russian icon in a haughty manner. Admittedly, the current aesthetes have reviewed their policy position on that score. Unfortunately, this has only been an initial step, for not infrequently the icons continue to be regarded as stand-alone valuable artifacts that could be placed either in a shrine, museum, expo or elsewhere, the reason for that apparently being the insufficient knowledge or insensitivity.

It positively amounts to a good deal of thoughtlessness to have this aspect of the church arts unwittingly separated from the complete phenomenon obviously made by the church and its functions, which needs to be taken as the arts synthesized, the genuine artistic environment where the church arts truly belong and can only be observed and admired as disparate pieces conceived to support a single goal. Even the most superficial glance at any ingredient of the church arts would make one easily see that they all are meant to come together to generate a single effect.

The interests of the country's culture would merely be well served if the attempts to forcefully separate some rays from the single source of creation and have those isolated and tagged for display were vehemently opposed and actively protested ... .

Whenever inside a shrine, we would confront the Platonic world of ideas, while in a museum we view the travesty of an icon rather than the icon itself...»

We all should particularly be thankful to the patriots that managed to save many of the consecrated artifacts in the 1930s when the drive was in full swing to have the Russian churches either razed to the ground or looted. Those experts succeeded in moving many of the Church furnishings over to museum depositories. However, the same people today come strongly against having the church artifacts moved to the original settings in order to help support the church's multifaceted activities, as they got used to regarding the consecrated religious articles as museum properties.

Water Basins of Moscow's Green Belt

The Moscow agglomeration is known to take up the central spot in the Russian Plain, which initially was completely covered with pine, fir and leaf trees. The settlers had incrementally penetrated into that wilderness to cultivate the newly appropriated lands. Moscow's location is typical of major old townships in the Russian Plain, with the high Borovitsky Hill on the Moskva river, (a tributary of the Oka river, a major river in the Volga-river basin) carrying the original settlement. The Moscow area is characterized by largely humid and moisture-containing geological environments with highly-diversified soils, by flat lands with lightly-pronounced elevations and depressions, abundance of surface waters, fast-growing needle-leaf vegetation, varied winds in terms of direction, force and speed patterns, extreme weathers ranging from freezing wintertime temperatures to summertime heat highs, as well as by short four-month summers. These circumstances bespeak the vulnerability of environments in the Moscow region, particularly given its low capacity for self-regeneration and self-cleaning. With the people living and working in these geographical latitudes for centuries, traditions have thereby been established for the man to know how to be ecologically-friendly, how to soundly use the surveyed natural riches, work to assure the environmental security and seek to take out the emerging imbalances.

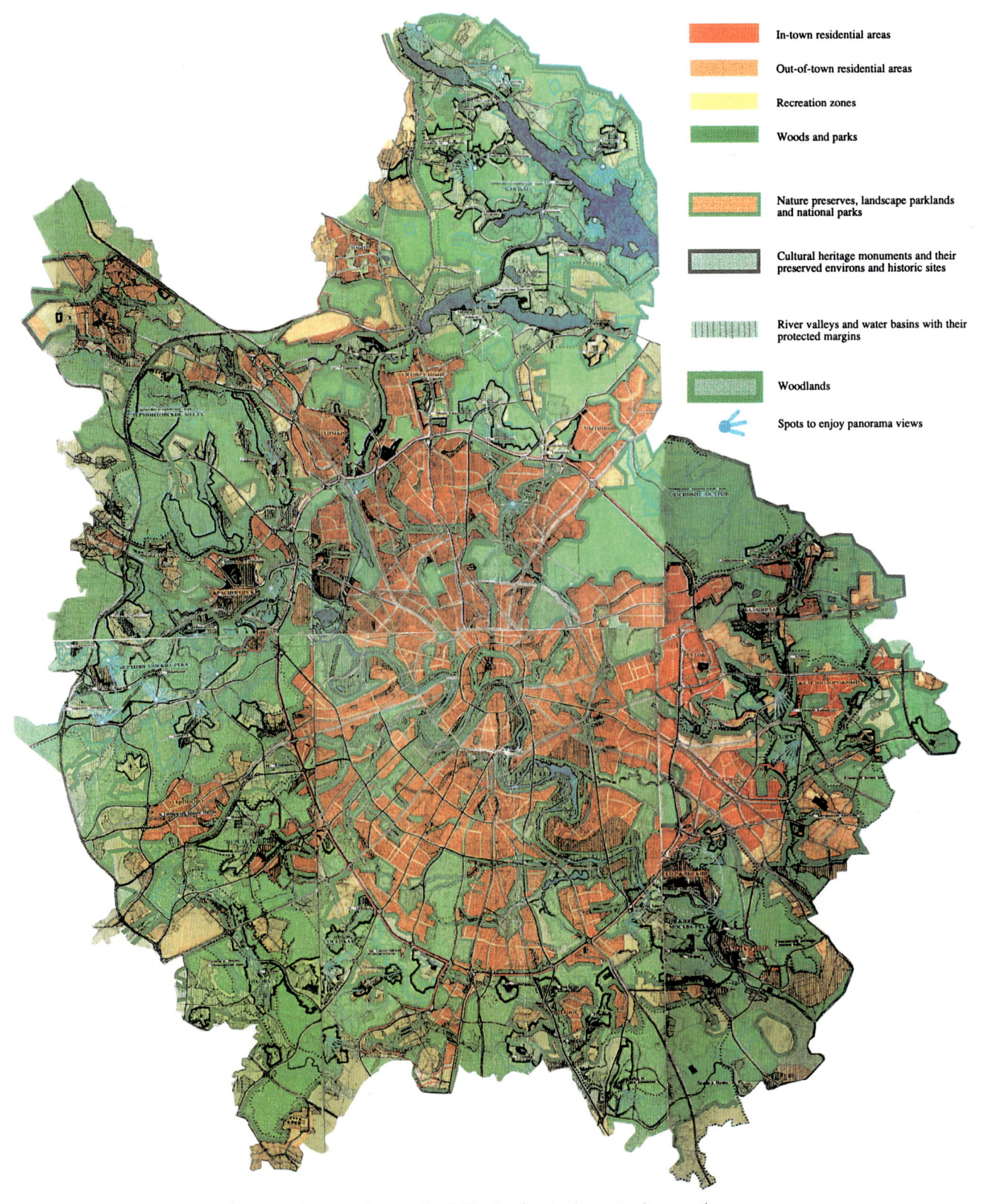

(red-orange)	In-town residential areas
(light orange)	Out-of-town residential areas
(yellow)	Recreation zones
(green)	Woods and parks
(orange/green)	Nature preserves, landscape parklands and national parks
(grey)	Cultural heritage monuments and their preserved environs and historic sites
(striped)	River valleys and water basins with their protected margins
(green pattern)	Woodlands
(arrow)	Spots to enjoy panorama views

Moscow and its protective green band. City-planning, development and preservation areas.

The existing rivers and streams certainly play the most crucial role in the life of the region. As many as a total of over six kilometres of streams and rivers are estimated to be running across each square kilometre of the Moscow region's territory. With the local rivers generally running from the north-west to south-east, the nature of their valleys is extremely varied, though they are clearly integrated into a single network of meandering rivers, rivulets streams and their tributaries. Not a single settlement could be found outside of this permeating system of flowing waters. Not a single old or new town could be found that was not built on a river.

Given the conditions of Moscow environs, the interdependence of rivers and woods has always been understood. With rivers giving life to the local woods and the woods enabling the rivers to survive, people finally came up with a theory of integrated ecology. The dis-

Near Moscow.

The Istra river. New Jerusalem.

covered extent of integration, as a matter of fact, comes to be present in any and all segments of varied geographical zones, with the Moscow region being particularly vulnerable to man-made intrusions that easily leave long-lasting scars.

The 20th century with its large-scale urban development projects and industry-building drives is known to have primarily been focused on boosting the engineering and manufacturing capacities: as many as 936 small rivers and streams within Moscow's confines have been taken into subterranean tubes, 40 percent of the city's territory has turned out to be devoid of natural streams and the overall number of streams has drastically dwindled. However, it would be wrong to believe that the water basins in Moscow environs have not developed to acquire new promising features. Moscow is one of just a few larger cities with water supply being totally tied up to the waters carried by the regional rivers. Coming to exist in the 1930s was the Moskva-Volga canal to connect the existing water basins, provide water supply and make a navigable waterway. Created in the 1960s was a huge system of large artificial lakes grown out of the smaller Ruza, Istra, Ozerna, Yauza and other rivers. The existing system of dams makes the Moskva river fully manageable, with the spring-water highs and inundations being completely ruled out as a consequence. Moscow's initial industrial facilities – the 18th-century mills and 19th – 20th-century manufacturing plants and factories – had gradually become the city's prominent industrial sites. Given that significant segments of the Moskva-river are now found to be within the city confines, with the industrial zones sitting on the river's downstream reaches as well on the Kliazma, Yauza, Pekhorka and other rivers, the larger rivers at present could mostly be admired from aboard boats, barges or cars crossing the bridges.

Overall, the following two frameworks have come into existence: man-made geometrical star-like structure on the one hand, and the natural pattern, which could be likened with a tree and its branches, on the other.

Unlike other major European cities, Moscow environs have proved to be much more vulnerable, with the desertification trend in the lands around Russia's capital city being increasingly noticeable. Tremendous shifts have come to occur within the confines of a predominantly closed area, with the environmental in-town and out-of-town conditions largely growing to become indistinguishable.

These sort-of commonized transformations have also transpired through Moscow preserving large-sized parks (measuring three to five thousand hectars in area) and even a whole national park (the Losiny Ostrov Wood measuring eleven thousand hectars).

Moscow's peripheral rivers and their tributaries, which have not been driven to flow through subterranean tubes, are known to have been giving their waters to near-river woods, parks and gardens (the Setun, Likhoborka, Chermianka and other rivers). Within a built-up agglomerative band, starting 10 – 15 kilometres from Moscow and stretching in width out to 40 kilometres from the capital city's beltway, one can now see an out-of-town populated space, which looks like a rural area and yet comes to be quite different from it.

Compared against major European cities, Moscow is 2.5 – 3 times less populated, with its relevant indicator merely standing at 95 dwellers per hectare of city land. The research has indicated that over the past 250 years the city limits have been pushed back whenever the average land-per-dweller indicator has dropped below 100 square metres. In addition, some constant value was eventually found to indicate the difference between the densities of «in-town» and «out-of-town» populations, the latter generally believed to be living in the countryside. Throughout the last two and a half centuries, the city population density level has on average been fifty times that of the out-of-town density level, though, admittedly, the current out-of-town population density indicator in actual numbers comes to be much higher than the one standing for the 18th-century Moscow's in-town population density.

The regularities and trends of the out-of-town spaces being built up have now turned out to be internationally focused by town and city builders, which obviously make one of the phenomena or genies of urbanization. The most common impacts of urban development projects in the countryside include rapid (five-seven years) degradation and erosion of the woodland, isolated forests, woods and wood strips in the city's environs, with the local nature being unable to adapt to a new set of conditions. As the transformations proceed unchecked, some form of desertification has incrementally been setting in. The content of vegetation within the capital city's peripheral band, stretching 1.5 – 2 kilometres wide, is about the same as that found in downtown Moscow.

With the Moscow Region's area being 42 percent filled with woodland and parkland, the out-of-town lands within 20 – 25 kilometres of the city limits merely hold green patches totaling 30 – 32 percent of the area in question. The territories, which truly could be referred to as forests (with 80 – 85 percent of the land covered by woods) are now 50 – 60 kilometres from Moscow, with forest «wedges» mostly lying between the principal national highways. The rivers and streams in the capital city's environs are seen to be drying out or getting polluted. Such crisis situations have generated

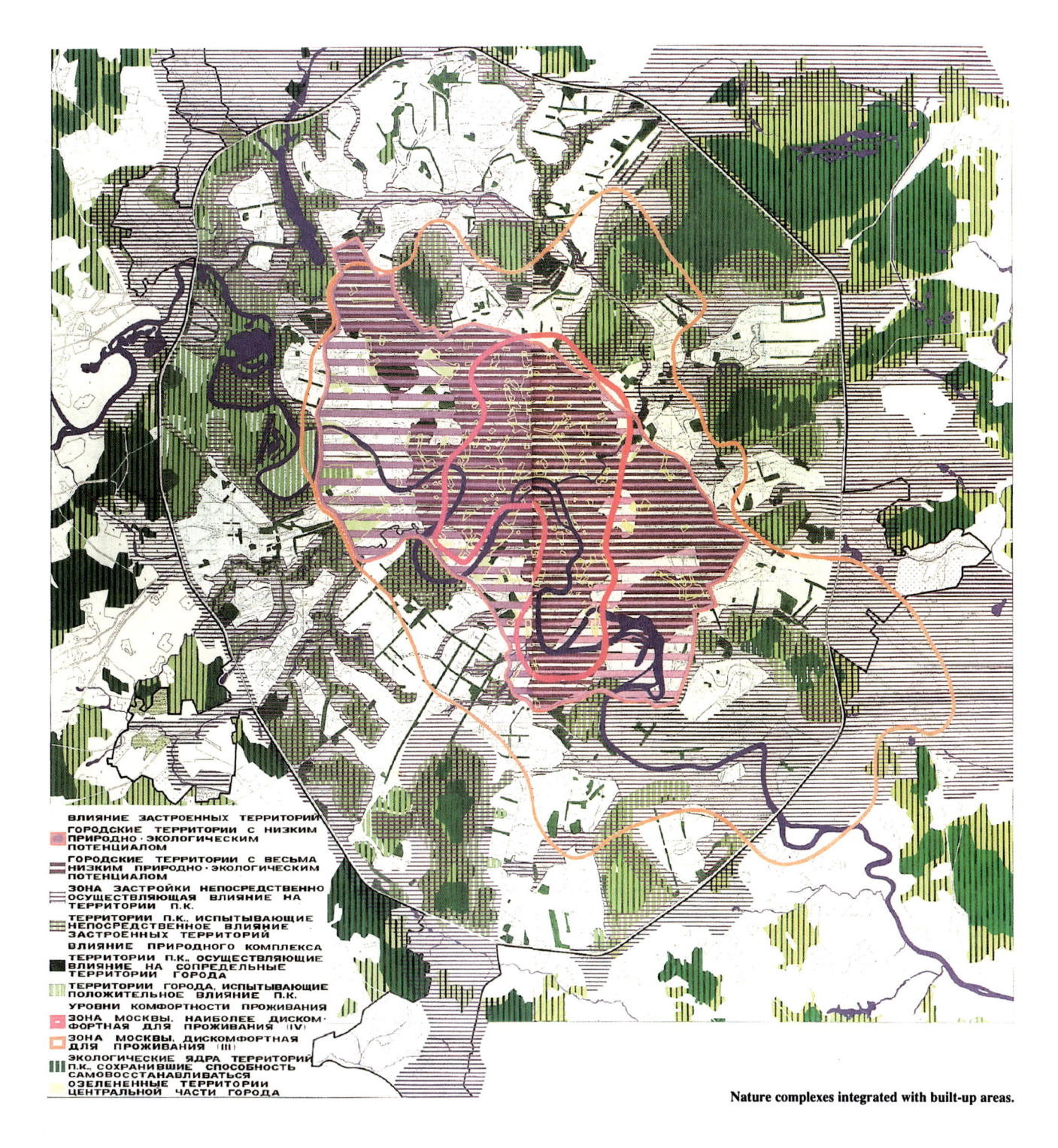

Nature complexes integrated with built-up areas.

a number of cures, with some of the remedies being aimed to take the streams into subterranean tubes, have them rerouted or merged.

The idea of creating protective green bands around the country's major cities was forwarded in the 18th century as some social utopia. However, as urban development projects and industrial efforts accelerated their advance, the city builders have come to realize the utility and true value of green belts maintained around major cities. Moscow appears to have been perfectly placed to have its abundantly wooded environs, the goal for city planners obviously being to preserve what had always been there.

The capital city's booming growth before and after the Second World War has fully revealed the commanding need for the city's environs to be appropriately shaped. The effort to just preserve the general content of rivers and woodland has proved to be by far insufficient. What is obviously needed today is a concerted effort of large numbers of people seeking to turn the empty and degraded plots of land into green segments that could in the long run be integrated to form huge parklands around the 21st-century cities.

Now, we have got a new concept of having Moscow provided with a band of woods and parks, which would indirectly help the in-town parks survive and enable the remote outlying woods to grow. The new concept is built upon the new perception of the existing water basins in the region, the largest ones being Moskvoretskoye and Kliazminskoye Lakes.

Until recently, the man-made ingredient in the integrated system of artificial and natural components of the habitats had been focused the most. The developing infrastructural and industrial facilities as well as major highways required that their functions should be appropriately provided for. The new vision for the Moscow and its green belt has been drafted to primarily focus the nature, with its network of rivers supporting the woods and woods safeguarding the local rivers. Given that the nature is unable to readily embrace the technological and industrial advance, it is the city itself that should be called upon to help out the lands surrounding Moscow.

Segments have been defined inside and outside Moscow where the existing water basins and parts or woods are expected to be maintained and grown to assure the desired nature content, which would include major rivers with their 1st, 2nd and 3rd-class tributaries, river valleys, adjacent terraces and slopes, near-river landscapes, hydro-engineering sites, natural and cultivated parks, as well as woods and forests.

Today, woods can only be observed along the watersheds between rivers and water basins, with each forest strip, park or garden holding at least two-three rivulets or streams. Nearly no major vegetation can now be seen masking the existing rivers in the region, which obviously affects the volumes of water flows. The newly-designed approach is aimed to rebuild the system of woods and water basins and eventually create an integrated green belt around Moscow.

The guidelines for rehabilitating the waters and woods of the Moscow Region and Moscow provide for a sequence of concerted efforts to conserve and restore the existing environment on a continual basis, make up for the losses sustained, reinforce the natural links, manage the city-generated impacts, build up new functions and enhance spiritual values shared by the people living in the area.

Preserving and restoring the available network of water basins, rivers, parks and woods in the heavily built-up areas of Moscow and the region positively amounts to a most awesome task. Moscow has been particularly badly hit in this regard, for it is only the smaller streams, running through a variety of parks and woods on the city's periphery, that could be substantively preserved. Kept in the older neighborhoods of Moscow were mainly the green strips running along the streams, which have now been turned into subterranean canals.

The smaller streams within Moscow's green belt have nearly been totally preserved. However, threatened the most today are the rivulets that run through built-up areas lying close to major highways. The rehabilitated streams in those urbanized areas around Moscow most certainly have a lot to do with the comprehensive drive to create the following five recreational complexes containing water basins and woods: Nizhne-Moskvoretsky, Verkhne-Moskvoretsky, Kliazmensky, Verkhne-Pekhorsky and Pekhorsky areas. The waters and green patches take up at least 60 percent of the capital city's protective belt and 27 percent of the land within Moscow's confines.

Needing the biggest attention today is the drive to recreate and grow green patches whose fragments continue to be held by the existing river and stream valleys. Unfortunately, in recent years those valleys, usually found between principal highways, have increasingly been built up with the cottages for the well-off Russians. The once abandoned townships and villages along the rivers have now been filled with new life and activity. Given the most conservative estimates, one hectare of the built-up land needs to be compensated for with at least six hectares of vegetation and water basins: parks meadows, rehabilitated cultivated landscapes, green strips along the existing dams, highways and roads, river and lake banks, canals and scattered woods in recreational zones. This strategy is certain to help restore the waters and woods and bring the trees and shrubs from the watersheds down into the valleys.

Laid bare in recent years also have been heads of the rivers that are running across heavily built up areas, with the river beds badly needing to be rehabilitated. River and stream sources (springs, lakes) are expected to be protected with vegetation and shelter-belts serving as green corridors.

The water basins, rivers and woods can hardly get restored with no external assistance, given that the ongoing man-made impacts have been too severe to be handled efficiently. The need is definitely there for focused steps to be taken in order to drain excessive waters from the swamped territories, reinforce the river and lake banks as well as ravine and hill slopes, put in check or canalize the valley-held drains, recreate and manage the natural flows and streams, build a system of antilandslide fortifications, overhaul the canalized subterranean and open streams, create a system of basins filled with cleaned-up sewage waters certified to be good enough for fish-breeding and washing down of the more polluted rivers. The entire range of measures to improve near-river territories, intercept and treat the polluted flows, rebuild the damaged landscape, ameliorate the river-valley lands, construct storage ponds or adjust water-basin beds is expected to assure rehabilitation of the region's waters, parks and woods.

Picture of Moscow's Ecology

No balanced and sound decisions aimed to draft and carry out a set of environmental security and human healthcare measures and take steps to prevent irrevocable trends, that might precipitate the degradation of rivers, streams, lakes, forests, cultivated land segments and other fixed assets, could be implementable unless the true knowledge is secured on the status of man-made pollution levels. That knowledge on the conditions of capital city's environment and its capacity to survive industrial and other man-made impacts in terms of timing, cost and veracity could best be provided by a remote-control orbiting vehicle supplemented with ground-based mobile platforms designed to take the relevant calibrated measurements of the local environment particulars. The orbit- and ground-origin reports are thereby made available to provide for truthfulness and completeness of the data reflecting the health of the local environment and the people.

The utilization of space-based vehicles to track the area and the levels of man-generated impacts appears to be the most promising strategy to find the true status of Moscow's ecology.

Activated to conduct automated observation of the Earth in the Moscow area are Resurs-01-type satellites from the NPP VNIIEM research and industrial facility, with the onboard prime-mission scanning equipment being designed to beam down the reports formatted in three spectral ranges. The observation imagery is built up from the onboard-sensor-produced data reflecting the make-up of the underlying surface and atmosphere emissions captured to support relatively broad spectral patterns.

The digital space-origin imagery processing techniques, designed by the Research Centre for Space Ecology, involve the use of dedicated modularly-based software applications developed to assure investigation of the imagery received. The resultant picture comes out to be either a multichromatic or black-and-white imaging map, with each color or shade of grey representing that or other status of the underlying surface segments, water basins or even the condition of atmosphere. The processing results come out more graphically on multichromatic maps.

The use of space-based Earth-ecology monitoring techniques in combination with the conventional ground-based methods to take measurements of the status of ecology at the specified sites allows to concurrently find out the conditions of water basins and other spots on the underlying surface, know the quality of atmosphere over large spaces, and precisely identify, delineate and even categorize the areas and shapes of degraded zones. Space-based Earth monitoring in a large number of cases enables the researchers to reveal the specifics of the growing fields of atmosphere pollution, which fail to be recorded and delineated with the use of conventional land-based environment-monitoring platforms that are limited in numbers and unable to produce the sufficient body of data to build up dependable ecology-status maps.

The knowledge thereby secured can be used to find solutions to the pressing ecology problems, to put in place the right-sized network of ground-based ecology-monitoring stations and develop local schemes to provide for comprehensive protection of the nature. Today, the concerted effort is well under way to handle a number of crucial environmental security problems, with the city-wide ecology-status maps being built-up on a continual basis, water basins and recreation zones improved and organized in the capital city's environs, vegetation and soil-pollution charts made readily available. Healthcare-focused ecology charts allow to cat-

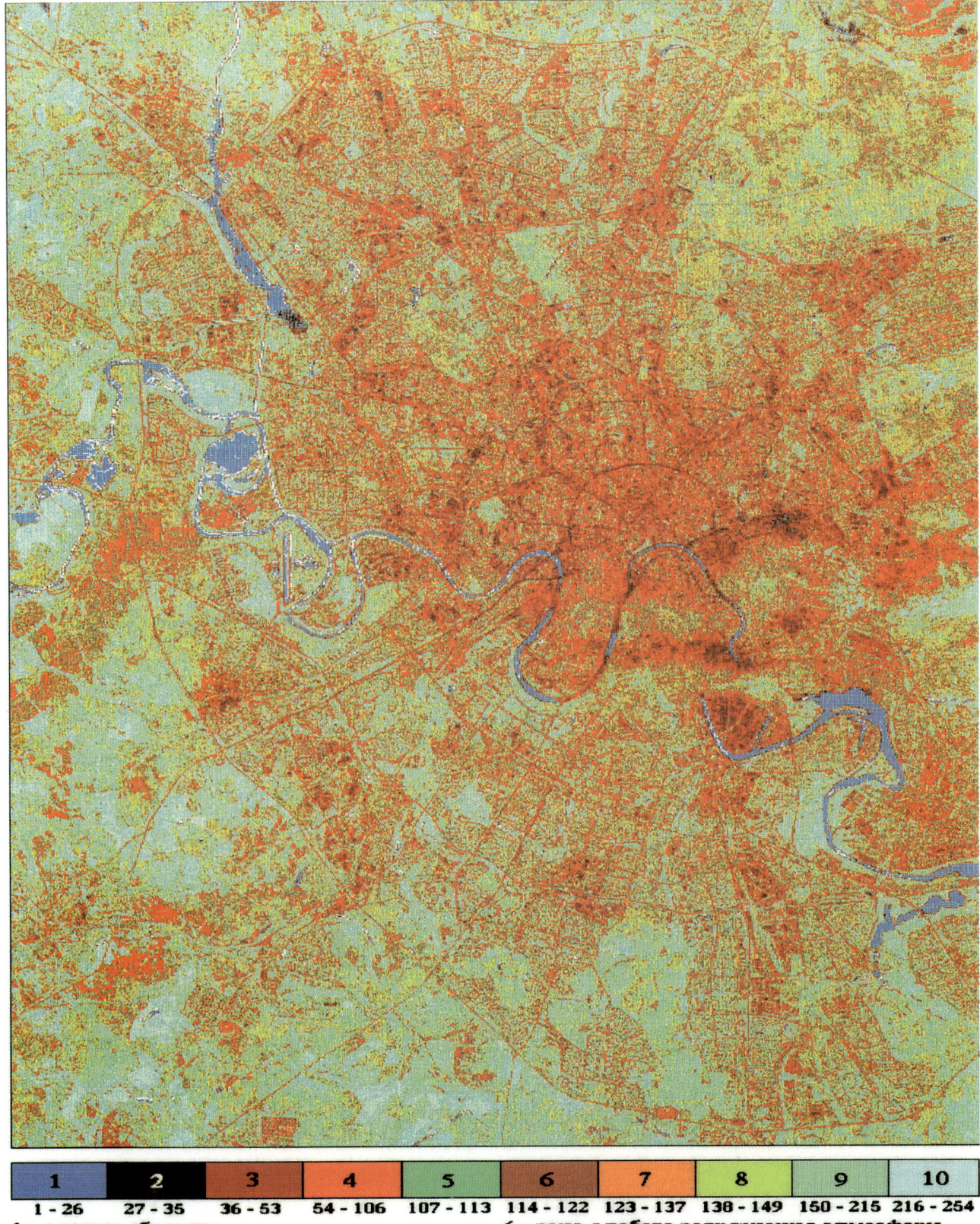

1	2	3	4	5	6	7	8	9	10
1 - 26	27 - 35	36 - 53	54 - 106	107 - 113	114 - 122	123 - 137	138 - 149	150 - 215	216 - 254

1 - водные объекты
2 - участки загрязненной воды
3 - основные источники загрязнения
4 - зона сильного загрязнения атмосферы
5 - зона умеренного загрязнения (зелёные насаждения)
6 - зона слабого загрязнения атмосферы
7 - зеленые массивы со смешанным составом древесной растительности
8 - редколесье, кустарники на открытых незастроенных участках
9 - редколесье, кустарники
10 - травянистые участки

В парковых зонах, таких как Лосиный остров, Сокольники и др., наблюдаются антропогенные изменения состояния лесных экосистем.

Moscow's ecology map pictured from space.

egorize the persisting zones of hazardous pollutions that are known to bear on the prevalent sickness rates.

While conducting the June 1996 space-based survey of Moscow, the IR-sensor imagery was secured in order to get an update on the size of wooded segments. The imagery filtering software was used to engage the spectrum's green segment and thereby reveal the vegetation-covered lands. Then, a sequence of steps was undertaken to generate a synthesized map, with the wooded area being made different from the surrounding spaces by the value of 100 brightness measuring units.

Following the in-depth investigation of the space imagery received, ten categories of areas have been eventually identified. Shown in magenta, blue and yellow-to-orange colors are the areas most vulnerable to varied pollution impacts, with the pollution levels being roughly in sync with the red-to-magenta intensities. The pollution values can be seen plunging as the magenta and red shades change to the dark-green and green colors. The recent chemical research findings on the issue have been proven by the reports beamed from the outer space.

The ecology-status maps for Moscow and its isolated districts contain the information on industrial pollution trails, hazardous aerosols in the atmosphere and their evolution patterns, conditions of the in-town water basins and parks. The space observation reports are now used to track the man-generated pollution effects and support comprehensive studies conducted to help improve the local environment, ameliorate the automobile-pool territories and reduce the hazardous impacts from the heavy-traffic thoroughfares.

1	2	3	4	5	6	7	8	9	10
1 - 26	27 - 35	36 - 63	54 - 106	107 - 113	114 - 122	123 - 137	138 - 149	150 - 215	216 - 254

Эколого-транспортная карта-схема г. Москвы из космоса.

Moscow's traffic-related ecology map seen from space.

CHAPTER THREE

Architectural Invitation to the 21st Century

The foundation-stone of the first stage in the construction of the «Moscow City» Complex

The model of the «Moscow City» Business Centre

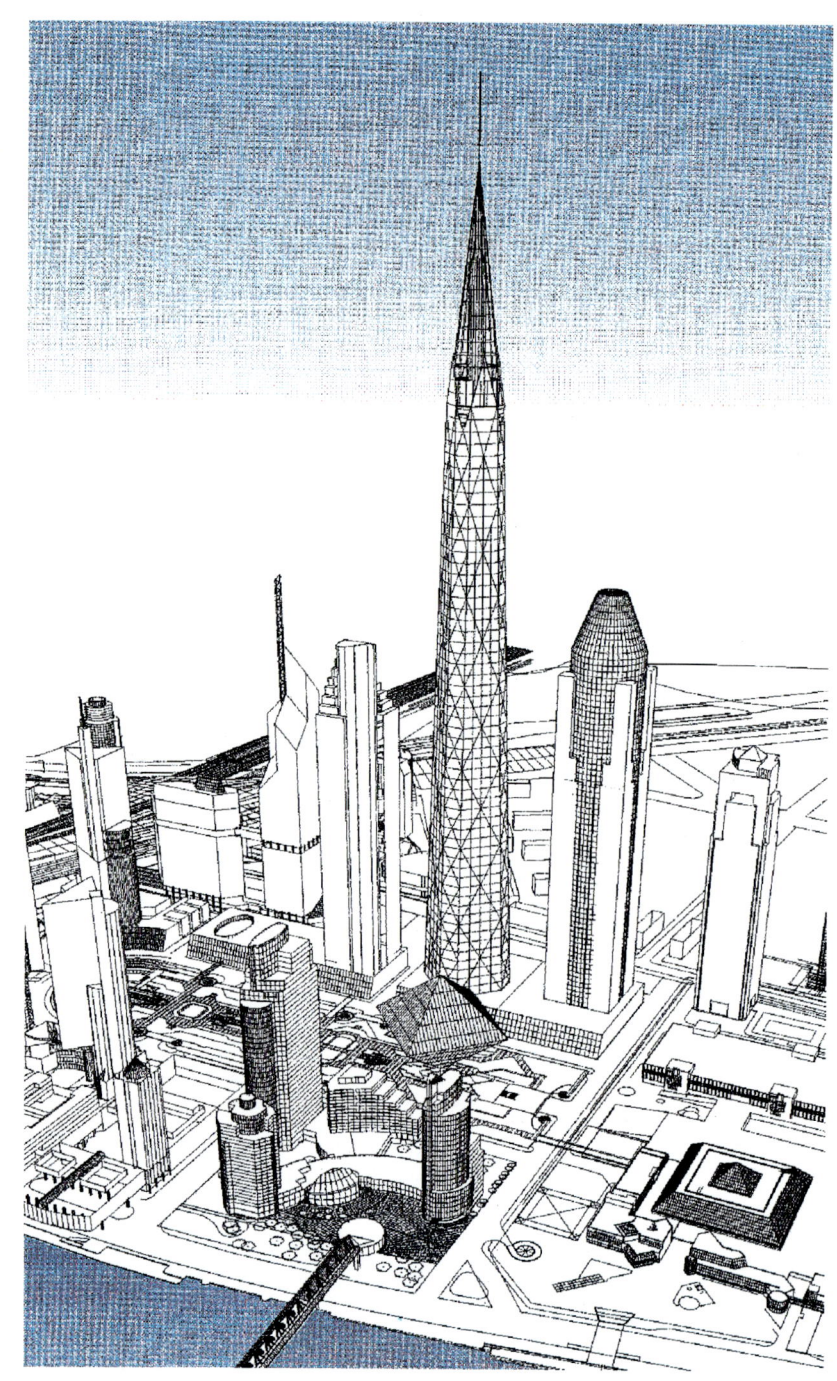

The concept of the «Moscow City» Business Centre on Krasnaya Presnya by architects
B. Tkhor, G. Sirota, S. Ghusaryov, O. Dubrovsky, T. Frolova, I. Raitburg and engineer V. Philin.

The design of community/business centre in the vicinity of «Yugo-Zapadnaya» subway station by architects V. Kuzmin, L. Pavlov, V. Prokhorov,
V. Krasnoshchokov and engineers E. Briling, V. Doshchinsky, V. Fadeyev, L. Grigoryevskaya, E. Krimova.

Downtown Moscow in the 21st Century

Nowadays there are good reasons to think of the further development of Moscow in general and its historic centre in particular. Among these reasons are the approaching significant date of the city's 850th anniversary and the coming end of the 20th century, now going down in history and carrying away many romantic illusions which have turned out to be deceptive. And finally they are the social-economic realities still new to us, which require a deeper comprehension of the city's philosophy and definition of modern laws of the environment as well as finding out the principles of future professional activities.

It is known that Moscow's centuries-long development has not been spontaneous. Its ancient plans already prove the fact that from the very beginning, nearly since the city's foundation, the town-building process has been subject to the most strict discipline and severe logic of the first settlement. This settlement has been basically preserved up to now. It has become the historical core of the present-day capital. Fortifications along the town boundaries provided external protection for its residents. As for the inside of the settlement, the shortest and most effective routes of communication were created to connect the main parts of the town – its administrative, commercial and residential quarters. Every patch of land was valued and therefore very densely built over. But the unique natural landscape that had initially determined the site for the foundation of the town, appreciably affected the formation of Moscow's picturesque image even in those ancient times.

Every epoch has left its noticeable trace, adding something new and vitally significant to the city's planning composition. For instance, the city-planning concept that Peter I attempted to implement in Moscow in the 17th and 18th centuries, has reached our days. The concept consisted in creating another metropolitan and government centre, comfortably positioned on the banks of the Yauza River. Palaces and administrative buildings appeared there as well as estates and a beautiful regular park with a cascade of ponds, fountains, sculptures, grottoes, pavilions, flower-beds and parterres. For more than a hundred years the Moscow Imperial residence was situated in this particular neighbourhood. However, the territory did not subsequently retain its special metropolitan status.

The long-term city development plans envisage successive continuation of the considerable historico-cultural, architectural and town-planning potential of this district. A project for its revival has been designed by the «Mosproyekt-2» Department.

But the true centre of Moscow has always been and continues to be the Kremlin around which the city structure has been gradually taking shape. Everything created by the generations of talented Russian and foreign architects and town-planners, expressed the capital's peculiar aspect, which in its turn reflected various phases of history, the change of social and economic structures and the evolution of architectural styles.

By analysing ancient engravings picturing views of Moscow, one can trace the way expressive architectural ensembles and monuments were gradually erected, cathedrals, estates and mansions were built, theatres, rows of stalls, stations, bridges and embankments were constructed, boulevards and parks appeared.

As far as the city-planning aspects of Moscow's development are concerned, it should be noted that since the edict «About working out a plan of Moscow» was issued in 1732, geodesic city-building and city-planning projects have been regularly drawn up and appropriate adjusting regulations have been periodically elaborated. The planning structure reflecting development of progressive ideas of the Russian town-building has also been constantly improved. For example, an edict was issued in 1742 «About building houses in Moscow according to plans and observing the fixed width of 8 sazhens (about 19 yd) for streets and 4 sazhens (about 9 yd) for lanes». Another edict «About preventing further construction of buildings on Moscow squares and demolishing previously built structures» was made in 1753. In 1762 a Construction Committee was established which worked on a new city reconstruction project. For the first time the project provided for building a circular system of streets in addition to the radial system which already existed. This was to be achieved by demolishing the White Town's fortress walls and creating a Boulevard Ring. The project also envisaged construction of a drainage canal with a river harbor in its eastern part. The canal still exists nowadays. The so-called post-fire project drawn up by the same Construction Committee and dated by the years 1813 – 1818 was of tremendous significance to Moscow. According to that project works were conducted on the construction of a circular boulevard in place of the former Earth Bank as well as the foundation of the squares Kaluzhskaya, Serpukhovskaya, Krasniye Vorota, Devichye Pole and a number of others, still existing at present. It was at that particular time that many large architectural ensembles were formed, such as Teatralnaya Square with the Bolshoy Theatre, the Manege, the building of the Moscow State University and others, which forever determined the peculiar character of the city's historical centre.

The construction of the first Russian railroad in 1851 which connected the Empire's two capitals, became an important factor that stimulated Moscow's further growth and formation. Since Moscow was the hub of the Russian railway system where all the trunk lines converged, the subsequent erection of Peterburgsky, Yaroslavsky, Ryazansky, Nizhegorodsky, Brestsky and Bryansky railway stations was also of great significance. By the end of the previous century Moscow turned into the greatest business, commercial, industrial and transportation centre in Russia, its population reaching 1 mln people. 15 years later it had more than 2 mln residents.

Moscow's development at the end of the century was not so much connected with working out a regular plan as with creating a system of city-building hubs to be used as starting points for building new quarters or reconstructing old, historically formed districts. By that time the unique aspect of the City of Moscow, Kitay-Gorod, took its shape. Kitay-Gorod housed numerous banks, wholesale stores, offices, trading houses, merchants' inns and restaurants, administrative quarters of firms and insurance companies. At the same time communication lines between the stations and Kitay-Gorod (Myasnitskaya, 1st Meshchanskaya, Novoslobodskaya, Tverskaya, Arbat, Vozdvizhenka, Pyatnitskaya streets) were being formed and newly built over. The new aspect of Moscow's downtown area and its main facade at the end of the 19th century were formed by the ensembles and panoramas which could be well observed not only traditionally from the riverside but when approached from the stations, too. The Cathedral of the Redeemer, built not far from the Kremlin, organically joined the historically formed system of Moscow architectural structures. Its massive bulk as well as the bulks of the Kremlin, the Pokrov and Kazan Cathedrals, seemed to attract the surrounding buildings and first of all the huge building of the Foundling Hospital, symmetrically positioned to the right of the Kremlin walls. The construction of the Cathedral of the Redeemer (designed by K. Ton) introduced decisive changes into the nature and scale of the historic centre. It gave a new tinge to the existing systems of verticals and Moscow's silhouette. New accents were added in a number of cases which

The model of community/business centre near «Yugo-Zapadnaya» subway station

increased the monumentality of the previously built structures. The bell towers that appeared along the banks of the river raised its significance in the city's ensemble, underlining the picturesque nature of the surrounding views. The ensemble of Red Square was gradually being formed, which included the Historical Museum, the Upper and Medium rows of stalls and the building of the Municipal Duma. The administrative/commercial complexes in Tretyakovsky Passage, Business and Boyar Yards, the building of the Northern Insurance Society and the Polytechnic Museum were constructed and the main semicircle of squares of the Moscow Centre was thus created, which fringed the boundaries of Moscow's most ancient nucleus, Kitay-Gorod.

At the end of the century the city's centre experienced one of the most radical changes in its history. An active building process was going on all over the vast territory of the city. The prevailing tendency of that process was to increase the number of storeys and housing density and to merge local construction hubs, thus turning Moscow into a single huge building site. Also, the construction of certain definite buildings was not so often inspired by the city administration as by private individuals, not only businessmen but philanthropists and patrons of arts, too. A great number of theatres, museums, art galleries and hospitals big enough to occupy entire blocks appeared in Moscow at that time. Multistorey tenement buildings became essential housing elements.

At the turn of the 20th century Moscow presented an impressive view of a city being rapidly urbanized. More than 3,000 five- to seven-storey buildings were constructed within a short period of the year 1911. Present-day Moscow still enjoys the social, technical and transport infrastructure created at the time of the formation of the Russian capital. All the railroads and stations including the 34 miles long inner circular line with 15 depots and four bridges across the Moskva River, streetcar tracks, water and electricity supply lines, as well as the sewerage, lighting and telephone communications systems, many of which are still in use today, were constructed at the beginning of the century.

The foresight of our predecessors, the scope of their projects and their ability to implement numerous city-building programmes in such spheres as education, medicine, technology, transport and others cannot but deserve high esteem. Thorough analysis of the social-economic machinery of that time as well as a deep research into Moscow's traditionally formed city-building standards and regulations are needed to ensure continuity of their application to present-day conditions. Knowledge of the city-building and planning laws of formation of Moscow's historical urban environment will help avoiding gross mistakes while carrying out construction and reconstruction work in the city.

In March 1918, following a bicentennial interval, Moscow again became the capital of Russia which gave an additional powerful impulse to the development of the city. It was in the 20s that the first socially oriented general plans of Moscow already appeared. In those plans special attention was paid to the development of the city centre. Therefore, process of their implementation, though having some positive results, generally caused considerable disturbance to its unique historical aspect. The reconstruction of society was to be symbolically expressed in huge prestigious structures and wide metropolitan avenues. It required destruction of everything that embodied the dark aspects of the capitalist past. The first highly symbolic step in that reconstruction consisted in moving workers from factory barracks to large apartments of the rental buildings situated downtown. This led to extreme overpopulation of the downtown quarters, moved the workers farther away from their jobs and, above all, produced an excessive number of communal apartments which turned into one of the city's worst social evils. For eighty years now, shared apartments have remained a complicated problem of the most prestigious central part of the city.

The city-building concept of the 30s, inspired with the belief in the omnipotence of technological progress, became the basis of the general plan of Moscow devised in 1935. However, the desire to achieve an ideal scheme and improve the established city structure led to irreversible losses of the historical legacy. The ten-year plan

New Arbat, viewed from Novinsky Boulevard.
The design of Arbatsky Boulevard
by architects M. Posokhin, G. Kalashnikov, E. Kerbel, N. Plekhanov.

of Moscow's reconstruction in 1951 – 1960 facilitated building up the territory outside the old city boundaries, along the main trunk lines. A significant event of that period was the erection of high-rises which consolidated in a picturesque manner the radial/circular structure of the city plan and defined the city's new expressive silhouette. The overall plan adopted in 1971 became an important city-building document that determined the general strategy of the city's development with due regard for the solution of social, economic, engineering, technical, environmental and other problems. It revived the idea of a regular radial/circular plan which took exaggerated shape owing to the construction of a circular motor way. The star-like symmetry of the city centre continued the geometrical concept which was entering into obvious disagreement with the size of the territory being developed. The inertia of natural progress could not be restricted by conditional boundaries and adjusted to the traditional radial-circular scheme. A few years later Moscow overstepped the circle outlined by the general plan. Greater Moscow's future design must obviously envisage expedient city-building on the entire territory of the forest-park concentric zone, stretching for 6 to 9 miles outside the present-day city border, as well as its regular utilization.

The memorable 50s, 60s and 70s witnessed the construction in Moscow of tremendous architectural ensembles, huge buildings and structures which proclaimed new styles and largely formed Moscow's new panorama. Among those structures were the University on the Lenin Hills, the Central Stadium in Luzhniky, the Kremlin Palace of Congresses, Kalinin Avenue, the Rossiya Hotel, the building of the Council for Mutual Economic Aid, the House of the Council of Ministers of Russia, the Olympic constructions and a great many others.

The active implementation of the housing programme as a primary objective brought considerable excess to the 1971 general plan estimates: number of Moscow residents reached 9 mln people and the total figure, including population of the nearest adjoining towns, exceeded 11 or 12 mln. So, much land, specially reserved for greenery and infrastructural development, was wasted in the process. Ineffective use of the territory for industrial construction considerably worsened the ecological situation within the city. The planned withdrawal of unhealthy and irrelevant industrial enterprises was not executed. On the contrary, the need to retain the production potential caused a time-lagging increase by 20 per cent in the number of workers with the employment of manpower from other regions. In the 70s, the problem of the city's transport infrastructure became considerably aggravated. However, the one-sided approach to the city reconstruction still practised nowadays, which attaches primary importance to the problem of transport communication routes, seems to be erroneous, as they are streets, not blocks and living quarters, that acquire decisive significance in this case.

**New Arbat, viewed in front of the Kremlin.
The design of Arbatsky Boulevard
by architects M. Posokhin, G. Kalashnikov, E. Kerbel, N. Plekhanov.**

The separate street system designs proposed by the Moscow Research and Planning Institute of the Genplan Department are not linked to the plan's other sections. Those designs solve the problem of improving communication routes to the prejudice of the established city environment. Besides, there is obvious lack of balance in the availability of all city service facilities. This refers both to outlying living quarters and to the downtown and medium sections of Moscow, too. Attempts to correct this unbalanced city development were made while the general plan was being worked on in the years 1988 – 1992. «The Main Guidelines of the City-Building Development of Moscow and the Moscow Region for the Period till 2010» devised by the Research and Planning Institute of Genplan comprise a great amount of statistics, computations and planning materials for the overall plan's further development. However, there are many serious omissions there as well, which should be paid attention to. First of all, it is the lack of objective, detailed analysis of the actual situation in Moscow and of the reasons for the constant failure to carry out a number of points of the 1971 general plan, which substantially hinders outlining the problems that arose yesterday and that the city is facing today. It also hampers research into various ways of their effective solution. But the main drawback consists in the absence of a clear and reasonable planning concept, a strict city-building policy and a consistent strategy of architectural and spatial development of the picturesque image of Moscow as an entity.

All these omissions were pointed out to the authors in the Moscow Administration's special act of August 6, 1996 «About the Progress in Implementation of the Main Guidelines of the City-Building Development of Moscow City». The act contains instructions to devise the long-awaited package of laws of Moscow on city-building and first of all the law «About the Overall Plan of the Development of Moscow City», which will allow strengthening the legal basis for coordination and effective solution of long-term and primary tasks of the city development and for cooperation in this process of the representative and executive powers as well as authorities of certain specific branches and local government bodies.

As regards the city's downtown area, its development is largely predetermined by «The Detailed Planning Project of the Central Part of Moscow within the Garden Ring» that was devised in the late 80s. Its «Main Guidelines» were approved by the act of the Moscow Administration of September 17, 1991. «The Main Guidelines of the Detailed Planning Project» are a city-planning and regulating document which defines the basic trend and general outlines of the overall reconstruction of the capital's historical centre for the period till the end of the first decade of the 21st century.

One of its most important peculiarities is that it specially singles out the city's historical nucleus in the whole structure of its downtown section and regards that nucleus as an integral city-building formation within the system of the city's other historical parts, as a separate unit of overall reconstruction and regeneration. Also, since the Kremlin and Red Square present the main ensemble of the city's spatial landscape and planning structure whose composition is linked to the system of historical dominants, their retention is treated as the primary task of the centre's reconstruction. The main components of the approach, metropolitan planning establishments dealing with the overall reconstruction of the central Moscow apply to their work today, are: successive development of city-building principles, architectural and artistic traditions, assistance to the growth of the historical and cultural potential and city-forming significance of separate pieces of architecture and the historical city environment as well as their proper utilization. The top priority tasks now are reconstruction, renewal and renovation of the centuries-old buildings, while new construction is conducted by mastering methods of environmental planning. The organizing structures that control and coordinate city-building and planning activities, are being drastically reformed.

Development of the established city centre's spatial landscape system includes reconstruction of the historical environment, creation of new community complexes as well as planting greenery and carrying out general improvement on the territories adjoining the embankments of the Moskva and the Yauza Rivers and the Drainage Canal. The primary reconstruction envisages:

– city-building regeneration of the main freeways, historical streets and lanes within the area of the historical centre's nucleus;

– reconstruction of squares surrounding the Kremlin and Kitay-Gorod; retention by Kitay-Gorod of its long-established cultural, commercial and business functions with active development of educational museum establishments and recreation/catering complexes, especially in the neighbourhood of Nikolskaya Street which will become a pedestrian precinct;

– formation of squares (Triumphalnaya, of Kursky Station, Taganskaya, of Paveletsky Station, Serpukhovskaya, Sukharevskaya and others) along the Boulevard and Garden Rings, including the construction of a system of large community and commercial/business centres. The most important city-building and artistic problem is thus solved, which is the completion of the city historical centre's system of ensembles. The city-building renewal of areas with highly valued historical environment and dense concentration of pieces of architecture will favour reanimation of their former functional activity for the benefit of residents and visitors of the centre, their inclusion into the city centre's system and improvement of artistic and aesthetic qualities of the city's historical nucleus.

And qualities like compatibility of scales, close coordination between new buildings and existing rarities and observing the proper number of storeys within the general building composition of central streets should be considered the main architectural principle of this work.

Only in the past few years, the elaboration of reconstruction drafts for mini-districts within the Garden Ring exposed 500 structures liable to immediate construction and reconstruction, which were later included into the Moscow Administration's complex

The design of Arbatsky Boulevard.

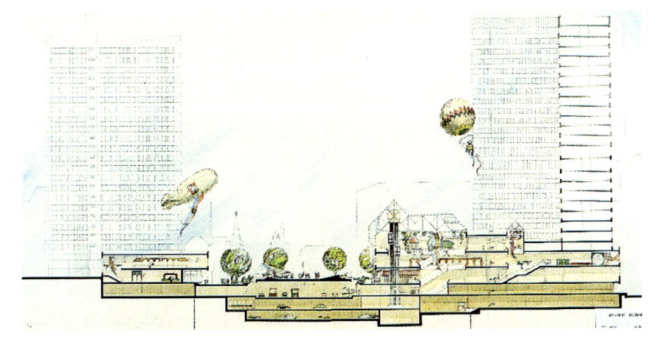

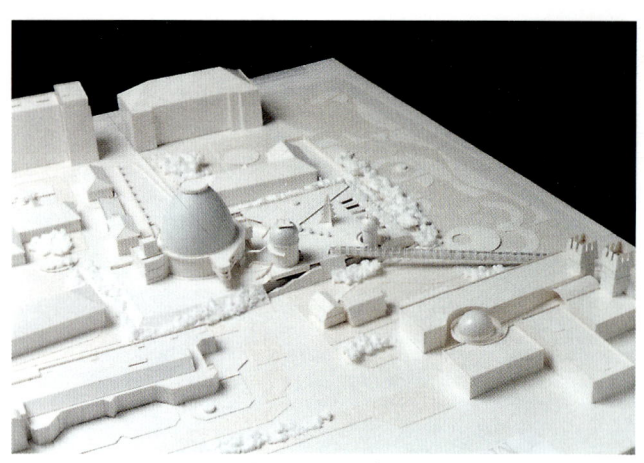

Reconstruction design of the Moscow Planetarium.

acts. The number of realized drafts, specifically aimed city-building programmes and proposals from planning establishments is constantly growing, which facilitates creation of a favourable investment climate, actual positive changes in the city centre's appearance and decoration of the Moscow streets and lanes.

The following main trends can be pointed out in this respect:

– revival of sacred places, such as cathedrals and monasteries, re-creation of gone cathedrals (Cathedral of the Kazan Virgin on Red Square and the Cathedral of the Redeemer could serve as examples);

– restitution of lost qualities to the unique structures of the metropolitan centre (the renewal and reconstruction of the Bolshoy and Maly Theatres, the Petrovsky Mall, the Metropole, the Savoy and the National Hotels could be pointed out as examples);

– resumption of small-scale construction, since it has been mastered, for building numerous commercial establishments, meant for service and business purposes.

An important social objective both for the centre and for the city as a whole is the elimination of communal housing and providing a separate apartment for every family, apartments downtown to be given preferably to native Muscovites. The success of the reconstruction is closely linked to the implementation of the proposals concerning the withdrawal of a number of manufacturing enterprises not functionally connected with the centre. The Central Administrative District is suggested to be cleared of a total of more than 300 industrial enterprises, separate workshops and scientific organizations, which will make it possible to free in excess of 268 acres of the city land to be used for housing construction and building service esablishments. The withdrawal is hampered by the fact that many enterprises turn into joint-stock companies and privatize their basic funds, the compensation for which is sometimes too meaningful for the investors.

The development of the system of cultural and educational functions in a city scale must be based on the previously built complexes and structures, situated in the Kremlin, Kitay-Gorod, in main avenues, streets and boulevards, with active utilization of various pieces of architecture and the established environment in such historical neighbourhoods as the Kadashevskaya Housing Estate, the Ivanovskaya Hill and Zayauzye. We have come to understand the necessity of consolidation and development of traditional shopping streets for the sake of forming an extensive system of overall service rendered to residents and visitors of the downtown area, with the largest shopping centres, such as the «Detsky Mir» Children's Department Store, the «GUM» State Department Store and the «TSUM» Central Department Store, to be turned into shopping/exhibitional and recreation complexes. Priority will be given to the development of specialized and multifunctional centres of culture and service, including recreation and educational establishments.

The downtown housing construction totaling 700,000 – 950,000 square yards, with the existing housing resources stabilized, will, by estimate, bring the total available housing to 6,300,000 – 6,500,000 square yards of overall dwelling space. Large-scale major reconstruction of the old housing, including floor-replacement and replanning apartments for separate family dwelling, will provide comfortable, up-to-date life conditions in the reconstructed buildings, totalling 2,600,000 – 3,000,000 square yards of dwelling space. The city's hotel-lodging resources must increase more than twice. The centre's «Detailed Planning Project» envisages priority in the development and improvement of the passenger transport system, including construction of new subway lines, building alternate exits and additional stations on the lines already in operation and introduction of small-size transport facilities to carry out internal transportation of passengers from large transport terminals and parking lots to zones of intensive public activities. Freight traffic is proposed to be barred from the Moskva and Yauza central riverside drives, and in the future from the Garden Ring, too. Building new power substations and reconstruction of outdated ones as well as construction of new city communication routes are planned to provide technical support for the overall reconstruction of the downtown area within the Garden Ring.

The main principles of the functional and planning arrangement of downtown construction and general technical and economic indices, formulated in the «Detailed Planning Project», serve as a basis for further planning stages and for realizing reconstruction draft projects in separate mini-districts to be followed by implementing composite plans both in areas controlled by municipal departments and in the entire area within the Garden Ring. They are needed to bring efficiency and flexibility to the activities of the administrations of the Municipal Department and the Central Administrative District, to facilitate implementation of their social and economic programmes and adjustment of long-term reconstruction and improvement tasks in the sphere of city-building.

In accordance with «The Main Guidelines of the Detailed Planning Project of the Centre» and «The City-Building Concept of the Reconstruction of the Central Administrative District of Moscow», which comprise all the spheres of the city centre's long-term development, specific designs are being devised and implemented concerning the top priority overall reconstruction in such neighbourhoods as Sretenka, Tverskaya, Nikitskaya, Arbat, Bolshaya Yakimanka Streets, Kitay-Gorod, the Kadashevskaya and Ovchinnikovskaya Embankments and in a number of other places.

Bearing in mind Moscow's imperishable legacy, it is necessary to learn the art of creating architectural city-building ensembles, compatible in scale, and to master the skill of working out large planning compositions, which the previous generations had a perfect command of. The large-scale construction work being carried out in downtown Moscow today, such as the re-creation of the Cathedral of the Redeemer, the construction of the community/shopping centre on Manezhnaya, the reconstruction and development of Teatralnaya Square and on a great number of other projects, presents good evidence to the effect that such an urge does exist and is supported by the understanding of how much today is dependent on the architect working in a concrete historical setting, upon his high proficiency, background, feeling of tact and responsibility to the past and the future of the great city.

Like any other city leading an active life and thus having a lot of problems, Moscow does not only require constant improvement of the centuries-old city environment but also new construction and functional transformations of ancient territories. However, strict and detailed regulation is needed of the entire structure of the city life, of each and every possible and impossible action by experts. Any display of violence or chaos, which is another extreme, are inadmissible here. The policy of monitoring and conservation does not prove its value either. Purposeful creative activities are needed so as to combine professional knowledge and experience with cooperation on the part of the population which is indeed concerned about the results. Like any other city, Moscow needs possibilities of self-regulation which do not exclude long-term forecasts in the main basic directions. This

Ceremony of the consecration and laying of a capsule into the concrete basement of the re-created Church of the Redeemer in January 7, 1995.

must be fully realized by the designers drafting the laws «About the General Plan of the Development of Moscow City», «About the Basic Principles of City-Building in Moscow City», «About Dividing the Territory of Moscow into City-Building Zones» and the like, which are to serve as a legal basis for acts of the law and documents to regulate Moscow's development and city-building in the coming decades.

Now as never before, Moscow which is nearing the turn of the new millennium, needs daring and inspiring ideas reaching out towards the far future. Here is a good example of what happens when there are none. The greatest building projects being implemented in downtown Moscow at the present time, such as the re-creation of Cathedral of the Redeemer, construction of the underground shopping/recreation centre on Manezhnaya Square, reconstruction and development of Teatralnaya Square and a number of others were not provided for by Moscow's previous general plan, while the appearance of such huge structures does disturb the usual scene, drastically change the smart looks of the city and require considerable changes in the entire surrounding infrastructure. While looking forward to the future, we probably do not have to deny the previous findings. For instance, why not return to the proposals made by the experts of the «Mosproyekt-2» Department, such as the creation of a single city-building ensemble to include Cathedral of the Redeemer, the Kremlin and the Foundling Hospital as the future complex of the Parliament Centre of the Russian Federation. According to the authors' design, the formation of such an ensemble within the city's historical nucleus would embrace the integral city-building space of the Cathedral being re-created to revive the people's spirituality, of the Kremlin to symbolize state power, of the Rossiya Hotel complex and the building of the Imperial Foundling Hospital to stand for the 18th century's humanistic ideas, which would turn into a Parliament centre with all the necessary conference halls and utility rooms totalling 155,000 square yards.

Compositional integrity and coordination with the Kremlin ensemble are also characteristic features of the ancient building pattern in Zamoskvorechye, where development of tourist and cultural functions, as well as those of recreation and communication of people of similar interests is planned for the future.

Some interesting proposals have been worked out for the Lefortovo neighbourhood. For a long time now, its appearance has been determined by complexes of historical buildings. Thus, the tremendous building of Catherine's Palace, created by architect Rinaldi, as well as the park adjoining the Yauza River, both occupy a key position and compositionally dominate over the whole architectural planning structure of the surrounding building pattern. Bearing in mind the location in this neighbourhood of several large technical engineering educational and planning institutes, authors of the design suggest that the Russian Academy of Technical Engineering Sciences be positioned in the palace and a national scientific, educational and cultural centre be thus created. The value of the Lefortovo Palace Complex from the point of view of city-building reaches far beyond the scope of the park itself and refers to the vast areas adjoining the Yauza River's both banks. The thorough historical and city-building examination of this territory and the adjoining quarters permitted making proposals concerning social and functional renewal of the Lefortovo palace/park ensemble, its transport service and environmental protection. Complete restoration of the imperial palaces and the park and charging them with renovated metro-

Re-creation of the Cathedral of the Redeemer. Summer of 1996.
Architects M. Posokhin, A. Denisov and others.

Interior of the Cathedral of the Redeemer.
Watercolour by K. Ukhtomsky, the 19th century.

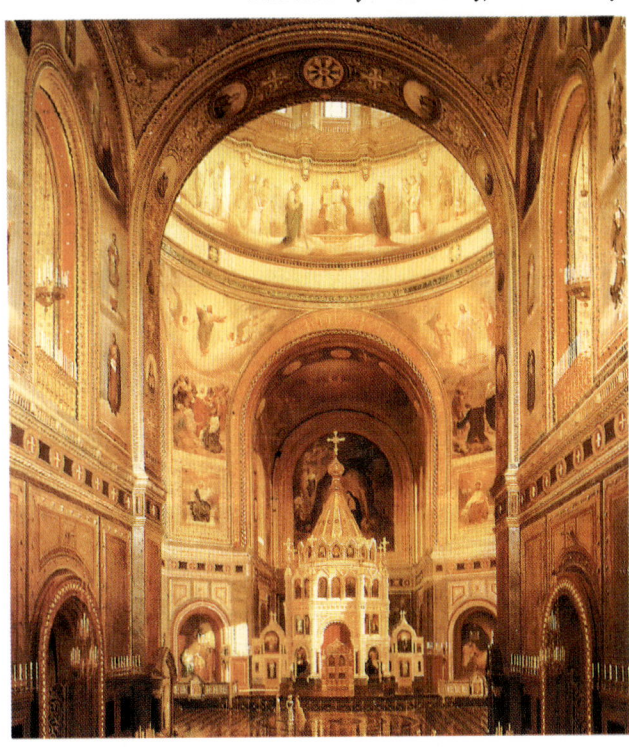

politan functions in the coming years will become a city-scale objective of national importance as one of Moscow's high priority programmes.

Architects and city-builders devising projects specifically meant for the city centre must anticipate the far future and use it to check their decisions. They must be able to manipulate not only the category of space but of time, too. For instance, the project of creating a pedestrian boulevard in place of present-day New Arbat Freeway, yet unclaimed, seems to be obviously advantageous. It envisages creation of a vast green zone with walkways, cascades of fountains, shopping places and all sorts of entertainment. The stream of noisy city traffic will be driven underground, with the freeway lowered a few yards below the surface and multilevel parking lots and bus stops positioned under the carriage-way, which will considerably reduce the density of the traffic and pedestrian flows in one of the busiest downtown sections. This design has received approval from Moscow's Mayor U. M. Luzhkov and acknowledgement to the effect that the implementation of such a concept as well as active utilization of multilevel underground space below Tverskaya Street, Taganskaya and Kudrinskaya Squares will be most effective both in the solution of long-pending transport and environmental problems and in the creation of a unique natural atmosphere, reasonable from the artistic point of view, in the very centre of Moscow. Future construction of a system of boulevards along the Garden Ring is also planned, similar to those which existed here a long time ago.

It is becoming evident nowadays that many realized proposals of Moscow's previous general plans are rejected by the living organism of the ancient city. For instance, two huge bridges across the Moskva River, Moskvoretsky Bridge and Bolshoy Ustyinsky Bridge, do not actually participate in the city's dynamic life. The intensive traffic flow near the Kremlin walls and the unique value of the city environment have come into obvious conflict here. Experts are in search of the most effective solution to the problem, such as turning Moskvoretsky Bridge into a pedestrian one to link up Red Square and Zamoskvorechye, and lining it with rows of stalls, viewing platforms, cafes and the like. As regards Bolshoy Ustyinsky Bridge, it will be of greater use if a free passage through Novokuznetskaya Street is accomplished to open the way to the Boulevard Ring from the southern part of the city, along Dubininskaya Street.

The centre's environmental programme will include rehabilitation of the Moskva River and the Drainage Canal. The creation of an integral pedestrian system to link up the Boulevard Ring, the Cathedral of the Redeemer, the Island, the Canal's pedestrian embankments, Moskvoretsky Bridge, Red Square and the Russian Community Centre being built on Shlyuzovaya embankment as well as the launching within this system of many entertainment, shopping and recreation enterprises will considerably enlarge the Moscow centre's resources in the sphere of tourism and recreation.

While building new pieces of architecture and developing the city structure, certain attention must be paid to the historically established natural landscape and the environmental problems. The state of the city vegetation has long been arousing concern. And it is not just a matter of decoration. Plants serve as the city's lungs and what the centre really needs is not separate trees but tracts of greenery, shadowy boulevards, parks and gardens which have been largely lost now. A proper combination of nature and architecture must be found by means of careful restoration of fragments of the remaining natural landscapes. The development of a concept of Moscow's architectural and artistic aspect will facilitate the process of forming a comfortable atmosphere compatible with human nature, including colour patterns of facades, advertizing, street design, arrangement of recreation pedestrian zones and improvement of industrial territories.

The time has come for thorough ascertainment and active development of the available reserves within the city and its centre, which means efficient correction of the existing city-building documents, and for intensive search for architectural, planning, artistic and image-bearing decisions that 21st century Moscow deserves.

Revival of the Brattsevo Estate

One of the primary objectives of the revival project for the estate Brattsevo is to perform a number of working operations aimed at preserving and renewing that unique natural and architectural complex. And re-creation of the village of Brattsevo and its historical environment will make it possible to simulate a return to the 18th and 19th centuries and feel the atmosphere that existed around the Cathedral of the Virgin's Shroud.

The ensemble of the estate includes the mansion-house, presenting a piece of architecture of the 18th and the early 19th centuries, the utility buildings of the late 19th century, two habitable park outbuildings, the rotunda-pavilion, the ponds, the bigger and the smaller stone bridges, the water tower, the garden section with a system of ravines and two dwelling houses built in 1954 – 1956.

The mansion situated in the central part of the garden ensemble has been relatively well preserved as it has never been in abeyance. Now it houses the recreation centre of the Theatrical Workers' Union of the Russian Federation. A proposal has been made to clear the building of the lodgings and the public catering unit so as to use it as a house of arts, for holding exhibitions of theatrical costumes and paintings and hosting musical and poetic evenings.

At present the recreation centre can simultaneously house 200 vacationers. To retain this housing capacity it is proposed, on the one hand, to perform reconstruction of the two dwelling buildings constructed in 1954 – 1956 and use them for housing the lodgings and all the utility and service premises necessary to provide comfortable staying and adequate recreation. On the other hand, re-creation of the large habitable park outbuilding, previously lost, to house additional lodgings will allow both making up for the loss of dwelling space in the mansion and compositional completion and arrangement of the front space of the yard. The utility buildings of the late 19th century should be used as administrative premises of the house of arts.

Renewal of the park rotunda will also be performed as well as of the bigger and the smaller stone bridges. Major repairs and reconstruction of the water tower will be executed, which is to be preserved as a background element. The greenhouse will also be restored later on, which will house a winter garden.

The re-creation of the village of Brattsevo will bring back the feeling of human scale. The renewed Cathedral of the Virgin's Shroud and the country houses, being a striking contrast to the surrounding rectilinear building pattern, will be in perfect harmony with the nature of the park. All of this will create a new qualitative level of the environment.

The village complex being restored is situated within the city territory and surrounded by high-rise apartment buildings and a children's hospital. The landscape peculiarities of the area permit no intrusion by massive building structures but require support in the city-building situation. All this has inspired the creation of an integral village complex, not a scattered one. The Cathedral of the Virgin's Shroud will be its centre with the surrounding single-storey houses to underline its beauty and large scale as compared to the high-rises.

The historical materials still preserved in the archives are used to re-create the village's central nucleus, which comprises the Cathedral and the parish buildings that include the houses of the priest, the clergy and the psalm-readers, the Sunday-school and the lodge. The housing estate consists of 64 separately positioned cottages with an area of 120 to 360 square yards each.

A hotel complex will be erected beyond the circular motor way, in the vicinity of the Skhodnya River, to separate the Mitinskaya Municipal Zone from the monument of architecture and as if to accomplish the city-building and planning decision of the garden ensemble. The landscape peculiarities of the river's right bank make it possible to position there a complex of low buildings gradually gaining height up to 13 yards to be level with the tree-tops, with the greatest attention being paid to the field of view opening from the estate to the western slope of the river's flood-lands. Reducing dimensions of the buildings while approaching the river-

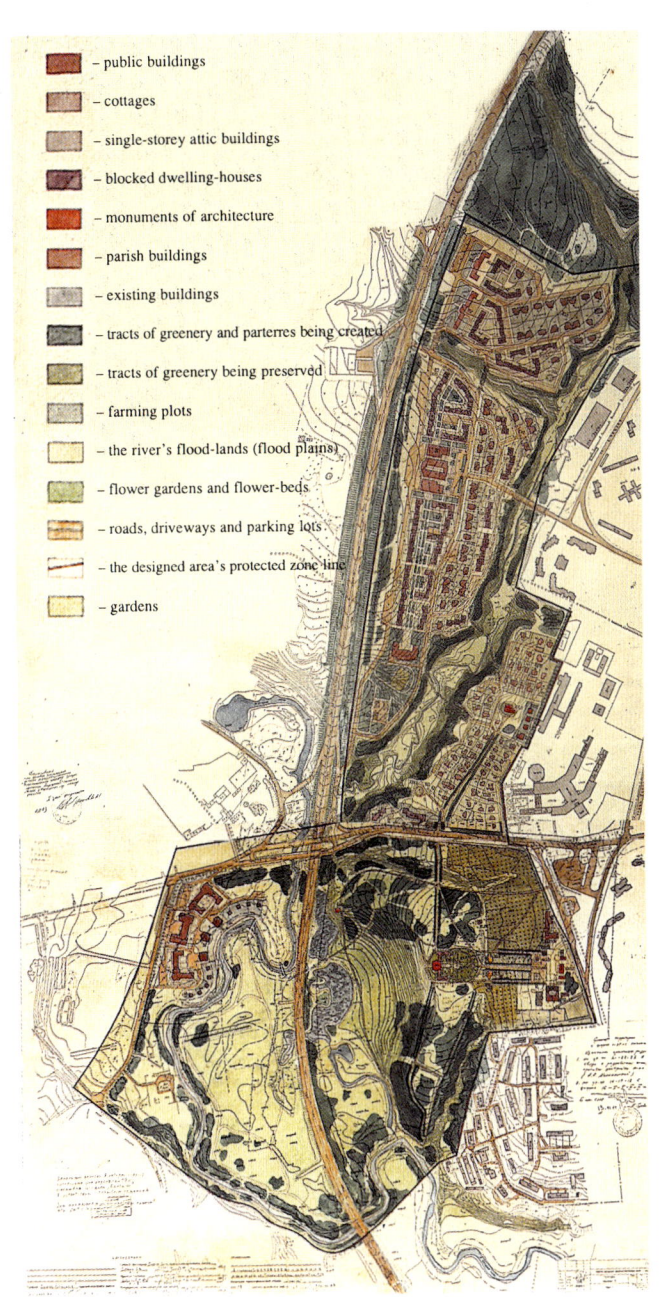

- public buildings
- cottages
- single-storey attic buildings
- blocked dwelling-houses
- monuments of architecture
- parish buildings
- existing buildings
- tracts of greenery and parterres being created
- tracts of greenery being preserved
- farming plots
- the river's flood-lands (flood plains)
- flower gardens and flower-beds
- roads, driveways and parking lots
- the designed area's protected zone line
- gardens

«Brattsevo» Estate in the General Plan.

bed as well as arranging the yard space directed towards the estate and the river's flood-lands, allow an organic accomplishment of the ensemble and make up for possible expenditures on the landscape's regeneration. Specially cleared patches with the best viewing characteristics are provided for the main points to be viewed.

Construction of the hotel complex to house 150 rooms for comfortable staying and fruitful work will also partially make up for the lack of hotel rooms in the Tushinsky District. The complex will comprise: 3 large buildings linked up with viaducts with a variety of service and utilities, 3 isolated buildings with suites as well as single- and double-room cottages down the riverside providing for a long-term independent stay. The small-size housing complex will consist of blocked 2- and 3-storey buildings, 104 of which will be cottages and 127 will be isolated houses.

The area of the new building project is located outside large residential quarters, so the service establishments are situated far enough both from the cottages and from the village and the garden ensemble being restored. They are concentrated in Yan Rainis Boulevard, in V. Latsis and Skhodnenskaya Streets. This brought about the creation of the estate's own infrastructure and a consumer service network including the post office, the telegraph, the laundry reception centre, the medical aid station and the police station.

Construction of a lyceum for 200 students and a kindergarten for 80 children will facilitate solving the problem of children's schooling within the territory of the village, provide their safe movement and meet the normative requirements. The shopping/sports complex which will serve as the village's community centre with all the necessary social institutions, will also be the place of leisure and recreation.

Such a complex of low buildings is a kind of dwelling different in quality, form and content, which makes it possible to combine the normative environmental and aesthetic requirements applied to modern dwelling in an urbanized overpopulated city. Its city-building decision ensures the creation of quiet enclosed space, characteristic of Moscow's 19th century building pattern, with patios and landscape architecture arranged in a laconic way.

One of the top-priority objectives of the project is the restoration of the park, which is to include transplanting some species of trees, planting greenery in wasted areas, clearing the further growth, founding a new orchard, making partial improvements of the ponds, renewing and clearing them, and building dams.

A network of roads and foot-paths will appear within the tract of vegetation down the Skhodnya River and its tributaries (including the flood-lands and valley slopes) after it has been cleared of less valuable species. The improvement of the park will turn it into a recreation zone for the residents of the designed neighbourhood.

Dwelling houses, mainly cottages, will be built in place of the old large gardens. The greenery will be of the farm type, lawns with spots of trees and bushes prevailing. A 33-yard wide sanitary protection zone will appear along the circular motor way.

«Brattsevo» Estate. Its present state and the building project including the renewal of the Cathedral of the Virgin's Shroud, designed by architects I. Voskresensky, A. Kukushkin, V. Babanov, K. Gorodov and N. Shilov.

«Brattsevo» Estate. The building project including renewal of the Cathedral of the Virgin's Shroud.

The system of ponds was situated in the lower section of the park, on the first terrace above the flood-lands of the Skhodnya River. To restore that system it is necessary to carry out improvement of the ponds, renew the main dam, build a new conduit, dam-bridges between the ponds and a spillway dam with an earth dike. Image of the bridge between the first and the second ponds is known from the photographs and watercolours, the other two bridges can be restored by analogy. The boating station is being newly designed. Its position has been chosen so as not to disturb the general composition of the late 18th century pond.

The measures and recommendations proposed by the project will ensure preservation and restoration of the natural environment as well as impart new significance to the monuments of architecture and the art of gardening.

Future of the Inner Circular Railroad Line

Bearing in mind the inevitability of Moscow's development, the City Council, considering the construction of a circular railroad at the end of the previous century, decided on the project of a 51 versts (34 miles) long circle to run a long way from the city so as to preserve the vacant lands as a reserve for the future city expansion.

The construction continued from 1902 to 1908. The main aim of building the Circular Railroad Line was to ensure freight transportation within the city territory with no obstruction of the railway traffic, to provide interception of freights and their distribution in all the radial directions. The installations built along the Line included 4 bridges across the Moskva River and 73 artificial structures: over- and underpasses through all the main entrance roads and railroad lines, «steam locomotive and car sheds», i. e. locomotive depots, water towers, forging shops, dwelling houses for the workers and a telegraph station. The European technical standard of the Circular Line was highly estimated by the foreign press which regarded it as a «railroad phenomenon».

Passengers were transported both with the aim of excursions and sightseeing and for the purpose of taking wealthy people to their country houses, with the fares being relatively high. 16 stations (designed by architect A. N. Pomerantsev) were constructed and equipped with heating and electricity.

At present the 34 miles long Circular Railroad Line ensures passage of freight traffic from 10 radial directions and provides railroad transport for those Moscow enterprises which are somehow tied to it, though the specifications of the bridges across the Moskva River did not allow its electrification and made it necessary to continue the use of diesel traction. The Line has 15 dumping depots including 11 local depots and 3 freight depots. Even with the construction of the Moscow Outer Circular Railroad Line in 1942, running 25 – 30 miles away from Moscow, the Inner Circular Line has been in use up to now passing the largest amount of freights within the Moscow Railroad Junction.

In 1917 the Circular Railroad became the city boundary. The transportation of passengers did not last long. The suburbs moved closer and trips to the country began to involve more distant places. However, in the mid 20s, local construction was of minor character, so the Railroad retained its countrified nature. As it was said in the guidebooks, «stations of the Moscow Circular Railroad were mostly situated in vacant lots and on virgin land».

The «New Moscow» plan did not only outline the prospects of building another dumping junction within a distance of 12 versts (8 miles) of the Circular Railroad but also devised the concept of passenger traffic along the Line and anticipated the appearance of entrance tracks close to the city centre, running through tracts of greenery.

Moscow's general plans contained two main approaches which either stayed at peace or came into conflict, they were city expansion by developing new lands and reconstruction of the existing city structure. The expansion of Moscow's city boundary took place approximately with 25 year-intervals (in 1917, 1935, 1960, 1985), each time the city area to resident ratio became less than 120 square yards per person, which presents evidence of certain stability in understanding the idea of city space.

According to the 1935 General Plan of Moscow's reconstruction, the Circular Railroad turned out to be situated within the city boundary though it retained its out-of-town nature: parks and tracts of greenery were planned in the vicinity to separate the Line from the main bulk of the city.

Development of Moscow's railroad traffic including that of the Circular Railroad Line was encouraged by a belt of industrial enterprises, municipal services and warehouses being shaped alongside, which was also in full conformity with the ideological guidelines that regarded the Railroad as a «red, proletarian» installation. The war intensified industrial development of the area within its zone. In the new conditions, the issue of large-scale passenger traffic on the Circular Railroad was debated in 1943, 1946, 1947, 1949, 1960, 1966, 1983 and 1996.

At present, 90 years after its construction, the Circular Railroad Line, meaning its Inner Circle, is no more located in the outlying part of Moscow, but in its medium section. It divides the city area in the following manner: in the north the medium section is separated from the outlying zone and in the south the medium section is separated from the central historical area. 20 out of the 34 miles of the Railroad are lined with industrial zones, 6 miles are surrounded with residential quarters and an 8 mile-section runs through recreation areas. 13 subway stations turned out to be situated near the Inner Circular Railroad. 4 of the 8 stations of the railroad commuter service are located within a distance of 450 yards of the Line, the other 4 are up to 800 yards away from it.

Since 1959, the Inner Circle has belonged to the Moscow regional branch of the Moscow Railroad Network. It provides transportation service for 160 enterprises, 120 of which are serviced from the depots located along the Circle. The total daily freight turnover exceeds 580 cars (in 1993). All the stations except Cherkizovo and Kozhukhovo are linked to the radial directions with 24 junction lines. Until recently, the Inner Circle executed up to 40 per cent of the total freight transportation, occupying more than 60 per cent of the Moscow railroad junction's territory. However, freight transportation has been considerably reduced lately, and does not exceed 30 per cent of 1980's maximum amount. Even if the volume of production is regained, transportation of freights will not exceed 50 per cent of 1980's amount until the year 2010. The technical condition of the Inner Circle is unsatisfactory. The surrounding area of 40,000 – 48,000 acres with more than 1.2 mln residents, where mainly industrial enterprises are situated with 1.1 mln jobs, has been developed in an extremely extensive and irrational way. The nature of the adjoining neighbourhood is not actually urban, the intensity of its development is 3 – 4 times lower than that of the city as a whole, manufacturing and housing resources are increasingly deteriorating. The lack of service facilities makes this area radically different not only from the downtown quarters but from Moscow's outlying zone, too, where complex districts of modern multistorey buildings have appeared since the 80s.

The Inner Circular Railroad has become sort of a significant demarcation line to divide the city space. The time wasted on movement between two neighbouring districts makes 0.5 – 1 hour. The lack of contact between the districts arising from the Circle's existence brings about the situation when 750,000 residents live in the districts, where contact with industrial areas is somehow complicated, while the industrial areas with up to 500,000 jobs are short of intensive contact with the residential quarters.

Discomfort and unattractiveness of the city atmosphere are aggravated by the deteriorating environmental situation. The appearance of some neighbourhoods, the condition of buildings along the branch lines, the existence of huge single-storey warehouses and garage structures arouse doubts that areas like these belong to the capital.

The zone affected by the Inner Circle comprises 17,500 acres of Moscow's natural complex as well as the territories where monuments of history and culture are located. They are Lossiny Island, a natural park which constitutes Moscow's pride and greatest value, the Botanical Gardens of the Russian Academy of Sciences, Izmailovsky Park, parks of the All-Russian Exhibition (the former Exhibition of National Economic Achievements), Luzhniky, the Vorobyovy Hills, Poklonnaya Hill and Pokrovskoye-Glebovo Park. The Inner Circle zone includes Krutitskoye Coaching Inn, Simonov, Danilov, Donskoy, Andreyevsky and Novodevichy Monasteries, Sviblovo, Izmailovo, Neskuchnoye Estates, Mamonova Country House, Studenets, Pokrovskoye-Streshnevo, Mikhalkovo, Petrovskoye-Razumovskoye, the historical village of Phily and Hodinskoye Field, more than 10 memorial cathedrals.

When big industrial enterprises and warehouses with large freight turnover appeared in abundance around the Inner Circle, certain specific proposals were made by the 1951 General Plan of Moscow and the feasibility study of the 1961 General Plan. Those proposals envisaged creation of 5 circular freeways, with their different purposes to ensure integrity of the whole city. In addition to the Boulevard and the Garden Rings, another three were planned: the third one – Camer-Collezhskoye, the fourth one – Parkovoye – to run mainly along the Inner Circular Railroad, and the fifth one to go through the outlying area of the city.

Transportation was to be carried out mainly along the fourth (Parkovoye) circle (37 per cent). Its name – Parkovoye (having something to do with parks) – originated from its peculiar trace, which was to link up all the greatest parks and forest-parks.

Positioning the freeway along the Inner Circular Railroad and the park zones (outside residential quarters) would have allowed free passage of intensive traffic flows, high concentration of freight traffic, moving nonstop at speeds up to 50 mph, and flyover crossing. Moscow's industrial belt was to obtain a considerable increase in automobile traffic capacity, which was to be regarded as «the most acceptable city-building decision».

Problem of reconstruction of the Inner Circle of the Moscow Railroad Network was attended to in the 90s, when new approaches to the reformation of the city environment appeared as a result of general changes of the situation in the country as a whole. Moscow now is the capital of Russia with the status of a subject of the Russian Federation entitled to its own borders. Primary significance is attached to the stable development of the city, whose resources are limited, within its territorial borders, this development proceeding from a thorough examination of the environmental situation. The city-forming tendencies have also been changed (the concept of Moscow being the centre of socialist industry brought about the construction in the city of such tremendous enterprises as the ZIL, the AZLK, the «Serp i Molot» and a number of other plants). No other European capital can equal Moscow's scope of industrial pollution. Its «red» industrial belt being photographed from space assumes a «black-red» tint, which is the colour of ecological disaster.

With all the elements of the city-building situation changed, Moscow has been faced with the necessity of structural reorganization of its city-forming basis and advanced development of its «third» sector, which comprises management, finances, high technologies, culture and social services, that is development of its metropolitan functions under new conditions.

Newly set or actually brought back are the tasks of restoring the environment humane for man and attractive not only for investors but for residents and visitors of the capital, too, the tasks of creating an ecologically safe city, relatively homogeneous in comfortability but heterogeneous in conditions, an international centre of business, culture, information science, high technologies, of preserving unique objects, nature and landscape art.

Production zones, occupying 16 per cent of Moscow's total area, present the city's special potentiality. Their utilization now is the least effective (being 3 times lower than the advisable standard). The building pattern lacks order and consists of single- and 2-storey houses. The zones are ecologically dangerous and account for 40 per cent of the total pollution of the environment.

Industrial zones of Moscow's so-called medium section also bear certain significance for the city. They possess developed infrastructure but have a high degree of capital consumption and an extremely unfavourable state of the environment. They were formed mainly during the first half of the 20th century and their livelihood has been ensured by the Inner Circle of the Moscow Railroad Network. The adjoining areas present a frozen mixture of freight depots, stational workshops, former workmen's settlements and blocks. The residential quarters are badly in need of reconstruction and lack social infrastructure.

The long existence of the Inner Circle and its original position in the outskirts around Moscow, largely vacant at the beginning of the 20th century, gave it the actual status of a certain ecological boundary. Running from the south through the Moskva River's flood-lands, the Circle outlined a certain natural unity of the central part of the Moskva's valley with the northern section of the territory between the Moskva and the Yauza Rivers. The intensively developing historical centre and as intensively developing outlying areas are separated by another zone along the Inner Circle, different in quality, which is marked with sources of air and geochemical pollution. The Circle singled out the lowest part of present-day Moscow with the worst condition of all the other city districts. Minor rivers along the Circle are tunnelled, the lands excluded from the ecosystem as well as those occupied by pollution sources make close to 95 per cent, with only 5 per cent of the territory possessing average reproducing functions.

Such an effective boundary as the Inner Circle with its present-day utilization, being surrounded by large industrial and production zones, increasingly affects the inward, central areas where even small vacant lots, including those of the natural complex, are densely built over. On the other hand, the withdrawal into the outlying belt of the business, scientific and other centres of city-wide significance is being hampered and the inner sections of the city forest-parks are being reduced. The social-economic field of the city environment, as far as transport, information, management, infrastructural, public, business, social, cultural and other ties are concerned, has outgrown the boundary marked by the Inner Circle of the Moscow Railroad Network.

Concepts of the Inner Circle's operation within the future city structure are determined by the urgent needs of the capital and by what it is expedient to utilize or destroy at this hard time.

To keep the Inner Circle for further performance of freight transportation, including that of transit nature, pending the end of the industrial paralysis, when the freight traffic intensity regains its pre-perestroika level, actually means to preserve for a long period of time the inactive branch lines and the extensive way of industrial construction allowing only pre-perestroika technologies, trends and objectives as well as certain definite manufacturing quality typical of any average industrial centre. To ensure transit freight transportation, reconstruction and additional construction are needed of the Moscow Outer Circle running through the territory of the Moscow region and serving the purpose of freight interception outside the capital.

Arranging passenger traffic in addition to freight transportation, due to its reduction, creates prospects for the establishment in Moscow of an additional circular communication route. But riding commuter trains within the city territory, which is a habit with suburban residents, is quite uncomfortable for Muscovites who are used to the subway. Creation of so-called agglomeration centres at the circular/commuter transfer junctions would favour concentration of shopping and service functions, thus clearing the area of the historical centre, however their suburban nature would still be retained. Commuter inconveniences, difficult approaches to stations, long time-intervals typical of commuter railroads are unattractive and not comfortable enough as a way of getting around Moscow.

A highway along the Inner Circle specially aimed at the distribution of freights among consumers, actually avoiding the centres of built-up neighbourhoods, would more likely be able to encourage creation of new terminals and gas stations without attracting investments from the «third» sector.

With the lack of circular communications in Moscow taken into account, one cannot but appreciate the Inner Circle as the city's unique potentiality. Its transformation into a freeway including total dismantlement of the tracking, withdrawal of loading and dumping facilities and rearrangement of freight depots will bring about a 10 per cent increase in automobile transportation.

This option is the most attractive from the point of view of the city environment. The circular freeway would link together the forming centres on Gagarin Square, in Luzhniky, near Kiyevsky Station, the Moscow City International Centre, the Krasnopresnensky Centre, the new Vladikino Centre and the All-Russian Exhibition Centre.

The western section of the Inner Circle will obtain functions of a metropolitan city centre, the northern part will become a significant recreation/tourist link-up (stretching down the Likhoborka River, the Botanical Gardens of the Russian Academy of Sciences, the territory of the All-Russian Exhibition Centre, across the Yauza River and Losiny Island and along Izmailovsky Park). The southeastern section of the Circle will largely retain its industrial and business functions and may be supplemented with business and community centres.

Formation of an adequate city environment along the new circular freeway will intensify utilization of the adjoining territories. Vacant lots, idle spots and lands sparsely built over can be used to position enterprises and establishments withdrawn from the historical centre, including automobile transportation enterprises from the well organized expensive areas. The circular freeway following the outlying belt's boundary will attract business and public establishments. The total number of jobs will grow 1.5 – 2 times, but those will be highly qualified and well paid jobs.

Boulevards and pedestrian zones can be constructed over underground sections of the freeway. Bridges are expedient on road embankment sections, with the space underneath used for transfer junctions, shopping centres and multilevel parking lots. In the future, surface sections of the freeway can be driven underground, too, thus creating conditions for safe utilization of the city territory.

The reconstruction of the Inner Circle is a matter of long time, still it is an urgent necessity. The city can acquire a true Parkovoye (park) circle, a circle of wonderful centres, of the Moskva River scope and forest-parks.

Naturally, implementation of this project is only possible by stages. At present, it is expedient to «break» the Inner Circle, preserving those of its sections which are linked with the operation of the most significant enterprises, but excluding freight transit. Existing radial railroad entrances will be terminated at those sections.

The advantage of a detached railroad, possessed by the Inner Circle, can be realized by using it for construction of a surface Metro with further creation of multilevel transfer junctions. Liable to the termination of railroad traffic in the first place may be the Kanatchikovo – Smolenskaya section, which accords with the forming trend of the city centre's expansion.

Reconstruction of the Inner Circle's northern section, adjoining the Likhoborka River, is of special significance. It must be part of the measures aimed at the rehabilitation of the river and the area of the surrounding natural complex. Particular caution should be exercised during the reconstruction of the territory on Lossiny Island.

The Inner Circular Line must become an integral part of the 21st century Moscow and the neighbourhoods to appear around it will bear the ancient names of places, former villages and forests, which are dear to each and every Muscovite.

New Tretyakovka and Artists' Club

The project of reconstruction of the Tretyakov State Picture Gallery/Artists' Central Club (designed by architects S.B. Tkachenko and M.D. Khazanov) is the result of long and hard preparatory planning work by the architects of the design studio, which absorbed the main functional, planning, volumetric and spatial ideas, that had been previously put forward in the professional circles and by the Tretyakov State Picture Gallery's authorities, concerning reconstruction and transformation of the existing building. The proposals (developed in several versions) do not only envisage the necessary enlargement of the exhibitional and utility spaces of the Gallery and the addition of a large concert hall to expand the function spectrum of the Tretyakov State Picture Gallery/Artists' Central Club but mainly concern the development of a new image of the cultural centre being renewed, according with its multifunctional social purpose and capable of making the centre of the city still more beautiful.

The desire to link in the most organic way the structure being renewed with the surrounding parklike territory, to include it into panorama of the embankment, to connect it with the river and the Garden Ring has predetermined the intricate volumetric composition of the new complex. During its detailed development the following factors were taken into consideration: inclusion into the composition of the existing right-angled strict-shaped building; need to specially outline the facade facing the river and the city centre; designing the entrance to the halls of the Gallery which is not actually outlined in any way now; early division of the pedestrian flow to select those going to the Tretyakov Gallery/Artists' Club when they are still in the vicinity of the Garden Ring; adding sophistication to the structure's silhouette and inclusion into its system of some high-rise features of the Moskva River embankments; creation of an integral architectural ensemble of exhibition buildings to reflect the architectural aesthetics of the 90s, which combines expressive simplicity of form and capabilities of the new building techniques with the Moscow architecture's traditional trends.

The inclusion into the volumetric building structure of a multigenre, carefully designed concert hall has made it possible to outline and volumetrically expose the Picture Gallery's lateral axis as well as to form the facades, facing the embankment and the park, with the main entrances vividly expressed. The new exhibition spaces in the upper part of the building, which is being additionally built, will be naturally lit through arcade-type glazed arched ceilings of the style close to post-modernism. Cylindrical transparent surfaces do not only have prototypes in the Moscow architecture (the GUM arcades, etc.), they sort of enter into a dialogue with the wonderful cable-stayed structures of Krimsky Bridge designed by architect A. Vlasov. Besides, as regards the image aspect, these ceilings inspire visual associations with the famous Crystal Palace, which is one of post-modernists' favourite masterpieces. The Palace was designed by D. Packstone, who was the father of many techniques, forms and motives in the architecture of exhibition pavilions of the second half of the 19th and the 20th centuries.

Project of the Artists' Central Club reconstruction and the Tretyakov Gallery in Krimskaya Embankment by architect S. Tkachenko.

Parts of the building facing the embankment, the Garden Ring and the park entrance are proposed to be surrounded with elegant gallery-bridges to serve as connections between round staged towers. This part of the complex is intended both for those coming to the Museum and concerts and for visitors of the Park of Arts. Authors' mini-exhibitions, trade fairs, artistic cafes, bars, souvenir, antique and book stores will be located here. These expressive small-size constructions constitute a formal transition from the huge bulk of the main structure to the park design. They can also be associated with the Kremlin towers, which can be viewed on the opposite bank of the river, or with the steeples of the Stalin hills, or with a funny children's play town. Their peculiar position, which is actually free relative to the main structure, has made it possible for the authors of the project to coordinate, from the planning point of view, the new exhibition complex with the adjoining structures (Gorky Park of Culture and Rest, the school of arts, the buildings on the spit, etc.).

Children's Wonderpark in Moscow

The idea to create a «Disney Land» in Russia arose nearly 40 years ago. It originated due to the fact that N. S. Khrushchov could not get to the Disney Land during his visit to the USA. The security service produced reasons of safety to account for the refusal, as it was difficult to provide adequate protection for the head of the Soviet State.

The Moscow architects received an order from the Government to create an amusement park of our own. A large group of architects and artists fulfilled the first stage of the work on the specially allotted territory of Nizhniye Mnevniky Island, formed by the bend of the Moskva River in the north-western part of the capital. The configuration of the island inspired authors of the project with the idea to design the park in the shape of a map of our Motherland, where the wealth of traditions, the variety of folklore and, of course, the achievements of all the Union Republics of the USSR could be demonstrated in miniature. In 1960, the «Tekhnika Molodyozhy» («The Youth's Technology») Magazine wrote, "The cold seas of the Arctic Ocean will rim the «Wonderland» with a blue fringe in the North. Visitors of the Black Sea coast in the Crimea and the Caucasus will be fascinated by the luxuriant vegetation of the subtropics. The impressive model of Siberia will give one a clear view of this wonderful and extremely rich part of our Motherland. The old, grey-haired, mighty Urals will demonstrate the riches of the «Mistress of the Copper Mountain». There was Moscow in the project, too, presented as a huge model, a Tajik aul, the «Lunnik» (resident of the Moon) attraction which had the form of a terrestrial globe, the Underwater Kingdom and many others. The project received approval and 800 mln roubles were assigned for the implementation of its first stage. It had been thought out to the slightest detail. The authors adopted many interesting features of the Disney Land but also managed to generate some ideas, harmonious with our history and culture, and introduce them into the design. Nevertheless, only a few years later no one seemed to care about it any more. It was forgotten and the group of the designers, busy with their every-day work, fell apart. The idea has been brought back to life only now, that the time of changes has set in.

In 1988, on the initiative of the famous artist, academician Z. Tseretely, architect V. Ivanov, one of the authors of the previous project of the «Wonderpark», who had by that time become director of the Institute of Genplan of Moscow, prepared an appeal to the Government and head of the Moscow Administration B. N. Yeltsin, proposing the resumption of the work. As a result, the chief architect of Moscow received direct instructions to organize realization of a project of a children's park.

The work began with gathering the necessary information on Disney parks which had appeared in great number in many countries of the world. Some of the parks were visited by the authors for the purpose of familiarization with their work. Talks were held with representatives of the administration of the Disney Land park in the USA and a number of foreign companies concerning the prospects of their participation in the project.

Various variants of the park's possible design were examined. It was actually a competitive examination of different versions, which went on until the moment when the results of the work were submitted for consideration to the City-Building Council of the Moscow Architectural Committee. The Council in which representatives of the Moscow community took part, such as cultural workers, writers, cosmonauts, artists and scriptwriters, considered 2 ver-

Project of the Children's Wonderpark in Nizhniye Mnevniky Island by architects L. Vavakin, Z. Tseretely, V. Shalimov, V. Ivanov, A. Sorokin and engineers A. Velkin and A. Rodin.

sions of the compositional decision of the Children's Wonderpark. One of them presented a Miracle-City, designed as a circular structure to be surrounded by a wall-shaped building, whose 4 sections were to contain information on the 4 elements: Water, Earth, Air and Fire. The rest of the island was to be occupied by the park.

The second version constituted a more complicated composition within the park tract of the island, which consisted of 5 building complexes (to stand for the number of continents), forming a semicircle around the central pavilion.

The decision taken during the discussion was in favour of the second version, which allowed visitors of the park to be shown the wealth of material culture of the Earth's continents. And the interior contents of the central pavilion were to be arranged in accordance with the proposal of the first variant, entitled «Man in the world, the world in Man». Further work was continued in compliance with this decision. It included more detailed realization of the first stage of the construction.

At present, there is a fully designed concept and a project of the Wonderpark, including the programme of top-priority measures. Famous pieces of architecture of Europe, Asia, Africa, America and Australia, diminished in size, are to demonstrate the riches of the world. The Wonderpark's attractions, protected against unfavourable weather conditions, will be operating all the year round to ensure the optimum payback of the running expenses.

The complexes will be linked together by surface and underground connections. Visitors of the Park, having bought tickets, will be easily getting around the zones using monorails or underground mini-trains. Such a decision allows the green space of the park within the island's territory to be freely visited by Muscovites, with the beaches, sports grounds, cafes, restaurants, equestrian sport centre and a branch of the Moscow Zoo at their service. Thus, to use the recreation facilities of Nizhniye Mnevniky people will not necessarily have to buy tickets. Hotel complexes are planned to be built in the western and eastern sections of the island for the use of visitors of the Wonderpark and recreation zones.

Project of the Children's Wonderpark. The main square.

At the present time, the area of the island, which makes 875 acres of land, is actually vacant of any major constructions, with the exception of several buildings in its eastern part, where some warehouses and the remaining structures of the settlement, previously located in Nizhniye Mnevniky, are situated. The western part of the island is occupied with old greenhouses and vegetable fields. That is why the first stage of the construction of the Wonderpark is planned to take place in the western section. Bearing in mind the need for sources of funds to finance the construction of the Park, a large supermarket is planned to be built near the hotel complex, intended for customers coming to do shopping with their children. For this purpose, the interior space of the supermarket is planned to include special playrooms, where parents will be able to leave their children for a few hours without caring about the way they will spend this spare time. These properly designed rooms will house playing machines and sports equipment.

Out of the total number of attractions belonging to the Wonderpark, several pavilions are intended to be built simultaneously with the construction of the hotel and the shopping centre. Those pavilions are supposed to mark the beginning of the complex, named «Europe is Our Common Home». Visitors of the «Ancient Moscow» pavilion will see some life-size patterns of old Moscow designed by Appolinary Vasnetsov. The «Russian Winter» pavilion will give one a chance to take a ride on a troika through a blizzard even in the summer time. The «Fairy Tale House» will demonstrate all the wealth of fairy tale folklore of the peoples of Russia.

These pavilions and a number of other facilities, too, will form Moscow Square, designed in the shape of an amphitheatre, where outdoor public festivities will take place and carnivals and festivals will be opened. This square will be the starting point of the bulk of the complex «Europe is Our Common Home». Ancient Moscow, the Colosseum, the Cathedral of Notre Dame and a small part of Venice will also be here. And the most famous structures of America, Africa and Australia will make it possible for people to see all wealth of the world architecture and to acquaint themselves with cultures of various nations of the world. The project contains the design of another complex, the 6th one, having the appearance of a green field. It is the Country of the Future, where children's vivid imagination will be able to create pictures of the future in their minds.

The monorail, running over the Park in a transparent tube and connecting each complex with the central pavilion to form a transparent hemisphere, stands for the idea that life on the Earth can only be secured by joint effort of all peoples and by ensuring peace among all the nations on all the continents.

Many foreign experts who have got acquainted with the project suppose that the authors have succeed in finding a concept, novel and effective in form, attractive in its commercial prospects and capable of drawing the attention of many countries of the world.

It is only natural that the idea of creating the Park has its opponents, too. As a rule, the main argument they resort to is the wrong timing of the construction of such an expensive complex in the country's present-day complicated economic situation. The answer to this can be that they have always declared in this country that children are our hope for the future. However, despite a great number of loud slogans proclaiming the privileged position of children in our Motherland, it is easy to make sure that children are destitute and, as compared to civilized countries, deprived of many incentives to inspire their fantasy and reveal their creativeness. That is exactly the effect American psychologists observe, analyzing the way children behave after visiting Disney parks, and asserting that artist Disney succeeded in finding wonderful means and forms, not only arousing a child's creative tendencies but also strengthening the family due to children's and their parents' mutual emotions. And the family is the initial element of the state, as they used to say quite recently.

The Moscow Administration has done a great deal so as to have a Wonderpark constructed in Moscow. A fund of the project has been established, which envisages concessionary terms of its realization and exploitation. Appropriate project documentation has been developed concerning the Park as a whole and the first stage of the construction in particular. A business plan has been worked out showing commercial solvency of the top-priority measures in the course of the construction. Now implementation of this interesting project has become a matter of investment and business initiative.

About the Future of Lefortovo

The continuous study of Lefortovo's unique status from the point of view history, culture and landscape makes one treat the matter of the future fate of this Moscow neighbourhood quite seriously and make better use of its rich potentialities so as to keep up the traditions and restore the high significance of the place in the centuries-old history of the capital.

Lefortovo Housing Estate appeared on the banks of the Yauza River in the late 17th century. Assuming the state power in 1689, Peter I chose this particular place outside the Kremlin walls to establish the second metropolitan centre, which became the starting point of the great reforms that took place in Russia and were based on the strong desire for European civilization and openness. As for the city-building aspect, this idea was expressed in the foundation on the banks of the river of an integral landscaping architectural ensemble, which predetermined the scale and architecture of St. Petersburg.

In 1697 – 1699, on Peter's initiative, F. Lefort's palace was erected on the right bank of the Yauza River, which for a long time served as a place to host assemblies, gala ceremonies and diplomatic receptions. The Cathedral of 17 Sts. Peter and Paul on the left bank, in Soldatskaya Housing Estate, where the regiment under command of Lefort was stationed, still exists nowadays. It was constructed in 1711 for the money granted by Peter I and with his personal participation. Meanwhile, Admiral-General F. Golovin, one of Peter's associates, had an estate with a large garden built on the same bank of the Yauza, opposite to Lefort's palace. Peter I took possession of those lands in 1720 and at his desire planning of the walkways and ponds was done by Dr. N. Bidloo, which has reached our days.

Later on, architect A. Rinaldi designed Catherine's Palace. The tremendous palace was built within the territory of the Imperial garden in 1773 – 1776 and is still in existence.

For more than 100 years, until the early 19th century, the Lefortovo palaces served as the main Imperial residence in Moscow. During the coronations that were held in the Uspensky Cathedral of the Kremlin, the palaces would house the Imperial Courts of Catherine I, Peter II, Anna Ioannovna, Yelizaveta Petrovna, Peter III, Catherine the Great, Pavel Petrovich and Alexander I.

Starting from the late 17th and up to the early 20th century, the best Russian architects were successively and continuously creating the Lefortovo palace ensemble. They were D. Aksamitov, M. Fontana, F.-B. Rastrelli, D.V. Ukhtomsky, A. Rinaldi, K. Blank, D. Quarenghi, F. Kamporezhi, M.F. Kazakov, I.V. Yegotov, D. Gilyardi, M.F. Shestakov, I.I. Pozdeev, I.E. Bondarenko and I.P. Mashkov.

Names of a great number of our famous compatriots are associated with the Lefortovo neighbourhood. They are Peter the Great's associates F. Lefort, P. Gordon, A.D. Menshikov, F.A. Golovin, N. Bidloo, physician-in-ordinary G. Lestok, chancellor A.A. Bezborodko, great poet A.S. Pushkin, artists P.A. Fedotov and K.F. Youon, composers A.N. Skryabin and A.P. Borodin, writer A.I. Kuprin, famous philanthropist Princess N.B. Shakhovskaya and many others.

Extensive historical materials of the Russian state archives of Moscow and St. Petersburg as well as those of Holland, Germany and Poland reflect various periods of the formation and prosperity of the Imperial palaces near the Yauza River and confirm the unique significance for Moscow of this landscaping architectural monument of our culture.

The art of gardening under Peter I bore a vivid imprint of his personal tastes and reorganization ambitions, of his desire to obtain access to the All-European culture. A garden, as he saw it, was not just of mere architectural or sanitary significance, it was first of all a place for education and instruction. While the palace park was still in the process of creation, its compositional decision already contained a certain intention of ideological nature, which was to add a European civilized element to the visitors' world outlook and their attitude to nature.

The first experiments of the Moscow park near the Yauza River were later continued in St.Petersburg, where they were considerably expanded. There are good reasons to think that Peter's Moscow park, when revived, can equal the Summer Garden in St.Petersburg, the gardens in Peterhof, Strelnya, Oraniyenbaum and Yekaterinhof. The analogy being continued, the Yauza can be compared with the famous Moika River in St.Petersburg and Catherine's Palace with the legendary Hermitage. Thus, the functional renewal of the palace park must be first of all directed at the continuation of the traditions that originated as far back as three centuries.

For a long time now, the appearance of the neighbourhood has been determined by the leading complexes of historical buildings, such as Catherine's Palace. The Palace and the Yauza park occupy a key position and compositionally dominate over the whole architectural and spatial structure of the surrounding building pattern.

Bearing in mind the location in the area of several largest technical engineering educational and planning institutes, such as the Moscow State University of Technology, Central Institute of Aviation Engineering, Russian Research Institute of Oil Industry, Moscow Construction Engineering Institute, Moscow Power Engineering Institute, Russian Electromechanical Institute, Moscow Research Institute of Architectural Planning, etc., with the total number of students, teaching and research staff exceeding 30,000, it would be expedient to have the Russian Academy of Technical Engineering

Sciences positioned in Catherine's former palace and a national scientific, educational and cultural centre thus created. The building could house a large scientific and technical library and a reference room, it could serve as a place to host international contacts.

Creation of a community centre on the basis of the administrative building of Catherine's Palace (No 1, Krasnokazarmennaya

The Lefortovo park (in its present condition)

The revival and functional renewal of the Lefortovo Park (a proposed version)

   I. The Palace garden ensemble
  II. The «Catherine's Palace» Russian Academy of Technical Engineering Sciences
 III. The «Palace Garden» multifunctional community centre
 IV. The complex of the General Military Hospital named after Peter the Great
  V. The Museum of General and Local History called «Relieve me of my sorrows»

Street) also seems expedient and feasible. Withdrawal of private apartments and new construction to replace the adjoining industrial structures make it possible to create considerable spaces to be used as various clubs, renting and reference libraries, cafes, musical, dancing and concert halls, a theatre, a movie-hall, a hotel, a restaurant, sales points, health improvement salons, etc., which would increase the number of local residents, visiting the palace garden all the year round, and favour educational and recreation procedures with children and adults as well as arranging tourist service of the city.

The garden itself should be regarded as a functional piece of art, where people take walks, have a rest, do thinking, enjoy themselves, study, celebrate, play music, dance, etc. To keep up these traditions summer reading-rooms, observatories, concert stages, green banqueting rooms, grottos, pavilions, sports and play grounds, fountains, greenhouses, hotbeds and so on should be newly created in the garden.

A detailed historical city-building study of the area of the Lefortovo palace complex, the park and the adjoining quarters on both banks of the Yauza has been conducted as well as a research into the social, functional, transport and environmental situation, which has permitted working out proposals on the social and functional renewal of the whole neighbourhood.

The city-building isolation of the Bolshoye Lefortovo district is emphasized by the existence of the surrounding railroads of the Kurskoye and Kazanskoye directions, that were built in the 1960s in a roundabout way to avoid the area of the most valuable historical buildings. The inner logic of the planning system formed in this area is centred on the large ensemble of the Imperial palaces and the park, positioned in the middle and equal in scope and significance to the Kremlin ensemble. The existence in Moscow of 2 centres, which originated in different historical periods, is a sure certainty. The forming Government/business ensemble in Krasnopresnenskaya Embankment, including the White House, the City and the like, may in the future become the third centre of attraction in Moscow. Development of the metropolitan business and historical centre would be favoured by the creation of a new short subway line to link up the most significant business, cultural and Government facilities.

Thus, it is evident that the project of revival and functional renewal of Lefortovo comprises a wide range of problems which are impossible to be solved by local effort. Adequate restoration of the Imperial palaces and the garden and entrusting them with renewed metropolitan functions must become an all-Moscow task of national significance to be put on the list of the city's top-priority programmes. It should be remembered that in 1999 Petrovo-Lefortovo will celebrate its tercentenary. It was the Yauza neighbourhood of all places that the Russian capital moved to 300 years ago and it was here that the establishment of the new Russian State system started. Perhaps, it is high time to begin preparing for the celebration of the anniversary which must increase the interest of Russians in this part of the capital, worthy of becoming a scientific, cultural and educational centre of Russia.

The Bridge between the Past and the Future

Among the Moscow subway bridges, Smolensky Bridge seems to have the finest appearance. Unlike the monstrous subway bridge near the Vorobyovy Hills, which resembles a boa constrictor that has devoured an elephant, or Philyevsky and Kolomensky bridges which are merely utilitarian, Smolensky Bridge looks like an ordinary respectable foot/highway bridge of the 50s. Its beautifully designed arch and granite-faced abutments, surmounted with massive cast iron vases, blend well with the monumental building pattern of Smolenskaya and Taras Shevchenko Embankments.

Everybody who has ever ridden along that bridge is sure to remember the wonderful sights one can view, looking through the train windows in the directions of Krasnaya Presnya and the Vorobyovy Hills. Those views, especially on a fine day, must have made many people fairly annoyed with the train moving too rapidly to see them as much as they wanted.

The desire to make the bridge accessible to pedestrians, too, as well as the idea to make use of the idle technical zones over the subway bridge access tunnels have become the original reasons for the order, given by the «Metrostroy» Subway Construction Department to Design Shop No 5 of the «Mosproyekt-2» Department. The order concerned the development of a reconstruction concept for the subway bridge, including possible ways of utilization for commercial purposes of the adjoining city areas.

Three versions of possible architectural decisions were designed under the leadership of architect S.B. Tkachenko. All of them proceed from the sound conviction that a further increase in the housing density of the downtown area is inevitable and providing that area with convenient pedestrian communication routes is necessary. The basic idea of the projects is to create a continuous

Smolenskaya Embankment
(a version of the reconstruction by architects S. Tkachenko and O. Dubrovsky)

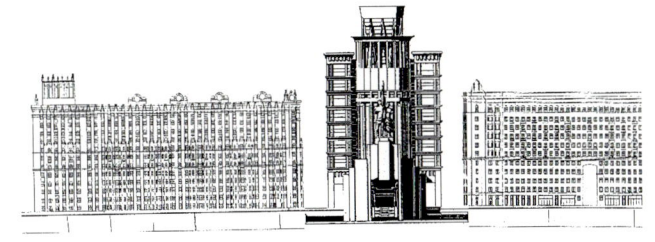

The reconstruction project of Smolensky Subway Bridge including the sculpture «The Worker and the Kolkhoznitsa» (a woman collective farmer) by V. Mukhina

«overflowing» system of buildings and other constructions with the subway bridge to link them together. This must be an extensive building complex combining business, show, hotel, residential, exhibition, shopping, cultural, utility, and service functions. Apart from multistorey surface structures, the proposals envisage possible development of multilevel underground space to be used for parking lots, storage and engineering facilities.

The project versions are structurally formed following a single three-section pattern, which adequately expresses the peculiarities of the city-building situation. The sections include: the office/shopping complex on Smolenskaya Embankment being developed as far as the 1st Smolensky Lane, the bridge, and the office/shopping complex on Taras Shevchenko Embankment and along the 1st and 2nd Borodinskaya Streets.

The city-building decision concerning the neighbourhood of Smolenskaya Embankment is of particular interest. Creating an adequate, architecturally formed pedestrian connection between the complex and the ground in front of «Smolenskaya Radialnaya» Subway Station of the Filyovskaya Line, the group of authors brought back into professional use the idea, long ago generated by I.V. Zholtovsky, whose famous house «with a turret» had been built in the vicinity. The size of that turret, which was slightly turned relative to the surface of the house's side elevation, exactly corresponded to the red lines of the planned yet unbuilt parade square in front of the subway station and of the passage to link it with the embankment.

Each version makes the bridge accessible to pedestrians with the subway traffic continued. However, the ways to achieve it are different.

Version No 1 (by architect I.I. Voznesensky) envisages construction of a moving foot-way running through a glass tube, lit during night-time and providing adequate panoramic view. Version No 2 (by architect I.V. Bilashenko) transforms the bridge into a kind of viewing attraction. A high metal arch is proposed to be constructed over the existing bridge span (thrice as high as the bridge itself), along which small cable cars like those of a cable railroad or a viewing wheel will move. A broad view of the whole western part of the city, including that of the complex on Poklonnaya Hill in the background, will open in front of the passengers' eyes. Version No 3 (by architect O.L. Dubrovsky) proposes the simplest and the most natural decision, which is expanding the bridge structure to build isolated sidewalks on both sides of the subway tracks. In other words, if this version is realized, people will be able just to stroll down the bridge, the way they do along the other Moskva River bridges.

Though the engineering data (functional and building areas, etc.) and the basic city-building decisions of the designed versions are actually the same, their architectural aspects are quite different.

In Version No 1, the aspect submits to the bridge's flat contour, as if visually prolonged into the depth of the building pattern. In the office complexes on both river banks, lateral separation prevails as well as gradual stepped climbing, only interrupted with regular appearance of small steeple turrets, necessary to connect the foot-way, moving along the bridge, with the surface. Those turrets resemble the bridge abutments and are a match for the general aspect decision. The office/shopping complex in the vicinity of Smolenskaya Embankment, though emphasized by its elliptical, stepped shape, is lower than the height accent of the complex on the opposite bank, which is a round tower, surmounted with a transparent funnel-shaped structure. According to this version, it is this particular tower that is included into the system of verticals of the Embankment (such as the Toko Bank, the Council for Mutual Economic Aid, the Ukraine Hotel, the International Centre of Information, etc.). On the whole, the architectural design of the complex has been devised in a very strong and modern manner.

Version No 2 expresses the idea of the bridge as well, from the point of view of plasticity, but is based on different formal principles. Its composition brings numerous historical associations and at the same time presents an original piece of creative work on the part of the author. The office complexes remind one of the famous Viennese house and the imposing Roman aqueducts. Their aspects are combined by the theme of the arch, which is a diminished repetition in shape of the new high arch of the cable road bridge. This version is beautiful from the point of view of rhythm and proportions. The stepped tower is quite expressive. The same as in the previous version, it is positioned in the vicinity of Taras Shevchenko Embankment. The problem of approach to the complex from Smolenskaya Subway Station has been solved in a peculiar way, too. It takes the form of an imposing arch, similar in shape to that of the bridge. Through that arch one

The reconstruction project of Smolensky Subway Bridge by architects S. Tkachenko and O. Dubrovsky.

can view the expressive line of the complex's arch substructures that precede the bridge. Those substructures can already be seen from the I.V. Zholtovsky house.

Version No 3 looks the least urbanized, still it seems to match in the most adequate way the peculiarities of the existing building pattern and the architecture of this city neighbourhood. It has made a serious attempt to return from piece-work planning, that has been a dominating tendency in Moscow in the past 5 years, to the creation of extensive city ensembles. Bearing in mind the large size of the buildings in Smolenskaya Embankment and the flat and wall-like nature of their facades, the authors have put forward a daring proposal to break the monotony by re-creation, above the bridge's eastern abutment, of the front section of the famous USSR pavilion at the 1937 World Fair in Paris (designed by architect B.M. Iofan), surmounted with the sculpture «The Worker and the Kolkhoznitsa».

It is common knowledge that V.I. Mukhina's outstanding composition needs an adequate pedestal, good enough to emphasize its plastic merits. Placing it into the context of the Moskva River embankment undoubtedly deserves attention. One cannot but notice that the picturesque nature of this city area and its spirit, formed in the years of Stalinism, largely correspond to the heroic pathos of the sculpture and can serve it as a good background. By positioning the Iofan pavilion above the subway bridge's abutment and carefully restoring its specifications as far as the height and volume are concerned, the authors have created the optimum conditions for Mukhina's duet to be exposed to view. In its turn, the monumental bulk of the pavilion, accomplished by the sculpture, has become capable of compositionally «uniting» the buildings on Smolenskaya Embankment and imparting the quality of artistic sense to the whole ensemble.

As distinct from the previous versions, whose architecture was based on the principle of contrast to the established environment, Version No 3 comes closer to the search for a compromise of styles. The architectural forms of its office/shopping elements situated on the river banks seem to be subject to the influence of the Soviet architectural style of the 1930s – 1940s, the so-called Ar Deko with its tendency to geometrical ornamentation and rhythmical experiments. Resorting to this layer of the Moscow architectural legacy in this case is especially well-grounded, as it is this particular layer, that the Iofan pavilion stylistically belongs to. Meanwhile, the aesthetics of the complexes on the river banks is quite contemporary and leaves no doubts as to the time of their creation. So, this version seems to constitute one of the real ways of forming the new «Moscow style».

The thorough, highly professional, comprehensive development of Version No 3 presents one of its most significant merits. All nuances have been adjusted with point accuracy, all basic components have been taken into account, such as the height of the river bank, the height of the front section of the 1937 pavilion, the height of the buildings on both embankments and, finally, even the height of the Zholtovsky house, situated at a distance. The perfection of this project from the point of view of accuracy and coordination of the slightest details should be specially underlined as for a long time now most of the constructions being realized have unfortunately lacked this particular quality, for which the city has to pay a dear price.

Even a brief survey of the developed versions of the reconstruction concept for Smolensky Subway Bridge and the adjoining territories convincingly proves, that with the implementation of the project Moscow can obtain another outstanding ensemble and, thus, can further increase its wealth and prosperity.

The Kremlin. Ivan the Great Bell-Tower.

Epilogue

The present publication is an integral component of the Jubilee Publishing Programme that is being implemented in line with the Government of Moscow Plan. Its four books reflect the results of the architectural city-building studies of the recent past, describe actual designs and theoretical concepts devised in several Moscow General Plans, and keep record of their practical implementation. This publication portrays the entire history of Moscow in concert with the descriptions of the greatest architectural and city-building monuments created over a long period of the city existence.

On November 9, 1994 Russia's President Boris El'tsin issued a Decree on Celebrating the Jubilee as a popular feast. Moscow Mayor Yuriy Luzhkov headed the Commission for the preparation for this remarkable date. A lot of events were scheduled, among them the meeting of the largest world cities mayors, theatrical performances and marches along Moscow streets, competitions and presentations of jubilee awards to Muscovites. Rallies, exhibitions, concerts will take place everywhere. Work aimed at restoration of historical ensembles and regeneration of the city's historical environment will have been completed in the central squares around the Kremlin and in Kitay-Gorod.

The Jubilee will become an asset of the whole mankind, and the fact that UNESCO included it in the list of calendar events to be celebrated by the entire world community proves it.

Contents of Volume Two

BOOK THREE

Socialist Reconstruction of Moscow 1917 – 1992......9

FOREWORD......2

INTRODUCTION......11
Natural Landscape Evolution (*K.N. Nenarokova*)......12
Panorama of Moscow Life in the Early Years
of the 20th Century (*M.V. Nashchokina*) 17
Preservation of Cultural Heritage (*A.S. Trofimov*) 26
The Icon of Our Lady with the Orb (*V.V. Filatov*) 29
Moscow's Super Problem (*G.Ya. Mokeyev*)......32

**Chapter One. Moscow in the First Years
of the Soviet Era 1917 – 1930**......37
Two Worlds: The Bolsheviks Versus the Church
(*archpriest V. Tsypin*)......46
Bolsheviks Take Care of Cultural Heritage (*A.S. Trofimov*)......56
Moscow – Capital of the Soviet Russia
(*N.N. Bronovitskaya, Yu.P. Bocharov*)......61
Lenin Plan for Monumental Propaganda (*Yu.A. Bychkov*)......63
Defining the Guidelines (*V.A. Vinogradov*)......65
Transformation Gets a Boost (*N.D. Glushchenko*)......67
The General Plan «New Moscow» (*N.N. Bronovitskaya,
Yu.P. Bocharov, N.D. Glushchenko*)......69
The First All-Russian Agricultural Show (*A.S. Longinov*)......73
The «Greater Moscow» Plan (*N.N. Bronovitskaya,
Yu.P. Bocharov, N.D. Glushchenko*)......74
Guidelines for the Growth of Soviet Capital (*N.D. Glushchenko*)....76
Architectural Romanticism of the 1920s (*M.G. Barhin*)......78
Architectural Chimeras (*G.Ya. Mokeyev*)......82

**Chapter Two. Stalin's Reconstruction
of the USSR Capital 1930 – 1953**......89
Mysterious Pages of History of the 30s......94
The 1935 General Plan of Moscow Reconstruction
(*Yu.P. Bocharov*)......96
The First Steps of Reconstruction
(*Yu.P. Bocharov, N.D. Glushchenko*)......113
The Destiny of Sukhareva Tower (*V.B. Murav'ev*)......118
Moscow's Municipal Economy in War Years
(*N.D. Glushchenko*)......120
The Wartime Moscow (*K.M. Simonov*)......122

Wonders of Kazan and Tikhvin Icons of Our Lady
(*archpriest B. Kirilov*)......124
The 1951 General Plan and its Implementation
(*N.D. Glushchenko*)......127
The All-Union Agricultural Exhibition (VSKhV)
(*N.D. Glushchenko*)......130
Soviet Architecture over 30 Years of the Russian Federation
(*V.A Shkvarikov*)......131

**Chapter Three. On the Way Towards a Model
Communist City, 1954 – 1985**......135
Resolutions on Architectural Over-Indulgence
(*N.D. Glushchenko*)......140
General Plan for Moscow Development. Feasibility
Fundamentals. Year of 1961 (*A.Yu. Becker*)......142
Development of Capital's Downtown and Competition of 1967
(*Yu.P. Bocharov, I.G. Lezhava*)......145
Energetic Struggle for Ancient Moscow Begins
(*A.S. Trofimov*)......148
General Plan of Development of 1971
(*L.V. Vavakin*)......154
In Defense of the Historic Moscow (*A.A. Savin*)......160
All-Russian Society for Protection of Historic
and Cultural Monuments (*N.D. Glushchenko*)......163
«Monuments of Motherland» (*N.N. Vizzhilin*)......165
«Nasty» Commission (*N.M. Moleva*)......167
General Plans of the 1935 and 1971
Public Criticism (*G.Ya. Mokeyev, V.A. Vinogradov*)......170

**Chapter Four. Reconsideration
of City-Building Priorities 1986 – 1991**......175
A New City-Building Concept of Moscow Development
(*L.V. Vavakin*)......177
A Concept of Regeneration of Historical Moscow
(*V.A. Vinogradov, G.Ya. Mokeyev*)......182
Social Foundations of City Functioning:
from the Quality of Environment to the Quality of Life
(*T.M. Dridze*)......188
Engineer and Geological Aspects of Preservation
of Moscow Architectural Monuments (*E.M. Pashkin*)......194

BOOK FOUR
RENAISSANCE OF NEW RUSSIA'S CAPITAL 199

INTRODUCTION (*V.A. Vinogradov*) 202

Chapter One. REGENERATION OF HISTORIC MOSCOW 203
Democratization of the Society and
New City-Building Policy (*L.V. Vavakin*) 206
Reconstruction of Historical City
and Professional Ethics (*A.P. Kudryavtsev*) 209
Conservation of Woods and Parks Protection Belt
(*A.T. Melamed, K.N. Nenarokova*) 216
Renaissance of the Historical Centre of Moscow
(*M.M. Posokhin*) 218
The Resurrection of the Cathedral (*T.A. Knyazeva*) 223
The Rebirth of the Morozovs' Mansion in Spiridonovka
(*N.S. Datieva*) 228
Reconstruction of the Old Gostiny Dvor
(*M.V. Nashchokina*) 230

Chapter Two. MOSCOW ON THE EVE OF BIMILLENIUM OF THE CHRISTIAN CIVILIZATION 235
Building New Architectural Ensembles (*L.V. Vavakin*) 236
The Greater Ascension Church at the Nikitsky Gates
(*O.I. Zhurin*) 240
The Saint Tatiana the Martyr Church at Moscow University
(*O.I. Zhurin*) 241
Recreating the Spiritual and Enlightening Complex
at Krylatskoye (*O.I. Zhurin*) 242
Arts and Religion (*N.D. Nedovich*) 243
Water Basins of Moscow's Green Belt
(*K.N. Nenarokova*) 244
Picture of Moscow's Ecology
(*Yu.V. Novikov, T.I. Marshalkin*) 248

Chapter Three. ARCHITECTURAL INVITATION TO THE 21ST CENTURY 251
Downtown Moscow in the 21st Century
(*M.M. Posokhin*) 253
Revival of the Brattsevo Estate (*A.N. Kukushkin*) 258
Future of the Inner Circular Railroad Line
(*K.N. Nenarokova*) 260
New Tretyakovka and Artists' Club (*M.V. Nashchokina*) 262
Children's Wonderpark in Moscow (*L.V. Vavakin*) 263
About the Future of Lefortovo (*Z.V. Kharitonova*) 265
The Bridge between the Past and the Future
(*M.V. Nashchokina*) 266

EPILOGUE 270

Edited and printed by «Moscow Textbooks» JSC

Publishing House: «Moscow Textbooks» JSC. **General director S.M.LINOVICH**
© Concept: V.A.VINOGRADOV
© Design and model: G.A.KOMAROV, V.A.VINOGRADOV
Authors: V.A.VINOGRADOV (leading),
Yu.P.BOCHAROV, G.A.KOMAROV, T.A.KORYUKINA, G.Ya.MOKEEV
Russian text editiors: N.D.GLUSHCHENKO, T.A.KORYUKINA
Translation: G.I.GOROV
English text editor: S.K.FOMIN
Jacket photo: V.A.SVERDLOV from the original by G.A.KOMAROV
Photos in the text: N.N.ALEXEEV, V.M.RUDCHENKO, E.V.SHVED,
A.P.KUDRYAVTSEV, S.B.LEONOV, K.N.NENAROKOVA,
A.I.EPIFANOV, A.N.KUKUSHKIN, Z.V.KHARITONOVA, A.KULESHOV,
Yu.P.BOCHAROV, L.V.VAVAKIN, L.N.LAVRENYOV, I.G.LEZHAVA
Computer imposing: K.S.DONCHUK, M.A.NOVOSEL'TSEV
Art editor: Ya.B.MALOGOLOVKINA
Proof-reading: N.M.ABRAMOVA, A.A.TALALAEVSKAYA
Colour separation: N.V.BALASHOV, V.N.KOZLYAEV
Montage: M.A.PAVLOVA
Printing: V.A.MAKHOV

First fly-leaf: Moscow centre in the 17th century. Reconstruction. V. Nedelin
Second fly-leaf: Present-day Moscow centre. Model

MOSCOW. 850TH ANNIVERSARY
Edit.No. 071230 of 27.10.95
Signed for printing on 02.07.97
Format 60 X 90 $^1/_8$. Bleached paper
Offset printing. Physical printer's sheets 34
Run of 10 000 copies. Order No. 5950

Printed by «Moscow Textbooks» JSC
15, Ul. Zorge Moscow, 125252
Post-printing works:
Order of the Work Red Banner
GUPP «Children's Book» of Roskompechat
49, Sushchevsky Val, Moscow, 127018

Moscow Government Telecommunications and Mass-Media Committee

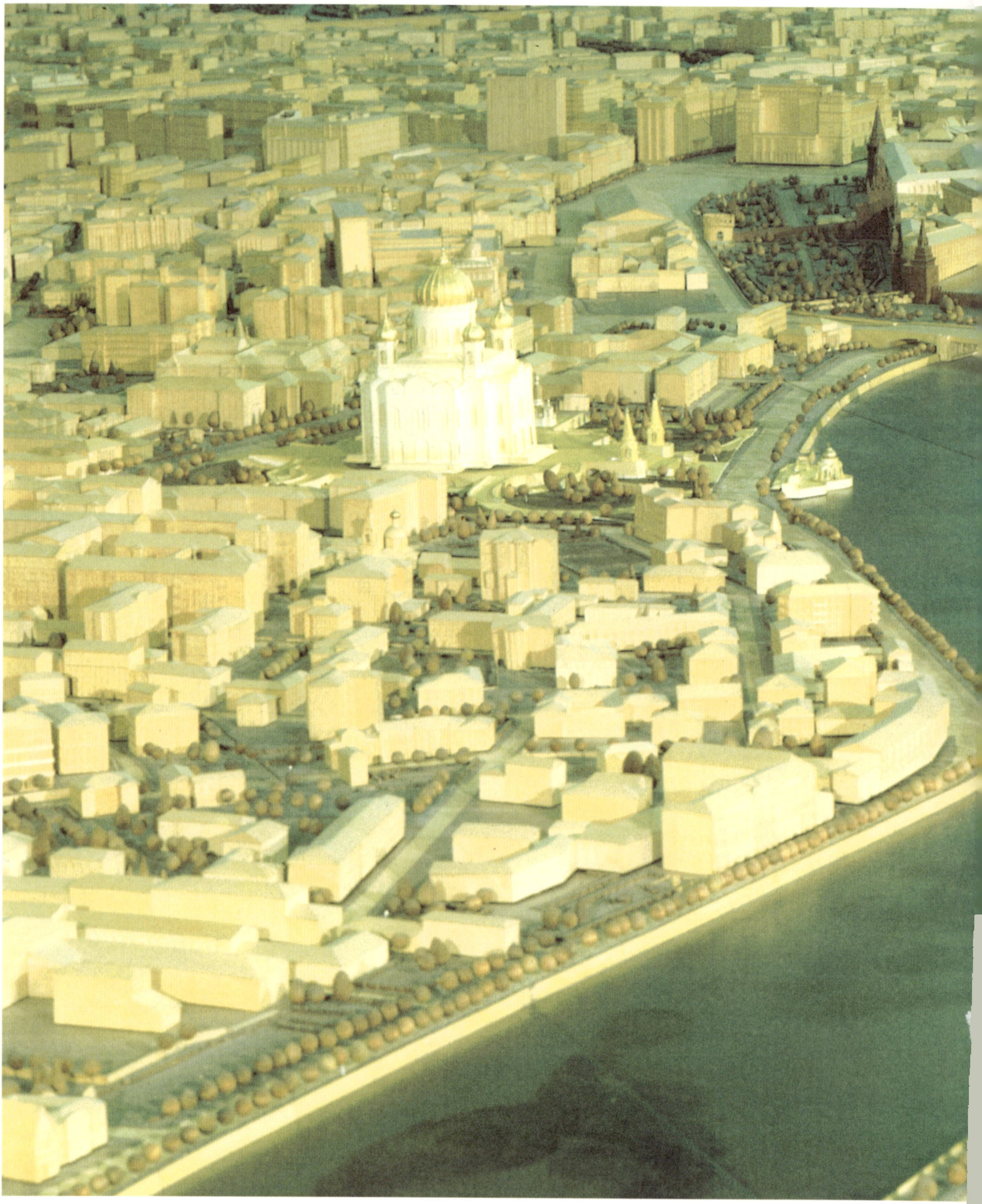